# Books in the Nonprofit and Public Management Series

James S. Bowman, *Ethical Frontiers in Public Management* (paperback), 0-7879-0002-8

David G. Carnevale, *Trustworthy Government: Leadership and Management Strategies for Building Trust and High Performance,* 0-7879-0062-1

Steven Cohen and William Eimicke, *The New Effective Public Manager: Achieving Success in a Changing Government* (2nd ed., revised and expanded), 0-7879-0087-7

Steven Cohen and William Eimicke, *The Effective Public Manager: Achieving Success in a Changing Government* (3rd ed.), 0-7879-5938-3

Stephen E. Condrey, *Handbook of Human Resource Management in Government,* 0-7879-4099-2

Philip J. Cooper and Chester A. Newland, *Handbook of Public Law and Administration,* 0-7879-0930-0

Terry L. Cooper, *The Responsible Administrator: An Approach to Ethics for the Administrative Role* (4th ed.), 0-7879-4133-6

Paul Epstein, *Results That Matter: How Performance Measurement and Civic Collaboration Empower Communities,* 0-7879-6058-6

H. George Frederickson, *The Spirit of Public Administration,* 0-7879-0295-0

Patricia W. Ingraham, James R. Thompson, and Ronald P. Sanders, *Transforming Government: Lessons from the Reinvention Laboratories,* 0-7879-0931-9

Patricia Keehley, Steven Medlin, Sue MacBride, and Laura Longmire, *Benchmarking for Best Practices in the Public Sector: Achieving Performance Breakthroughs in Federal, State, and Local Agencies* (LSI), 0-7879-0299-3

Carol W. Lewis, *The Ethics Challenge in Public Service* (2nd ed.), 0-7879-6756-4

Russell M. Linden, *Seamless Government: A Practical Guide to Re-Engineering in the Public Sector,* 0-7879-0015-X

Russell M. Linden, *Seamless Government Workbook: A Hands-On Guide to Implementing Organizational Change,* 0-7879-4035-6

Russell M. Linden, *Seamless Government: A Practical Guide to Re-Engineering in the Public Sector* (book and workbook set), 0-7879-4486-6

Russell M. Linden, *Seamless Government Workbook* (ten-pack set), 0-7879-4487-4

Russell M. Linden, *Working Across Boundaries: Making Collaboration Work in Government and Nonprofit Organizations,* 0-7879-6430-1

Roy T. Meyers, *Handbook of Government Budgeting,* 0-7879-4292-8

David Osborne and Peter Plastric, *The Reinventor's Fieldbook: Tools for Transforming Your Government,* 0-7879-4332-0

James L. Perry, *Handbook of Public Administration* (2nd ed., revised), 0-7879-0194-6

Dennis D. Pointer and James E. Orlikoff, *The High-Performance Board: Principles of Nonprofit Organization Governance,* 0-7879-5697-X

Hal G. Rainey, *Understanding and Managing Public Organizations* (3rd ed.), 0-7879-6561-8

John Clayton Thomas, *Public Participation in Public Decisions: New Skills and Strategies for Public Managers,* 0-7879-0129-6

# UNDERSTANDING AND MANAGING PUBLIC ORGANIZATIONS

# UNDERSTANDING AND MANAGING PUBLIC ORGANIZATIONS

### THIRD EDITION

Hal G. Rainey

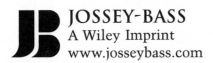

JOSSEY-BASS
A Wiley Imprint
www.josseybass.com

Published by Jossey-Bass
A Wiley Imprint
989 Market Street, San Francisco, CA 94103-1741   www.josseybass.com

Jossey-Bass books and products are available through most bookstores. To contact Jossey-Bass directly call our Customer Care Department within the U.S. at 800-956-7739, outside the U.S. at 317-572-3986, or fax 317-572-4002.

Jossey-Bass also publishes its books in a variety of electronic formats. Some content that appears in print may not be available in electronic books.

**Library of Congress Cataloging-in-Publication Data**

Rainey, Hal G. (Hal Griffin), date.
  Understanding and managing public organizations / Hal G. Rainey — 3rd ed.
      p. cm. — (The Jossey-Bass nonprofit and public management series)
Includes bibliographical references and index.
  ISBN 0-7879-6561-8 (alk. paper)
  1. Public administration. I. Title. II. Series.
  JF1351.R27 2003
  351—dc21

                                                           2003006234

Printed in the United States of America
THIRD EDITION
HB Printing          10 9 8 7 6 5

# THE JOSSEY-BASS
# NONPROFIT AND PUBLIC MANAGEMENT SERIES

# CONTENTS

**PART THREE: STRATEGIES FOR MANAGING
AND IMPROVING PUBLIC ORGANIZATIONS**

# TABLES, FIGURES, AND EXHIBITS

## Tables

## Figures

# Exhibits

# PREFACE

The previous editions of this book reviewed the literature on management and organization theory and suggested applications to the public sector grounded in evidence from research on public organizations and the people in them. The book has thus been valuable to practicing managers, to scholars, and to students in the field, having served primarily and widely as a text in courses for master of public administration students and in seminars for doctoral students in public administration and public affairs programs. The revisions in this third edition seek to enhance the book's usefulness in such courses.

Reviewers of the first edition suggested greater integration among the chapters and the addition of an organizing framework for the material. I therefore presented in the first chapter of the second edition a conceptual framework that links the chapters and topics in the book. This framework emphasizes a fundamental challenge for leaders and members of organizations, that of integrating and coordinating the components and domains of the organization, including its environment, its strategy- and decision-making processes, its goals and values, its culture, its structure, its authority and power relationships, its tasks, its communication processes, and of course its people—the organization's leaders, teams, and groups, and their motivations, work attitudes, and behaviors. As the book illustrates, the field of management and organizational theory has developed no comprehensive theory or scientific solution that achieves this integration. Nevertheless, the book's chapters describe concepts and insights from the organization and management literature that support leaders' and managers' efforts to think and act comprehensively, to integrate the myriad topics and issues they face. The final chapter illustrates how to use the framework to approach various management challenges, such as privatization of public services, in an integrative, comprehensive fashion.

The rest of the book's chapters flesh out the conceptual framework by reviewing the theories, research, and practices associated with major topics in the field of organizations and their management. As described in Chapter One, the field of public management and leadership has continued to develop rapidly since publication of the previous editions. Accordingly, many chapters and topics in this edition have been expanded to cover new material and new developments. For example, the chapters on motivation (Nine and Ten) and leadership (Eleven) include additional coverage of recent research and thought on those topics, such as the theory of goal setting as a motivational procedure, social learning theory, self-efficacy, and charismatic leadership. This edition also covers a lot of the most recent research on such topics as how public managers lead and behave, effective performance in government agencies, public service networks and third-party government, the nature of public service motivation, organizational commitment in public organizations, differences between public and private managers' perceptions of the personnel systems with which they work, organizational culture in public organizations, and many other topics. It addresses such developments as the continued progress of the National Public Management Research Conferences, the Government Performance Project, the O'Toole-Meier model of public management, and the recent stream of research on governance. The chapters on the major topics of the book show that researchers have published a profusion of studies on these and other topics since the second edition appeared, thus raising a major challenge for one who seeks to review and interpret them all.

In addition, previous editions of this book have analyzed, as does this one, the distinctions between public organizations and their members, on the one hand, and other types of organizations, leaders, and employees, such as those in the business sector, on the other. Chapter Three presents a conceptual analysis of these distinctions: What do we mean when we refer to these different types of organizations and the people who work for them? How do we define them and study their differences? Subsequent chapters describe a large number of research articles and other forms of evidence that compare public and private organizations in terms of the topics that these chapters cover. Although I have tried to keep track of comparisons of public, private, and nonprofit organizations on a continuing basis, I have been surprised at how many studies of this type have appeared in recent years. Assembling these studies, describing them, and interpreting them for the reader has posed another serious challenge, but a welcome one because one of the book's objectives is to provide the most comprehensive compilation and review possible of such research-based comparisons of public and private (and public and nonprofit) organizations.

Another goal and challenge of the previous editions of the book was to cover important developments in the practice and contemporary context of general management and public management. The previous editions covered such topics as Total Quality Management, the influence of the best-selling book *Reinventing Government* (Osborne and Gaebler, 1992) and the REGO movement it spawned, including the federal government's National Performance Review; and the management of privatization and contracting-out programs, among others. This edition reports on research evaluating the influence of these developments on governments at all levels in the United States and in other nations. It also covers more recent developments, such as the New Public Management movement around the world, the George W. Bush administration's President's Management Agenda, the human capital movement in government and the Human Capital Crisis, and some of the developments related to the new emphasis on homeland security.

Such coverage is provided in part to make this edition of the book even more interesting and useful than the previous editions for practicing managers and professionals, and for students interested in such roles. This edition also offers a lot of suggestions for those who are faced with practical leadership and management challenges, including managing relations with the media (Chapter Five), enhancing one's power and authority (Chapter Seven), motivating employees (Chapter Ten), managing and leading organizational culture (Chapter Eleven), managing conflict (Chapter Twelve), leading organizational change (Chapter Thirteen), and other topics. In addition, it gives examples of how these insights and concepts are used in the field. For instance, Chapter Eight begins with a description of the major structural transformation the U.S. Internal Revenue Service has recently undergone, and of the structural changes made at a national laboratory in response to public concerns about its safety. Chapter Ten points out that many of the efforts to reform pay systems in government would have been much more effective if they had been informed by a clear understanding of a number of motivation theories. Chapter Thirteen shows how strategies for leading organizational change have led to successful large-scale change in government agencies, and how not applying such strategies has led to failure in other instances. Ultimately, the book pursues the theme that effective leadership involves the well-informed, thoughtful, integrative use of a variety of management concepts and points rather than the hot pursuit of catchy phrases and glib advice. Illustrating this theme, many students of military strategy and history express great admiration for Carl Von Clausewitz's classic treatise *On War* (1986). Clausewitz essentially takes the position that he cannot advise an individual commander on how to conduct a specific campaign because such situations are so highly varied and contingent. Rather, he aims to provide general perspective and insight on how to conceive of the nature and enterprise of war. Even persons who loathe military force and military analogies might accept the point that people facing practical challenges often profit from general understanding and insight as much as from detailed prescriptions.

## Audience

As mentioned earlier, the primary audience for previous editions of *Understanding and Managing Public Organizations* included graduate students and scholars interested in public management and applications of organization theory to the public sector. Reviewers of the previous editions said that practitioners would be unlikely to delve into the detailed reviews of research and theory the book provides. I concede this point, but begrudgingly. This assumption underestimates many practicing leaders and managers—certainly many of those whom I have encountered. Many of them, given the time and opportunity, are among the most thoughtful and reflective students of leadership and management. They may dislike abstruse and ponderous academic discourse, because they are inclined to action and strive for practical results. They may also find quick advice and bright ideas attractive, because they do not have a great deal of time to read. In addition, they are not likely to spend long periods in management courses; instead, they usually receive shorter doses of training and consultation that they use to search for new ideas and solutions. Yet when practicing managers do enroll in long courses in academic settings, they often lead their classes in insight and in interest in new concepts and broad perspectives. They often spurn "war stories" and how-to manuals.

Thus, the lines between practicing managers, students, and management scholars often blur. Sometimes practicing managers seek degrees in long-term academic programs and play the role of student. Often they teach or help to teach courses. My colleague Larry O'Toole points out that many academics act as practitioners or quasi-practitioners in their service on commissions and in their research and consulting activities. Therefore, although the primary goal of this book is to serve students and scholars interested in research and theory, it can also serve practicing managers and leaders. I cling to the belief that this book can function as a reference for busy managers who want a review of basic topics in the field, who might find the conceptual framework and some of the suggestions and examples useful, or who might value the book in other ways.

## Organization

The best overview of the organization of the book can be obtained by reviewing the table of contents. Part One covers the dynamic context of public organizations. Its five chapters introduce the basic objectives and assumptions of the book and the conceptual framework mentioned earlier. Chapter One discusses the current context of public management in practice and in scholarship, and the challenges this context raises for applying organization and management theory to public organizations. Chapter Two summarizes the history of organization and management theory, describing the development of some of the most important concepts and issues in the field, which are developed further in later chapters. In addition, this historical review shows that most of the prominent organization and management theorists have been concerned with developing the general theory of organizations and have not been particularly interested in public organizations as a category. Their disinterest in public organizations justifies the effort made in this book to apply organization theory to public organizations, and indicates the challenges involved. Chapter Three defines public organizations and distinguishes them from private ones. It also provides an introductory overview of the assertions about the nature of public organizations made in later chapters. Chapters Four and Five review the literature on organizational environments, particularly the political and institutional environments of public organizations.

Part Two focuses on key dimensions of organizing and managing. These seven chapters concentrate on major topics in organization theory and management, including goals and effectiveness, power, strategy, decision making, structure and design, and the people in organizations (including discussions of values, motivation, work-related behaviors and attitudes, leadership, organizational culture, teams and groups, communication, and conflict). They describe current research on these topics and discuss how it applies to public organizations.

Part Three covers strategies for managing and improving public organizations. Chapter Thirteen addresses organizational change and development. Chapter Fourteen, the last chapter of the book, presents, as noted earlier, ideas for achieving organizational excellence in the public sector, and includes discussion of recent developments such as the total quality movement and increased privatization. Finally, the chapter illustrates how the conceptual framework may be used to pursue a comprehensive management strategy that addresses both new initiatives and long-standing challenges.

# Acknowledgments

I still owe thanks to all the people mentioned in the first two editions, and the list has grown even longer. It defies enumeration here. Despite my concern about leaving out anyone, I must leave out a great many people anyway. I offer thanks to all those who have discussed this edition of the book with me and made suggestions, including Barry Bozeman, Richard Chackerian, Delmer Dunn, Patricia Ingraham, Ed Kellough, Ken Meier, Larry O'Toole, Bart Wechsler, and many others. As were the first two editions, this book is dedicated primarily to my son, Willis, my daughter, Nancy, and my wife, Lucy.

Jay Eungha Ryu and Young Han Chun, doctoral students in the School of Public and International Affairs at the University of Georgia, provided invaluable research assistance for this book. They energetically searched for relevant research and provided notes and reviews on it, advice on how to integrate it into the book, and many additional suggestions and insights. So many were their suggestions and contributions that I could not take advantage of them all and must hold these students blameless for any shortcomings of this book. Another doctoral student, Sergio Fernandez, also provided valuable research assistance and advice. These three people also served as friends and supporters as their often addlepated professor struggled with the challenges that this third edition involved.

The assumptions and arguments made in each edition of this book amount to acknowledgment of the contributions of numerous authors, both those I have cited and those I was unable to draw in due to time and space limitations. These arguments include the assertion that most public organizations are important institutions that provide crucial services. They currently face a measure of public scorn, pressures to perform better with less money, and increasing demands for an elaborate array of functions and services. These pressures are aggravated by misunderstandings, oversimplifications, myths, and outright lies about the nature and performance of public organizations and employees in the United States and many other countries. Public organizations are often highly effective, well-managed entities with hardworking, high-performing employees, yet they face distinctive pressures and constraints in addition to the typical challenges all organizations face, and these constraints can lead to dysfunction and poor performance. The review of insights and concepts about organizations and management provided in this book seeks to support those who strive to maintain and advance the effective management of public organizations. The book thus acknowledges all those who strive with sincerity to provide public, social, or altruistic service.

*July 2003*                                                                              Hal G. Rainey
*Athens, Georgia*

# THE AUTHOR

*Hal G. Rainey* is Alumni Foundation Distinguished Professor in the Department of Public Administration and Policy of the School of Public and International Affairs at the University of Georgia. He has published numerous articles on management in the public sector, with an emphasis on leadership, incentives, organizational change, organizational culture and performance, and the comparison of organization and management in the public, private, and nonprofit sectors.

The first edition of *Understanding and Managing Public Organizations* won the Best Book Award of the Public and Nonprofit Sectors Division of the Academy of Management in 1992. In 1995 Rainey received the Charles H. Levine Award for Excellence in Research, Teaching, and Service, conferred jointly by the American Society for Public Administration and the National Association of Schools of Public Affairs and Administration. He has served as chair of the Public and Nonprofit Sectors Division of the Academy of Management and as chair of the Public Administration Section of the American Political Science Association. He received his B.A. degree (1968) in English from the University of North Carolina at Chapel Hill and his M.A. degree (1973) in psychology and Ph.D. degree (1977) in public administration from the Ohio State University.

In 1991 Rainey served on the Governor's Commission on Effectiveness and Economy in Government of the state of Georgia. As a commissioner, he served on the Task Force on Privatization. In 1995 he served on the Athens–Clarke

County Consolidation Charter Overview Commission of Athens–Clarke County, Georgia. Before entering university teaching and research, Rainey served as an officer in the U.S. Navy and as a VISTA volunteer.

# UNDERSTANDING
# AND MANAGING
# PUBLIC ORGANIZATIONS

# PART ONE

# THE DYNAMIC CONTEXT OF PUBLIC ORGANIZATIONS

CHAPTER ONE

# THE CHALLENGE OF EFFECTIVE PUBLIC ORGANIZATION AND MANAGEMENT

When terrorists crashed jets into the twin towers of the World Trade Center and forced the term *9/11* into the American vocabulary, the attack ignited a drive in the United States and other nations to organize ourselves to repel such atrocities in the future. Within a year, the president proposed and Congress established the new Department of Homeland Security, which involved a vast reorganization of the federal government to bring together twenty-two existing federal agencies and 170,000 employees into this new agency.

The attack also drew attention to the people, the essential component of any organization, who work in public service. Around the nation citizens donned baseball caps and T-shirts bearing the initials of the New York City Fire Department and the New York Police Department. Wearing these caps and shirts, people came together in vigils and ceremonies to commemorate all of the people lost in the attack, but also to pay tribute to the self-sacrificing heroism of the emergency personnel who rushed into the burning buildings at the cost of their lives. Commentators and journalists around the world praised the leadership of the mayor of New York during the crisis.

Intense public discourse swirled around questions about how these terrible events could have been prevented. Journalists and public officials demanded to know whether the terrorists' success exposed weaknesses in the way agencies such as the CIA, the FBI, and the Immigration and Naturalization Service were organized and managed. Congress launched a special investigation into these apparent lapses. An FBI agent received national publicity and testified before Congress after she alleged that a memorandum warning of suspicious activities had not made its way up the hierarchy of the FBI and had not received serious attention at higher levels. Thus, an organizational and managerial problem—inadequate communication and handling of crucial information that needs to move up and through organizational channels—allegedly contributed to the September 11 disaster.

In state and local governments in the United States, and in the governments of other nations, similar inquiries sought to assess how effectively these governments were organized to combat terrorism. One of the great organizational challenges in responding to the threat of terrorism involved how to coordinate disparate and far-ranging organizations.

As Congress, the president, the media, experts, and interest groups deliberated over how to design the new Department of Homeland Security, they debated many questions long familiar to public administration scholars and practitioners. How much authority should the leaders of the new agency have? Should the employees of this agency have employment rights and protections under the civil service rules of the U.S. government? If so, would the agency's leaders be deprived of the flexibility they would need to hire, remove, and transfer employees, and hence impede the performance of the new agency? How should the new agency be structured so as to bring together the necessary activities and coordinate them while at the same time dividing up responsibilities in the appropriate way? The debate over these questions illustrated the issues and values that infuse the processes of organizing and managing in government. These issues include how to ensure the effectiveness of the organization and its accountability within the political system, and how to protect the public interest. These concerns about power and authority and about democratic processes and values translated into specific practical concerns in the organization and management of the new agency. The president asked for flexibility in the hiring, assigning, and discharge of employees of the Department of Homeland Security. This involved relaxing the rules of the federal civil service system that govern such processes and provide civil service employees with various protections. Public employee unions and some members of Congress opposed the loss of these protections for employees of the new agency. The president and others argued that flexibilities would help the leaders and managers of the new agency rapidly place the best people in jobs, motivate them, move them around, and remove them if necessary. The opponents of these flexibilities pointed to the threat of abuses by superiors in the agency and to the need to protect the rights of the employees.

In sum, the response to one of the greatest crises in American history focused on the organization and management of government activities and the people in them (Wise and Nader, 2002). The response thus illustrated a central theme of this book: government organizations and the people in them perform crucial functions, and their effective organization and management are essential to the well-being of the nations and communities they serve. While the September 11 attacks underscore this point in a dramatic and terrible way, the topic has a long history. Governments in the United States and in other nations, and the organizations within those governments, have followed a continuing pattern of organizing, reorganizing, reforming, and striving to improve performance (Kettl, 2002; Light, 1997; Pollitt and Bouckaert, 2000). In the process, they have operated within a context of constitutional provisions, laws, and political authorities and processes that have heavily influenced their organization and management.

# Toward Improved Understanding and Management of Public Organizations

All nations face decisions about the roles of the government and private institutions in their society. September 11 slowed some parts of an antigovernment trend around the world during the last several decades that has influenced decisions about the role of public organizations. This trend has spawned a movement in many countries to curtail government authority and replace it with greater private activity. This skepticism about government implies that there are sharp differences between government and privately managed organizations. During this same period, however, numerous writers have argued that there has been too little sound analysis of such differences. They have contended that the elaborate body of knowledge we have on management and organizations has paid too little attention to the public sector. At the same time, they have said, the large body of scholarship in political science and economics that focuses on government bureaucracy has had too little to say about managing that bureaucracy. This critique has elicited a wave of research and writing on public management and public organization theory by experts and researchers who have been working to provide more careful analyses of organizational and managerial issues in government.

This chapter elaborates on these points to develop another central theme of this book: we face a dilemma in combining our legitimate skepticism about public organizations with the recognition that they play indispensable roles in society. We need to maintain and improve their effectiveness. We can profit by studying major topics from general management and organization theory and by examining the rapidly increasing evidence of their successful application in the public sector. The evidence indicates that the governmental context strongly influences organization and management, often sharply constraining performance. Just as often, however, governmental organizations and managers perform much better than is commonly acknowledged. Examples of effective public management abound. These examples usually reflect the efforts of managers in government who combine managerial skill with effective knowledge of the public sector context. Experts continue to research and debate the nature of this combination, however, as more evidence appears rapidly and in diverse places. This book seeks to base its analysis of management in public organizations on the most careful and current review of this evidence to date.

## Ambivalence Toward Government

The proposal to bestow vast authority and responsibility on the massive new Department of Homeland Security is strikingly ironic given the prevailing opinion about public organizations and their actions during the last several decades. Nations around the world have pursued privatization policies by selling state-owned enterprises to private operators. In the United States, contracting out of government services to the private sector has increased sharply at all levels of government (Savas, 2000). Antigovernment sentiment has swept the United States. Opinion surveys have revealed seething resentment of taxes and the widespread conviction that government operates in wasteful and ineffective ways. Angry criticisms have focused on the government with such intensity that the term *bureaucrat bashing* has come into use. Both Jimmy Carter and Ronald Reagan attacked the federal bureaucracy in their election campaigns. President Carter pressed for deregulation of industry, reduction of federal red tape, and major civil service reforms to combat alleged sloth and inefficiency among federal employees. President Reagan more aggressively impugned government and sought reductions in funding and authority for many federal programs and agencies. When Bill Clinton won the presidency from George Bush, the change suggested some weakening of the antigovernment trend, because Clinton was the more liberal and progovernment of the two candidates. Nevertheless, President Clinton initiated the National Performance Review (NPR), a major review of the operations of the federal government, claiming that the federal government worked poorly and needed a drastic overhaul. In addition to eliciting many presidential directives and congressional actions aimed at achieving such reforms (described in Chapter Fourteen), the NPR cut employment in the federal workforce by about 11 percent, or over 324,000 employees. George W. Bush has led the drive to strengthen the role of government in homeland security and antiterrorism, but at the same time has pushed for privatization of social security. He issued the *President's Management*

*Agenda,* which announced as one of his major priorities increased "competitive sourcing," in which federal agencies would open their functions to competition from private sector providers.

These presidential policies, mirrored by similar ones at other levels of government in the United States and in many other nations, reflect the assumption that government activities differ from those of the private sector and that government performs less effectively and efficiently than private sector organizations. In the United States, these beliefs have served as fundamental principles of the political economy. Many political ideologues and economic theorists have treated them as truisms, and surveys have found that the majority of citizens accept them.

Americans regard government with more ambivalence than hostility, however. Government in the United States, at all levels, stands as one of the great achievements of the nation and as one of the most significant institutions in human history. No major nation operates without a large, influential public sector. Government in the United States accounts for a smaller proportion of the gross national product than do governments in most of the other major nations of the world, including economically successful ones. Taxes in the United States are low by international standards; as a percentage of the gross domestic product, the taxes levied by governments in the United States are among the lowest of the major industrialized nations. The contention that government in the United States is a massively ineffective, expensive, wasteful, overweening institution is not supported by international comparisons. Americans show an implicit recognition of this fact. Some of the same surveys that find waning faith in government also find fundamental support for a strong governmental role (Lipset and Schneider, 1987; Katz, Gutek, Kahn, and Barton, 1975). Even as the antigovernment trend just described has played out, demands for a strong and active government have continued and, as illustrated repeatedly in the chapters to follow, government organizations and employees have often responded by performing very well.

Hirschman (1982) has argued that sentiments for and against government activity wax and wane cyclically in the United States and other countries. It remains to be seen whether September 11 will lead to a fundamental shift in the way Americans regard their government. Certainly they will continue to play out the time-honored paradox of conferring massive funding and responsibility on government agencies and officials even as they castigate and ridicule them (Whorton and Worthley, 1981; Sharkansky, 1989). Thus, the United States will continue to struggle with a complex version of the dilemma faced by all nations. We know that both government and private activities have strengths and weaknesses and that both are crucial. The challenge lies in designing the proper mix and balance of the two and in doing what we can to attain effective management of both (Lindblom, 1977).

# General Management and Public Management

This book proceeds on the argument that a review and explanation of the literature on organizations and their management, integrated with a review of the research on public organizations, supports understanding and improved management of public organizations. As this approach implies, these two bodies of research and thought are related but separate, and their integration poses a major challenge for those interested in public management. The character of these fields and of their separation needs clarification. We can begin that process by noting that scholars in sociology, psychology, and business administration have developed an elaborate body of knowledge in the fields of organizational behavior and organization theory.

## Organizational Behavior, Organization Theory, and Management

The study of organizational behavior had its primary origins in industrial and social psychology. Researchers of organizational behavior typically concentrate on individual and group behaviors in organizations, analyzing motivation, work satisfaction, leadership, work-group dynamics, and the attitudes and behaviors of the members of organizations. Organization theory, conversely, is based more in sociology. It focuses on topics that concern the organization as a whole, such as organizational environments, goals and effectiveness, strategy and decision making, change and innovation, and structure and design. Some writers treat organizational behavior as a subfield of organization theory. The distinction is primarily a matter of specialization among researchers; it is reflected in the relative emphasis each topic receives in specific textbooks (Daft, 2001; Hellriegel, Woodman, and Slocum, 2000) and in divisions of professional associations.

Organization theory and organizational behavior are covered in every reputable, accredited program of business administration, public administration, educational administration, or other form of administration, because they are considered relevant to management. The term *management* is used in widely diverse ways, and the study of this field includes the use of sources outside typical academic research, such as government reports, books on applied management, and observations of practicing managers about their work. While many elements—finance, information systems, inventory, purchasing, production processes, and others—play crucial roles in effective management, this book concentrates on organizational behavior and organization theory. We can further define this concentration as the analysis and practice of such functions as leading, organizing, motivating, planning and strategy making, evaluating effectiveness, and communicating.

A strong tradition, hereafter called the "generic tradition," pervades organization theory, organizational behavior, and general management. As discussed in Chapter Three, most of the major figures, both classical and contemporary, in this field have applied their theories and insights to all types of organizations. They have worked to build a general body of knowledge about organizations and management. Some have pointedly rejected any distinctions between public and private organizations as crude stereotypes. Many current texts on organization theory and management contain applications to public, private, and nonprofit organizations (Daft, 2001).

In addition, management researchers and consultants frequently work with public organizations and use the same concepts and techniques they use with private businesses. They have argued that their theories and frameworks apply to public organizations and managers because management and organization in government, nonprofit, and private business settings face similar challenges and follow generally similar patterns.

## Public Administration, Economics, and Political Science

The generic tradition offers many valuable insights and concepts, as this book illustrates repeatedly. Nevertheless, there is a body of knowledge specific to public organizations and management. We have a huge government, and it entails an immense amount of managerial activity. City managers, for example, have become highly professionalized. We have a huge body of literature and knowledge on public administration. Economists have developed theories of public bureaucracy (Downs, 1967), political scientists have written extensively about it (Hill, 1992; Meier, 2000; Stillman, 1996), and they usually depict the public bureaucracy as quite different from private business. Political scientists concentrate on the political role of public organizations and on the relationships that these organizations have with legislators, courts, chief executives, and interest groups. Economists analyzing the public bureaucracy emphasize the absence of economic markets for its outputs. They have usually concluded that this absence of markets makes public organizations more bureaucratic, inefficient, change-resistant, and susceptible to political influence than private firms (Barton, 1980; Breton and Wintrobe, 1982; Dahl and Lindblom, 1953; Downs, 1967; Niskanen, 1971; Tullock, 1965).

In the 1970s, authors began to point out the divergence between the generic management literature and the literature on the public bureaucracy and to call for better integration of these topics (Allison, 1983; Bozeman, 1987; Hood and Dunsire, 1981; Lynn, 1981, 1996; Meyer, 1979; Perry and Kraemer, 1983; Pitt and Smith, 1981; Rainey, Backoff, and Levine, 1976; Wamsley and Zald, 1973;

Warwick, 1975). These authors noted that organization theory and the organizational behavior literature offer elaborate models and concepts for analyzing organizational structure, change, decisions, strategy, environments, motivation, leadership, and other important topics. In addition, researchers tested these frameworks in empirical research. Because of their generic approach, however, they paid too little attention to the issues raised by political scientists and economists concerning public organizations. For instance, they ignored the internationally significant issue of whether government ownership and economic market exposure make a difference for management and organization.

Critics also faulted the writings in political science and public administration for too much anecdotal description and too little theory and systematic research (Perry and Kraemer, 1983; Pitt and Smith, 1981). Scholars in public administration generally disparaged as inadequate the research and theory in that field (McCurdy and Cleary, 1984; Kraemer and Perry, 1989; White and Adams, 1994). In a national survey of research projects on public management, Garson and Overman (1981, 1982) found relatively little funded research on general public management and concluded that the research that did exist was highly fragmented and diverse.

Neither the political science nor the economics literature on public bureaucracy paid as much attention to internal management—designing the structure of the organization, motivating and leading employees, developing internal communications and teamwork—as did the organization theory and general management literature. From the perspective of organization theory, many of the general observations of political scientists and economists about motivation, structure, and other aspects of the public bureaucracy appeared oversimplified.

## Issues in Education and Research

Concerns about the way we educate people for public management also fueled the debate about the topic. In the wake of the upsurge in government activity during the 1960s, graduate programs in public administration spread among universities around the country. The National Association of Schools of Public Affairs and Administration began to accredit these programs. Among other criteria, this process required master of public administration (M.P.A.) programs to emphasize management skills and technical knowledge rather than provide a modified master's program in political science. This approach implied the importance of identifying how M.P.A. programs compare to master of business administration (M.B.A.) programs in preparing people for management positions. At the same time, it raised the question of how public management differs from business management.

These developments coincided with expressions of concern about the adequacy of our knowledge of public management. In 1979 the U.S. Office of Personnel Management (1980) organized a prestigious conference at the Brookings Institution that featured statements by prominent academics and government officials about the need for research on public management. It sought to address a widespread concern among both practitioners and researchers about "the lack of depth of knowledge in this field" (p. 7). Around the same time, various authors produced a stream of articles and books arguing that public sector management involves relatively distinct issues and approaches. They also complained, however, that too little research and theory and too few case exercises directly addressed the practice of active, effective public management (Allison, 1983; Chase and Reveal, 1983; Lynn, 1981, 1987, 1996). More recently, this concern with building research and theory on public management has developed into something of a movement, as more researchers have converged on the topic. Beginning in 1990, a network of scholars have come together for a series of National Public Management Research Conferences. These conferences have led to the publication of books containing research reported at the conferences (Bozeman, 1993; Brudney, O'Toole, and Rainey, 2000; Frederickson and Johnston, 1999; Kettl and Milward, 1996) and of many professional journal articles. In 2000, the group formed the Public Management Research Association to promote research on the topic. Later chapters of this book cover many of the products of their research.

## Ineffective Public Management?

On a less positive note, recurrent complaints about inadequacies in the practice of public management have also fueled interest in the intellectual version of ambivalence about public organizations and their management that tends to be shown by public and political officials. We generally recognize that large bureaucracies—especially government bureaucracies—have a pervasive influence on our lives (Chackerian and Abcarian, 1984). They often blunder, and they can harm and oppress people, both inside and outside the organizations (Adams and Balfour, 2001; Denhardt, 1999; Hummel, 1994). We face severe challenges in ensuring both the effective operation of these organizations and our control over them through democratic processes. Some analysts contend that our efforts to maintain this balance often create disincentives and constraints that prevent many public administrators from assuming the managerial roles that managers in industry typically play (Warwick, 1975; Lynn, 1981; National Academy of Public Administration, 1986; Ban, 1995; Gore, 1993; Thompson, 1993). Some of these authors argue that too many public managers fail to engage seriously the challenges of motivating their subordinates, effectively designing their organizations and work processes, and otherwise actively managing their responsibilities. Both elected and politically appointed officials face short terms in office, complex laws and rules that constrain the changes they can make, intense external political pressures, and sometimes their own amateurishness. Many concentrate on pressing public policy issues and, at their worst, exhibit political showmanship and pay little attention to the internal management of the agencies and programs under their authority. Middle managers and career civil servants, constrained by central rules, have little authority or incentive to manage.

Experts also complain that too often elected officials charged with overseeing public organizations show too little concern with effectively managing them. Elected officials have little political incentive to attend to "good government" issues such as effective management of agencies. Some have little managerial background, and some tend to interpret managerial issues in ways that would be considered outmoded by management experts. Many legislators and politically elected or appointed executives adhere to an "administrative orthodoxy" (Warwick, 1975; Knott and Miller, 1987). They believe that sound management in government agencies requires a strict hierarchy of accountability, strict accounting and control, elaborate reporting requirements, and tightly specified procedures. This orientation conflicts sharply with contemporary management thought and the practices of many of the most successful business firms.

## The Dilemmas of Improving Public Management

Concerns about ineffective public management have led to a continuing series of efforts to reform and improve it, at all levels of government in the United States and in nations around the world (Kettl, 2002; Osborne and Gaebler, 1992; Pollitt and Bouckaert, 2000). Later chapters describe many of these efforts. Ironically, in view of the complaints about political leaders paying too little attention to management, when they have paid attention it often has not worked or has backfired significantly. The reforms have often taken on a negative, control-oriented character, especially in the United States, where political leaders often justify such reforms by connecting them to public stereotypes and resentments of the government bureaucracy and its bureaucrats. This has in turn raised serious concerns about damage to the public service.

Having attacked the federal bureaucracy in their election campaigns, Presidents Carter and Reagan moved to control and curtail it. Carter administration officials developed the Civil Service Reform Act of 1978 as a management-improvement initiative, and the original objectives of the framers of the initiative were very positive and enlightened (Pfiffner and Brook, 2000). Ultimately, however, the act's provisions emphasized steps to make it easier to discipline and fire federal employees, to base their pay more directly on performance, and to make it easier for politically appointed agency heads to select and transfer the career civil service managers who work under them. Even so, administration officials attracted little political support for a "good government" initiative. They found they could mobilize support most effectively by stressing the difficulty of firing lazy, incompetent civil servants. Newspapers seized on this angle enthusiastically (Kettl, 1989). Later, surveys found that the act had resulted in high levels of insecurity and discouragement among federal managers.

President Reagan attacked federal agencies even more aggressively than President Carter did and worked for cuts in their authority, funding, and staffing. Reagan administration officials sought to increase the president's authority over federal agencies and to squelch resistance to his initiatives from career civil servants. These officials increased the number of political appointees to high levels within federal agencies. In effect, this demoted career civil servants by placing administration loyalists in positions above them (Volcker Commission, 1989). In addition, aggressive funding cutbacks disrupted many agencies (Rubin, 1985). Some agencies floundered when politically appointed executives were indicted for illegal actions.

Experienced observers began to warn of a crisis in the public service and a need for revitalization (Volcker Commission, 1989; Thompson, 1993; Denhardt and Jennings, 1987). Surveys found serious morale problems, with large percentages of career managers reporting that they intended to leave government and that they would advise their own children against a career in federal service. Other surveys found that students showed little interest in public service careers. Paul Volcker, who chaired the Federal Reserve Board during the Carter and Reagan administrations, served as chair of the National Commission on the Public Service (1989), also called the Volcker commission, which brought together a panel of distinguished public servants to direct an analysis of the crisis and recommend remedies. The commission's report recommended steps to improve public support for public service; to improve pay, performance, recruiting, and training; and to improve relations between political appointees and career civil servants.

The concerns about the state of the civil service were heightened by incidents that suggested that the pressures on the public sector and public agencies seriously affected their performance. For example, the explosion of the space shuttle *Challenger* in 1986 was the greatest disaster to befall the American space program up to that point. Analysts blamed the catastrophe in part on political pressures on the National Aeronautics and Space Administration (NASA) that overpowered professional criteria in the agency's decision-making processes (Kettl, 1988, p. 143; Romzek and Dubnick, 1987).

Nevertheless, in many ways the pattern continued. As described earlier, the NPR under the Clinton administration drew on the justification that the federal government needed vast improvements in its management. Vice President Gore (1993), in leading the NPR, expressed positive regard for federal employees and said the federal administrative system, not the people, caused the problems. The NPR included a major cutback in federal employment, however, and by the end of the Clinton administration federal managers were expressing concerns about understaffing in relation to the workload they faced (Light, 2002a; National Council of Social Security Management Associations, 2002).

Not surprisingly, the George W. Bush administration did not have many nice things to say about the Clinton reforms. As further discussed in Chapter Fourteen, the second President Bush was the first president to have a management degree, and early in his administration he indicated an interest in management by issuing the *President's Management Agenda* (U.S. Office of Management and Budget, 2002). In this report, the Bush administration attacked the Clinton administration's elimination of 324,580 employees as a poorly planned, across-the-board cutback in which people were let go without assessing their importance to agency missions. The *Agenda* announced five primary government-wide initiatives: Strategic Management of Human Capital, Competitive Sourcing, Improved Financial Performance, Expanded Electronic Government, and Budget and Performance Integration. The U.S. Office of Management and Budget (2002) then issued "agency scorecards" to twenty-six major federal agencies based on discussions with experts in government and universities. The scorecards used a "traffic light" grading system for each of the five government-wide initiatives. Green meant success, yellow meant mixed results, and red meant unsatisfactory. Of the 130 "traffic lights" awarded to the twenty-six agencies on the five initiatives, only 19 were yellow, 1 was green, and the rest were red.

The trend has played out at other levels of government as well. In 1996, the state of Georgia attracted national attention when Governor Zell Miller led a reform initiative in which newly hired state government employees would not receive civil service job protections that state employees had had for many years (West, 2002). Governor Miller's public calls for reform echoed those of Jimmy Carter at the federal level almost twenty years earlier, emphasizing the need to shake up a stodgy bureaucracy and slothful bureaucrats. Around the same time, Governor Jeb Bush sought similar reforms in Florida using similar justifications.

In all these reform efforts, there were positive features and messages as well as negative ones. The political leaders often emphasized the value of good public servants and the objective of protecting good workers from those who shirked their duties. The leaders of the reform efforts probably harped on bad management to get public attention and support, and to get the attention of public employees, who might resist changes as they are allegedly notorious for doing. All of the efforts nevertheless show the continuing tendency to justify reforms by claiming that public management is in very bad shape.

As suggested earlier, many informed observers worry that this tendency to harp on bad public management can demoralize and damage the public service. In 2002, a second Volcker Commission convened to renew efforts to revitalize the public service. Also, a successful businessman donated a large amount of money to support the formation of the Partnership for Public Service. The Partnership is a nonprofit organization devoted to promoting public service through such steps as improving recruitment for government work. It joined the U.S. Senate Governmental Affairs Committee (U.S. Senate, Committee on Governmental Affairs, 2000, 2001) and the U.S. General Accounting Office (2002a, 2002b) in calling for a response to a "human capital crisis" in the federal government. Using the term *human capital* to emphasize the crucial value of the human beings in an organization, those associated with this movement have pointed out that a huge percentage of the federal workforce will become eligible for retirement in the near future. They have also pointed to surveys of good students in universities that have found that only one out of ten rates the federal government as a good place to work. In addition, rapid changes in information technology and other areas have changed the skills and personnel needed in all types of organizations, and increased competition for people with the necessary skills. All of these challenges, aggravated by the sharp cuts in the federal workforce in the 1990s, appear to be contributing to a crisis in the federal service, according to the members of this movement. Similar challenges face state and local governments (Walters, 2002) and European nations as well (Office of Economic Cooperation and Development, Public Management Committee, 2002).

Significantly, by the middle of 2002, surveys were finding declining morale and work satisfaction among federal managers and employees (Light, 2002a). They also found, as they have for years, that many public managers and employees also criticized the management systems in which they worked, thus underscoring the point that reforms often target problems that public employees themselves complain about. The problems in public service do not arise simply because some political leaders and reformers say unflattering things about the public bureaucracy and public employees. The agonies and ironies of the repeated attempts at reform and improvement reflect ongoing dilemmas in controlling and managing public organizations. Still, the negative turns that many reforms take tend to damage the reforms themselves and the public service they aim to reform. An objective of this book is to assess and disseminate valuable concepts about organizations and management that can support more effective management and more positive and effective management reforms.

## Effective Public Management

For pursuing the objective just mentioned, there is plenty of help available. The sharp criticisms of government and government agencies and employees that predominated public discourse about them in the 1980s and persisted in various ways through the 1990s evoked a counterattack from authors who argued that public bureaucracies perform better than is commonly acknowledged (Doig and Hargrove, 1987; Downs and Larkey, 1986; Goodsell, 1994; Milward and Rainey, 1983; Tierney, 1988). Others described successful governmental innovations and policies (Holzer and Callahan, 1998; Poister, 1988b; Schwartz, 1983). Wamsley and his colleagues (1990) called for increasing recognition that the administrative branches of governments in the United States play as essential and legitimate a role as the other branches of government. Many of these authors pointed to evidence of excellent performance by many government organizations and officials, and to the difficulty of proving that the private sector performs better. Attacks on government agencies often misplace the blame, targeting the public bureaucracy for problems that arise from legislative or interest-group pressures. In addition, government bureaucracy serves as an easy target because of public stereotypes and misunderstanding. For example, years ago a Roper poll asked a representative sample of Americans how much of every $100 spent on the social security program goes to administrative costs. The median estimate was about $50; the actual figure is about $1.30 (Milward and Rainey, 1983). More recently, administrative costs of the Social Security Administration have equaled only 0.8 percent of total benefits paid out to 140 million beneficiaries (Eisner, 1998), so the agency has evidently cut its costs even further, and further eroded the accuracy of negative stereotypes about inefficient public bureaucracy.

In response to this concern, as well as to the concerns about the adequacy of the literature and of our knowledge about effective public management, the literature continued to burgeon in the 1990s and into the new century. As later chapters show, a genre has developed that includes numerous books and articles about effective leadership, management, and organizational practices in government agencies (Ban, 1995; Barzelay, 1992; Behn, 1994; Borins, 1998; Cohen and Eimicke, 1998; Cooper and Wright, 1992; Denhardt, 2000; Doig and Hargrove, 1987; Hargrove and Glidewell, 1990; Holzer and Callahan, 1998; Ingraham, Thompson, and Sanders, 1998; Jones and Thompson, 1999; Light, 1998; Linden, 1994; Osborne and Gaebler, 1992; Popovich, 1998; Rainey and Steinbauer, 1999; Riccucci, 1995; Thompson and Jones, 1994; Wolf, 1993, 1997). In addition, books are appearing that defend the value and performance of government in general (Glazer and Rothenberg, 2001; Light, 2002b; Neiman, 2000; Esman, 2000). It remains to be seen whether the terrible events of September 11 will lead to a change in the general public orientation toward government (Hirschman, 1982). Clearly, however, a movement is under way that asserts that government organizations can and do perform well, and that we need continued inquiry into when they do, and why.

## The Challenge of Sustained Attention and Analysis

The controversies just described reflect fundamental complexities of the American political and economic system. That system has always subjected the administrative branch of government to conflicting pressures over who should control and how, whose interests should be served, and what values should predominate (Waldo, [1947] 1984). Management involves paradoxes that require organizations and managers to balance conflicting objectives and priorities. Public management often involves particularly complex objectives, and especially difficult conflicts among them.

In this debate over the performance of the public bureaucracy and about whether the public sector represents a unique or a generic management context, both sides are correct, in a sense. General management and organizational concepts can have valuable applications in government; however, unique aspects of the government context must often be taken into account. In fact, the examples of effective public management given in later chapters show the need for both. Managers in public agencies can effectively apply generic management procedures, but they must also skillfully negotiate external political pressures and administrative constraints to create a context in which they can manage effectively. The real challenge involves identifying how much we know about this process, and when, where, how, and why it applies. We need researchers, practitioners, officials, and citizens to devote sustained, serious attention to developing our knowledge of and support for effective public management and effective public organizations.

## Organizations: A Definition and a Conceptual Framework

As we move toward a review and analysis of research relevant to public organizations and their management, it becomes useful to clarify the meaning of basic concepts about organizations and to develop a framework to guide the sustained analysis this book will provide. Figure 1.1 presents a framework for this purpose. Figure 1.2 elaborates on some of the basic components of this framework, providing more detail about organizational structures, processes, and people.

Writers on organization theory and management have argued for a long time over how best to define *organization,* and have reached little consensus. It is not a good use of time to worry over a precise definition, so here is a provisional one that employs elements of Figure 1.1. This statement goes on too long to serve as a precise definition; it actually amounts to more of a perspective on organizations:

> An organization is a group of people who work together to pursue a *goal.* They do so by attaining resources from their *environment.* They seek to transform those resources by accomplishing *tasks* and applying *technologies* to achieve effective *performance* of their goals, thereby attaining additional resources. They deal with the many uncertainties and challenges associated with these processes by *organizing* their activities. Organizing involves *leadership* processes, through which leaders guide the development of *strategies* for achieving goals and the establishment of structures and processes to support those strategies. *Structures* are the relatively stable, observable assignments and divisions of responsibility within the organization, achieved through such means as hierarchies of authority, rules and regulations, and specialization of individuals, groups, and subunits. The division of responsibility determined by the organizational structure divides the organization's goals into components on which the different groups and individuals can concentrate—hence the term *orga*nization, referring to the set of organs that make up the whole. This division of responsibility requires that the individual activities and units be coordinated. Structures such as rules and regulations and hierarchies of authority can aid coordination. *Processes* are less physically observable, more dynamic activities that also play a major role in the response to this imperative for coordination. They include such matters as determining power relationships, decision making, evaluation, communication, conflict resolution, and change and innovation. Within these structures and processes, *groups* and *individuals* respond to *incentives* presented to them, making the contributions and producing the products and services that ultimately result in effective performance.

While this perspective on organizations and the framework depicted in the figures seem very general and uncontroversial, they have a number of serious implications that could be debated at length. Mainly, however, they simply set forth the topics that the chapters of this book cover and indicate their importance as components of an effective organization. Management consultants working with all types of organizations claim great value and success for frameworks about as general as this one, as ways of guiding decision makers through important topics

**FIGURE 1.1. A FRAMEWORK FOR ORGANIZATIONAL ANALYSIS.**

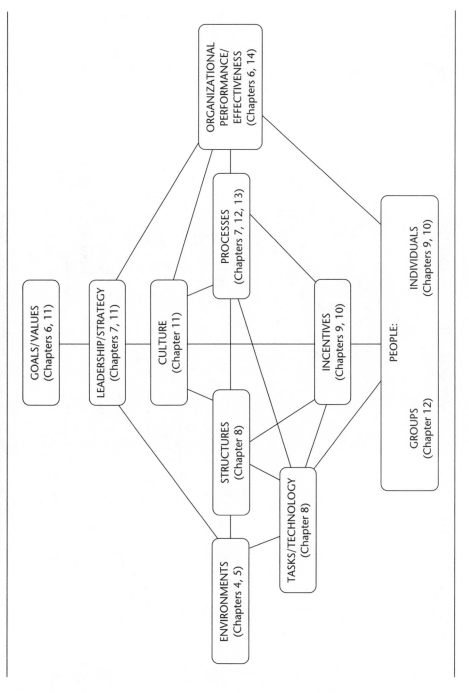

**FIGURE 1.2. A FRAMEWORK FOR ORGANIZATIONAL ANALYSIS (ELABORATION OF FIGURE 1.1).**

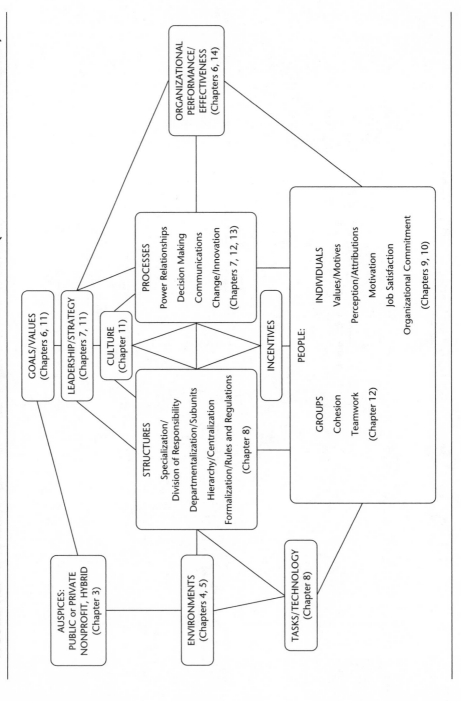

and issues. Leaders, managers, and participants in organizations need to develop a sense of what it means to organize effectively, and a sense of which aspects of an organization they should think about most in trying to improve the organization or organize some part of it or some new undertaking. The framework presented here offers one of many approaches to organizing one's thinking about organizing, and the chapters to come elaborate its components. The final chapter provides an example of applying the framework to organizing for and managing a major trend, the contracting out of public services.

# Summing Up Some Key Points

This chapter has advanced the following points and assumptions for the book.

The terrorist attacks on September 11 and the major emphasis on an organizational response to them illustrate the crucial roles that public organizations play. They also contrast sharply with an antigovernment trend in the public's attitudes and actions in the United States and in many other nations. Many people assume that government organizations cannot perform as effectively or efficiently as private ones. Yet this assumption is not grounded in sound evidence, and it runs against some important themes in organization theory and management.

In the United States, this antigovernment trend involves a measure of ambivalence. Citizens support a strong role for government in many ways and make many demands on government and government agencies. They support the delegation of large amounts of authority and funding to government agencies and officials. These pressures indicate the continuing need to improve the performance of government agencies.

We can improve public management and the performance of public agencies by learning from the literature on organization theory, organizational behavior, and general management and applying it to government agencies and activities. The literature on organizations and management has not paid enough attention to public sector organizations and managers. This book integrates research and thought on the public sector context with the more general organizational and management theories and research.

This integration has important implications for the debates on whether public management is basically ineffective or often excellent, and on how to reform and improve public management and education for people who pursue it. A sustained, careful analysis, drawing on available concepts, theories, and research, and organized around the general framework presented in this chapter, can contribute to advancing our knowledge of these topics.

CHAPTER TWO

# UNDERSTANDING THE STUDY OF ORGANIZATIONS

## A Historical Review

L arge, complex organizations and literature about them have existed for many centuries, but they have proliferated tremendously within the last two centuries. Most of the large body of research and writing available today appeared fairly recently. This chapter reviews major developments in the research, theory, and thinking about organizations and management over the last century. Exhibit 2.1 (at the end of the chapter) provides a summary of the developments reviewed in this chapter.

This book's analysis of public organizations begins with this review for a number of reasons. It illustrates the generic theme mentioned in the previous chapter. It shows that the major contributors to this field have usually treated organizations and management as generally similar in all contexts, not drawing much of a distinction between the public and private sectors. The generic emphasis has much value, and this book draws upon it. It also sets the stage for the controversy over whether public organizations can be treated as a reasonably distinct category. Later chapters show evidence supporting the claim that they are distinctive in important ways.

Managers need to be aware of the historical developments summarized in this chapter. The review covers terms, ideas, and names that serve as part of the vocabulary of management, and well-prepared managers need to develop a sound understanding of them. For example, managers regularly refer to *Theory X* and *Theory Y, span of control,* and other concepts the review covers.

In addition, this historical overview illustrates a central theme in the study and practice of management—the important role of theory and expert opinion. The review provided here shows that the different bodies of theory about how to organize and manage have strongly influenced, and been influenced by, the way managers and organizations behave. Some of the general trends involve profoundly important beliefs about the nature of human motivation and of successful organizations. The review shows that management theory and practice have evolved over the past century. Theories about the motives, values, and capacities of people in organizations have evolved, and this evolution has in turn prompted additional theories about how organizations must look and behave in response to the increasing complexity and rapid change in the contexts in which they operate. Theories and expert opinion have moved away from emphasis on highly bureaucratized organizations with strong chains of command, very specific and unchanging job responsibilities, and strong controls over the people in them, and toward more flexible, "organic" organizations, horizontal communications, and a virtual crescendo of calls for participation, empowerment, teamwork, and other versions of more decentralized, adaptive organizations. The description in Chapter One of presidents and governors calling for more flexibility in managing people in government reflects this general trend in some ways, but it also raises the question of how government organizations can respond to this trend.

The review thus shows that theories are not impractical abstractions but frameworks of ideas that often play a major role in management practice. It illustrates why the framework in Figures 1.1 and 1.2 looks as it does, and it shows that the framework actually reflects many of the major developments in the field over the century.

## The Systems Metaphor

Figures 1.1 and 1.2 and the accompanying definition of organization in Chapter One implicitly reflect one major organizing theme for these developments: how the field has moved from early approaches (now considered "classical" views) that emphasized a single appropriate form of organization and management, toward more recent approaches that reject this "one best way" concept. Recent perspectives emphasize the variety of organizational forms that can be effective under the different contingencies, or conditions, that organizations face.

This trend in organization theory borrows from the literature on general systems theory. This body of theory has developed the idea that there are various types of systems in nature that have much in common. Analyzing these systems, according to systems theorists, provides insights about diverse entities and a common language for specialists in different fields (Daft, 2001, pp. 11–15; Kast and Rosenzweig, 1973, pp. 37–56; Katz and Kahn, 1966, pp. 19–29).

A system is an ongoing process that transforms certain specified *inputs* into *outputs;* these in turn influence subsequent inputs into the system in a way that supports the continuing operation of the process. One can think of an organization as a system that takes in various resources and transforms them in ways that lead to attaining additional supplies of resources (the definition in Chapter One includes this idea). Systems have *subsystems,* such as communications systems or production systems within organizations, and *throughput processes,* which are sets of internal linkages and processes that make up the transformation process. The outputs of the system lead to *feedback,* the influences that the outputs have on subsequent inputs. The systems theorists, then, deserve credit (or blame) for making terms such as *input* and *feedback* part of our everyday jargon. Management analysts have used systems concepts—usually elaborated far beyond the simple description given here—to examine management systems and problems.

A major trend among organizational theorists in the past century has been to distinguish between *closed* systems and *open* or *adaptive* systems. Some systems are closed to their environment; the internal processes remain the same regardless of environmental changes. A thermostat is part of a closed system that transforms inputs, in the form of room temperature, into outputs, in the form of responses from heating or air conditioning units. These outputs feed back into the system by changing the room temperature. The system's processes are stable and machine-like. They respond consistently in a programmed pattern.

One can think of a human being as an open or adaptive system. Humans transform their behaviors to adapt to their environment when there are environmental changes for which the system is not programmed. Thus, the human being's internal processes are open to the environment and able to adapt to shifts in it.

Some organization theorists have expressed skepticism about the usefulness of the systems approach (Meyer, 1979), but others have found it helpful as a metaphor for describing how organization theory has evolved during this century. These theorists say that the earliest, "classical" theories treated organizations and employees as if they were closed systems.

## Classical Approaches to Understanding Organizations

These early theories, and the advice they gave to managers, emphasized stable, clearly defined structures and processes, as if organizational goals were always clear and managers' main challenge was to design the most efficient, repetitive, machinelike procedures to maximize attainment of the organization's goals. Some organization theorists also characterize this view as the "one best way" approach to organization.

## Frederick Taylor and Scientific Management

In a *New Yorker* cartoon published in 1990, a lady has walked into an office where a man is kneeling on top of filing cabinets and reaching down into the drawers of the cabinet and filing papers. The lady says, "According to our time-and-motion studies, you handle your time very well, but a lot of your motion is wasted." The cartoon assumes that at the end of the twentieth century any intelligent person would know the meaning of a time-and-motion study. This technique became well-known because of the scientific management school.

Frederick Taylor (1919) is usually cited as one of the pioneers of managerial analysis. He was the major figure in the scientific management school, which in Taylor's own words involved the systematic analysis of "every little act" in tasks to be performed by workers. Taylor asserted that scientific management involved a division of labor that was relatively new in historical terms. Whereas for centuries work processes had been left to the discretion of skilled craftspeople and artisans, scientific management recognized a division of responsibility between a managerial group and a group that performed the work. The role of management was to gather detailed information on work processes, analyze it, and derive rules and guidelines for the most efficient way to perform the required tasks. Workers were then to be selected and trained in these procedures so they could maximize their output, the quality of their work, and their own earnings.

Taylor and others developed procedures for analyzing and designing tasks that are still in use today. They conducted time-motion studies, which involved the detailed measurement and analysis of physical characteristics of the workplace, such as the placement of tools and machinery in relation to the worker and the movements and time that the worker had to devote to using them. The objective was to achieve the most efficient physical layout for the performance of a specified task. Analytical procedures of this sort are still widely used in government and industry.

Taylor's determination to find the "one best way" to perform a task was such that he even devoted himself to finding the best way to design golf greens and golf clubs. He designed a putter that the golfer stabilized by cradling the club in his or her elbows. The putter proved so accurate that the U.S. Golf Association banned it (Hansen, 1999).

Taylor's emphasis on the efficient programming of tasks and workers provoked controversy even in its heyday. In later years critics attacked his work for its apparent inhumanity and its underestimation of psychological and social influences on worker morale and productivity. Some of this criticism is overdrawn and fails to give Taylor credit for the positive aspects of his pioneering work. Taylor actually felt that his methods would benefit workers by allowing them to increase their earnings and the quality of their work. In his own accounts of his work he said that he originally became interested in ways of encouraging workers without supervisors' having to place pressure on them. As a manager, he had been involved in a very unpleasant dispute with workers, which he attributed to the obligation to put them under pressure (Burrell and Morgan, 1980, p. 126). He wanted to find alternatives to such situations.

Yet Taylor did emphasize pay as the primary reward for work. He stressed minute specialization of worker activities, as if the worker were a rather mindless component of a mechanistic process. He did not improve his image with later organizational analysts when he used as an illustration of his techniques a description of his efforts to train a Scandinavian worker, whom he said was as dumb as an ox, in the most efficient procedures for shoveling pig iron. Though the value of his contribution is undeniable, as a guiding conception of organizational analysis, scientific management severely oversimplified the complexity of the needs of humans in the workplace.

## Max Weber: Bureaucracy as an Ideal Construct

Also in the early decades of the century, Max Weber's writings became influential, in a related but distinct way. Organization theorists often treat Weber as the founder of organizational sociology—the analysis of complex organizations. His investigations of bureaucracy as a social phenomenon provided the most influential early analysis of the topic (Gerth and Mills, 1946).

The proliferation of organizations with authority formally distributed among bureaus or subunits is actually a fairly recent development in human history. Weber undertook to specify the defining characteristics of the bureaucratic form of organization, which he saw as a relatively new and desirable form in society. He saw the spread of such organizations as part of a movement toward more legal and rational forms of authority and away from authority based on tradition (such as monarchical power) or charisma (such as that possessed by a ruler like Napoleon). The bureaucratic form was distinct even from the administrative systems of the ancient Orient (such as in Mandarin China) and from other systems regarded as similar to modern systems. In traditional feudal or aristocratic systems, Weber said, people's functions were assigned by personal trustees or appointees of the ruler. Further, their offices were more like avocations than modern-day jobs; authority was discharged as a matter of privilege and the bestowing of a favor.

The bureaucratic form was distinct in its legalistic specification of the authorities and obligations of office. Weber wrote that the fully developed version of bureaucracy had the following characteristics:

1. Fixed, official jurisdictional areas are established by means of rules. The rules distribute the regular activities required by the organization among these fixed positions or offices, prescribing official duties for each. The rules distribute and fix the authority to discharge the duties, and they also establish specified qualifications required for each office.
2. There is a hierarchy of authority, involving supervision of lower offices by higher ones.
3. Administrative positions in the bureaucracy usually require expert training and the full working capacity of the official.
4. Management of subunits follows relatively stable and exhaustive rules, and knowledge of these rules and procedures is the special expertise of the official.
5. The management position serves as a full-time vocation, or career, for the official.

Weber regarded this bureaucratic form of organization as having technical advantages compared to administrative systems in which the officials regarded their service as an avocation, often gained by birthright or through the favor of a ruler, to be discharged at the official's personal discretion. In Weber's view, the existence of qualified career officials, a structured hierarchy, and clear, rule-based specifications of duties and procedures made for precision, speed, clarity, consistency, and reduction of costs. In addition, the strict delimiting of the duties and authority of career officials and the specification of organizational procedures in rules supported the principle of the objective performance of duties. Duties were performed consistently, and clients were treated without favoritism; the organization was freed from the effect of purely personal motives. With officials placed in positions on the basis of merit rather than birthright or political favoritism, constrained by rules defining their duties, and serving as career experts, bureaucracies represented the most efficient organizational form yet developed, from Weber's perspective.

Weber did express concern that bureaucratic routines could oppress individual freedom (Fry, 1989) and that problems could arise from placing bureaucratic experts in control of major societal functions. Nevertheless, he described bureaucracy as a desirable form of organization, especially for efficiency and the fair and equitable treatment of clients and employees. He thus emphasized a model of organization involving clear and consistent rules, a hierarchy of authority, and role descriptions. For this reason, Weber is often grouped with the other classic figures as a proponent of what would later be characterized as the closed-system view of organizations.

## The Administrative Management School: Principles of Administration

Also in the first half of the century, a number of writers began to develop the first management theories that encompassed a broad range of administrative functions that we now include under the topic of management, and the proper means of discharging those functions. They sought to develop principles of administration to guide managers in such functions as planning, organizing, supervising, controlling, and delegating authority. This group became known as the administrative management school (March and Simon, 1958).

The members of the administrative management school emphatically espoused one proper mode of organizing. They either implied or directly stated that their principles would provide effective organization. The flavor of their work and their principles are illustrated in prominent papers by two of the leading figures in this group, Luther Gulick and James Mooney. In "Notes on the Theory of Organization," Gulick (1937) discussed two fundamental functions of management, the division of work and the coordination of work. Concerning the division of work, he discussed the need to create clearly defined specializations. Specialization, he said, allows the matching of skills to tasks and the clear, consistent delineation of tasks. He noted certain limits on specialization. No job should be so narrowly specialized that it does not take up a full work day, leaving the worker idle. Certain technological conditions, or traditions or customs, may constrain the assignment of tasks; and there are certain tasks, such as licking an envelope, that involve steps so organically interrelated that they cannot be divided.

Once a task has been properly divided, coordinating the work then becomes imperative. On this matter, Gulick proposed principles that were much clearer than his general points about specialization. Work can be coordinated through organization or through a dominant idea or purpose that unites efforts. Coordination through organization should be guided by several principles. First is the *span of control*—the number of subordinates reporting to one supervisor. The span of control should be kept narrow, limited to between six and ten subordinates per supervisor. Effective supervision requires that the supervisor's attention not be divided between too many subordinates. Gulick also proposed the principle of *one master*—each subordinate should have only one superior. There should be no confusion as to who the supervisor is. A third principle is *technical efficiency through the principle of homogeneity*—tasks must be grouped into units on the basis of their homogeneity. Dissimilar tasks should not be grouped together. In addition, a specialized unit must be supervised by a homogeneous specialist. Gulick gave examples of problems resulting from violation of this principle in government agencies: in an agricultural agency, for instance, the supervisor of the pest control division must not be given supervisory responsibility over the agricultural development division.

In the same paper, Gulick sought to define the job of management and administration through what became one of the most widely cited and influential acronyms in general management and public administration: POSDCORB. The letters stand for planning, organizing, staffing, directing, coordinating, reporting, and budgeting. These are the functions, he said, for which principles needed to be developed in subsequent work.

In "The Scalar Principle," Mooney (1930) presented a generally similar picture of the effort to develop principles. He said that an organization must be like a scale, a graded series of steps, in terms of levels of authority and corresponding responsibilities. The principle involved several component principles. The first of these was leadership. Under this principle, Mooney said, a "supreme coordinating authority" at the top must project itself through the entire "scalar chain" to coordinate the entire structure. This was to be accomplished through the principle of delegation, under which higher levels assign authority and responsibility to lower levels. These processes accomplished the third principle of functional definition, under which each person is assigned a specific task.

These two papers reflect the characteristics of the administrative management school. If certain of the principles seem vague, that was typical, as critics would later point out. In addition, these two authors clearly emphasize formal structure in the organization and the hierarchical authority of administrators. While some of the principles are vaguely discussed, some of them are quite clear. Tasks should be highly specialized. Lines of hierarchical authority must be very clear, with clear delegation down from the top and clear accountability and supervisory relations. Span of control should be narrow. There should be unity of command; a subordinate should be directly accountable to one superior. Like Weber and Taylor, these authors tended to emphasize consistency, rationality, and machinelike efficiency. They wrote about organizations as if they could operate most effectively as closed systems, designed according to the one proper form of organization.

The historical contribution of this group is undeniable; the tables of contents of many contemporary management texts reflect the influence of these theorists' early efforts to conceive the role of management and administration. In some highly successful corporations, top executives have made this literature required reading for subordinates (Perrow, 1970b).

Gulick identified very strongly with public administration. He and other members of the administrative management school played important roles in the work of various committees and commissions on reorganizing the federal government, such as the Brownlow Committee in 1937 and the Hoover Commission in 1947. The reforms these groups proposed reflected the views of the administrative management school; they were aimed at such objectives as grouping federal agencies according to similar functions, strengthening the hierarchical authority of the chief executive, and narrowing the executive's span of control.

The immediate influence of these proposals on the structure of the federal government was complicated by political conflicts between the president and Congress (Arnold, 1995). They had a strong influence, however, especially on the development of an orthodox view of how administrative management should be designed in government. Some scholars argue that the influence has continued across the years. They contend that structural developments in public agencies and the attitudes of government officials about such issues still reflect an orthodox administrative management school perspective (Golembiewski, 1962; Knott and Miller, 1987; Warwick, 1975, pp. 69–71). The influence of the administrative management school on these reform efforts can be considered the most significant direct influence on practical events in government that organization theorists have ever had. Nevertheless, critics later attacked the views of the administrative management theorists as too limited for organizational analysis. As described later, researchers began to find that many successful contemporary organizations violate the school's principles drastically and enthusiastically.

Before turning to the reaction against the administrative management perspective, however, we should note the context in which the administrative management theorists as well as the preceding early theorists worked. The administrative management theorists' work was related to the broad progressive reform movement earlier in that century (Knott and Miller, 1987). Those reformers sought to eradicate corruption in government, especially on the part of urban political machines and their leaders. They sought to institute more professional forms of administration through such means as establishing the role of the city manager. In addition, the growth of government over the earlier part of the century had led to a great deal of sprawling disorganization among the agencies and programs of government; there was a need for better organization. In this context, the administrative management theorists' emphasis on basic organizational principles appears not only well justified but absolutely necessary.

It is also important to acknowledge that these early theorists did not advance their ideas as simplemindedly as some later critics depict it. Although Luther Gulick came to be characterized in many organization theory texts as one of the foremost proponents of highly bureaucratized organizations, he wrote a reflection on administrative issues from World War II in which he drew conclusions about the efficiency of democracy. He argued that the democratic system of the United

States actually gave it advantages over the seemingly more authoritarian and hierarchical axis powers. The more democratic process required more participation and cooperation in problem solving and thus led to better planning and implementation of plans than in the authoritarian regimes (Van Riper, 1998). Gulick thus suggested that more democratic processes may look less efficient than more authoritarian ones, even though they can produce more efficient and effective results. It will be evident in later sections that Gulick's thinking thus foreshadowed much of contemporary management theory. (Gulick also played an important role in the development of park and recreational programs, and reportedly suggested to William Naismith that he invent an indoor game to keep young people in condition during cold weather. Naismith then invented basketball.)

Another very original thinker, Mary Parker Follett, wrote very approvingly of the effort to develop administrative principles, and scholars sometimes classify her as a member of this school. She wrote, however, a classic essay on "the giving of orders" (Follett, [1926] 1989) that had very original and forward-looking implications. In the essay, she proposed a cooperative, participative process for giving orders, in which superiors and subordinates develop a shared understanding of the particular situation and what it requires. They then follow the "law" of the situation rather than having a superior impose an order on a subordinate. Follett's perspective both foreshadowed later movements and influenced them in the direction of the kind of participatory and egalitarian management described later. It also foreshadowed contemporary developments in feminist organization theory (Morton and Lindquist, 1997; Guy, 1995; Hult, 1995).

Still, the several contributions covered so far concentrated on a relatively limited portion of the framework for organizational analysis given in Figures 1.1 and 1.2 and the definition of organization in Chapter One. They emphasized the middle and lower parts of the framework, particularly organizational structure. They paid some attention to tasks and to incentives and motivation, but they were quite limited in comparison to the work of later authors. Additional developments would rapidly begin to expand the analysis of organizations, with increasing attention paid to the other components in Figures 1.1 and 1.2.

## Reactions, Critiques, and New Developments

Developments in the emerging field of industrial psychology led to a sharp reaction against Taylor's ideas about scientific management and the principles of the administrative management school. These developments also led to a dramatic change in the way organizational and managerial analysts viewed the people in organizations. Researchers studying behavior and psychology in industry began to develop more insight into psychological factors in work settings. They analyzed the relationships between such factors as fatigue, monotony, and worker productivity. They studied working conditions, analyzing variables such as rest periods, hours of work, methods of payment, routineness of work, and the influence of social groups in the workplace (Burrell and Morgan, 1980, p. 129).

## The Hawthorne Studies: The Discovery of Human Beings in the Workplace

A series of experiments beginning in the mid-1920s at the Hawthorne plant of the Western Electric Company provided a more subtle view of the psychology of the workplace than previous theorists had produced. The Hawthorne studies involved a complex series of experiments and academic and popular reports of their results over a number of years. Controversy continues over the interpretation and value of these studies (Burrell and Morgan, 1980, pp. 120–143); however, most organization theorists describe them as pathbreaking illustrations of the influence of social and psychological factors on work behavior, conditions that often have stronger effects than factors such as pay or the physical conditions of the workplace. An employee's work-group experiences, a sense of the importance of one's work, and attention and concern on the part of supervisors are among a number of important social and psychological influences on workers.

The leaders of the project identified several major experiments and observations as the most significant in the study (Roethlisberger and Dickson, 1939). In one experiment, the researchers lowered the level of illumination in the workplace and found that productivity nevertheless increased, because the workers responded to the attention of the researchers. In another study, they improved the working conditions in a small unit through numerous alterations in rest periods and working hours. Increases in output were at first taken as evidence that the changes were influencing productivity. When the researchers tested that conclusion by withdrawing the improved conditions, however, they found that, rather than falling off, output remained high. In the course of the experiment, the researchers had consulted the workers about their opinions and reactions, questioned them sympathetically, and displayed concern for their physical well-being. Their experiment on the physical conditions of the workplace had actually altered the social situation in the workplace, and that appeared to account for the continued high output.

In observing another work group, the researchers found that it enforced strict norms regarding group members' productivity. To be a socially accepted member of the group, a worker had to avoid being a "rate buster," who turns out too much work; a "chiseler," who turns out too little; or a "squealer," who says something to a supervisor that could be detrimental to another worker. This suggested to the researchers a distinction between the formal organization, as it is officially presented in organization charts and rules, and the informal organization. The informal organization develops through unofficial social processes within the organization, but it can involve norms and standards that are just as forceful influences on the worker as formal requirements.

The Hawthorne studies were widely regarded as the most significant demonstration of the importance of social and psychological factors in the workplace up to that time, and they contributed to a major shift in research on management and organizations. The emphasis on social influences, informal processes, and the motivating power of attention from others and a sense of significance for one's work constituted a major counterpoint against the principles of administrative management and scientific management.

## Chester Barnard and Herbert Simon: The Inducements-Contributions Equilibrium and the Limits of Rationality

A successful business executive turned organization theorist and an academic who would become a Nobel laureate provided additional major contributions that weighed against the administrative management school and moved research in new directions. These contributions added substantially to the attention that organization theorists paid to organizational processes (especially decision making), people, environments, leadership, and goals and values.

Encouraged by the members of the Harvard group who were responsible for the Hawthorne studies and related work (Burrell and Morgan, 1980, p. 148), Chester Barnard wrote *The Functions of the Executive* (1938). It became one of the most influential books in the history of the field.

Barnard's definition of an organization—"a system of consciously coordinated activities or forces of two or more persons" (1938, p. 73)—illustrates the sharp difference between his perspective and that of the classical theorists. Barnard focused on how leaders induce and coordinate the cooperative activities fundamental to an organization. He characterized an organization as an "economy of incentives," in which individuals contribute their participation and effort in exchange for incentives that the organization provides. The executive cadre in an organization must ensure the smooth operation of this economy. The executive must keep the economy in equilibrium by ensuring the availability of the incentives to induce the contributions from members that earn the resources for continuing incentives, and so on. (Notice that the definition of organization in Chapter One speaks of leaders' and organizations' seeking to gain resources from the environment to translate into incentives. This reflects the influence of Barnard's perspective.)

Barnard offered a rich typology of incentives, including not just money and physical and social factors but also power, prestige, fulfillment of ideals and altruistic motives, participation in effective or useful organizations, and many others. (Chapter Nine provides a complete listing of the possible incentives he named.)

Barnard also saw the economy of incentives as being interrelated with other key functions of the executive—specifically, communication and persuasion. The executive must use communication and persuasion to influence workers' subjective valuations of various incentives. The executive can, for example, raise the salience of major organizational values. The persuasion process requires a communication process, and Barnard discussed both at length. He also distinguished between formal and informal organizations, but he saw them as interrelated and necessary to each other's success. He thought of the informal organization as the embodiment of the communication, persuasion, and inducement processes that were essential to the cooperative activity he saw as the essence of organization. Some authors now cite Barnard's ideas on these topics as an early recognition of the importance of organizational culture, a topic that has received a lot of attention in management in recent years (see, for example, Peters and Waterman, 1982).

Barnard's divergence from the classical approaches is obvious. Rather than stating prescriptive principles, he sought to describe the empirical reality of organizations. He treated the role of the executive as central, but he deemphasized formal authority and formal organizational structures, suggesting that those factors are not particularly important to understanding how organizations really operate. Compared to other authors up to that time, Barnard offered a more comprehensive analysis of the organization as an operating system, to be analyzed as such rather than bound by a set of artificial principles. His approach was apparently exhilarating to many researchers, including one of the preeminent social scientists of the century, Herbert Simon.

Simon attacked the administrative management school much more directly than Barnard had. In an article entitled "The Proverbs of Administration" in *Public Administration Review* (1946), he criticized the administrative management school's principles of administration as vague and contradictory. He compared them to proverbs because he saw them as prescriptive platitudes, such as "Look before you leap," that are useless because they are unclear. Often, too, they are countered by a contradictory proverb: "He who hesitates is lost." The principle of specialization, for example, never specified whether one should specialize by function, clientele, or place. Specialization also contradicts the principle of unity of command, which requires that a subordinate report to a superior within his or her specialization. But if a school has an accountant, who is obviously a specialist, that accountant must report to an educator. The two principles conflict.

Similarly, the principle of span of control also conflicts with unity of command. In a large organization, narrow spans of control require many hierarchical levels. There must be many small work units, with a supervisor for each. Then there must be many supervisors above those supervisors to keep the span of control narrow at that level, and so on up. This makes communication up, down, and across the organization very cumbersome, and it makes it difficult to maintain clear, direct hierarchical lines of authority.

Simon called for a more systematic examination of administrative processes to develop concepts and study their relationships. Researchers, he said, should determine when individuals in administrative settings should choose one or the other of the alternatives represented by the principles. As indicated by his critique, such choices are seldom clear. Such limits on the ability of organizational members to perform well and to be completely rational are major determinants of organizational processes and their effects. Simon argued that these limits on rationality and ability must be more carefully analyzed. In sum, he argued for a more empirical and analytical approach to organizational analysis, with decision making as the primary focus.

Hammond (1990) contends that Simon's critique of Gulick and others in the administrative management school overlooked major strengths of that approach. As mentioned earlier, the administrative management school did seek to analyze challenges that managers constantly face, challenges that later researchers have not really found answers for and that have a continuing influence on organizational structures in government. Still, most organization theorists agree that Simon's rejection of the school's principles had the stronger influence on subsequent work in the field and changed its direction.

Simon pursued his ideas further in *Administrative Behavior* (1948). As the title indicates, he emphasized analysis of actual behavior rather than stating formal prescriptions or principles. He drew on Barnard's idea of an equilibrium of inducements and contributions and extended it into a more elaborate discussion of an organization's need to provide sufficient inducements to members, external constituencies, and supporters for it to survive. (The definition and framework in Chapter One also reflect the influence of Simon's perspective.)

Like Barnard, Simon was concerned with the complex process of inducement and persuasion and with abstract incentives such as prestige, power, and altruistic service in addition to material incentives. He emphasized the uncertainties and contradictions posed by the classical principles purporting to guide administrative decisions. He displayed a continuing interest in a fundamental question: Amid such uncertainty and complexity, how are administrative choices and decisions made? The classical principles of administration were based on the assumption that administrators could and would be rational in their choice of the most efficient mode of organization. Much of economic theory assumed the existence of "economic man"—an assumption that firms and individuals are strictly rational in maximizing profits and personal gain. Simon observed that in administrative settings, there are usually uncertainties. "Administrative man" is subject to cognitive limits on rationality. Strictly rational decisions and choices are impossible in complex situations, because information and time for making decisions are limited, and human cognitive capacity is too limited to process all the information and consider all the alternatives. Whereas most economic theory assumed maximizing behavior in decision making, Simon coined a new concept. Rather than maximize, administrators "satisfice." Satisficing involves choosing the best of a limited set of alternatives so as to optimize the decision within the constraints of limited information and time. Thus, an administrator does not make maximally rational decisions, because that is essentially impossible. The administrator makes the best possible decision within the constraints imposed by the available time, resources, and cognitive capacity.

This conception of the decision-making process challenged a fundamental tenet of economic theory. It influenced subsequent research on decision making in business firms, as amplified by *A Behavioral Theory of the Firm* by Richard Cyert and James March (1963; see Exhibit 2.1). It provided a major step toward more recent approaches to organizational decision making, as we will see later. With James March, Simon later published another influential book, *Organizations* (March and Simon, 1958), in which they further elaborated the theory of an equilibrium between inducements and worker contributions. They presented an extensive set of propositions about factors influencing the decision by an employee to join and stay with an organization and, once in it, to produce. Simon's conception of decision making in administrative settings appears to be the foremost reason that he was later awarded the Nobel Prize in economics, however.

## Social Psychology, Group Dynamics, and Human Relationships

Another important development began in the 1930s when Kurt Lewin, a psychological theorist, arrived in the United States as a refugee from Naziism. An immensely energetic intellectual, Lewin become one of the most influential social scientists of the century. He developed *field theory* and *topological psychology*, which sought to explain human actions as functions of both the characteristics of the individual and the conditions impinging on the individual at a given time. This may not sound original now, but it differed from other prominent approaches of the time, such as Freudian psychology, which emphasized unconscious motives and past experiences.

Lewin's emphasis on the field of forces influencing an individual's actions drew on his interest in group behaviors and change processes in groups and individuals (Back, 1972, p. 98). He studied power, communication, influence, and "cohesion" within groups, and he developed a conception of change that has been valuable to analysts of groups and organizational change for years.

Lewin argued that groups and individuals maintain a "quasi-stationary equilibrium" in their attitudes and behaviors. This equilibrium results from a balance between forces pressing for change and those pressing against change. To change people, you must change these forces. Groups exert pressures and influences on the individuals within them. If a person is removed from a group and persuaded to change an attitude but is then returned to the same field of group pressures, the change is unlikely to last. One must alter the total field of group pressures, through a three-phase process. The first phase is "unfreezing," or weakening, the forces against change and strengthening the forces for change. Next, the "changing" phase moves the group to a new equilibrium point. Finally, the "refreezing" phase firmly sets the new equilibrium through such processes as expressions of group consensus.

One of Lewin's better-known experiments in group dynamics illustrates his meaning. Lewin conducted "action research," which involved analysis and sometimes manipulation of ongoing social processes of practical importance, such as race relations and group leadership. During World War II, Lewin sought to aid the war effort by conducting research on methods of encouraging consumption of underutilized foods as a way of conserving resources. He conducted an experiment in which he attempted to convince housewives that they should use more beef hearts in preparing meals. He assembled the housewives in groups and presented them with information favoring the change. They then discussed the matter, aired and resolved their concerns about the change ("unfreezing"), and came to a consensus that they should use more beef hearts. In groups in which the housewives made a public commitment to do so, more of them adopted the new behavior than in groups where the members made no such public commitment. The group commitment is an example of "refreezing," or setting group forces at a new equilibrium point.

As the intellectual leader of a group of social scientists interested in research on group processes, Lewin was instrumental in establishing the Research Center for Group Dynamics at MIT and the first National Training Laboratory, which served for years as a leading center for training in group processes. These activities produced an interesting set of diverse, sometimes opposing influences on later work in the field.

Lewin's efforts were among the first to apply experimental methods (such as using control groups) to the analysis of human behavior. The work of Lewin and his colleagues set in motion the development of experimental social psychology, which led to elaborate experimentation on group processes. Some of the important experiments on groups were relevant to organizational behavior. In another classic experiment conducted by members of this group, Lester Coch and John R. P. French (1948) compared different factory work groups faced with a change in their work procedures. One group participated fully in the decision to make the change, another group had limited participation, and a third group was simply instructed to make the change. The participative groups made the change more readily and more effectively, with the most participative group doing the best. These sorts of projects were instrumental in making *participative decision making*, or PDM, a widely discussed and utilized technique in management theory and practice. Numerous experiments of this sort contributed to the growing literature on industrial psychology and organizational behavior.

Interestingly, Lewin's influence also led to an opposing trend in applied group dynamics. The National Training Laboratory conducted training in group processes for governmental and industrial organizations. After Lewin's death, the group dynamics movement split into two movements. In addition to the researchers who emphasized rigorous experimental research on group concepts, a large group continued to emphasize industrial applications and training in group processes. They tended to reject experimental procedures in favor of learning through experience in group sessions. Their work contributed to the development of the field of organization development (described in Chapter Thirteen). It also led to the widespread use of T-groups, sensitivity sessions, and encounter-group techniques during the 1960s and 1970s (Back, 1972, p. 99). The work of Lewin and his colleagues substantially influenced analysts' conceptions of the components of Figures 1.1 and 1.2, especially those concerned with processes of change and decision making and those concerned with people, especially groups.

## The Human Relations School

The Hawthorne experiments and related work and the research on group dynamics were producing insights about the importance of social and psychological factors in the workplace. They emphasized the potential value of participative management, enhancing employee self-esteem, and improving human relations in organizations. Numerous authors began to emphasize such factors.

The psychologist Abraham Maslow developed a theory of human needs that became one of the most influential theories ever developed by a social scientist. Maslow argued that human needs fall into a set of major categories, arranged in a "hierarchy of prepotency." The needs in the lowest category dominate a person's motives until they are sufficiently fulfilled, and then those in the next-highest category dominate, and so on. The categories, in order of prepotency, were physiological needs, safety needs, love needs, self-esteem needs, and self-actualization needs. The self-actualization category referred to the need for self-fulfillment, for reaching one's potential and becoming all that one is capable of becoming. Thus, once a person fulfills his or her basic physiological needs, such as the need for food, and then fulfills the needs at the higher levels on the hierarchy, he or she ultimately becomes concerned with self-actualization. This idea of making a distinction between lower- and higher-order needs was particularly attractive to writers emphasizing human relations in organizations (for more detail on Maslow's formulation, see Chapter Nine).

Douglas McGregor, for example, published a book whose title foretells its message: *The Human Side of Enterprise* (1960). McGregor had been instrumental in bringing Kurt Lewin to MIT, and the influence of both Lewin and Maslow was apparent in his conceptions of "Theory X" and "Theory Y." He argued that management practices in American industry were dominated by a view of human behavior that he labeled Theory X. This theory held that employees were basically lazy, passive, resistant to change and responsibility, and indifferent to organizational needs. Hence management must take complete responsibility for directing and controlling the organization. Managers must closely direct, control, and motivate employees. McGregor felt that Theory X guided organizational practices in most industrial organizations and was at the heart of classic approaches to management such as scientific management.

Theory Y involved a diametrically different view of employees. Drawing on Maslow's conception of higher-level needs for self-esteem and self-actualization, McGregor defined Theory Y as the view that employees are fully capable of self-direction and self-motivation. Underutilized though this theory was, management based on this approach would be more effective, because individual self-discipline is a more effective form of control than authoritarian direction and supervision. McGregor advocated management approaches that would allow more worker participation and self-control, such as decentralization of authority, management by objectives, and job enlargement.

Theory Y clearly rejected the classical approach to organization; that rejection was emphatic in other major works of the time that placed a similar value on releasing human potential in the workplace. Argyris (1957), for example, argued that there were inherent conflicts between the needs of the mature human personality and the needs of organizations. When management applies the classical principles of administration, healthy individuals will experience frustration, failure, and conflict. Healthy individuals desire relative independence, activeness, and use of their abilities. These motives clash with the classical principles, such as those that call for narrow spans of control, a clear chain of command, unity of direction, and narrow specialization. These principles foster dependence on superiors and organizational rules, promote passiveness due to reduced individual discretion, and limit workers' opportunities to use their abilities. Argyris, too, called for further development of such techniques as participative leadership and job enlargement to counter this problem.

Like the classical theorists before them, the proponents of human relations theories in turn became the targets of scathing criticism. Critics complained that they concentrated too narrowly on one dimension of organizations—the human dimension—and were relatively inattentive to other major dimensions, such as organizational structure, labor union objectives, and environmental pressures. They argued that the human relations types were repeating the mistake of proposing one best way of approaching organizational and managerial analysis, that they always treated interpersonal and psychological factors as the central, crucial issues. Some critics also grumbled about the tendency of these theories to always serve the ends of management, as if the real objective were to get workers to acquiesce in the roles management imposed on them. Even where the motives were pure, some critics asserted, the approach was often naive.

Probably the most damaging critique of the human relations approach was concerned with its lack of empirical support, that is, the lack of evidence that improved human relations would lead to improved organizational performance (Perrow, 1970b). The upsurge in empirical research that occurred in the 1950s and 1960s produced evidence of considerable conflict in some very successful organizations. Research also produced little evidence of a strong relationship between individual job satisfaction and productivity.

Like the criticisms of the classical approaches, these criticisms tended to be overblown and a bit unfair. They often overlooked the historical perspective of the writers, underestimating the significance of what they were trying to do at the time. The insights that these organizational analysts provided remain valuable—and dangerous to ignore. Examples still abound of management practices that cause damage because of inattention to the factors emphasized by the human relations theorists. When improperly implemented, scientific management techniques have created ludicrous situations in which workers slow down or disguise their normal behaviors when management analysts try to observe them.

For example, a consulting firm once tried to implement a management improvement system in a large state agency in Florida. The system involved a detailed analysis of work procedures through a process similar to time-motion methods. The process involved having observers spot-check employees at random intervals to note their activities. If an employee was idle, the observer would record that fact. A university professor went to the office of a midlevel administrator in the agency to discuss a research project. Finding the administrator on the phone, the professor began to back out of his office, in case the administrator wanted privacy for the phone call. The administrator beckoned her back in, explaining that he was not on the phone; he was sitting there trying to think. He was holding the phone to his ear to be sure that the observer would not happen by and record him as being idle. Another administrator was not so careful. After working late into the night on a project and coming in early to complete it, he finally finished and sat back to take a break, without thinking. Too late! The observer happened by and checked his record sheet. Idle!

Another example involved a management trainee in a large manufacturing firm who was assigned to work with the firm's systems engineers on the design of the assembly line. One step in the production process involved having an employee sit and watch two glass water tanks, through which refrigerator compressors would be dragged by a wire. If there was a leak in the compressor, an air bubble would be released, and the employee would remove the compressor as defective. The management trainee expressed disgust at the incompetence of the employees, who were constantly failing at this simple task, where all they had to do was sit and watch two tanks of water for eight hours. As a solution, the systems designers changed the procedure so that an employee would sit directly facing a tank and would have to watch only one tank. The management trainee expressed even more disgust to find that the employees were so stupid that they could not even handle this simple task! Later, representatives from this company contacted a university, looking for consultants to help them deal with the problems of absenteeism and vandalism on the assembly line. As these examples illustrate, even several decades after the human relations material began to appear, there are still plenty of instances of unenlightened management attitudes that could be improved by some reading in the human relations literature.

## Open-Systems Approaches and Contingency Theory

Criticism of the human relations approach, increasing attention to general-systems theory, and new research findings forced a more elaborate view of organizations. Researchers found that organizations successfully adopt different forms under different circumstances or contingencies. Organizational analysts became convinced that different forms of organization can be effective under certain contingencies of tasks and technology, organizational size, environment, and other factors. The effort to specify these contingencies and the organizational forms matched to them made *contingency theory* the dominant approach in organizational analysis in the 1960s and 1970s. The contingency perspective still provides a guiding framework, although researchers have either moved beyond the earlier versions of it or moved in different directions (Daft, 2001, pp. 24–29).

Around the middle of the twentieth century, researchers associated with the Tavistock Institute in Great Britain began conducting research on *sociotechnical systems,* emphasizing the interrelationships between technical factors and social dimensions in the workplace (Burrell and Morgan, 1980, pp. 146–147). For example, Trist and Bamforth (1951) published an analysis of a change in work processes in a coal-mining operation that is now regarded as a classic study. They found that the technical changes in the work process changed the social relationships within the work group. They depicted the organization as a system with interdependent social and technical subsystems that tend to maintain an equilibrium. In response to disturbances, the system moves to a new point of equilibrium, a new ongoing pattern of interrelated social and technical processes. Additional studies by the Tavistock researchers further developed this view that organizations are systems that respond to social, economic, and technological imperatives that have to be satisfied for effective operation of the system—that is, that there are group and individual characteristics, task requirements, and interrelations among them that must be properly accommodated in the design of the organization.

With their consistent emphasis on organizations as ongoing systems seeking to maintain equilibrium in response to disturbances, Tavistock researchers also began to devote attention to the external environments of organizations. In a widely influential article entitled "The Causal Texture of Organizational Environments," Emery and Trist (1965) noted the increasing flux and uncertainty in political, social, economic, and technological settings in which organizations operate and discussed the influence on the internal operations of organizations of the degree of "turbulence" in their environment. Thus, the emphasis moved toward analysis of organizations as open systems facing the need to adapt to environmental variations.

In the United States, the most explicit systems approach to organizational analysis appeared in a very prominent text by Daniel Katz and Robert L. Kahn (1966), *The Social Psychology of Organizations.* They showed how the systems language of inputs, throughputs, outputs, and feedback could be usefully applied to organizations. In analyzing throughput processes, for example, they differentiated various major subsystems, including maintenance subsystems, adaptive subsystems, and managerial subsystems. Scholars regard Katz and Kahn's effort as a classic in the organizational literature (Burrell and Morgan, 1980, p. 158), but it also provides an example of the very general, heuristic nature of the systems approach. Because of its very general concepts, organizational researchers increasingly treated systems theory as a broad framework for organizing information, as a "macroparadigm" (Kast and Rosenzweig, 1973, p. 16), but not as a clearly articulated theory. The metaphor of organizations as open, adaptive systems remained powerful, however, as an expression of the view of organizations as social entities that adapt to a variety of influences and imperatives.

Besides the efforts to apply systems concepts to organizations, research results supported the view that organizations adopt different forms in response to contingencies. (Chapter Eight provides further description of the studies cited in the following paragraphs.) In England, Joan Woodward (1965) conducted a path-breaking study of British industrial firms. She found that the firms fell into three categories on the basis of the production process or "technology" they employed: small-batch or unit production systems were used by such organizations as ship-building and aircraft manufacturing firms, large-batch or mass-production systems were operated by typical mass-manufacturing firms, and continuous production systems were used by petroleum refiners and chemical producers. Most importantly, she concluded that the successful firms within each category showed similar management-structure profiles, but those profiles differed among the three categories. The successful firms within a category were similar on such dimensions as the number of managerial levels, the spans of control, and the ratio of managerial personnel to other personnel, yet they differed on these measures from the successful firms in the other two categories. This indicated that the firms within a category had achieved a successful fit between their structure and the requirements of the particular production process or technology with which they had to deal. The firms appeared to be effectively adapting structure to technology.

Another very influential study, reported by Burns and Stalker (1961) in *The Management of Innovation,* further contributed to the view that effective organizations adapt their structures to contingencies. Burns and Stalker analyzed a set of firms in the electronics industry in Great Britain. The industry was undergoing rapid change, with new products being developed, markets for the products shifting, and new information and technology becoming available. The firms faced considerable flux and uncertainty in their operating environments. Burns and Stalker classified the firms into two categories on the basis of their managerial structures and practices: *organic* and *mechanistic* organizations. Their descriptions of the characteristics of these two groups depict mechanistic organizations as bureaucratic organizations designed along the lines of the classical approaches. The name of the category also has obvious implications: these were organizations designed to operate in machinelike fashion. Burns and Stalker argued that the organic type, so named to underscore the analogy with living, flexible organisms, performed more successfully in the rapidly changing electronics industry. In these organizations there was less emphasis on communicating up and down the chain of command, on the superior controlling subordinates' behavior, and on strict adherence to job descriptions and organizational charts. There was more emphasis on networking and lateral communication, on the supervisor as facilitator, and on flexible and changing work assignments. Such organizations adapted and innovated more effectively under changing and uncertain conditions because they had more flexible structures and emphasized flexibility in communication, supervision, and role definition. The mechanistic form can be more successful under stable environmental and technological conditions, however, where its emphasis on consistency and specificity makes it more efficient than a more loosely structured organization. Thus, Burns and Stalker also emphasized the need for a proper adaptation of the organization to contingencies.

Another important research project heavily emphasized organizations' environment as a determinant of effective structure. Paul Lawrence and Jay Lorsch (1967) studied U.S. firms in three separate industries that confronted varying degrees of uncertainty, complexity, and change. The researchers concluded that the firms successfully operating in uncertain, complex, changing environments had more highly differentiated internal structures. By differentiated structures, they meant that the subunits differed a great deal among themselves, in their goals, time frames, and internal work climates. Yet these highly differentiated firms also had elaborate structures and procedures for integrating the diverse units in the organization. The integrating structures included task forces, liaison officers and committees, and other ways to integrate the diverse units. Successful firms in more stable, certain environments, on the other hand, showed less differentiation and integration. Lawrence and Lorsch concluded that successful firms must have internal structures as complex as the environments in which they operate.

Other researchers continued to develop the general contingency perspective and to analyze specific contingencies. Perrow (1973) published an important analysis of organizational technology. He proposed two basic dimensions for the concepts of technology: the predictability of the task (the number of exceptions and variations encountered) and the analyzability of the problems encountered (the degree to which, when one encounters a new problem or exception, one can follow a clear program for solving it). Routine tasks are more predictable (there are fewer exceptions or variations) and more analyzable (exceptions or variations can be resolved through an established program or procedures). Organizations with routine tasks have more formal, centralized structures. They use more rules, formal procedures, and plans. Organizations with nonroutine tasks, where tasks have more exceptions and are harder to predict and where exceptions are harder to analyze and resolve, must have more flexible structures. They use more formal and informal meetings than rules and plans. (Chapter Eight describes a study confirming these relationships in public organizations.)

At about the same time, James Thompson (1967) published *Organizations in Action*, a very influential book that further developed the contingency perspective. Drawing on Herbert Simon's ideas about bounded rationality and satisficing, Thompson depicted organizations as reflecting their members' striving for rationality and consistency in the face of pressures against those qualities. He advanced numerous propositions about how organizations use hierarchy, structure, units designed to buffer the environment, and other arrangements to try to "isolate the technical core"—that is, to create stable conditions for the units doing the basic work of the organization. Thompson suggested that organizations will try to group subunits on the basis of their technological interdependence—their needs for information and exchange with each other in the work process (see Chapter Eight). Organizations, he proposed, will also adapt their structures to their environment. Where environments are shifting and unstable, organizations will adopt decentralized structures, with few formal rules and procedures, in order to provide flexibility for adapting to the environment (Chapter Four provides further description). One of Thompson's important achievements was to provide a driving logic for contingency and open-systems perspectives by drawing on Simon's ideas. Organizations respond to complexity and uncertainty in their technologies and their environments by adopting more complex and flexible structures. They do so because the greater demands for information processing strain the bounded rationality of managers and the information processing capacity of more formal bureaucratic structures. Clear chains of command and vertical communication up and down them and strict specialization of tasks and strict rules and procedures can be too slow and inflexible in processing complex information and adapting to it.

In the 1990s, probably without realizing it, an executive of one of the major computer corporations in the world expressed this kind of logic. His corporation was suffering operating losses and was losing out in competition with smaller, more innovative firms. The corporation, the executive said, had been taking too long to make decisions and to respond to new conditions. It had too many levels, and innovations required too many reviews and approvals within the hierarchy. The corporation, he said, was trying to decentralize into many smaller, more independent units that could respond to markets and competitors more rapidly. The executive said that the corporation had to push authority down in its organizational structure so that decisions could be made rapidly by the people with the necessary information.

Through the 1960s and 1970s, an upsurge in empirical research on organizations extended and tested the open-systems and contingency-theory approaches and added new contingencies to the set. Many of these studies took place in public and nonprofit organizations. Peter Blau and his colleagues (Blau and Schoenherr, 1971) reported a series of studies—of government agencies, actually—showing relationships between organizational size and structure. These and other studies added size to the standard set of contingencies. Hage and Aiken (1969) reported on a series of studies of social welfare agencies that provided evidence that routineness of tasks, joint programs among organizations, and other factors were related to organizational structure and change. In England, a team of researchers (Pugh, Hickson, and Hinings, 1969) conducted what became known as the Aston studies, a major effort at empirical measurement of organizations, and developed an empirical taxonomy, grouping organizations into types based on the measured characteristics. They interpreted differences in their taxonomic categories as the results of differences in age, size, technology, and external auspices and control. (Chapter Eight discusses important implications of these studies for theories about public organizations.) Child (1972) pointed out that in addition to the other contingencies that contingency theorists emphasized, managers' strategic choices play an important role in adapting organizational structure. These and numerous other efforts had by the mid-1970s established the contingency approach—the argument that organizational structures and processes are shaped by contingencies of technology, size, environment, and strategic choice—as the central school or movement in organization theory. Authors began to translate the contingency observations into prescriptive statements for use in "organizational design" (Galbraith, 1977; Starbuck and Nystrom, 1981; Mintzberg, 1989; Daft, 2001).

Like the other theories covered in this review and in later chapters, contingency theory soon encountered criticisms and controversies. Researchers disputed how the key concepts should be defined and measured. Different studies produced conflicting findings. Some studies found a relation between technology and structure, some did not (Hall, 2002, pp. 87–91). The basic idea that organizations must adapt to conditions they face, through such responses as adopting more flexible structures as they contend with more environmental uncertainty, still serves as a central theme in organization theory (Daft, 2001; Donaldson, 2001; Scott, 2003) and management practice (Peters, 1987).

The developments in organizational research reviewed here have produced an elaborate field with numerous professional journals carrying articles reporting analyses of a wide array of organizational topics. These journals and a profusion of books cover organizational structure, environment, effectiveness, change, conflict, communication, strategy, technology, interorganizational relations, and related variables.

In the last two decades, the field has moved in new directions, many of which represent extensions of contingency and open-systems theories, with increased or redirected emphasis on organizational environments (compare Scott, 2003). Later chapters describe how organization theorists have developed *natural selection* and *population ecology* models for analysis of how certain organizational forms survive and prosper in certain environmental settings while others do not (Aldrich, 1979; Hannan and Freeman, 1989; Hall, 2002; Scott, 2003). Other theorists have analyzed external controls on organizations, with emphasis on organizations' dependence on their environments for crucial resources (Pfeffer and Salancik, 1978).

The research and theory on people and groups in work settings described earlier have similarly led to a proliferation of closely related work, in organizational behavior and organizational psychology, including a similar trend toward elaborate empirical studies and conceptual development during the 1960s and 1970s. Thousands of articles and books have reported work on employee motivation and satisfaction, work involvement, role conflict and ambiguity, organizational identification and commitment, professionalism, leadership behavior and effectiveness, task design, and managerial procedures such as management by objectives and flextime.

As the different fields have progressed, relatively new topics have emerged. In the last decade a major trend toward adopting Total Quality Management programs in industry and government has swept the United States. This wave developed out of writings earlier in the century by some key American authors such as W. Edwards Deming and Joseph Juran that had been embraced by the Japanese but virtually ignored in the United States until recently (note that the historical overview in this chapter has said nothing about these authors). The topic of organizational culture has received a lot of attention and is featured in Figures 1.1 and 1.2. While some important earlier authors such as Barnard and Philip Selznick (see Exhibit 2.1) had devoted attention to related themes, organizational culture surged to prominence in the management literature in the 1980s. Advances in technology, especially computer, information, and communications technology, have presented organizations and managers with dramatic new challenges and opportunities, and researchers have been pressing to develop the theoretical and research grounding needed to understand and manage these developments. The increasing presence in the workforce of women and racial and ethnic groups that were severely underrepresented in the past has given rise to a body of literature focusing on diversity in organizations (Golembiewski, 1995; Ospina, 1996) and feminist organization theory (Hult, 1995). Later chapters give more attention to many of these recent topics.

## The Quiet Controversy over the Distinctiveness of Public Organizations and Management in Organization Theory

The rich field of organization theory provides many valuable concepts and insights on which this book draws. It also raises an important issue for those interested in public organizations and public management: Have the characteristics of public organizations and their members been adequately covered in this voluminous literature? Has it paid sufficient attention to the governmental and political environments of organizations, which seem so important for understanding public organizations? As mentioned in Chapter One and further described in later chapters, there has been a literature on public bureaucracies for many years, but the historical review provided here illustrates the inattention on the part of most of the organization theorists to this literature. In fact, many organization theorists have paid so little attention to a distinction between public and private organizations that any controversy over the matter remains quiet in most major journals on organization theory and outside of public administration journals. Implicitly, many organization theorists convey the message that we need no real debate, because the distinction lacks importance.

The analysts discussed in the preceding historical review have either concentrated on industrial organizations or sought to develop generic concepts and theories that apply across all types of organizations. For example, even though Peter Blau, a prominent organization theorist, published an organizational typology that included a category of "commonweal organizations" very similar to what this book calls public organizations, he published empirical studies that downplayed such distinctiveness of organizational categories (Blau and Scott, 1962). Blau and Schoenherr (1971) examined government agencies for his studies of organizational size, but he drew his conclusions as if they applied to all organizations. So have replications of Blau's study (Beyer and Trice, 1979), even though Argyris (1972, p. 10) suggested that Blau may have found the particular relationship he discovered because he was studying organizations governed by civil service systems. Such organizations might respond to differences in size in different ways than do other organizations, such as business firms. When the contingency theorists analyzed environments, they typically concentrated on environmental uncertainty, especially as a characteristic of business firms' market environments, and showed very little interest in political or governmental dynamics in organizational environments.

Providing a more classical example of this tendency, Weber argued that his conception of bureaucracy applied to government agencies and private businesses alike (Meyer, 1979). Major figures such as James Thompson (1962) and Herbert Simon (Simon, Smithburg, and Thompson, 1950) have stressed the commonalities among organizations and have suggested that public agencies and private firms are more alike than different. The contributions to organization theory and behavior described in this review were aimed at the worthy objective of developing theory that would apply generally to all organizations. With some clear exceptions (Blau and Scott, 1962; Scott, 2003, p. 341–344), the theorists repeatedly implied or aggressively asserted that distinctions such as public and private, market and nonmarket, and governmental and nongovernmental offered little value for developing theory or understanding practice. Herbert Simon continued to offer such observations until the end of his life. He contended that public, private, and nonprofit organizations are essentially identical on the dimension that receives more attention than virtually any other in discussions of the unique aspects of public organizations—the capacities of leaders to reward employees (Simon, 1995, p. 283, n. 3). Simon (1998, p. 11) also bluntly asserted that it is false to claim "that public and nonprofit organizations cannot, and on average do not, operate as efficiently as private businesses" (Simon, 1998, p. 11). So, one of the foremost social scientists of the twentieth century shows little sympathy for the distinction we have to develop in the next chapter.

Even so, research and writing about public bureaucracies had been appearing for many decades when many of these studies were published, and they were related to organizational sociology and psychology in various ways. They developed separately from organizational sociology and psychology, however. Political scientists or economists did the writing on public bureaucracies. They usually emphasized the relationship between the bureaucracy and other elements of the political system. The economists concerned themselves with the effects of the absence of economic markets for the outputs of public bureaucracies (Downs, 1967; Niskanen, 1971). The organizational sociologists and psychologists described in this chapter, while interested in environments, paid relatively little attention to these political and economic market issues. As noted, they worked much more intensively on internal and managerial dimensions—organizational structure, tasks and technology, motivation, and leadership.

Authors interested in the management of public organizations began to point to this gap between the two literatures (Rainey, 1983). As mentioned in Chapter One and described in more detail in Chapter Three, various authors cited in this book mounted a critique of the literature on organization theory, saying that it offered an incomplete analysis of public organizations and the influences of their political and institutional environments (Wamsley and Zald, 1973; Warwick, 1975; Meyer, 1979; Hood and Dunsire, 1981; Pitt and Smith, 1981; Perry and Kraemer, 1983). Yet they also complained that the writings on public bureaucracy were too anecdotal and too discursively descriptive, lacking the systematic empirical and conceptual analyses common in organization theory. Also, the literature on public bureaucracies showed too little concern with internal structures, behavior, and management, topics that had received extensive attention from researchers in organizational sociology and psychology and from general management analysts. Researchers began to provide more explicit organizational analyses of the public bureaucracy, of the sort described in this book. As Chapter One mentioned, recently a profusion of books and articles have provided many additional contributions. But all of this activity has actually dramatized, rather than fully resolved, the question of whether we can clarify the meaning of public organizations and public management and show evidence that such categories have significance for theory and practice. Thus the next chapter turns to the challenge of formulating a definition and drawing distinctions.

## EXHIBIT 2.1. MAJOR DEVELOPMENTS IN ORGANIZATION AND MANAGEMENT THEORY IN THE TWENTIETH CENTURY.

I. *Classic Theories.* Implied a "one best way" to organize and a "closed-system" view of organizations and the people in them.

  A. *Max Weber (Rational-Legal)*
- Provided one of the early influential analyses of bureaucracy. Defined its basic characteristics, such as hierarchies of authority, career service, selection and promotion on merit, and rules and regulations that define procedures and responsibilities of offices.
- Argued that these characteristics grounded bureaucracy in a rational-legal form of authority and made it superior to organizational forms based on traditional authority (such as aristocracy) or charismatic authority. Of these alternatives, bureaucracy provides superior efficiency, effectiveness, and protection of clients' rights.
- Also argued that bureaucracies are subject to problems in external accountability since they are very specialized and expert in their areas of responsibility and may be subject to self-serving and secretive behaviors.

  B. *Frederick Taylor (Scientific Management)*
- Most prominent figure in the Scientific Management movement.
- Advocated the use of systematic analyses, such as "time-motion" studies, to design the most efficient procedures for work tasks (usually consisting of high levels of specialization and task simplification).
- Argued that management must reward workers with fair pay for efficient production so that workers can increase their well-being through productivity. This implies that simplified, specialized tasks and monetary rewards are primary motivators.

  C. *Administrative Management School*
Sought to develop "principles of administration" that would provide guidelines for effective organization in all types of organizations. The principles tended to emphasize specialization and hierarchical control:
- Division of Work. Work must be divided among units based on task requirements, geographic location, or interdependency in the work process.
- Coordination of Work. Work units must be coordinated back together, through other principles:
  *Span of Control.* A supervisor's "span of control" should be limited to five to ten subordinates.
  *One Master.* Each subordinate (and subunit) should report directly to only one superior.
  *Technical Efficiency.* Units should be grouped together for maximum technical efficiency based on work requirements, technological interdependence, or purpose.
- The Scalar Principle. Authority must be distributed in an organization like locations on a scale; as you move higher in the hierarchy, each position must have successively more authority, with ultimate authority at the top.

II. *Redirections, New Directions, and New Insights.* Toward the middle of the century, new authors challenged the previous perspectives and moved the field in new directions.

  A. *Human Relations and Psychological Theories*

    1. *Hawthorne Studies: Motivating Factors*
While studying physical conditions in the workplace, researchers found that weaker lighting in the workplace did not reduce productivity as predicted. They concluded that the attention they paid to the workers during the study increased the workers' sense of importance, the attention they paid to their duties, and their

## EXHIBIT 2.1. MAJOR DEVELOPMENTS IN ORGANIZATION AND MANAGEMENT THEORY IN THE TWENTIETH CENTURY, Cont'd.

communication, and this raised their productivity. Other phases of the research indicated that the work group played an important role in influencing workers to attend to their job and be productive. The studies have come to be regarded as a classic illustration of the importance of social and psychological factors in motivating workers.

2. *Maslow: The Needs Hierarchy*

   Maslow held that human needs and motives fall into a hierarchy, ranging from lower-order to higher-order needs—from physiological needs (food, freedom from extremes of temperature) to needs for safety and security, love and belonging, self-esteem, and finally self-actualization. The needs at each level dominate an individual's motivation and behavior until they are adequately fulfilled, and then the next level of needs will dominate. The highest level, self-actualization, refers to the need to fulfill one's own potential. The theory influenced many other theories, largely due to its emphasis on the motivating potential of higher-order needs.

3. *McGregor: Theories X and Y*

   Drawing on Maslow's theory, McGregor argued that management in industry was guided by "Theory X," which saw workers as passive and without motivation and dictated that management must therefore direct and motivate them. Rejecting the emphasis on specialization, task simplification, and hierarchical authority in the scientific and administrative management movements, McGregor argued that management in industry must adopt new structures and procedures based on "Theory Y," which would take advantage of higher-order motives and workers' capacity for self-motivation and self-direction. These new approaches would include such structures and procedures as job enrichment, management by objectives, participative decision making, and improved performance evaluations.

4. *Lewin: Social Psychology and Group Dynamics*

   Driven out of Europe by Naziism, Kurt Lewin came to the United States and led a group of researchers in studies of group processes. They conducted pathbreaking experiments on the influence of different types of leaders in groups and the influence of groups on groups members' attitudes and behaviors (for example, they documented that a group member is more likely to maintain a commitment if it is made in front of the group).

   This work influenced the development of the field of social psychology and of the group dynamics movement. The group dynamics movement actually developed in two directions. One involved a wave of experimental research on groups in laboratories and organizational settings. For example, a classic study by Coch and French (1948) found that work groups in factories carried out changes more readily if they had participated in the decision to make the change; this study contributed to the growing interest in participative decision making in management. The second direction involved the widespread use of group processes for personal and organizational development, using such methods as encounter groups, "T-groups," and "sensitivity groups."

   Lewin developed ideas about attitude and behavior change, based on "force field analysis" and the concept of "unfreezing, moving, and refreezing" group and individual attitudes and behaviors. These ideas are still used widely in the writing about and practice of organizational development.

## EXHIBIT 2.1. MAJOR DEVELOPMENTS IN ORGANIZATION AND MANAGEMENT THEORY IN THE TWENTIETH CENTURY, Cont'd.

B. *Chester Barnard and Herbert Simon*
  1. *Chester Barnard*
     Barnard's sole book, *The Functions of the Executive* (1938), became one of the most influential management books ever written. Departing from the emphases of the administrative management school, he argued the importance of "informal" organizational structures. An organization is an economy of incentives, in which the executive must obtain resources to use in providing incentives for members to participate and cooperate. The executive must stimulate cooperation and communication and must draw on a complex array of incentives, including not just financial incentives but such rewards as fulfilling mutual values, conferring prestige, affirming the desirability of the group, and others (see Table 9.2).
  2. *Herbert Simon*
     In his 1946 *Public Administration Review* article "Proverbs of Administration," Simon drew on Barnard's insights to attack the administrative management school. He criticized their "principles" as being more like vague proverbs, in some cases too vague to apply and in some cases contradictory. He called for greater analysis of administrative conditions and behaviors to determine when different principles actually apply.

     His book *Administrative Behavior* (1948) pursued these points and called for the scientific study of administrative behavior, with decision making as the central focus. He observed that actual administrative decision making is less rational than many economic theorists had assumed, in that decision makers are less likely to pursue clearly identified and precisely valued goals—with an exhaustive review of alternatives and consistent selection of the path that will maximize goal attainment with minimal expenditure of resources—than such theorists had believed. Instead, administrators' ability to act rationally is often limited by incomplete knowledge and information, limited skills and mental abilities, the inability to predict or antici-pate events, and other factors. Instead, they select the best available alternatives after a limited search, using available rules of thumb. Simon later referred to this as "satisficing."

     Cyert and March, in a study of business firms reported in *A Behavioral Theory of the Firm* (1963), provided evidence supporting Simon's observations. With others, March's later work along these lines would lead to development of the "garbage can model" of decision making, one of the most prominent current perspectives (see Chapter Seven).

     March and Simon's *Organizations* (1958) provided elaborate conceptual frameworks and hypotheses about behavior in organizations, especially about individuals' decisions to join an organization and actively participate in it. Their work influenced the development of empirical research on organizational behavior. Pursuing his interest in decision making, Simon became a leader in research on artificial intelligence, the use of computers to make complex decisions.

     Simon's insights about bounded rationality and satisficing, based on his analysis of administrators' challenges in making decisions under conditions of complexity and uncertainty, influenced the development of open-systems and contingency theory (described later). In part because his ideas challenged basic assumptions in much of economic theory, he won the Nobel Prize for economics in 1978.

## EXHIBIT 2.1. MAJOR DEVELOPMENTS IN ORGANIZATION AND MANAGEMENT THEORY IN THE TWENTIETH CENTURY, Cont'd.

C. *Organizational Sociology and Bureaucratic Dysfunction*

Following in the tradition of Weber, sociologists began studying the characteristics of organizations and bureaucracies.

1. *Merton (1940): Bureaucratic Structures and Member Personalities*

Some of these authors began to observe that the bureaucratic characteristics Weber had regarded as good could actually lead to bad, or dysfunctional, conditions when they interacted with human characteristics, such as personalities. Merton (1940), for example, observed that specialization, elaborate rules, and an emphasis on adhering to the rules can lead to "trained incapacity," in which people have trouble with problems that do not fit within the rules or their specialization. Also, "displacement of goals" can occur, in which people worry so much about adhering to the rules that their behavior conflicts with the goals of the organization. In addition, people in different departments may pursue the goals of their department more than those of the overall organization.

2. *Victor Thompson: Bureaupathology*

Victor Thompson, a public administration scholar, argued that bureaucratic organizations can cause "bureaupathology" in their members, who may become overly concerned with protecting the authority of their office and too impersonal in their relations with clients and other members of the organization.

3. *Selznick: Leadership and Institutionalization*

Many other scholars studied other organizational processes. Selznick, in *TVA and the Grass Roots* (1966), analyzed the ways in which organizations and their leaders develop relationships with external environments, through such processes as "cooptation," or drawing external groups into the decision-making processes of the organization to gain their support. In *Leadership and Administration* (1957), he analyzed the ways in which leaders develop their organizations as "institutions," by influencing the organizational environment, setting major directions for the organization, and supporting these efforts through recruiting, training, and other enhancements of the organization's capacity.

4. *Kaufman: Socialization*

In his study *The Forest Ranger* (1960), Kaufman analyzed the ways in which the U.S. Forest Service developed the commitment of forest rangers and coordinated the activities of its widely dispersed employees through socialization processes that developed shared values and through accepted rules and procedures.

III. *Relatively Recent Developments*

A. *Organizational Behavior and Organizational Psychology*

The analysis of humans in organizations just described has led to the development of an elaborate body of theory and research on topics such as the psychology of individuals in organizations, work motivation, and work-related attitudes such as job satisfaction (Chapter Ten), leadership (Chapter Eleven), and group processes in organizations (Chapter Twelve). The group dynamics movement described earlier has contributed to developing a body of knowledge about organizational development (Chapter Thirteen). These bodies of research, theory, and practice provide an understanding of human behavior and psychology in organizations that far exceeds what the "classic" theories can offer.

B. *Organization Theory and Design*

The stream of sociological research on organizations described here contributed to a burgeoning field of theory and research on large organizations that has taken many directions and covered many topics in recent years.

## EXHIBIT 2.1. MAJOR DEVELOPMENTS IN ORGANIZATION AND MANAGEMENT THEORY IN THE TWENTIETH CENTURY, Cont'd.

1. *Adaptive Systems and Contingency Theory*
   One major development—the adaptive-systems perspective—has supplanted the classic view of organizations as machinelike, closed systems with one proper way of organizing. This perspective regards organizations as being varied in their characteristics because of their needs to adapt to the conditions they face. Contingency theories developed the idea that organizations vary between more bureaucratized, highly structured entities and more flexible, loosely structured entities, depending on such contingencies as the nature of their operating environment, their tasks and technologies, their size, and the strategic decisions made by their leadership. The following are examples of influential adaptive systems and contingency-theory studies and analyses:
   - Burns and Stalker (1961), in their research on firms in Great Britain, found that the managerial and structural characteristics of the most successful firms were different in different industries. In industries where the operating environments (competitors, prices, products, technologies) of the firms were stable and predictable, "mechanistic" organizations with classic bureaucratic structures performed well. In industries where these environments were rapidly changing and complex, more flexible, loosely structured, "organic" organizations performed best.
   - Joan Woodward (1965), in studying firms in Great Britain, found that the most effective firms in particular industries did not have the same structural characteristics as the most effective firms in other industries. Rather than there being one best pattern of organization for all industries, the study indicated that the most effective pattern depended on the requirements raised by technological aspects of the work in each industry.
   - Lawrence and Lorsch (1967), in a study of businesses in the United States, found that the best-performing firms have structures that are as complex as their environment. Firms in environments with low levels of uncertainty (more predictable, less complex) operate well with less complex internal structures. Firms in more uncertain, less predictable, more complex environments have higher levels of differentiation (variation among units) and integration (arrangements for coordinating units, such as task forces or liaison roles).
   - Peter Blau and his colleagues (1971) conducted a series of studies that showed that organizational size has an important relationship to organizational structure.
   - Katz and Kahn (1966) published an influential book analyzing organizations as systems.
   - James Thompson (1967) published a highly influential analysis of organizations that integrated the closed- and open-systems perspectives. Drawing on Simon's observations about the challenges of decision making under conditions of bounded rationality, Thompson observed that "dominant coalitions" in organizations strive to set up closed-system conditions and rational decision-making processes, but that as tasks, technologies, environmental conditions, and strategic decisions produce more complexities and uncertainties, organizations must adapt by adopting more flexible, decentralized structures and procedures.

2. *Extensions to Organization Theory*
   Later discussions describe many extensions to the adaptive-systems perspective, such as new theories about the effects of organizational environments (Chapter Four) and more dynamic or adaptive management processes such as organizational culture and market-type arrangements (Chapter Eleven).

CHAPTER THREE

# WHAT MAKES PUBLIC ORGANIZATIONS DISTINCTIVE

The overview of organization theory in Chapter Two brings us to a fascinating and important controversy. Leading experts on management and organizations have spurned the distinction between public and private organizations as a crude oversimplification or an unimportant issue. Other very knowledgeable people have called for the development of a field that recognizes the distinctive nature of public organizations and public management. Meanwhile, policymakers around the world struggle with decisions involving trillions of dollars worth of assets about the privatization of state activities and the proper roles of the public and private sectors. Figure 1.2 asserts that government organizations' status as public bodies has a major influence on their environment, goals, and values, and hence on their other characteristics. This characterization sides with those who see public organizations and managers as sufficiently distinct to deserve special analysis.

This chapter discusses important theoretical and practical issues that fuel this controversy, and develops some conclusions about the distinction between public and private organizations. First, it examines in depth the problems with this distinction. It then describes the overlapping of the public, private, and nonprofit sectors in the United States, which erodes simple distinctions among them. The discussion then turns to the other side of the debate: the meaning and importance of the distinction. If they are not distinct from other organizations, such as businesses, in any important way, why do public organizations exist? Answers to this question point to the inevitable need for public organizations and to their distinctive attributes. Still, given all the complexities, how can we define public organizations and managers? This chapter discusses some of the confusion over the meaning of *public* and then describes some of the best-developed ways of defining the category and conducting research to clarify it. After analyzing some of the problems that arise in conducting such research, the chapter concludes with a description of the most frequent observations about the nature of public organizations and managers. The remainder of the book examines the research and debate on the accuracy of these observations.

# Public Versus Private: A Dangerous Distinction?

Many authors caution against making oversimplified distinctions between public and private management (Bozeman, 1987; Murray, 1975; Simon, 1995, 1998). Objections to such distinctions deserve careful attention because they provide valuable counterpoints to invidious stereotypes about government organizations and the people who work in them. They also point out realities of the contemporary political economy and raise challenges that we must face when clarifying the distinction.

## The Generic Tradition in Organization Theory

A distinguished intellectual tradition bolsters the generic perspective on organizations—that is, the position that organization and management theorists should emphasize the commonalities among organizations in order to develop knowledge that will be applicable to all organizations, avoiding such popular distinctions as public versus private and profit versus nonprofit. As serious analysis of organizations and management burgeoned early in the twentieth century, leading figures argued that their insights applied across commonly differentiated types of organizations. Many of them pointedly referred to the distinction between public and private organizations as the sort of crude oversimplification that theorists must overcome. From their point of view, such distinctions pose intellectual dangers: they oversimplify, confuse, mislead, and impede sound theory and research.

The historical review of organization theory in the last chapter illustrates how virtually all of the major contributions to the field were conceived to apply broadly across all types of organizations, or in some cases to concentrate on industry. Throughout the evolution described in that review, the distinction between public and private organizations received short shrift.

In some cases, the authors either clearly implied or aggressively asserted that their ideas applied to both public and private organizations. Max Weber claimed that his analysis of bureaucratic organizations applied to both government agencies and business firms. Frederick Taylor applied his scientific management procedures in government arsenals and other public organizations, and such techniques are widely applied in both public and private organizations today. Similarly, members of the administrative management school sought to develop standard principles to govern the administrative structures of all organizations. The emphasis on social and psychological factors in the workplace in the Hawthorne studies, McGregor's Theory Y, and Kurt Lewin's research pervades the organizational development procedures that consultants apply in government agencies today (Golembiewski, 1985).

Herbert Simon (1946) implicitly framed much of his work as being applicable to all organizational settings, both public and private. Beginning as a political scientist, he coauthored one of the leading texts in public administration (Simon, Smithburg, and Thompson, 1950). It contains a sophisticated discussion of the political context of public organizations. It also argues, however, that there are more similarities than differences between public and private organizations. Accordingly, in his other work he concentrated on general analyses of organizations (Simon, 1948; March and Simon, 1958). He thus implied that his insights about satisficing and other organizational processes apply across all types of organizations. In his more recent work shortly before his death, he emphatically asserted that public, private, and nonprofit organizations are equivalent on key dimensions . He said that public, private, and nonprofit organizations are essentially identical on the dimension that receives more attention than virtually any other dimension in discussions of the unique aspects of public organizations—the capacities of leaders to reward employees (Simon, 1995, p. 283, n. 3). He stated that the "common claim that public and nonprofit organizations cannot, and on average do not, operate as efficiently as private businesses" is simply false (Simon, 1998, p. 11). Thus, the leading intellectual figure of organization theory clearly assigned relative unimportance to the distinctiveness of public organizations.

Chapter Two also showed that contingency theory regards the primary contingencies affecting organizational structure and design to be environmental uncertainty and complexity, the variability and complexity of organizational tasks and technologies (the work that the organization does and how it does it), organizational size, and the strategic decisions of managers. Thus, even though this perspective emphasizes variations among organizations, it downplays any particular distinctiveness of public organizations. James Thompson (1962), a leading figure among the contingency theorists, echoed the generic refrain—that public and private organizations have more similarities than differences. During the 1980s, the contingency perspective evolved in many different directions, some involving more attention than others to governmental and economic influences (Scott, 2003). Still, the titles and coverage in management and organization theory journals and in excellent overviews of the field (Daft, 2001; Hall, 2002) reflect the generic tradition.

## Findings from Research

Objections to distinguishing between public and private organizations draw on more than theorists' claims. Studies of variables such as size, task, and technology in government agencies show that these variables may influence public organizations more than anything related to their status as a governmental entity. These findings agree with the commonsense observation that an organization becomes bureaucratic not because it is in government or business but because of its large size.

Major studies that analyzed many different organizations to develop taxonomies and typologies have produced little evidence of a strict division between public and private organizations. Some of the prominent efforts to develop a taxonomy of organizations based on empirical measures of organizational characteristics have failed to show any value in drawing a distinction between public and private or have produced inconclusive results. Haas, Hall, and Johnson (1966) measured characteristics of a large sample of organizations and used statistical techniques to categorize them according to the characteristics they shared. A number of the resulting categories included both public and private organizations.

This finding is not surprising, because organizations' tasks and functions can have much more influence on their characteristics than their status as public or private. A government-owned hospital, for example, obviously resembles a private hospital more than it resembles a government-owned utility. Consultants and researchers frequently find in both the public and the private sectors organizations with highly motivated employees as well as severely troubled organizations. They often find that factors such as leadership practices influence employee motivation and job satisfaction more than whether the employing organization is public, private, or nonprofit.

Pugh, Hickson, and Hinings (1969) classified fifty-eight organizations into categories based on their structural characteristics; they had predicted that the government organizations would show more bureaucratic features, such as more rules and procedures, but they found no such differences. They did find, however, that the government organizations showed higher degrees of control by external authorities, especially over personnel procedures. The study included only eight government organizations, all local government units with functions similar to those of business organizations (for example, a vehicle repair unit and a water utility). Consequently, the researchers interpreted as inconclusive their findings regarding whether government agencies differ from private organizations in terms of their structural characteristics. Studies such as these have consistently found the public-private distinction inadequate for a general typology or taxonomy of organizations (McKelvey, 1982).

## The Blurring of the Sectors

Those who object to the claim that public organizations make up a distinct category also point out that the public and private sectors overlap and interrelate in a number of ways, and that this blurring and entwining of the sectors has advanced even farther in recent years (Cooper, 2003, p. 11; Haque, 2001; Kettl, 1993, 2002; Moe, 2001; Weisbrod, 1997, 1998).

*Mixed, Intermediate, and Hybrid Forms.* A number of important government organizations are designed to resemble business firms. A diverse array of state-owned enterprises, government corporations, government-sponsored corporations, and public authorities perform crucial functions in the United States and other countries (Seidman, 1983; Musolf and Seidman, 1980; Walsh, 1978). Usually owned and operated by government, they typically perform business-type functions and generate their own revenues through sales of their products or by other means. Such enterprises usually receive a special charter to operate more independently than government agencies. Examples include the U.S. Postal Service, the Resolution Trust Corporation, the National Parks Service, port authorities in many coastal cities, and a multitude of other organizations at all levels of government. Such organizations are sometimes the subjects of controversy over whether they operate in a sufficiently businesslike fashion while showing sufficient public accountability. The magnitude of the resources involved in these hybrid arrangements is striking. In 1996, the U.S. comptroller general voiced concern over the results of audits by the General Accounting Office (GAO) of federal loan and insurance programs. These programs provide student loans, farm loans, deposit insurance for banks, flood and crop insurance, and home mortgages. The programs are carried out by government-sponsored enterprises such as the Federal National Mortgage Association ("Fannie Mae"). The comptroller general said that the GAO audits indicated that cutbacks in federal funding and personnel have left the government with insufficient financial accounting systems and personnel to monitor these liabilities properly. The federal liabilities for these programs total $7.3 trillion. Since the comptroller general made his assessment, experts have continued to point to accountability issues that these organizations pose, because they tend to have relative independence from political and regulatory controls and can use their resources to gain and even extend their independence (Koppel, 2001; Moe, 2001).

On the other side of the coin are the many nonprofit, or third-sector, organizations that perform functions similar to those of government organizations. Like government agencies, many nonprofits obviously have no profit indicators or incentives and often pursue social or public service missions, often under contract with the government (Weisbrod, 1997). To further complicate the picture, however, experts on nonprofit organizations observe a trend toward "commercialization" of nonprofits, by which they try to make money in businesslike ways that may jeopardize their public service missions (Weisbrod, 1998). Finally, many private, for-profit organizations work with government in ways that blur the distinction between them. Some corporations, such as defense contractors, receive so much funding and direction from government that some analysts equate them with government bureaus (Weidenbaum, 1969; Bozeman, 1987).

***Functional Analogies: Doing the Same Things.***  Obviously, many people and organizations in the public and private sectors perform virtually the same functions. General managers, secretaries, computer programmers, auditors, personnel officers, maintenance workers, and many other specialists perform similar tasks in public, private, and hybrid organizations. Organizations located in the different sectors—for example, hospitals, schools, and electric utilities—also perform the same general functions. The New Public Management movement that has spread through many nations in recent decades has taken various forms but has often emphasized the use in government of procedures similar to those purportedly used in business and private market activities, on the basis of the assumption that government and business organizations are sufficiently similar to make it possible to use similar techniques in both settings (Barzelay, 2001; Ferlie, Pettigrew, Ashburner, and Fitzgerald, 1996; Kettl, 2002).

***Complex Interrelations.***  Government, business, and nonprofit organizations interrelate in a number of ways (Kettl, 1993, 2002; Weisbrod, 1997). Governments buy many products and services from nongovernmental organizations. Through contracts, grants, vouchers, subsidies, and franchises, governments arrange for the delivery of health care, sanitation services, research services, and numerous other services by private organizations. These entangled relations muddle the question of where government and the private sector begin and end. Banks process loans provided by the Veterans Administration and receive social security deposits by wire for social security recipients. Private corporations handle portions of the administration of Medicare by means of government contracts, and private physicians render most Medicare services. Private nonprofit corporations and religious organizations operate facilities for the elderly or for delinquent youths using funds provided through government contracts and operate under extensive government regulation. In thousands of examples of this sort, private businesses and nonprofit organizations become part of the service delivery process for government programs and further blur the public-private distinction. Chapters Four, Five, and Fourteen provide more detail on these situations and their implications for organizations and management (Moe, 1996, 2001; Provan and Milward, 1995).

***Analogies from Social Roles and Contexts.*** Government uses laws, regulations, and fiscal policies to influence private organizations. Environmental protection regulations, tax laws, monetary policies, and equal employment opportunity regulations either impose direct requirements on private organizations or establish inducements and incentives to get them to act in certain ways. Here again nongovernmental organizations share in the implementation of public policies. They become part of government and an extension of it. Even working independently of government, business organizations affect the quality of life in the nation and the public interest. Members of the most profit-oriented firms argue that their organizations serve their communities and the well-being of the nation as much as governmental organizations do. As noted earlier, however, observers worry that excessive commercialization is making too many nonprofits too much like business firms. According to some critics, government agencies also sometimes behave too much like private organizations. One of the foremost contemporary criticisms of government concerns the influence that interest groups wield over public agencies and programs. According to the critics, these groups use the agencies to serve their own interests rather than the public interest.

## The Importance of Avoiding Oversimplification

Theory, research, and the realities of the contemporary political economy show the inadequacy of simple notions about differences between public and private organizations. For management theory and research, this realization poses the challenge of determining what role a distinction between public and private can play. For practical management and public policy, it means that we must avoid oversimplifying the issue and jumping to conclusions about sharp distinctions between public and private.

That advice may sound obvious enough, but violations of it abound. During the intense debate about the Department of Homeland Security at the time of this writing, a *Wall Street Journal* editorial warned that the federal bureaucracy would be a major obstacle to effective homeland security policies. The editorial repeated the simplistic stereotypes about federal agencies that have prevailed for years. The author claimed that federal agencies steadfastly resist change and aggrandize themselves by adding more and more employees. The editorial advanced these claims even at a time when the Bush administration's *President's Management Agenda* pointed out that the Clinton administration had reduced federal employment by over 324,000 positions and criticized the way the reductions were carried out. Surveys also have shown that public managers and business managers often hold inaccurate stereotypes about each other (Stevens, Wartick, and Bagby, 1988; Weiss, 1983). For example, the increase in privatization and contracting out has led to more and more controversy over whether privatization proponents have made oversimplified claims about the benefits of privatization, with proponents claiming great successes (Savas, 2000) and skeptics raising doubts (Donahue, 1990; Hodge, 2000; Kuttner, 1997; Sclar, 2000).

For all the reasons just discussed, clear demarcations between the public and private sectors are impossible, and oversimplified distinctions between public and private organizations are misleading. We still face a paradox, however, because scholars and officials make the distinction repeatedly in relation to important issues, and public and private organizations do differ in some obvious ways.

## Public Organizations: An Essential Distinction

If there is no real difference between public and private organizations, can we nationalize all industrial firms, or privatize all government agencies? Private executives earn massively higher pay than their government counterparts. The financial press regularly lambastes corporate executive compensation practices as absurd, and claims that these compensation policies squander many billions of dollars. Can we simply put these business executives on the federal executive compensation schedule and save a lot of money for these corporations and their customers? Such questions make it clear that there are some important differences in the administration of public and private organizations. Scholars have provided useful insights into the distinction in recent years, and researchers and managers have reported more evidence of the distinctive features of public organizations.

### The Purpose of Public Organizations

Why do public organizations exist? We can draw answers to this question from both political and economic theory. Even some economists who strongly favor free markets regard government agencies as inevitable components of free-market economies (Downs, 1967).

***Politics and Markets.*** Decades ago, Robert Dahl and Charles Lindblom (1953) provided a useful analysis of the raison d'être for public organizations. They analyzed the alternatives available to nations for controlling their political economies. Two of the fundamental alternatives are political hierarchies and economic markets. In advanced industrial democracies, the political process involves a complex array of contending groups and institutions that produces a complex, hydra-headed hierarchy, which Dahl and Lindblom called a *polyarchy.* Such a politically established hierarchy can direct economic activities. Alternatively, the price system in free economic markets can control economic production and allocation decisions. All nations use some mixture of markets and polyarchies.

Political hierarchy, or polyarchy, draws on political authority, which can serve as a very useful, inexpensive means of social control. It is cheaper to have people relatively willingly stop at red lights than to work out a system of compensating them for doing so. However, political authority can be "all thumbs" (Lindblom, 1977). Central plans and directives often prove confining, clumsy, ineffective, poorly adapted to many local circumstances, and cumbersome to change.

Markets have the advantage of operating through voluntary exchanges. Producers must induce consumers to engage willingly in exchanges with them. They have the incentive to produce what consumers want, as efficiently as possible. This allows much freedom and flexibility, provides incentives for efficient use of resources, steers production in the direction of consumer demands, and avoids the problems of central planning and rule making inherent in a polyarchy. Markets, however, have a limited capacity to handle types of problems for which government action is required (Lindblom, 1977; Downs, 1967). Such problems include the following:

- *Public goods and free riders.* Certain services, once provided, benefit everyone. Individuals have the incentive to act as free riders and let others pay, so government imposes taxes to pay for such services. National defense is the most frequently cited example. Similarly, even though private organizations could provide educational and police services, government provides most of them because they entail general benefits for the entire society.

- *Individual incompetence.* People often lack sufficient education or information to make wise individual choices in some areas, so government regulates these activities. For example, most people would not be able to determine the safety of particular medicines, so the Food and Drug Administration regulates the distribution of pharmaceuticals.

- *Externalities or spillovers.* Some costs may spill over onto people who are not parties to a market exchange. A manufacturer polluting the air imposes costs on others that the price of the product does not cover. The Environmental Protection Agency regulates environmental externalities of this sort.

Government acts to correct problems that markets themselves create or are unable to address—monopolies, the need for income redistribution, and instability due to market fluctuations—and to provide crucial services that are too risky or expensive for private competitors to provide. Critics also complain that market systems produce too many frivolous and trivial products, foster crassness and greed, confer too much power on corporations and their executives, and allow extensive bungling and corruption. Public concern over such matters bolsters support for a strong and active government (Lipset and Schneider, 1987). Conservative economists argue that markets eventually resolve many of these problems and that government interventions simply make matters worse. Advocates of privatization claim that government does not have to perform many of the functions it does and that government provides many services that private organizations can provide more efficiently. Nevertheless, American citizens broadly support government action in relation to many of these problems.

***Political Rationales for Government.***   A purely economic rationale ignores the many political and social justifications for government. In theory, government in the United States and many other nations exists to maintain systems of law, justice, and social organization; to maintain individual rights and freedoms; to provide national security and stability; to promote general prosperity; and to provide direction for the nation and its communities. In reality, government often simply does what influential political groups demand. In spite of the blurring of the distinction between the public and private sectors, government organizations in the United States and many other nations remain restricted to certain functions. For the most part, they provide services that are not exchanged on economic markets but are justified on the basis of general social values, the public interest, and the politically imposed demands of groups.

Moore (1995, p. 54) has suggested that public managers strive to create "public value" in the form of services whose benefits to specific clients outweigh the costs of production while at the same time assuring citizens and their representatives that something of value has been created. Bozeman (2002a) proposes a concept of "public value failure" as a supplement to the concept of market failure. He argues that market failure concepts have tended to concentrate on market efficiency and utilitarianism, while public value failure concentrates instead on failures of the public and private sectors to fulfill core public values. Bozeman suggests a number of instances in which this can occur. For example, mechanisms for articulating and aggregating values fail when core public values are skirted because of flaws in policymaking processes. For example, if public opinion strongly favor⁻ gun control but no such policies are enacted, the disjunction between public opinion and policy outcomes fails to maximize public values about democratic representation. In another example, the public and private sectors may produce a situation involving threats to human dignity and subsistence, such as an international market for internal human organs leading impoverished individuals to sell their internal organs merely to survive. Interesting and important, the concepts of public value and public value failure further illustrate the relatively abstract nature of the rationales for government and its organizations, and in turn become significant aspects of the context for understanding and managing government organizations.

## The Meaning and Nature of Public Organizations and Public Management

While the idea of a public domain within society is an ancient one, beliefs about what is appropriately public and what is private, in both personal affairs and social organization, have varied among societies and over time. The word *public* comes from the Latin for "people," and dictionaries define it as pertaining to the people of a community, nation, or state (Guralnick, 1980). The word *private* comes from the Latin word that means to be deprived of public office or set apart from government as a personal matter. In contemporary definitions, the distinction between public and private often involves three major factors (Benn and Gaus, 1983): *interests* affected (whether benefits or losses are communal or restricted to individuals); *access* to facilities, resources, or information; and *agency* (whether a person or organization acts as an individual or for the community as a whole). These dimensions can be independent of one another and even contradictory. For example, a military base may purportedly operate in the public interest, acting as an agent for the nation, but deny public access to its facilities.

***Approaches to Defining Public Organizations and Public Managers.*** The multiple dimensions along which the concepts of public and private vary make for many ways to define public organizations, most of which prove inadequate. For example, one time-honored approach defines public organizations as those that have a great impact on the public interest (Dewey, 1927). Decisions about whether government should regulate have turned on judgments about the public interest (Mitnick, 1980). In a prominent typology of organizations, Blau and Scott (1962) distinguished between *commonweal* organizations, which benefit the public in general, and *business* organizations, which benefit their owners. The public interest, however, has proved notoriously hard to define and measure (Mitnick, 1980). Some definitions directly conflict with others; for example, defining the public interest as what a philosopher king or benevolent dictator decides versus what the majority of people prefer. Most organizations, including business firms, affect the public interest in some sense. Manufacturers of computers, pharmaceuticals, automobiles, and many other products clearly have tremendous influence on the well-being of the nation.

Alternatively, researchers and managers often refer to auspices or ownership, an implicit use of the agency factor mentioned earlier. Public organizations are governmental organizations, and private organizations are nongovernmental, usually business firms. Researchers using this simple dichotomy have kept the debate going by producing impressive research results (Mascarenhas, 1989). The blurring of the boundaries between the sectors, however, shows that we need further analysis of what this dichotomy means.

***Agencies and Enterprises as Points on a Continuum.***  Observations about the blurring of the sectors are hardly original. Half a century ago, in their analysis of markets and polyarchies, Dahl and Lindblom (1953) described a complex continuum of types of organizations, ranging from *enterprises* (organizations controlled primarily by markets) to *agencies* (public or government-owned organizations). For enterprises, they argued, the pricing system automatically links revenues to products and services sold. This creates stronger incentives for cost reduction in enterprises than in agencies. Agencies, conversely, have more trouble integrating cost reduction into their goals and coordinating spending and revenue-raising decisions, because legislatures assign their tasks and funds separately. Their funding allocations usually depend on past levels, and if they achieve improvements in efficiency, their appropriations are likely to be cut. Agencies also pursue more intangible, diverse objectives, making their efficiency harder to measure. The difficulty in specifying and measuring objectives causes officials to try to control agencies through enforcement of rigid procedures rather than through evaluations of products and services. Agencies also have more problems related to hierarchical control, such as red tape, buck passing, rigidity, and timidity, than do enterprises.

More important than these assertions in Dahl and Lindblom's oversimplified comparison of agencies and enterprises is their conception of a continuum of various forms of agencies and enterprises, ranging from the most public of organizations to the most private (see Figure 3.1). Dahl and Lindblom did not explain how their assertions about the different characteristics of agencies and enterprises apply to organizations on different points of the continuum. Implicitly, however, they suggested that agency characteristics apply less and less as one moves away from that extreme, and the characteristics of enterprises become more and more applicable.

***Ownership and Funding.***  Wamsley and Zald (1973) pointed out that an organization's place along the public-private continuum depends on at least two major elements, ownership and funding. Organizations can be owned by the government

# FIGURE 3.1. AGENCIES, ENTERPRISES, AND HYBRID ORGANIZATIONS.

The continuum between government ownership and private enterprise. Below the line are arrangements colloquially referred to as public, government-owned, or nationalized. Above the line are organizational forms usually referred to as private enterprise or free enterprise. On the line are arrangements popularly considered neither public nor private.

| | Private nonprofit organizations totally reliant on government contracts and grants (Atomic Energy Commission, Manpower Development Research Corporation). | Private corporations reliant on government contracts for most revenues (some defense contractors, such as General Dynamics, Grumman). | Heavily regulated private firms (heavily regulated privately owned utilities). | Private corporations with significant funding from government contracts but majority of revenues from private sources. | Private corporations subject to general government regulations such as affirmative action, Occupational Safety and Health Administration regulations. | Private Enterprise |
|---|---|---|---|---|---|---|
| | | | Government ownership of part of a private corporation | | | |
| Government Agency | State-owned enterprise or public corporation (Postal Service, TVA, Port Authority of NY). | Government-sponsored enterprise, established by government but with shares traded on stock market (Federal National Mortgage Association). | | Government program or agency operated largely through purchases from private vendors or producers (Medicare, public housing). | | |

Source: Adapted and revised from Dahl and Lindblom, 1953.

or privately owned. They can receive most of their funding from government sources, such as budget allocations from legislative bodies, or they can receive most of it from private sources, such as donations or sales within economic markets. Putting these two dichotomies together results in the four categories illustrated in Figure 3.2: publicly owned and funded organizations, such as most government agencies; publicly owned but privately funded organizations, such as the U.S. Postal Service and government-owned utilities; privately owned but governmentally funded organizations, such as certain defense firms funded primarily through government contracts; and privately owned and funded organizations, such as supermarket chains and IBM.

This scheme does have limitations; it makes no mention of regulation, for example. Many corporations, such as IBM, receive funding from government contracts but operate so autonomously that they clearly belong in the private category. Nevertheless, the approach provides a fairly clear way of identifying core categories of public and private organizations.

***Economic Authority, Public Authority, and "Publicness."*** Bozeman (1987) draws on a number of the preceding points to try to conceive the complex variations across the public-private continuum. All organizations have some degree of political influence and are subject to some level of external governmental control.

## FIGURE 3.2. PUBLIC AND PRIVATE OWNERSHIP AND FUNDING.

|  | Public Ownership | Private Ownership |
|---|---|---|
| Public Funding (taxes, government contracts) | Department of Defense<br>Social Security<br>Administration<br>Police departments | Defense contractors<br>Rand Corporation<br>Manpower Development<br>Research Corporation<br>Oak Ridge National<br>Laboratories |
| Private Funding (sales, private donations) | U.S. Postal Service<br>Government-owned<br>utilities<br>Federal Home Loan<br>Bank Board | General Motors[a]<br>IBM<br>General Electric<br>Grocery store chains<br>YMCA |

[a]These large corporations have large government contracts and sales, but attain most of their revenues from private sales and have relative autonomy to withdraw from dealing with government.

*Source:* Adapted and revised from Wamsley and Zald, 1973.

Hence, they all have some level of "publicness," although that level varies widely. Like Wamsley and Zald, Bozeman uses two subdimensions—political authority and economic authority—but treats them as continua rather than dichotomies. Economic authority increases as owners and managers gain more control over the use of their organization's revenues and assets, and decreases as external government authorities gain more control over their finances.

Political authority is granted by other elements of the political system, such as the citizenry or governmental institutions. It enables the organization to act on behalf of those elements and to make binding decisions for them. Private firms have relatively little of this authority. They operate on their own behalf and only for as long as they support themselves through voluntary exchanges with citizens. Government agencies have high levels of authority to act for the community or country, and citizens are compelled to support their activities through taxes and other requirements.

The publicness of an organization depends on the combination of these two dimensions. Figure 3.3 illustrates Bozeman's depiction of possible combinations. As in previous approaches, the owner-managed private firm occupies one extreme (high on economic authority, low on political authority), and the traditional government bureau occupies the other (low on economic authority, high on political authority). A more complex array of organizations represents various combinations of the two dimensions. Bozeman and his colleagues have used this approach to design research on public, private, and intermediate forms of research and development laboratories and other organizations. Later chapters describe the important differences they found between the public and private categories, with the intermediate forms falling in between (Bozeman and Loveless, 1987; Crow and Bozeman, 1987; Emmert and Crow, 1988; Coursey and Rainey, 1990). Also employing a concept of publicness, Antonsen and Jorgensen (1997) compared sets of Danish government agencies high on criteria of publicness, such as the number of reasons their executives gave for being part of the public sector (as opposed to being in the public sector as a matter of tradition or for economies of scale). The agencies high on publicness showed a number of differences from those low on this measure, such as higher levels of goal complexity and of external oversight.

Even these more complex efforts to clarify the public-private dimension do not capture its full complexity. Government and political processes influence organizations in many ways, through laws, regulations, grants, contracts, charters, franchises, direct ownership (with many variations in oversight), and numerous other ways (Salamon and Elliot, 2002). Private market influences also involve many variations. Perry and Rainey (1988) suggest that future research can continue to compare organizations in different categories, such as those in Table 3.1.

### FIGURE 3.3. "PUBLICNESS": POLITICAL AND ECONOMIC AUTHORITY.

Economic
Authority

    Private firm
    managed by owner

           Closely held
           private firm,
           professionally
           managed

                    Corporation with                Government-
                    shares traded                   industry
                    publicly on stock             research
                    market                       cooperative

                          Corporation         Research
                          heavily reliant      university
                          on government
                          contracts

                Private               Government-
                nonprofit             sponsored
                organization        enterprise

        Professional                     Government
        association                     corporation
                                or government
  Small                                 organization
  voluntary                           funded through
  association                         user fees

                                            Government
                                          agency
                                        (funded from
                                        taxes)

                                                  Political
                                                  Authority

*Source:* Adapted from Bozeman, 1987.

# TABLE 3.1. TYPOLOGY OF ORGANIZATIONS CREATED BY CROSS-CLASSIFYING OWNERSHIP, FUNDING, AND MODE OF SOCIAL CONTROL.

| | Ownership | Funding | Mode of Social Control | Representative Study | Example |
|---|---|---|---|---|---|
| Bureau | Public | Public | Polyarchy | Meier (2000) | Bureau of Labor Statistics |
| Government corporation | Public | Private | Polyarchy | Walsh (1978) | Pension Benefit Guaranty Corporation |
| Government-sponsored enterprise | Private | Public | Polyarchy | Musolf and Seidman (1980) | Corporation for Public Broadcasting |
| Regulated enterprise | Private | Private | Polyarchy | Mitnick (1980) | Private electric utilities |
| Government enterprise | Public | Public | Market | Barzelay (1992) | Government printing office that must sell services to government agencies |
| State-owned enterprise | Public | Private | Market | Aharoni (1986) | Airbus |
| Government contractor | Private | Public | Market | Bozeman (1987) | Grumann |
| Private enterprise | Private | Private | Market | Williamson (1975) | IBM |

*Source:* Adapted and revised from Perry and Rainey, 1988.

Although this topic needs further refinement, these analyses of the public-private dimension of organizations clarify important points. Simply stating that the public and private sectors are not distinct does little good. The challenge involves conceiving and analyzing the differences, variations, and similarities. In starting to do so, we can think with reasonable clarity about a distinction between public and private organizations, although we must always realize the complications. We can think of assertions about public organizations that apply primarily to organizations owned and funded by government, such as typical government agencies. At least by definition, they differ from privately owned firms, which get most of their resources from private sources and are not subject to extensive government regulations. We can then seek evidence comparing these two groups, and in fact such research often shows differences, although we need much more evidence. The population of hybrid and third-sector organizations raises complications about whether and how differences between these core public and private categories apply to those hybrid categories. Yet we have increasing evidence that organizations in this intermediate group—even within the same function or industry—differ in important ways on the basis of how public or private they are. Designing and evaluating this evidence, however, involve some further complications.

## Problems and Approaches in Public-Private Comparisons

Defining a distinction between public and private organizations does not prove that important differences between them actually exist. We need to consider the supposed differences and the evidence for or against them. First, however, some intriguing challenges in research on public management and public-private comparisons need to be considered, because they figure importantly in sizing up the evidence.

The discussion of the generic approach to organizational analysis and contingency theory introduced some of these challenges. Many factors, such as size, task or function, and industry characteristics, can influence an organization more than its status as a governmental entity. Research needs to show that these alternative factors do not confuse analysis of differences between public organizations and other types. Obviously, for example, if you compare large public agencies to small private firms and find the agencies more bureaucratic, size may be the real explanation. Also, one would not compare a set of public hospitals to private utilities as a way of assessing the nature of public organizations. Ideally, an analysis of the public-private dimension requires a convincing sample, with a good model that accounts for other variables besides the public-private dimension. Ideally, studies would also have huge, well-designed samples of organizations and employees, representing many functions and controlling for many variables. Such studies require a lot of resources and have been virtually nonexistent with the exception of one recent example (which found differences among public, nonprofit, and private organizations, as described in Chapter Eight; see Kalleberg, Knoke, Marsden, and Spaeth, 1996; Kalleberg, Knoke, and Marsden, 2001). Instead, researchers and practitioners have adopted a variety of less comprehensive approaches.

Some writers theorize on the basis of assumptions, previous literature and research, and their own experiences (Dahl and Lindblom, 1953; Downs, 1967; Wilson, 1989). Similarly, but less systematically, some books about public bureaucracies simply provide a list of the differences between public and private, based on the authors' knowledge and experience (Gawthorp, 1969; Mainzer, 1973). Other researchers conduct research projects that measure or observe public bureaucracies and draw conclusions about their differences from private organizations. Some concentrate on one agency (Warwick, 1975), some on many agencies (Meyer, 1979). Although valuable, these studies examine no private organizations directly.

Many executives and managers who have served in both public agencies and private business firms make emphatic statements about the sharp differences between the two settings (Blumenthal, 1983; Hunt, 1999; Rumsfeld, 1983; IBM Endowment for the Business of Government, 2002; Weiss, 1983). Quite convincing as testimonials, they apply primarily to the executive and managerial levels. Differences might fade at lower levels. Other researchers compare sets of public and private organizations or managers. Some compare the managers in small sets of government and business organizations (Buchanan, 1974, 1975; Kurland and Egan, 1999; Rainey, 1979, 1983; Porter and Lawler, 1968). Questions remain about how well the small samples represent the full populations and how well they account for important factors such as tasks. More recent studies with larger samples of organizations still leave questions about representing the full populations. They add more convincing evidence of distinctive aspects of public management (Hickson and others, 1986; Kalleberg, Knoke, Marsden, and Spaeth, 1996; Kalleberg, Knoke, and Marsden, 2001; Pandey and Kingsley, 2000) or provide refinements to our understanding of the distinction without finding sharp differences between public and private managers on their focal variables (Moon and Bretschneider, 2002).

To analyze public versus private delivery of a particular service, many researchers compare public and private organizations within functional categories. They compare hospitals (Savas, 2000, p. 190), utilities (Atkinson and Halversen, 1986), schools (Chubb and Moe, 1988), airlines (Backkx, Carney, and Gedajlovic, 2002), and other types of organizations. Similarly, other studies compare a function, such as management of computers or the innovativeness of information technology in government and business organizations (Bretschneider, 1990; Moon and Bretschneider, 2002). Still others compare state-owned enterprises to private firms (Hickson and others, 1986; Mascarenhas, 1989; MacAvoy and McIssac, 1989). They find differences and show that the public-private distinction appears meaningful even when the same general types of organizations operate under both auspices.

Studies of one functional type, however, may not apply to other functional types. The public-private distinction apparently has some different implications in one industry or market environment, such as hospitals, compared to another industry or market, such as refuse collection (Hodge, 2000). Yet another complication is that public and private organizations within a functional category may not actually do the same thing or operate in the same way (Kelman, 1985). For example, private and public hospitals may serve different patients, and public and private electric utilities may have different funding patterns.

In some cases, organizational researchers studying other topics have used a public-private distinction in the process and have found that it makes a difference (Chubb and Moe, 1988; Hickson and others, 1986; Kalleberg, Knoke, Marsden, and Spaeth, 1996; Kurke and Aldrich, 1983; Mintzberg, 1972; Tolbert, 1985). These researchers have no particular concern with the success or failure of the distinction per se; they simply find it meaningful.

A few studies compare public and private samples from census data, large-scale social surveys, or national studies (Brewer and Selden, 1998; Houston, 2000; Kalleberg, Knoke, Marsden, and Spaeth, 1996; Light, 2002a; Smith and Nock, 1980; U.S. Office of Personnel Management, 2000). These have great value, but such aggregated findings often prove difficult to relate to the characteristics of specific organizations and the people in them. In the absence of huge, conclusive studies, we have to piece together evidence from more limited analyses such as these. Many issues remain debatable, but we can learn a great deal from doing so.

## Common Assertions About Public Organizations and Public Management

In spite of the difficulties, the stream of assertions and research findings continues. During the 1970s and 1980s, various reviews compiled the most frequent arguments and evidence about the distinction between public and private (Fottler, 1981; Meyer, 1982; Rainey, Backoff, and Levine, 1976). There has been a good deal of progress in research, but the basic points of contention have not changed substantially. Exhibit 3.1 shows a recent summary and introduces many of the issues that later chapters examine. The table and the discussion of it that follows pull together theoretical statements, expert observations, and research findings. Except for those mentioned, it omits many controversies about the accuracy of the statements (these are considered in later chapters). Still, it presents a reasonable depiction of prevailing issues and views about the nature of public organizations and management that amounts to a theory of public organizations.

Unlike private organizations, most public organizations do not sell their outputs in economic markets. Hence, the information and incentives provided by

## EXHIBIT 3.1. DISTINCTIVE CHARACTERISTICS OF PUBLIC MANAGEMENT AND PUBLIC ORGANIZATIONS: A SUMMARY OF COMMON ASSERTIONS AND RESEARCH FINDINGS.

### I. Environmental Factors

I.1. Absence of economic markets for outputs; reliance on governmental appropriations for financial resources.

I.1.a. Less incentive to achieve cost reduction, operating efficiency, and effective performance.

I.1.b. Lower efficiency in allocating resources (weaker reflection of consumer preferences, less proportioning of supply to demand).

I.1.c. Less availability of relatively clear market indicators and information (prices, profits, market share) for use in managerial decisions.

I.2. Presence of particularly elaborate and intensive formal legal constraints as a result of oversight by legislative branch, executive branch hierarchy and oversight agencies, and courts.

I.2.a. More constraints on domains of operation and on procedures (less autonomy for managers in making such choices).

I.2.b. Greater tendency for proliferation of formal administrative controls.

I.2.c. Larger number of external sources of formal authority and influence, with greater fragmentation among them.

I.3. Presence of more intensive external political influences.

I.3.a. Greater diversity and intensity of external informal political influences on decisions (political bargaining and lobbying; public opinion; interest-group, client, and constituent pressures).

I.3.b. Greater need for political support from client groups, constituencies, and formal authorities in order to obtain appropriations and authorization for actions.

### II. Organization-Environment Transactions

II.1. Public organizations and managers are often involved in production of public goods or handling of significant externalities. Outputs are not readily transferable to economic markets at a market price.

II.2. Government activities are often coercive, monopolistic, or unavoidable. Government has unique sanctioning and coercion power and is often the sole provider. Participation in consumption and financing of activities is often mandatory.

II.3. Government activities often have a broader impact and greater symbolic significance. There is a broader scope of concern, such as for general public interest criteria.

II.4. There is greater public scrutiny of public managers.

II.5. There are unique expectations for fairness, responsiveness, honesty, openness, and accountability.

### III. Organizational Roles, Structures, and Processes

The following distinctive characteristics of organizational roles, structures, and processes have been frequently asserted to result from the distinctions cited under I and II. More recently, distinctions of this nature have been analyzed in research with varying results.

III.1. Greater goal ambiguity, multiplicity, and conflict.

III.1.a. Greater vagueness, intangibility, or difficulty in measuring goals and performance criteria; the goals are more debatable and value-laden (for example, defense readiness, public safety, a clean environment, better living standards for the poor and unemployed).

III.1.b. Greater multiplicity of goals and criteria (efficiency, public accountability and openness, political responsiveness, fairness and due process, social equity and distributional criteria, moral correctness of behavior).

III.1.c. Greater tendency of the goals to be conflicting, to involve more trade-offs (efficiency versus openness to public scrutiny, efficiency versus due process and social equity, conflicting demands of diverse constituencies and political authorities).

III.2. Distinctive features of general managerial roles

III.2.a. Recent studies have found that public managers' general roles involve many of the same functions and role categories as those of managers in other settings but with some distinctive features: a more political, expository role, involving more meetings with and interventions by external interest groups and political authorities; more crisis management and "fire drills"; greater challenge to balance external political relations with internal management functions.

## EXHIBIT 3.1. DISTINCTIVE CHARACTERISTICS OF PUBLIC MANAGEMENT AND PUBLIC ORGANIZATIONS: A SUMMARY OF COMMON ASSERTIONS AND RESEARCH FINDINGS, Cont'd.

III.3. Administrative authority and leadership practices.

    III.3.a. Public managers have less decision-making autonomy and flexibility because of elaborate institutional constraints and external political influences. There are more external interventions, interruptions, constraints.

    III.3.b. Public managers have weaker authority over subordinates and lower levels as a result of institutional constraints (for example, civil service personnel systems, purchasing and procurement systems) and external political alliances of subunits and subordinates (with interest groups, legislators).

    III.3.c. Higher-level public managers show greater reluctance to delegate authority and a tendency to establish more levels of review and approval and to make greater use of formal regulations to control lower levels.

    III.3.d. More frequent turnover of top leaders due to elections and political appointments causes more difficulty in implementing plans and innovations.

    III.3.e. Recent counterpoint studies describe entrepreneurial behaviors and managerial excellence by public managers.

III.4. Organizational structure.

    III.4.a. Numerous assertions that public organizations are subject to more red tape, more elaborate bureaucratic structures.

    III.4.b. Empirical studies report mixed results, some supporting the assertions about red tape, some not supporting them. Numerous studies find some structural distinctions for public forms of organizations, although not necessarily more bureaucratic structuring.

III.5. Strategic decision-making processes.

    III.5.a. Recent studies show that strategic decision-making processes in public organizations can be generally similar to those in other settings but are more likely to be subject to interventions, interruptions, and greater involvement of external authorities and interest groups.

III.6. Incentives and incentive structures.

    III.6.a. Numerous studies show that public managers and employees perceive greater administrative constraints on the administration of extrinsic incentives such as pay, promotion, and disciplinary action than do their counterparts in private organizations.

    III.6.b. Recent studies indicate that public managers and employees perceive weaker relations between performance and extrinsic rewards such as pay, promotion, and job security. The studies indicate that there may be some compensating effect of service and other intrinsic incentives for public employees and show no clear relationship between employee performance and perceived differences in the relationship between rewards and performance.

III.7. Individual characteristics, work-related attitudes and behaviors.

    III.7.a. A number of studies have found different work-related values on the part of public managers and employees, such as lower valuation of monetary incentives and higher levels of public service motivation.

    III.7.b. Numerous highly diverse studies have found lower levels of work satisfaction and organizational commitment among public than among private managers and employees. The level of satisfaction among public sector samples is generally high but tends consistently to be somewhat lower than that among private comparison groups.

III.8. Organizational and individual performance.

    III.8.a. There are numerous assertions that public organizations and employees are cautious and not innovative. The evidence for this is mixed.

    III.8.b. Numerous studies indicate that public forms of various types of organizations tend to be less efficient in providing services than their private counterparts, although results tend to be mixed for hospitals and utilities. (Public utilities have been found to be efficient somewhat more often.) Yet other authors strongly defend the efficiency and general performance of public organizations, citing various forms of evidence.

*Source:* Adapted from Rainey, Backoff, and Levine, 1976, and Rainey, 1989.

economic markets are weaker in or absent from them. Some scholars theorize (as many citizens believe) that this reduces incentives for cost reduction, operating efficiency, and effective performance. In the absence of markets, other governmental institutions (courts, legislatures, the executive branch) use legal and formal constraints to impose greater external governmental control of procedures, spheres of operations, and strategic objectives. Interest groups, the media, public opinion, and informal bargaining and pressure by governmental authorities exert an array of less formal, more political influences. These differences arise from the distinct nature of transactions with the external environment. Government is more monopolistic, coercive, and unavoidable than the private sector, with a greater breadth of impact, and it requires more constraint. Therefore, government organizations operate under greater public scrutiny and are subject to unique public expectations for fairness, openness, accountability, and honesty.

Internal structures and processes in government organizations reflect these influences, according to the typical analysis. Also, characteristics unique to the public sector—the absence of the market, the production of goods and services not readily valued at a market price, and value-laden expectations for accountability, fairness, openness, and honesty as well as performance—complicate the goals and evaluation criteria of public organizations. Goals and performance criteria are more diverse, they conflict more often (and entail more difficult trade-offs), and they are more intangible and harder to measure. The external controls of government, combined with the vague and multiple objectives of public organizations, generate more elaborate internal rules and reporting requirements. They cause more rigid hierarchical arrangements, including highly structured and centralized rules for personnel procedures, budgeting, and procurement.

Greater constraints and diffuse objectives allow managers less decision-making autonomy and flexibility than their private counterparts have. Subordinates and subunits may have external political alliances and merit-system protections that give them relative autonomy from higher levels. Striving for control because of the political pressures on them but lacking clear performance measures, executives in public organizations avoid delegation of authority and impose more levels of review and more formal regulations.

Some observers contend that these conditions, aggravated by rapid turnover of political executives, push top executives toward a more external, political role with less attention to internal management. Middle managers and rank-and-file employees respond to the constraints and pressures with caution and rigidity. Critics and managers alike complain about weak incentive structures in government, lament the absence of flexibility in bestowing financial rewards, and point to other problems with governmental personnel systems. Complaints about difficulty in firing, disciplining, and financially rewarding employees generated major civil service reforms in the late 1970s at the federal level and in states around the country and have continued ever since. As noted in Chapter One, this issue of the need for flexibility to escape such constraints became the most important point of contention in the debate over the new Department of Homeland Security in 2002.

In turn, expert observers assert, and some research indicates, that public employees' personality traits, values, needs, and work-related attitudes differ from those of private sector employees. Some research finds that public employees place lower value on financial incentives, show somewhat lower levels of satisfaction with certain aspects of their work, and differ in some other work attitudes from their private sector counterparts. Along these lines, as Chapter Ten describes, a growing body of research on public service motivation over the last decade suggests special patterns of motivation in public and nonprofit organizations that can produce levels of motivation and effort comparable to or higher than those among private sector employees (Perry, 1996, 2000; Houston, 2000; Francois, 2000).

Intriguingly, the comparative performance of public and nonpublic organizations and employees figures as the most significant issue of all and the most difficult one to resolve. It also generates the most controversy. As noted earlier, the general view has been that government organizations operate less efficiently and effectively than private organizations because of the constraints and characteristics mentioned previously. Many studies have compared public and private delivery of the same services, mostly finding the private form more efficient. Efficiency studies beg many questions, however, and a number of authors defend government performance strongly. They cite client satisfaction surveys, evidence of poor performance by private organizations, and many other forms of evidence to argue that government performs much better than generally supposed. As Chapters Six and Fourteen elaborate, in recent years numerous authors have claimed that public and nonprofit organizations frequently perform very well and very innovatively, and offer evidence or observations about when and why they do.

This countertrend in research and thinking about public organizations actually creates a divergence in the theory about them. One orientation treats government agencies as inherently dysfunctional and inferior to business firms, and another perspective emphasizes the capacity of public and nonprofit organizations to perform well and innovate successfully. Both perspectives tend to agree on propositions and observations about many characteristics of public and nonprofit organizations, such as the political influences on public agencies.

This discussion and Exhibit 3.2 provide a summary characterization of the prevailing view of public organizations that one would attain from an overview of the literature and research. Yet for all the reasons given earlier, it is best for now to regard this as an oversimplified and unconfirmed set of assertions. The challenge now is to bring together the evidence from the literature and research to work toward a better understanding and assessment of these assertions.

CHAPTER FOUR

# ANALYZING THE ENVIRONMENT OF PUBLIC ORGANIZATIONS

The historical overview in Chapter Two should have made clear why organizational environment became one of the most important concepts in the study of management and organizations. The early contributors to the study of organizations concentrated on the middle parts of the framework in Figure 1.1—on structures, mainly, with limited attention to certain aspects of tasks, processes, incentives, and people. They placed little emphasis on an organization's environments or its managers' responses to them. Contemporary researchers and experts now regard organizational environments, and the challenges of dealing with them, as absolutely crucial to analyzing and leading organizations. This is certainly true for public organizations, because they are often more open than other organizations to certain types of environmental pressures and constraints. Public organizations tend to be subject to more directions and interventions from political actors and authorities who seek to direct and control them.

Management experts now exhort managers to monitor and analyze their environments, and consultants regularly lead executives and task forces through such analyses as part of strategic planning sessions (described further in Chapter Seven). In spite of all the attention to organizational environments, however, the management field provides no exact science for analyzing them, in part because the concept is complex and difficult in various ways. Public organizations are often embedded in larger governmental structures. The Food and Drug Administration, for example, operates as a subunit of the U.S. Department of Health and Human

Services, which in turn is a component of the U.S. federal government. The larger units of government impose systemwide rules on all agencies in the government, covering such administrative processes as human resources management, purchasing and procurement, and the budgeting process. In many agencies, different subunits operate in very different policy areas and often have stronger alliances with legislators and interest groups than with the agency director (Radin, 2002, p. 35; Seidman and Gilmour, 1986; Kaufman, 1979). All this can make it hard to say where an agency's environment begins and ends.

In addition, members of an organization often *enact* its environment (Scott, 2003, p. 141; Weick, 1979, p. 169). They consciously or unconsciously choose which matters to pay attention to and what to try to change. They make choices about the organization's *domain,* or field of operations, including the geographic areas, markets, clients, products, and services on which the organization will focus. Decisions about an organization's domain determine the nature of its environment. For example, some years ago leaders of the Ohio Bureau of Mental Retardation adopted a "deinstitutionalization" policy, moving patients out of the large treatment facilities operated by the agency and into smaller, private sector facilities. This changed the boundaries of the agency, its relations with its clients, and the set of organizations with which the agency worked. Organizations can sometimes create or shape their environments as much as they simply react to them. This complicates the analysis of environments, but it makes it all the more important.

These complications about the concept of an organization's environment may explain a rather surprising disappearing act that the concept has performed in the work of some major organization theorists. Authors who developed and championed the concept (Aldrich, 1979), have more recently produced books that mention the term sparingly and do not treat it as a primary concept, with no explanation of its demise (Aldrich, 1999; Baum and McKelvey, 1999). The term appears much less frequently in the titles of articles in prominent journals. Actually, as described shortly, most of the contemporary analyses of organizations and management employ concepts relevant to organizations' relations with their operating contexts or environments. Authors may increasingly feel that new concepts, such as networks, stakeholders, boundaries, and others discussed in this chapter, have more value than the concept of an organizational environment. In addition, prominent authors still employ the concept of organizational environment in important ways (Daft, 2001, chap. 4 and 5; Hall, 2002; Kalleberg, Knoke, Marsden, and Spaeth, 1996, chap. 6; Scott, 2003, chap. 6).

## General Dimensions of Organizational Environments

One typical approach to working through some of the complexity of environmental analysis is simply to lay out the general sectors or clusters of conditions, such as those in Exhibit 4.1, that an organization encounters. Consultants and experts often use such frameworks to lead groups in organizations through an *environmental scan* (described in Chapter Seven) as part of a strategic planning project or in a general assessment of the organization. For example, the U.S. Social Security Administration (2000) used an environmental scan in their efforts to develop a major vision statement.

Anyone can provide examples of ways in which such conditions influence organizations. Technological and scientific developments gave birth to many government agencies, such as the Environmental Protection Agency and the Nuclear Regulatory Commission. Technological developments continually influence the operation of government agencies; they must struggle to keep up with advances in computer technology, communications, and other areas. Congress passed legislation mandating vast changes at the U.S. Internal Revenue Service largely as a result of difficulties the agency had in developing and adapting to new information technologies for processing tax returns (Bozeman, 2002b). Demographic trends currently receive much attention, as analysts project increasing percentages of women and minorities in government employment. This raises the challenge

## EXHIBIT 4.1. GENERAL ENVIRONMENTAL CONDITIONS.

- *Technological conditions:* the general level of knowledge and capability in science, engineering, medicine, and other substantive areas; general capacities for communication, transportation, information processing, medical services, military weaponry, environmental analysis, production and manufacturing processes, and agricultural production.
- *Legal conditions:* laws, regulations, legal procedures, court decisions; characteristics of legal institutions and values, such as provisions for individual rights and jury trials as well as the general institutionalization and stability of legal processes.
- *Political conditions:* characteristics of the political processes and institutions in a society, such as the general form of government (socialism, communism, capitalism, and so on; degree of centralization, fragmentation, or federalism) and the degree of political stability (Carroll, Delacroix, and Goodstein, 1988). More direct and specific conditions include electoral outcomes, political party alignments and success, and policy initiatives within regimes.
- *Economic conditions:* levels of prosperity, inflation, interest rates, and tax rates; characteristics of labor, capital, and economic markets within and between nations.
- *Demographic conditions:* characteristics of the population such as age, gender, race, religion, and ethnic categories.
- *Ecological conditions:* characteristics of the physical environment, including climate, geographical characteristics, pollution, natural resources, and the nature and density of organizational populations.
- *Cultural conditions:* predominant values, attitudes, beliefs, social customs, and socialization processes concerning such things as sex roles, family structure, work orientation, and religious and political practices.

of managing diversity in the workplace (Ospina, 1996; Selden, 1997). Mainly due to the increasing size of the population of retired Americans, the Social Security Administration (SSA) projected that the beneficiaries of its main programs will increase from about 50 million people to more than 60 million between 1999 and 2010. Due to this increase and changes in laws about Social Security, such as legislation requiring more services to beneficiaries with disabilities, the agency projected the need for an increase of 15,000 to 20,000 work years of employee effort during this period if the agency continued to use its current procedures (U.S. Social Security Administration, 2000, p. 6). Public administrators attend carefully to legal developments, such as changes in public officials' legal liability for their decisions (Cooper, 2000; Koenig and O'Leary, 1996; Rosenbloom and O'Leary, 1997; Rosenbloom, Kravchuck, and Rosenbloom, 2001). As for the political dimensions of organizational environments, much of the rest of this book, but especially this and the next chapter, pertains to such influences.

Another common approach to analyzing environments is to list specific elements of an organization's environment, such as important stakeholders, or organizations and groups that have an important interest in the organization (Harrison and Freeman, 1999). A typical depiction of such elements of the environment might include competitors, customers, suppliers, regulators, unions, and associates. Similarly, Porter (1998) analyzes the major influences on competition within an industry: industry competitors, buyers, suppliers, new entrants, and substitutes. Consultants working with organizations on strategy formulation sometimes use such frameworks in a *stakeholder analysis,* to identify key stakeholders of the organization and their particular claims and roles (Bryson, 1995).

## Research on Environmental Variations

Organizational researchers have also produced more specific evidence about the effects of environments. Selznick (1966; see also Hall, 2002) helped lead this trend with a study of a government corporation, the Tennessee Valley Authority (TVA). He found that environmental influences play a crucial role in *institutionalization* processes in organizations. Values, goals, and procedures become strongly established, not necessarily because managers choose them as the most efficient means of production, but in large part as a result of environmental influences and exchanges. The TVA, for example, engaged in *co-optation,* absorbing new elements into its leadership to avert threats to its viability. The U.S. government established the TVA during the New Deal years to develop electric power and foster economic development along the Tennessee River. TVA officials involved local organizations and groups in decisions. This gained support for the TVA, but it also brought in these groups as strong influences on the organization's values and priorities.

In some cases, these groups shut out rival groups, putting the TVA in conflict with other New Deal programs with which it should have been allied. Thus, an organization's needs for external support and its consequent exchanges with outside entities can heavily influence its primary values and goals.

Later research made the importance of the external environment increasingly clear. Prominent studies that led to the emergence of contingency theory found more and more evidence of the impact of environmental uncertainty and complexity (Donaldson, 2001). Burns and Stalker (1961), for example, studied a set of English firms and classified them into two categories. *Mechanistic* firms emphasized a clear hierarchy of authority, with direction and communication dependent on the chain of command, and specialized, formally defined individual tasks. Other firms were more *organic,* with less emphasis on hierarchy and more lateral communication and networking. Tasks were less clearly defined and changed more frequently. Managers in these firms sometimes spurned organizational charts as too confining or even dangerous. The mechanistic firms succeeded in stable environments—those with relative stability in products, technology, competitors, and demand for their products. In such a setting, they could take advantage of the efficiencies of their more traditional structures. Other firms, such as electronics manufacturers, faced less stable environmental conditions, with rapid fluctuations in technology, products, competitors, and demand. The more organic firms, which were more flexible and adaptive, succeeded in this setting.

Lawrence and Lorsch (1967) studied firms in three industries whose environments exhibited different degrees of uncertainty as a result of more or less rapid changes and greater or lesser complexity. As changes in the environment became more rapid and frequent, and as the environment became more complex, these conditions imposed more uncertainty on decision makers in the organizations. The most successful firms had structures with a degree of complexity matching that of the environment. Firms in more stable environments could manage with relatively traditional, hierarchical structures. Firms in more unstable, uncertain environments could not.

In addition, different subunits of these firms faced different environments. As these different environments imposed more uncertainty on the subunits' managers, the successful firms became more *differentiated.* That is, the subunits differed more and more from one another in their goals, the time frames for their work, and the formality of their structure. This increased the potential for conflict and disorganization, however. Successful firms in more uncertain environments responded with higher levels of *integration.* They had more methods for coordinating the highly differentiated units, such as liaison positions, coordinating teams, and conflict-resolution processes. This combination of differentiation and integration made the successful firms in more uncertain environments more internally complex. The authors' general conclusion advanced one of the prominent components of the contingency idea: organizations must adopt structures that are as complex as the environments they confront.

As many studies of this sort accumulated, James Thompson (1967) synthesized the growing body of research in a way that provided additional insights. Organizations must contend with the demands of their tasks and their environments. They do so by trying to isolate the *technical core*, their primary work processes, so that their work can proceed smoothly. They use *buffering* methods to try to provide stable conditions for the technical core. For example, they use *boundary-spanning units*—such as inventory, personnel recruitment, and research and development units—to try to create smooth flows of information and resources. Yet environmental conditions can strain this process. In more complex environments, with more geographical areas, product markets, competitors, and other factors, organizations must become more internally complex. They do so by establishing different subunits to attend to the different environmental segments. More unstable environments create a need for greater decentralization of authority to these subunits and a less formal structure. The shifting environment requires rapid decisions and changes, and it takes too long for information and decisions to travel up and down a strict hierarchy.

Researchers have debated the adequacy of contingency theory (Hall, 2002, p. 285) and many have moved off in other directions. Yet recent books still emphasize the importance and implications of contingency theory perspectives on organizational environments (Daft, 2001; Donaldson, 2001). An organization's structure must be adapted to environmental contingencies as well as other contingencies. In simple, homogeneous, stable environments, organizations can successfully adopt mechanistic and centralized structures. In more complex and unstable environments, successful organizations must be organic and decentralized, partitioned into many departments with correspondingly elaborate integrating processes, and processes for managing the organization's boundaries and relation with the environment .

Scholars have also further developed contingency-theory concepts into carefully conceived environmental dimensions. Exhibit 4.2 illustrates prominent examples that researchers still use (Berman, Wicks, Kotha, and Jones, 1999). Clearly these dimensions apply to public organizations. Tax resentment and pressures to cut government spending in recent decades show the importance of environmental *capacity* (munificence or resource scarcity) for public organizations. The federal government has a regionalized structure, reflecting the influence of environmental heterogeneity and dispersion. Even organization theorists who attach little significance to the public-private distinction agree that public organizations face particular complications in *domain consensus and choice* (Miles, 1980; Hall, 2002; Van de Ven and Ferry, 1980; Meyer, 1979). Jurisdictional boundaries and numer-

## EXHIBIT 4.2. DESCRIPTIVE AND ANALYTICAL DIMENSIONS OF ORGANIZATIONAL ENVIRONMENTS.

*Aldrich (1979)*

Capacity: the extent to which the environment affords a rich or lean supply of necessary resources

Homogeneity-heterogeneity: the degree to which important components of the environment are similar or dissimilar

Stability-instability: the degree and rapidity of change in the important components or processes in the environment

Concentration-dispersion: the degree to which important components of the environment are separated or close together, geographically or in terms of communication or logistics

Domain consensus-dissensus: the degree to which the organization's domain (its operating locations, major functions and activities, and clients and customers served) is generally accepted or disputed and contested

Turbulence: the degree to which changes in one part or aspect of the environment in turn create changes in another; the tendency of changes to reverberate and spread

*Dess and Beard (1984)*

Munificence: the availability of needed resources

Complexity: the homogeneity and concentration of the environment

Dynamism: the stability and turbulence of the environment

ous authorities, laws, and political interests complicate decisions about where, when, and how a public organization operates. Research strongly supports the observation that public status influences strategic domain choices (Mascarenhas, 1989), although later chapters show how public managers often gain considerable leeway to maneuver.

*Turbulence* and *interconnectedness* characterize the environments of most public organizations. Studies of public policy implementation provide numerous accounts of policy initiatives that had many unanticipated consequences and implications for other groups. Public managers commonly encounter situations in which a decision touches off a furor, arousing opposition from groups that they would never have anticipated reacting (Chase and Reveal, 1983; Cohen and Eimicke, 1998). Similarly, environmental *stability*, *dynamism*, and *change rates* have major implications for public organizations. Rapid turnover of political appointees at the top of agencies and rapid external shifts in political priorities have major influences on public organizations and the people in them. For example, researchers find evidence that turbulence and instability in the environments of public agencies affect the morale of their managers and influence their acceptance of reforms (Ban, 1987; Golden, 2000; Rubin, 1985).

These environmental concepts are useful for enhancing our understanding of public organizations. As this discussion shows, however, no conclusive, coherent theory of organizations explains how these dimensions are related to one another and to organizations. In addition, organization theorists have defined these concepts at a very general level. Certainly they apply to public organizations, but to really understand public organizations we need to add more specific content to the environmental dimensions. There is a body of useful research and writing on public bureaucracies that can help in this task, to which this discussion will turn after a review of recent trends in research by organizational theorists relevant to the analysis of organizational environments.

## Recent Trends in Research on Organizational Environments

Some of the most prominent recent research in organization theory concentrates on organizational environments and moves beyond contingency theory (Aldrich, 1999, chap. 3; Hall, 2002, chap. 12). *Population ecology* theorists, for example, analyze the origin, development, and decline of populations of organizations using biological concepts (Hannan and Freeman, 1989). Just as biologists analyze how certain populations of organisms develop to take advantage of a particular ecological niche, population ecologists analyze the development of populations of organizations within certain niches (characterized by their unique combinations of available resources and constraints).

Some population ecology theorists reject the contingency-theory depiction of organizations as rational, speedy adapters to environmental change. Indeed, they see environments as selecting organizational populations in a Darwinian fashion (Hannan and Freeman, 1989). The population ecology perspective analyzes how populations of organizations go through processes of variation, selection, and retention. Variation involves the continuing appearance of new forms of organization, both planned and unplanned. Then the selection process determines which forms of organization will survive and prosper, based on their fit with the environment or their capacity to fill an environmental niche. A niche is a distinct combination of resources and constraints that supports the particular form of organization. Retention processes serve to continue the form through such environmental influences as pressures on the organizations to maintain past practices, and through such internal processes as employees developing common outlooks. Critics have raised questions about this perspective, arguing, for example, that its broad biological analogies devote no attention to human strategic decisions and motives in organizations (Van de Ven, 1979), and that its proponents have applied it mostly to populations of small organizations, leaving questions about how it applies to huge government agencies and business firms.

Aldrich (1999) advances an *evolutionary* perspective on populations of organizations that he describes as more general and overarching than the population ecology perspective but that obviously draws upon it. He says that the approach also has important connections to the perspectives described later in this chapter. It includes the processes of *variation, selection,* and *retention,* with elaborations. All three of these processes can operate on organizations from external or internal sources. Variations in routines, procedures, and organizational forms can be *intentional,* as individuals seek solutions to problems, or *blind,* as a result of mistakes or surprises. In addition, there is a fourth process, *struggle,* in which individuals, organizations, and populations of organizations contend with each other over scarce resources and conflicting incentives and goals. Aldrich does not undertake to describe specific implications or offer advice for managers, but his perspective goes even farther than the population ecology approach to provide insights about ways in which organizational populations are integral to processes of social change; show much more diversity of form than some research, such as the contingency approaches, recognized; and continually emerge and evolve. Both the population-ecology and the evolutionary perspectives, however, offer insights about historical and environmental forces that influence organizational change and survival, reminding us that any model for organizational analysis should remain sensitive to growth, decline, or other variations in organizational forms. For example, observers of very innovative public executives have argued that these executives appeared to engage in an "uncommon rationality" in which they "see new possibilities offered by an evolving historical situation" and take advantage of political and technological developments that offer such possibilities (Doig and Hargrove, 1990, pp. 10–11).

*Resource-dependence* theories analyze how organizational managers try to obtain crucial resources from their environment, such as materials, money, people, support services, and technological knowledge. Organizations can adapt their structures in response to their environment, or they can change their niches. They can try to change the environment by creating demand or seeking government actions that can help them. They can try to manipulate the way the environment is perceived by the people in the organization and those outside it. In these and other ways, they can pursue essential resources. These theorists stress the importance of internal and external political processes in the quest for resources. Chapter Six discusses how their analysis of resources in connection with internal power relationships applies to public organizations (Pfeffer and Salancik, 1978, pp. 277–278; Daft, 2001).

*Transaction-costs* theories analyze managerial decisions to purchase a needed good or service from outside, as opposed to producing it within the organization

(Williamson, 1975, 1981). Transactions with other organizations and people become more costly as contracts become harder to write and supervise. The organization may need a service particular to itself, or it may have problems supervising
contractors. Managers may try to hold down such costs under certain conditions
by merging with another organization or permanently hiring a person with whom
they had been contracting. These theories, which are much more elaborate than
summarized here, have received much attention in business management research
and have implications for government contracting and other governmental issues
(Aldrich, 1999; Bryson, 1995). Yet they usually assume that managers in firms
strive to hold down costs to maximize profits. Governmental contracting involves more political criteria and accountability, and different or nonexistent profit
motives, so at one point Williamson (1981) expressed uncertainty as to whether
transaction cost economics applies to nonmarket organizations. More recently,
however, he examined public bureaucracy from the perspective of transaction cost
economics (Williamson, 1999). He concluded that the public bureaucracy, like
other alternative modes of governance (such as markets, firms, and hybrids), is
well suited to some transactions and poorly suited to others. Williamson argued
that public bureaucracy handles "sovereign transactions," such as foreign affairs,
more effectively and efficiently than other modes, such as firms and markets.

Studies of *institutionalization* processes hark back to the work of Selznick (1966).
They analyze how certain values, structures, and procedures become institutionalized (widely accepted as the proper way of doing things) in and among organizations. Tolbert and Zucker (1983) showed that many local governments reformed
their civil service systems by adopting merit systems, because merit systems had
become widely accepted as the proper form of personnel system for such governments. In addition, the federal government applied pressures for the adoption
of merit systems. Meyer and Rowan (1983) argued that organizations such as
schools often adopt structures on the basis of "myth and ceremony." They do
things according to prevailing beliefs and not because the practices are clearly the
means to efficiency or effectiveness. DiMaggio and Powell (1983) showed that organizations in the same field come to look like one another as a result of shared
ideas about how that type of organization should look. Dobbin and his colleagues
(1988) found that public organizations have more provisions for due process, such
as affirmative action programs, than do private organizations. These studies have
obvious relevance for public organizations. Pfeffer (1982) suggested that this approach is particularly applicable to the public sector, where performance criteria
are often less clear. There, beliefs about proper procedures may substitute more
readily for firmly validated procedures linked to clear outcomes and objectives.
Public and nonprofit managers encounter many instances where new procedures
or schemes, such as a new budgeting technique, become widely implemented as

the latest, best approach—whether or not anyone can prove that it is. In addition, some of the research mentioned earlier shows how external institutions such as government impose structures and procedures on organizations. Some of these theorists disagreed among themselves over these different views of institutionalization—whether it results from the spread of beliefs and myths or from the influence of external institutions such as government (Scott, 1987).

Partly to resolve such divergence in concepts of institutionalism, researchers drew distinctions between types of institutionalization processes that lead to institutional *isomorphism,* a wonderfully tortured bit of jargon that refers to organizations and other institutions becoming similar or identical to each other in form (Dimaggio and Powell, 1983; Scott, 2003, p. 134–141). This institutionalization of similar forms can come from *coercive isomorphism,* in which they have to comply with similar laws and regulations. *Normative isomorphism* comes from compliance with professional and moral norms such as those imposed through accreditation or certification processes by professional associations. *Mimetic isomorphism* occurs when organizations and other entities imitate each other, based on a prevailing orthodoxy or culturally supported beliefs about the proper structures and procedures. Frumkin and Galaskiewicz (2003) used the data from the National Organizations Survey, a nationally represented sample of organizations, to examine whether public, private, and nonprofit organizations tended to differ in the incidence of these types of institutionalization processes. They found that coercive, normative, and mimetic effects were stronger for government establishments than for business establishments.

These developments show how elaborate and diverse the work on organizational environments has become, and each one provides insights. In fact, scholars are currently arguing more and more frequently that there is a need to bring these models together rather than argue about which is the best one (Aldrich, 1999; Hall, 2002, p. 314). Obviously they all deal with processes that influence organizations in some combination, and all are true to some degree.

# The Political and Institutional Environments of Public Organizations

The work on organizational environments provides a number of insights, many of them applicable to public organizations. The preceding review of the literature on organizational environments also shows, however, why people interested in public organizations call for more complete attention to public sector environments. The contingency-theory researchers express environmental dimensions very generally. They pay little attention to whether government ownership makes a difference or whether it matters if an organization sells its outputs in economic markets. They depict organizations, usually business firms, as autonomously adapting to environmental contingencies. Political scientists, however, have for a long time regarded as obvious that external political authorities often directly mandate the structures of public agencies, regardless of environmental uncertainty (Warwick, 1975; Pitt and Smith, 1981). The most current perspectives on organizational environments bring government into the picture, but they also express their concepts very generally, subsuming governmental influences under broader concepts.

## Major Components and Dimensions

Public executives commenting on public management and political scientists and economists writing about public organizations typically depict organizational environments in ways similar to the conceptual framework shown in Exhibit 4.3. (Brudney, Hebert, and Wright, 1999; Downs, 1967; Dunn, 1997; Dunn and Legge, 2002; Meier, 2000; Hood and Dunsire, 1981; Lynn, Heinrich, and Hill, 2000; Pitt and Smith, 1981; Stillman, 1996; Wamsley and Zald, 1973; Warwick, 1975; Wilson, 1989). One also needs to recognize that the environmental pressures on public organizations, as with all organizations, are becoming more global in nature (Welch and Wong, 2001a, 2001b). The rest of this chapter discusses the top part of the table, concerned with general values and institutions. The next chapter covers the bottom portion, dealing with institutions, entities, and actors.

## General Institutions and Values of the Political Economy

Chapter Two defined public agencies as organizations owned and funded by government. They operate under political authority and without economic markets for their outputs. The political system of the nation and its traditions, institutions, and values heavily influence the exercise of this political authority. The U.S. Constitution formally states some of these values and establishes some of the nation's primary public institutions and rules of governance. Legislation and court cases have further defined and applied them. Rosenbloom and O'Leary (1997) observed that the personnel systems in government are "law-bound." That observation applies to many other aspects of management and organization in government agencies as well.

Other values and rules receive less formal codification but still have great influence. For example, Americans have traditionally demanded that government agencies operate with businesslike standards of efficiency, although the Constitution nowhere explicitly expresses this criterion (Waldo, [1947] 1984). Relatedly, the nation maintains a free-enterprise system that affords considerable autonomy

## EXHIBIT 4.3. MAJOR ENVIRONMENTAL COMPONENTS
## FOR PUBLIC ORGANIZATIONS.

*General Values and Institutions of the Political Economy*

Political and economic traditions
Constitutional provisions and their legislative and judicial development
    Due process
    Equal protection of the laws
    Democratic elections and representation (republican form)
    Federal system
    Separation of powers
Free-enterprise system (economic markets relatively free of government controls)

*Values and performance criteria for government organizations*

    Competence
        Efficiency
        Effectiveness
        Timeliness
        Reliability
        Reasonableness
    Responsiveness
        Accountability, legality, responsiveness to rule of law and governmental authorities,
            responsiveness to public demands
        Adherence to ethical standards
        Fairness, equal treatment, impartiality
        Openness to external scrutiny and criticism

*Institutions, Entities, and Actors with Political Authority and Influence*

Chief executives
    Executive staff and staff offices
Legislatures
    Legislative committees
    Individual legislators
    Legislative staff
Courts
Other government agencies
    Oversight and management agencies (GAO, OMB, OPM, GSA)
    Competitors
    Allies
    Agencies or governmental units with joint programs
Other levels of government
    "Higher" and "lower" levels
    Intergovernmental agreements and districts
Interest groups
    Client groups
    Constituency groups
    Professional associations
Policy subsystems
    Issue networks
    Interorganizational policy networks
    Implementation structure
News media
General public opinion
Individual citizens with requests for services, complaints, and other contacts

to businesses and considerable respect for business values (Waldo, [1947] 1984; Lindblom, 1977). These values are not clearly and specifically codified in the Constitution. According to MacDonald (1987), the Constitution actually lacks some of the provisions necessary for a free-enterprise system, in part because some of the framers considered certain economic activities, such as trading debt instruments, to be immoral. Full development of the necessary governmental basis for a free-enterprise system required the actions of Alexander Hamilton, the first secretary of the treasury. Among other steps, he established provisions for the use of government debt as a source of capital for corporations. MacDonald, a conservative, would almost certainly disavow the conclusion that the private enterprise system in the United States was largely created through the efforts of a government bureaucrat, using government funding. More generally, however, these examples illustrate the existence, through formally codified instruments and less formally codified conditions, of general values and institutional arrangements that shape the operation of public authority.

These general values and institutional arrangements in turn influence the values, constraints, and performance criteria of public organizations. They sound abstract, but they link directly to practical challenges and responsibilities for public organizations and managers.

## Constitutional Provisions

The Constitution places limits on the government and guarantees certain rights to citizens. These include provisions for freedom of expression and the press, equal protection under the law, and protections against the denial of life, liberty, or property without due process of law. The provisions for freedom of association and expression and freedom of the press empower media representatives, political parties, and interest groups to assess, criticize, and seek to influence the performance of government agencies, in ways discussed in the next chapter.

Such provisions as those for equal protection and due process also have major implications for the operations of public organizations. The equal protection provisions, for example, provided some of the underlying principles and precedents for affirmative action requirements. The requirement for legal due process requires administrative due process as well and acts as one major form of control over public bureaucracies and bureaucrats (West, 1995, chap. 2). Agencies are often required to give notice of certain actions and to adhere to disclosure rules, to hold open hearings about their decisions, and to establish procedures for appealing agency decisions. For example, the Administrative Procedures Act requires federal agencies to adhere to certain procedures in rule making (and other legislation has established similar requirements at other levels of government). When the Department of Education makes rules about student loans or the SSA makes rules about claims for coverage under its disability programs, the agencies have to adhere to such rule-making procedures. If the SSA denies or revokes an applicant's disability coverage, the applicant has the right to adjudication procedures, which may involve a hearing conducted by an administrative law judge. These requirements strongly influence the agency's management of disability cases and the work of individual caseworkers. Generally, the requirement for all the appeals and hearings conflicts with the agency's goal of minimizing costs and maximizing efficiency of operations. More subtly, it raises complex issues about how efficiency relates to the fair handling of individual cases by individual caseworkers (Mashaw, 1983). Chapters Eight and Ten show evidence that rules and procedures for disciplining and firing employees in the public service, based in part on due process principles, create one of the sharpest differences between public and private organizations confirmed by research. These examples illustrate how general constitutional principles that seem abstract actually translate into a set of immediate challenges in organizational behavior and management.

Democratic elections are another feature of the political system in the United States and other countries that has direct implications for organization and management. The electoral process produces regular, or at least frequent, changes in chief executives, legislative officials, and the political appointees that come and go with them. These changes in leadership often mean frequent changes in the top-level leadership of public agencies—every two years for many agencies—and often bring with them shifts in priorities that mean changes in agencies' focus and sometimes in their power, their influence, and the resources available for their people and subunits.

The Constitution also establishes a federal system that allocates authority to different levels of government in ways that influence the organization and management of public agencies. State governments require that local governments establish certain offices and officers, such as sheriffs and judges, thereby specifying major features of the organizational structure of those governments. State legislation may mandate a formula to be used in setting the salaries of those officials. Many federal programs operate by granting or channeling funds to states and localities, often with various specifications about the structure and operations of the programs at those levels.

A particularly dramatic example of the way societal values and institutions can influence public organizations comes from the provision in the Constitution for separation of powers. As indicated in Exhibit 4.3 and discussed shortly, government agencies face various pressures for efficient, effective operations. Separation of powers, however, represents a system that is explicitly designed with less emphasis on efficiency than on constraining the power of government authorities

(Wilson, 1989). In the *Federalist Papers,* James Madison discussed the constitutional provision for dividing power among the branches of government as a way of constraining power. He pointed out that a strong central executive authority might be the most efficient organizational arrangement. But the government of the United States, he wrote, was instead being purposefully designed to constrain authority by dividing it among institutions. In one of the great exercises of applied psychology in history, he pointed out that if humans were angels, no such arrangements would be necessary. But because they are not, and because power can corrupt some people and oppress others, the new government would set ambition against ambition, dividing authority among the branches of government so that they would keep one another in check. Lower levels of government in the United States are designed with similar patterns of divided authority. For the organization and management of agencies, these arrangements have dramatic implications, because they subject the organizations and their managers to multiple authorities and sources of direction that are in part designed to conflict with one another. From its inception, the American political system has thus embodied a dynamic tension among conflicting values, principles, and authorities.

The controversy over whether this system works as intended never ends. Nevertheless, the political authorities and actors representing these broader values and principles impose on public organizations numerous performance criteria, such as those listed in Exhibit 4.3. Authors use various terms to express the diversity of these criteria. Fried (1976), for example, refers to democracy, efficiency, and legality as the major performance criteria for the public bureaucracy in the United States. Rosenbloom, Kravchuck, and Rosenbloom (2001) consider law, management, and politics to be the three dominant sources of administrative criteria. Putnam (1993) seeks to evaluate the performance of government according to its responsiveness to its constituents and its efficiency in conducting the public's business. Exhibit 4.3 uses Meier's (2000) distinction between *competence* and *responsiveness* criteria.

## Competence Values

Public organizations operate under pressure to perform competently. Demands for efficiency come from all corners. Newspapers and television news departments doggedly pursue indications of wasteful uses of public funds at all levels of government. Political candidates and elected officials attack examples of waste, such as apparently excessive costs for components of military weaponry. The U.S. General Accounting Office (GAO), auditors general at the state and local levels, and other oversight agencies conduct audits of government programs, with an emphasis on efficiency. Special commissions, such as the Grace Commission (organized under the Reagan administration), investigate wasteful or inefficient practices in government. Similar commissions have been appointed in many states to examine state government operations and attack inefficiency. The Clinton administration's National Performance Review (described more fully in Chapter Fourteen) emphasized streamlining federal operations and reduced federal employment by over 324,000 jobs. Inefficiency in federal operations served as one of the justifications for its formation.

But efficiency was not necessarily the highest priority in the design of the U.S. government, as just described. External authorities, the media, interest groups, and citizens also demand effectiveness, timeliness, reliability, and reasonableness, even though these criteria may conflict with efficiency. Efficiency means producing a good or service at the lowest cost possible while maintaining a constant level of quality. These additional criteria are concerned with whether a function is performed well, on time, dependably, and in a logical, sensible way. Government often performs services crucial to individuals or to an entire jurisdiction. People want the job done; efficiency is often a secondary concern. Also, in government the connection between a service and the cost of providing it is often difficult to see and analyze. Evidence that police, firefighters, emergency medical personnel, and the military lack effectiveness or reliability draws sharp responses that may relegate efficiency to a lesser status. In the aftermath of the September 11 attacks, federal spending for military action in Afghanistan and Iraq, and for homeland security, increased sharply even though a federal budget surplus turned into a deficit during this period. Clearly the imperative of security against terrorism outweighed considerations of frugality and efficiency.

Sometimes one element of the political system stresses some of these criteria more vigorously than others (Pitt and Smith, 1981). This can increase conflicts for public managers, because different authorities emphasize different criteria. For example, the judiciary often appears to emphasize effectiveness over administrative efficiency because of its responsibility to uphold legal standards and constitutional rights. Judges rule that certain criteria must be met in a timely, effective way, virtually regardless of cost and efficiency. The courts have ordered that prisons and jails and affirmative action programs must meet certain standards by certain dates. They protect the right of clients of public programs to due process in decisions about whether they can be denied benefits. This increases the burden on public agencies, forcing them to conduct costly hearings and reviews and to maintain extensive documentation. The courts in effect leave the agencies to worry about efficiency and cost considerations. The press and legislators, meanwhile, criticize agencies for slow procedures and expensive operations.

Casework by members of Congress, state legislators, and city council members can also exert pressure for results other than efficiency. (In this context, casework means action by an elected official to plead the case of an individual citizen or group who makes a demand of an agency.) A congressional representative or staff member may call about a constituent's late social security check. A city council member may call a city agency about a complaint from a citizen about garbage collection services. While these requests can promote effective, reasonable responses by an agency, responding to sporadic, unpredictable demands of this sort can tax both the agency's efficiency and its effectiveness.

## Responsiveness Values

The responsiveness criteria in Exhibit 4.3 often conflict sharply with competence criteria and also with each other. Public managers and organizations remain accountable to various authorities and interests and to the rule of law in general (Radin, 2002; Rosen, 1998; West, 1995). They must comply with laws, rules, and directives issued by government authorities and provide accounts of their compliance as required. Rosen (1998) describes a long list of different mechanisms, procedures, and institutions for accountability. In addition, Romzek and Dubnick (1987; Romzek, 2000) point out that public managers and organizations are subject to different types of accountability that have different sources and that exert different levels of direct control over administrators. Hierarchical and legal accountability exert high degrees of control. The hierarchical form involves imposition of rules, procedures, scrutiny, and other controls from within an agency. Legal accountability, in Romzek and Dubnick's definitions, involves high levels of control from external sources, in the form of oversight and monitoring by external authority. Professional and political accountability involve lower degrees of direct control over individual administrators. Professional accountability involves internal controls in an organization by allowing considerable discretion to administrators and expecting them to be guided by the norms of their profession. Political accountability also involves a lot of individual leeway to decide how to respond, but to external political sources such as legislators or other political stakeholders. The administrator decides whether or not to respond to an influence attempt by such a person or group. Obviously these forms of accountability can overlap and work in combinations, and the relative emphasis they receive can have dramatic consequences. Romzek and Dubnick attribute a disaster that befell the U.S. space program, the Challenger explosion, to a shift away from professional accountability in NASA to more emphasis on political and hierarchical accountability.

Public organizations and their managers are often expected to remain open and responsive in various ways. Saltzstein (1992) points out that bureaucratic responsiveness can be defined in at least two ways, as responsiveness to the public's wishes or as responsiveness to the interests of the government, and that much of the discourse on the topic takes one or the other of these perspectives. These conflicting pressures sometimes coincide with accountability, in the sense of responding to directives and requests for information from government authorities. Yet public agencies also receive requests for helpful, reasonable, and flexible responses to the needs of clients, interest groups, and the general public. Because they are public organizations, their activities are public business, and citizens and the media demand relative openness to scrutiny (IBM Endowment for the Business of Government, 2002; Wamsley and Zald, 1973). For some programs, the enabling legislation requires citizen advisory panels or commissions to represent community groups, interest groups, and citizens. Administrative procedures at different levels of government require public notice of proposed changes in government agencies' rules and policies, often with provisions for public hearings at which citizens can attempt to influence the changes. The courts, legislatures, and legal precedent also require that agencies treat citizens fairly and impartially by adhering to principles of due process through appeals and hearings. The Freedom of Information Act and similar legislation at all levels of government require public agencies to make records and information available upon request under certain circumstances. Other legislation mandates the privacy of clients' records under certain circumstances.

A related criterion, *representativeness*, pertains to various ways in which officials should represent the people, and another means of making government bureaucracy responsive to the needs of citizens. Representativeness is a classic issue in government and public administration, with discourse about the topic dating back for centuries. The topic has taken on even more momentum recently, because of the rise of such issues as equal employment opportunity, affirmative action, and more recently, diversity. One view of representativeness holds that identifiable ethnic and demographic groups should be represented in government roughly in proportion to their presence in the population. The advisory groups mentioned previously also reflect representativeness criteria in another sense. One important and currently lively line of inquiry pursues the distinction between *passive* representation, which simply refers to whether members of different groups are present in governmental entities and agencies, and *active* representation. Active representation occurs when the members of a group actually serve as advocates for the group in decisions about programs and policies. Selden (1997, p. 139; see also Selden, Brudney and Kellough, 1998) reports evidence that where districts of the Farmers Home Administration have higher percentages of minority supervisors, more rural housing loans go to minorities. Keiser, Wilkins, Meier, and Holland (2002) point out that passive representation has been found to lead to active representation for race but not for gender. They then report evidence of conditions under which passive representation will lead to active representation for gender in educational contexts. For example, in schools with more female administrators, female teachers were associated with more educational success for girls. Similarly, Dolan (2000) reports evidence that female federal executives express attitudes more supportive of women's issues when they work in agencies with high percentages of women in leadership positions. Brudney, Hebert, and Wright (2000) report evidence that among agency heads in the fifty states, the administrators' values and perceived organizational role sets influence their tendency to display active representation. Other researchers are examining representativeness issues at local government levels as well (Miller, Kerr, and Reid, 1999; Schumann and Fox, 1999). These criteria add to the complex set of objectives and values that public managers and organizations must pursue and seek to balance. In federal agencies and many state and local government organizations, support for diversity is a criterion in the performance evaluations of many executives and managers, so representativeness in this sense joins the list of values and goals they need to pursue.

Later chapters describe additional examples and evidence of how conflicting values and criteria such as those just discussed influence public organizations and pose very practical challenges for public managers. External authorities and political actors intervene in management decisions in pursuit of responsiveness and accountability, and impose structures and constraints in pursuit of equity, efficiency, and effectiveness. Sharp conflicts over which values should predominate—professional effectiveness or political accountability, for example—lead to major transformations of organizational operations and culture (Maynard-Moody, Stull, and Mitchell, 1986; Romzek, 2000). Before examining these effects on major dimensions of organization and management, however, Chapter Five considers in more depth the elements in the lower portion of Exhibit 4.3, the institutions, entities, and actors that seek to impose these values and criteria, and their exchanges of influence with public organizations.

CHAPTER FIVE

# THE IMPACT OF POLITICAL POWER AND PUBLIC POLICY

For a research project on public organizations, a college professor interviewed the Secretary of the Florida Department of Community Affairs (DCA). DCA manages programs for management of emergencies (such as hurricanes), housing and community development, planning for growth, and ecological protection that often include grants for which localities can apply. DCA thus has a great influence on the constituencies of many political officials and, as one might expect, gets a lot of attention from those officials. During the interview, the DCA secretary's administrative assistant came in and handed her a note. The secretary told the interviewer that even though she had agreed to take no phone calls during the interview, she would have to interrupt the interview to return a phone call. She showed the interviewer the note. It was a message from one of the most powerful state senators. It said, "This is my <u>SECOND</u> phone call to you and you have not returned my call." The administrative assistant explained that the senator had told her to write the note that way, to put *second* in all capitals and underline it. The director felt that she had better return the call right away. Government executives often have to be very responsive to elected officials.

Chapter Two defined public organizations as those the government owns and funds and therefore has authority to direct and control. Chapter Four reviewed organization theorists' ideas about the crucial relationship between organizations, including public organizations, and their environments. It also argued that public organizations' environments impose a relatively distinctive set of values and criteria on them, through direction and influence by government institutions and entities (see the bottom half of Exhibit 4.3). This chapter provides a brief, summary description of the sources of authority and influence—the power—of these entities over public organizations.

A complex literature analyzes these topics, but it is impossible to cover this literature fully in a brief chapter. Nevertheless, for the analysis of public organizations we need to cover insights gained from studies of public bureaucracy in order to integrate them with the topics in general management and organization theory covered in later chapters. In addition, public managers need to understand and deal with the political entities discussed here. So, it is important to highlight some of the key points and issues.

Power and influence relationships are seldom simple, unidirectional, or entirely clear. Analyses of public organizations certainly illustrate these complexities. Wood and Waterman (1994, pp. 18–22) point out that for years scholars analyzing public bureaucracies often characterized them as being out of the control of their political masters. Some scholars have depicted regulatory agencies as "captured" by the interests they were supposed to regulate. Others have concluded that "iron triangles," or tight alliances of agencies, interest groups, and congressional committees, dominate agency policies and activities and close out other authorities and actors. These accounts describe bureaucracies as operating relatively independently of presidents, courts, and legislative bodies (except for special committees with which they might be allied).

A peculiar popular myth about public bureaucracies sees them as existing either for no reason and against everyone's better judgment or only for the selfish interests of the bureaucrats. In fact, a public agency that no one wants or that only the bureaucrats want is the easiest target for elimination. Still, such popular views persist, and they correspond to very important political developments. Recent U.S. presidents, governors, and mayors have launched efforts to control bureaucracies, seeking to wrest from them their allegedly excessive power or to streamline and reduce them (Arnold, 1995; Durant, 1992; Pfiffner and Brook, 2000; U.S. Office of Management and Budget, 2002; Walters, 2002; West, 2002).

Writers on public management often emphasize an opposing view, however. As mentioned in Chapter One, some experts on public management worry that elaborate constraints on public managers deprive them of authority to carry out their jobs and frustrate them professionally (National Academy of Public Administration, 1986). Thus the discussion on bureaucratic power has fallen into two conflicting camps, one in which bureaus and bureaucrats are seen as independent and influential and one in which they are regarded as impotent (Kingdon, 1995; Wood and Waterman, 1994).

Recently, evidence has mounted that both of these views have some merit, that bureaucratic power can more accurately be described as a dynamic mixture of both of these conditions. Researchers and government executives report numerous cases in which federal agencies have shown marked responsiveness to the authority of the president, the Congress, and the courts (Golden, 2000; IBM Endowment for the Business of Government, 2002; Rubin, 1985; Wood and Waterman, 1994); conversely, Wood and Waterman (1994) also show evidence of "bottom-up" processes in which federal agencies initiate policy relatively independently. Similarly, recent studies of public management and leadership provide accounts of proactive behaviors by leaders of public agencies (Behn, 1994; Doig and Hargrove, 1987; Hargrove and Glidewell, 1990; Riccucci, 1995). Dunn (1997) describes respectful relations between government executives and their political superiors, and Dunn and Legge (2002) find that many local government managers espouse a partnership model for their relations with elected officials. The relative power of public organizations, their leaders, and the governmental institutions to which they are formally accountable is dynamic and depends on various conditions such as the salience of a particular issue, agency structure, agency expertise, public attitudes and support, and other factors. This chapter reviews many of the formal powers of the external actors that influence public organizations, and as many of these dynamic factors as possible, because of their essential role in the fundamental organizational process of gaining financial resources, grants of authority, and other resources from the environment. (Exhibit 5.1 summarizes many of these formal powers and other bases of influence.) As Norton Long (1949, p. 257) declared in a classic essay, "the lifeblood of administration is power."

# Public Organizations and the Public

Public organizations need support from what political scientists call *mass publics*, or broad, diffuse populations, and especially from *attentive publics*—more organized groups that are interested in specific agencies.

## Public Opinion and Mass Publics

General public opinion influences the management of public organizations more than much of the management literature acknowledges. Two types of mass opinion figure importantly: attitudes toward government in general and attitudes toward particular policies and agencies. Chapter One described the antigovernment trend of the last several decades and how elected officials responded with

## EXHIBIT 5.1. SOURCES OF POLITICAL AUTHORITY AND INFLUENCE OF INSTITUTIONS, ENTITIES, AND ACTORS IN THE POLITICAL SYSTEM.

*Chief Executives*
Appointment of agency heads and other officials
Executive staff and staff offices (for example, budget office)
Initiating legislation and policy directions
Vetoing legislation
Executive orders and directives

*Legislative Bodies*
Power of the purse: final approval of the budget
Authorizing legislation for agency formation and operations
Approval of executive appointments of officials
Oversight activities: hearings, investigations
Authority of legislative committees
Initiating legislation

*Courts*
Review of agency decisions
Authority to render decisions that strongly influence agency operations
Direct orders to agencies

*Government Agencies*
Oversight and management authority (GAO, OMB, OPM, GSA)
Competitors
Allies
Agencies or government units with joint programs

*Other Levels of Government*
"Higher" and "lower" levels
Intergovernmental agreements and districts

*Interest Groups*
Client groups
Constituency groups
Professional associations

*Policy Subsystems and Policy Communities*
Issue networks
Interorganizational policy networks

*News Media*
Constitutional protections of freedom of the press
Open meetings laws, Sunshine laws

*General Public Opinion*
Providing (or refusing to provide) popular support

*Individual Citizens*
Requests for services, complaints, other contacts

efforts to reform government bureaucracies. As noted in Chapter One, when President Carter reformed the civil service system, changing pay and disciplinary procedures and provisions for appointing senior executives, he promoted the reform as a means of motivating federal workers and making it easier to fire lazy ones. President Reagan more aggressively attacked the federal bureaucracy, cutting agency budgets and staffing, and sought to diminish the authority of career federal administrators (Aberbach and Rockman, 2000; Durant, 1992; Golden, 2000; Rubin, 1985). Morale in the federal service suffered. Surveys revealed that many career civil servants intended to leave the service and would discourage their children from pursuing a career in federal service (Volcker Commission, 1989). As part of the National Performance Review, the Clinton administration cut about 324,000 federal jobs between 1993 and 2000. The George W. Bush administration issued the *President's Management Agenda,* which called for improved management due to severe deficiencies in management in federal agencies. Both of these recent initiatives seemed clearly to be designed in part to show the public that the president would reform the inefficient federal bureaucracy. The general climate of unfavorable public opinion about the public bureaucracy thus had significant effects on the morale and work behaviors of government employees, the structure of the federal government, and the functioning of major federal agencies.

A sharp public outcry in 1989 against a proposed pay raise for members of Congress, federal judges, and federal executives provided another good example of the effects of general public opinion on government employees and organizations. In opinion polls, more than 80 percent of the public opposed the increase. Ralph Nader and the National Taxpayers' Union fought the raise aggressively, exhorting voters to write to and call their representatives to object to it. Congress overwhelmingly voted down the raise. After its defeat, stories in the *New York Times* and elsewhere reported bitter reactions by federal managers, including many who would not even have been in positions to receive the raise. They expressed sharp disappointment over the symbolic rejection of their value to the society.

In state and local governments across this country and in other nations, unfavorable public attitudes about government have provided some of the support for various reforms (Peters and Savoie, 1994). Some reforms have targeted government pay systems, seeking changes that would tie a government employee's pay more closely to his or her performance. The reforms have been justified as a way to remedy allegedly weak motivation and performance on the part of public employees (Ingraham, 1993; Kellough and Lu, 1993; Gabris, 1987). In Georgia and Florida, for example, the governors proposed during the 1990s that merit system protections for state employees be abolished, in part so it would be easier to fire them and to tie their pay more closely to their performance (West, 2002; Kellough and Nigro, 2002). Walters (2002) points out that Governor Miller in Georgia promoted the reforms to the public in the same way Jimmy Carter had argued for similar reforms during his presidency—by connecting them to the stereotype of the inefficient bureaucrats who could not be fired. These sorts of reforms have been undertaken in various nations, and have been particularly prevalent in English-speaking countries in recent decades (Kettl, 2002; Peters and Savoie, 1994; Pollitt and Bouckaert, 2000). They reflect the decline in general public support for government spending and programs.

## Ambivalence and Paradoxes in Public Opinion

As the surge in patriotic sentiment and praise for the New York City firefighters and police after September 11 showed, public attitudes about government exhibit marked ambivalence and this ambivalence influences public managers and their agencies (Lipset and Schneider, 1987; Whorton and Worthley, 1981). Surveys have often found that respondents say they would like lower taxes but do not want public spending reduced for most types of services (Ladd, 1983; Beck, Rainey, and Traut, 1990). Surveys have also found that when respondents are asked how they feel about federal agencies in general, they give unfavorable responses. When asked, however, for a specific evaluation of how they were treated by a particular agency in a specific instance, they give much more favorable responses (Katz, Gutek, Kahn, and Barton, 1975).

Ambivalent public attitudes contribute to the challenges of public management. In the absence of economic markets as mechanisms for measuring need and performance, public officials and public organizations often struggle with difficult questions about what the public wants. In recent decades, elected officials have often responded with reforms and decisions that directly influence structures, behavior, and management in public organizations. Nations cycle in and out of periods of antigovernment sentiment (Hirschman, 1982). At the time of this writing, it remains to be seen whether the events of September 11 and its aftermath will change the climate in the United States. Nevertheless, these examples illustrate the influence on public management of general public sentiment.

## Public Opinion and Agencies, Policies, and Officials

The general level of public support for a particular agency's programs affects the agency's ability to maintain a base of political support. Certain agencies hold a more central place than others in the country's values (Meier, 2000; Wamsley and Zald, 1973), and the public regards their work as more crucial. The Department of Defense, police departments, and fire departments typically retain strong general public support because of the importance people attach to national defense and personal security. Some social programs, such as those perceived to involve welfare payments to the poor, receive weaker support in public opinion polls.

Hargrove and Glidewell (1990) have proposed a classification of public agencies and managerial jobs that places a heavy emphasis on public opinion. They classify public management jobs on the basis of how the public perceives the agency's clientele (for example, public sentiment toward prisoners and welfare dependents is usually negative), the level of respect the public has for the professional authority of the agency and its head (for example, a scientific or medical professional basis usually gets more respect), and its general level of support for the mission and purpose of the agency. This chapter returns to such factors later when discussing the sources of authority for public agencies and managers.

# Media Power: Obvious and Mysterious

The importance of public opinion bolsters the power of the news media. Congressional committees or state legislative committees summon agency executives before them to explain the events surrounding an embarrassing news story about an agency. Whistle-blowers who go public with news about agency misconduct or incompetence have often received such harsh treatment that the federal government has made special provisions to protect them (Rosen, 1998). Bad press can sledgehammer an agency or an official, damaging budgets, programs, and careers. A survey of persons who served as high-level executives in various presidential administrations found that the vast majority of them regarded media coverage as having a significant impact on public policy. Most of them had tried to get media coverage for their agency, and three quarters of them reported spending at least five hours a week on matters pertaining to the press and media coverage (Graber, 2003, p. 245).

Close media scrutiny of government plays an indispensable role in governance. The news media also report aggressively on scandals in private business, yet they appear to place more emphasis on scrutiny of government. Government is often more accessible, and it is more appropriate to watch it carefully, because government spends the taxpayers' money. In cities around the country, local news reporters regularly chase down stories about governmental waste or abuse. For example, in some cities they have searched the parking lots of bars and restaurants during normal working hours to take pictures of the license tags of any government vehicles parked there. In one city a television station carried stories about the high costs of the furniture in the office of one of the county commissioners. Major television networks have news segments and special series that regularly broadcast allegations of government waste.

News reporters usually take a strong adversarial stance. They want to avoid seeming naive or co-opted. They need to focus on serious problems and generate an audience by reporting on controversial issues. The Volcker Commission (1989) report describes how Carter administration officials had trouble attracting interest in their proposals for civil service reforms until they developed a twenty-six-foot chart illustrating the tortuous steps it took to fire a bad federal employee. The news media immediately focused on this issue and provided more coverage. This attention apparently led the president to emphasize the negative, punitive aspects of the reforms in trying to build support for them. Thus, media coverage influenced the tenor of reforms that shaped the personnel practices of the federal government and influenced the morale of employees throughout the public sector.

If anything, news coverage of government appears to be increasingly negative. Patterson (2001) carefully documents that since 1960 news coverage has become much less descriptive (reporters no longer present only the facts) and much more interpretive of developments. During the same period, coverage of candidates during presidential elections has become much more negative.

Instances in which unfavorable press coverage damages a person, program, or agency make concern about media coverage part of the lore of government (Linsky, 1986). Officials and experts from Washington speak of managing in a "goldfish bowl" (Allison, 1983; Cohen and Eimicke, 1995; IBM Endowment for the Business of Government, 2002), with media attention playing a stronger role in government than it does in business management (Blumenthal, 1983). For years observers have worried that some federal executives devote more time to creating a splash in the media than to performing well as managers (Lynn, 1981). Many public employees appear to feel that they will not get into much trouble for poor performance but will get into a *lot* of trouble for creating bad publicity (Lynn, 1981; Warwick, 1975; Downs, 1967). City and county officials will pack an auditorium to listen to consultants speak on how to handle media relations, and they regularly complain about unfair media coverage.

This apparent power of the media has mysterious qualities. The potential damage from bad coverage is often unclear. Ronald Reagan earned a reputation as the "Teflon president" by maintaining popularity in spite of sharp criticism in the media. As an additional irony, much of the worry over press coverage amounts to worrying over an entity in which the general public expresses little confidence. Public opinion polls find that public confidence in journalists and the news media is lower than public confidence in many other institutions and has been declining in recent decades (Patterson, 2001). For a long time, many experts argued that the media exercise little influence over public voting patterns and attitudes about specific issues. Some experts on the news media now argue that the media exert a powerful influence on public attitudes, but in a diffuse way. Media coverage develops a climate that pervades the informational environment, and this in turn influences public opinion (Murray, Schwartz, and Lichter, 2001; Lichter, Rothman, and Lichter, 1986). In addition, some experts conclude that journalists develop a shared view of what constitutes news, and this leads to a version of the news that is generally shared by the different news organizations (Patterson, 2001).

Media attention also varies. Some agencies regularly get more media attention than others. Hood and Dunsire (1981) found that the foreign affairs office and the treasury get particularly high levels of press coverage in Britain, while other central government departments get relatively little attention. The media often seriously neglect administrative issues. Yet public officials also know that media attention can shift unpredictably. In one large state, where the department of administration ordinarily received little public attention, the director decided to change the set of private health insurance plans from which the state's employees chose their coverage. Many employees disliked the new set of plans. An outburst of complaints from state employees caused a sudden wave of coverage in the newspapers and television news around the state. A legislative committee soon called the director before special hearings about the changes.

Officials at higher levels and in political centers (capitals and large cities) often pay a great deal of attention to media strategies. Many city governments issue newsletters, televise city council meetings, and use other methods of public communication. Some federal and state agencies invest heavily in issuing public information. Even so, many public managers resist suggestions that they should devote time to media relations, regarding themselves as professionals rather than as "politicians." More active approaches, however, usually prove to be the most effective (Graber, 2003). Various experts have offered advice on how to deal with the media. Exhibit 5.2 summarizes typical recommendations.

# Interest Groups, Clients, and Constituencies

The support of organized groups also determines the political well-being of public agencies. The role of organized interests in American politics generates continuing controversy. Special-interest politics poses the danger that the system will become (or has already become) too fragmented into self-interested groups, making it resistant to central coordination and hence unmanageable (Lowi, 1979). Critics say that the system favors richer, more powerful groups over the disadvantaged and allows private interests to control major domains of public policy. Influence peddling abounds in this system and creates ethical dilemmas for many public managers. Some face temptations, for example, to go easy on industries that they regulate in order to enhance their chance of acquiring a lucrative job in them.

## EXHIBIT 5.2. GUIDELINES FOR MANAGING RELATIONS WITH THE NEWS MEDIA.

Experts on managing relations between government agencies and the news media propose such guidelines as the following:

- Understand the perspective of the media—their skepticism, their need for information and interesting stories, their time pressures.
- Organize media relations carefully—spend time and resources on them and link them with agency operations.
- Get out readable press releases providing good news about the agency; be patient if the media respond slowly.
- Respond to bad news and embarrassing incidents rapidly, with clear statements of the agency's side of the story.
- Seek corrections of inaccurate reporting.
- Use the media to help boost the agency's image, to implement programs, and to communicate with employees.
- To carry all this off effectively, make sure that the agency performs well, and be honest.

The Community Relations Office of the City of Claremont, California, published the following guidelines for managing relations with reporters:

- Prepare an agenda on each subject the media may be interested in. Include a list of three to five points you want to "sell" the reporter.
- Write or verbally deliver "quotable quotes" of ten words or less.
- Listen carefully to the question. The reporter may have made incorrect assumptions, and you will need to give clearer background information before answering the question.
- Avoid an argument with the reporter.
- If interrupted in midthought, proceed with your original answer before answering the new question.
- Challenge any effort to put words into your mouth.
- Don't just answer the question; use the question as a springboard to "sell" your agenda.
- If you do not know the answer, say so. Do not speculate.
- If you cannot divulge information, state why in a matter-of-fact way.
- Be positive, not defensive.
- Always tell the truth.

*Source:* First half adapted from Cohen and Eimicke, 1995; Chase and Reveal, 1983; and Garnett, 1992. Second half adapted from Larkin, 1992.

Yet public managers also recognize that interest-group activities are not all bad. They play an important role in the current system and provide government with important information. Legislation requires that public managers consult with interested groups and their representatives. Often these groups voice reasonable demands—help our industry so we do not have to lay people off, help us with the economic development of your jurisdiction, help defend the country with this new weapons system, support education, aid the disadvantaged. Sometimes demands from different groups are reasonable but sharply conflicting.

Given the importance of these groups, many public managers have to culti-vate their support. More generally, many authors have pointed out that because public agencies need political support for their funding and for authorization to act, their leaders have to nurture political constituencies (Chase and Reveal, 1983; Doig and Hargrove, 1987; Graber, 2003; Hargrove and Glidewell, 1990; Meier, 2000; Radin, 2002; Rourke, 1984; Wildavsky, 1988;). Strong support from con-stituencies helps an agency defend itself against budget cuts or even secure bud-get increases from legislative bodies. It can also help agencies defend themselves against unwanted directives from legislators and chief executives. Constituent groups can promote an agency in ways that it cannot properly pursue itself. In-terest groups can block an agency's actions, sometimes popping up unexpect-edly as a manager tries to act.

What kind of group support bolsters an agency? Apparently, the most effec-tive support comes from well-organized, cohesive groups that are strongly com-mitted to the agency and its programs. Conversely, *capture* of an agency by a constituency can damage the agency and bias it toward the self-interested prior-ities of that group (Rourke, 1984; Wilson, 1989). Critics have accused some reg-ulatory agencies of being captives of the industries or professions they supposedly regulate, and they complain that other agencies are captured by the clientele who receive their services (allegedly, the Forest Service has been captured by timber in-terests and the Bureau of Mines by mining interests). Agencies appear to have the most flexibility when they have the support of multiple groups; they can then sat-isfy some groups, if not all, and even have them confront one another about their conflicting demands (Chase and Reveal, 1983; Meier, 2000; Rourke, 1984).

Studies over the last two decades have reported that managers in state and local government agencies often see interest-group involvement with their agency as ben-eficial and appropriate. State and local agency managers regard interest groups as having less influence on the operations of their agency than the chief execu-tive (the governor or mayor) or the legislature. When groups do exert influence, they often provide useful information about policy issues and group positions (Abney and Lauth, 1986; Brudney and Hebert, 1987; Elling, 1983). Abney and Lauth (1986) found additional evidence that agency managers at the urban level see interest-group involvement as appropriate when it focuses directly on the agency and inappropriate when it is channeled through the city council or the mayor. The managers may be too forgiving of interest-group influences, but the findings also suggest a more positive or at least necessary side of interest groups. Experienced public managers see maintaining relations with these groups as a necessary part of their work, often frustrating but also challenging and sometimes helpful. Public managers have to be accessible to such groups, seriously attentive to what they have to say, patient and self-controlled when the groups are harshly critical, and honest (Chase and Reveal, 1983; Cohen and Eimicke, 1995).

## Legislative Bodies

Congress, state legislatures, city councils, and county commissions exercise as much formal, legal authority over public organizations as does any other entity. Formal authority always operates in a political context, which may weaken it or bolster it in practical terms.

### Formal Authority

Legislative bodies have substantial formal powers, including authority to control agency budgets, to pass legislation that authorizes and directs agency actions, and to oversee agency activities through hearings, investigations, and other means.

*Power of the Purse.* Legislative bodies provide the money needed to operate public agencies. They exercise the final power of approval over budget allocations to agencies. They can fund new initiatives or cut and curtail agency activities aggressively.

*Legislation.* Government agencies are usually born through legislation, especially at the federal and state levels. (At local levels, the agencies of a city government are often required under state guidelines.) Such legislation states the basic missions and duties of the agencies and authorizes their activities. Additional legislation can give an agency new duties. Its policies and programs can be extended, given to some other agency, reformed, or abolished.

Some scholars observe that legislation often transmits vague, idealized directives to agencies. For example, legislation directs various regulatory agencies to promote "just" and "reasonable" practices in the public interest and for the common welfare (Woll, 1977). According to Lowi's (1979) prominent argument, these broad grants of authority give the agencies considerable discretion, and hinder central, purposeful control of the agencies and the public policy process. Diffuse directives also add to the influences that impose vague, multiple, often conflicting goals on government agencies.

Conversely, legislatures sometimes do the opposite, delving into the precise details of agency management and procedures and engaging in micromanagement. They sometimes reform the general structure of the executive branch, combining certain departments and splitting others apart. They sometimes dictate the organizational structure of major agencies, including what subunits they establish. They produce legislation governing the details of personnel procedures for the agencies within their jurisdiction or precisely dictate other administrative procedures. For example, state legislatures sometimes include in legislation detailed specifications about the types of computer records a state regulatory agency must maintain. The U.S. Internal Revenue Service Restructuring and Reform Act of 1998 (RRA98) specified many of the main features of the agency's structure and procedures, such as its new operating divisions, flexibilities in personnel administration, and sanctions for specific forms of misconduct by IRS employees. This example, however, actually illustrates a complex interplay between the legislative and administrative branches that may create the appearance of legislative direction when in fact the agency is the source of some of the ideas. In actuality, many of the provisions of RRA98, such as the agency's new structure and its provisions for personnel administration, were proposed by task forces and executives in the agency, and then written into the legislation.

**Oversight.** Legislative bodies regularly conduct hearings, audits, and investigations into agency activities (Rosen, 1998). Hearings are a normal part of the appropriations process and of the process of developing legislation. Investigatory and oversight agencies are established under the authority of the legislative branch to carry out inquiries into agency activities and performance. The General Accounting Office at the federal level and auditors general or similar offices in the states conduct audits to support legislative oversight.

Congressional oversight at the federal level has intensified in recent decades and has increasingly focused on administrative processes, apparently in response to presidents' efforts to control the bureaucracy (West, 1995). Wood and Waterman (1994) report evidence that congressional oversight can significantly influence the outputs and actions of federal agencies. They show, for example, that it led to a sharp increase in enforcement actions by the Environmental Protection Agency's hazardous waste compliance division during one period in the 1980s.

**Committees.** Particular legislative committees oversee particular agencies, conducting hearings about them, examining their operations, and developing legislation pertaining to them. Names of some committees correspond almost exactly to the names of major federal and state agencies. City councils often have a committee structure as well, with committees corresponding to the major departments and functions of the city government. Harold Seidman, one of the leading experts on federal administrative reforms, argues that if one wants to reform the federal bureaucracy, one must first reform Congress. Congressional committees jealously guard their authority over agencies (Seidman and Gilmour, 1986). An appropriations committee chair once objected to extending the president's power to veto legislation, saying, "We don't want the agencies taking orders from the president. We want them to take orders from us" (Miller, 1990).

## Informal Influence

Legislative influences can be relatively informal as well, rather than codified into law. For example, legislators call administrators on the phone to press them for information or to ask for certain actions. State and federal administrators trying to relocate their agencies' offices or facilities to save money or to reorganize their operations frequently hear from outraged legislators whose districts will lose facilities and jobs. During the 1960s, the U.S. Department of Labor sought to better organize diverse work-training programs run by various bureaus by bringing them under the authority of a newly created Manpower Administration. In committee hearings, powerful members of Congress told the head of this new agency that he should leave the Bureau of Apprenticeship and Trades (BAT) alone and not bring it into the new structure (Ruttenberg and Gutchess, 1970). Labor unions wanted to maintain a strong influence on BAT and had lobbied members of Congress to oppose moving BAT into the new structure. Similarly, legislators press for the hiring or against the firing of political friends and allies in agencies (Warwick, 1975). None of these actions is necessarily formally authorized, and some are quite improper. They illustrate an additional dimension of legislative influence on the bureaucracy and show why legislators strive to defend their alliances and influences with the bureaucracy.

## Limits on Legislative Power

Some experts insist that, even armed with all these powers, legislative bodies exert little real control over administrative agencies (Woll, 1977). The agencies are specialized and staffed with experts who know much more about their functions than do legislators and their staffs. Legislators often have little incentive to be aggressive in supervising agency performance (Meier, 2000; Ripley and Franklin, 1984). Such "good government" activities offer little political advantage, because constituents often cannot see the results. In addition, tough oversight of agencies could jeopardize relationships with them, removing them as potential sources of favors for constituents. Agencies also have independent sources of support from interest groups and from parts of the legislative bodies and executive branches that they can play off against other parts. As mentioned previously, however, recent evidence suggests that although legislative influence is a complicated subject, legislative bodies clearly influence agencies significantly in many instances (Wood and Waterman, 1994).

Legislative authority also varies across jurisdictions. Certain states, such as Florida, have relatively powerful legislatures that are based on the state's legal and institutional arrangements. The authority and power of city councils and county commissions vary from place to place depending, for example, on whether there is a "strong mayor" or "weak mayor" government in a city.

# The Chief Executive

Presidents, governors, and mayors rival the legislative branch for the status of strongest political influence on agencies. Presumably, chief executives have the greatest formal power over the public bureaucracies in their jurisdictions. Yet, as with legislative bodies, the influence patterns are complex and dynamic, and chief executives face similar challenges in taming the unwieldy bureaucracy.

## Appointments

Chief executives appoint heads of executive agencies and usually an additional array of patronage positions within those agencies. Wood and Waterman (1994) found that the appointment of a new agency head was often strongly related to a change in agency actions and outputs in the direction of the president's preferences. The chief executive's ability to influence agencies through these appointments varies by agency, jurisdiction, and political climate, however. President Reagan mounted an aggressive effort to influence federal agencies through appointments. He filled the top positions of some major agencies with executives committed to reducing the regulatory role, size, and influence of the federal bureaucracy. As a result, certain agencies sharply curtailed their staff and activities (Golden, 2000; Rubin, 1985). Administration officials also added new levels of political appointees at the top of agencies. This added layers between the top executives and the highest-level career civil servants, effectively demoting career service managers. These steps had so much impact that the Volcker Commission (1989) called for reductions in the number of appointments the president can make. This example illustrates the potential power that the authority to make appointments gives a chief executive. In certain states and localities, many major or cabinet-level agency executives are independently elected and thus not beholden to the chief executive. Jurisdictions also vary in the degree to which they have patronage appointments within agencies.

## Executive Staff Offices

The executive offices of the U.S. president and of governors and mayors around the country give chief executives various resources that can bolster their influence. Units within an executive office can represent special constituencies and functions.

A governor might have an office of minority affairs or veterans' affairs as a way of demonstrating concern for that constituency. Other subunits might concentrate on press relations or relations with the legislature. Some governors and local executives have inspectors general in their executive offices to conduct investigations into allegations of improprieties in agencies.

## Budgeting Authority

The most significant of the staff offices are those that wrestle with budgets—the Office of Management and Budget in the Executive Office of the President and similar offices on the staffs of mayors and governors. The legislative branch ultimately approves the budget, but the chief executive assembles agency budget requests and submits them to the legislature for approval. The chief executive tries to hammer his or her priorities into the budget by proposing extensions or cuts in funding for programs. The executive's influence over the budget depends on many factors—anticipated tax revenues, programs needing attention, developments in the political climate (such as strong midterm election results for the chief executive's party or strong popularity ratings). The legislative body may fight back, of course, putting money back into programs that the chief executive tries to cut, and vice versa. Agency officials engage in various ploys to maintain their funding and avoid cuts (Wildavsky, 1988). Their ability to do so depends on factors already described, such as group support. Yet through this process the chief executives have significant potential influence on public policy and public agencies.

## Policy Initiatives and Executive Orders

Chief executives have certain formal powers to tell agencies what to do through directives and executive orders (Cooper, 1996). For example, some of the original equal employment opportunity (EEO) initiatives were implemented through executive orders from President Eisenhower and later presidents. They directed federal agencies and private companies holding federal contracts to establish EEO programs. Chief executives can also prompt agencies to develop programs and policies that the executive will support through the budgeting process.

Many of the proposals developed by the Clinton administration's National Performance Review were implemented through presidential executive orders. The president ordered agencies to reduce rules and red tape, to develop customer service standards, and to establish "reinvention laboratories" to develop innovative new processes, among other actions. Cooper (1996) argues that executive orders can be very useful to presidents, and some of these actions illustrate their effects. Agencies responded rapidly in carrying out some of the actions the president directed as part of the National Performance Review. Cooper also notes, however, that executive orders can complicate the roles of agency executives, because they sometimes conflict with other legal mandates for the agency. They become part of the complex, often conflicting influences on agencies and their leaders. In one virtually comical instance, President Clinton issued an executive order directing all federal agencies to reduce their rules by 50 percent.

# The Courts

As with the other institutions surrounding public organizations, some experts say that the courts exert powerful controls over the public bureaucracy, while others see them as ineffectual. Various experts point to the courts as the strongest ultimate check on the power of the public bureaucracy, while others see bureaucratic power overwhelming the courts.

The federal and state courts operate under fairly conservative principles (Cooper, 2000, pp. 63–67; Woll, 1977). Courts overrule the actions of agencies for two main reasons. They can stop an agency from going beyond the intent of the legislation that created it. They can also prevent an agency from violating correct procedures, such as those required under the due process of law provisions of the Constitution and related legal precedents. These standards actually focus the courts on preventing agency actions rather than on proactively directing policies and programs. In addition, a number of relatively conservative legal principles strengthen the position of public agencies in disputes with citizens or groups. Examples of these include provisions that make public officials immune to many types of liability or require citizens with complaints against agencies to exhaust all possible remedies that they can seek through the agency before a court will hear their complaint. Also, for the courts to settle a dispute, someone has to initiate a lawsuit; this is expensive and can take a long time. Agencies win a lot of suits because they have highly specialized personnel and legal expertise at their disposal (Meier, 2000).

In a sweeping critique of contemporary governmental processes in the United States, Lowi (1979) cites vague legislation as a major problem in weakening judicial oversight of the bureaucracy. To achieve compromise among diverse interests in the legislative process, Congress and other legislative units give diffuse grants of authority to agencies, passing legislation that communicates only very general objectives and standards. Courts then have difficulty enforcing adherence to congressional intent. The sheer size and complexity of the administrative branch of government, the wide range of specializations it encompasses, and the technical complexity of many of the policy issues that come before the courts make it extremely difficult for the courts to exercise strong control over bureaucratic actions (Stewart, 1975).

Yet under the right circumstances, the courts wield immense authority and can be very aggressive in the oversight of administrative agencies (O'Leary and Straussman, 1993; Rosenbloom and O'Leary, 1997). Through injunctions they can force or block an agency's actions. They can make an agency pay damages, thus making administrators very careful about assessing the legal implications of their rules and procedures. Limitations on judicial interventions concerning, for example, citizens' ability to sue government officials and exhaustion of administrative remedies have relaxed over time (Meier, 2000). A ruling making it easier for citizens to sue social workers when children under their supervision suffer child abuse has changed the procedures and expenses of agencies across the country. In surveys, administrators report that court decisions influence the allocation of funds at state and local levels for education, prisons, hospitals, and other services (Meier, 2000).

Congress has moved toward including more specific standards in some legislation (Wilson, 1989), and court rulings sometimes focus powerfully on one particular aspect of an agency's operations. Courts sometimes intervene in particular agency activities, often due to some constitutional principle such as due process of law or equal protection of the law. On occasion, courts have in effect taken over schools and prisons in certain jurisdictions. Lawsuits to force agencies to comply with legislation requiring environmental impact statements prior to any major building project have delayed many projects in many agencies. The courts wait in the background, in a sense, directly intervening in day-to-day operations of public organizations only on occasion. Yet they pose an ominous background presence. Administrators frequently take actions and establish procedures expressly because of what a court has done or *might* do.

Recent research has strengthened the position that courts have a significant influence on agency operations (O'Leary, 1994; Wood and Waterman, 1994). O'Leary (1994) cites numerous examples of a "new partnership" between judges and public managers that entails significant judicial influence over agencies and their operations as well as extensive interaction with agencies' managers and staff. She has reviewed research on these developments in relation to personnel administration in agencies and found evidence of such interaction. Her research provides evidence that the courts sometimes dictate which issues an agency must attend to. Courts can diminish the authority of administrators, in part by dictating where they must devote agency resources. This can decrease the budgetary discretion of administrators (and can involve a judge's refusal to defer to an administrator's expertise). Court orders can also influence staff morale, sometimes demoralizing people in the agency and sometimes boosting their enthusiasm about their work. These examples and findings provide the beginnings of a body of research that needs much more development. The material from organization theory and organizational development reviewed in other parts of this book shows that the legal and judicial environment have not received much attention from organizational researchers (O'Leary and Straussman, 1993). These examples, however, show how the governmental and legal institutions surrounding public organizations can directly influence organizational design and effectiveness and the behavior of the people within organizations. They also reveal that most public managers and employees need a sound knowledge of the judicial environment (Rosenbloom and O'Leary, 1997; Cooper, 1996, 2000), and they raise a number of important research questions for scholars.

# Other Agencies and Levels of Government

Public organizations both work together and fight with one another. The participants in this contest represent all the different levels of government, the various agencies, and certain oversight bodies concerned with personnel administration, budgeting, and central purchasing. Later chapters describe many examples of ways in which this affects management within public organizations.

In the U.S. federal system of government, higher levels of government direct and regulate the lower levels in various ways. Some federal programs, such as social security, are actually carried out by state personnel following federal guidelines. Behind this generally cooperative structure, however, patterns of mutual influence operate.

Grants from higher levels of government exert some of this influence. Merit systems have disseminated throughout the personnel departments of state and local governments in the United States, in part because federal grants were made available to set up such systems. Federal laws can mandate that federal money for programs be matched in certain ways by states and localities. For example, states must contribute to Medicare payments for individuals, adding to the amounts paid by the federal government. With these funding arrangements come influences on state and local governments' structures and procedures.

Laws and regulations, whether or not they are attached to grants or other funding instruments, also exert such influences. State and federal environmental protection regulations and growth and economic development mandates dictate how programs must be managed by lower levels of government. Federal legislation sometimes directs a federal agency to do certain things in every state unless the states do them in a way that meets certain minimum standards established by the federal government. An example of this is the federal government's policy regarding mine safety regulations, under which it must oversee mine safety within a state unless the state can finance and manage the program itself, at least at the level required by federal standards.

The relationships between the different levels of government may be very smooth in many instances, but the lower levels do not necessarily accept higher-level influences and requirements lying down. During the Reagan administration, some state governments refused to carry out directives from the Social Security Administration requiring them to review the cases of many disability payment recipients and deny payments to some of them under more stringent rules. During a later administration, many states were slow to comply with federal laws requiring that they increase their share of Medicare payments (Tolchin, 1989). Localities also work hard to influence state and federal legislation that may bear significantly on their activities. Associations such as the League of Cities lobby at the state and federal levels for legislation that they feel they need.

Organizations at a given level of government also cooperate and compete in many ways. Johnson (1989) describes how, as of the late 1980s, the "intelligence community" of the U.S. government involved more than forty federal agencies with responsibilities for intelligence operations. The delivery of many local services in the United States often involves a complex network of joint agreements and contracts among localities. State and federal agencies typically have overlapping responsibilities and engage in joint planning and activity. The EEO Coordinating Commission was established to coordinate the various agencies at the federal level that had responsibilities for carrying out affirmative action and EEO policies. Agencies also compete with each other for the time and attention of higher-level executives (Chase and Reveal, 1983) and over turf, seeking to block other agencies and authorities from gaining control over their programs (Wilson, 1989).

## Public Managers' Perceptions of the Political Environment

Later chapters describe a variety of studies that pertain to how public managers respond to these components of their political environments and how those environments influence public organizations. Some studies mentioned earlier, however, provide evidence of how public managers perceive various aspects of the political context, such as the relative influence of chief executives, legislatures, and interest groups (Abney and Lauth, 1986; Brudney and Hebert, 1987; Elling, 1983). These studies indicate that state agency managers see their legislatures as the most influential, with the governor coming second (although there are variations among the states in the relative power of the governor and the legislature). Local managers see the chief executive—the mayor—as the most influential actor. State and local agency managers rate interest groups as much less influential than legislatures and chief executives but often see them as valuable contributors to decision making.

Aberbach, Putnam, and Rockman (1981; see also Aberbach and Rockman, 2000) provide a similar account of the strong influence of the legislative branch at the federal level. They analyzed contacts between administrative officials and other actors in the federal systems of the United States and five other industrial democracies. In the United States they found much higher levels of contact between civil service administrators in agencies and congressional committee members than either of these two groups had with the executive heads of the agencies. The civil service managers had even more contacts with constituent groups than with Congress, however. Aberbach, Putnam, and Rockman referred to this pattern as the "end run" model, because it involves civil servants and legislators going around executive agency heads, and they discovered that it occurs more often in the United States than in any of the other countries they studied.

Studies identifying how public managers perceive the nature of their own political activities are rare, but Olshfski (1990) identifies three conceptions of politics that emerge in state agency executives' descriptions of their political activities: *political astuteness,* the understanding of the political system and the processes of government and their own departments; *issue politics,* the political activities, such as bargaining and coalition building, necessary to advance an issue or achieve an objective; and *electoral politics,* the knowledge and activity related to gaining general political support for themselves, an elected official, or their departments.

# The Public Policy Process

Analyses of public policy have burgeoned over the last several decades, and so has the recognition that public organizations play an essential role in the formation and implementation of public policy. The policymaking and policy implementation processes are an extremely important aspect of the environment of public organizations and public managers.

## Many Arenas, Actors, Levels, and Instruments

Government activity at all levels encompasses a diverse array of functions and policy domains. Without any standard nomenclature, scholars and government officials refer to policy categories such as defense, health, science and technology, social welfare and poverty, environmental protection, energy, economic and fiscal policy (including tax policy), agricultural policy, industrial development policy, educational policy, and regulatory policy. Government activities at state and local levels, sometimes referred to as service delivery rather than public policy, include a similarly diverse list: industrial development, zoning and land use, police and firefighting services, transportation (including streets and roads), garbage collection, prisons and jails, parks and recreation, and many others. As mentioned earlier, state and local governments are also part of the policymaking process for major federal policies. Within these policy areas and spanning them, many specific programs operate at various levels of scope, size, and complexity. All these institutions, levels, authorities, and groups play a part in shaping policy and carrying it out. O'Toole (2000) observes that research on public policy implementation, once very active, slowed down during the last decade, in part because the factors that influence policy implementation are so numerous and complex. Adding to these complexities, governmental policies draw many private for-profit and nonprofit organizations into the processes of making and carrying out public policy. Many government programs operate largely through grants, purchases, and contracts with nongovernmental organizations, such as weapons manufacturers or private nonprofit organizations that seek, for example, to help troubled youths. Besides contracts and grants, governments utilize many additional instruments or "tools" of government action, such as loan programs, regulations, insurance programs, vouchers, user charges, permits, and tax policies (Salamon and Elliot, 2002).

## Policy Subsystems

For a long time, political scientists have observed that this complex public policy system has operating within it an array of subsystems that handle different areas of policy. Also for a long time, political scientists described these domains as being dominated by "iron triangles," which are alliances of congressional committees, administrative agencies, and interest groups that control major policy areas such as defense and environmental policy. Key people in the committees, agencies, and interest groups in the triangle exchange political favors and support. Authorities outside the triangle, even the president, can wield little influence over it. This situation has long been lamented as one of the fundamental problems of government in the United States. Ronald Reagan complained about iron triangles in one of his last public statements as president.

Although the iron triangle analogy refers to a very significant problem, political scientists now point out that it oversimplifies the true complexity and dynamism of these coalitions. Competition and conflict among groups and agencies may flare within the so-called triangles, making them much less solid than the analogy implies. Lawyers may fight doctors over a change in legislation on malpractice suits. One group of large corporations may line up on the other side of an issue from another group of equally large corporations. In addition, as problems change, different groups, organizations, and individuals move in and out of the policy arena. The iron triangle analogy fails to depict the instability and flux in the process. It also suggests that grim power politics is the driving force behind patterns of influence in the public sector (Kingdon, 1995).

To better characterize the situation, scholars began to coin new terms. Heclo (1978) referred to "issue networks" of experts, officials, and interests that form around particular issues and that can shift rapidly. Milward and Wamsley (1982) described what they call policy networks, or complex and shifting aggregations of groups, experts, public and private organizations, governmental authorities, and others whose interplay shapes the formation and implementation of policy. Others referred to subgovernments' implementation structures (Hjern and Porter, 1981), public service industries, policy subsystems (Rainey and Milward, 1983), and policy communities (Kingdon, 1995). These subsystems or networks prove unwieldy and resistant to external control or coordination with other networks. Yet the depiction of the problem as one of staunch control by self-serving bureaucrats, politicians, and private interests oversimplifies the problem. Often the difficulties in coordination and control result largely from the flux and complexity of the issues, interests, and participants involved in the process.

## Privatization, the Hollow State, and Networks

Because government and government agencies at all levels have increasingly contracted out portions of their functions and used the tools or instruments just described, government now delivers more programs and services through organizations that are not formally owned or operated by government. These developments involve increased sharing of power with these nongovernmental organizations, with government providing a proxy to private organizations to carry out its programs and policies (Kettl, 1993, 2002). Privatization has continued to expand in many policy areas, such as human and social service programs (Smith and Lipsky, 1993), environmental and energy programs, and prisons.

These developments complicate the lines of accountability and make public managers responsible for organizational activities they can control indirectly, through contracts and grants or other mechanisms. In some cases, private and nonprofit contractors and grant recipients, instead of providing a competitive private sector alternative, become part of the political lobby for the programs with which they are involved (Smith and Lipsky, 1993). In other cases, government officials use private contractors to justify the pursuit of certain political and social objectives that they might not be able to justify through the normal legislative process. Moe (1996) argues that in these ways, privatization may involve more of a governmentalization of the private sector than a privatization of government.

In some policy areas, privatization has extended so far that government has become "hollow," with private contractors taking over most or all of its authority and activity (Milward and Provan, 2000; Milward, Provan, and Else, 1993; Provan and Milward, 2001). Mental health programs, for example, may be provided by networks of private or nonprofit organizations, with government funding but virtually no involvement by government employees and fairly high autonomy on the part of the providers in making decisions about services and programs. Government policies and programs are increasingly carried out by networks of government agencies, private firms, and nonprofit organizations that are supposed to collaborate in the delivery of the program or policy (Kettl, 2002). The proliferation of such networks, or of interdependent groups of organizations or parts of organizations that have no formal hierarchical or superior-subordinate relations to each other, raises complex issues about their design, management, and evaluation that later chapters discuss (Milward and Provan, 2000; Provan and Milward, 2001; O'Toole, 1999). Obviously they make contract management and the management of other network or third-party arrangements more important skills for many public managers (see Chapter Six). Accordingly, Chapter Fourteen covers the management of privatization in considering managerial excellence in the public sector.

## The Agenda-Setting Process and the Agenda Garbage Can

Public policy researchers also help characterize the complex context of public management by analyzing how certain matters gain prominence on the public agenda while others languish outside of public notice. Kingdon (1995) says that this process resembles the "garbage can model" of decision making developed by March and his colleagues (Cohen, March, and Olsen, 1972). As described in more detail in Chapter Seven, the garbage can model depicts decision making in organizations as being much less systematic and rational than is commonly supposed. People are not sure about their preferences or about how their organization works. Streams of problems, solutions, participants, and choice opportunities flow along through time, sometimes coming together in combinations that shape decisions. (An example of a choice opportunity is a salient problem that has to be addressed by a newly formed committee with sufficient authority to have a chance at getting something done.) The process is more topsy-turvy than the organizational chart might suggest. Sometimes solutions actually chase problems, as when someone has a pet idea that he or she wants to find a chance to apply. Sometimes administrators simply look for work to do. Choice opportunities are like garbage cans in which problems, solutions, and participants come together in a jumbled fashion.

Kingdon revises this view when he applies it to public policy, referring to streams of problems, policies, and politics flowing alongside one another and sometimes coming together at key points to shape the policy agenda. Problems come to the attention of policymakers in various ways: through indicators, such as unemployment figures or figures on budget deficits; through events, such as crises that focus their attention on them; and through feedback, such as citizen complaints and reports on the operation of programs. Policies develop within the policy community as various ideas and alternatives emerge from the "policy primeval soup." Like microorganisms in a biological primeval soup, they originate, compete, evolve, and prosper or perish. They are evaluated in think tanks, conferences, staff meetings in legislative bodies and government agencies, and interest-group activities. They may be partially tried out in programs or legislation, and a long period of "softening up" often follows the original proposal, in which the alternative becomes more and more acceptable. Some alternatives have a long history of implementation, shelving, alteration, and retrial. For example, various versions of public works and job-training camps have appeared at different levels of government since the days of the Civilian Conservation Corps during the New Deal and the Job Corps during the Johnson administration's War on Poverty. At times, events in these streams converge to open windows of opportunity in which political forces align in support of a policy alternative for a particular problem, moving this combination to a central place on the public agenda.

In Kingdon's portrayal, the agenda-setting process appears difficult to predict and understand, but not wildly out of control. The processes of gestation and evaluation focus considerable scrutiny on ideas and alternatives and their workability. Still, this analysis illustrates the dynamism of the policymaking environment in which public managers must operate. In later chapters, the idea of identifying windows of opportunity figures usefully in the discussion of managing change in public organizations. Many of the challenges facing a public manager turn on effective assessment of the political feasibility of particular actions and alternatives and of the array of political forces shaping or curtailing various opportunities.

Public managers, especially at higher levels, must skillfully manage their relationship with the external authorities, actors, networks, and policy processes described in this chapter. They also have to operate effectively within the pattern of interventions and constraints from their environments. The next chapters examine major dimensions in organizing and managing in the public sector. At many points, the discussion illustrates and shows evidence of how the political and institutional environments of public organizations affect their characteristics and the behaviors of the people who work in them.

PART TWO

# KEY DIMENSIONS OF ORGANIZING AND MANAGING

CHAPTER SIX

# ORGANIZATIONAL GOALS AND EFFECTIVENESS

One hates to draw on a topic as horrible as war to make a point, but the Gulf War in the early 1990s and the war in Iraq over a decade later illustrated an important one about the effectiveness of government and government organizations. In the years after the American withdrawal from Vietnam, authors became talk show celebrities for writing books about the shortcomings of the U.S. military (for example, Luttwak, 1984). In the months leading up to the Gulf War, journalists worried that the U.S. forces' weapons and equipment would malfunction in the desert sands, and that the United States could suffer thirty to forty thousand casualties in a war against Iraqi forces. Journalists and commentators expressed similar concerns prior to the war in Iraq. When the wars were over, one had to conclude that the United States and allies had achieved so much success so rapidly, and with so few American casualties, that the outcomes appeared spectacularly successful, by military standards. Many Americans opposed the war, the Iraqi people suffered horribly, each of the American lives lost was a tragedy, and there were almost certainly plenty of mistakes to criticize. The American military forces, however, did not blunder as critics would have led one to expect. Similarly, when U.S. forces were assigned the goal of destroying terrorist forces in Afghanistan, again observers worried that the operation would be extremely protracted and damaging to the United States. Again, while the operation did not achieve total success in a number of ways, its general speed and overpowering effectiveness displayed the fearsome capabilities of the U.S. military. In industrialized democracies, we criticize government sharply as a way of controlling it, often to the point of convincing ourselves that government organizations and their employees bungle constantly and hopelessly. Quite often, however, their effectiveness proves striking, even frightening.

Organizations are goal-directed, purposive entities, and their effectiveness in pursuing those goals influences the quality of our lives and even our ability to survive. Virtually all of management and organization theory is concerned with performance and effectiveness, at least implicitly. Virtually all of it is in some way concerned with the challenge of getting an organization and the people in it to perform well. This chapter first discusses major issues about organizational goals and the goals of public organizations, including observations that other authors have made about how public organizations' goals influence their other characteristics. Then the chapter reviews the models of organizational effectiveness that researchers have developed and discusses their implications for organizing and managing public organizations.

As previous chapters have discussed, beliefs about the performance and effectiveness of public organizations, especially in comparison to private organizations, have played a major role in some of the most significant political changes and government reforms in recent history, in nations around the world. Executives and officials in government, business, and nonprofit organizations emphasize goals and effectiveness in a variety of ways. One can hardly look at the annual report or the Web site of an organization without encountering its mission statement, which expresses the organization's general goals. Very often one also sees statements of core values that express general objectives, and on the Web sites of many government agencies, one can review the organization's strategic plan or performance plan, which expresses its specific goals and performance measures. All of the major federal agencies have strategic plans with goals statements or "performance plans" or both on their Web sites and in their annual reports. The Government Performance and Results Act (GPRA) of 1993 directed each federal agency to develop such plans, and subsequent reports of their performance in relation to the goals. Web sites now make available copies of all the federal agencies' strategic plans and performance plans.

For example, on the Web site for the Social Security Administration (SSA), which in money paid out is the largest federal program, one can review the 2003 performance plan (U.S. Social Security Administration, 2003). The plan proclaims this mission for the agency: "To promote the economic security of the nation's people through compassionate and vigilant leadership in shaping and managing America's social security programs." It further states five strategic goals:

- To promote valued, strong, and responsive social security programs and conduct effective policy development, research and program evaluation
- To deliver customer-responsive, world-class service
- To ensure the integrity of social security programs, with zero tolerance for fraud and abuse
- To be an employer that values and invests in each employee
- To strengthen public understanding of the social security programs

The plan further states a number of more specific goals that refine these strategic ones. For example, the plan states that by 2004, nine out of ten people who do business with the SSA will rate the overall service as "good," "very good," or "excellent," with most rating it as excellent. The plan also states that by 2005, 67 percent of the public's interactions with SSA will be available either electronically via the Internet or through automated telephone service. It further sets the goal of maintaining at 99.8 percent the accuracy rate for avoiding overpayments and underpayments in the main social security program (Old-Age, Survivors, and Disability Insurance).

These expressions of the goals of the SSA raise the question of how useful they are and how much influence they will have on the agency's effectiveness. Clearly many officials and executives think such expressions have value. One now finds strategic plans and performance plans of this sort at all levels of government (Berman and Wang, 2000), in part because state legislatures have passed legislation similar to the GPRA, requiring state agencies to prepare such plans. This huge national investment in stating goals and performance measures reflects one of the strongest trends in public management in the last two decades. Authors and officials have increasingly emphasized themes such as "managing for results" that involve stating goals and measurements that reflect effectiveness in achieving the goals (Abramson and Kamensky, 2001; Osborne and Gaebler, 1992). There is also a movement emphasizing the integration of such goals and performance measures with governmental and agency budgets (Grizzle and Pettijohn, 2002). Melkers and Willoughby (1998) report that forty-seven of the fifty states have some form of requirement for performance-based budgeting.

This concentration on goals and performance measures involves interesting basic assumptions. It assumes that public organizations will perform better if the people in them clarify their goals and measure progress against them. This assumption usually links to the idea that government agencies need to perform a lot better, and that they can do so by becoming more like business firms, which presumably have clearer goals and performance measures. These assumptions sound reasonable enough, but Radin (2000) points out that these and others undergirding the GPRA and related approaches at other levels of government may not work well in the fragmented, pluralistic institutional and political environments of government agencies described in the last chapter. The multiple authorities and actors in the system do not necessarily agree on the goals and performance criteria for public organizations, and they often do not support a rational, goal-oriented approach to decision making.

Still, the importance attached to goals, performance, and effectiveness makes it interesting and important to examine the way organization and management theorists have dealt with these topics. Ironically, in relation to the emphasis that public officials have been placing on goals and measures, when one turns to the literature on organizational goals and effectiveness, one finds something of a muddle, although a very insightful one. Experts in the field have not developed clear, conclusive ways of defining organizational goals and defining and assessing effectiveness. Their use of the somewhat unusual-sounding concept of organizational effectiveness reflects some of the complications. Referring simply to organizational success bears less of an implication that the activities of the organization brought about the success. Referring to effectiveness suggests not only that the organization had good results but also that it brought about these results through its own management, design, and other features.

Many other terms for performing well also have limitations. In assessing business firms, most investors look carefully at their profitability. Yet sophisticated investors realize that short-term profitability may in some cases mask long-term problems. In addition, consumer advocates and environmental groups object to assessments of business performance that disregard concerns for the environment and ethical concerns for the consumer. In addition, profitability does not apply to government and nonprofit organizations. As with the generic approach in general, researchers have to consider the need for a general body of knowledge on organizational effectiveness that is not restricted to certain sectors or industries. As described shortly, in response to such complications, researchers have attempted a number of different approaches to organizational goals and effectiveness.

# General Organizational Goals

An organizational goal is a condition that an organization seeks to attain. The discussion here recites many problems with the concept of goals, but organization theorists have developed some useful insights and distinctions about them. For example, the mission statements that have become so popular in recent decades represent what organization theorists would call official goals (Perrow, 1961). Official goals are formal expressions of general goals that present an organization's major values and purposes, such as those for the SSA described earlier. One tends to encounter official goals in mission statements and annual reports, where they are meant to enhance the organization's legitimacy and motivate and guide its members. Operative goals are the relatively specific immediate ends an organization seeks, reflected in its actual operations and procedures. People in organizations often consider goals important as expressions of guiding organizational values that can stimulate and generally orient employees to the organization's mission. In addition, clarifying goals for individuals and work groups can improve efficiency and productivity. The discussion of motivation in Chapter Ten reviews the research that shows that providing workers with clear, challenging goals can enhance their productivity. Nevertheless, the concept of a goal has many complications, with important implications for organizing and managing and for the debate over whether public and private organizations differ.

These complications include the problem that goals are always multiple (Rainey, 1993). A goal is always one of a set of goals that one is trying to achieve (Simon, 1973). The goals in a set often conflict with one another—maximizing one goal takes away from another goal. Short-term and long-term goals can conflict with each other. For example, while business firms supposedly have clearer, more measurable goals than public and nonprofit organizations, such firms have to try to manage conflicts among goals for short-term and long-term profits, community and public relations, employee and management development, and social responsibility (such as compliance with affirmative action and environmental protection laws). Goals are arranged in chains and hierarchies, and this makes it hard to express a goal in an ultimate or conclusive way. One goal leads to another or is an operative goal for a higher or more general goal. Many of the concepts related to organizational purpose—such as goals, objectives, values, incentives, and motives—overlap in various ways, leaving us with no conclusive or definitive terminology. Distinctions among these concepts are relatively arbitrary.

These complications appear to be related to a divergence among organization theorists, between those who take the concept of goals very seriously and those who reject it as relatively useless (Rainey, 1993). These complications present a problem for both theorists and practicing managers. The later discussion of models of effectiveness points out that these sorts of complications impede the assessment of organizational effectiveness—it can be difficult to say what an organization's goals really are and to measure their achievement. It is important for leaders and managers to help the organization clarify its goals, but these complications make that a very challenging process. The next chapter discusses some of the procedures that members of organizations can use to clarify the organization's goal statements.

## Goals of Public Organizations

The complications also contribute to an interesting anomaly in the debate over the distinctiveness of public organizations. They imply that all organizations, including business firms, have vague, multiple, and relatively intangible goals. Without a doubt, however, the most often repeated observations about public organizations are that their goals are particularly vague and intangible compared to those of private business firms and that they more often have multiple, conflicting goals (see III.1.a in Exhibit 3.2; Rainey, 1993). Previous chapters illustrated the meaning of this observation. Public organizations produce goods and services that are not exchanged in markets. Government auspices and oversight imposed on these organizations include such multiple, conflicting, and often intangible goals as the constitutional, competence, and responsiveness values discussed in Chapters Four and Five (see Exhibit 4.3). In addition, authorizing legislation often assigns vague missions to government agencies and provides vague guidance for public programs (Lowi, 1979; Seidman and Gilmour, 1986). With such mandates, coupled with concerns over public opinion and public demands, agency managers feel pressured to balance conflicting, idealized goals. Conservation agencies, for example, receive mandates and pressures both to conserve natural resources and to develop them (Wildavsky, 1979, p. 215). Prison commissioners face pressures both to punish offenders and to rehabilitate them (DiIulio, 1990). Police chiefs must try to find a balance between keeping the peace, enforcing the law, controlling crime, preventing crime, and assuring fairness and respect for citizen rights, and operating efficiently and with minimal costs (Moore, 1990).

In addition, many observers go on to assert that these goal complexities have major implications for public organizations and their management. Some researchers emphasize the effect of these complexities on work attitudes and performance. Buchanan (1974, 1975) found that federal agency managers reported lower organizational commitment, job involvement, and work satisfaction than did managers in private business. He also found that the federal managers reported a weaker sense of having impacts on their organizations and a weaker sense of finding challenge in their jobs. He concluded that the vagueness and value conflicts inherent in public organizations' goals were among several reasons the federal managers reported lower commitment, involvement, and satisfaction. He argued that the diffuseness of agencies' objectives made it harder to design challenging jobs for the public sector managers and harder for them to perceive the impact of their work, which in turn weakened federal managers' commitment and satisfaction. Other studies have found more positive attitudes among managers in government than Buchanan observed, but his conclusions suggest the kinds of problems that vague and conflicting organizational goals may cause.

Boyatzis (1982), in a study of the competencies of a broad sample of managers, found that public managers displayed weaker "goal and action" competencies—those concerned with formulating and emphasizing means and ends. He concluded that the difference must result from the absence in the public sector of clear goals and performance measures such as sales and profits.

Other observations concern effects on organizational structure (pervasiveness of rules, number of levels) and hierarchical delegation. Some scholars have asserted that the goal ambiguity in public agencies and the consequent difficulties in developing clear and readily measurable performance indicators lead to performance evaluation on the basis of adherence to proper procedure and compliance with rules (Barton, 1980; Dahl and Lindblom, 1953; Lynn, 1981; Meyer, 1979; Warwick, 1975). Under accountability pressures and scrutiny by legislative bodies, the chief executive, oversight agencies, courts, and the media, higher-level executives in public agencies demand compliance with rules and procedures mandated by Congress or oversight agencies or contained in their chartering legislation. Executives and managers in public agencies also tend to add even more rules and clearance requirements in addition to externally imposed rules and procedures; plus, they add more hierarchical levels of review and generally resist delegation in an effort to control the units and individuals below them. The absence of clear, measurable, well-accepted performance criteria thus induces a vicious cycle of "inevitable bureaucracy" (Lynn, 1981) in which the demand for increased accountability increases the emphasis on rule adherence and hierarchical control. Some authors add the observation that these conditions breed a paradox in which the proliferation of rules and clearance requirements fails to achieve control over lower levels (Warwick, 1975; Buchanan, 1975). Rules provide some protections for people at lower levels, through civil service protections and the safety of strict compliance with other administrative rules. Superiors' efforts to control lower-level employees through additional rules and reporting requirements add to bureaucratic complexity without achieving control.

In this way, goal ambiguity also supposedly contributes to a weakening of the authority of top leaders in public organizations. Because they cannot assess performance on the basis of relatively clear measures, their control over lower levels is weakened. The absence of clear performance measures also allegedly contributes to a weakening of their attentiveness to developing their agencies. Because they cannot simply refer to their performance against unambiguous targets to justify continued funding, they must play more political, expository roles to develop political support for their programs. Blumenthal (1983), reflecting on his experiences as a top federal and business executive, begins his account of the differences between these roles with the observation that there is no bottom line in government. Media relations, general appearance and reputation, and political relations external to the agency figure more importantly in how others assess an executive's performance than do concrete indicators of the performance of his or her agency. Allison (1983) provides an account of the similar observations of experienced public officials about the absence of a bottom line and of accepted and readily measurable performance indicators in public agencies.

Later chapters examine some of the research findings that support or fail to support these observations. For example, several surveys covering different levels of government, different parts of the United States, and different organizations have asked managers in government agencies and business firms to respond to questions about whether the goals of their organization are vague, hard to define, and hard to measure. The results have showed no particular differences between the government managers and the business managers in their responses to such questions Rainey, 1983; Rainey, Pandey, and Bozeman, 1995). In addition, Bozeman and Rainey (1998) report evidence that government managers in their study were more likely than business managers to say that their organizations had too many rules; this is not consistent with the claim that government managers like to create more and more rules and red tape. In spite of conflicting assertions and findings such as these, the main point is that many observers claim that the goals of public organizations have a distinct character that influences their other characteristics and their management. The findings just mentioned do not necessarily prove that there are no such differences, but they certainly complicate the debate. They illustrate the importance for researchers and managers of clarifying just what is meant by these repeated references to the vague, conflicting, multiple goals of public agencies and of proving or disproving their alleged effect on organizations and management in government.

Regardless of these complications in the analysis of the goals of public agencies, it is still very important and useful for agency leaders and managers to try to clarify their organization's goals and assess its effectiveness in achieving them. The Web sites of many public agencies, and the next chapter, provide many examples of efforts at clarifying goals and missions, and an expanding literature on public management provides many more (Behn, 1994, p. 50; Denhardt, 2000; Hargrove and Glidewell, 1990, p. 95; Meyers, Riccucci, and Lurie, 2001). Chapter Ten describes a stream of research in psychology that has found that work groups perform better when given clear, challenging goals (Wright, 2001, forthcoming). In seeking to clarify goals, however, managers need to be aware of the attendant complications and conflicts. They also need to be aware of the concepts and models for assessing organizational effectiveness that researchers have developed, as well as of the controversies over the strengths and weaknesses of the models and the trade-offs among them.

# Models for Assessing Organizational Effectiveness

The people who study organizational effectiveness agree on many of the preceding points, but they have never come to agreement on one conclusive model or framework for assessing effectiveness (Daft, 2001; Hall, 2002;). The complexities just described, as well as numerous others, have caused them to try many approaches.

## The Goal Approach

When organization theorists first began to develop models of organizational effectiveness, it appeared obvious that one should determine the goals of one's organization and assess whether it achieves them. As suggested already, however, organizations have many goals, which vary along many dimensions and often conflict with one another. Herbert Simon (1973) once pointed out that a goal is always embedded in a set of goals, which a person or group tries to maximize simultaneously—such as to achieve excellence in delivery of services to clients but also keep the maintenance schedule up, keep the members happy and motivated, maintain satisfactory relations with legislators and interest groups, and so on. Many different coalitions or stakeholders associated with an organization—managers, workers, client and constituency groups, oversight and regulatory agencies, legislators, courts, people in different subunits with different priorities for the organization, and so on—can have different goals for the organization.

One can also state goals at different levels of generality, in various terms, and in various time frames (short-term versus long-term). Goals always link together in chains of means and ends, in which an immediate objective can be expressed as a goal but ultimately serves as a means to a more general or longer-term goal. In addition, researchers and consultants can have a hard time specifying an organization's goals because the people in the organization have difficulty stating or admitting the real goals. Organizations have not only formal, publicly espoused goals but also actual goals. In their annual reports, public agencies and business firms often make glowing statements of their commitment to the general welfare as well as to their customers and clients. An automobile company might express commitment to providing the American people with the safest, most enjoyable, most efficient automobiles in the world. A transportation agency might state its determination to serve all the people of its state with the safest, most efficient, most effective transportation facilities and processes possible. Yet the actual behavior of these organizations may indicate more concern with their economic security than with their clients and the general public. The goal model, in simplified forms, implies a view of management as a rational, orderly process. Earlier chapters have described how management scholars increasingly depict managerial decisions and contexts as more turbulent, intuitive, paradoxical, and emergent than a rational, goal-based approach implies.

All of these complications cause organizational effectiveness researchers to search for alternatives to a simple goal model. The discussion of strategy in Chapter Four demonstrated, however, that experts still exhort managers to identify missions, core values, and strategies. This may depart from a strict goal-based approach, but when you tell people to decide what they want to accomplish and to design strategies to achieve those conditions, you are talking about goals, even if you devise some other names for them. Goal clarification also plays a key role in managerial procedures described in later chapters, such as management by objectives (MBO).

Experts continue to suggest various terminologies and procedures for identifying organizational goals, and the goal model has never really been banished from the search for effectiveness criteria. These prescriptive frameworks, however, illustrate many of the complexities of goals mentioned earlier. Morrisey (1976), for example, illustrates the multiple levels and means-ends relationships of goals. He suggests a framework for public managers to use in developing MBO programs that he describes as a funnel in which the organization moves from greater generality to greater specificity by stating goals and missions, key results areas, indicators, objectives, and finally, action plans. Gross (1976) suggests a framework involving seven different groups of goals—satisfying interests (such as those of clients and members), producing output, making efficient use of inputs, investing in the organization, acquiring resources, observing codes (such as laws and budgetary guidelines), and behaving rationally (through research and proper administration). Under each of these general goals he lists multiple subgoals. Obviously, managers and researchers have difficulty clearly and conclusively specifying an organization's goals.

For similar reasons, researchers have grappled with complications in measuring effectiveness. As usual, they have encountered the problem of choosing between subjective measures and objective measures. Some have asked respondents to rate the effectiveness of organizations, sometimes asking members for the ratings, sometimes comparing members' ratings of their own units in the organization with the ratings provided by other members (such as top managers or members of other units). Sometimes they have asked people outside the organization for ratings. Others have developed more objective measures, such as profitability and productivity indicators, from records or other sources. Some researchers have developed both types of evidence, but they have found this expensive. They have also sometimes found that the two types of measures may not correlate with each other. In one frequently used variant of the goals approach, researchers have not sought to determine the specific goals of a specific organization; rather, they have measured ratings of effectiveness on certain criteria or goals that they assume all organizations must pursue, such as productivity, efficiency, flexibility, and adaptability. Mott (1972), for example, studied the effectiveness of government organizations (units of NASA; the State Department; the Department of Health, Education, and Welfare; and a state mental hospital) by asking managers in them to rate the quantity, quality, efficiency, adaptability, and flexibility of their divisions.

## The Systems-Resource Approach

Partly because of difficulties with goal models, Yuchtman and Seashore (1967) developed a systems-resource model. They concentrated on whether an organization can attain valued resources from its environment to sustain itself. They placed effectiveness criteria in a hierarchy, with the organization's ability to exploit external resources and opportunities as the ultimate criterion. They regarded this criterion as being ultimately immeasurable by itself: it has to be inferred by measuring the next-highest, or penultimate, criteria, which they identified in a study of insurance companies. These criteria included such factors as business volume, market penetration, youthfulness of organizational members, and production and maintenance costs. They developed these factors by using statistical techniques to group together measures of organizational activities and characteristics such as sales and number of policies in force. Drawing on a survey they conducted in the same companies, they also examined the relationships between lower-order, subsidiary variables, such as communication and managerial supportiveness, and the penultimate factors.

Not many researchers have followed this lead with subsequent research efforts. Critics have raised questions about whether the approach confuses the conception and ordering of important variables. Some of the penultimate factors could just as well be called goals, others seem to represent means for achieving goals, and some of the factors seem more important than others. Critics have complained that the analytical techniques bunched together unlike factors inappropriately. Others have pointed out that the criteria represent the interests of those in charge of the organizations, even though other actors, such as customers and public interest groups, might have very different interests.

Still, insights from the study influenced later developments in thinking about effectiveness. The study found that some subsidiary variables were related to later readings on penultimate variables. This shows that effective procedures now can lead to effective outcomes later and emphasizes the importance of examining such relationships over time. Some subsidiary measures are linked strongly to certain penultimate factors but not to others. This shows that one can point to different dimensions of effectiveness, with different sets of variables linking with them.

Also, while few researchers have reported additional studies following this model, at least one such study applied it to public agencies. Molnar and Rogers (1976) analyzed county-level offices of 110 public agencies, including various agricultural, welfare, community development, conservation, employment, and planning and zoning agencies. They argued that the resource-dependence model, which is applied to business firms, needs modification for public agencies, for reasons similar to those discussed earlier in this book—absence of profit and of sales in markets, which blurs the link between inputs and outputs; consequent evaluation by political officials and other political actors; and an emphasis on meeting community or social needs that rivals emphases on internal efficiency.

Rogers and Molnar had people in the agencies rate their own organization's effectiveness and the effectiveness of other organizations in the study. To represent the systems-resource approach for public agencies, they examined how many resources (equipment, funds, personnel, meeting rooms) an agency provided to other agencies in the study ("resource outflow") and how many they received from other agencies ("resource inflow"). They also calculated a score for how much resources flowing in exceeded resources flowing out. They found that the higher the level of resources flowing into an agency, the higher the level of resources flowing out. The more effective agencies thus appeared better able to develop effective exchanges with other agencies, using their own resources to attract resources. Of course, the effectiveness of public agencies involves many additional dimensions, but this study offers an interesting analysis of one means of examining it.

## Participant-Satisfaction Models

Another approach involves asking participants about their satisfaction with the organization. This approach focuses on whether the members of an organization feel that it fulfills their needs or that they share its goals and work to achieve them. This approach can figure importantly in managing an organization, but it has serious limitations if participation is conceived too narrowly. Participants include not just employees but also suppliers, customers, regulators and external controllers, and allies. Some of the more recent studies of effectiveness ask many different participants from such categories for ratings of an organization (Cameron, 1978). Others have tried to build in more ethical and social-justice considerations by examining how well an organization serves or harms the most disadvantaged participants (Keeley, 1984). The participant-satisfaction approach thus adds crucial insights to our thinking about effectiveness, but even these elaborated versions of the approach encounter problems in handling the general social significance of an organization's performance. Organizations also affect the interests of the general public or society and of individuals not even remotely associated with the organization as participants.

## Human Resource and Internal Process Models

These approaches to organizational effectiveness assess it by referring to such factors as internal communications, leadership style, motivation, interpersonal trust, and other internal states assumed to be desirable. Likert (1967) developed a four-system typology that follows this pattern, assuming that as one enhances open and employee-centered leadership, communication, and control processes, one achieves organizational effectiveness. Blake and Mouton's managerial grid (1984) involves similar assumptions, as do many organization development approaches.

Some who take positions quite at odds with the human relations orientation nevertheless share this general view. Management systems experts who concentrate on whether an organization's accounting and control systems work well make similar assumptions. These orientations have played an important role in the debate over what public management involves. Some writers see inadequacies in public management primarily because of weak management systems and procedures of the sort that purportedly exist in superior form in industry (U.S. General Accounting Office, 2003; Crane and Jones, 1982). They call for better accounting and control systems, better inventory controls, better purchasing and procurement, and better contracting procedures. These human resource and internal process approaches do not involve complete conceptions of organizational effectiveness, but public managers often employ them, and experts assessing public organizations apply them.

## The Government Performance Project

An example of such an application, and one of the most elaborate initiatives in assessing effectiveness of governments and government agencies, the Government Performance Project (GPP) received considerable professional and public attention at the turn of the twenty-first century. It involved one of the most widely applied, if not *the* most widely applied, efforts ever undertaken to assess effectiveness of government entities. In 1996, supported by a grant from the Pew Charitable Trusts, researchers at the Maxwell School of Citizenship and Public Affairs at Syracuse University, in partnership with representatives of *Governing* magazine, developed a process for rating the management capacity of local and state governments and federal agencies in the United States. In spite of its name, the GPP does not measure performance directly, but rather evaluates the capacity of management systems in government entities and thus represents a variant of an internal process model. The GPP evaluates five management system areas: financial management, human resources management, capital management, information technology management, and managing for results. The assessments also seek to determine how well these management systems are integrated in a government or government agency. Figure 6.1 illustrates this basic framework.

As Figure 6.1 implies, the assessment procedure is based on the assumption that governments and government organizations perform well when they have strong management capacity in the areas indicated in the figure. The framework provides general criteria for each of the five management areas. Panels of experts helped to choose measures and indicators for these criteria. For example, criteria for financial management include a multiyear perspective on budgeting; mechanisms that preserve fiscal health; sufficient availability of financial information to policymakers, managers, and citizens; and appropriate control over financial operations. Human resources management criteria include provisions for strate-

## FIGURE 6.1. CONCEPTUAL FRAMEWORK
## OF THE GOVERNMENT PERFORMANCE PROJECT.

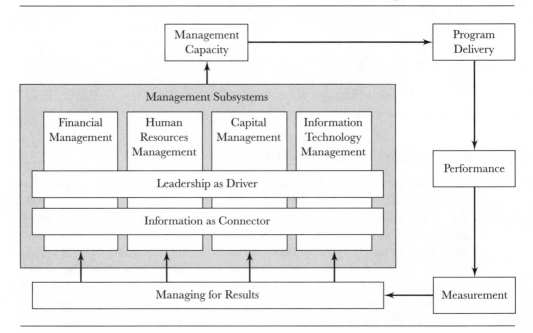

gic analysis of human resource needs, ability to obtain needed employees and a skilled workforce, and ability to motivate employees. Information technology (IT) management includes such criteria as whether IT systems support managers' information needs and strategic goals, and support communication with citizens and service delivery to them, as well as the adequacy of planning, training for, procuring, and evaluating IT systems. Criteria for managing for results include engagement in results-oriented strategic planning, use of results in policymaking and management, use of indicators to measure results, and communication of results to stakeholders.

The GPP assessed these capacities in federal agencies, state governments, and city and county governments, assigning letter grades (that is, A, B, C) for each of the five management capacities and for overall capacity. The procedures for assessing these capacities were not available to the public as of the end of 2002. The Web site describes the procedures as follows:

> The GPP grades governments based on the analysis of information it collects from the following resources and procedures: criteria-based assessment, comprehensive self-report surveys, document and Web site analysis, extensive follow-up and validation, statistical checks and comparisons, journalistic interviews with managers and stakeholders, and journalist/academic consensus. Surveys are distributed in March, governments return completed surveys and submit documents by June, analysis occurs during July to November, grading takes place in November, and grades and results are released at the end of January.

Actually, both the academics and the journalists assigned grades to the government organizations, but their grades were similar. The academics assigned grades on the basis of analysis of the information gathered in the process just described, while the journalists relied more on interviews with the organizations. The researchers in charge of the project could not release the exact procedures for assessment because consulting firms were offering to work with government organizations on ways to get better grades, and the researchers felt that publication of the exact procedures could bias the process. The journalists relied on more subjective, journalistic methods.

In 1998, the project studied and rated management activities in fifty states and fifteen federal agencies. The state results were published in the February 1999 issue of *Governing* and the federal results were published in the February 1999 issue of *Government Executive* magazine. In 1999, the GPP assessed the management capacity of the top thirty-five U.S. cities by revenue and five federal agencies. The city results were published in the February 2000 issue of *Governing* and the federal results were published in the March 2000 issue of *Government Executive*. Furthermore, the release was covered by two national newspapers, the *Christian Science Monitor* and *USA Today;* more than 250 regional newspapers; and more than two hundred radio and television stations.

An interesting and ambitious project, the GPP nevertheless evades easy evaluation because one cannot review the actual assessment procedures. The assessments do not directly measure outcomes, impacts, or results for the organizations reviewed by the GPP, so as a version of an internal process model it does not directly address the actual effectiveness of government organizations in achieving goals and results.

## Toward Diverse, Conflicting Criteria

Increasingly, researchers tried to examine multiple measures of effectiveness. Campbell (1977) and his colleagues, for example, reviewed various approaches to effectiveness, including those described earlier, and developed a comprehensive list of criteria (see Exhibit 6.1). Obviously, many dimensions figure into effectiveness. Even this elaborate list does not capture certain criteria, such as effectiveness in contributing to the general public interest or the general political economy.

### EXHIBIT 6.1. ORGANIZATIONAL EFFECTIVENESS DIMENSIONS AND MEASURES.

| | |
|---|---|
| 1. Overall effectiveness | 16. Planning and goal setting |
| 2. Productivity | 17. Goal consensus |
| 3. Efficiency | 18. Internalization of organizational goals |
| 4. Profit | 19. Role and norm congruence |
| 5. Quality | 20. Managerial interpersonal skills |
| 6. Accidents | 21. Managerial task skills |
| 7. Growth | 22. Information management and communication |
| 8. Absenteeism | 23. Readiness |
| 9. Turnover | 24. Utilization of environment |
| 10. Job satisfaction | 25. Evaluations by external entities |
| 11. Motivation | 26. Stability |
| 12. Morale | 27. Value of human resources |
| 13. Control | 28. Participation and shared influence |
| 14. Conflict/cohesion | 29. Training and development emphasis |
| 15. Flexibility/adaptation | 30. Achievement emphasis |

*Source:* Campbell, 1977, pp. 36–39.

As researchers try to incorporate more complex sets of criteria, it becomes evident that organizations pursue diverse goals and respond to diverse interests, which imposes trade-offs. Cameron (1978) reported a study of colleges and universities in which he gathered a variety of types of effectiveness measures. Reviewing the literature, he noted that effectiveness studies use many types of criteria, including organizational criteria such as goals, outputs, resource acquisition, and internal processes. They also vary in terms of their universality (whether they use the same criteria for all organizations or different ones for different organizations), whether they are normative or descriptive (describing what an organization should do or what it does do), and whether they are dynamic or static. He also noted different sources of criteria. One can refer to different constituencies, such as the dominant groups in an organization, many constituencies in and out of an organization, or mainly external constituents. The sources also vary by level, from the overall, external system to the organization as a unit, organizational subunits, and individuals. Finally, one can use organizational records or individuals' perceptions as sources of criteria.

In his own study of educational institutions, Cameron (1978) drew on a variety of criteria: objective and subjective criteria; measures reflecting the interests of students, faculty, and administrators; participant criteria; and organizational criteria (see Table 6.1). Cameron developed profiles of different educational institutions according to the nine general criteria and found them to be diverse. One institution scored high on student academic and personal development but quite low on student career development. Another had the opposite profile—low on the first two criteria, high on the third. One institution scored high on community involvement, the others scored relatively low. These variations show that even organizations in the same industry or service sector often follow different patterns of effectiveness. They may choose different strategies, involving somewhat different clients, approaches, and products or services. In addition, these differences show that effectiveness criteria can weigh against one another. By doing well on one criterion, an organization may show weaker performance on another. Cameron points out that a university aiming at distinction in faculty research may pay less attention to the personal development of undergraduates than a college more devoted to attracting and placing undergraduates.

# The Competing Values Approach

Quinn and Rohrbaugh (1983) draw this point about conflicting criteria into their competing values framework. They had panels of organizational researchers review the criteria in Table 6.1 to distill the basic dimensions out of the set. The panels' responses indicated that the criteria grouped together along three value

## TABLE 6.1. EFFECTIVENESS DIMENSIONS FOR EDUCATIONAL INSTITUTIONS.

| Perceptual Measures | Objective Measures |
|---|---|
| **1.** *Student educational satisfaction* | |
| Student dissatisfaction | Number of terminations |
| Student complaints | Counseling center visits |
| **2.** *Student academic development* | |
| Extra work and study | Percentage going on to graduate school |
| Amount of academic development | |
| **3.** *Student career development* | |
| Number employed in major field | Number receiving career counseling |
| Number of career-oriented courses | |
| **4.** *Student personal development* | |
| Opportunities for personal development | Number of extracurricular activities |
| Emphasis on nonacademic development | Number in extramurals and intramurals |
| **5.** *Faculty and administrator employment satisfaction* | |
| Faculty and administrators' satisfaction with school and employment | Number of faculty members and administrators leaving |
| **6.** *Professional development and quality of the faculty* | |
| Faculty publications, awards, conference attendance | Percentage of faculty with doctorates |
| Teaching at the cutting edge | Number of new courses |
| **7.** *System openness and community interaction* | |
| Employee community service | Number of continuing education courses |
| Emphasis on community relations | |
| **8.** *Ability to acquire resources* | |
| National reputation of faculty | General funds raised |
| Drawing power for students | Previously tenured faculty hired |
| Drawing power for faculty | |
| **9.** *Organizational health* | |
| Student-faculty relations | |
| Typical communication type | |
| Levels of trust | |
| Cooperative environment | |
| Use of talents and expertise | |

*Source:* Adapted from Cameron, 1978, p. 630. See original table for numerous additional measures for each dimension.

dimensions (see Figure 6.2). The first dimension, organizational focus, ranges from an internal emphasis on the well-being of the organization's members to an external focus on the success of the entire organization. The second dimension is concerned with control as opposed to flexibility. The third involves relative concentration on means (such as good planning) or ends (such as achieving productivity goals). Quinn and Rohrbaugh point out that these dimensions reflect fundamental dilemmas that social scientists have debated for a long time—means versus ends, flexibility versus control and stability, internal versus external orientation.

The dimensions combine to represent the four models of effectiveness shown in Figure 6.2. The human relations model emphasizes flexibility in internal processes and improving cohesion and morale as a means of developing the people in an organization. The internal process model also has an internal focus, but it emphasizes control, through maintaining sound information, auditing, and review systems, as a means to stability. At the external end, the open-systems model emphasizes responsiveness to the environment, with flexibility in structure and

## FIGURE 6.2. THE COMPETING VALUES FRAMEWORK.

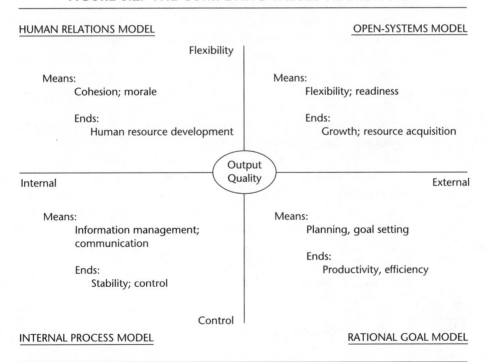

*Source:* Quinn and Rohrbaugh, 1983. Reprinted by permission of the authors. Copyright © 1983, Institute of Management Sciences.

process as a means to achieving growth and acquiring resources. The rational goal model emphasizes careful planning to maximize efficiency.

Quinn and Rohrbaugh recognize the contradictions between the different models and values. They argue, however, that a comprehensive model must retain all of these contradictions, because organizations constantly face such competition among values. Organizations have to stay open to external opportunities yet have sound internal controls. They must be ready to change but maintain reasonable stability. Effective organizations and managers balance conflicting values. They do not always do so in the same way, of course. Quinn and Cameron (1983) drew amoeba-like shapes on the diagram in Figure 6.2 to illustrate the different emphases that organizations place on the values. An organization that heavily emphasizes control and formalization would have a profile illustrated by a roughly circular shape that expands much more widely on the lower part of the diagram than on the upper part. For an organization that emphasizes innovation and informal teamwork, the circle would sweep more widely around the upper part of the chart, showing higher emphasis on morale and flexibility. This contrast again underscores the point that different organizations may pursue different conceptions of effectiveness.

Quinn and Cameron also point out that effectiveness profiles apparently shift as an organization moves through different stages in its life cycle. In addition, major constituencies can impose such shifts. They describe how a unit of a state mental health agency moved from a teamwork and innovation profile to a control-oriented profile because of a series of newspaper articles criticizing the unit for lax rules, records, and rule adherence.

Still, the ultimate message is that organizations and managers must balance or concurrently manage competing values. Rohrbaugh (1981) illustrates the use of all the values with a measure of the effectiveness of an employment services agency. Quinn (1988) has developed scales for managers to conduct self-assessments of their own orientation within the set of values, for use in training them to manage these conflicts. The competing values framework expresses the values in a highly generalized form and does not address the more specific, substantive goals of particular agencies or the explicit political and institutional values imposed on public organizations. Nevertheless, it provides valuable insights into the effectiveness of public organizations, especially on the point that the criteria are multiple, shifting, and conflicting.

## The Balanced Scorecard

An approach to assessing organizational performance and effectiveness that has achieved considerable prominence incorporates multiple dimensions and measures into the process. Kaplan and Norton (1996, 2000) developed the Balanced

Scorecard to prevent a narrow concentration on financial measures in business auditing and control systems. Devised for use by business firms, this model has been used by government organizations in innovative ways.

The Balanced Scorecard requires an organization to develop goals, measures, and initiatives for four perspectives (Kaplan and Norton, 1996, p. 44):

- The financial perspective, in which typical measures include return on investment and economic value added
- The customer perspective, involving such measures as customer satisfaction and retention
- The internal perspective, involving measures of quality, response time, cost, and new product introductions
- The learning and growth perspective, in which goals and measures focus on such matters as employee satisfaction and information system availability

Responding to the National Performance Review's emphasis on setting goals and managing for results, a task force applied the Balanced Scorecard in developing a model for assessment of the federal government procurement system carried out in major federal agencies (Kaplan and Norton, 1996, pp. 181–182). Interestingly, Kaplan and Norton also describe applications in the public sector that were in effect before descriptions of their model were published. Sunnyvale, California, a city repeatedly recognized for its excellence in management, has for more than twenty years produced annual performance reports stating goals and performance indicators for each major policy area. Charlotte, North Carolina, issued an objectives scorecard in 1995 reporting on accomplishments in "focus areas," including community safety, economic development, and transportation. The report also provided performance measures from four perspectives, including the financial, customer service, internal work efficiency, and learning and growth perspectives (Kaplan and Norton, 1996, pp. 181–185). The Texas State Office of the Auditor has developed its own version of the approach, adding a focus on mission for their public sector context, because financial results in public institutions do not play the central role they do in private firms. Their model includes concentrations on mission, customer focus, internal processes, learning and knowledge, and financial matters (Kerr, 2001).

Other agencies, influenced by the approach, have developed their own versions. In the major reforms at the Internal Revenue Service described in Chapters Eight and Thirteen, the agency adopted a "balanced measures" approach. The model includes goals and measures in the areas of business process results, customer satisfaction, and employee satisfaction. The executives leading the reforms regularly reviewed reports from consulting firms that had conducted customer satisfaction and employee satisfaction surveys.

The Balanced Scorecard and related approaches raise plenty of issues that can be debated. For example, an emphasis on serving "customers" has grown in the field of public administration over the last decade. This trend has sparked some debate and controversy over whether government employees should think of citizens and clients as customers. In addition, the long-term success of balanced measurement systems remains to be seen. As indicated previously, some of the related approaches involve simply trying to measure employee satisfaction, and some measures of work satisfaction do not really assess learning and growth in the organization as Kaplan and Norton proposed. The Balanced Scorecard and similar balanced measurement approaches do, however, emphasize the important and valuable point that people in public organizations need to develop well-rounded and balanced measures of effectiveness that combine attention to results and impacts, internal capacity and development, and the perspectives of external stakeholders, including so-called customers.

## Effectiveness in Organizational Networks

Government programs and policies have always involved complex clusters of individuals, groups, and organizations, but such patterns of networking have become even more prevalent in recent decades (Henry, 2002; Kettl, 2002; Raab, 2002; Vigoda, 2002). A variety of developments have fueled this trend, including increased privatization and contracting out of public services, greater involvement of the nonprofit sector in public service delivery, and complex problems that exceed the capacity of any one organization, as well as other trends (O'Toole, 1999). The growing significance of networks raises challenges for research, theory, and practice in public administration, especially in relation to the effectiveness of public organizations and public management. O'Toole (1999, p. 44) defines networks as "structures of interdependence involving multiple organizations or parts thereof, where one unit is not merely the formal subordinate of the others in some larger hierarchical arrangement." Such situations do not involve typical or traditional chains of command and hierarchical authority. For managers, the lines of accountability and authority are loosened, and the management of a network requires more reliance on trust and collaboration than programs operated within the hierarchy of one organization (O'Toole, 1999). Managers also face varying degrees of responsibility to activate, mobilize, and synthesize networks (McGuire, 2002).

In addition to altering the roles of managers, networks bring up new questions about assessing effectiveness and achieving it, and researchers have developed new and important insights about such matters. For example, Provan and

Milward (1995) analyzed the mental health services of four urban areas in the United States. They found that these services were provided by networks of different organizations, each of which provided some type of service or part of the package of mental health services available in the area. Quite significantly, virtually none of the organizations was a government organization. The government—the federal government for the most part—provided most of the funding for the mental health services in these areas, but networks of private and nonprofit organizations provided the services.

The researchers pointed out that for such networks of organizations, a real measure of effectiveness should not be focused on any individual organization. Instead, one must think in terms of the effectiveness of the entire network. Provan and Milward focused on clients in measuring the network's effectiveness, using responses from clients, their families, and caseworkers concerning the clients' quality of life, their satisfaction with the services of the network, and their level of functioning. They then examined the characteristics of the network in relation to these measures of effectiveness. They found that the most effective of the four mental health service networks was centralized and concentrated around a primary organization. The government funds for the system went directly to that agency, which played a strong central role in coordinating the other organizations in delivering services. This finding runs counter to the organic-mechanistic distinction discussed in earlier chapters, which suggests that decentralized, highly flexible arrangements are most appropriate (Provan and Milward, 1995, pp. 25–26).

More recently, Milward and Provan (1998, 2000) have developed the findings of their study into principles about the governance of networks. They conclude that a network will most likely be effective when a powerful core agency integrates the network, the mechanisms for fiscal control by the state are direct and not fragmented, resources are plentiful, and the network is stable. In addition, they have further developed ideas about how one must evaluate networks, pointing out that assessing the effectiveness of networks requires evaluation on multiple levels. Evaluators must assess the effectiveness of the network at the community level, at the level of the network itself, and at the level of the organization participating in the network. Given the continuing and growing importance of networks, we can expect continuing emphasis on developing concepts and frameworks such as these.

# Managing Goals and Effectiveness

A reason to review this material on goals and effectiveness fairly early in the book, before the chapters that follow, is to raise basic issues concerning the goals of public organizations that allegedly influence their operations and characteristics. In addition, the concepts and models of effectiveness provide a context and basic theme for the topics to be discussed. The complications with these concepts and the absence of a conclusive model of effectiveness raise challenges for researchers and practicing managers alike. The next chapter and later chapters show how important these challenges are, however, and provide examples of how leaders have addressed them. Later chapters provide examples of mission statements and expressions of goals and values that members of public organizations have developed. The next chapter discusses strategic management, decision making, and power relationships that are part of the process of developing and pursuing goals and effectiveness. Later chapters discuss topics such as organizational culture and leadership, communication, motivation, organizational change, and managing for excellence—all topics that relate to goals and effectiveness. As Figures 1.1 and 1.2 in Chapter One indicate, a central challenge for people in public organizations is the coordination of such issues and topics in pursuit of goals and effectiveness.

## Effectiveness of Public Organizations

As noted at the outset of this book and this chapter, beliefs about the effectiveness of public organizations, and about their performance in comparison to business firms, are important parts of the culture of the United States and other countries. These beliefs and perceptions have influenced some of the major political developments in recent decades, and one could argue that they have helped shape the history of the United States and other nations. The preceding sections show, however, that assessing the effectiveness of organizations involves many complexities. Assessing the performance of the complex populations of organizations is even more complicated.

Chapter Fourteen returns to the topics of the effectiveness of public organizations and their effectiveness compared to private organizations. It argues that public organizations often operate very well, if not much better than suggested by the widespread public beliefs about their inferior performance indicated in public opinion polls. Chapter Fourteen makes this argument before covering additional ideas about the effective leadership and management of public organizations, claiming that public managers and leaders often perform well in managing goals and effectiveness.

CHAPTER SEVEN

# FORMULATING AND ACHIEVING PURPOSE

## Power, Strategy, and Decision Making

During the administration of the first President George Bush, major news-papers carried reports on a controversial aide to the secretary of the Depart-ment of Housing and Urban Development (HUD) who had gained power in the department. The reports claimed that the aide had little background in hous-ing policy and had received her appointment because she came from a prominent family. According to the reports, the secretary of HUD had inattentively allowed her to make heavy use of his autopen—an apparatus that automatically signs the secretary's name—to influence major decisions on funding and agency policies. She garnered support from members of Congress by channeling projects and grants to their constituencies. She also allegedly used the authority of the secre-tary to move trusted associates into key positions in the agency, where they could give her early information about the unit heads' plans so she could devise ways to overrule them and channel their projects toward her supporters. In spite of her maneuvering, however, when she was nominated for the position of assistant sec-retary of HUD, Congress would not confirm her appointment because of her lack of credentials and qualifications. Ultimately, her influence on spending decisions in a housing rehabilitation program received intense scrutiny from federal audi-tors and news reporters and brought a deluge of bad publicity and legal problems (Maitland, 1989; Waldman, Cohn, and Thomas, 1989).

In a similar but less serious episode years later, the inspector general (IG) of the U.S. Department of Health and Human Services drew criticism over allegations that she had driven many experienced, long-term career civil servants out of the IG office into retirement or into positions in other agencies. Critics claimed that she had ousted these career officials by treating them abrasively and giving them trivial duties. Defenders claimed that the IG was simply assuring the loyalty of her staff. Whether or not the criticisms were valid, the coverage of these criticisms, even in the *Wall Street Journal*, an often conservative periodical, indicates the care that governmental executives need to exercise in using their power and authority (Lueck, 2002).

In 1997–1998, the Congress was developing legislation mandating major reform and restructuring of the Internal Revenue Service. A Senate committee held hearings in which taxpayers testified about serious abuses by IRS revenue agents. The hearings received extensive coverage in the media. Senators used the hearings to justify writing into the IRS legislation requirements for immediate termination of any IRS agent who committed any of a set of specified abuses of taxpayers. An investigation by the U.S. General Accounting Office would later find that most of the allegations about abuses were exaggerated or inaccurate. Nevertheless, IRS employees referred to the set of termination provisions as the "deadly sins," and uncertainty over how they would be enforced led to a sharp drop in tax collection and enforcement actions, and a decline in morale. Conversely, in interviews with researchers, some executives within IRS observed that the situation probably strengthened the power and authority of the new IRS commissioner to carry out the reforms mandated by Congress, by convincing IRS employees and stakeholders of the need for drastic change to improve the agency's relations with political officials, citizens, and taxpayers. As described further in later chapters, the commissioner would later receive praise from all major stakeholders—the major union, members of Congress, the press, professional groups, and others—for his leadership of the reform process and the skillful way in which he developed and used his authority in the change process.

People in organizations have varying degrees of power and authority. Whether or not people like to think about attaining power, they need to consider the matter because only with some power can they pursue valuable goals and patterns of effectiveness of the sort discussed in the last chapter. Also, people may abuse power, using it in destructive or improper ways, and others have to use their power to stop the abuses. As the examples just presented indicate, the very definition and identification of what constitutes an abuse depends on the distribution of power among those who want to influence that definition.

Also, people need power and authority to participate in making decisions and in carrying them out, as with the decisions in the IRS about how to carry out the reforms. Organizations exist, in a sense, as ongoing systems of decision making.

Herbert Simon (1948), a Nobel Laureate in economics as well as one of the most influential scholars in organization theory and public administration, treated decision making as the central concept in organizations and management.

As described in earlier chapters, the most prominent trend in decision making in public organizations in the last two decades involves strategic planning. The Government Performance and Results Act of 1993 (GPRA) requires all federal agencies to create strategic plans. Most states have similar legislation, and many local governments have developed strategic plans. The framework presented in the first chapter indicates that organizational leadership teams lead the development of strategies aimed at achieving goals. When effective, the strategy-building process links the organizational environment, goals and values, structure, processes, and people in the pursuit of organizational performance and effectiveness. To develop and carry out strategies, the members of the organization must exert their influence within it. They have to manage and work with internal power relationships and decision-making processes. As earlier chapters have emphasized, all of the topics and parts of the framework and definition from Chapter One are related to each other and mutually influential. This chapter describes concepts, theories, and research that experts and scholars on organizations have developed about three of these topics—power, strategy, and decision making—and suggests applications and examples for public organizations and their management.

# Power and Politics Inside Organizations

As the examples show, external power and politics influence internal power and politics. Political scientists have long recognized the role of external politics in determining the power of public organizations, and that units within the government bureaucracy engage in power struggles and turf warfare (Meier, 2000; Wilson, 1989). Yet aside from case descriptions, political scientists have paid little attention to power relationships within individual public organizations. Writers on management have started looking at power within organizations only recently, but they have done more to analyze it than political scientists have. As discussed in other chapters, early management theories depicted managers as basing their decisions on rational choices and optimal alternatives. Researchers increasingly realized, however, that politics and power relationships figure importantly in all organizations (Pfeffer, 1981, 1992; Hall, 2002). Some theorists have made a point of claiming that the politics in business firms and the politics in government agencies are very similar to each other (Yates, 1985). They have warned managers of the dangers of overlooking power and politics within their organizations, and they have exhorted managers to assess these dimensions of their settings. They have also discussed power in a positive sense, as necessary to performing effectively and, when shared, as a means of motivating people (Kanter, 1987; Block, 1987).

Over the years, scholars and other observers have claimed that the many rules and controls imposed on public organizations by external authorities and political actors weaken the authority of public sector managers. Political alliances among people in agencies, interest groups, and legislators further weaken the authority of higher-level executives. This situation suggests that in spite of the claims of management writers that business firms resemble public agencies in such matters, issues of power and influence are more complex for government managers. At the same time, rather paradoxically, observers typically depict the public bureaucracy as quite powerful. So, although they are constrained in many ways, public managers clearly can attain considerable power and authority within their organizations.

Public managers also vary in power, just as agencies do. Agency power can be enhanced by a number of factors: strong, well-organized constituencies; skillful leadership; organizational esprit de corps or cohesion (a relatively strong commitment to the agency and its role, as with the Forest Service or the Peace Corps); and expertise—specialized technical knowledge required for the delivery of a service that the public values highly (Meier, 2000; Rourke, 1984). These factors in turn determine the power of people and units within public organizations.

## Bases of Power in Organizations

The HUD official's inability to attain sustained, successful power raises the question of how one does so. Social scientists usually refer to French and Raven's typology of the bases for power in groups (1968): *reward* power is the power to confer or withhold rewards that others want, such as pay; *coercive* power comes from the ability to take forceful action against another person; a person has *referent* power over others if they see him or her as someone they wish to be like, as a standard for them to emulate; *expert* power derives from the control of knowledge, information, and skills that others need; and a person holds *legitimate* power if others accept his or her authority to tell them what to do.

These types of power have important implications for managers. One might think of coercive power as the ultimate mode of influence. The capacity to tax, arrest, imprison, and execute individuals is a fundamental attribute of government. These powers justify strong controls on public organizations, which often have a coercive character themselves. As for their own leadership behaviors, however, public managers need to recognize that management theorists have long emphasized the relative clumsiness and costliness of coercive power (Etzioni, 1975).

Forcing and threatening people require costly vigilance and oversight and can make enemies.

Managers may have authority to coerce, but their real challenge lies in finding ways to reward (Barnard, 1938). As Chapter Ten describes, public managers face particular constraints on their power over certain rewards. They may have some legitimate authority because of their rank and position, but they also have to maintain a less formal legitimacy in the eyes of their subordinates and external authorities. Managers must invest heavily in setting a good example and performing well in order to obtain referent power and expert power. For all the politics that surrounds public managers, experienced officials and observers still report that a public administrator's skill, integrity, experience, and expert knowledge can give him or her a positive form of power over both members of the organization and external authorities.

The HUD official described earlier rewarded certain supporters, illustrating the importance of political alliances. Yet her relatively coercive treatment of some agency officials probably contributed to her ultimate troubles. Also, she allegedly abused legitimate power (the secretary's autopen) and she lacked sufficient legitimate, expert, and referent power to sustain her position. Later chapters provide examples of more effective approaches that also involve development of constituencies but entail a more effective vision of a contribution to society, a vision sustained by a reputation for expertise and integrity (Chase and Reveal, 1983; Cohen and Eimicke, 1995; Doig and Hargrove, 1987; Hunt, 1999; IBM Endowment for the Business of Government, 2002).

## Dependency and Strategic Contingencies

In analyzing power, organization theorists have also drawn on the concept of dependency—how much a person or group must rely on another person or group for resources. Groups and units that have the most to do with obtaining key resources for their organization gain power. Studies of business firms have found that their members rate the sales and production divisions of their firms as the most powerful units (Kenny and others, 1987; Perrow, 1970a). Businesses depend on these units to produce and sell the products essential to bringing in money. Other people can also depend on a person or unit for information, completed tasks, and services.

Similarly, power accrues to units that manage *strategic contingencies,* or the factors and events that figure crucially in the operations of the organization and its ability to achieve goals (Hickson and others, 1971; Daft, 2001). Units that handle the biggest problems facing the organization gain power. Earlier chapters discussed the central role of environmental uncertainty in recent analyses of organizations;

strategic contingencies include circumstances that impose major uncertainties on an organization, and those who handle these uncertainties become important. Nothing illustrates the influence of a strategic contingency more than the intense national concern with terrorism and homeland security since the attack on the World Trade Center, and the amount of attention the federal government has paid to the formation of the Department of Homeland Security to confront this contingency.

The study by Kenny and his colleagues (1987) further suggests that these concepts apply to public organizations, but with important distinctions. They analyzed major decisions in thirty public and private organizations in Great Britain. The private organizations included manufacturing and service firms. The public group included local governments, health districts, and state-owned enterprises such as a chemical manufacturer and an airline (both nationalized in the United Kingdom). The researchers asked managers of both types of organizations which internal and external units were involved in major decision making and how much influence these units had. The two groups had similar patterns of unit involvement. For example, accounting, auditing, and production units were most frequently involved in making major decisions. In the public organizations, however, external government agencies became involved much more often. Sales, marketing, and production units had a great deal of influence in both groups. In the public organizations, adjudication units—committees or commissions that decide on resources and policies, such as a health services district commission—had the strongest influence rating. Yet this type of unit approached having the lowest rating in the private organizations. Surprisingly, external government agencies were also rated as having little influence in the public organizations, in spite of their frequent involvement, but as being very influential in the private organizations. The authors suggest that this might mean that public sector managers take for granted the influence of external agencies, while business managers react more sharply to government interventions.

Overall, the study indicates that units that produce and distribute primary goods and services wield strong influence in both types of organizations. Even in public organizations with a high market or client orientation, such as those in the study—government manufacturers, a health district, and so on—the institutional authority of government affects internal influence patterns and external agencies often become involved. The strong role of adjudication units in public organizations reflects the authority conferred on them by the institutions of government. In the organizations studied, those units also handle key strategic dependencies by representing external constituencies and making policy decisions. Later we will see that the same researchers also found that the strategic decision-making processes of the public organizations also reflect the effects of their public sector status.

## Power at Different Organizational Levels

Management experts also consider how people at different levels and in different units obtain power. Daft (2001) points out that top managers have a variety of sources of power. They have considerable authority by virtue of their formal position, such as authority to control key decisions. They can also influence allocation of resources. In government agencies, in spite of external constraints and politics, the agency heads usually exert considerable influence over funding for subunits and allocation of other key resources, such as personnel. Top managers can control *decision premises*—fundamental values or principles that guide decision making—and information (Simon, 1948). A new director of the law enforcement department in a large state found a strong emphasis on hierarchical authority and communication in the department. He wanted to develop a climate of more open communication, in which employees could express their opinions and make suggestions. The director made it clear to his managers that the agency would adopt these orientations through open-door policies, improved communications, and other steps. This position became a guide for decision making by the other managers. The director established guidelines on how to respond when an employee asks to speak to a manager—"You listen!" The basic premise behind the agency's decision-making procedure now guides subsequent, more specific decisions. (Later chapters provide further examples of managers' efforts to communicate major values and premises to others.)

Top managers can also take advantage of *network centrality*. They occupy the center of networks of information, personal loyalty, and resource flows. The HUD official placed loyal associates in key positions to develop an information network. This worked effectively until deficits in other dimensions of her power eroded her position (Maitland, 1989).

Lower-level members of an organization can have substantial power as well. They may serve as experts on key tasks. They can obtain influence through effort, interest, informal coalitions (such as those formed by groups of friends), or formal organizations (such as unions). They can use rules and other organizational norms to their advantage. In his analysis of "street-level" government service providers, Lipsky (1980) points out that they have considerable autonomy. Civil service rules, vague performance measures, and extensive rules governing service delivery constrain higher officials' authority over them.

Middle managers have some of the influence potential of both executives and lower-level employees. Management experts interested in empowerment as a means of making managers more effective have lately focused increased attention on these managers (Kanter, 1987; Block, 1987). These authors often focus on business firms, but empowerment also has intriguing implications for public agencies.

Middle managers occupy positions below corporate vice presidents or major division and department heads. In government, this would include those below assistant secretaries or major bureau heads, such as managers in GS 13–15 positions in the federal government.

Kanter (1987) argues that middle managers in business firms have so little power that they cannot perform effectively. Many rules and routines govern their work, and there are few rewards for innovation. They rarely participate in important conferences or task forces. They lack resources and support to do useful things, such as rewarding excellent subordinates or pursuing a promising initiative. Higher-level managers must bestow a positive form of power on these middle managers. They must relax rules, increase participation, assign important tasks, and reward innovation (Kanter, 1987). This sharing of power *expands* power, giving more people in the organization the capacity and incentive to do good work. Later chapters describe how excellent corporations and effective leaders employ such policies.

Empowerment has developed into such a widely used concept that it has achieved buzzword status and is even referred to satirically in *Dilbert* cartoons. In one, the boss announces that empowerment is the management concept of the era and that he is empowering the employees. Dilbert and a fellow worker immediately start trying to fire one another, while another employee rejoices over never having to work hard again. While obviously meant to be amusing, the cartoon makes a point that many management experts make—empowering people in the workplace requires careful preparation, in such forms as training people and providing resources and organizational conditions to support their new roles (see, for example, Yukl, 2001, pp. 106–109). In addition, research on empowerment in a government human services agency found that empowerment is multidimensional. It can involve such provisions as involvement in agency decisions, skill development, job autonomy, and encouragement of creativity and initiative. The effectiveness of these different provisions depends on the values and preferences of the employees. (Petter and others, 2002).

Interestingly, Kanter's analysis of problems in industry sounds like the complaints about heavy constraints on managers in government. The proposed solution, however, sometimes contrasts sharply with common approaches in government. Elected officials and top agency executives often impose *more* rules to try to improve performance and maintain control (Wilson, 1989; Lynn, 1981; Warwick, 1975), as the Senate did in the IRS example at the beginning of this chapter. President Reagan aggressively sought to *dis*empower career federal civil servants (Durant, 1992; Golden, 2000), and political officials have made more recent efforts to exert strong controls over the bureaucracy (Hedge and Johnson, 2002). As these efforts indicate, the accountability pressures in government complicate empowerment approaches. Government officials face a serious challenge in finding ways to allow civil servants sufficient authority and participation to maintain a competent and motivated public service (Volcker Commission, 1989; National Academy of Public Administration, 1986). In addition, officials continue various efforts to build more flexibility into governmental management systems. In 2001, the Bush administration launched such an initiative by advancing Freedom to Manage legislation (Bush, 2001). The legislation stated the objective of providing federal managers with "tools and flexibility" to manage areas such as personnel, budgeting, and property management and disposal.

## Power Among Subunits

Pfeffer and Salancik (1978; Pfeffer, 1992) apply similar thinking to the analysis of power distributions among subunits. A department or bureau has more power when there is greater dependency on it, when it has more control over financial resources and greater centrality to the important activities of the organization, when there is less *substitutability* of services (when others have few or no alternatives to dealing with the unit for important needs), and when it has a larger role than other units in coping with important uncertainties facing the organization.

## Getting and Using Power

When they draw practical suggestions from this literature, management writers offer advice such as this (Daft, 2001):

- Move into areas of great uncertainty or strategic contingencies facing the organization and play an important role in managing those areas.
- Increase other departments' dependence on your own by making them depend on you for key resources and information. Incur obligations by doing additional work for others.
- Provide resources for the organization by bringing in money and other resources from external sources.
- Build coalitions and networks with others by building trust and respect through helpfulness and high motivation. Involve many people, including those who disagree with you.
- Influence the premises behind decision-making processes by such means as influencing the flow of information about one's department and shaping the agendas of important meetings.
- Enhance the legitimacy and prestige of your position and department.
- Be reasonably aggressive and assertive, but be quiet and subtle about power issues—do not make loud claims or demands about power.

Suggestions as general as these certainly apply in most management settings. For public management, they need to be interpreted in light of the points made here about legitimate authority and external political authority.

# Decision Making in Organizations

Decision-making issues are closely related to power issues, because power determines who gets to decide. The literature often suggests that, as with power issues, public organizations should have distinct decision-making processes because of factors different from those faced by private organizations, such as political interventions and constraints and more diverse, diffuse objectives (Nutt, 1999, 2000). The most recent evidence supports such assertions. Although this evidence shows that the general decision-making processes of public organizations often resemble those of private organizations, it also indicates that major decisions in public organizations involve more complexity, dynamism, intervention, and interruption than those in their private counterparts. These conditions help to explain why demands for accountability and efficiency that have led to schemes for rationalizing government decision-making processes have often failed. At the same time, however, public employees engage in much routine decision making that can be highly standardized. This raises another key challenge for public managers—deciding when to try to standardize and rationalize decision-making processes. Concepts from general organization theory help in the analysis of this issue.

Many contemporary management scholars (such as Daft, 2001) have analyzed decision-making processes according to a contingency-theory perspective of the sort described in Chapters One and Two. In some situations, managers can successfully adopt highly rationalized decision-making processes. Other situations involve too much uncertainty for such structured approaches and require more complex, intuitive decision making.

## Rational Decision-Making Models

Rationality has various meanings and dimensions, but in the social sciences, a *strictly* rational decision-making process would involve the following components:

1. Decision makers know all the relevant goals clearly.
2. Decision makers clearly know the values used in assessing those goals and targeting levels of attainment for them, so they also know their preferences among the goals and can rank order them.

3. Decision makers examine all alternative means for achieving the goals.
4. Decision makers choose the most efficient of the alternative means for maximizing the goals.

These strict conditions are seldom met except in the most simple of situations, but we know that simple situations that require decisions come up all the time. A bureau chief receives a careful committee report that demonstrates that three alternative vendors can sell the bureau identical copying machines. The bureau chief chooses the least expensive machine. To do otherwise would invite others to question the chief's competence, ethics, or sanity.

***Rational Decision-Making Techniques in Public Organizations.*** Public agencies apply techniques akin to those of scientific management when they have consultants or in-house experts analyze work processes to design more efficient, effective work procedures. The public service centers of the Social Security Administration, for example, needed a system for keeping track, to prevent misplacement, of the huge number of client file folders that move around to various employees who process the clients' claims. Consultants working with the agency developed a system for putting bar codes on the file folders so that the codes can be read into the computer with a scanner wand at each work location. This scan records the folder's location and creates a record of the location of each file within the system.

Similarly, management science techniques have wide applications in government (Downs and Larkey, 1986). These techniques involve mathematical models or other highly structured procedures for decision making. Linear programming, for example, uses mathematical formulas to determine how many units of output can be produced with given levels of inputs and thus the best mix of inputs for a production process. Other mathematical techniques support design of workflows and queuing processes. Many discussions of such techniques emphasize the greater difficulty of achieving successful applications in government because of such factors as vague performance criteria and political interventions (Drake, 1972; Morse and Bacon, 1967). In many technical areas of government work, however, these techniques have applications that are just as useful as those in industry.

Many of the proposals for improving government operations over the past several decades have advocated approaches that involve elements of rational decision making (Downs and Larkey, 1986; Lynn, 1981). Lyndon Johnson issued a presidential directive ordering that the planning and program budgeting system (PPBS) be implemented in the budgeting processes of federal agencies. PPBS involves a systematic process of organizing budget requests according to major programs, with the plans and objectives for those programs specified and justified. Advocates proposed PPBS as a reform of previous budgeting techniques that concentrated on the items or activities to be funded and paid little attention to program objectives. The Department of Defense had used the system with some success prior to President Johnson's order. Problems in implementing PPBS more widely led, however, to the order's cancellation a few years later.

When Jimmy Carter campaigned for president, he proposed the use of zero-based budgeting techniques as a way of exerting greater control over federal spending. These techniques involve looking at the requests for funding of various activities as if their funding levels were zero. The idea is to force a systematic, rational review of major commitments and possible reallocations rather than simply taking existing programs for granted. The procedure never came into use in any significant way.

Others have proposed that the public sector can use management by objectives techniques as well as the private sector does (Rodgers and Hunter, 1992). These techniques involve careful negotiation and specification of primary objectives for individuals and units, with performance evaluations concentrating on whether those objectives have been achieved (Swiss, 1991). As with the techniques discussed previously, debate goes on over prospects for using such a systematic and explicit technique in public organizations (Bowsher, 1990).

Some public organizations use elements of these techniques, but attempts to implement them widely have not been successful. Apparently the public sector conditions of diffuse goals, political complications, and highly complex programs often overwhelm such highly rationalized procedures. The GPRA requires federal agencies to produce strategic plans and performance plans that state their objectives, with reports on their success in accomplishing the objectives. This requirement involves a version of a rational process, and Radin (2000) poses difficult questions about whether such a process can prove successful within the political and institutional context of government in the United States.

***Rationality Assumptions and the Behaviors of Public Managers and Officials.***
Another role that the concept of rationality has played in analyzing public organizations revolves around its use to interpret the behavior of public managers and other government officials. "Public choice" economists have developed a body of theory using approaches typical in economics to analyze how citizens and officials make political decisions. They argue, for example, that in political just as in economic contexts, individuals rationally maximize utility. Voters vote in their own self-interest, and political officials in essence try to buy votes by providing the government programs and services that voters want. Because no market process ensures that one has to pay directly for the goods and services one receives, groups

of voters use the political system to benefit themselves at the expense of others. They demand that their elected officials give them services and subsidies that *they* need, sometimes shifting to other voters much of the burden of paying for them. When these theorists turn to the public bureaucracy, they suggest similar problems. In some of the most prominent, widely cited academic works on public bureaucracies, they suggest that government organizations strive for ever greater budgets (Niskanen, 1971) and tend toward rigidity (Downs, 1967) and information distortion (Tullock, 1965).

Evidence about these assertions has accumulated, and some of it supports them. Clearly, these assertions refer to serious challenges for public managers and potential shortcomings of public agencies. The evidence and careful assessment of the assertions, however, also indicate that they are oversimplified and, as depictions of many bureaucrats and public bureaucracies, simply inaccurate (Blais and Dion, 1991; Bendor and Moe, 1985). Chapters Thirteen and Fourteen return to questions about the performance of government agencies and their managers. While acknowledging the severe performance problems that public agencies and managers sometimes exhibit, those chapters also present evidence and assertions that public agencies and their managers often perform very well.

***The Limits of Rationality.*** Chapter Two describes how Herbert Simon (1948) advanced his observations about constraints on managers' ability to follow highly rational procedures, especially in complex decision-making settings (see also Jones, 1999). Simon argued that for large-scale decisions, the deluge of relevant information and uncertainties overloads the cognitive capacity of managers to process it. Managers strive for rationality—they are *intendedly rational*. But cognitive limits, uncertainties, and time limits cause them to decide under conditions of *bounded rationality*. They do not maximize in accordance with rationality assumptions; they "satisfice." They undertake a limited search among alternatives and choose the most satisfactory of them after as much consideration as they can manage within the constraints imposed by their situation. Cyert and March (1963) studied business firms and found that they approached major decisions largely as Simon had suggested. Rather than making decisions in highly rational modes, managers in the firms followed satisficing approaches. They engaged in "problemistic searches"—that is, they started searching for alternatives and solutions in relation to problems that came up rather than in a systematic, explicitly goal-oriented way. They also engaged in "sequential attention to alternatives," turning from possibility to possibility, looking at one alternative until they saw some problem with it and then turning to another. They tended to use benchmarks and rules of thumb rather than careful explication of goals and a strategy for maximizing them. For example, without conclusive evidence to justify doing so, they might set a target of a 5 percent profit increase per year for the next five years, simply because that is almost what they have achieved in the past.

## Contingency Perspectives on Decision Making

Current views of management typically follow this pattern of regarding strictly rational approaches to decision making as applicable within relatively limited domains of managerial activity. Where tasks and the operating context afford relatively stable, clear, simple conditions, managers find such approaches feasible. As conditions become more complex and dynamic, however, the deluge of information and uncertain conditions overwhelms procedures that require highly explicit statements of goals and painstaking analysis of numerous alternatives. More intuitive and experience-based judgment then comes into play, supplementing or supplanting highly rational procedures.

James Thompson (1967; Daft, 2001, p. 426) suggested a contingency framework to express these variations. Decision-making contexts vary along two major dimensions: the degree to which the decision makers agree on goals, and the degree to which they understand means-ends or cause-effect relationships—that is, the degree to which they have well-developed technical knowledge about how to solve the problems and accomplish the tasks. Where both goal agreement and technical knowledge are high, very rational procedures apply. The earlier example about the Social Security Administration's file tracking system illustrates a situation in which everyone agreed on the goals. Everyone wanted more efficient, effective file tracking procedures. In addition, the consultants had well-developed ways of analyzing the efficiency and effectiveness of the new file tracking system. A rational procedure served very well.

The Internal Revenue Service deals each year with the problem of receiving a flood of tax returns and extracting and sorting them correctly. State departments of motor vehicles and the U.S. Social Security Administration process many routine applications and claims every day. In decisions about activities such as these, management science techniques and other forms of highly rationalized analysis have valuable applications (as long as they are properly implemented, in a humane and communicative fashion). For example, the U.S. Navy once effectively implemented a planned maintenance system with elaborate scheduling charts that directed when the various pieces of machinery and equipment on a ship should receive maintenance. Instruction cards detailed the maintenance tasks to be performed and included a system for recording the completion of tasks. In effect, the ships followed a strict recipe for maintenance.

At the other end of the scale, where decision makers have no clear consensus on goals and little clarity as to the technical means of achieving them, one can hardly follow a simple blueprint. Measurement, mathematical models and analysis, and strict guidelines for decisions become more tenuous. Under these conditions, managers engage in more bargaining and political maneuvering and more intuitive, judgmental decision making.

## Incremental Decision-Making Processes

Much more in political science than in management, scholars have debated whether government decision-making processes follow an *incremental* pattern. This perspective on public sector decisions has features similar to those of the bounded rationality perspective and has similar intellectual origins. Incrementalism in decision making means concentrating on increments to existing circumstances, or relatively limited changes from existing conditions. Those who regard the policymaking process as having this characteristic argue that major, wrenching changes to federal budget categories seldom receive much consideration. Instead, the officials formulating the budget concentrate on the limited increments, up and down, proposed in any given year. Policymakers restrict the size of the changes they propose. The bigger the change, the more opposition they stir up and the more complex becomes the task of analyzing the change.

Political scientists have debated intensively over whether incrementalism accurately characterizes the policymaking and budgeting processes. In addition, they debate its desirability. Some argue that incremental processes stimulate useful bargaining among active political groups and officials, and guard against ill-considered radical changes. Others complain that they make the policymaking and budgeting processes too conservative and shortsighted and too supportive of existing coalitions and policies.

The debate has become mired in difficulties about what is meant by an increment—how large a change has to be to be large. It has led to the conclusion, however, that policy and budgetary changes tend to be incremental but are not always. Fairly drastic cuts in some portions of the federal budget during the Reagan administration, along with fairly sharp increases in military spending, illustrate that regardless of how one identifies an increment, cuts or increases can greatly affect public managers and their agencies (Rubin, 1985). More generally, however, the decision-making processes of public organizations play out within these larger incremental policymaking processes. Policy changes that agencies initiate or that influence them involve a complex interplay of political actors tugging and hauling over any significant change.

In fact, these aspects of the governmental context lead to prescriptions for using incremental approaches as the most feasible alternative. Charles Lindblom's article "The Science of Muddling Through" (1959) is a classic statement of this perspective. He notes that the requirement for political consensus and compromise results in vague goals for public policies and programs. In addition, public administrators carrying out these policies must maintain political support through public participation and consensus building. They have to remain accountable to elected officials, who usually have less experience than they do. As a result, stated goals and ends for policies provide little clarity, and means become inseparable from ends. Administrators find it difficult or politically unacceptable to state a precise societal impact for which a program aims. They must identify a package of means and ends that can achieve political consensus and support. Far-reaching, original procedures and goals evoke particularly strong opposition and usually must be modified if support is to be maintained. In addition, the need for political support often outweighs such criteria as efficiency and substantive impact. Thus, in formulating their packages of means and ends, administrators must strive for satisfactory decisions—that is, they must satisfice—after examining a relatively limited set of alternatives. Often they rely heavily on past practice. A good deal of intelligence may enter the decision-making process through the involvement of many groups, experts, and officials. Generally, however, the approach involves avoiding major departures and concentrating on relatively limited, politically feasible steps. One can see why critics worry about the implications of such an approach (Rosenbloom, 2001). It can lead to unduly conservative decisions, and it can favor politically influential groups over disadvantaged and less organized groups.

*Mixed Scanning.* Etzioni (1967, 1986) proposed an approach aimed at reaching a compromise between the extreme versions of rational decision making and incrementalism. He argued that administrators and other officials make both decisions that have large-scale, long-term implications and decisions of more limited scope. The latter decisions often follow major directions already selected by the former. Etzioni suggested that decision makers strive, through "mixed scanning," to recognize the points at which they concentrate on broader, longer-range alternatives and those at which they focus on more specific, incremental decisions that are a part of larger directions. Decision makers need to mix both perspectives, taking the time to conduct broad considerations of many major issues and alternatives to prevent the shortsightedness of incrementalism. Yet such broad scans cannot involve all the comprehensive analysis required by highly rational models; thus, more intensive analysis must follow on decisions within areas of pressing need.

*Logical Incrementalism.* Quinn (1990) suggested a pattern of logical incrementalism in which long-range strategic decisions set a framework for incremental steps aimed at carrying out the broader objectives. Focused mainly on business organizations, the approach involves careful consideration of long-range, general priorities. Implementing these priorities, however, involves limited, experimental steps. Decision makers must recognize that the priorities need adaptation and that compromise remains important. These suggestions are consistent with some prescriptions for successful large-scale change in organizations discussed in Chapter Thirteen.

### An Incremental Model of Decision-Making Processes Within Organizations.

Political scientists usually apply the concept of incrementalism to the process of creating broad public policy. Mintzberg, Raisinghani, and Theoret (1976) studied twenty-five major decisions in organizations and formulated an incremental model of decision-making processes. The model depicts decisions, even major ones, as involving numerous small, incremental steps moving through certain general phases. "Decision interrupts" can occur at any of these phases, causing the process to cycle back to an earlier point. The *identification* phase involves recognizing the problem and diagnosing it through information gathering. Then, in the *development* phase, a search process that identifies alternatives is followed by design of a particular solution. Finally, in the *selection* phase, the solution is evaluated, and through an authorization step the organization makes a formal commitment to the decision.

This process seldom flows smoothly. Decision interrupts at any of the steps make the decision-making process choppy and cyclical rather than smooth and carefully directed. An internal interruption may block diagnosis of a problem. Even when a solution has been designed, a new option may pop up and throw the process back. For example, a new executive may come in and refuse to authorize a decision that is otherwise ready for implementation, or an external interruption such as a government mandate may cause higher executives to push a proposal back for further development.

This incremental decision-making model has been used in research comparing private managers with managers from public and nonprofit organizations. Schwenk (1990) used it to analyze managers' perceptions about decision processes in their organizations. He found that compared to private business managers, public and nonprofit managers reported more interruptions, recycling to earlier phases, and conflicts in the decision processes in their organizations. This evidence of differences in decision-making processes between public and private organizations is consistent with the results of other research, such as the study by Hickson and others (1986) discussed later in this chapter.

## The Garbage Can Model

The tendency to regard major organizational decisions as complex and dynamic rather than smoothly rational now dominates the management literature. It reaches its apex in the *garbage can model*. This metaphor comes from the observation that decisions are made in organizations when particular decision-making opportunities or requirements arise. Like garbage cans, these instances have a diverse array of material cast into them in a disorderly fashion. As noted earlier, James March participated in research validating Simon's observations about constrained rationality in organizational decisions (Cyert and March, 1963). March and his colleagues also observed that organizational decisions involve much more internal political activity than is generally supposed, with extensive bargaining and conflict among coalitions (March, 1962; Pfeffer, 1982).

These observations evolved into the garbage can model, which holds that in organizational decision-making processes, participation, preferences, and technology (know-how, techniques, equipment) are ambiguous, uncertain, and rapidly changing. These conditions tend to occur especially in "loosely coupled" organizations such as universities and many government agencies (Weick, 1979; March and Olsen, 1986). The members and units have loose control and communication with one another. It is often unclear who has the authority to decide what and for whom. In addition, people may loosely engage even with very important issues, because other matters preoccupy them. People come and go in the organization and in decision-making settings such as committees. Problems and potential solutions come and go as well as conditions change. Choice opportunities also come up—a committee may look for decisions to make, or a manager may look for work to do. A solution may go looking for a problem: a promising alternative may become available that virtually begs for some type of application, or a person or group may have a pet technique that they want to find a way to use. Thus, problems, decision-making participants, solutions, and choice opportunities flow along in time relatively independent of one another.

Decision making occurs when these elements come together in a way that is conducive to making a decision—the right problem arises when the right decision-making participants are receptive to an available solution, all coming together in a choice opportunity. The model emphasizes that the linkages between these elements are more temporal than consequential; that is, they result as much from coincidence as from rational calculation (March and Olsen, 1986).

The model has considerable intuitive appeal; anyone who has worked in a complex organization knows of chaotic or accidental decisions. In addition, a number of studies have found that the model accurately depicts decision-making processes in a variety of organizations. March and Olsen (1986) stress that they intend the model not as a replacement for other perspectives on decision making but as a supplement to them, thus implying that they do not claim that it perfectly accounts for all decision-making processes and contexts. They do not rule out relatively rational approaches in certain instances. In addition, they point out that the model does not imply that all decisions involve unavoidable bedlam and chaos. Dominant values and norms, historical contexts, leaders with a firm sense of mission, and other factors can guide or bias decisions in systematic ways.

The proponents of the model do not state very clearly just where and when it applies. Early on in their theoretical work, they suggested (without explaining) that the model applies mainly to public and educational organizations (March and Olsen, 1976; Cohen, March, and Olsen, 1972). Most of the applications apparently have concentrated on educational and military organizations and courts. Yet at times the proponents also suggest that it applies to business firms and generally to all organizations (March and Olsen, 1986, p. 12). Critics have attacked the garbage can model for remaining too metaphorical, imprecise, and internally contradictory to support scientific progress (Bendor, Moe, and Shotts, 2001), although not surprisingly the developers of the perspective disagree (Olsen, 2001). Still, the model has important implications for public management. As discussed shortly, Hickson and his colleagues (1986) found that this type of decision-making process occurs more frequently in public organizations than in private firms.

# Strategic Management

Although most experts on managerial decision making emphasize the rather chaotic nature of the process, by no means do they deny that managers do and should engage in purposeful, goal-oriented actions. As described in earlier chapters and in earlier sections of this chapter, the topic of strategic management has advanced prominently in recent decades, and government agencies at all levels engage in strategic planning (Berry and Wechsler, 1995). The concept of strategy comes from the idea of military strategy, of using the resources and strengths of a military force to achieve goals—military victory, usually—by forming plans and objectives and executing them. The concept is more attractive than similar rubrics, such as planning and business policy, because of this emphasis on assessing one's own general goals, one's strengths and weaknesses, and the external threats and opportunities that one faces in deploying one's forces to best advantage in pursuit of those goals.

## Prescriptive Frameworks for Strategic Management

Management consultants and experts propose a variety of approaches for developing strategy. Bryson and Roering (1996) provide an excellent summary of eight major approaches to strategic planning that provides more depth and detail on the models mentioned in this discussion. Bryson (1995) concludes that managers can apply virtually all of them in the public sector (although with several provisos, discussed shortly). Some of the models, such as that of the Boston Consulting Group, focus on high-level corporate decisions about the relative priority of the corporation's business activities. The Boston Consulting Group's "portfolio model" exhorts executives to treat the mix of business units in a large corporation as if they represented stocks in an individual's portfolio of assets. Executives assess the business units in the corporation on two dimensions—market growth and size of market share. The units high on both of these dimensions are "stars"; they should receive priority attention and reinvestment of profits. Units with small shares in slow-growing markets—low on both key dimensions—are "dogs" and candidates for divestiture. Mixed situations provide opportunities for strategic shifting of resources. A unit with a high market share in a slowly growing market brings in a lot of money but does not have strong growth prospects. These activities should be treated as "cash cows" and used to provide resources for units that provide growth opportunities. Units that are in a rapidly growing market but not yet in command of a large share of it should be considered for infusions of resources from other units, especially the cash cows. The approach sounds cutthroat, but it actually emphasizes *synergy*—the effective meshing of all the activities in an organization to produce overall gains beyond what the activities would gain as the sum of their independent operations.

Ring (1988) applied a modified portfolio model to public sector strategy making. He used "tractability of the problem" and "public support" as the key dimensions. Where problems are manageable and public support is high, public managers can seek to gain resources that they can then use to deal with more difficult policy problems in settings where public support is high but the problem is very difficult to solve. Where public support and tractability are both low, public managers simply seek to shift the priority away from those problems. Similarly, Rubin (1988) suggests that strategic patterns will differ according to whether the time horizon for the policy issue is long or short and whether the policy plays out within a disruptive or an anticipated environment.

Other approaches emphasize different levels and issues (Bryson, 1995). *Strategic planning systems* propose methods for formulating and implementing strategic decisions and allocating resources to back them up across units and levels of an organization. *Stakeholder management* approaches analyze how key stakeholders evaluate an organization and form strategies to deal with each stakeholder. (Stakeholders include individuals or groups who have a major interest in an organization, such as unions, customers, suppliers, and regulators.) *Competitive analysis* approaches analyze major forces acting on an industry, such as the power of buyers and suppliers, the prospects for substitute products, and competition in its markets. The aim is to gain competitive advantage through such strategies as differentiating oneself from competitors and selecting the segments of an industry in which one should compete (Porter, 1998). *Strategic issues management* focuses on identifying major issues that appear crucial to an organization's ability to achieve its objectives and deciding how a working group in the organization will respond to these issues and resolve them. *Process strategies* and *strategic negotiation* approaches treat strategic decision making as a highly political process and prescribe ways of managing the constant bargaining required. Similarly, *logical incrementalism,* as described earlier, emphasizes the incremental nature of strategic decisions and ways to guide bargaining along a consistent path. (For more detail, see Bryson, 1995, and Bryson and Roering, 1996.)

## Applications of Strategic Management in the Public Sector

Numerous frameworks for strategic management in the public sector are now available (Bryson, 1995; Bryson and Roering, 1996; Nutt and Backoff, 1992). They tend to involve a version of the Harvard Policy and Stakeholder model of strategic planning (Berry and Wechsler, 1995), which focuses on such procedures as strategic issue management, stakeholder analysis, environmental scanning, and SWOT analysis (described shortly). The procedures prescribed by scholars and consultants usually begin with a planning and organizing phase. A strategic management group (SMG) typically manages the process and must agree on who will be involved, how the strategic analysis will proceed, and what the group expects to achieve. Usually the procedure requires a structured group process and a facilitator—a consultant skilled in helping groups make decisions. The facilitator often asks members of the group to list their views about important points, such as stakeholders, opportunities, and threats. Then the group members follow a procedure for synthesizing their views, such as the nominal group technique described in Chapter Twelve.

The SMG usually begins with a preliminary assessment of the history and current status of the organization to produce a general statement of the organization's mission, such as those provided in Exhibit 7.1. Bryson (1995) suggests that for public organizations this step requires a careful review of the organization's mandates—the requirements imposed by external authorities through legislation and regulations. This review can clarify what external authorities dictate and can also provide insights about new approaches. For example, representatives of a public hospital who interpret their mandate as forbidding competition with private health services may find upon review that they have the authority to do so.

## EXHIBIT 7.1. VISION, MISSION, AND
## GOAL STATEMENTS OF GOVERNMENT ORGANIZATIONS.

From U.S. Department of Transportation
2002 Strategic Plan

### Vision

A visionary and vigilant Department of Transportation leading the way to
transportation excellence and innovation in the twenty-first century

### Mission

Serve the United States by ensuring a safe transportation system that furthers our
vital national interests and enhances the quality of life of the American people

### Strategic Goals

*Safety:* Promote public health and safety by working toward the elimination of transportation-related deaths and injuries

*Mobility:* Shape an accessible, affordable, reliable transportation system for all people, goods,
and regions

*Economic growth:* Support a transportation system that sustains America's economic growth

*Human and natural environment:* Protect and enhance communities and the natural environment affected by transportation

*National security:* Ensure the security of the transportation system for the movement of people and goods, and support the National Security Strategy

### Organizational Excellence Goal

Advance the Department's ability to manage for results and innovation

From U.S. Department of Education
2002 Strategic Plan

*Goal One:* Create a culture of achievement

1.1 Link federal education funding to accountability for results
1.2 Increase flexibility and local control
1.3 Increase information and options for parents
1.4 Encourage the use of scientifically based methods within federal education programs

*Goal Two:* Improve student achievement

2.1 Ensure that all students read on grade level by the third grade
2.2 Improve mathematics and science achievement for all students
2.3 Improve the performance of all high school students
2.4 Improve teacher and principal quality

*Goal Three:* Develop safe schools and strong character

3.1 Ensure that our nation's schools are safe and drug-free and that students are free of
    alcohol, tobacco, and other drugs
3.2 Promote strong character and citizenship among our nation's youth

*Goal Four:* Transform education into an evidence-based field

4.1 Raise the quality of research funded or conducted by the Department
4.2 Increase the relevance of our research in order to meet the needs of our customers

## EXHIBIT 7.1. VISION, MISSION, AND
## GOAL STATEMENTS OF GOVERNMENT ORGANIZATIONS, Cont'd.

*Goal Five:* Enhance the quality of and access to postsecondary and adult education

5.1 Reduce the gaps in college access and completion among student populations differing by race and ethnicity, socioeconomic status, and disability while increasing the educational attainment of all

5.2 Strengthen accountability of postsecondary institutions

5.3 Establish effective funding mechanisms for postsecondary education

5.4 Strengthen historically black colleges and universities, Hispanic-serving institutions, and tribal colleges and universities

5.5 Enhance the literacy and employment skills of American adults

*Goal Six:* Establish management excellence

6.1 Develop and maintain financial integrity and management and internal controls

6.2 Improve the strategic management of the Department's human capital

6.3 Manage information technology resources, using e-gov, to improve service for our customers and partners

6.4 Modernize the student financial assistance programs and reduce their high-risk status

6.5 Achieve budget and performance integration to link funding decisions to results

6.6 Leverage the contributions of community- and faith-based organizations to increase the effectiveness of Department programs

6.7 By becoming a high performance, customer-focused organization, earn the President's Quality Award

Working toward the mission statement, the SMG typically reviews trends in the operating environment, using a framework like those described in Chapter Four. It may also conduct a stakeholder analysis at this point and develop idealized visions of how it wants the organization to be in the future. Ultimately, the mission statement expresses the general purpose of the organization and its major values and commitments.

Next, the SMG members assess the strengths and weaknesses of the organization and look outward to the environment and forward to the future to identify opportunities and threats facing the organization. This assessment of strengths, weaknesses, opportunities, and threats is called a SWOT analysis. The SMG can choose from an array of techniques for this analysis (Nutt and Backoff, 1992). A typical approach involves the nominal group technique mentioned earlier. From the SWOT analysis, the SMG develops a list of *strategic issues*—conflicts among opposing forces or values that can affect the organization's ability to achieve a desired future (Nutt and Backoff, 1992). Then the group develops plans for managing these issues (Nutt and Backoff, 1992; Ring, 1988; Eadie, 1996). A wide variety of public sector organizations now use this approach to strategic planning (Bryson, 1995; Boschken, 1988; Wechsler and Backoff, 1988).

## Analytical Research on Managerial Strategies in the Public Sector

In addition to recommending procedures, researchers have studied the strategies that public organizations actually pursue and how their strategic decisions actually develop. Some of these studies show the effects of government ownership on strategy. In their study of strategic decisions in thirty British organizations, Hickson and his colleagues (1986) found that strategic decision-making processes in publicly owned service and manufacturing organizations differed from those in private service and manufacturing firms. The public organizations followed a "vortex-sporadic" decision-making process. This involves more turbulence, more shifting participation by a greater diversity of internal and external interests, more delays and interruptions, and more formal and informal interaction among participants. The type of decision made a great difference, as did the distinction between service and manufacturing organizations. The results, however, indicate that the public sector context does impose on internal strategic decision making the sorts of interventions and constraints described in earlier chapters. The findings are consistent with other analyses of the distinctive context of strategic planning in the public sector, which observe that strategic planners in the public sector must consider a broader scope of impact and a more diverse and attentive set of stakeholders (Nutt and Backoff, 1995, 1999), and considerations of market volatility and competition that apply in the private sector need to be replaced by considerations of need for governmental action and responsiveness (Nutt and Backoff, 1995, 1999). Nutt (1999) has also identified distinctive patterns of assessing alternatives in the public sector.

Mascarenhas (1989) studied 187 public and private offshore drilling firms in thirty-four countries to analyze their strategic domains (markets served, product type, customer orientation, and technology applied). The government-owned firms operated mainly in domestic markets, with narrow product lines and stable customer bases. Publicly traded private firms (those whose stock is traded on exchanges) were larger, operated in many geographical markets, and offered a wider range of products. Privately held firms were more like the state-owned firms but had less stable customer bases. The nationality and size of the firms also made a big difference, but the ownership distinctions persisted even with controls for those factors. The results support the point, mentioned in Chapter Three, that public organizations tend to have greater constraints on their strategic domains.

Other studies have analyzed important variations in strategy within the public sector. Wechsler and Backoff (1986) studied four state agencies in Ohio and found that they pursued four types of strategies. The Department of Natural Resources followed a developmental strategy. This agency had diverse tasks, constituencies, and independent funding sources. The managers had relative independence to pursue a strategy of enhancing the capabilities, resources, and general performance of the organization. Stronger external forces shaped the transformational strategy of the Department of Mental Retardation. Professional experts and legal rights groups advocated deinstitutionalization of the mentally retarded—getting them out of large hospitals and into normal living conditions. The agency also faced constant budgetary pressures. It responded by transforming itself from a manager of hospitals to a monitor and regulator of client services delivered through community-based programs and contracts. The Department of Public Welfare received intense criticism in the media and from legislators and faced increasing human service needs and potential cutbacks in funding, so its managers followed a protective strategy. They strengthened internal controls, lowered the agency's public profile ("getting the agency out of the newspapers"), mended relations with legislators, and worked to protect funding levels. The Public Utilities Commission, which regulates utility pricing decisions, adopted a political strategy. Nuclear energy issues and increasing fuel prices led to more political activity by consumer advocates. The agency's decisions became more favorable to consumers, reflecting a shift in response to changing configurations of stakeholders.

Boschken (1988) found that a private sector model of strategic variations applied well to government enterprises. Miles and Snow's prominent typology (1978) suggests that *defenders* react to stable environments by trying to protect their hold on their markets and their customers, emphasizing efficiency and centralization. *Analyzers*, operating in moderately changing contexts, take a similar approach but seek to innovate moderately, allowing looser control of innovative efforts. *Prospectors* are found in contexts of growth and dynamism; they seek opportunities and take risks, employing more decentralized and organic management. *Reactors* may appear in any context. They simply drift without clear purpose, responding to conditions as they arise. Boschken (1988) found this framework useful in analyzing the strategic behaviors of port authority organizations for various cities on the West Coast. Public authorities fall between public agencies and business firms. Nevertheless, the study suggests that the very general frameworks for the private sector can be useful in government.

Berry and Wechsler (1995) conducted a national survey of state agencies and found that even by the early 1990s the majority of agencies, about 60 percent, employed strategic planning. The leaders of the agencies had initiated the process at their level rather than due to directives from a higher level such as a governor, primarily to set program and policy direction. Berry and Wechsler concluded that the evidence indicated that strategic planning was a successful public sector management innovation.

These studies show that strategic orientation varies considerably among public organizations. Public managers, like private managers, engage in a variety of purposeful efforts to respond to their environment and achieve their objectives. This general perspective stands in sharp contrast to negative stereotypes of public managers as passive and inattentive to long-term purposes, which often get drawn into respectable academic theory. The research and writing also suggest that we can develop generalizations about power, decision making, and strategy formulation in the public sector.

## Issues for Managers and Researchers

There are more observations about the general features of the public sector context than there is consensus about how to deal with the variations within it. The assertions in the literature about the general characteristics of public organizations that distinguish them from their private counterparts can be summarized as follows:

- There are more political intrusions into management in public organizations and there is a greater infusion of political criteria.
- A more elaborate overlay of formal, institutional constraints governs the management process, involving more formal laws, rules, and mandated procedures and policies.
- Goals and performance criteria are generally more vague, multiple, and conflicting for public organizations.
- Economic market indicators are usually absent, and the organizations pursue idealized, value-laden social objectives.
- The public sector must handle particularly difficult social tasks, often under relatively vague mandates from legislative bodies.
- Public organizations must jointly pursue all of the complex goals described earlier—accountability, responsiveness, representativeness, openness, efficiency, and accountability.

The literature on power in organizations reminds us that power is elusive and complex and that thinking too much in terms of power relationships can be deluding. Yet the best-intentioned of managers have to consider means of exerting influence for the good ends they seek. We now have a considerable literature on the power of bureaucracies in general, with a growing set of case studies of effective public managers and how they gain and use influence within the political system (Olshfski, 1990; Doig and Hargrove, 1987; Allison, 1983; Lewis, 1980; Kotter and Lawrence, 1974). We do not, however, have many studies of large samples of public managers that analyze their power and influence within the system and what causes variations in it. Both managers and researchers, then, face the question of what to make of the current state of knowledge on this topic.

Pulling together the material from organization theory and political science suggests some answers. For one thing, public administrators apparently face relatively sharp constraints on their power and influence as a result of their particular context. High-level executives such as politically elected executives and appointed cabinet officers must share authority over their administrative units with legislators and other political authorities. Their authority over their subordinates and organizations is constrained by rules and procedures imposed by other units, such as those governing civil service procedures, purchasing, procurement and space-allocation decisions, and budgeting decisions. At lower managerial levels, managers' authority is further overshadowed by the stronger formal authority and resource control of other institutional authorities. Kingdon (1995) reports a survey in which federal officials rated the president and Congress as having much more influence over the policy agenda than administrative officials.

Within this disadvantaged setting, however, administrative officials have varying degrees of influence. Given the assertions of the literature on organizational and bureaucratic power, one would expect that administrative officials, although always subject to the shifting tides of political, social, and technical developments, have greater influence under the following conditions:

- When they play important roles relative to major policy problems and to obtaining resources for their agency—when they are in key budgetary decision-making roles or in policymaking positions central to the agency's mandates and to the support of major constituencies.
- When they have effective political support from committees and actors in the legislative branch, in other components of the executive branch, and in interest and constituency groups.
- When they have strong professional capabilities and credentials. Some agencies are dominated by a particular professional group, such as attorneys, foreign service officers, police officers, or military officers. Managers without strong credentials and abilities in these specializations will need other strengths, such as excellent preparation or a reputation as a strong generalist manager.
- When they have excellent substantive knowledge of government and its operations and institutions (for example, the legislative and administrative lawmaking processes) and of the policies and programs of the agencies in which they work.
- When they achieve or have the capacity to achieve a reputation for general stature and competence, including high energy, intelligence, integrity, and commitment to serving the public.

Public managers have to consider these power and influence issues because they are directly related to the autonomy and authority they exercise in decision-making processes and to the nature of the decision-making process itself. The evidence and analysis discussed in this chapter and earlier suggest more political intrusions and institutional constraints on decision making in public organizations than in private organizations. Executives who have had experience in business and government echo these observations (Perry and Kraemer, 1983).

More explicitly, Ring and Perry (1985) synthesized literature and research on management strategy for public organizations and came to a similar conclusion. They found that existing research and observations indicate that public sector strategic decision making takes place under such conditions as the following:

- Policy ambiguity (policy directives that are more ill-defined than those in business firms)
- Greater openness to the participation and influence of the media and other political officials and bodies, and greater attentiveness from a more diverse array of them
- More artificial time constraints due to periodic turnover of elected and appointed officials and mandated time lines from courts and legislatures
- Shaky coalitions (relative instability in the political coalitions that can be forged around a particular policy or solution)

Besides the implications of the political science literature and these observations, research findings increasingly validate this general scenario. A number of studies show more constraints, interruptions, interventions, and external contacts in the public sector than in the private sector. Porter and Van Maanen (1983) compared city government administrators with industrial managers and found that city administrators feel they have less control over how they allocate their own time, feel more pressed for time, and regard demands from people outside their organization as a much stronger influence on how they manage their time. The study by Hickson and his colleagues (1986) described earlier emphasizes the more turbulent pattern of participation, delay, interruption, and participation in public sector decision making.

Ring and Perry (1985) also suggest some of the consequences of this context for strategic management. They say that because public managers must often shoot for more limited objectives, they are more likely to have to follow incremental decision-making patterns, and thus their strategies are more likely to be emergent than intended (that is, their strategic decisions and directions are more likely to emerge from the decision-making process than to follow some originally intended direction). Effective public managers must maintain greater flexibility in their orientation toward staff assignments and controls and avoid premature commitments to a given set of objectives. According to Ring and Perry, they must straddle competing demands for efficiency, equity, high moral standards, and political responsiveness to constituent groups by showing open-mindedness, shunning dogmatism, and skillfully integrating competing viewpoints. They must effectively "wield influence rather than authority" and minimize discontinuities in the process. These suggestions from Ring and Perry are noticeably similar to suggestions for garbage can management, but they give more explicit attention to the external political context surrounding major decisions in public organizations.

The question of political influences on decisions raises one final issue addressed in the organizational literature on decision making: Which contingencies determine that decisions must be less structured and systematically rational? As illustrated in earlier examples, many decisions in public organizations are not pervaded with politics and institutional constraints but take place much as they might in a business firm. A challenge facing practitioners and researchers alike is the clarification of where, when, and how deeply the political environment of public organizations affects their decision-making processes. Researchers on public management have not clarified when such contingencies occur. Public managers appear to have more encapsulated, internally manageable decision-making settings (where rational decision-making processes are often more appropriate) when tasks and policy problems are clear, routine, and tractable, and at levels of the organization and in geographical locations that are remote from political scrutiny; when issues are minimally politically salient or enjoy consistent public support; when legislative and other mandates are clear as opposed to "fuzzy" (Lerner and Wanat, 1983); and when administrative decision makers gain stronger authority to manage a situation autonomously, without political intervention. Given the present state of research and knowledge, researchers and managers alike have to struggle to analyze such variations in decision-making contexts to determine the most appropriate approaches.

This theme of appropriately assessing and managing the political context in relation to other organizational contingencies comes up again in later chapters. The next chapter addresses additional issues about structure and technology in public organizations, issues related to decision-making processes and influence within the political environment, which in turn relate to later questions about human behavior and performance in public organizations.

CHAPTER EIGHT

# ORGANIZATIONAL STRUCTURE, DESIGN, TECHNOLOGY, AND INFORMATION TECHNOLOGY

The U.S. Internal Revenue Reform and Restructuring Act of 1998 (known as RRA98) directed the IRS to redesign its structure. The IRS had operated for about half a century with the same geography-based structure; that is, the agency was organized on the basis of geographic regions and further subdivided into districts. Most of the important auditing, enforcement, and tax collection work occurred in the thirty-three geographic districts. The directors of these thirty-three districts had a lot of authority over what happened in their districts, and often had considerable prestige and presence there as well. Most of the tax returns they received were sent to be processed at one of ten major service centers located around the nation.

As part of the set of reforms that RRA98 mandated, IRS executives led a major transformation in the agency's structure, to a customer-focused design. The new commissioner of the IRS, Charles Rossotti, proposed the design as a version of similar approaches used by major banks. Large banks face a variety of demands from different clusters of their customers. Individual retail customers want checking accounts and small loans. Small businesses and self-employed persons have additional needs for business loans and payroll services. Very large corporations have further needs for support of their larger loans and payroll services, pension plans, and stock and bond offerings. The large banks have often designed their structures into divisions to address the needs of these different sets of customers.

The IRS developed a similar plan. The agency reorganized into four main operating divisions:

- A wage and investment division, for taxpayers filing their individual income tax returns.
- A small business and self-employed division.
- A large and medium-sized business division.
- A tax-exempt and government entities division, which has no analogue in the example about large banks; it deals with issues of concern to nonprofit organizations and tax-exempt pension programs.

The IRS also established an agency-wide shared services division that handles many of the common service and support needs of the other parts of the agency, such as maintenance of personal computers and payroll processing. Many business firms and other organizations have recently established a division of this sort to handle widely shared common services.

Redesigning the IRS represented a huge undertaking, because the organization employs more than 100,000 people, processes more than 425 million tax returns per year, and handles well over a trillion dollars in revenue each year. The reorganization required several years and involved numerous design teams working on plans for the new organization. The new divisions came into operation in 2000 and 2001, and the success of the new design remains to be evaluated, but clearly the reorganization worked in the sense of firmly establishing the new structure.

Another example is the Brookhaven National Laboratory (BNL) on Long Island, which serves as an important scientific resource for the nation and the world (see www.bnl.gov). Scientists at BNL conduct leading research in physics, biology, chemistry, medicine, environmental science, and other areas. One major facility at BNL, the Relativistic Heavy Ion Collider, allows scientists to conduct experiments in which they use this massive particle accelerator to stage collisions between large subatomic particles, and to study the results of the collisions for evidence about the fundamental characteristics of atomic particles and matter. Although scientists at BNL take pride in the lab's research in part because of its peacetime applications (as opposed to nuclear research for military applications), environmentalists and local residents have worried for a long time about the danger of environmental pollution from the lab. During the 1990s, the discovery and disclosure of a small leak of tritium, a radioactive substance, caused a public outcry. Although scientists at the lab considered the leak extremely minor and not at all dangerous, the news of the leak aggravated the longstanding worries about the lab. Demonstrators conducted protests at the entrance to the lab compound. Celebrities, such as a supermodel and a famous actor, pled in public for the closing of the lab and claimed that it caused cancer in local residents. They and other activists prevailed upon political leaders in the area to do something about BNL.

Amid the controversy, the secretary of energy cancelled the contract for the management of the lab. The lab is a government-owned, contractor-operated organization. Years ago, when the federal government established national laboratories, the management of the labs was contracted out. Under these contracts, private business firms or consortia of universities would manage the labs. Brookhaven had been managed for more than fifty years under a contract with a consortium of major universities. After the secretary of energy cancelled the contract, the Department of Energy entered into a new contract with a partnership between a university and a major research institute, who provided the new management team for the lab.

Soon, the administrative structure at BNL changed significantly. The main organizational departments, called directorates, included directorates for the major scientific programs where the scientists conducted research, such as the directorate for high energy and nuclear physics, and for life sciences. There were also administrative directorates, such as the directorate for finance and administration. The new management group added additional administrative directorates, one for environment, safety, health, and quality, which oversees environmental protection and safety procedures at BNL, and one for community involvement, government, and public affairs. The directors who headed the directorates met regularly as a group with the director of the lab, the top administrator, and often voted on major issues. Scientists at the lab pointed out that the addition of the new administrative directorates meant that the administrative functions were receiving increased emphasis and influence. For example, more directors of administrative directorates meant more votes for administrative functions in the meetings with the lab director.

Soon the new management group also introduced requirements that employees working at BNL had to complete Web-based training programs in laboratory safety procedures and waste disposal and environmental protection procedures. Many of the scientists grumbled about these requirements, because they saw them as unnecessary training in elementary procedures that they already followed. They felt that the new rules and procedures wasted time and resources because they tied up employees in completing the training instead of working on research. In addition, scientists at BNL often get grants from other sources to conduct research, and overhead expenses taken out of their grants increased to pay for the added administrative functions and the additional training.

In effect, then, the new administrative directorates and the added administrative rules and procedures increased the importance of administrative controls and influences relative to scientific research priorities. Why did this occur? The new laboratory director explained that something had to be done to respond to the public controversy and outcry about the environmental dangers at BNL. While the scientists at the lab grumbled about the new procedures, they expressed great respect for the director, a former university president and a scientist himself. The scientists acknowledged that he had to do something to respond to the political and public relations pressures on the lab.

These examples illustrate why the historical overview in Chapter Two and the discussion of organizational environments in Chapter Four show that so many factors, such as environmental complexity, public sector status (including political oversight and mandates), goals, and leadership affect organizational structures and their design. Management researchers use the term *structure* to refer to the configuration of the hierarchical levels and specialized units and positions within an organization, and to the formal rules governing these arrangements. They use *technology* and *tasks* to refer to the work processes of an organization that often serve as major influences on the design of organizational structure.

As the historical review in Chapter Two showed, the concept of organizational structure has played a central role in organization and management theory from the beginning. Researchers have analyzed organizational technologies and tasks as important elements affecting the best structure. In spite of the constraints placed on them, public managers have considerable authority over the structure of their organizations and make many decisions in relation to technology and tasks, so current thinking on these topics is important to effective public management.

This chapter first discusses the interesting division of opinion about whether public organizations have distinctive structural characteristics, such as more red tape than private organizations. It then examines the importance of organizational structure and its relation to political power, strategy, and other topics. Next, it describes major concepts and findings from the research on organizational structure, technology, and design. Organization theorists have generally addressed structure from a generic perspective, devoting little attention to the distinctive structural attributes of public organizations, even though some important studies have concentrated on public agencies. These general points apply to most organizations, however, and the discussion here gives examples specifically involving public organizations. The chapter concludes by turning more directly to the evidence about whether public organizations differ in structure and design from private organizations.

# Do Public Organizations Have Distinctive Structural Characteristics?

Novels, essays, and popular stereotypes have all bemoaned the absurdity and inhumanity of government bureaucracies. Their observations often focus on structural matters, such as rigid rules and hierarchies. More formal scholarship often follows suit. In a virtual tradition among some economists, government bureaucracies play the role of villain, sometimes threatening both prosperity and freedom. In probably the most widely cited book on bureaucracy ever published, Downs (1967) argues that government bureaucracies inevitably move toward rigidity and hierarchical constraints. He states a "law of hierarchy" that holds that large government organizations, with no economic markets for their outputs, have more elaborate and centralized hierarchies than do private business firms. Downs's law represents a broad consensus that government bureaucracies have exceedingly complex rules, red tape, and hierarchies, even in comparison to large private sector organizations (Barton, 1980; Bozeman, 2000; Dahl and Lindblom, 1953; Lindblom, 1977; Sharkansky, 1989).

An opposite consensus also exists, however. Organization theorists' research on organizational structure offers the best-developed concepts and empirical findings on the topic. Yet as the first several chapters of this book pointed out, most organization theorists have not regarded public organizations as a particularly distinctive category. They have usually adopted a generic perspective that contends that their concepts of structure apply broadly across many types of organizations and that distinctions such as public and private are oversimplified and based on crude stereotypes. Many organization theorists regard other factors, such as organizational size, environmental complexity, and technology, as more important influences on structure than public or private status. Mainstream organization theory in effect sharply disputes the view among some economists and political scientists—that public bureaucracies have excessive red tape and highly centralized and elaborate hierarchies.

We will further examine the evidence in this controversy later in this chapter. First, however, we will review the concepts and insights about organizational structure developed by organization theorists and how they apply to public organizations—because they do. Most of the research comparing public and private organizations' structures uses these concepts and methods from organization theory. After reviewing these concepts, we will turn to the evidence comparing public and private organizational structures, which will show some very interesting developments in this research, some of them quite recent. To some people, carefully examining research on the structures of public bureaucracies and business firms sounds about as inviting as reading the telephone book. But if you like to base your thinking on well-developed evidence instead of on stereotypes and the half-baked assertions we hear in popular discourse, following and interpreting the research on this topic are intriguing challenges.

## The Development of Research on Structure

We have already seen examples of the influence of political actors and government authorities on the structures of public agencies: legislation and political pressures that force structural changes; rules and clearances imposed on federal managers by oversight agencies; micromanagement by legislators who specify rules and organizational structure; legislators and interest groups jealously guarding the structural autonomy of an agency, preventing its reorganization under the authority of another organization; and President Reagan's demotion of federal career civil servants by creating new positions above them. Presidents have created new agencies and placed them outside existing agencies to keep them away from those agencies' powerful political and administrative coalitions (Seidman and Gilmour, 1986). John Kennedy placed the Peace Corps outside the State Department, and Lyndon Johnson kept the youth employment training programs of the Office of Economic Opportunity away from the Department of Labor. Interest group pressures have led to the removal of bureaus from larger agencies. Due to such pressures, Congress removed the Department of Education from the Department of Health, Education and Welfare, which then became the Department of Health and Human Services (HHS) (Radin and Hawley, 1988). Later, similar political pressures led Congress to remove the Social Security Administration (SSA) from HHS.

Interestingly, however, early in this century, public administration experts leading the development of the field did not emphasize such political dynamics in their most prominent analyses of government organizations. The school's proponents argued that its principles of administration applied equally well in government and business organizations. After all, the object was to make government more efficient, more businesslike, and less "political."

Luther Gulick (1937; see also Chapter Two of this book) and others in the administrative management school advocated such administrative principles as highly specialized, clearly described task assignments; clear chains of command and authority (with "unity of command," where each person has "one master"—one supervisor—and therefore receives clear directions); a centralized authority structure, with authority residing mainly at the top of the organization; and narrow "spans of control" to help maintain clear lines of authority (a span of control is the number of subordinates reporting to a superior; a narrow span of control means relatively few people report to any given supervisor).

These principles were to guide decisions about structure that would maximize efficiency and performance. Even though it tended to downplay distinctions between government and business, this drive toward developing efficient, effective structure drew strength from important issues in government at the time. A reform movement in the later part of the nineteenth century and the earlier decades of the twentieth attacked government corruption and mismanagement, particularly in urban areas. Reformers saw these principles guiding the efficient structuring of organizations as a means of purging political patronage and slovenly management (Knott and Miller, 1987).

Later, government growth during the New Deal and after World War II brought a vast proliferation of government agencies. Gulick and other proponents of the principles of the administrative management school influenced major proposals for reorganizing the sprawling federal bureaucracy and played an important role in major developments in the structure of the federal government in this century. For example, some of the reforms proposed grouping various federal agencies under larger "umbrella" agencies as a means of narrowing the chief executive's span of control. Some experts have argued that many government officials continue to hold the general view of proper organization espoused by the administrative management school (Knott and Miller, 1987; Warwick, 1975; Seidman and Gilmour, 1986).

As explained in Chapter Two, the classic approach to structure came under criticism as research on organizations burgeoned during the middle of the twentieth century. The contingency perspective on organizational structure rejected the quest for one common set of principles to guide organizational design. Contingency theorists contended that an organization's structure must be adapted to key contingencies facing the organization, such as environmental variations and uncertainty, the demands of technology or the production process, the size of the organization, and strategic decisions by managers and coalitions within the organization.

A profusion of empirical studies in the 1960s and 1970s added to this perspective, seeking to define and measure structural concepts. By the 1970s, research journals were filled with empirical studies analyzing these concepts. The activity led to the fairly typical version of contingency frameworks that we will examine next, and to the topic of *organizational design*, which we will take up after that.

During the 1980s and 1990s, the literature on organizations and the practice of management within them moved still further in the direction described in Chapter Two—away from bureaucratized, mechanistic structures and toward flexible, organic structures. Management mavens touted extremely loose and informal structure as the ideal (Peters, 1988). Many large corporations launched initiatives to decentralize their structure and make themselves more flexible, and business periodicals carried stories about "bureaucracy-busting" executives. By the turn of the new century, experts on organizational design were describing how many corporations had adopted "lateral," "horizontal," or "team-based" structures in the quest for high levels of flexibility and adaptability.

The public sector followed the lead of the private sector in these directions. The National Performance Review (described in Chapters One and Fourteen) reduced the federal workforce by 324,000 positions, particularly in oversight staff and middle management. In addition, the president ordered a 50 percent reduction in agency rules, eliminated the federal personnel manual as a symbolic gesture toward reducing personnel rules, and took other steps toward decentralizing and loosening up the bureaucratic structure of the federal government. The Winter Commission, which proposed ways of revitalizing state and local public service, also proposed reducing bureaucratic rules and decentralizing procedures. Among other proposals, the commission called for "flattening" the bureaucracy by eliminating middle layers in public agencies, and "deregulating" government by eliminating many personnel rules and decentralizing procedures (Thompson, 1993). Within a few years, state governments began efforts to eliminate layers of middle management (Walters, 1996) and to loosen the rules that gave public employees merit system protections in their jobs (Walters, 2002). The George W. Bush administration included in the *President's Management Agenda* an emphasis on "e-government" and "competitive sourcing" that would involve competition between providers, for most federal activities (U.S. Office of Management and Budget, 2002). These priorities would make the structure of federal agencies more complex in various ways, but proponents argued that they would also make federal agencies more flexible and adaptive. These trends show that organizational structure and its design and management remain key challenges for public managers.

# Structural Dimensions and Influences

Researchers trying to work out clear definitions and measures of organizational structure have run into many complications. For example, you can measure structural features objectively (by counting the number of rules, for example) or subjectively (by asking people how strictly they must follow the rules). In addition, organizations can be very complex, with different units having markedly different structures, and this makes it hard to develop an overall measure of an organization's structure.

## Dimensions of Structure

While the issue is a complex one, research has produced concepts that help clarify the topic of structure. Researchers typically use such dimensions as the following to define organizational structure (Daft, 2001; Hall, 2002; Kalleberg, Knoke, Marsden, and Spaeth, 1996; Kalleberg, Knoke, and Marsden, 2001).

*Centralization.* The degree of centralization in an organization is the degree to which power and authority concentrate at the organization's higher levels. Some researchers measure this dimension with questions about the location of decision-making authority (asking, for example, whether decisions have to be approved at higher levels).

*Formalization.* Formalization is the extent to which an organization's structures and procedures are formally established in written rules and regulations. Some researchers measure this element by asking employees how much they have to follow established rules, whether they must go through "proper channels," and whether a rule manual exists (Hage and Aiken, 1969; Pandey and Scott, 2002). Others determine whether the organization has organization charts, rule manuals, and other formal instructions (Pugh, Hickson, and Hinings, 1969; Kalleberg, Knoke, Marsden, and Spaeth, 1996).

*Red Tape.* Red tape consists of burdensome administrative rules and requirements. Sociologists and psychologists who study organizations have not used this concept a great deal, but as described later, scholars in public administration have recently refined and applied the concept in research on organizations (Bozeman, 2000; Pandey and Scott, 2002).

*Complexity.* Organizational complexity is measured in terms of the number of subunits, levels, and specializations in an organization. Researchers break down this dimension further into subdimensions (Hall, 2002). Organizations vary in *horizontal differentiation,* or the specialized division of labor across subunits and individuals. To measure horizontal differentiation, some researchers have simply counted the number of subunits and individual specializations in an organization (Blau and Schoenherr, 1971; Meyer, 1979). *Vertical differentiation* refers to the number of hierarchical levels in an organization—its "tallness" or "flatness."

## Influences on Structure

The research has also analyzed a number of factors that influence organizational structure, concentrating on the following.

*Size.* Various studies have shown that larger organizations tend to be more structurally complex than smaller ones, with more levels, departments, and job titles (for example, Pugh, Hickson, and Hinings, 1969; Kalleberg, Knoke, Marsden, and Spaeth, 1996). Blau and Schoenherr (1971) also concluded, however, that the rate at which complexity increases with size falls off at a certain point; organizations that reach this point grow larger without adding new departments and levels as rapidly as they did before. In addition, this research indicates that larger organizations tend to have less administrative overhead. So, contrary to stereotypes and popular books about bureaucracy (Parkinson, 1957), larger organizations often have smaller percentages of their personnel involved in administrative work.

Argyris (1972) criticized the findings about public organizations in some studies of organizational size. He noted that Blau studied government agencies controlled by civil service systems and applied the results to *all* organizations in drawing his conclusions. Civil service regulations may have caused these organizations to emphasize task specialization and narrow spans of control and thus grow in the patterns that Blau observed. Business organizations might not follow these patterns, however. In contrast to the findings of a study of state employment agencies by Blau and Schoenherr (1971), Beyer and Trice (1979), studying a set of federal agencies, found no direct relationship between size and vertical or horizontal differentiation. Ultimately, they concluded that increased size increases the division of labor, which in turn increases vertical and horizontal complexity. In addition, the relationships among size, division of labor, and vertical and horizontal differentiation were stronger in federal units doing routine work than in those doing nonroutine work. Thus, larger public organizations tend toward somewhat greater structural complexity (more levels and subunits, greater division of labor) than smaller ones. Much larger organizations almost certainly show more complexity than much smaller ones, but the effects of size are not clear-cut.

Other researchers have reported further evidence that size has little clear influence on structure. Reviewing this research, Kimberly (1976) pointed out that size is actually a complex variable with different components, such as number of employees and net assets. Since different researchers use different measures of size, it is difficult to consolidate their findings and draw conclusions from them. Even so, in the National Organizations Study (Kalleberg, Knoke, Marsden, and Spaeth, 1996), touted by its authors as the first analysis of organizations based on a national probability sample, size figured as one of the important correlates of organizational structural characteristics.

*Environment.* Chapter Four showed that the effects of organizational environment dominate many current analyses of organizational structures, including those based on the contingency perspective. One of the central arguments of this perspective is that a formalized, centralized structure performs well enough in a simple, stable environment, where it can take advantage of specialization and clear patterns of communication and authority. As the environment presents more changes and more uncertainty, however, strict rules, job descriptions, and chains of command become more cumbersome and managers are unable to evolve and process information rapidly enough. Therefore, rules and assignments have to become more flexible. Communication needs to move laterally among people and units, not strictly up and down a hierarchy. People working at lower levels must be given more authority to decide without having to ask permission up the chain of command. As its environment becomes more fragmented, an organization must reflect this complexity in its own structure, giving the people in the units that confront these multiplying environmental segments the authority they need to respond to the conditions they encounter. Although in some ways it is superceded by more recent perspectives on organizations (Aldrich, 1999), this general perspective still exerts a great influence on current prescriptions for managers (Daft, 2001; Galbraith, Downey, and Kates, 2002).

More recent approaches, such as institutional models, contend that organizations adopt rules and structural arrangements because of prevailing beliefs about their appropriateness or because of influences from external institutions such as government. As we have seen, a number of researchers have advanced claims and evidence that governmental ownership and funding have important influences on the structures of public organizations.

***Technology and Tasks.*** A number of studies indicate that an organization's structure also depends on the nature of its work processes, or technologies and tasks. Researchers use a wide variety of definitions of technology and tasks, such as the interdependence required by and the routineness of the work. The effects on structure depend on which of these definitions one uses (Tehrani, Montanari, and Carson, 1990).

In a much-respected book, *Organizations in Action,* Thompson (1967) analyzes technology in terms of the type of interdependence among workers and units the work requires. Organizations such as banks and insurance companies have *mediating* technologies. They deal with many individuals who need largely the same set of services, such as checking accounts or insurance policies. Their work involves *pooled* interdependence because it pools together such services and sets of clients. They establish branches that have little interdependence with one another and formulate standardized rules and procedures to govern them. *Long-linked technologies,* such as typical assembly line operations, have a *sequential* pattern of interdependence. One unit completes its work and passes the product along to the next unit, which completes another phase of the work, and so on. Plans and schedules become an important coordination tool for these units. Units with *intensive* technologies have a *reciprocal* pattern of interdependence. The special units in a hospital or a research and development (R&D) laboratory need to engage in a lot of back-and-forth communication and adjustment in the process of completing the work. These units must be close together and coordinated through mutual adjustments and informal meetings. Thompson contended that organizations may have all these forms of interdependence. They will first organize together those persons and units that have reciprocal interdependence and require high levels of mutual adjustment. Then they will organize together those units with sequential interdependence, and then group units with pooled interdependence (such as the branches of a bank around a city). Analyzing many studies of structure, Tehrani, Montanari, and Carson (1990) found some support for Thompson's observations. Tehrani and others concluded that studies have tended to find that organizational units with high interdependence were much less likely to have a lot of standardized work procedures than organizations with low interdependence.

One can find examples of public organizations that follow the patterns that Thompson described. The SSA operates regional service centers around the country that process beneficiaries' claims, or applications for social security benefits. These centers provide an example of pooled interdependence and mediating technology. For a long time, within these centers, employees and units that processed the claims were organized as a long-linked technology. One large unit would perform one step or phase in the processing of a claim, such as claims authorization, in which a specialist assures that the client's claim is legal and acceptable. Then the claim would be delivered to another department in the service center where another specialist would perform the next phase of processing the claim, which involved calculating the amount the beneficiary would receive in monthly social security payments. Then the claim would go through several more steps in processing, such as recording and filing the claim in the beneficiary's record. As the population of beneficiaries grew and became more complex, however, and as the social security eligibility rules became more complex, the people working on different parts of the claims processing procedure needed to communicate with one another more and more about individual cases. This created backlogs as they sent cases back and forth between units. As Chapter Thirteen describes, the agency reorganized to establish modular work units, which brought together people from the different phases in single units. They could thus communicate and adjust more rapidly—an example of a more intensive technology. Other factors besides work processes influenced the reorganization, but Thompson's ideas about interdependence clearly apply.

Another very influential perspective on technology, developed by Perrow (1973), argues that work processes vary along two main dimensions: the frequency with which exceptions to normal procedures arise and the degree to which these exceptions are analyzable (that is, the degree to which they can be solved through a rational, systematic search). If a machine breaks down, often a clear set of steps can lead to fixing it. If a human being breaks down psychologically, usually few systematic procedures lead as directly to diagnosis and treatment.

Organizational technologies can rank high or low on either of these two main dimensions. *Routine* technologies involve few exceptions and provide clear steps in response to any that occur (high analyzability). In such cases, the work is usually programmed through plans and rules, because there is little need for intensive communication and individual discretion in performing the work. For examples of routine technology, researchers usually point to the work of many manufacturing personnel, auditors, and clerical personnel. At the opposite extreme, nonroutine technologies involve many exceptions, which are less analyzable when they occur. Units and organizations doing this type of work tend toward flexible, "polycentralized" structures, with power and discretion widely dispersed and with much interdependence and mutual adjustment among units and people. Units engaged in strategic planning, R&D, and psychiatric treatment apply such nonroutine technologies.

Between these extremes, Perrow suggests, are two intermediate categories, *craft* technology and *engineering* technology. Craft technology involves infrequent exceptions but offers no easily programmed solutions when they occur. Government budget analysts, for example, may work quite routinely but with few clear guidelines on how to deal with the unpredictable variations that may arise, such as unanticipated shortfalls. These organizations tend to be more decentralized than those with routine technologies. Engineering technology involves many exceptions but also offers analyzable responses to them. Engineers may encounter many variations, but often they can respond in systematic, programmed ways. Lawyers and auditors often deal with this type of work. When an Internal Revenue Service (IRS) auditor examines a person's income tax return, many unanticipated questions come up about whether certain of the person's tax deductions can be allowed. The auditor can resolve many of the questions, however, by referring to written rules and guidelines. Organizations with engineering technologies tend to be more centralized than those with nonroutine technologies, but more flexibly structured than those with routine technologies. Tehrani, Montanari, and Carson (1990) also found support for Perrow's observations. They reviewed numerous studies that showed that organizational units with routine technologies had more formal rules and procedures and fewer highly educated and professional employees.

Perrow's analysis clearly has applications to public organizations. In a study of state employment agencies, Van de Ven, Delbecq, and Koenig (1976) used questionnaire items about task variability and task difficulty based on Perrow's work.

The questions asked about how much the work involves the same tasks and issues, how easy it is to know whether the work is being done correctly, and similar issues. The researchers found relationships between the structures and coordination processes in organizational units and the nature of their tasks. Some units, such as units that handled applications for unemployment compensation, had tasks low in uncertainty (low in variability and difficulty). The employees mainly filled out and submitted application forms for the persons who came in to seek unemployment compensation. These units had more plans and rules and fewer scheduled and unscheduled meetings than other units, and relatively little horizontal communication among individuals and units. Other units had tasks higher in task uncertainty, such as the unemployment counseling bureau, which helped unemployed people seek jobs. This task involved many variations in the characteristics of the clients—in their needs and skills, for example—and often there was no clearly established procedure for responding to some of these unique variations. In this bureau, employees relied little on plans and rules and had more scheduled and unscheduled meetings and more horizontal communication than other units. Units that were intermediate on the task dimensions fell in the middle ranges on the structural and coordination dimensions. So, in many government agencies, in spite of the external political controls, subunits tend toward more flexible structures when they have uncertain, nonroutine, variable tasks.

Yet Perrow himself pointed out that organizations doing the same work can define the nature of it differently. Job Corps training centers for disadvantaged youths in the 1960s were first operated by personnel from the U.S. Office of Economic Opportunity, who adopted a nurturant approach to running the centers. Serious disciplinary problems led to the transfer of some of the centers to the Department of the Interior, after which the staff increasingly emphasized strict rules and discipline and highly structured routines. The same organization in effect altered its definitions of the same task. Similarly, many organizations have purposely tried to transform routine work into more interesting, flexible work to better motivate and utilize the skills of the people doing it. The SSA changed to modular work units partly for such reasons.

Also complicating the analysis of technology, various studies have found weak relationships between structure and technology, sometimes finding that size influences structure more than technology does. Research indicates that technology shows stronger effects on structure in smaller organizations than in larger ones (Tehrani, Montanari, and Carson, 1990). Similarly, the effects of task characteristics on structure are strongest within task subunits; that is, the task of a bureau within a larger organization has a stronger relationship to the structure of that bureau than to the structure of the larger organization. In sum, size, technology, structure, and other factors have complex interrelationships.

*Information Technology.* Increasingly, organizational researchers and managers have to try to assess the influence of information technology (IT) on organizational design. The advent and dissemination of computers, the Internet, e-mail, and other forms of information and communication technology have transformed organizations and working life within them and continue to have dramatic effects. A later section of this chapter reviews recent literature on the effects of IT.

*Strategic Choice.* Managers' strategic choices also determine structure. Managers may divide up an organization into divisions and departments designed to handle particular markets, products, or challenges that have been chosen for strategic emphasis. The examples at the beginning of this chapter about the IRS reorganizing for a more customer-oriented structure was part of a major strategic reorientation that IRS leadership sought to develop, and the changes in structure at BNL—the new directorates and new rules and procedures—represented strategic decisions about how to respond to intense challenges and pressures from the environment.

# Organizational Design

Work on contingency theory led to the development of literature offering guidelines for managers and others engaged in designing organizations (Galbraith, 1977, 2002; Mintzberg, 1979, 1983; Daft, 2001). Although these authors usually do not consider the distinctiveness of public organizations, many of the concepts they discuss apply in public management.

## Design Strategies

Jay Galbraith (1977) proposed a set of techniques for designing and coordinating activities in organizations that is based on an information processing approach. Organizations face varying degrees of uncertainty depending on how much more information they need than they actually have. As this uncertainty increases, the organizational structure must process more information. Organizations employ a mix of alternative modes for coordinating these activities. First they use the organizational *hierarchy of authority*, in which superiors direct subordinates, answering their questions and specifying rules and procedures for managing the information processing load. As uncertainty increases, it overwhelms these approaches. The next logical strategy, then, is to set *plans and goals* and allow subordinates to pursue them with less referral up and down the hierarchy and with fewer rules. They can also narrow *spans of control* so that superiors must deal with fewer subordinates and can process more information and decisions.

Many contemporary organizations operate under such great uncertainty that these basic modes become overloaded, so they must pursue additional alternatives. First, managers can try to reduce the need for information. They can engage in *environmental management* to create more certainty through more effective competition for scarce resources, through public relations, and through cooperation and contracting with other organizations. They can create *slack resources* (that is, create a situation in which they have extra resources) by reducing the level of performance they seek to attain, or they can create *self-contained* tasks, such as profit centers or groups working independently on individual components of the work. Alternatively, managers can increase information processing capacity by investing in *vertical information systems,* such as computerized information management systems, or by creating *lateral relations,* such as task forces or liaison personnel. Thus, managers have to adopt coordination modes in response to greater uncertainty and information processing demands. In recent work, Galbraith (2002; Galbraith, Downey, and Kates, 2002) exemplifies the movement among organizations and organization design experts toward increasing emphasis on flexibility and rapid adaptation to complex and quickly changing challenges. He emphasizes processes for lateral coordination, including *e-coordination,* greater utilization of teams, and methods of designing *reconfigurable* organizations amenable to continuous redesign, as well as *virtual corporation* models, where an organization contracts out "all activities except those at which it is superior" (Galbraith, 2002, p. 135).

## Mintzberg's Synthesis

Mintzberg (1979) presented one of the most comprehensive reviews of the literature on structure, summarizing the set of structural alternatives that managers can pursue. While his synthesis has grown somewhat dated in relation to the sorts of developments that Galbraith recently covered, many of the fundamental challenges for organization designers remain the same and Mintzberg's review still provides a valuable analysis of alternatives and distinctions. He began by setting forth his own scheme for describing the major components of organizations. They have an operating core, including members directly involved in the organization's basic work— police officers, machine operators, teachers, claims processors, and so on. The strategic apex consists of the top managerial positions—the board of directors, chief executive officer, president, and president's staff. The middle line includes the managers who link the apex to the core through supervision and implementation— the vice presidents down through the supervisors. Finally, two types of staff units complete the set of components. The technostructure consists of analysts who work on standardizing work, outputs, and skills—the policy analysts and program evaluators, strategic planners, systems engineers, and personnel training staff. The support staff units support the organization outside the work flow of the operating core—for example, mail room, food service, and public relations personnel.

**Design Parameters.**  Organizations establish structures to divide and then coordinate work within and among these units through the design of four different structural categories: positions, superstructures, lateral linkages, and decision-making systems.

*Design of Positions.*  Individual positions can be established through *job specialization*, *behavior formalization* (written job descriptions, written work instructions, general rules), and *training and indoctrination* (in which individuals learn the skills they will apply using their own judgment).

*Design of Superstructures.*  The different positions must be coordinated through the design of the organization's superstructure. All organizations do this in part through *unit grouping*, based on any of a number of criteria: knowledge and skill (lawyers, engineers, social workers), function (police, fire, and parks and recreation employees; military personnel), time (night shift, day shift), output (the products produced by the different divisions of a corporation), clients (inpatients or outpatients; beneficiaries of insurance policies), or place (the regional offices of business firms, the federal government, and many state agencies; precincts in a city police department).

Managers choose among these bases or some combination of them. We have little conclusive scientific guidance for those choices, but Mintzberg offers suggestions about criteria for grouping. It can follow *work-flow interdependencies,* where natural phases in the work require certain people to communicate closely or to be located near one another. *Process interdependencies* make it useful to group together people who perform the same type of work (attorneys, claims eligibility experts) so they can learn from one another and share tools and materials. Because of *scale interdependencies,* certain units may become large enough to need their own functional categories—their own set of attorneys, for example. Also, *social interdependencies* may make it useful to group individuals to facilitate social relations, morale, and cohesiveness. Military units that have trained together are often kept together for these reasons.

*Design of Lateral Linkages.*  Mintzberg suggests that coordination also requires linking operations laterally. For this purpose, organizations can use *performance-control systems, action-planning systems,* or *liaison devices.* Performance-control systems specify general results to be attained as indications that operations are effectively coordinated. For example, as described in Chapter Thirteen, in large service centers operated by the SSA, employees are organized into "modules." A module is a work unit that includes all the personnel required to handle a client's application for social security benefits (as well as other types of services), including people who authorize the benefits, people who calculate what the benefit payment will be, file clerks, typists, and other specialists. Administrators keep track of the average time the modules take in handling clients' requests—for example, how many days, on average, does each module take to complete the handling of a client's application? They can compare these times across modules and to national standards. A low average time (that is, fast processing of the requests) indicates effective coordination within the module. Good average times for all the modules suggest that the service center is effectively coordinated, that all modules are performing well. When a module falls behind the others and has backlogs of applications and slower times, however, this indicates a possible coordination problem, not just in the module but among the modules. Sometimes a module may have an overload of particularly difficult cases or some personnel problems such as high absenteeism or a lot of newer employees who need training. The slower time for the module may thus indicate that the assignment of cases and personnel is not effectively coordinated among the modules, and administrators may shift some of the caseload to other modules or transfer some personnel among modules temporarily so as to coordinate better the work of the modules. Thus, the performance-control information provides evidence about coordination within and among units. (Of course, simple reviews of limited performance information, such as time taken to complete the processing of an application, can have serious pitfalls as an evaluation system, and managers must be sensitive to these weaknesses.)

An action-planning system, by contrast, specifies not the general result or standard but the details about actions that people and groups are to take. In the modules just mentioned, the applications from clients are placed in file folders that move from point to point in the modules as different people do their part of the work on the case. The filing clerks are trained in a system for moving and keeping track of the files—there are many thousands of them for each module—so they will not be lost—and can be located at any given time. As the clerks move the files around the module, they log them in when they arrive at certain points, using a bar code scanner similar to those used in supermarkets. The careful specification of the actions of the file clerks in this file-tracking system is essential to coordinating the different specialists in the module and to assessing the coordination of the work among all the modules.

Liaison devices include such arrangements as having a person serve in a special position as "ambassador" to another unit, keeping track of developments there and facilitating communication with the other unit. Task forces or standing liaison committees can also address problems of coordination. One of the service centers used a task force to respond to a major coordination problem. The first three digits of a person's social security number indicate where that person was born or where he or she was when the number was issued. In the service centers, cases are usually assigned to modules on the basis of these first three digits. That alone can create coordination problems, because certain regions of the country produce more cases that are difficult to handle than other regions. Modules assigned to certain geographical areas may thus get more difficult cases than other modules. One service center considered moving its modules to "terminal digit case allocation"—that is, allocating cases on the basis of the last four digits of the social security number to achieve a fairer distribution. Yet moving to this new allocation system required extensive coordination among the modules because they had to transfer all the files among themselves to redistribute them according to the new system. The director of the center appointed a task force to consider and plan the new system. The task force was highly representative, with people from all levels and many different modules and units. Empowered by the director to plan and implement the new system as they saw fit, the task force effectively managed the transition to the new system.

*Design of Decision-Making Systems Through Decentralization.* Organizations can also decentralize. *Vertical decentralization* involves pushing decision-making authority down to lower levels. *Horizontal decentralization* involves spreading authority out to staff analysts or experts or across individuals involved in the work of the organization.

**Types of Organizational Structures.** Mintzberg also proposes a typology of five types of organizational structures, based on the employment of these design alternatives and shifts in the roles of the components described earlier. *Simple structures* are usually adopted by new, small government agencies, small corporations run by an entrepreneur, and other new, small, aggressive organizations headed by strong leaders. They tend toward vertical and horizontal centralization and coordination by means of direct supervision from a strong strategic apex. *Machine bureaucracies* include the prototypical large bureaucracies in the public and private sectors. They evolve from simple structures as growth, age, or external control leads to greater emphasis on standardizing work processes. The technostructure becomes more important as experts and staff specialists assume roles in this process. Mintzberg suggests a subcategory—*public* machine bureaucracies—consisting of government agencies that assume this form because they are required to standardize for political oversight. Alternatively, simple structures with a strong professional component (law firms, research organizations) evolve toward *profes-*

*sional bureaucracies,* with a profession that dominates their operating core, coordination primarily through standardization of skills (through professional training) rather than standardization of tasks, and general decentralization. Machine bureaucracies may further evolve into *divisionalized forms* as further growth leads to economies of scale for product-oriented subunits. It becomes more cost-effective to break the organization up into product divisions with their own versions of the various functional components—for example, their own manufacturing and marketing divisions. Mintzberg (1989) observed that public machine bureaucracies cannot do this. Without profit and sales measures by which their general performance can be monitored, and because they operate under more intensive, political oversight, public machine bureaucracies face more constraints than their private counterparts on their ability to decentralize to relatively autonomous divisions. Finally, an *adhocracy,* such as NASA or an innovation-oriented firm, has a very organic structure, with great emphasis on fluid communication and flexibility, largely through decentralization to project teams.

## Major Design Alternatives

***Functional Structures.*** Management writers also contrast the pros and cons of the major design alternatives from which organizations choose (Daft, 2001; Galbraith, 2002). *Functional structures,* the classical prototype, organize according to major functions—marketing and sales, manufacturing, finance, R&D. The advantages include economies of scale within the functional units (all the attorneys in the legal department can use the same law library; the manufacturing personnel share plants and machinery). Departments concentrate on their functions and enhance their specialized skills. Yet this may weaken coordination with other functions to ensure overall product quality or the implementation of needed changes.

***Product and Hybrid Structures.*** As organizations grow, producing more diverse products and competing in more diverse, rapidly changing markets, the functional structure proves too slow in responding to changes and too hierarchical to allow rapid coordination across functional divisions. Large corporations, such as the major automobile manufacturers, thus adopt *product structures,* with separate divisions each responsible for its own product line. Each division possesses its own units to perform major functions such as sales and manufacturing (for example, the Oldsmobile, Chevrolet, and Buick divisions of General Motors or, in a high-technology firm, divisions for medical instruments, personal computers, and electronic instruments). This approach sacrifices some of the advantages of the functional form, but it provides for more rapid responses to environmental changes (in product technology, customer demands, competitors) and greater concentration on the quality of the products rather than on individual functions. In fact, many corporations actually employ *hybrid structures*, with major product divisions (for example, chemicals, fuels, lubricants; see Daft, 2001) but also some major functional units (finance, human resources).

***Matrix Designs.*** During the last century, some firms developed a *matrix structure* in response to demands for both high-quality products in highly technical areas (product emphasis) and rapid and reliable production (functional emphasis). The sort of mixing or cross-hatching of different types of responsibility and authority characteristic of matrix organizations evolved into different alternatives, but still occurs quite frequently. Military weapons manufacturers, for example, faced pressure to produce highly technical weapons systems according to demanding standards, and to do so within sharp time constraints. Matrix structures purposely violate the classic prescriptions for "one master" and clear chains of authority. High-level managers share authority over the same activities, with some exercising functional authority (vice presidents for product development, manufacturing, marketing, procurement) and others having responsibility for the particular products or projects that cross all those functions. Thus, one manager may have responsibility for pushing the completion of a particular aircraft project, while others may share responsibility for the particular functions involved in getting the craft built. The authority of the product executives crosses all the functions, while the functional executives have authority over their functions across all the products. Diagrammed, this structure appears as a matrix of two sets of executives with crosshatched lines of authority. It offers the advantage of the ability to share or shift personnel or other resources rapidly across product lines and to coordinate the organization's response to dual pressures from the environment. It requires a heavy investment in coordination, liaison activities, and conflict resolution, however. Successful matrix designs often require a lot of training and good interpersonal skills on the part of managers, because they typically produce high levels of stress and conflict that must be resolved.

Some structures in the public sector have been equated with matrix structures. Simon (1983) describes the use of a matrix management arrangement at the U.S. Consumer Product Safety Commission. This commission was organized into functional bureaus, including the Bureau of Engineering, the Bureau of Economics, the Bureau of Biomedical Science, and so on. Each bureau had partial responsibility for developing regulations issued by the commission, but none had overall responsibility. The matrix arrangement involved six functional directorates and the Office of Program Management. The Office of Program Management had a program manager for each of a set of new product-oriented programs, including a chemical products program, an electrical products program, and a children's products program. These program managers chaired program teams made up of representatives from the various functional directorates. The teams managed the overall development of regulations for the products for which their programs were responsible, and they coordinated the work of the functional directorates pertaining to those programs. The commission's executives felt that the matrix arrangement would improve productivity, morale, effective use of resources, communication, and accountability, but it also increased stress and turf battles, and evoked some resistance, as matrix arrangements usually do.

The executive director of the commission observed that public managers face particular challenges in adopting matrix designs. He felt that private executives have more authority over rewards and have profit targets to use as incentives for cooperation. Public executives can impose fewer sanctions and have weaker authority to reassign those who resist a new design. Here again we see that a design developed in industry has potential value in government but requires skillful implementation within the constraints imposed by the public sector. Swiss (1991) provides further examples of the use of matrix organization in city governments.

***Market and Customer-Focused Designs.*** According to Galbraith (2002), many corporations have moved toward a *market structure,* where the main organizational units are organized on the basis of their orientation to groupings of customers, markets, or industries. The IRS reorganization described at the beginning of the chapter exemplifies a *customer-focused* version of this alternative. The more frequent adoption of this structural form has been driven by the rise of the service industry, which increases the value of knowledge of market segments and customers, and by the increasing tendency to contract out functions and services, which reduces demands for large-scale production operations that used to force an organization toward functional divisions or large-scale product divisions.

***Geographical Designs.*** Organizations have employed *geographical structures,* such as the emphasis on geographic regions and districts in the original IRS structure described at the beginning of the chapter. Although the IRS has moved away from that alternative, organizations continue to utilize it, sometimes as part of a hybridized combination with another structural emphasis, as in the case of a *global matrix structure* for a business firm's international operations (Daft, 2001, p. 497). This alternative can reduce transportation and logistics costs and challenges. It can bring services closer to customers and allow service delivery on site, and it can enhance the perception that the organization is local (Galbraith, 2002, p. 36). In addition, organizations often face major geographical imperatives, because of such developments as globalization and internationalization of organizational activities. Such developments virtually require emphasis on geography in organizational design, through such obvious alternatives as headquarters or centers of operation on different continents or in different nations (Daft, 2001, chap. 13).

***Process Structures.*** Still another contemporary approach to organizational design involves the *process structure,* in which divisions are organized around processes such as the new product development process, in which product development teams focus on new-product projects, and customer acquisition and maintenance processes, in which customer service teams focus on segments or groupings of customers.

Given all these alternatives, it should not be surprising that structures in organizations show a great deal of variation. These alternatives actually serve as prototypes that organizational designers choose among and blend using heavy doses of pragmatism, because obviously no scientific method exists for designing organizations. As discussed earlier, management experts currently propose that many organizations should adopt highly adaptive, permeable, fluid, loosely arranged structures, and they observe that organizations increasingly attempt to do so.

The literature on organization structure and design provides many illustrations of the employment of teams, including shifting teams in "reconfigurable" organizations, and of designs for lateral and horizontal coordination in and among organizations. The heavy emphasis on accountability of public organizations to external authorities may impede the use of some flexible structures in government agencies, but these alternatives are often applicable in some form. A geologist with the U.S. Geological Survey, for example, currently works with officials of the nation of Afghanistan to develop that war-ravaged nation's geological resources, such as water, oil, and mineral deposits. A project assessing the potential for such resources and their development will involve an ad hoc team representing different organizational units, including experts on water resources, mineral resources, oil and gas resources, and other resources and related issues (such as earthquakes). The team will be flexible and "reconfigurable" over time. In many other instances as well the more contemporary design alternatives apply to government and its organizations.

# Organizational Structures in Public Organizations

The question of alternative designs for public organizations brings us back to whether public organizations have distinctive structures. As mentioned earlier, some academic theories and observations suggest that public organizations are inherently different from private organizations, because governmental oversight and the absence of performance indicators such as sales and profits cause them to emphasize rules and hierarchy. If this is true, it suggests that public organizations cannot adopt some structural forms, such as decentralized and flexible designs, or that they can do so only with great difficulty. Conversely, many organization theorists regard public sector status as unimportant (in part because their research has often found little evidence that public organizations have distinctive structures). Pugh, Hickson, and Hinings (1969), for example, predicted that government organizations in their sample would show higher levels of formalization (they used a measure called "structuring of activities"), but they did not. Over the years, additional studies have concurred. Buchanan (1975) also sought to test the proverbial red-tape differences by comparing federal managers to business managers on a "structure salience" scale. Unexpectedly, the public managers perceived that a lower level of salience was assigned to structure in their organizations. Bozeman and Loveless (1987) found that public sector R&D units differed only slightly from private sector R&D units in the amount of red tape with which they had to contend. Langbein (2000) analyzed the results of a 1994 survey of 2,750 members of the Institute of Electrical and Electronic Engineers and compared those who worked in the public sector to those employed in the private sector on the degree to which they felt they had discretion—autonomy in decision making—in their work. She found no significant difference between the two groups (although she concluded that conditions that the engineers perceive as constraining discretion, such as disagreement among higher-level authorities, were more likely to prevail in the public sector). Kurland and Egan (1999) analyzed a small sample of organizations, comparing responses from members of two public agencies to those in seven private firms, and found little difference between the two sets of employees on perceptions about the formalization of their jobs and their communication patterns.

Yet other evidence suggests that public organizations do differ. Although Pugh, Hickson, and Hinings (1969) did not find greater "structuring of activities" in government organizations, in those organizations authority was more concentrated at the top of or outside the organization, especially concerning personnel procedures. The researchers concluded that an organization's size and technological development act as the main determinants of how the organization structures its activities, but government ownership exerts an influence independent of size and technology, causing this concentration of authority at the top or with external authorities. The study included only eight public organizations, all local government units with tasks similar to those of many business firms, including a local water department and a manufacturing unit of a government agency. This might explain why these organizations did not show as much bureaucratic structuring as anticipated. It also indicates, however, the effects of government ownership even on organizations that are much like business firms. A public manager would probably comment that the researchers simply observed the effects of civil service systems.

Mintzberg (1979) cited this evidence from Pugh, Hickson, and Hinings when he designated public machine bureaucracies as a subtype within the machine bureaucracy category in his typology of structures. He argued that many public bureaucracies tend toward the machine bureaucracy form because of external governmental control. Other studies have come to similar conclusions. Warwick (1975) concluded from his case study of the U.S. Department of State that public bureaucracies inherently incline toward elaborate hierarchies and rules. Meyer (1979) analyzed a national sample of state and local finance agencies and found their vertical hierarchies to be very stable over time. Political pressures forced frequent changes in their subunit composition, however, and pressures from the federal government led to formalization of their personnel systems. Meyer concluded that public bureaucracies have no alternative to elaborate hierarchies. Their managers' political strength and skill, however, determine how well they can defend themselves from external forces that can strip away their subunits and assign them to some other organization.

Holdaway, Newberry, Hickson, and Heron (1975) found, in a study of Canadian universities, that higher degrees of government control are related to correspondingly higher levels of formalization, standardization of personnel procedures, and centralization. Chubb and Moe (1990) reported that public school employees in the United States perceive more externally imposed formal constraints on personnel procedures and school policies than do private school employees. Rainey's sample of middle managers in state agencies (1983) perceived more organizational formalization, particularly concerning going through channels and adhering to standard operating procedures, than did middle managers in business firms. This study and a number of others found that government managers report much stronger constraints on the administration of extrinsic rewards such as pay and promotion under the existing personnel rules for their organizations than do business managers. Chapters Nine and Ten cite various studies that have found this difference at all levels of government. Also indicating the effects of public sector status on personnel procedures, Tolbert and Zucker (1983) showed how federal pressures influenced the diffusion of civil service personnel systems across governments in the United States. Light (2002a) compared the results from a survey of 673 U.S. federal employees to those of a survey of 505 private employees and found that federal employees perceived more layers of supervisors in their organizations. Zaffane (1994) compared survey responses of 474 public sector managers and 944 private sector managers in 238 organizations operating in Australia. The public managers perceived more emphasis on rules and regulations in their organizations than did their private counterparts.

Studies by professional associations and government agencies, and the testimony of public managers, paint a similar picture. A National Academy of Public Administration (1986) report lamented the complex web of controls and rules governing federal managers' decisions and the adverse effects of these constraints on their capacity and motivation to manage. The report complained that managers in charge of large federal programs often face irritating limits on their authority to make even minor decisions. The head of a program involving tens of millions of dollars might have to seek the approval of the General Services Administration before he or she can send an assistant to a short training program. Very large surveys of federal employees have found that a large percentage of federal managers and executives say they do not have enough authority to remove, hire, promote, and determine the pay of their employees. Large percentages have also expressed the opinion that federal personnel and budgeting rules create obstacles to productivity (U.S. Office of Personnel Management, 1979, 1980, 1983). Executives who have served in both business and government say similar things about the constraints on the authority of managers in government positions imposed by overarching rules and oversight agencies (Allison, 1983; Blumenthal, 1983; Chase and Reveal, 1983; IBM Endowment for the Business of Government, 2002). The National Performance Review during the Clinton administration sought to enact a number of reforms aimed at reducing rules and red tape in the federal government. President Clinton issued an executive order instructing all federal agencies to reduce their rules by 50 percent (an order that appears to have had virtually no impact), and other initiatives sought to decentralize and reduce the rules and constraints in federal human resource management and procurement procedures. These efforts reflect a widespread conviction that government organizations are subject to extensive and excessive rules and hierarchical controls.

Research on red tape also generally supports this view. Sociologists and psychologists who study organizations have not made much use of the concept of red tape, probably because they regard it as a vague, colloquial idea that supports crude stereotypes about organizations. Because the problem of red tape has been a classic and proverbial topic in government, however, researchers in public administration have done more in recent years to develop the concept. It derives from the practice in the British civil service of binding official documents in red tape and generally refers to cumbersome organizational rules and procedures, frequently associated with government. A topic of satire and ridicule at least since Charles Dickens wrote an essay about it, the red tape problem has over the years led to many initiatives aimed at reducing red tape in government. These efforts have tended to make little headway, often because one person or group may regard a rule as burdensome and absurd, while another person or group defends it as an essential protection of the public interest (Kaufman, 1977). Bozeman (2000) and others have developed the concept for use in research, however, and their research tends to support the generalization that public organizations have more red tape than private ones—a finding consistent with the findings about greater levels of formalization in public organizations. Bozeman defines red tape as "rules, regulations, and procedures that . . . entail a compliance burden but do not advance the legitimate purposes the rules were intended to serve" (p. 12). Thus, red tape differs from formalization (formal rules and procedures) in that red tape involves excessive and unduly expensive or burdensome rules and regulations. Bozeman also develops concepts for dimensions and types of red tape, such as *rule inception red tape*, which originates when the rule is established because of such problems as inaccurate forecasts about the effects of the rule, or because managers make excessive attempts at control. *Rule-evolved red tape* occurs when rules drift away from their original form because of how they are implemented or because they are incompatible with other rules. Pandey and Scott (2002) and Pandey and Kingsley (2000) further show empirical evidence that red tape should be regarded as a concept distinct from formalization.

Most important, when surveys have asked government and business managers about the extent of red tape in their organizations, the public managers have consistently reported higher levels than the business managers (Rainey, Pandey, and Bozeman, 1995). In other studies in which public and private managers have responded to questions about how long it takes to finish certain administrative functions, such as hiring a new person, firing an employee, or purchasing a piece of equipment, the public managers have reported longer times than the business managers (Scott and Falcone, 1998; Bozeman and Rainey, 1998).

All of these studies and reports provide increasing evidence that public sector status influences an organization's structure in a number of ways, particularly in regard to rules and structural arrangements over which external oversight agencies have authority, such as personnel and purchasing procedures. The stream of research does show some inconsistencies, however, on such dimensions as formalization, in which some studies find differences between the two sectors and some do not. A very interesting and important interpretation of these inconsistencies involves a distinction between formalization and red tape in general and formalization and red tape in such areas as personnel and purchasing, where government agencies are subject to control by external authorities that impose the rules on them. This interpretation takes on importance because it contrasts with the common assertion that a lot of rules and red tape originate inside public bureaucracies because bureaucrats have an affinity for rules and because higher-level government bureaucrats issue profusions of rules in attempts to control lower level bureaucrats (for example, Downs, 1967; Lynn, 1987; Warwick, 1975).

Bozeman and Bretschneider (1994) provide explicit evidence of these patterns. They analyzed them in R&D laboratories based on the labs' public or private status and on the amount of government funding they received. The government labs had highly structured personnel rules. The private labs did not, even when they received high levels of government funding. The labs did, however, receive more contacts and communications from government officials when they received more public funding. This suggests that government funding brings with it a different pattern of governmental influence than does governmental ownership. Ownership brings with it the formal authority of oversight agencies to impose rules, usually governing personnel, purchasing, and accounting and budgeting procedures. Bretschneider (1990) provided more evidence in an analysis of decisions about computer systems in public and private organizations. Managers in the public organizations experienced longer delays in getting approval to purchase computer equipment and in the processing of those purchases. The delays apparently reflect the procurement rules imposed by central procurement agencies such as the General Services Administration. In sum, these studies provide evidence, consistent with the pattern that began to emerge with the Pugh, Hickson, and Hinings (1969) study, that government ownership often subjects organizations to central oversight rules over such matters as personnel, purchasing, and budgeting and accounting procedures.

More recent survey evidence supports this observation more strongly than ever. Rainey, Facer, and Bozeman (1995) reported results of surveys in several different states, involving all levels of government and many different organizations, at different points across a fifteen-year period, and compared the responses of public and private managers to numerous questions about constraints under personnel rules. They asked whether the rules made it hard to fire a poor manager or reward a good manager with higher pay, and similar questions. The differences between the public and private managers were huge by the standards of survey research. Roughly 90 percent of the public managers agreed that their organization's personnel rules make it hard to fire poor managers and hard to reward good managers with higher pay, while 90 percent of the business managers disagreed. These differences shape the context of leadership and motivation in public organizations discussed in later chapters.

Another recent study provides further evidence of distinctive structural characteristics of public organizations, with findings based on a large representative sample of work organizations in the United States (Kalleberg, Knoke, Marsden, and Spaeth, 1996; Kalleberg, Knoke, and Marsden, 2001). The study also supports the interpretation that higher levels of rules and formalization in public organizations tend to concentrate in areas such as personnel and purchasing, which are subject to controls by external authorities. The researchers undertook the National Organizations Study (NOS) project in part because the samples in most studies of organizations are not large, representative ones, because such samples are expensive and hard to attain. Chapter Three, in the section headed "Findings from Research," described a study by Pugh, Hickson, and Hinings (1969) that sought to develop a taxonomy of organizations. Pugh and others did not find that the public organizations in their sample differed sharply from their sample of private organizations, although they did find some distinctive attributes of the public organizations. The researchers included only eight public organizations in their sample of nearly sixty organizations, however, and they expressed reservations about their findings for the public organizations. The NOS, by contrast, surveyed a carefully designed representative sample consisting of 725 work organizations. About 94 of these organizations were state, local, or federal government agencies. Status as a public agency turned out to be one of the strongest correlates of structural characteristics in the study.

The NOS researchers asked the respondents in the organizations they surveyed to reply to questions aimed at measuring the structural characteristics of their organizations, including decentralization and formalization (defined earlier in this chapter). Status as a public organization was among the variables most strongly related to these two structural characteristics. The public organizations tended to be less decentralized (thus more centralized) and more formalized (Marsden, Cook, and Kalleberg, 1994; Kalleberg, Knoke, and Marsden, 2001). In addition, the method of measuring formalization makes this finding consistent with the evidence mentioned earlier about the formalization of personnel rules and procedures in public organizations that appears to result from government civil service personnel systems. The researchers followed a procedure similar to that of Pugh, Hickson, and Hinings (1969) in which they asked whether the organization had written documentation for various important organizational matters. In the NOS, almost all of the questions used to measure formalization asked about written documentation of personnel matters—documentation on fringe benefits, hiring and firing procedures, personnel evaluation, and the requirement for written job descriptions and written performance records (Marsden, Cook, and Kalleberg, 1994; Kalleberg, Knoke, and Marsden, 2001). Thus, this study of a nationally representative sample of organizations, while not intended as a study of public organizations, provides evidence of the tendencies toward distinctive structural characteristics on the part of public organizations in the United States.

All this evidence supports the interpretation that the heavier dose of rules and regulations in public organizations originates mostly from external sources and not from the bureaucrats within the agencies. Adding to this evidence, Bozeman and Rainey (1998) report a survey that shows that managers in government, compared to business managers, would prefer their organizations to have fewer rules. This contradicts the view that managers in government generate excessive rules.

As indicated earlier, researchers have also found distinctive structural characteristics of public organizations that are not tied to rules imposed by oversight agencies. Tolbert (1985) found differences in the subunit structures of public and private universities related to external influences from public and private institutions and the universities' dependence on them for resources. Crow and Bozeman (1987) and Emmert and Crow (1987, 1988) report that public R&D units differ from private units in the size and structure of the administrative component of the organization and the way the research teams were organized. The public labs actually had more team-based organization. This again emphasizes that government organizations vary a great deal from one another, and that by no means do all follow a rigid bureaucratic pattern. In fact, these government labs appeared to respond more directly than the private labs to task contingencies of the sort discussed earlier.

## The Macrostructure of Public Organizations

The evidence of the influence of government ownership on the structures of public organizations brings up another structural topic, one that needs much additional attention from both researchers and managers. Structure *within* public organizations cannot easily be separated from structures *outside* the organization that are an inherent part of government. In other words, the internal structures of public agencies reflect, in part, the jurisdictional structures of the government body under which they operate. Legislatures, oversight agencies, and other governmental institutions impose systemwide rules and configurations on all the agencies within their jurisdiction (Warwick, 1975; Meyer, 1979; Hood and Dunsire, 1981). In addition, different units of government differ in the structural arrangements of their major institutional attributes, such as their formal, constitutional powers. In some states the governor has less formal power than in others, and the legislature has more formal authority. The governor of Florida, for example, appoints fewer of the cabinet officers of the state government than do governors in other states. Instead, some of these officers have to run for independent election, and consequently the agencies they head tend to have more independence from the governor than in other states. Meyer (1979) found that independently elected heads of finance agencies more effectively defend their agencies against the loss of subunits than do political appointees. Such characteristics of the complex macrostructural terrain support the observation that public organizations operate within larger structures that heavily influence their own.

## Summing Up the Literature on Structure

The researchers on organizational structure who reject a public-private distinction have shown us that structure is multidimensional and that both types of organization vary widely on different structural dimensions. Often these variations are related to the major contingencies of size, strategy, technology and tasks, and environmental uncertainty and complexity. Obviously, technological similarities cause government-owned electric utilities, hospitals, railroads, airlines, R&D labs, and manufacturing units to show stronger structural similarities to private or nonprofit versions of the same types of organizations than to other types of government organizations. The same holds true for organizations or organizational units engaged in similar tasks, such as R&D labs and legal offices. Indeed, the general structure of subunits of public organizations often resembles the structure of their private sector counterparts more than it resembles that of other units in the parent organization. Also, relatively small, independent organizations usually have simpler structures than larger organizations, so a smaller unit of government may exhibit less red tape or hierarchical complexity than a large private firm. Obviously, government agencies respond to environmental complexities and uncertainties just as private organizations do, as the examples at the beginning of this chapter illustrate. Thus we can see that it is incredibly simplistic to treat all public organizations as a uniform mass that is inherently subject to intensive red tape and bureaucracy.

Research on the structures of government organizations and research comparing government and business organizations, however, supports a balanced conclusion. This research suggests that public organizations generally tend toward higher levels of internal structural complexity, centralization, and formalization—especially in such areas as personnel and purchasing—than do private organizations. Size, task, technology, and environmental contingencies make a difference, often figuring more importantly than public or private ownership. Within given task categories, however, public organizations tend toward stable hierarchies and centralized and formalized rules, especially rules pertaining to the functions governed by oversight agencies—personnel, purchasing and procurement, and budgeting and accounting. Government organizations may not have more formalized and elaborate rules than private organizations of similar size, but they often have more centralized, formalized rules for functions such as personnel and procurement. Comparisons of government and nongovernment organizations engaged in the same type of work tend to support such conclusions.

Still, wide variations are likely. For example, R&D labs or other special units may have even more general structural flexibility under government ownership. In addition, government ownership and influence are multidimensional in that hybrid organizations such as public enterprises may be owned by government but privately funded and exempt from some central rules and controls. Privately owned organizations with extensive public funding often show heavy governmental influences on certain aspects of their structures; for example, defense contractors have small armies of government auditors on site, making sure their spending and record-keeping practices adhere to government regulations. Here again, government rules tend to follow from government ownership or funding.

All managers must deal with structural complexity and with external influences on their authority. Public managers usually face more elaborate structural arrangements and constraints, however, and must learn to work with them. Their understanding of the elaborate macrostructural patterns in government, of the structures of their own agencies, and of the origins and purposes of these arrangements can serve as a valuable component of their professional knowledge as public managers. Among other challenges, they must find ways to reward and encourage people working within these complex structures, even when the personnel rules they must follow do not readily provide much flexibility. The next chapter further considers that topic. Later chapters discuss how public managers can and do make valuable changes, in part through effective knowledge of the structure of government and its agencies and in part through effective applications of the general body of knowledge on organizational structure.

# Information Technology and Public Organizations

The most rapidly developing topic related to technology in recent years has been IT, with the developments coming so fast that everyone has difficulty keeping up with them and developing conclusive interpretations about their effects on organizations. The rapid advent of computer applications, the Internet, and other forms of information and communication technology have major implications for organizations and their management, but people have trouble saying exactly what effects they have and why. As for effects on public organizations, especially until recently, research has been scarce (Kraemer and Dedrick, 1997).

Experts on IT tend to report that the more salient effects in industry include the extension of computing technology into design and production applications, such as *computer-aided design*, in which computer programs carry out design functions, and *computer-aided manufacturing*, in which computers actually control machinery that carries out the manufacturing process. *Computer-integrated manufacturing* links together the machinery and the design and engineering processes through computers. Ultimately, an integrated information network links all major components of the organization, including inventory control, purchasing and procurement, accounting, and other functions, in addition to manufacturing and production. These developments, according to expert observers, support an evolution from mass production to mass customization, where manufacturers and service organizations produce large quantities of goods and services that are more tailored to the preferences of individual customers than previously possible. In addition, observers suggest that computerized integration of production processes has effects on organizational structures and processes. Computer-integrated manufacturing reportedly moves organizations toward fewer hierarchical levels, tasks that are less routine and more craftlike, more teamwork, more training, and more emphasis on skills in cognitive problem solving than in manual expertise (Daft, 2001, pp. 205–209).

Computer technology and the Internet have also become more influential in organizational decision-making processes. For many years organizations have been using computers to store large data sets and retrieve information from them, but more recently the capacity for active utilization of that data has advanced, so that computer-based *management information systems* (MIS) have become very common. A MIS typically provides middle-level managers with ready access to data they can use in decision making, such as sales and inventory data for business managers, and client processing and status data for managers in public and nonprofit organizations. Decision support systems provide software that managers can use interactively. Such a system may, for example, provide models that enable managers to assess the effects of certain decisions or changes they may be considering. Many government organizations currently utilize *geographic information systems* (GIS), which provide information about facilities or conditions in different geographic locations. A GIS might allow a planner to designate any particular geographic location in a city and pull up on the computer screen a diagram showing all the underground utility infrastructure, such as pipelines and electric cables, at that location. State employment training agencies have used a GIS to store and retrieve data on clients and potential clients at different locations in the state, for use in planning the location of their facilities and programs. An *executive information system* provides MIS-type support, but at a more general, strategic level, for the sorts of decisions required at higher executive levels.

Computers, the Internet, electronic mail, and other forms of information and communication technology make possible more elaborate and interactive networking of people and organizational units, both within and between organizations. Some organizations have moved away from traditional hierarchical and departmental reporting relationships to forms of virtual organization and dynamic network organization, in which a central hub coordinates other units that formally belong to the same organization, as well as organizations formally outside the hub organization (such as contractors or agencies with overlapping responsibility for public agencies), via e-mail and the Internet. Advances in IT reportedly lead to smaller organizations, decentralized organizations, better coordination internally and with external entities, more professional staff and professional departments for developing and maintaining the information systems, and more employee participation.

No one has precise knowledge of just how widely and deeply these generalizations apply to government organizations, but examples clearly indicate that they definitely apply in certain cases. Concerning evolution toward smaller organizations, for example, few Americans are aware that during the 1970s and 1980s the SSA went through Project 17,000, in which the agency eliminated 17,000 jobs, due largely to the computer taking over large portions of the processing of client claims that human beings had formerly handled. As for effects on professional staff, governments and government agencies, like business firms, have increasingly appointed *chief information officers* (CIOs) to lead the development and maintenance of IT and information systems (IS), with staff to support the CIO. The National Academy of Public Administration (2001) as well as other officials and organizations have pointed out that government requires more and more highly trained and skilled IT professionals, and has faced difficult challenges in recruiting them.

Concerning internal and external coordination, most large government agencies, like business firms and nonprofit organizations, now have an intranet, an Internet-based network within the organization with access restricted to designated organizational members. To maintain security of data about individual citizens and about such sensitive matters as national security, these intranet arrangements usually require elaborate provisions for controlled access. Some government employees now carry with them devices that periodically inform them of newly assigned access codes for their agency's intranet because the codes are changed periodically as a security precaution.

All federal agencies and virtually all state and local government agencies of any reasonable size now have Web sites that provide a lot of information to clients and citizens, and more and more public services are handled through the Internet and Web site–based operations, just as more and more business organizations relate to customers and suppliers through e-commerce. For example, because of federal laws that resulted from abuses of human beings in research projects in the past, the Centers for Disease Control requires researchers proposing research on human subjects to go through a "human subjects review" of their proposal. Researchers can now obtain forms for such a review and submit the required information via the agency's Web site. Congress has directed the IRS to increase sharply the number of tax returns submitted electronically. The IRS should do so whether or not Congress requires it, because in customer satisfaction studies of federal agencies, the IRS has gotten much higher customer satisfaction ratings from taxpayers who filed electronically than from those who filed through surface mail (American Customer Satisfaction Index, 2001).

Some governmental executives and managers have actively encouraged employees to contact them with questions and comments. For example, as part of the

National Performance Review during the Clinton years, the administration encouraged federal agencies to establish or designate "reinvention laboratories," or organizational units that would try new ways of improving and streamlining the agency's services and administrative procedures. In one such unit in the Department of Defense, the leaders invited employees to submit questions and suggestions to them via e-mail and promised to respond to each e-mail within several days. During his widely praised service as commissioner of the IRS, Charles Rossotti developed a reputation for reading, and frequently responding to, e-mail from employees at many organizational levels.

These examples indicate that IT has provided significant improvements and opportunities for government, its employees, and the clients of government agencies. As one might expect, however, IT raises many challenges for managers in government, some of which are daunting. Some of these issues are new, but some involve application of the topics covered in this book and challenges similar to those encountered in managing any significant operation or initiative. Executives and managers confront challenges in strategic planning for IT itself and in integrating IT into more general plans and strategies, as well as in procurement and purchasing, creating organizational structure and designs to incorporate IT and adapt to it, training, recruiting, and many other areas (Barrett and Green, 2001).

Fountain (2001; Dawes, 2002) has analyzed developments in and challenges of IT in government using a technology enactment framework based on an institutional perspective similar to the one described in Chapter Four. The framework treats IT developments as emerging from interactions among objective technologies such as computer hardware and software, organizational forms such as bureaucracies and networks, and institutional arrangements such as cultural and legal conditions. These components of the framework combine to influence the way technological initiatives play out. The framework helps to explain why even very similar technological initiatives can have very different outcomes, because of different organizational and institutional influences on their implementation. Fountain also describes how such influences raise formidable challenges for successful utilization in government, given the strong, often entrenched organizational and institutional influences. She describes the complications encountered by officials in the numerous agencies involved in trying to develop the International Trade Data System, an IS on international trade that linked all the different agencies with responsibilities related to it. The differences among the agencies in their cultures, missions, stakeholders, standard practices, and other characteristics caused the project to founder. Fountain concluded that this and other examples suggest the impediments to major IT initiatives linking and coordinating diverse agencies and programs, and the likelihood that developments in IT applications will involve more modest projects and changes. Other authors have also argued that the bureaucratic characteristics and political contexts of government agencies will impede and slow down adoption of IT (Nye, 1999).

Also illustrating and analyzing challenges in IT adoption in government, Bozeman (2002b) chronicled the agonies of the IRS in trying to modernize the tax system with computer and IT. One glaring example of the problem took the form of a "meltdown" at one of the large centers where IRS employees process tax returns. A visiting official found tax returns, including checks in payment of taxes, stuffed in the trash cans in the restroom. The new equipment designed by contractors for automated reading and processing of the tax returns did not work. Employees, fearful of discipline for not finishing enough tax returns fast enough, resorted to discarding the returns. News of such breakdowns and failures in the new systems brought a tidal wave of criticism. In 1996, one congressman referred to the agency's efforts as "a four billion dollar fiasco" (Bozeman, 2002b). Bozeman pointed out that the disaster was not as disastrous as critics sometimes claimed, because the IRS was still successfully using much of the equipment and hardware years later. The problems were severe, however, and Bozeman described how many of them arose from management lapses, such as failures in project management and in management of relations with contractors. The IRS continues to struggle with the challenges of tax systems modernization, but with new resources, personnel, and prospects for success.

In addition to these major cases and examples, researchers in public administration have conducted surveys covering larger numbers of organizations. These studies also show a mixed picture of the progress and influence of IT initiatives in public organizations, but they provide valuable evidence, including evidence of both success and progress. Bretschneider (1990), for example, added survey results to the evidence of particular challenges for public managers and IT professionals. He found that public organizations tend to be more information intensive than private firms—they have to engage in more information processing. Even so, he found that managers in government agencies report longer delays in procuring computer equipment than do private managers, due to more red tape, procurement rules, and accountability requirements in the public agencies. Conversely, Bretschneider and Wittmer (1993) report evidence of innovativeness in IT adoption by government agencies. In comparing IT conditions in government agencies to those in business firms, they found that the government organizations reported having more microcomputers per employee than the business firms. This appears to result from the more information-intensive task environment in public organizations, and the evidence tends to contradict the view that public agencies tend to lag behind private firms in IT adoption and utilization (Moon and Bretschneider, 2002). Somewhat similarly, Rocheleau and Wu (2002) surveyed municipal government IS managers and compared their responses to those of IS managers in business firms and found that the government managers rated IT and IT training more important than business managers did. Conversely, the business managers reported higher levels of spending on IT, IT training, and IT personnel in their organizations.

Moon and Bretschneider (2002) report survey results that indicate that public sector managers engage in higher levels of IT innovativeness in response to higher levels of red tape (as measured by survey items about the level of burdensome rules and procedures). Public managers may regard red tape as a transaction cost and try to minimize it through proactive adoption of IT. In addition, Moon and Bretschneider found evidence that more entrepreneurial and risk-receptive leadership in the organization has a positive relationship to IT innovativeness.

Other studies reflect on IT influences in addition to its utilization. On the basis of a mail survey of government program managers in the 450 largest U.S. counties, Heintze and Bretschneider (2000) analyzed the impact of IT implementation on organizational structures and performance. They found that the managers reported that IT implementation has little impact on organizational structures, in the sense of increasing management levels and numbers of decision makers. In addition, the managers perceived that any structural changes caused by IT implementation in public agencies have little impact on organizational performance (measured as improved ease of communication and improved technical decision making). However, the managers tended to regard IT adoption as having a direct positive impact on improving technical decision making (as opposed to an impact on decision making by way of influences on structure). While Heintze and Bretschneider note that county government managers may have different responses to developments in IT than state and federal managers, the lack of perceived structural effects of IT is striking.

Moon (2002) found generally similar results when he analyzed the data on 2,899 municipal governments with populations of more than ten thousand from the 2000 E-government Survey conducted by the International City/County Management Association and Public Technology Inc. Moon found that most municipal governments surveyed have their own Web sites and intranet. However, few have well-developed e-government strategic plans. Most of the municipal governments were in early stages of evolution in e-government utilization, using it mainly for simple information dissemination or two-way communication with citizens and stakeholders. Few governments reported being at the more advanced stages of development that involve using e-government for service provision and financial transaction. In findings similar to those of Heintze and Bretschneider, Moon reports that only a small portion of the governments reported that e-government programs enhance cost saving, downsizing, and entrepreneurial activities. A higher portion, however, reported improvements in work environment, general efficiency, and effective procurement. Although larger governments showed more active engagement with e-government, Moon concludes that in general municipal governments are not aggressively utilizing IT and that IT innovations are not contributing strongly to cost savings, revenue generation, and downsizing. Nevertheless, Moon concludes with an optimistic assessment of the future of municipal e-governments.

Lee and Perry (2002) analyze the impact of state governments' IT investments on Gross State Product (GSP), using data on all fifty states from 1990 to 1995. They report evidence that IT investment in state government boosts states' economic performance. Also, different IT management structures have different effects on performance. When a CIO oversees the entire IT operation, the impact on GSP is higher. One reason for this relationship is that "the CIO's technical expertise seems to facilitate better decisions regarding the design, modernization, use, sharing, and performance of IT resources" (p. 98). Compared to the studies described earlier, these findings indicate a much more positive effect of IT investments. Lee and Perry point out that their results may differ from previous ones because they control for the "productivity paradox," a much-debated absence of evidence that the dissemination of computer technology has generally enhanced productivity in organizations and in the economy (although Lee and Perry cite recent studies that do find productivity gains). Participants in the debate have suggested various explanations of the paradox, such as poor measurement procedures that fail to detect the effect, lagged or delayed effects that take time to show up, and mismanagement of the IT investments. The authors' analysis takes these possibilities into account, and they argue that previous studies might have found more positive impacts of IT investments if they had done so.

Additional evidence about IT adoption in state agencies comes from Hinnant's (2001) recent survey of 789 state government program managers in ten functional areas. He shows that a specific type of Internet-based technology needs to be congruent with the organization's task environment. Health and social service and law enforcement organizations are more likely to adopt IT technologies that electronically link the nonprofit and private sectors, while financial organizations are less likely to adopt the sector-spanning technologies. These findings are not surprising because the former two functions require strong and direct relationships between clients and stakeholders. Financial and budget organizations, conversely, have fewer needs for links with the nonprofit and private sectors. They show increased acceptance of Internet-based technologies that facilitate their interactions with stakeholders and clients, because these organizations' core tasks involve collecting information and money from clients. In addition, acceptance of Internet-based technologies increases when stakeholders are involved in their development. Acceptance also increases due to the motivation to share information

with external stakeholders and, as Moon and Bretschneider (2002) found, to reduce organizational red tape. In addition, as another less-than-optimistic note in
this stream of research, Hinnant also reports a frequent perception that state government agencies have weak capacity for implementing more advanced forms
of Internet-based technologies.

The conflicting findings in these observations and studies about IT in government include both encouraging and discouraging messages, but they almost
certainly provide a realistic perspective on the topic. Organizing and managing
any major new initiative, and especially highly technical ones such as IT projects,
should be expected to involve severe challenges for leaders and professionals in
any setting. As some of the authors observe, the challenges may be even more formidable in the public sector. Indications of prospects for improved service delivery, efficiency, communication, and general effectiveness, however, should motivate
anyone concerned with public service—which should include literally everyone—
to confront the challenges and take advantage of the possibilities.

CHAPTER NINE

# UNDERSTANDING PEOPLE IN PUBLIC ORGANIZATIONS

## Values and Motives

Obviously the people in an organization are crucial to its performance and to the quality of work life within it. Yet despite evidence of their value and effectiveness, the people in public organizations have served as targets of stereotypes and reform efforts for centuries. Fueled by myths and oversimplifications, these stereotypes have made prejudice against government employees one of the socially acceptable forms of bigotry in the United States and other nations. Criticism of government is essentially an industry in the United States, and in some ways an indispensable one. Industries need raw materials to produce their outputs, and government employees often serve as such resources for the legion of critics who make their living in whole or in part by criticizing government. One of numerous examples of this prejudice occurred during the 1990s when a popular cartoon strip expressed a long-standing stereotype one Sunday morning by depicting a government employee who "made civil service history" by going to work for a couple of hours on a holiday. Over the past two decades, surveys of government managers have found that the unfavorable public image of government weakens public employees' morale and their sense that public service is a respected occupation (U.S. Merit Systems Protection Board, 1987; Volcker Commission, 1989; Perry and Miller, 1990; Light, 2002a). At the same time, however, some of these same managers, as well as other experts, have expressed concern about the challenges they face in trying to motivate public employees because of such factors as elaborate protections for employees faced with disciplinary actions. Such constraints are one reason that a prominent public management scholar has argued that the problem of motivating employees is one of the most important issues in the field of public management (Behn, 1995). Certainly many elected officials in government accept this view, because various reform efforts in recent decades have focused on how to increase government employees' motivation and productivity.

This chapter and the next one are concerned with the people in public organizations. They emphasize the motivation and work-related values and attitudes (such as job satisfaction) of public employees. This chapter defines motivation and discusses it in the context of public organizations. It then reviews concepts basic to the analysis of motivation and work attitudes, including concepts about people's needs, values, and motives that serve as essential components of motivation theories and techniques. The discussion covers the values and motives that are particularly important in public organizations, such as the desire to perform a public service, and values and attitudes about pay, security, work, and other matters that often distinguish public sector managers and employees from those in other settings.

The next chapter describes the major theories of work motivation. It also summarizes techniques that organizations use to enhance employee motivation. It then describes research on major work-related attitudes, such as job satisfaction, organizational commitment, and professionalism. The discussions of all of these topics consider applications and examples in public organizations.

# Motivation and Public Management

Human motivation is a fundamental topic in the social sciences, and people's motivation to work is similarly a basic topic in the field of organizational behavior (OB). The framework presented in Figures 1.1 and 1.2 indicates that the people in an organization, and their behaviors and attitudes, are interrelated with such factors as organizational tasks, organizational structures and processes, leadership processes, and organizational culture. With all of these factors impinging on people, motivating employees and stimulating effective attitudes in them become crucial and sensitive challenges for managers. This and the next chapter show that, as with many topics in management and OB, the basic research and theory provide no conclusive science of motivation. Leaders have to draw on the ideas and apply the available techniques pragmatically, blending their experience and judgment with the insights the literature provides.

These two chapters show that OB researchers and management consultants often treat motivation and work attitudes as internal organizational matters influenced by such factors as supervisory practices, pay, and the nature of the work. Such factors figure importantly in public organizations; however, motivation in public organizations, like the other organizational attributes discussed in this book, is also greatly affected by the public sector environment. The effects of this environment require public managers to possess a distinctive knowledge of motivation that links OB with political science in ways essential to the analysis and practice of management.

The effects of the political and institutional environment of public organizations on the people in those organizations show up in numerous ways. In recent decades, governments at all levels in the United States and in other nations have mounted efforts to reform civil service systems and government pay systems (Ingraham, 1993; Peters and Savoie, 1994; Gore, 1993; Thompson, 2000; U.S. Office of Management and Budget, 2002). Typically, the reformers have sought to correct allegedly weak links between performance and pay, promotion, and discipline, claiming that these weak links undermine motivation and hence performance and efficiency. These reforms have come about not just because of public attitudes but also because government managers have for years complained about having insufficient authority over pay, promotion, and discipline (Macy, 1971; U.S. Office of Personnel Management, 1983, 1999, 2001). The reforms also reflect, then, the constraints on public managers that earlier chapters have described. That such reforms have often foundered or backfired (Ingraham, 1993; Kellough and Lu, 1993; Perry, Petrakis, and Miller, 1989) raises the possibility that these constraints are inevitable in the public sector (Rainey, Facer, and Bozeman, 1995). Many analysts and experienced practitioners regard the constraining character of government personnel systems as the critical difference between managing in the public sector and managing in a private organization (Thompson, 1989), and for decades government officials and agencies have sought to decentralize government personnel systems to provide them with more flexibility in human resource management (Gore, 1993; U. S. Office of Personnel Management, 2001).

If anything, the focus on the management and motivation of public employees intensified as the new century began. A *human capital movement* got under way in the federal government, with implications for the other levels of government. This emphasis on human capital reflects the belief that the human beings in an organization and their skills and knowledge are the organization's most important assets, more important than other forms of capital such as plants, machinery, and financial assets. Accordingly, organizations must invest in the development of their human capital. Concerns about an impending crisis in human capital have also driven this movement. Many federal managers and professionals at all levels of government will be eligible for retirement within a short period of years, and surveys have indicated that many young people do not see government as an attractive place to work. Technological advancements and other trends have been creating the need for government personnel with more and different types of advanced education and skills. Government has to compete with the private sector for such people, and private organizations often have more flexibility in competing for them and paying them more. The U.S. General Accounting Office, the U.S. Office of Personnel Management, and the U.S. Office of Management and Budget have all joined in trying to develop human capital policies and models and to get federal agencies to adopt them (see, for example, U.S. General Accounting Office, 2002a, 2002b). The topic spilled over into the debate over the legislation authorizing the Department of Homeland Security. Senator Voinovich of Ohio had been championing human capital legislation that would require each federal agency to appoint a chief human capital officer, to engage in strategic planning for human capital, and to engage in other steps to maintain and develop human capital. These requirements were included in the Department of Homeland Security legislation and extended to all federal agencies in that legislation.

The issue of homeland security raised other questions about people in public organizations as well. One of the central issues in that debate was whether the employees of the new department would have the same civil service protections as other federal employees. The Bush administration opposed such protections and wanted more flexibility to transfer, hire, fire, and discipline the employees, to enhance capacity to respond rapidly to national security needs. Public employee unions and their allies in the House and Senate opposed such flexibilities and called for more typical civil service protections. Ultimately, a compromise had to be hammered out before this historic legislation could pass the House and Senate.

These developments all suggest that managing people in government raises challenges very different from those faced by business and nonprofit organizations. As with other topics in this book, however, another side argues that government differs little from business in matters of motivation. Businesses also have problems motivating managers and employees, because of union pressures, selfish and unethical behaviors, ineffective bonus and merit-pay systems, and other problems. Business managers worry about the paperwork involved in firing an employee and about the potential for wrongful termination suits (Bryant, 1996). Ban (1995, p. 58) described an amusing incident in which a government manager who had worked in a business firm shocked his peers by saying that he liked working for government because it is easier to fire incompetent employees than in a business firm. In addition, Nobel Laureate Herbert Simon (1995), one of the most influential contributors to public administration theory and arguably the world's preeminent behavioral scientist, once proclaimed that reward practices in public, private, and nonprofit firms do not differ: "Everything said here about economic rewards applies equally to privately owned, nonprofit, and government-owned organizations. The opportunity for, and limits on, the use of rewards to motivate activities towards organizational goals are precisely the same in all three kinds of organizations" (p. 283, n. 3).

In addition, high motivation exists in many government organizations. Executives coming to government from business typically mention how impressed they are with how hard government employees work and how capable they are (Volcker Commission, 1989; Hunt, 1999; IBM Endowment for the Business of Government, 2002). In surveys, government managers have mentioned frustrations of the sort just discussed but have also reported high levels of work effort and satisfaction (see, for example, Light, 2002a).

Specialists in public personnel administration have for a long time argued that the claim that you cannot fire a government employee is a myth and that one certainly can do so by following the proper procedures (Ban, 1995, p. 157). A report by the U.S. Office of Personnel Management (1999) concludes that no one can provide evidence that managers in government are less likely than managers in business to discharge poorly performing employees, and that the turnover rates—the rates at which employees leave the organizations voluntarily or by dismissal—in both the public and the private sector do not appear to differ very much. In sum, experts differ over the accuracy of the claim that government personnel systems constrain managers much more than those in business firms and that this leads to lower motivation among government employees.

In this debate over whether there are similarities or differences in managing people in the public and private sectors, both sides are right in a sense. Public managers often do face unique challenges in motivating employees, but they can also apply a great deal from the general motivation literature. The challenge is to draw from the ideas and insights in the literature while taking into consideration the public sector context discussed in other chapters and while basing one's conclusions on as much actual evidence as possible. The next section reviews the assertions about the public sector context discussed in earlier chapters before the discussion turns to the concept of motivation itself.

# The Context of Motivation in Public Organizations

Previous chapters have presented observations and research findings that suggest a unique context for motivation in public organizations (Perry and Porter, 1982):

- The absence of economic markets for the outputs of public organizations and the consequent diffuseness of incentives and performance indicators in the public sector
- The multiple, conflicting, and often abstract values that public organizations must pursue
- The complex, dynamic political and public policy processes by which public organizations operate, which involve many actors, interests, and shifting agendas

- The external oversight bodies and processes that impose structures, rules, and procedures on public organizations, including civil service rules governing pay, promotion, and discipline, and rules that affect training and personnel development
- The external political climate, including public attitudes toward taxes, government, and government employees, which turned sharply negative during the 1970s and 1980s

Earlier chapters have also related these conditions to various characteristics of public organizations that in turn influence motivation:

- Sharp constraints on some public leaders and managers that limit their motivation and ability to develop their organization. Politically elected and appointed top executives and their appointees turn over rapidly. Institutional oversight and rules limit their authority. Lower-level public employees can develop external political alliances with interest groups and legislators, thus enhancing their independence.
- The relatively turbulent, sporadic decision-making processes in public organizations, which can influence managers' and employees' sense of purpose and their perception of their impact (Hickson and others, 1986; Light, 2002a).
- The relatively complex and constraining structures in many public organizations, including constraints on the administration of incentives (Rainey, Facer, and Bozeman, 1995; Thompson, 1989).
- Vague goals, both for individual jobs and for the organization; a weak sense of personal significance within the organization on the part of employees; unstable expectations; and uncohesive collegial and work groups—all the result of the preceding factors (Buchanan, 1974, 1975; Perry and Porter, 1982). Many observers argue that people at the lower and middle levels of public organizations often become lost in the elaborate bureaucratic and public policy system. They work under elaborate rules and constraints that, paradoxically, fail to hold them highly accountable (Warwick, 1975; Barton, 1980; Lipsky, 1980; Michelson, 1980; Lynn, 1981).
- Differences in the types of people who choose to work in public management, in light of the constraints on pay and performance in public service. These differences often include higher levels of public service motivation (Crewson, 1995b; Perry and Wise, 1990).

Some of these observations are difficult to prove or disprove. For others we have increased evidence, which later sections and the next chapter present. As we examine this evidence, it is important to examine how organizational researchers have treated the concept of motivation and its measurement.

# The Concept of Work Motivation

A substantial body of theory, research, and experience provides a wealth of insight into motivation in organizations (Pinder, 1998; Rainey, 2000). Yet in scrutinizing the topic, scholars have increasingly shown its complexity. Everyone has a sense of what we mean by *motivation*. The term derives from the Latin word for "move," as do the words *motor* and *motif*. We know that forces move us, arouse us, direct us. Work motivation refers to a person's desire to work hard and work well—to the arousal, direction, and persistence of effort in work settings. Managers in public, private, and nonprofit organizations use motivational techniques all the time. Yet debates about motivation have raged for years, because the simple definition just given leaves many questions about what it means to work hard and well, what determines a person's desire to do so, and how one measures such behavior.

## Measuring and Assessing Motivation

Motivation researchers have struggled with different ways of measuring motivation, none of which provides an adequately comprehensive measurement (Pinder, 1998, 43–4). For example, the typical definition of *motivation*, such as the one just provided, raises complications about what we actually mean by motivation. Is it an attitude or a behavior, or both? Must we observe a person exerting effort? As Exhibit 9.1 shows, researchers have tried to measure motivation in different ways that imply different answers to these questions. Some researchers have asked about behavior and attitudes (items 1 through 4 in Exhibit 9.1). At least one study (Guion and Landy, 1972) has tried to develop measures based on observations by a person's coworkers. As the set of examples in the exhibit implies, OB researchers have attempted very few measures of general work motivation. One of the few available general measures—section 1 in the exhibit—relies on questions about how hard one works and how often one does some extra work. Researchers have reported successful use of this scale (Cook, Hepworth, Wall, and Warr, 1981). One study using this measure, however, found that respondents gave very high ratings to their own work effort. Most reported that they work harder than others in their organization. They gave such high self-ratings that there was little difference among them (Rainey, 1983). This example illustrates the problem of asking people about their motivation. It also reflects the cultural emphasis on hard work in the United States, which leads people to report that they do work hard. Many people apparently want to think they work hard and feel that they do. If, however, as in the study just cited, most respondents report that they work harder than their colleagues, there must be organizations in which everyone works harder than

## EXHIBIT 9.1. QUESTIONNAIRE ITEMS
## USED TO MEASURE WORK MOTIVATION.

1. *Job Motivation Scale* (Patchen, Pelz, and Allen, 1965)

   This questionnaire, one of the few direct measures of job motivation, poses the following questions:

   > On most days on your job, how often does time seem to drag for you?
   > Some people are completely involved in their job—they are absorbed in it night and day. For other people, their job is simply one of several interests. How involved do you feel in your job?
   > How often do you do some extra work for your job that isn't really required of you?
   > Would you say that you work harder, less hard, or about the same as other people doing your type of work at [name of organization]?

2. *Work Motivation Scale* (Wright, forthcoming)

   > I put forth my best effort to get the job done regardless of the difficulties.
   > I am willing to start work early or stay late to finish a job.
   > It has been hard for me to get very involved in my current job. (Reversed)
   > I do extra work for my job that isn't really expected of me.
   > Time seems to drag while I am on the job. (Reversed)

3. *Intrinsic Motivation Scale* (Lawler and Hall, 1970)

   Intrinsic motivation refers to the motivating effects of the work itself. Researchers have measured it with items such as these:

   > When I do my work well, it gives me a feeling of accomplishment.
   > When I perform my job well, it contributes to my personal growth and development.
   > I feel a great sense of personal satisfaction when I do my job well.
   > Doing my job well increases my self-esteem.

4. *Reward Expectancies* (Rainey, 1983)

   Some surveys, such as the Federal Employee Attitude Survey, use questions about reward expectations, such as those that follow, to assess reward systems but also as indicators of motivation:

   > Producing a high quality of work increases my chances for higher pay.
   > Producing a high quality of work increases my chances for a promotion.

5. *Peer Evaluations of an Individual's Work Motivation* (Guion and Landy, 1972; Landy and Guion, 1970)

   For this method of measuring motivation, fellow employees evaluate an individual's work motivation on the following dimensions:

   > Team attitude
   > Task concentration
   > Independence/self-starter
   > Organizational identification
   > Job curiosity
   > Persistence
   > Professional identification

everyone else. Obviously, motivation is hard to measure with simple questionnaires. Recently, however, Wright (forthcoming) reported the successful use of the questions in section 2 of Exhibit 9.1 in a survey of government employees in New York State. The respondents' answers to the items were consistent and the scale containing these items showed meaningful relations to other variables such as the respondents' perceptions of the clarity of their work goals and the organization's goals.

Partly due to the problems with general measures of motivation, researchers have used various alternatives, such as measures of intrinsic or internal work motivation (section 3 in Exhibit 9.1; see also Cook, Hepworth, Wall, and Warr, 1981). Researchers in OB define intrinsic work motives or rewards as those that are mediated within the worker—psychological rewards derived directly from the work itself. Extrinsic rewards are externally mediated and are exemplified by salary, promotion, and other rewards that come from the organization or work group. As the examples in Exhibit 9.1 indicate, questions on intrinsic motivation ask about an increase in feelings of accomplishment, growth, and self-esteem through work well done. Measures such as these assess important work-related attitudes, but they do not ask directly about work effort or direction. They implicitly assume that if one feels this way at work, one must be motivated to exert effort.

Researchers and consultants have used items derived from expectancy theory, described in the next chapter, as proxy measures of work motivation. Such items (see section 4 in Exhibit 9.1) have been widely used by consultants in assessing organizations and in huge surveys of federal employees used to assess the civil service system and efforts to reform it (U.S. Office of Personnel Management, 1979, 1980, 1983). Surveys have also found sharp differences between government and business managers on questions such as these (Rainey, 1983; Rainey, Facer, and Bozeman, 1995). This research has also shown, however, that worker expectations concerning rewards are not strongly related to self-reported motivation on general measures such as the Patchen, Pelz, and Allen (1965) scale. They are very useful questions, but they are not good indicators of general motivation. The effort to use such scales as indicators of motivation implicitly acknowledges the limitations of asking people to report their own level of motivation and effort.

If one cannot ask people directly about their motivation, one can ask those around them for their observations about their coworkers' motivation (see section 5 in Exhibit 9.1). Landy and Guion (1970) had peers rate individual managers on the dimensions listed in the table. Significantly, their research indicated that peer observers disagree a lot when rating the same person. This method obviously requires a lot of time and resources to administer, and few other researchers have used this very interesting approach. The method does provide a useful illustration of the many possible dimensions of motivation.

As an additional example of the different outcomes that can motivate employees, one of the classic distinctions in the theory of management and organizations concerns the difference between motivation to join an organization and stay in it, on the one hand, and motivation to work hard and do well within it, on the other. These two motivations have related but fairly distinct determinants. Chester Barnard (1938), and later James March and Herbert Simon (March and Simon, 1958), in books widely acknowledged as prominent contributions to the field, analyzed this distinction. You might get people to shuffle into work every day rather than quit, but they can display keen ingenuity at avoiding doing what you ask them to do if they do not want to do it. Management experts widely acknowledge Barnard's prescience in seeking to analyze the ways in which organizational leaders must employ a variety of incentives, including the guiding values of the organization, to induce cooperation and effort (Williamson, 1990; Peters and Waterman, 1982; DiIulio, 1994).

## Rival Influences on Performance

Motivation alone does not determine performance. Ability figures importantly in performance. One person may display high motivation but insufficient ability, while another may have such immense ability that he or she performs well with little apparent motivation. The person's training and preparation for a certain task, the behaviors of leaders or coworkers, and many other factors interact with motivation in determining performance. A person may gain motivation by feeling able to perform well, or lose motivation through the frustrations brought on by lacking sufficient ability. Alternatively, a worker may lose motivation to perform a task he or she has completely mastered because it fails to provide a challenge or a sense of growth. As we will see, the major theories of employee motivation try in various ways to capture some of these intricacies. The points may sound obvious enough, but major reforms of the civil service and of government pay systems have frequently oversimplified or underestimated these concepts (Ingraham, 1993; Perry, Petrakis, and Miller, 1989; Rainey and Kellough, 2000).

## Motivation as an Umbrella Concept

The complexities of work motivation have given the topic the status of an umbrella concept that refers to a general area of study rather than a precisely defined research target (Campbell and Pritchard, 1983; Pinder, 1998). Indeed, Locke (1999), in an article reviewing and summarizing motivation research, proposes an elaborate, integrated model of work motivation that does not include the term *motivation*. Considerable research and theorizing about motivation continue, but they usually employ the term to refer to a general concept that incorporates many variables and issues (see, for example, Klein, 1989; Klein, 1990; Kleinbeck, Quast, Thierry, and Harmut, 1990). Locke and Latham (1990a), for example, present a model of work motivation that does not include a concept specifically labeled "motivation." Motivation currently appears to serve as an overarching theme for research on a variety of related topics, including organization identification and commitment, leadership practices, job involvement, organizational climate and culture, and characteristics of work goals.

# Needs, Values, Motives, and Incentives

The internal and external impetuses that arouse and direct effort—the needs, motives, and values that push us and the incentives, goals, and objectives that pull us—obviously play major roles in motivation. Every theory of work motivation discussed in Chapter Ten refers to these factors in some way. Classic debates have raged, however, over what to call them, what the proper set includes, and what roles they play. These debates, like the problems involved in defining and measuring motivation, raise serious challenges for both managers and researchers. If anything, the concepts of values, motives, and incentives have become even more prominent in management in recent years. Studies of leadership, change, and organizational culture—topics covered in later chapters—have increasingly emphasized the importance of shared values in organizations. So many organizations now publish statements of their organizational values that such statements are commonplace. Writers and consultants on leadership exhort leaders in organizations to learn to understand the values of the members of their work groups and organizations. DiIulio (1994) shows how particularly important this can be in public organizations by describing how members of the Bureau of Prisons display a strong commitment to the organization's values and mission in part because some of the bureau's long-term leaders have effectively promoted those values. But because this topic is so important, it raises the question of how managers (and scholars) can deal with all the complications involved in defining and understanding motivation, values, motives, and related concepts. This chapter approaches the problem by reviewing many of the efforts to specify and define important needs, values, motives, and incentives. This review provides a complex array of approaches to the problem, but it also gives a lot of examples and suggestions from which managers can draw.

Motivation theorists use the terms we have been using, such as *need, value, motive, incentive, objective,* and *goal,* in overlapping ways. We can, however, suggest definitions for them. A need is a resource or condition required for the well-being of an individual. A motive is a force acting within an individual that causes him or her to seek to obtain or avoid some external object or condition. An incentive is an external object or condition that evokes behaviors aimed at attaining or avoiding it. A goal is a future state that one strives to achieve, and an objective is a more specific, short-term goal, a step toward a more general, long-term goal. Rokeach (1973), an authority on human values, offered an often-quoted definition of a value as "an enduring belief that a specific mode of conduct or end-state of existence is personally or socially preferable to an opposite or converse mode of conduct or end-state of existence" (p. 5).

Many people would disagree with these definitions and switch some of them around. The challenge for public managers, however, is to develop a sense of the range of values, motives, incentives, and goals that influence employees, even in view of all the quandaries that researchers raise. The research on motivation tells us to expect no simple list, because goals, needs, values, and motives always occur in complex sets and interrelationships. They are linked—one value takes on importance as a means to achieving another more general or more important one. They are also grouped into sets, with workers pursuing all the members of a set simultaneously.

## Attempts to Specify Needs, Values, and Incentives

Tables 9.1 and 9.2 present some of the prominent lists and typologies from the research on needs, motives, values, and incentives. These lists illustrate the diversity among theorists and provide some of the most useful enumerations of these topics ever developed. Murray's typology of human needs (1938), for example, provides one of the more elaborate inventories of needs ever attempted, but even so, it fails to exhaust all possible ways of expressing human needs and motives. Maslow's needs hierarchy (1954), probably the most prominent theory of human needs, has significantly influenced the field of management. As described in Chapter Two, Maslow proposed five categories of needs, arranged in a "hierarchy of prepotency" from the most basic physiological needs through safety needs, social needs, and self-esteem needs, and up to the highest level, the self-actualization needs.

Researchers trying to determine whether individuals rank their needs as the theory predicts have found that Maslow's five-level hierarchy does not hold. Instead, the evidence points to a two-step hierarchy: lower-level employees show more concern with material and security rewards, while higher-level employees place more emphasis on achievement and challenge (Pinder, 1998). Analyzing the results of a large survey of federal employees, Crewson (1995b) found this kind of difference between the employees at lower General Schedule (GS) salary levels (GS 1–8) and the highest GS levels (GS 16 and above). He found that respondents

# TABLE 9.1. THE COMPLEXITY OF HUMAN NEEDS AND VALUES.

| Murray's List of Basic Needs (1938) | Maslow's Need Hierarchy (1954) | Alderfer's ERG Model (1972) | Rokeach's Value Survey (1973) | |
|---|---|---|---|---|
| | | | Terminal Values | Instrumental Values |
| Abasement | Self-actualization needs | Growth needs | A comfortable (prosperous) life | Ambitious (hard-working, aspiring) |
| Achievement | Esteem needs | Relatedness needs | An exciting (stimulating, active) life | Broad-minded (open-minded) |
| Affiliation | Belongingness/social needs | Existence needs | A sense of accomplishment (lasting contribution) | Capable (competent, effective) |
| Aggression | Safety needs | | A world at peace (free of war and conflict) | Cheerful (lighthearted, joyful) |
| Autonomy | Physiological needs | | A world of beauty (of nature and the arts) | Clean (neat, tidy) |
| Counteraction | | | Equality (brotherhood, equal opportunity for all) | Courageous (standing up for one's beliefs) |
| Defendance | | | Family security (taking care of loved ones) | Forgiving (willing to pardon others) |
| Deference | | | Freedom (independence, free choice) | Helpful (working for the welfare of others) |
| Dominance | | | Happiness (contentedness) | Honest (sincere, truthful) |
| Exhibition | | | Inner harmony (freedom from inner conflict) | Imaginative (daring, creative) |
| Harm avoidance | | | Mature love (sexual and spiritual intimacy) | Independent (self-reliant, self-sufficient) |
| Nurturance | | | National security (protection from attack) | Intellectual (intelligent, reflective) |
| Order | | | Pleasure (an enjoyable, leisurely life) | Logical (consistent, rational) |
| Play | | | Salvation (eternal life) | Loving (affectionate, tender) |
| Rejection | | | Self-respect (self-esteem) | Obedient (dutiful, respectful) |
| Sentience | | | Social recognition (respect, admiration) | Polite (courteous, well-mannered) |
| Sex | | | True friendship (close companionship) | Responsible (dependable, reliable) |
| Succorance | | | Wisdom (a mature understanding of life) | Self-controlled (restrained, self-disciplined) |
| Understanding | | | | |

## TABLE 9.2. TYPES OF INCENTIVES.

| Incentive Type | Definitions and Examples |
|---|---|
| **Barnard (1938)** | |
| Specific incentives | Incentives "specifically offered to an individual" |
|    Material inducements | Money, things, physical conditions |
|    Personal, nonmaterialistic inducements | Distinction, prestige, personal power, dominating position |
|    Desirable physical conditions of work | |
|    Ideal benefactions | "Satisfaction of ideals about nonmaterial, future or altruistic relations" (pride of workmanship, sense of adequacy, altruistic service for family or others, loyalty to organization, esthetic and religious feeling, satisfaction of hate and revenge) |
| General incentives | Incentives that "cannot be specifically offered to an individual" |
|    Associational attractiveness | Social compatibility, freedom from hostility due to racial, religious differences |
|    Customary working conditions | Conformity to habitual practices, avoidance of strange methods and conditions |
|    Opportunity for feeling of enlarged participation in course of events | Association with large, useful, effective organization |
|    Condition of communion | Personal comfort in social relations |
| **Simon (1948)** | |
| Incentives for employee participation | Salary or wage, status and prestige, relations with working group, promotion opportunities |
| Incentives for elites or controlling groups | Prestige and power |
| **Clark and Wilson (1961) and Wilson (1973)** | |
| Material incentives | Tangible rewards that can be easily priced (wages and salaries, fringe benefits, tax reductions, changes in tariff levels, improvement in property values, discounts, services, gifts) |
| Solidary incentives | Intangible incentives without monetary value and not easily translated into one, deriving primarily from the act of associating |
|    Specific solidary incentives | Incentives that can be given to or withheld from a specific individual (offices, honors, deference) |
|    Collective solidary incentives | Rewards created by act of associating and enjoyed by all members if enjoyed at all (fun, conviviality, sense of membership or exclusive-collective status or esteem) |

## TABLE 9.2. TYPES OF INCENTIVES, Cont'd.

| Incentive Type | Definitions and Examples |
| --- | --- |
| Purposive incentives | Intangible rewards that derive from satisfaction of contributing to worthwhile cause (enactment of a law, elimination of government corruption) |
| **Downs (1967)** | |
| General "motives or goals" of officials | Power (within or outside bureau), money income, prestige, convenience, security, personal loyalty to work group or organization, desire to serve public interest, commitment to a specific program of action |
| **Niskanen (1971)** | |
| Variables that may enter the bureaucrat's utility function | Salary, perquisites of the office, public reputation, power, patronage, output of the bureau, ease of making changes, ease of managing the bureau, increased budget |
| **Lawler (1971)** | |
| Extrinsic rewards | Rewards extrinsic to the individual, part of the job situation, given by others |
| Intrinsic rewards | Rewards intrinsic to the individual and stemming directly from job performance itself, which satisfy higher-order needs such as self-esteem and self-actualization (feelings of accomplishment and of using and developing one's skills and abilities) |
| **Herzberg, Mausner, Peterson, and Capwell (1957)** | |
| Job "factors" or aspects. Rated in importance by large sample of employees. | In order of average rated importance: security, interest, opportunity for advancement, company and management, intrinsic aspects of job, wages, supervision, social aspects, working conditions, communication, hours, ease, benefits |
| **Locke (1969)** | |
| External incentive | An event or object external to the individual which can incite action (money, knowledge of score, time limits, participation, competition, praise and reproof, verbal reinforcement, instructions) |

at the lower salary levels rated job security and pay as the most important job factors, while executive-level employees gave the highest rating to the importance of public service and to having an impact on public affairs. The executive-level employees also gave their lowest ratings to job security and pay. This suggests that the self-actualization motives among public sector executives focus on public service, a point to which we will return shortly.

Alderfer's typology of existence, relatedness, and growth needs (1972) provides still another example of an effort to specify basic human needs. On the basis of empirical research, Alderfer reduced Maslow's categories to this more parsimonious set.

As Crewson's analysis shows, this distinction between higher- and lower-order motives holds in public organizations. As described later, other surveys have also shown that lower-level public employees attach more importance to job security and benefits than public managers and executives, who say they consider these factors less important than accomplishment and challenging work. Managers coming into government often say they are attracted by the opportunity to provide a public service and to influence significant events. At the same time, as discussed shortly, prominent motivation theorists argue that employees at all levels can be motivated by higher-order motives and should be treated accordingly. Chapter Thirteen describes how that philosophy played a role in a major reorganization of the Social Security Administration. Another application of Maslow's theory in organizations involved the use of measures of need satisfaction based on Maslow's hierarchy (Porter and Lawler, 1968). As presented in Chapter Ten, one study comparing public and private managers found that public managers were somewhat less satisfied in many of the need categories.

Human values are also basic components of motivation. Rokeach (1973) developed two corresponding lists of values—instrumental values and terminal values (see Table 9.1)—and designed questionnaires to assess people's commitment to them. Sikula (1973a, 1973b) compared government and business executives using the Rokeach instrument, compiling responses from managers in twelve occupational groups. Six of the groups consisted of managers from industry, education, and government, including fifty-four executives in the U.S. Department of Health, Education and Welfare (HEW, now the Department of Health and Human Services). The other six groups consisted of people in nonmanagerial roles. The value profile of the HEW executives was generally similar to that of the other managerial groups, whose members all placed a higher priority on values related to competence (being wise, logical, and intellectual) and initiative (imagination, courage, sense of accomplishment) than the members of the other groups. Among the six managerial groups, the HEW executives placed the highest priority on being responsible, honest, helpful, and capable. They also gave higher ratings than any other group to the terminal values of equality, mature love, and self-respect, and they were lower than the other groups on the terminal values of happiness, pleasure, and a comfortable life. Sikula's limited sample leaves questions about whether the findings apply to all public managers. Yet the emphasis on service (helpfulness) and integrity and the de-emphasis on comfort and pleasure conform with other findings about public managers described later in this chapter and in the next one.

Researchers continue to use the Rokeach concepts and methods to study values among people in government and the nonprofit sector. Simon and Wang (2002), for example, used this approach to assess value changes over time in Americorps volunteers. Among other changes, they found increases in the ratings of freedom and equality among the volunteers after their service, compared to their expressed values prior to their service.

## Incentives in Organizations

Other researchers have analyzed incentives in organizations as a fundamental aspect of organized human activity. As described in Chapter Two, some very prominent theories about organizations have depicted them as "economies of incentives." Organizational leaders must constantly maintain a flow of resources into their organization to cover the incentives that must be paid out to induce people to contribute to the organization (Barnard, 1938; Simon, 1948; March and Simon, 1958). In analyzing these processes, these theorists developed the typologies of incentives outlined in Table 9.2, which provides about as thorough an inventory as anyone has produced (although Barnard used some very awkward terms). The typologies reflect the development across the twentieth century of an increasing emphasis in management theory on incentives besides material ones, such as personal growth and interest and pride in one's work and one's organization. Barnard, March, and Simon implied that all executives, in both public and private organizations, face these challenges of attaining resources and providing incentives.

Clark and Wilson (1961) and Wilson (1973) followed this lead in developing a typology of organizations based on the primary incentive offered to participants—*material, solidary* (defined as "involving community responsibilities or interests"), or *purposive* (see Table 9.2). Differences in primary incentives force differences in leadership behaviors and organizational processes. Leaders in solidary organizations, such as voluntary service associations, face more pressure than leaders in other organizations to develop prestige and worthy service projects to induce volunteers to participate. Leaders in purposive organizations, such as reform and social protest organizations, must show accomplishments in relation to the organization's goals, such as passage of reform legislation. A controversy that received a great deal of media coverage during 2002 illustrates this point. A leader of a feminist organization wrote a public letter to the Augusta National Golf Club, which hosts the prestigious Masters Tournament, protesting the club's exclusion of women from its membership and demanding that the club include female members. The president of the club rejected the demand and the dispute raged in the media for months. Regardless of the merits of the two sides of the dispute, the incident illustrates the need of a purposive organization—in this case, the feminist organization—to show activity related to its purpose.

Subsequent research on this typology of primary organizational incentives has concentrated on why people join political parties and groups; it has not specifically addressed public agencies. The concept of purposive incentives has great relevance for government, however. For many public managers, a sense of valuable social purpose can serve as a source of motivation. In addition to the Crewson (1995b, 1997) and DiIulio (1994) examples described earlier, large surveys of federal employees have found that sizeable percentages of them agree that the opportunity to have an impact on public affairs provides a good reason to stay in government service, especially at higher managerial and professional levels, and especially in certain agencies, such as the Environmental Protection Agency (U.S. Merit Systems Protection Board, 1987).

***Extrinsic and Intrinsic Incentives.*** The distinction between extrinsic and intrinsic incentives described in Table 9.2 figures importantly in research and practice related to motivation in organizations. Since the days of Frederick Taylor's pay-them-by-the-shovelful approach to rewarding workers (see Chapter Two), management experts have increasingly emphasized the importance of intrinsic incentives in work.

***The "Most Important" Incentives.*** The variety of incentives in Table 9.2 show why we can expect no conclusive rank-ordered list of the most important needs, values, and incentives of organizational members. There are too many ways of expressing these incentives, and employees' preferences vary according to many factors, such as age, occupation, and organizational level. Herzberg, Mausner, Peterson, and Capwell (1957) compiled the rankings shown in Table 9.2 from sixteen studies covering eleven thousand employees. Other studies have come to different conclusions, however. Lawler (1971), for example, disagrees with the Herzberg ranking, indicating that a wider review of research suggests that people rate pay much higher (averaging about third in importance in most studies). He argues that management scholars have often underestimated the importance of pay because they object to managerial approaches that rely excessively on pay as a motivator. He points out that pay often serves as a proxy for other incentives, because it can indicate achievement, recognition by one's organization, and other valued outcomes. Pay can serve as an effective motivating incentive in organizations, if pay systems are designed strategically (Lawler, 1990).

***Motives and Incentives in Public Organizations.*** In spite of these complications, there are some useful theories and research about the importance of certain motives and incentives in public organizations. Downs (1967) and Niskanen (1971), two economists who developed theories about public bureaucracies, proposed the inventories of public managers' motives listed in Table 9.2. They made the point that for public managers, political power, serving the public interest, and serving a particular government bureau or program become important potential motives. Downs developed a typology of public administrators on the basis of such motives. Some administrators, he argued, pursue their own self-interest. Some of these people are climbers, who seek to rise to higher, more influential positions. Conservers seek to defend their current positions and resources. Other administrative officials have mixed motives, combining concern with their own self-interest with concerns for larger values, such as public policies and the public interest. They fall into three groups of managers who pursue increasingly broad conceptions of the public interest. Zealots seek to advance a specific policy or program. Advocates promote and defend an agency or a more comprehensive policy domain. Statesmen pursue a more general public interest. As public agencies grow larger and older, they fill up with conservers and become rigid (because the climbers and zealots leave for other opportunities or turn into conservers). Among the mixed-motive officials, few can maintain the role of statesmen, and most become advocates. In the absence of economic markets for outputs, the administrators must obtain resources through budget allocation, and they have to develop constituencies and political supports for their agency. This pushes them toward the advocate role and discourages statesmanship.

Downs's book (1967) is almost certainly the most widely cited work ever written on government bureaucracy, but researchers have never really tested his theory in empirical studies. Its accuracy remains uncertain, then, but it does make the important point that public managers' commitments to their agencies, programs, and the public interest become important motives for them. They also face difficult decisions about the relative importance of these motives and the relationships among them.

Niskanen (1971) also was interested in how bureaucrats "maximize utility," as economists put it. He theorized that, in the absence of economic markets, bureaucrats pursuing any of the incentives listed in Table 9.2 do so by trying to obtain larger budgets. Even those motivated primarily by public service and altruism have the incentive to ask for more staff and resources and hence larger budgets.

Government bureaucracies therefore tend to grow inefficiently. Although this theory, too, has received scant empirical testing, public managers clearly do defend their budgets and usually try to increase them. Yet many exceptions occur, such as when agency budgets increase because of legislative adjustments to formulas and entitlements that agency administrators have not requested. Some agencies also initiate their own cuts in funding or personnel or accept such reductions fairly readily (Rubin, 1985; Golden, 2000). In the 1980s, the Social Security Administration launched a project to reduce its workforce by seventeen thousand, about 21 percent of its staff (U.S. General Accounting Office, 1986). As part of the National Performance Review, the major federal government reform initiative during the Clinton administration, federal agencies eliminated about 324,000 jobs in the federal civilian workforce (Thompson, 2000). Federal employment had been relatively stable in number of employees since about 1950, therefore declining as a percentage of the overall growing general U.S. workforce in the United States, and these reductions brought federal employment to its lowest level in decades. The reductions suggest that even if government managers are strongly motivated to aggrandize themselves with larger budgets and larger staffs, they are not very good at it. For reasons such as this, apparently, Niskanen's more recent work focuses on discretionary budgets—those parts of the organizational budget over which administrators have some discretion (see Blais and Dion, 1991). An increasing body of research finds mixed support, at best, for many of Niskanen's basic assumptions about the motives and capacities of bureaucrats to engage in budget maximizing (Bendor and Moe, 1985; Blais and Dion, 1991; Dolan, 2002).

Both of these theories reflect the tendency of some economists to argue that public bureaucracies incline toward dysfunction because of the absence of economic markets for their outputs (see, for example, Tullock, 1965; Barton, 1980). The theories may accurately depict problems to which public organizations are prone. Later chapters discuss the ongoing controversy over the performance of public organizations and point out that in fact they often perform very well.

***Attitudes Toward Money, Security and Benefits, and Challenging Work.*** Government does not offer the large financial gains that some people make in business, although civil service systems have traditionally offered job security and well-developed benefits programs. One might expect these differences to be reflected in public employees' attitudes about such incentives. We have increasing evidence that they do, although with many complications. Numerous surveys have found that government employees place less value than employees in business on money as an ultimate goal in work and in life (Houston, 2000; Jurkiewicz, Massey, and Brown, 1998; Karl and Sutton, 1998; Khojasteh, 1993; Kilpatrick, Cummings, and Jennings, 1964; Porter and Lawler, 1968; Lawler, 1971; Rawls, Ullrich, and Nelson,

1975; Rainey, 1983; Siegel, 1983; Wittmer, 1991). Some studies have found no difference between public and private employees in the value they attach to pay (Gabris and Simo, 1995). Such variations in research results probably reflect the way such attitudes vary by time period, organizational level, geographical area, occupation, and type of organization. Gabris and Simo used a sample containing only two public and two private organizations, so the sample may not be representative of the two sectors. Yet this possibility reminds us that we have to be careful, in designing research and drawing general conclusions, to take into account such factors as the organizational and professional level of the individuals.

Organizational level figures importantly in comparisons of attitudes about pay because, obviously, at top executive levels and in certain advanced professions, public sector salaries are usually well below those in the private sector. Below the highest organizational levels, however, pay levels are often fairly comparable in the public and private sectors. Studies have sometimes found that federal white-collar salaries were lower than private sector salaries for similar jobs, by about 22 percent according to one study (U.S. General Accounting Office, 1990). The federal government and many state and local governments conduct pay-comparability studies, however, and try to keep their pay levels competitive with those of the private sector. One can go to the Web site of the U.S. Office of Personnel Management and see the locality pay adjustments for different locations in the United States.

For such reasons, analyzing the comparability of pay between the two sectors can be complicated. Public employee unions often emphasize studies showing lower levels of pay in the public sector, but economists and other analysts often respond by pointing out that even where such differences exist, superior benefits in the public sector, such as greater job security and security of health and retirement benefits, eliminate the difference in total compensation. Differences between the two sectors tend to be concentrated at certain levels and in certain occupations and professions, and when all forms of compensation are taken into account, public sector compensation levels often appear comparable or superior to those in the private sector at lower organizational levels (Donahue, 2002). Gold and Ritchie (1993), for example, point out that average salaries for state and local government employees tend to be higher than average salaries for private sector employees in the same state. Yet public sector workers with higher skill levels and those at higher levels make less than comparable private sector employees. These differences are due to a different skill mix in the two sectors. The private sector has a higher proportion of blue-collar workers, and the public sector has a higher proportion of technical and professional workers, who tend to get higher pay than blue-collar workers. So, the higher average in the public sector is apparently due to the employment of a larger proportion of higher-paid technical and professional employees, although these same employees may make less than comparable employees in the private sector (Gold and Ritchie, 1993). Langbein and Lewis (1998) analyzed results of a survey of the Institute of Electrical and Electronic Engineers and compared the engineers in the public sector and in defense contractor firms to those in the nondefense-related private firms. They found evidence that the engineers in the public and defense contractor organizations had lower levels of productivity than the engineers in the nondefense-related firms, but the public and defense contractor engineers were significantly underpaid compared to the private sector engineers, even after controlling for productivity.

As this suggests, at the highest executive levels and for professions such as law, engineering, and medicine, the private sector offers vastly higher financial rewards, and the differences in these areas have been increasing (Volcker Commission, 1989; Gold and Ritchie, 1993; Kelman, 1989). Studies of high-level officials who entered public service have found that most of them took salary cuts to do so. Compensation did not influence their decision, however; challenge and the desire to perform public service were the main attractions (Crewson, 1995b; Hartman and Weber, 1980). In sum, many people who choose to work for government do not emphasize making a lot of money as a goal in life, even though at lower organizational levels many public employees do not work at markedly lower pay than people in similar private sector jobs. Because top executives and professionals in government work for much lower salaries than their private sector counterparts, they must be motivated by goals other than high earnings.

Nevertheless, pay issues can still have a very strong influence on the motivation of public sector employees. As pointed out earlier, pay can have a symbolic meaning, as a recognition of an employee's skill and performance (Lawler, 1990). Studies with limited samples have also found that some public managers attach higher importance to increases in their pay than do private sector managers. Apparently these midlevel public managers felt that they had little impact on their organizations and turned to pay rather than responsibility as a motive (Schuster, 1974).

Research also indicates that security and benefits serve as important incentives for many who join and stay with government, although the research results on this point are mixed. A major survey by Kilpatrick, Cummings, and Jennings (1964) found that vast majorities of all categories of public employees, including federal employees, cited job and benefit security (retirement, other protective benefits) as their motives for becoming a civil servant. Sixty-two percent of their sample of federal executives (GS 12 and above) held this view. A survey of about seventeen thousand federal employees by the U.S. Merit Systems Protection Board (1987) found that 81 percent considered annual leave and sick leave benefits as reasons to stay in government, and 70 percent saw job security as a good reason to stay. Houston (2000) and Jurkiewicz, Massey, and Brown (1998) also report surveys in which public employees placed higher value on job security or on security and stability in general than did private sector respondents to the surveys. As described earlier, however, a rough version of the Maslow needs hierarchy tends to apply. Compared to employees at lower salary levels, smaller percentages of the public sector executives, managers, and professionalized employees (such as scientists and engineers) responding to surveys attached a high level of importance to benefits and job security (Crewson, 1995b) and at least one study found that they placed lower value on job security than private sector respondents did (Crewson, 1997). Further complicating the picture, some surveys using small samples found no difference between public and private employees in the value they attached to job security (Gabris and Simo, 1995; Karl and Sutton, 1998). These variations in findings may result from variations in the samples, such as the types of organizations and the levels of the employees surveyed. It appears reasonable to conclude, however, that job security and other forms of security such as stable health and retirement benefits have served as significant incentives and attractive work factors for many public sector employees, although employees at higher salary, managerial and professional levels tended to attach less value to them in their responses to surveys.

As compared to employees at lower salary levels, managers and executives generally attach more value to intrinsic incentives, in that they report more attraction to opportunities for challenge and significant work. Some evidence indicates that public sector employees, especially managers, executives, and those at professional levels, give higher ratings of the importance of intrinsic incentives than do their private sector counterparts (Hartman and Weber, 1980). The large Federal Employee Attitude Surveys of the late 1970s and early 1980s asked newly hired employees to rate the importance of various factors in their decision to work for the federal government. Virtually all of the executive-level employees (97 percent of GS 16 and above) rated challenging work as the most important factor. Employees at lower GS levels rated job security and fringe benefits more highly than did the executives, but about 60 percent of them also rated challenging work as the most important factor. Rawls, Ullrich, and Nelson (1975) found that students headed for the nonprofit sector—mainly government—showed higher "dominance," "flexibility," and "capacity for status" ratings in psychological tests and a lower valuation of economic wealth than did students headed for the for-profit sector. The nonprofit-oriented students also played more active roles in their schools. Guyot (1960) found that a sample of federal middle managers scored higher than their business counterparts on a need-for-achievement scale and about the same on a measure of their need for power. We have some evidence, then, that government managers express as much or more concern with achievement and challenge than do private managers. Khojasteh (1993) found that intrinsic rewards such as recognition had higher motivating potential for a sample of public managers than for a sample of private managers. Crewson (1997) analyzed two large surveys that indicated that public sector employees placed more importance than private employees on intrinsic incentives such as helping others, being useful to society, and achieving accomplishments in work. Gabris and Simo (1995) found no differences between public and private employees on perceived importance of a number of extrinsic and intrinsic motivators, but they did find that the public sector employees placed more importance on service to the community. Karl and Sutton (1998) reported survey results showing that workers in both the public and the private sectors appear to be placing more importance on job security than in the past, but public sector workers report that they value interesting work more than private sector workers do, while the private sector workers place more importance than public sector respondents do on good wages. Jurkiewicz, Massey, and Brown (1998) report that public sector employees gave higher ratings than private employees to having the chance to learn new things and the chance to use their special abilities. Comparing a large sample of federal executives to a large sample of business executives, Posner and Schmidt (1996) found that the federal executives placed greater importance on such organizational goals as quality, effectiveness, public service, and value to the community. The business executives, however, attached more importance to morale, productivity, stability, efficiency, and growth than did the federal executives.

These studies suggest that challenging, significant work and the opportunity to provide a public service are often the main attractions for public managers. Perceptions of public service vary over time, however, with changes in the political climate, the economy, and generational differences (although Jurkiewicz and Brown, 1998, found few differences in motivational factors among three different age cohorts in government organizations). Surveys of career preferences among top students at leading universities have found that these students place a high priority on challenging work and personal growth. They see government positions as less likely than positions in private industry, however, to provide challenging work and personal growth (Sanders, 1989; Partnership for Public Service, 2002). They see government employment as providing superior opportunities for service to society, but they rated that opportunity as intermediate in importance. Their attitudes may reflect the antigovernment climate of the 1980s and 1990s, and general perceptions about government may change. The Partnership for Public Service, a nonprofit organization formed in 2001 to promote public service and prevent its apparent decline, has heavily emphasized the apparent challenges that these findings raise for recruiting talented young people into government service.

Somewhat surprisingly, however, researchers have found that younger workers in the public sector are expressing higher levels of general job satisfaction than younger workers in the private sector (Steel and Warner, 1990) and that employees entering the public sector show higher levels on certain measures of skill and quality than do those entering the private sector (Crewson, 1995a). These findings appear to apply to all of the broad populations of workers in the public and private sectors. They may indicate that government does provide generally superior working conditions than the private sector broadly conceived, because private employers can more readily fire, lay off, and otherwise impose difficulties on workers. The differences may not hold, however, for highly talented young people considering the public service as a career. Yet if the public sector can indeed attract high-quality employees, the challenge of providing them with challenging work becomes all the more important. The discussion of work-related attitudes such as organizational commitment in the next chapter returns to this issue, because scholars have debated whether it is particularly hard to provide challenging work in public organizations.

## The Motive for Public Service: In Search of the Service Ethic

The topic of challenging work in the public service and of motives for pursuing it brings us to the motive mentioned in discussions of why people want to work for government—the service ethic, the desire to serve the public, or as researchers on this topic now sometimes refer to it, public service motivation, or PSM. Interestingly, although this topic echoes again and again in research on public organizations, until recently it has not been the subject of nearly as much systematic research as one might expect. Public executives and managers tend to express a greater motivation to serve the public, as shown by Sikula's survey (1973a), described earlier. Similarly, Kilpatrick, Cummings, and Jennings (1964) found that federal executives, scientists, and engineers gave higher ratings than their counterparts in business to work-related values such as doing your best even if you dislike your work, doing work that is worthwhile to society, and helping others as main sources of occupational satisfaction. Rainey (1983) found that state agency managers rated the opportunity to engage in meaningful public service as more important than did managers in large business firms. As noted earlier, the Federal Employee Attitude Surveys found that high percentages of managers and executives entering the federal government rated public service and having an impact on public affairs as the most important reasons for entering federal service, with very low percentages of these groups rating salary and job security as important attractions (Crewson, 1995b). Findings such as these suggest the common characteristics of persons motivated by public service: they place a high value on work that helps others and benefits society as a whole, involves self-sacrifice, and provides a sense of responsibility and integrity. Public managers often mention such motives (Crewson, 1997; Hartman and Weber, 1980; Houston, 2000; Lasko, 1980; Kelman, 1989; Sandeep, 1989; Wittmer, 1991).

The general references to PSM earlier and in some of the surveys cited in this chapter leave many questions about what we mean by service motivation and how we can assess it. Rainey (1982) asked middle managers in state agencies and business firms to rate the value of various rewards of their work, including the opportunity to engage in a meaningful public service. The public managers rated this item much more highly than did business managers. These high ratings were strongly related to their job satisfaction, but only weakly related to their job involvement (see Table 9.1 for a definition of job involvement). This suggests that PSM differs from job involvement and other generic concepts developed in OB research in ways that we need to understand more fully. As indicated in Tables 9.1 and 9.2, many analyses of values, motives, and incentives in organizational research and the social sciences do not focus directly on PSM. Many pay virtually no attention to such motives. PSM is by no means restricted to government employees, but the topic should play a major part in the development of theories of public management and behavior in public organizations.

Researchers have begun to develop this topic with more detailed analysis and evidence. Perry and Wise (1990) suggested that public service motives can fall into three categories: *instrumental motives,* including participation in policy formulation, commitment to a public program because of personal identification, and advocacy for a special or private interest; *norm-based motives,* including desire to serve the public interest, loyalty to duty and to government, and devotion to social equity; and *affective motives,* including commitment to a program based on convictions about its social importance and the "patriotism of benevolence." They drew the term *patriotism of benevolence* from Frederickson and Hart (1985), who define it as an affection for all the people in the nation and a devotion to defending the basic rights granted by enabling documents such as the Constitution.

Perry (1996) provided evidence of the dimensions of a general public service motive and ways of assessing it. He analyzed survey responses from about four hundred people, including managers and employees in various government and business organizations and graduate and undergraduate students He analyzed the responses to questions such as those in Table 9.3 to see if the respondents answered them in ways that supported the conclusion that their public service motives fall into these dimensions (in technical terms, he analyzed the reliability of these subscales using a confirmatory factor analysis). Perry (2000) has also sought to elaborate and advance the theory of PSM. Criticizing general motivation theory because of its inability to explain important behavioral and cognitive phenomena in many public and nonprofit organizations, he proposed a theory that

## TABLE 9.3. DIMENSIONS AND QUESTIONNAIRE MEASURES OF PUBLIC SERVICE MOTIVATION.

| Dimension | Questionnaire Items |
|---|---|
| Attraction to Public Affairs | Politics is a dirty word. (Reversed)[a]<br>The give and take of public policymaking doesn't appeal to me. (Reversed)<br>I don't care much for politicians. (Reversed) |
| Commitment to the Public Interest | It is hard to get me genuinely interested in what is going on in my community. (Reversed)<br>I unselfishly contribute to my community.<br>Meaningful public service is very important to me.<br>I would prefer seeing public officials do what is best for the community, even if it harmed my interests.<br>I consider public service a civic duty. |
| Compassion | I am rarely moved by the plight of the underprivileged. (Reversed)<br>Most social programs are too vital to do without.<br>It is difficult for me to contain my feelings when I see people in distress.<br>To me, patriotism includes seeing to the welfare of others.<br>I seldom think about the welfare of people whom I don't know personally. (Reversed)<br>I am often reminded by daily events about how dependent we are on one another.<br>I have little compassion for people in need who are unwilling to take the first step to help themselves.<br>There are few public programs I wholeheartedly support. (Reversed) |
| Self-Sacrifice | Making a difference in society means more to me than personal achievements.<br>I believe in putting duty before self.<br>Doing well financially is definitely more important to me than doing good deeds. (Reversed)<br>Much of what I do is for a cause bigger than myself.<br>Serving citizens would give me a good feeling even if no one paid me for it.<br>I feel people should give back to society more than they get from it.<br>I am one of those rare people who would risk personal loss to help someone else.<br>I am prepared to make enormous sacrifices for the good of society. |

[a]"Reversed" indicates items that express the opposite of the concept being measured, as a way of varying the pattern of questions and answers. The respondent should disagree with such statements if they are good measures of the concept. For example, a person high on the compassion dimension should disagree with the statement, "I am rarely moved by the plight of the underprivileged."

*Source:* Perry, 1996.

accounts for motivational processes in government and voluntary organizations. He contends that such a theory must include four domains of critical variables that he elaborates in the article: sociohistorical context, motivational context, individual characteristics, and behavior.

But PSM involves additional dimensions. It appears to vary over time, with changes in the public image of government service, and to take different forms in different agencies and service areas. It is an elusive topic for analysis. Sociologists who have studied the altruistic motivations of civil rights workers found that these people have trouble putting into words the motives behind the sacrifices they make and the risks they take (Demerath, Marwell, and Aiken, 1971). Public managers' references to their own service motives often take a similarly diffuse form. Although complex, these motivations need more attention from managers and researchers. The constraints on extrinsic incentives in government jobs make intrinsic and public service incentives even more important, in part because managers have some influence over them (Cohen and Eimicke, 1995; Romzek, 1990).

Development of the concept of PSM takes on more importance in light of recent evidence linking it to other important factors in public organizations. Brewer and Selden (1998) analyzed the results of a large survey of federal employees about whistle-blowing (exposing wrongdoing), conducted by the U.S. Merit Systems Protection Board (MSPB). They found more public service–related motives among employees who engaged in whistle-blowing than among those who did not, especially when the whistle-blowers perceived the wrongdoing as a threat to the public interest. Naff and Crum (1999) found that the respondents to another large MSPB survey who expressed higher levels of PSM expressed higher job satisfaction, had higher performance ratings from their supervisors, and otherwise expressed more positive attitudes toward their work. Alonso and Lewis (2001), analyzing the results of two surveys of very large samples of federal employees, also found that one of the surveys indicated that employees with higher levels of PSM received higher performance ratings from their supervisors. Complicating matters, however, the other survey showed a negative relationship between the supervisor's performance ratings and the respondent's expression of PSM. Brewer, Selden, and Facer (2000) analyzed the responses concerning PSM from about seventy government employees and public administration students and concluded that the respondents fell into four categories of conceptions of public service: *Samaritans* express a strong motivation to help other people, *communitarians* are motivated to perform civic duties, *patriots* work for causes related to the public good, and *humanitarians* express a strong motivation to pursue social justice. This differentiation of conceptions of PSM makes the important point that PSM is likely to vary among individuals and organizations. Adding a distinctive contribution to this stream of research and theory, Francois (2000) has proposed a formal model that postulates that public sector organizational activities can operate as efficiently and effectively as private business organizations, where PSM acts as a basic incentive.

These studies vary in the way they conceive and measure PSM, and this accounts for some of the variations in their findings and directions. Still, the stream of research and theorizing has sufficient consistency and momentum to establish PSM as a viable topic in public administration as well as in related fields, as having significance and value in both research and practice.

In spite of the complexities in analyzing all the possible motives, values, and incentives in organizations, the research has produced evidence of their patterns among public sector employees and the differences between public sector and private sector employees. The evidence in turn suggests challenges for leaders and managers in the public sector. Even though many public employees may value intrinsic rewards and a sense of public service—often more highly than private sector employees value them—the next chapter describes some experts' concerns that the characteristics of the public sector context described in earlier chapters can impede leaders' effort to provide such rewards. Yet the next chapter and later ones also present examples of how public organizations and their leaders can and do provide rewarding experiences for employees and enhance their motivation. The next chapter also continues the analysis by examining theories that suggest how values and motives affect work motivation, techniques for increasing motivation, and other important work attitudes that are related to motivation.

CHAPTER TEN

# UNDERSTANDING PEOPLE IN PUBLIC ORGANIZATIONS

## Theories of Work Motivation and Work-Related Attitudes

Chapter Nine discussed motives, values, and incentives, which play essential roles in leadership, organizational culture, and employee motivation and performance. It also illustrated the complex array of values, motives, and incentives that researchers have identified. Both researchers and managers face the question of how these factors influence motivation. This chapter reviews the most prominent theories of motivation, which represent theorists' best efforts to explain motivation and to describe how it works. Some of the terms sound abstract, but the effort is quite practical—How do you explain the motivation of members of your organization and use this knowledge to enhance their motivation? No one has yet developed a conclusive theory of work motivation, but each theory provides important insights about motivation and can contribute to managers' ability to think comprehensively about it. The examples provided show that reforms in government have often revealed simplistic thinking about work motivation on the part of the reformers—thinking that could be improved by more careful attention to the theories described in this chapter.

Chapter Nine also pointed out that organizational behavior scholars now treat motivation as an umbrella term to refer to a set of attitudes and behaviors related to employee behavior, such as job satisfaction and organizational commitment. After reviewing the motivation theories, this chapter describes these important work-related attitudes.

This and the preceding chapter emphasize the complexity of motivation and the array of concepts and factors related to it because they reflect the state of our knowledge about these topics and the challenges that managers and scholars face in dealing with them. Managers and organizations invest heavily in efforts and procedures designed to motivate employees; this chapter briefly summarizes many of these techniques.

# Theories of Work Motivation

One way of classifying the theories of motivation that have achieved prominence is to distinguish between *content theories* and *process theories*. Content theories are concerned with analyzing the particular needs, motives, and rewards that affect motivation. Process theories concentrate more on the psychological and behavioral processes behind motivation, often with no designation of important rewards and motives. The two categories overlap, and the distinction need not be taken as confining. It serves largely as a way of introducing some of the major characteristics of the different theories.

## Content Theories

Exhibit 10.1 summarizes the needs, values, and incentives that play a part in prominent content theories of motivation. These theories go beyond the mere listing of factors that influence motivation (as did the theories described in Chapter Nine) to specify how such factors influence motivation.

*Maslow: Needs Hierarchy.* Abraham Maslow's theory of human needs and motives (1954), described in Chapters Two and Nine and in Exhibit 10.1, advanced some of the most widely influential ideas in social science. Contemporary scholars of work motivation do not accept the needs hierarchy as an adequate theory of motivation, but it contributed concepts that are now regarded as classic and continues to influence important intellectual developments (see, for example, Burns, 1978). Maslow's conception of self-actualization as the highest-order human need was his most influential idea. It has appealed widely to people searching for a way to express this ultimate human motive, to fulfill one's potential.

In later writings, Maslow (1965) further developed his ideas about self-actualization, going beyond the summary in Exhibit 10.1, and discussed the

## EXHIBIT 10.1. CATEGORIES OF NEEDS AND VALUES EMPLOYED IN SELECTED CONTENT THEORIES.

**Maslow's Needs Hierarchy (1954)**

*Physiological Needs:* Needs for relief from hunger, thirst, and fatigue and for defense from the elements

*Safety Needs:* Needs to be free of the threat of bodily harm

*Social Needs:* Needs for love, affection, and belonging to social units and groups

*Self-Esteem Needs:* Needs for sense of achievement, confidence, recognition, and prestige

*Self-Actualization Needs:* The need to become everything one is capable of becoming, to achieve self-fulfillment, especially in some area of endeavor or purpose (such as motherhood, artistic creativity, or a profession)

**Herzberg's Two-Factor Theory (1968)**

| *Hygiene Factors* | *Motivators* |
|---|---|
| Company policy and administration | Achievement |
| Supervision | Recognition |
| Relations with supervisor | The work itself |
| Working conditions | Responsibility |
| Salary | Growth |
| Relations with peers | Advancement |
| Personal life | |
| Relations with subordinates | |
| Status | |
| Security | |

**McClelland: Need for Achievement, Power, and Affiliation (1961)[a]**

*Need for Achievement:* The need for a sense of mastery over one's environment and successful accomplishment through one's own abilities and efforts; a preference for challenges involving moderate risk, clear feedback about success, and ability to sense personal responsibility for success. Purportedly stimulates and facilitates entrepreneurial behavior.

*Need for Power:* A general need for autonomy and control over oneself and others, which can manifest itself in different ways. When blended with degrees of altruism and inhibition, and low need for affiliation, can facilitate effectiveness at management.

*Need for Affiliation:* The need to establish and maintain positive affective relations, or "friendship" with others.

**Adams: The Need for Equity (1965)**

The need to maintain an equitable or fair balance between one's contributions to an organization and one's returns and compensations from it (determined by comparing the balance maintained by others to one's own); the need to feel that one is not overcompensated or undercompensated for one's contributions to the organization.

[a]McClelland and other researchers do not provide concise or specific definitions of the need concepts.

*Source:* Adapted from Rainey (1993).

relationship of this motive to work, duty, and group or communal benefits. Maslow was concerned that during the 1960s some psychologists interpreted self-actualization as self-absorbed concern with one's personal emotional salvation or satisfaction, especially through the shedding of inhibitions and social controls; he sharply rejected such ideas. Genuinely self-actualized persons achieve this ultimate state of fulfillment through hard work and dedication to a duty or mission that serves values higher than simple self-satisfaction, through work that benefits others or society. Genuine personal contentment and emotional salvation, he argued, are by-products of such dedication. In this later work, Maslow emphasizes that the levels of need are not separate steps from which one successively departs. Rather, they are cumulative phases of a growth toward self-actualization, a motive that grows out of the satisfaction of social and self-esteem needs and also builds on them.

Maslow's ideas have had a significant impact on many social scientists but have received little reverence from empirical researchers attempting to validate them. As described in Chapter Nine, researchers trying to measure Maslow's needs and test his theory have not confirmed a five-step hierarchy. Instead they have found a two-step hierarchy in which lower-level employees show more concern for material and security rewards, and higher-level employees place more emphasis on achievement and challenge (Pinder, 1998).

Critics also point to theoretical weaknesses in Maslow's hierarchy. Locke and Henne (1986) identify the dubious behavioral implications of Maslow's emphasis on need deprivation—that is, his contention that unsatisfied needs dominate behavior. Being deprived of a need does not tell a person what to do about it, and the theory does not explain how people know how to respond. Locke and Henne also complain that Maslow's concept of self-actualization is so hazy that it is hard to evaluate.

In spite of the criticisms, Maslow's theory has had a strong following among many other scholars and management experts. Maslow contributed to a growing recognition of the importance of motives for growth, development, and actualization among members of organizations. His ideas also influenced other developments in the social sciences and OB. For example, in a prominent book on leadership, James MacGregor Burns (1978) drew on Maslow's concepts of a hierarchy of needs and of higher-order needs such as self-actualization. Burns observed that transformational leaders—that is, leaders who bring about major transformations in society—do not engage in simple exchanges of benefits with their followers. Rather, they appeal to higher-order motives in the population, including motives for self-actualization that are tied to societal ends, involving visions of a society transformed in ways that fulfill such personal motives. As a political scientist, Burns concentrated on political and societal leaders, but writers on organizational leadership have acknowledged his influence on recent thought about transformational leadership in organizations (see Chapter Eleven). In addition, Maslow's work foreshadowed and helped to shape current discussions of organizational mission and culture, worker empowerment, and highly participative forms of management (see, for example, Block, 1987; Peters and Waterman, 1982; Lawler, 2000).

*McGregor: Theory X and Theory Y.* Douglas McGregor's ideas about Theory X and Theory Y (1960) also reflect the influence of Maslow's work and the penetration into management thought of an emphasis on higher-order needs. As described in Chapter Two, McGregor argued that industrial management in the United States has historically reflected the dominance of a theory of human behavior that he calls Theory X, which assumes that workers lack the capacity for self-motivation and self-direction and that managers must design organizations to control and direct them. McGregor called for wider acceptance of Theory Y, the idea that workers have needs like those Maslow described as higher-order needs—for growth, development, interesting work, and self-actualization. Theory Y should guide management practice, McGregor argued. Managers should use participative management techniques, decentralized decision making, performance evaluation procedures that emphasize self-evaluation and objectives set by the employee, and job enrichment programs to make jobs more interesting and responsible. McGregor's ideas offered only the rudiments of a theory, and researchers do not regard it as an adequately comprehensive theory of work motivation. Like Maslow's, however, McGregor's ideas have had profound effects on the theory and practice of management. Chapter Thirteen describes two examples of efforts to reform and change federal agencies that drew on McGregor's ideas about Theory Y.

*Herzberg: Two-Factor Theory.* Frederick Herzberg's two-factor theory (1968) also emphasized the essential role of higher-order needs and intrinsic incentives in motivating workers. From studies involving thousands of people in many occupational categories, he and his colleagues concluded that two major factors influence individual motivation in work settings. They called these factors *motivators* and *hygiene factors* (see Exhibit 10.1). Insufficient hygiene factors can cause dissatisfaction with one's job, but even when they are abundant they do not stimulate high levels of satisfaction. As indicated in Exhibit 10.1, hygiene factors are extrinsic incentives—including organizational, group, or supervisory conditions—or externally mediated rewards such as salaries. While hygiene factors can only prevent dissatisfaction, motivators are essential to increasing motivation. They include intrinsic incentives such as interest in and enjoyment of the work itself and a sense of growth, achievement, and fulfillment of higher-order needs.

Herzberg concluded that because motivators are the real sources of stimulation and motivation for employees, managers must avoid the negative techniques of controlling and directing employees and should instead design work to provide for the growth, achievement, recognition, and other elements people need, which are represented by the motivators. This approach requires well-developed job enrichment programs to make the work itself interesting and to give workers a sense of control, achievement, growth, and recognition, which produces high levels of motivation.

Herzberg's work sparked controversy among experts and researchers. He and his colleagues developed their evidence by asking people to describe events on the job that led to feelings of extreme satisfaction and events that led to extreme dissatisfaction. Most of the reports of great satisfaction mentioned intrinsic and growth factors. Herzberg labeled these motivators in part because the respondents often mentioned their connection to heightened motivation and better performance. Reports of dissatisfaction tended to concentrate on the hygiene factors.

Researchers using other methods of generating evidence did not obtain the same results, however (Pinder, 1998). Critics argued that when people are asked to describe an event that makes them feel highly motivated, they might hesitate to report such things as pay or an improvement in physical working conditions. Instead, in what social scientists call a social desirability effect, they might attempt to provide more socially acceptable answers. Critics also questioned Herzberg's conclusions about the effects of the two factors on individual behavior. These concerns about the limitations of the theory led to a decline in interest in it. Locke and Henne (1986), for example, found no recent attempts to test the theory and concluded that theorists no longer took it seriously. Nevertheless, the theory always receives attention in reviews of motivation theory because of its contribution to the stream of thought about restructuring work to make it interesting and to satisfy worker's needs for growth and fulfillment. While researchers have turned away from the theory because it does not provide a complete and well-validated explanation of motivation, its central theme contributes to the mainstream of current thinking about motivating people in organizations.

### McClelland: Needs for Achievement, Power, and Affiliation.

In its day, David McClelland's theory about the motivations for seeking achievement, power, and affiliation (friendly relations with others)—especially his ideas about the need for achievement—was one of the most prominent theories in management and OB. It elicited thousands of studies (McClelland, 1961; Locke and Henne, 1986). Need for achievement (*n Ach*), the central concept in his theory, refers to a motivation— a "dynamic restlessness" (McClelland, 1961, p. 301)—to achieve a sense of mastery over one's environment through success at achieving goals by using one's own cunning, abilities, and efforts. McClelland originally argued that *n Ach* was a common characteristic of persons attracted to managerial and entrepreneurial roles, although he later narrowed its application to predicting success in entrepreneurial roles (Pinder, 1998).

McClelland measured *n Ach* through a variety of procedures, including the Thematic Apperception Test (TAT). The TAT involves showing a standard set of pictures to individuals, who then make up brief stories about what is happening in each picture. One typical picture shows a boy sitting at a desk in a classroom reading a book. A respondent identified as low in *n Ach* might write a story about the boy daydreaming, while someone high in *n Ach* might write a story about the boy studying hard to do well on a test. Researchers have also measured *n Ach* through questionnaires that ask about such matters as work role preferences and the role of luck in outcomes.

McClelland (1961) argued that persons high in *n Ach* are motivated to achieve in a particular pattern. They choose fairly challenging goals with moderate risks, where outcomes are fairly clear and accomplishment reflects success through one's own abilities. Persons in roles such as research scientist, which requires waiting a long time for success and recognition, may have a motivation to achieve, but they do not conform to this pattern. As one example of the nature of *n Ach* motives, McClelland (1961) cited the performance of students in experiments in which they chose how to behave in games of skill. The researchers had the students participate in a ring-toss game. The participants chose how far from the target peg they would stand. The high–*n Ach* participants tended to stand at an intermediate distance from the peg, not too close but not too far away. McClelland interpreted this choice as a reflection of their desire to achieve through their own skills. Standing too close made success too easy and thus did not satisfy their desire for a sense of accomplishment and mastery. Standing too far away, however, made success a gamble, a matter of a lucky throw. The high–*n Ach* participants chose a distance that would likely result in success brought about by the person's own skills. McClelland also offered evidence of other characteristics of persons with high-*n Ach*, such as physical restlessness, particular concern over the rapid passage of time, and an aversion to wasting time.

McClelland claimed that measuring *n Ach* could determine the success of individuals in business activities and the success of nations in economic development (McClelland, 1961; McClelland and Winter, 1969). He analyzed the achievement orientation in the folktales and children's stories of various nations and produced some evidence that cultures high in *n Ach* themes also showed higher rates of economic development. He has also claimed successes in training managers in business firms in less developed countries to increase their *n Ach* and enhance the performance of their firm (McClelland and Winter, 1969). McClelland suggested achievement-oriented fantasizing and thinking as a means to improving the economic performance of nations. Others have also reported the use of achievement motivation training with apparent success in enhancing motivation and increasing entrepreneurial behaviors (Miner, 1980, p. 67).

McClelland (1975) later concluded that *n Ach* encouraged entrepreneurial behaviors rather than success in managerial roles. He argued, however, that his conceptions of the needs for power and affiliation did apply in predicting success in management roles (although there is much less empirical research about these needs to support his claims). McClelland concluded that the most effective managers develop high motivation for power, but with an altruistic orientation and a concern for group goals. This stage also involves a low need for affiliation, however, because too strong a need for friendship with others can hinder a manager.

Reviewers vary in their assessments of the state of this theory. Some rather positive assessments (Miner, 1980) contrast with others that focus only brief attention on it (Pinder, 1998) or criticize it harshly. Locke and Henne (1986) condemn the body of research on the theory as chaotic. They say that the status of the theory has become confused since McClelland narrowed the focus of *n Ach* to entrepreneurial behaviors, but most of the huge set of empirical studies of the theory have not focused on entrepreneurs. One finds little very recent research on the theory in major management or organizational journals.

Regardless of its prestige among scholars, this theory adds another important element to a well-developed perspective on motivation. Individuals vary in the general level and pattern of internal motivation toward achievement and excellence that they bring to work settings. These differences suggest the importance of employee selection in determining the level of motivation in an organization.

***Equity Theory.*** J. Stacy Adams (1965) argued that a sense of equity in contributions and rewards has a major influence on work behaviors. A sense of inequity brings discomfort, and people therefore act to reduce or avoid it. They assess the balance between their inputs to an organization and the outcomes or rewards they receive from it, and they perceive inequity if this balance differs from the balance experienced by other employees. For example, if another person and I receive the same salary, recognition, and other rewards, yet I feel that I make a superior contribution by working harder, producing more, or having more experience, I will perceive a state of inequity. Conversely, if the other person makes superior inputs but gets lower rewards than I get, I will perceive inequity in the opposite sense; I will feel overcompensated.

In either case, according to Adams, a person tries to eliminate such inequity. If people feel overcompensated, they may try to increase their inputs or reduce their outcomes to redress the inequity. If they feel undercompensated, they will do the opposite, slowing down or reducing their contributions. Adams advanced specific propositions about how workers react that depend on factors such as whether they receive hourly pay or are paid according to their rate of production. For example, he predicted that if workers are overpaid on an hourly basis, they will produce more per hour, to reduce the feeling that they are overcompensated. If they are overpaid on a piece-rate basis, however, they will slow down, to avoid making more money than other workers.

These sorts of predictions have received some confirmation in laboratory experiments. The theory proves difficult to apply in real work settings, however, because it is hard to measure and assess inequity, and some of the concepts in the theory are ambiguous (Miner, 1980). People vary in their sensitivity to inequity, and they may vary widely in how they react to the same conditions.

While this specific theory has not held up well, equity in contributions and rewards figures very importantly in management. As described later, more recent models of motivation include perceptions about equity as important components. Equity issues also play a role in debates about civil service reforms and performance-based pay plans in the public sector. Governments at all levels in the United States and in other countries have tried to adopt performance-based pay plans (Ingraham, 1993; Kellough and Lu, 1993). Supporters of such plans have often cited equity principles akin to those stressed in this theory. They have argued that people who perform better than others but receive no better pay perceive inequity and experience a loss of morale and motivation, and that the highly structured pay and reward systems in government tend to create such situations (Schay, 1988). More recently, the drive to implement pay-for-performance plans in government has slowed (Gore, 1993), and the more recently popular alternative involves "broadbanding" or "paybanding" systems. In these systems, a larger number of pay grades and pay steps within those grades are collapsed into broader bands or categories of pay levels. Better performers can be more rapidly moved upward in pay within these bands, rather than having to go through the previous, more elaborate set of grades and steps one at a time. People promoting and designing these plans also point to pay equity as a major justification for such plans. For example, the Internal Revenue Service implemented a carefully developed paybanding system for their middle managers, in part because some of these managers had commented in focus group sessions that they felt demoralized when they worked and tried very hard but received the same pay raises as other managers who did so little that they were "barely breathing" (Thompson and Rainey, 2003).

Equity theory has influenced a recently developing stream of research on justice in organizations (Rainey, 1997; Greenberg and Cropanzano, 2001). This research examines employees' perceptions of *distributive justice* in organizations, or the fairness and equity in distribution of rewards and resources, and of *procedural justice*, or the fairness with which people feel they and others are treated in organizational processes such as decision making that affects them, layoffs, or disciplinary actions. For example, are they given a chance to comment or have hearings about such decisions? Generally, researchers have found that perceptions of higher levels of justice in organizations tend to relate to positive work-related attitudes such as work satisfaction and satisfaction with supervision and leadership. Kurland and Egan (1999) compared perceptions of organizational justice on the part of public employees in two city agencies to those of employees in seven business firms. The public employees perceived lower levels of procedural and distributive justice than the private employees did. For the public employees, higher levels of perceived distributive and procedural justice were related to higher satisfaction with supervisors. For the private employees, only higher levels of procedural justice were related to higher satisfaction with supervisors. Lee and Shin (2000), conversely, compared employees in public and private R&D organizations in Korea, and found no differences between the two groups in perceptions of procedural justice, but the public employees perceived less distributive justice in relation to pay. More research along these lines with larger samples will be interesting and valuable, although it will be ironic if the civil service procedures that purportedly protect government employees do not serve to heighten their sense of procedural justice in their organizations. More research would support the analysis of why this might be the case.

For most managers, trying to ensure that people feel they are rewarded fairly in comparison to others is a major responsibility and challenge. A manager often finds it easier to rely heavily on the most energetic and competent people than to struggle with the problem of dealing with less capable or less enthusiastic ones. If a manager cannot or does not appropriately reward those on whom he or she places heavier burdens, these more capable people can become frustrated. Managers in government organizations commonly complain that the highly structured reward systems in government aggravate this problem. In work groups and team-based activities, too, the problem of a team member's not contributing as well as others can raise tensions. The OB literature does contain questionnaires for assessing fairness and equity to help in confronting such problems (Gordon, 2002, p. 135). Many of the motivational techniques described later in this chapter, and the leadership and cultural issues discussed in the next chapter, pertain to the challenge of maintaining equity in the work setting.

## Process Theories

Process theories emphasize how the motivational process works. They describe how goals, values, needs, or rewards operate in conjunction with other factors to determine motivation. The content factors—the particular needs, rewards, and so on—are not specified in the theories themselves.

## Expectancy Theory

Expectancy theory states that an individual considering an action sums up the values of all the outcomes that will result from the action, with each outcome weighted by the probability of its occurrence. The higher the probability of good outcomes and the lower the probability of bad ones, the stronger the motivation to perform the action. In other words, the theory draws on the classic utilitarian idea that people will do what they see as most likely to result in the most good and the least bad.

Although the theory draws on classic utilitarian ideas, it has assumed an important role in contemporary OB theory. Vroom (1964) stated the theory formally, with algebraic formulas (see Figure 10.1). The formula expresses the following idea: the force acting on an individual and causing him or her to work at a particular level of effort (or to choose to engage in a particular activity) is a function of the sum of the products of the perceived desirability of the outcomes associated with working at that level (or the *valences*) and the *expectancies* for the outcomes. Expectancies are the person's estimates of the probability that the expected outcomes will follow from working at a particular level. In other words, multiply the value (positive or negative) of each outcome by the expectancy (perceived probability) that it will occur, and sum these products for all the outcomes. A higher sum reflects higher expectancies for more positively valued outcomes and should predict higher motivation.

Researchers originally hoped that this theory would provide a basis for the systematic research and diagnosis of motivation: ask people to rate the positive or negative value of important outcomes of their work and the probability that desirable work behaviors would lead to those outcomes or avoid them, and use the expectancy formula to combine these ratings. They hoped that this approach would improve researchers' ability to predict motivational levels and analyze good and bad influences on them, such as problems due to beliefs that certain outcomes

## FIGURE 10.1. FORMULATIONS OF EXPECTANCY THEORY.

### A Formulation Similar to Vroom's Early Version

$$F_i = \Sigma(E_{ij}V_j)$$

where  $F$ = the force acting on an individual to perform act $i$

$E$ = the expectancy, or perceived probability, that act $i$ will lead to outcome $j$

$V$ = the valence of outcome $j$

and

$$V_j = \Sigma(V_k I_{jk})$$

where  $V$ = the valence of outcome $j$

$I$ = the instrumentality of outcome $j$ for the attainment of outcome $k$

$V$ = the valence of outcome $k$

### A Formulation Similar to Various Revised Formulations

Motivation = $f[EI \times EII(V)] = f[(E \rightarrow P) \times [(P \rightarrow O)(V)]]$

where  $EI = (E \rightarrow P)$ = expectancy I, the perceived probability that a given level of work effort will result in a given level of performance

$EII = (P \rightarrow O)$ = expectancy II, the perceived probability that the level of performance will lead to the attainment of outcome $j$

$V$ = the valence of outcome $j$

*Source:* Adapted from Rainey, 2000.

were unattainable or that certain rewards offered little value. A spate of empirical tests soon followed, with mixed results. Some of the studies found that the theory failed to predict effort and productivity. Critics soon began to point out weaknesses in the theory (Campbell and Pritchard, 1983; Pinder, 1998, pp. 351–359). They complained that it did not accurately represent human mental processes, because it assumed that humans make exhaustive lists of outcomes and their likelihoods and sum them up systematically. Researchers found it difficult to list on a questionnaire all the possible outcomes important to people in an organization and to measure their valences.

Nevertheless, expectancy theory still stands as one of the most prominent work motivation theories, and researchers have continued to propose various improvements on it (Evans, 1986). More recent versions relax the mathematical formula and simply state that motivation depends generally on the positive and negative values of outcomes and their probabilities, in ways we cannot precisely specify (see Figure 10.1). Some of these more recent forms of the theory have broken down the concept of expectancies into two types, as illustrated in the figure. Expectancy I (EI) perceptions reflect an individual's beliefs about the likelihood that effort will lead to a particular performance level. Expectancy II (EII) perceptions reflect the perceived probability that a particular performance level leads to a given level of reward. The distinction helps to clarify some of the components of motivational responses. For example, the Performance Management and Recognition System (PMRS), one of the many pay-for-performance plans adopted by governments during the 1980s, applied to middle managers in federal agencies (General Schedule salary levels 13–15). Under PMRS, a manager's superior would rate the manager's performance on a five-point scale, and the manager's annual salary increase would be based on that rating. PMRS got off to a bad start in many federal agencies, however. In some agencies, the vast majority of the managers received very high performance ratings and their EI perceptions strengthened. It became clear that they had a high likelihood of performing well enough to receive a high rating. Yet about 90 percent of the managers in some agencies received pay raises of 3 percent or less, and fewer than 1 percent received pay raises of as much as 10 percent. EII perceptions, then, naturally weaken. One may expect to perform well enough to get a high rating (EI), but performance at that level may not lead to a high probability of getting a significant reward (EII). PMRS, like many other performance-based pay plans in government, applies expectancy theory implicitly but fails to do so adequately (Perry, 1986; Perry, Petrakis, and Miller, 1989). Soon after its introduction, PMRS was canceled. The fundamental problem persists, moreover, in performance evaluation systems in the public and private sectors. During 2002, Kay Cole James, head of the U.S. Office of Personnel Management (OPM), repeatedly pointed out that about 90 percent of the members of the Senior Executive Service (SES) received the highest performance ratings. (The SES consists of the highest ranks of career executives in the U.S. federal civil service.) Ms. James called on the executives who made these ratings to accept more responsibility for making distinctions among the performance levels of the people they evaluated.

Some recent versions of the theory also draw in other variables. They point out, for example, that a person's self-esteem can affect EI perceptions. Organizational characteristics and experiences, such as the characteristics of the pay plan or the perceived equity of the reward system, can influence EII perceptions—as in the PMRS case. Some of the most recent versions bring together expectancy concepts with ideas about goal setting, control theory, and social learning theory, discussed in the following sections (Klein, 1989). These examples show how recent formulations of the theory provide useful frameworks for analyzing motivational plans and pinpointing the sources of problems.

*Expectancies as Dependent Variables.* In spite of the controversies over the theory, researchers and management consultants have used expectancy-type questions as dependent variables. Individuals' beliefs about the relationship between performance and pay and about job security, promotion, and other incentives often show significant relationships to other important attitudes, such as work satisfaction and self-reported work effort. Researchers use EI scales with items regarding beliefs about the relationship between effort and performance, asking whether effort will lead to high-quality and high-quantity output. For example, one item asks for agreement or disagreement with the statement "Trying as hard as I can leads to high-quality output." EII items ask about the link between performance and rewards, for example, "Producing a high-quality output increases my chances for promotion." Other EII items ask about the relationship of quantity, quality, and timeliness of output to rewards such as promotion, higher pay, job security, and recognition.

*Expectancy Theory and Public Organizations.* The PMRS and pay-for-performance examples show why expectancy theory has had important applications in the public sector. It has served as the implicit theoretical underpinning for reforms of many civil service and other government pay systems. In addition, expectancy questions of the sort just described have been used in major surveys of government employees that were intended in part as a means to evaluate some of the reforms (U.S. Office of Personnel Management, 1979, 1980, 1983). As described shortly, these and other surveys using expectancy items have found some consistent distinctions between public sector and private sector incentive structures (Rainey, Pandey, and Bozeman, 1995; Rainey, Facer, and Bozeman, 1995).

## Operant Conditioning Theory and Behavior Modification

Another body of research that has influenced motivation theory and practice and that has implications similar to those of expectancy theory applies operant conditioning and behavior modification concepts to the management of employees. This approach draws on the theories of psychologists such as B. F. Skinner, who argued that we can best analyze behavior by studying the relationships between observable behaviors and contingencies of reinforcement.

The term *operant conditioning* stems from a revision Skinner (1953) and others made to older versions of stimulus-response psychology. Skinner pointed out that we animals do not develop behaviors simply in response to stimuli. We emit behaviors as well, and those behaviors operate on our environment, generating consequences. We repeat or drop behaviors depending on the consequences. We acquire behaviors or extinguish them in response to the conditions or contingencies of reinforcement.

A reinforcement is an event that follows a behavior and changes the probability that the behavior will recur. (We might call this a reward or punishment, but Skinner apparently felt that the term *reinforcement* was a more objective one, because it assumes less about what goes on inside the subject.) Learning and motivation depend on *schedules* of reinforcements, referring to how regularly they follow a particular behavior. For example, a manager can praise an employee every time he or she does good work, such as completing a task on time, or the manager can praise the behavior once out of every several times it occurs. According to the operant conditioning perspective, such variations make a lot of difference.

Operant theory derives from what psychologists have called the *behaviorist* school of psychology. Behaviorism gained its label because it emphasizes observations of the overt behaviors of animals and humans without hypothesizing about what goes on inside them. In a classic debate in psychology, some theorists (the precursors to the expectancy theorists) argued that motivation and learning theories should refer to what goes on inside the organism. Behaviorists, such as Skinner, rejected the use of such internal constructs, arguing that because one cannot observe them scientifically, they can only add confusing speculation to the analysis of motivation. Skinner argued that one can scientifically analyze only those behaviors that are overtly observable. As described later, in recent years psychologists have worked toward reconciling operant behaviorism with cognitive concepts (Kreitner and Luthans, 1987; Pinder, 1998, p. 443; Bandura, 1978, 1997).

Skinner and other behaviorists analyzed relationships between reinforcements and behaviors and developed principles related to various types and schedules of reinforcement. For example, Skinner pointed out that a subject acquires a behavior more rapidly under a constant reinforcement schedule, but the behavior will extinguish (stop occurring) faster than one brought about using a variable-ratio schedule. Accordingly, the behaviorists would suggest that constant praise by the manager might have more immediate effects on the employee than intermittent praise, but the effects would fall off rapidly if the manager stopped the constant praise. Intermittent praise might be slower to take effect, but it would last longer. Behaviorists also point out that positive reinforcement works better than negative reinforcement or punishment. Exhibit 10.2 summarizes the concepts and principles from this body of theory.

*Behavior modification* refers to techniques that apply principles of operant conditioning to modify human behavior. The term apparently comes from the way in which the behaviorists studied the principles of reinforcement, by modifying and shaping behaviors. They would, for example, develop a behavior by reinforcing small portions of it, then larger portions, and so on, until they developed the full behavior (for example, inducing an anorexic patient to eat by first reinforcing related behaviors such as picking up a fork, and then eating a small amount, and so on). Behavior modification has come to refer broadly and somewhat

## EXHIBIT 10.2. CONCEPTS AND PRINCIPLES
## OF OPERANT CONDITIONING.

### Types of reinforcement

*Positive reinforcement:* Increasing a behavior by providing a beneficial stimulus, contingent on workers' exhibiting that behavior. Example: An agency director announces that she will reward her assistant directors in their performance appraisals for their efforts to help their subordinates with professional development. She praises and rewards those efforts in the appraisals. As a result, the assistant directors devote even more attention to their subordinates' professional development.

*Negative reinforcement:* Decreasing behavior by removing or withholding an aversive stimulus (withholding punishment). Example: A supervisor stops reprimanding an employee for arriving late when the employee arrives on time; the probability increases that the employee will thereafter arrive on time.

*Operant extinction:* The result of withholding or removing a positive reinforcement. Example: A new agency director replaces the one described above and ignores the assistant directors' efforts at promoting their subordinates' professional development. As a result, the assistant directors reduce their efforts.

*Punishment:* Application of an aversive stimulus to reduce occurrence of a behavior. Example: Docking the pay of a habitually late worker.

### Schedules of reinforcement

*Fixed schedule:* Applies the reinforcement on a regular basis or after a fixed period of time or a fixed number of occurrences of the behavior.

*Variable schedule:* Varies the time period or number of repetitions.

*Ratio schedule:* Applies reinforcements according to a designated ratio of reinforcements to responses, such as once for every five occurrences.

*Interval schedule:* Applies reinforcement after a designated time interval.

### These categories can be combined

A fixed-interval schedule—a weekly paycheck.
A variable-interval schedule—a bonus every so often.
A fixed-ratio schedule—piece-rate pay scales.
A variable-ratio schedule—intermittent praise for a behavior.

### Selected principles of reinforcement

Positive reinforcement provides the most efficient means of influencing behavior. Punishment is less efficient and effective in shaping behavior (Skinner, 1953).

A low-ratio reinforcement schedule—reinforcement after each occurrence of a behavior, for example—produces rapid acquisition of the behavior but more rapid extinction when the reinforcement stops.

Intermittent reinforcement, especially in highly variable intervals or according to a variable-ratio schedule (reinforcement after long, varying periods or after varied numbers of occurrences), requires more time for behavior acquisition, but extinction occurs more slowly when the reinforcements cease.

vaguely to a wide variety of techniques for changing behaviors, such as programs for helping people to stop smoking. Some of these techniques adhere closely to behaviorist principles; others may have little to do with them. Behavior modification practitioners claimed successes in psychological therapy, improvement of student behavior and performance in schools, supervision of mentally retarded patients, and rewarding the attendance of custodial workers (Bandura, 1969; Sherman, 1990). Many organizations, including public ones such as garbage collection services, have adopted variants of these techniques to improve performance and productivity.

As these examples show, managers and consultants have applied behavior modification techniques in organizations. The ideas about intermittent schedules just mentioned and noted in Exhibit 10.2, for example, lead some behavior modification proponents (Kreitner and Luthans, 1987) to prescribe such managerial techniques as not praising a desired behavior constantly. They advise praise on a varying basis, after a variable number of repetitions of the behavior. They might also prescribe periodic bonuses to supplement a worker's weekly paycheck, arguing that the regular check will lose its reinforcing properties over time but the bonuses will act as variable-interval reinforcements, strengthening the probability of sustained long-term effort. They have also offered useful suggestions about incremental shaping of behaviors by reinforcing successively larger portions of a desired behavior.

These kinds of prescriptions provide examples of those offered by practitioners of organizational behavior modification (OB Mod). OB Mod often involves this approach:

1. Measure and record desirable and undesirable behaviors, to establish baselines.
2. Determine the antecedents and consequences of these behaviors.
3. Develop strategies for using reinforcements and punishments—such as praise and pay increases—to change the behaviors.
4. Apply these strategies, following the reinforcement schedules mentioned earlier.
5. Assess the resultant behavioral change.

A number of field studies of such projects have reported successes in improving employee performance, attendance, and adherence to safety procedures (Pinder, 1998, pp. 432–443). A highly successful effort by Emery Air Freight, for example, received widespread publicity (Kreitner and Luthans, 1987). The project involved having employees monitor their own performance, setting performance goals, and using feedback and positive reinforcements such as praise and time off.

Yet controversy over explanations of the success of this project reflects more general controversies about OB Mod. Critics have argued that the success of the

Emery example, as well as other applications of OB Mod, was not the result of their using operant conditioning principles. They succeeded, according to the critics, because they included such steps as setting clear performance goals and making rewards contingent upon them (Locke, 1977). Therefore, the critics contend, these efforts do not offer any original insights derived from OB Mod. One might draw similar conclusions from expectancy theory, for example. Other criticisms focus on the questionable ethics of the emphasis on manipulation and control of people. Also, behavior modification and OB Mod appear to be most successful in altering relatively simple behaviors amenable to clear measurement. Even then, the techniques often involve practical difficulties, because of all the measuring and reinforcement scheduling required.

For their part, proponents of OB Mod, and behavior modification more generally, point to the successes of the techniques. They counter attacks on the ethics of their approach by arguing that they cut through a lot of obfuscating fluff about values and internal states and move right to the issue of correcting bad behaviors and augmenting good ones. ("Do you want smokers to be able to stop, anorexics to eat, and workers to follow safety precautions, or do you not?") Similarly, OB Mod advocates claim that their approach succeeds in developing a focus on desired behaviors (getting the filing clerk to come to work on time), as opposed to making attributions about attitudes ("The filing clerk has a bad attitude"), and an emphasis on strategies for positive reinforcement of desired behaviors (Kreitner and Luthans, 1987; Stajkovic and Luthans, 2001).

## Social Learning Theory

Social learning theory reflects both the limitations and the value of operant conditioning theory and OB Mod. Developed by psychologist Albert Bandura (1978, 1989, 1997) and others, social learning theory—and later, "social cognitive theory" (Bandura, 1986)—blends ideas from operant conditioning theory with greater recognition of internal cognitive processes such as goals and a sense of self-efficacy, or personal effectiveness. It gives attention to forms of learning and behavior change that are not tightly tied to some external reinforcement.

For example, individuals obviously learn by modeling their behaviors on those of others and through vicarious experiences. Humans also use anticipation of future rewards, mental rehearsal and imagery, and self-rewarding behaviors (such as praising oneself) to influence their behavior. Applications of such processes in organizational settings have included frameworks for developing leadership and self-improvement, and studies have suggested that the sorts of techniques just mentioned can improve performance. For example, Sims and Lorenzi (1992) proposed models and methods for motivating oneself and others through self-management that make use of some of the techniques just suggested—such as setting goals for oneself and developing the capacity of others to set their own goals, developing self-efficacy in oneself and others, and employing modeling and self-rewarding behaviors (such as self-praise). Sims and Lorenzi propose that this approach can support the development of more decentralized, participative, empowering leaders and teamwork processes in organizations.

## Goal-Setting Theory

Psychologist Edwin Locke and his colleagues have advanced a theory of goal setting that has been very successful in that it has been solidly confirmed by well-designed research (Pinder, 1998, pp. 365–383; Locke, 2000; Locke and Latham, 1990a). The theory simply states that difficult, specific goals lead to higher performance than easy goals, vague goals, or no goals (for example, "Do your best"). Difficult goals enhance performance by directing attention and action, mobilizing effort, increasing persistence, and motivating the search for effective performance strategies. Commitment to the goals and feedback about progress toward achieving them are also necessary for higher performance. Commitment and feedback do not by themselves stimulate high performance without difficult, specific goals, however. Research findings also indicate that while participation in setting a goal does not enhance commitment to it, expecting success in attaining the goal does enhance commitment. As the value of the goal increases, commitment to the goal increases. If money is contingent on the goal, that may lead to the setting of higher goals and to higher goal commitment. Individual differences also show strong relationships to the effectiveness of goal setting.

Locke and Latham (1990b) contend that assigning difficult, specific goals enhances performance because of the goals' influence on an individual's personal goals and his or her self-efficacy. Self-efficacy refers to a person's sense of his or her capability or effectiveness in accomplishing outcomes (Bandura, 1989). Assigned goals influence personal goals through a person's acceptance of and commitment to them. They influence self-efficacy by providing a sense of purpose and standards for evaluating performance, and they create opportunities for accomplishing lesser and proximal goals that build a sense of self-efficacy (Earley and Lituchy, 1991).

Although many studies support this theory, another reason for its success may be its compactness and relatively narrow focus (Pinder, 1998). The theory and much of the research that supports it concentrate on task performance in clear and simple task settings, which is amenable to the setting of specific goals. Also, a few studies have examined complex task settings (Locke and Latham, 1990a). However, some of the prominent contributions to organization theory in recent decades, such as the contingency theory and garbage can models of decision making (described in previous chapters), have emphasized that in many situations clear, explicit goals are quite difficult to specify. This suggests that in many of the most important settings, such as high-level strategy development teams, clear, specific goals may be impossible, or even dysfunctional. Similarly, precise goals can raise potential problems for public organizations, given their complex goal sets. Nevertheless, this body of research emphasizes the value of clear goals for work groups. Whether or not it applies precisely to higher-level goals for public agencies, developing reasonably clear goals remains one of the major responsibilities and challenges for public executives and managers. The literature on public management now offers numerous examples of leaders in public agencies who have developed effective goals (Behn, 1994; DiIulio, 1990; Moore, 1990; Allison, 1983). In addition, Wright (2001) has proposed a model of the motivation of government employees that emphasizes both goal-setting theory and social learning theory. He has also reported results of a survey of state government employees in New York State that show relations between goal concepts such as greater work goal clarity and self-reported work motivation (Wright, forthcoming).

# Recent Directions in Motivation Theory

As mentioned earlier, no theory has provided a conclusive general explanation of work motivation, and reviewers tend to agree that motivation theory is in a disorderly state (Landy and Becker, 1987; Locke, 1999; Pinder, 1998, pp. 466–472; Katzell and Thompson, 1990). Some theorists are calling for the development of separate theories to apply to different settings or dependent variables. Pinder (1998, p. 469) argues that the effort to develop and evaluate the existing motivation theories as general, universal theories is fruitless. He proposes the development of "middle range" theories that apply to limited combinations of people and situations. This would involve the development of a taxonomy of motivational settings (the motivational attributes of a work setting), combined with a taxonomy of motivational types (the motivation-related attributes of individuals in a work group), and the development of the middle-range theories to be applied within such categories. Similarly, Landy and Becker (1987) reject the quest for a universal theory and contend that the existing theories should be treated as theories that apply to different combinations from a set of dependent variables (choice, effort, satisfaction, performance, and withdrawal).

Others have tried to integrate some of the theories just described (Katzell and Thompson, 1990). There has been a good deal of attention to the integration of goal-setting theory and expectancy theory (Evans, 1986; Klein, 1989; Landy and Becker, 1987; Locke and Latham, 1990b), sometimes including other theories, such as control theories. Klein (1990) proposes a feasibility theory of motivation—emphasizing the availability of resources for task performance—that brings in need theory and draws on expectancy theory. Because of the success of goal-setting theory, there has been a strong trend toward including goal-related concepts in theories and integrating them with other cognitive concepts, such as those from social learning theory (Bandura, 1997; Pervin, 1989; Locke and Latham, 1990a, 1990b). For the time being, however, motivation theory remains a body of interesting and useful but partial efforts to apprehend a set of phenomena too complex for any single theory to capture.

## Motivation Practice and Techniques

The state of motivation theory just described confronts both managers and researchers with the problem of what to make of it. The theorists lament their inability to provide a universal, conclusive work motivation theory, but that is quite a demanding standard. As illustrated earlier by the use of expectancy theory to analyze the PMRS, the individual theories provide useful frameworks for thinking about motivation and trying to lead and manage it. Taken together, they make up a broader, looser, but still valuable framework for analyzing motivational issues in practical settings. The content theories remind us of the importance of intrinsic incentives and equity and provide concepts for expressing them. This may seem obvious enough, but civil service and pay reforms in government in the last several decades have concentrated heavily on extrinsic incentives, to the virtual exclusion of the intrinsic incentives the content theorists emphasize.

Expectancy and operant conditioning theories emphasize an analysis of what is rewarded and punished in organizations and work settings. Kerr (1989), in an article now considered a classic, pointed out that leaders in organizations very frequently fail to reward the behaviors they say they want and in fact reward those they say they do not want. The theories just discussed provide concepts and suggestions for analyzing such reward practices. The theories direct attention to rewards and disincentives rather than to dubious assumptions or attributions about a person's reasons for behaving as he or she does.

Also, in spite of the travails of the theorists, organizations need motivated members, and they address this challenge in numerous ways. Exhibit 10.3 provides a description of many of the general techniques used to motivate employees, several of which have a large literature devoted to them. Real-world practice often loosely reflects theory, stressing pragmatism instead. Far from making theory irrelevant, however, the practices of organizations often justify the apparently

## EXHIBIT 10.3. METHODS COMMONLY USED TO ENHANCE WORK MOTIVATION IN ORGANIZATIONS.

*Improved performance appraisal systems.* Reforms involving the use of group-based appraisals (ratings for a work group rather than an individual), or appraisals by a member's peers.

*Merit pay and pay-for-performance systems.* A wide variety of procedures for linking a person's pay to his or her performance.

*Broadbanding or paybanding pay systems.* Pay systems in government and other settings have often had numerous pay grades and pay steps within those grades. A person would move step-by-step up these categories, usually moving only one step per year. Broadbanding systems collapse many of these steps and grades into broader "bands" or ranges of pay. This enables a supervisor to move a well-performing person to a higher pay level, faster.

*Bonus and award systems.* One-time awards for instances of excellent performance or other achievements.

*Profit-sharing and gain-sharing plans.* Sharing profits with members of the organization (usually possible only in business organizations, for obvious reasons). Employee stock owner-ship plans are roughly similar, providing a means of rewarding employees when the organization does well.

*Participative management and decision making.* These involve a sustained commitment to engage in more communication and sharing of decisions, through teams, committees, task forces, general meetings, open-door policies, and one-to-one exchanges.

*Work enhancement: job redesign, job enlargement, and rotation.* Usage varies, but job redesign usually means changing jobs to enhance control and interest for the people doing the work. Job enlargement, or "horizontal loading," involves giving employees a greater variety of tasks and responsibilities at the same skill level. Job restructuring, or "vertical loading," involves giving employees more influence over decisions normally made by superiors, such as work scheduling, or, more generally, enlarging employees' sense of responsibility by giving them control of a complete unit of work output (for example, having work teams build an entire car or having caseworkers handle all the needs of a client). These approaches may involve job sharing and rotation among workers and various team-based approaches.

*Quality of Work Life (QWL) programs and Quality Circles (QCs).* Organizations of all types have tried QWL programs, which typically involve efforts to enhance the general working environ-ment of an organization through representative committees, surveys and studies, and other procedures designed to improve the work environment. Quality circles, used successfully in Japanese companies, are teams that focus directly on improving the quality of work processes and products.

---

obvious advice of the theorists and experts, because organizations frequently have trouble achieving desirable motivational strategies on their own (Kerr, 1989). For example, surveys find that fewer than one-third of employees in organizations feel that their pay is based on performance (Katzell and Thompson, 1990). As illustrated in the earlier example about PMRS, these techniques often involve im-plicit motivational assumptions and theories that could be improved through more careful analysis.

## Incentive Structures and Reward Expectancies in Public Organizations

The challenge of tying rewards, especially extrinsic rewards, to performance is even greater in many public organizations than it is in private ones. Chapter Eight described numerous studies that demonstrate that organizations under government ownership usually have more highly structured, externally imposed personnel procedures than private organizations have. The civil service systems and centralized personnel systems in government jurisdictions apparently account for these effects.

Of course, public organizations also vary among themselves in how much such systems affect them. The U.S. General Accounting Office, for example, has a relatively independent personnel system and uses a pay-for-performance plan. Government enterprises often have greater autonomy in their personnel procedures than typical government agencies. In demonstration projects, some government agencies have adopted pay-for-performance plans (Schay, 1988) and paybanding systems (Thompson and Rainey, 2003), with apparent success. Debate continues over whether pay constraints are an inherent feature of government (Gabris, 1987; Ingraham, 1993). Significantly, the Civil Service Reform Act of 1978 (Pfiffner and Brook, 2000) sought to loosen the constraints on pay and other personnel rules and procedures in the federal government, but then about fifteen years later the Clinton Administration's National Performance Review (Gore, 1993) launched still another initiative to decentralize federal personnel rules, including those governing pay and other incentives. The U.S. Office of Personnel Management (2001) has for years sought to provide flexibilities in the rules and procedures of the federal system, yet federal managers still call for more of them (Rainey, 2002). Nevertheless, the evidence indicates that at present public organizations more often have more formalized, externally imposed personnel systems than private organizations do.

This evidence of more formalized personnel rules does not in itself prove that people in public organizations perceive them as such. Chapter Eight also described surveys revealing that public managers, in comparison to their private sector counterparts, report more formalized personnel procedures and greater structural constraints on their authority to administer extrinsic rewards such as pay, promotion, and discipline, and to base these on performance (Rainey, Facer, and Bozeman, 1995; U.S. Office of Personnel Management, 1979, 1980, 1983; Elling, 1986). Recently, Ban (1995) reported on extensive interviews with federal managers; again, they consistently described the federal personnel rules and procedures as constraining and cumbersome.

The perceptions of the public managers in these studies may reflect shared stereotypes. Business managers may have personnel problems that are just as serious as those faced by public sector managers, despite the stereotype of a stronger relationship between rewards and performance in private business than in government. Interestingly, the OPM has issued a report about a study that found no evidence that federal agencies have lower discharge rates than private firms, and little evidence that an inordinate number of poor performers remain employed in the federal service. Even if that is the case, these findings indicate that the perception among public managers of having greater difficulty with such matters currently forms part of the culture at all levels of government in the United States.

The existence of formalized personnel systems and managers' perceptions of constraints under them do not prove that public employees see no connection between extrinsic rewards and their performance. For years, expert observers (Thompson, 1975) have pointed out that some public managers find ways around formal constraints on rewards by isolating poor performers, giving them undesirable assignments, or establishing linkages between rewards and performance in other ways. Ban (1995) describes how managers in different federal agencies respond differently to the federal personnel rules depending on the culture of the agency. In some agencies the managers resist the strictures of the rules more aggressively and try to manipulate them in constructive ways. In other agencies the managers abide more strictly by the rules.

Nevertheless, a number of surveys have indicated that public employees perceive weaker relationships among performance and pay, promotion, and disciplinary action than private employees do (Porter and Lawler, 1968; Rainey, 1979, 1983; Lachman, 1985; Rainey, Traut, and Blunt, 1986; Solomon, 1986; Coursey and Rainey, 1990). These studies used expectancy-theory questionnaire items about such relationships and found that public sector samples rated them as weaker. Similarly, the OPM (U.S. Office of Personnel Management, 1979) surveys found that sizable percentages of federal employees feel that pay, promotion, and demotion do not depend on performance. Again, these results may reflect shared stereotypes. In fact, there are some conflicting findings. Analysts in the OPM compared results from their survey question about pay and performance to results from a similar item on a large survey of private sector workers; they found little difference in the percentages of employees who expect to get a pay raise for good performance.

## Self-Reported Motivation Among Public Employees

The reforms of the civil service system and numerous writers on public organizations assume that these differences in incentive structure diminish motivation among public employees. One can more readily make that claim than prove it. As noted earlier, organizational researchers have difficulty measuring motivation. A few studies have compared public and private managers and employees on scales of self-reported motivation, however, and have found no large differences. Rainey (1979, 1983), using the Patchen scales described in Chapter Nine, found no differences in self-reported motivation between middle managers in public and private organizations. Virtually all of the public and private managers said they work very hard. Baldwin (1990) also found no difference in self-reported motivation between groups of public and private managers. Rainey (1983) found no difference in responses to expectancy items about the connection between performing well and intrinsic incentives such as the feeling of accomplishing something worthwhile, although the public managers perceived stronger connections between performance and the sense of engaging in a meaningful public service. Bozeman and Loveless (1987) reported somewhat higher levels of positive work climate in public R&D labs than in private labs. Wright's (forthcoming) study of the motivation of state government employees did not compare them with private sector respondents, but the level of self-reported motivation they expressed clearly indicated that they claim to work very hard. Brehm and Gates (1997) also analyzed surveys of government employees of various types and found that they reported that they work hard and that their supervisors tended to agree. In addition, the very large surveys of public employees and managers mentioned earlier found that they report high levels on measures related to motivation. They report very high work effort, a strong sense of challenge in their job, a strong sense of their organization's being important to them, high ratings of their organization's effectiveness, and high general work satisfaction (National Center for Productivity and Quality of Working Life, 1978; U.S. Office of Personnel Management, 1979; U.S. Merit Systems Protection Board, 1987).

Similarly, in spite of the stereotype of the cautious government bureaucrat (Downs, 1967; Warwick, 1975), public managers have claimed in response to surveys that they feel open to change and to new ways of doing things (Rainey, 1983). Many federal employees express skepticism about prospects for changing their organization, but most federal managers and executives (65 to 75 percent) see change as possible (U.S. Office of Personnel Management, 1979). Bellante and Link (1981) report a study showing that more risk-averse people join the public sector. Their measures of risk aversion, however, included smoking and drinking less, using automobile seat belts, and having higher medical and automobile insurance coverage. These could just as well serve as indicators of the sort of dutiful, public service–oriented, somewhat ascetic individuals suggested in studies of work-related values (Kilpatrick, Cummings, and Jennings, 1964; Sikula, 1973a) and do not themselves indicate aversion to professional and managerial risks. Golembiewski (1985; Golembiewski, Proehl, and Sink, 1981) reviewed 270 organizational development efforts in public organizations and concluded that more than 80 percent of them were apparently successful. Bozeman and Kingsley (1998) found no differences between managers in public and private organizations in their perceptions of the degree to which the leaders of the organization engaged in risk taking and encouraged a risk-taking culture (although they did find that more managers perceived that political influence on their organizations from elected officials diminished the risk-taking orientation in both types of organizations). Roessner (1983) noted scant evidence concerning the comparative innovativeness of public and private organizations but found no indication of private sector superiority in rates of diffusion of technological innovations. Light's (2002a) comparison of survey responses of federal employees to those of private sector employees appears to illustrate some of the complications in coming to conclusions about innovativeness and receptivity to change among government employees. The federal employees were more likely than their private sector counterparts to express pessimism about whether their organizations encouraged risk taking, about whether they trusted their organizations, about the morale of their coworkers, and about whether their job was a dead end. At the same time, they were just as likely as the private sector respondents to express satisfaction with the chance to accomplish something worthwhile, and more likely to say that they would choose to work in the same sector if they had the choice. These results appear to indicate that working in government often involves many frustrations and constraints of the sort discussed in earlier sections and chapters, but it also involves intrinsic rewards and other encouragements that lead many of the people in public service to continue to cope with the frustrations, to seek improvements and accept changes, and to devote effort and energy to their tasks and missions.

Self-reports about one's efforts and about these other factors have obvious limitations. The research indicates, nevertheless, that although many public employees and managers perceive relatively weak connections between performance and extrinsic rewards such as pay and promotion, they report attitudes and behaviors consistent with high motivation.

## Other Motivation-Related Work Attitudes

As noted earlier, motivation as a general topic covers numerous dimensions, including a variety of work-related attitudes such as satisfaction, commitment, involvement, and professionalism. Motivational techniques often aim at enhancing these attitudes as well as work effort. Researchers have developed many of these concepts about work attitudes, often distinguishing them from motivation in the sense of work effort. Increasingly, in the United States and in other nations, business, government, and nonprofit organizations have concerned themselves with encouraging their employees' positive work-related attitudes and with conducting surveys of them (Brief, 1998; Gallup Organization, 2003; U.S. Office of Personnel Management, 2003). As described in the discussion of the Balanced Scorecard in Chapter Six, some government agencies regularly measure the work satisfaction of their people. In 1999, the Department of Defense conducted a huge survey of the work satisfaction and other work attitudes of active duty military personnel (U.S. General Accounting Office, 2000).

These work-related attitudes have importance in their own right, but they are also interesting because researchers have used some of them to compare public and private managers. The following sections define and discuss major concepts of work attitudes, then later sections describe the research on their application in the public sector and in comparisons to the private sector.

*Job Satisfaction.* Thousands of studies and dozens of different questionnaire measures have made job satisfaction one of the most intensively studied variables in organizational research, if not the most studied. Job satisfaction concerns how an individual feels about his or her job and various aspects of it (Gruneberg, 1979), usually in the sense of how favorable—how positive or negative—those feelings are. Job satisfaction is often related to other important attitudes and behaviors, such as absenteeism, the intention to quit, and actually quitting.

Years ago, Locke (1983) pointed out that researchers had published about 3,500 studies of job satisfaction without coming to any clear agreement on its meaning. Job satisfaction nevertheless continues to play an important role in recent research (Cranny, 1992). The different ways of measuring job satisfaction illustrate different ways of defining it. Some studies use only two or three summary items, such as the following:

- In general, I like working here.
- In the next year I intend to look for another job outside this organization.

General or global measures ask questions about enjoyment, interest, and enthusiasm to tap general feelings in much more depth. They often employ multiple-item scales, with the responses to be summed up or averaged, such as the following from the Minnesota Satisfaction Questionnaire (Weiss, Dawis, England, and Lofquist, 1967):

- I definitely dislike my work [reversed scoring].
- My job is pretty uninteresting [reversed scoring].
- I feel happier in my work than most other people.
- I find real enjoyment in my work.
- Most days I am enthusiastic about my work.

Specific, or facet, satisfaction measures ask about particular facets of the job. The following examples are from Smith's Index of Organizational Reactions (1976):

*Supervision:* "Do you have the feeling you would be better off working under different supervision?"

*Company identification:* "From my experience, I feel this organization probably treats its employees _____" [five possible responses, from "poorly" to "extremely well"].

This index also includes scales for kind of work, amount of work, coworkers, physical work conditions, financial rewards, and career future. Porter's Needs Satisfaction Questionnaire (1962) asks respondents to rate thirteen factors concerned with fulfillment of a particular need, rating how much of each factor there is now and how much there should be. The degree to which the "should be" rating exceeds the "is now" rating measures need dissatisfaction, or the inverse of satisfaction. The following are examples of the items included:

*Security needs:* "The feeling of security in my management position."

*Social needs:* "The opportunity, in my management position, to give help to other people."

*Self-actualization needs:* "The opportunity for personal growth and development in my management position."

Porter's questionnaire, which is not used very frequently anymore, employs categories based on Maslow's needs theory. Some of the research on public sector work satisfaction described later used this method.

*Determinants of Job Satisfaction.* Different measures of job satisfaction use different definitions of it, and this complicates the research on the topic. Different studies using different measures—and hence different definitions—often come to conflicting conclusions about how job satisfaction is related to other variables. Partly because of these variations, researchers do not agree on a coherent theory or framework of what determines job satisfaction. Research generally finds higher job satisfaction associated with better pay, sufficient opportunity for promotion, consideration from supervisors, recognition, good working conditions, and utilization of skills and abilities. Even so, some studies report contradictory findings for almost any possible determinant.

This situation actually makes sense, because it is obviously unrealistic to try to generalize about how much any single factor affects a worker's satisfaction. Any particular factor in a given setting contends with other factors in that setting. Various studies suggest the importance of individual differences between workers: level of aspiration, level of comparison to alternatives (whether the person looks for or sees better opportunities elsewhere), level of acclimation (what a person is accustomed to), educational level, level in the organization and occupation, professionalism, age, tenure, race, gender, national and cultural background, and personality (values, self-esteem, and so on). The influence of any one of these elements, however, depends on other factors. For example, tenure and organizational level usually correlate with satisfaction. Those who have been in an organization longer and are at a higher level report higher satisfaction. This makes sense. Unhappy people leave; happy people stay. People who get to higher levels should be happier than those who don't. Yet some studies find the opposite. In some organizations, longer-term employees feel undercompensated for their long service. Some people at higher levels may feel the same way or may feel that they have hit a ceiling on their opportunities. Career civil servants sometimes face this problem (Rainey, 1983).

Researchers also look at job characteristics and job design as determinants of job satisfaction. The most prominent approach, by Hackman and Oldham (1980), also draws on Maslow's need-fulfillment theory. These researchers report higher job satisfaction for jobs higher on the dimensions measured by their Job Diagnostic Survey, which includes the following subscales: skill variety, task identity, task significance, autonomy, feedback from the job, feedback from agents, and dealing with others. Hackman and Oldham's findings conform to a typical position among management experts, that more interesting, self-controlled, significant work, with feedback from others, improves satisfaction.

Besides looking at the person and the job, researchers have analyzed factors extrinsic to the work itself: pay, promotion, job security, supervision, work-group characteristics, participation in plans and decisions, and organizational structure and climate. These factors often influence satisfaction, but they too depend on the other factors in a given setting.

*Consequences of Job Satisfaction.* Controversy also persists regarding the consequences of job satisfaction. For years authors regularly pointed out that job satisfaction showed no consistent relationship to individual performance (Pinder, 1998). They typically cited Porter and Lawler's interpretation of this evidence (1968), which pointed out that good performance is just as likely to lead to higher satisfaction as satisfaction is likely to lead to better performance. A good performer who receives better rewards as a result of his or her good performance experiences heightened satisfaction. Yet a good performer who doesn't get better rewards experiences dissatisfaction, thus dissolving any positive link between satisfaction and performance. The link between performance and rewards, they concluded, plays a key role in determining the performance-satisfaction relationship. Though many individual studies have reported weak relationships between satisfaction and performance, some meta-analytical studies—analyses of many studies to look for general trends in their results—suggest that the relationship of job satisfaction to performance is generally stronger than this typical interpretation suggests (Petty, McGee, and Cavender, 1984).

Researchers have also pointed out that satisfaction shows fairly consistent relationships with absenteeism and turnover. These behaviors cost organizations a lot of money, so because satisfaction helps to explain them, they are important variables. Although fairly consistent, these relationships have not proved extremely strong either. Obviously, practical factors such as health and family problems influence these behaviors. Satisfaction shows a stronger relationship with the expressed intention of turnover, but this does not always predict turnover very well.

In spite of these complexities, job satisfaction figures very importantly in organizations. Distinct from motivation and performance, it can nevertheless influence them, as well as other important behaviors, such as turnover and absenteeism. Some studies have also found work satisfaction to be related to life satisfaction and physical health (Gruneberg, 1979).

*Role Conflict and Ambiguity.* In an influential book published some years ago, Kahn and his colleagues (1964) argue that characteristics of an individual's role in an organization determine the stress that the employee experiences in his or her work. These ideas about organizational role characteristics do not currently appear to be attracting much research attention, but they are relevant and interesting to anyone working in an organization or profession. A number of "role senders" seek to impose expectations and requirements on the person through both formal and informal processes. These role senders might include bosses, subordinates, coworkers, family members, or anyone else who seeks to influence the person's role. If these expectations are ambiguous and conflicting, the stress level increases. Other researchers later developed questionnaire items to measure role conflict and role ambiguity (Rizzo, House, and Lirtzman, 1970; House and Rizzo, 1972). Role ambiguity refers to a lack of necessary information at a given organizational position. The role ambiguity questionnaire asks about clarity of objectives, responsibilities, amount of authority, and time allocation in the person's job. Role conflict refers to the incompatibility of different role requirements. A person's role might conflict with his or her values and standards or with his or her time, resources, and capabilities. Conflict might exist between two or more roles that the same person is expected to play. There might be conflict among organizational demands or expectations, or conflicting expectations from different role senders. The survey items on role conflict ask whether there are adequate labor and other resources to carry out assignments, whether others impose incompatible expectations, and whether the respondent has to buck roles in order to carry out assignments.

The two role variables consistently showed relationships to job satisfaction and some similar measures, such as job-related tension (Miles and Petty, 1975; Miles, 1976), but they were not so consistently related to measures of job performance (Schuler, 1977, p. 164). They also showed a relationship to a number of other organizational factors, such as participation in decision making, leader behaviors, and formalization. Individual characteristics such as need for clarity and perceived locus of control (whether the individual sees events as being under his or her control or as being controlled externally) also influence how much role conflict and ambiguity a person experiences. These concepts are important by themselves, because managers increasingly concern themselves with stress management and time management. Managing one's role can play a central part in these processes. In addition, however, research on public managers has also employed role questionnaires.

***Job Involvement.*** In observing increasingly technical, professional, and scientific forms of work, researchers find differences among individuals in their involvement in their work. For some people, especially advanced professionals, work plays a very central part in their lives. Researchers measure job involvement by asking people whether they receive major life satisfaction from their jobs, whether their work is the most important thing in their life, and similar questions. Job involvement is distinct from general motivation and satisfaction but resembles intrinsic work motivation (Cook, Hepworth, Wall, and Warr, 1981). It figures importantly in the work attitudes of highly professionalized people who serve in crucial roles in many organizations. The concept has also played an interesting role in the research on public managers, as described shortly.

***Organizational Commitment.*** The concept of organizational commitment has also figured in research on public and private managers (discussed later in this chapter). Individuals vary in their loyalty and commitment to the organizations in which they work. Certain people may consider the organization itself to be of immense importance to them, as an institution worthy of service, as a location of friends, as a source of security and other benefits. Others may see the organization only as a place to earn money. Professionals such as doctors, lawyers, and scientists often have loyalties external to the organization—to the profession itself and to their professional colleagues.

Scales for measuring organizational commitment ask whether the respondent sees the organization's problems as his or her own, whether he or she feels a sense of pride in working for the organization, and similar questions (Mowday, Porter, and Steers, 1982). Studies also show the complex, multidimensional nature of commitment. For example, Angle and Perry (1981) show the importance of the distinction between *calculative commitment* and *normative commitment* to organizations. Calculative commitment is based on the perceived material rewards the organization offers. In normative commitment, the individual is committed to the organization because he or she sees it as a mechanism for enacting personal ideals and values.

Balfour and Wechsler (1996) further elaborated the concept of organizational commitment in a model for the public sector based on a study of public employees. Their evidence suggested three forms of commitment. *Identification commitment* is based on the employee's degree of pride in working for the organization and on the sense that the organization does something important and does it competently. *Affiliation commitment* derives from a sense of belonging to the organization and of the other members of the organizations as "family" who care about one another. *Exchange commitment* is based on the belief that the organization recognizes and appreciates the efforts and accomplishments of its members. Balfour and Wechsler's study contributes to an interesting stream of research and thought on public organizations, to which we will return later (Cho and Lee, 2001; Fletcher and Williams, 1996; Moon, 2000; Steinhaus and Perry, 1996; Zaffane, 1994). In addition, we will return to the point that their study and others suggest ways that public sector leaders and managers can enhance commitment and other work experiences in their organizations.

**Professionalism.** For years, sociological researchers have studied the way in which highly trained specialists control complex occupations. Technological advances have made certain valuable types of work increasingly complex and difficult to apprehend. Specialists in these areas must have advanced training and must maintain high standards. Only specialists, however, have the qualifications to establish and police the standards. From the point of view of society and of large organizations, these factors raise problems involving monopolies, excessive self-interest, and mixed loyalties. Government and business organizations also face challenges in managing the work and careers of highly trained professionals.

Researchers have offered many definitions of the term *profession*, typically including these elements:

- Application of a skill based on theoretical knowledge
- Requirement for advanced education and training
- Testing of competence through examinations or other methods
- Organization into a professional association

- Existence of a code of conduct and emphasis on adherence to it
- Espousal of altruistic service

Occupational specializations that rate relatively highly on most or all of these dimensions are highly "professionalized." Medical doctors, lawyers, and highly trained scientists are usually considered advanced professionals without much argument. Scholars usually place college professors, engineers, accountants, and sometimes social workers in the professional category. Often they define less-developed specializations, such as library science and computer programming, as semiprofessions, emerging professions, or less professionalized occupations.

In turn, management researchers analyze the characteristics of individual professionals, because they play key roles in contemporary organizations. They point out that, as a result of their selection and training, professionals tend to have certain beliefs and values (Filley, House, and Kerr, 1976):

- Belief in the need to be expert in the body of abstract knowledge applicable to the profession
- Belief that they and fellow professionals should have autonomy in their work activities and decision making
- Identification with the profession and with fellow professionals
- Commitment to the work of the profession as a calling, or life's work
- A feeling of ethical obligation to render service to clients without self-interest and with emotional neutrality
- A belief in self-regulation and collegial maintenance of standards (that is, a belief that fellow professionals are best qualified to judge and police one another)

Members of a profession vary on these dimensions. Those relatively high on most or all are highly professional by this definition.

The characteristics of professions and professionals may conflict with the characteristics of large bureaucratic organizations. Belief in autonomy may conflict with organizational rules and hierarchies. The situation at the Brookhaven National Laboratory described at the beginning of Chapter Eight is an example of such conflict. The scientists chaffed under the new rules and procedures imposed upon them by administrators seeking to enhance safety and public accountability. Emphasis on altruistic service to clients can conflict with organizational emphases on cost savings and standardized treatment of clients. Identification with the profession and desire for recognition from fellow professionals may dilute the impact of organizational rewards, such as financial incentives and organizational career patterns. Professionals might prefer an enhanced professional reputation to salary increases, and they might prefer their professional work to moving "up" into management.

Without moving up, however, they hit ceilings that limit pay, promotion, and prestige. Some studies in the past have found higher organizational formalization associated with higher alienation among professionals (Hall, 2002).

Conflicts between professionals and organizations do not appear to be as inevitable as once supposed, however. Certain bureaucratic values, such as emphasis on the technical qualifications of personnel, are compatible with professional values (Hall, 2002). For example, professionals may approve of organizational rules on qualifications for jobs. Professionals in large organizations may be isolated in certain subunits, such as laboratories, where they are relatively free from organizational rules and hierarchical controls (Larson, 1977; Bozeman and Loveless, 1987; Crow and Bozeman, 1987). Certain professionals, such as engineers and accountants, may want to move up in organizations in nonprofessional roles (Schott, 1978; Larson, 1977). Some empirical studies have found that, for some professionals, professional commitment is positively correlated with organizational commitment (Bartol, 1979). Golden (2000) describes how professionals in certain federal agencies during the Reagan administration disagreed with many of the policies of the Reagan appointees who headed their agency, but regarded it as their professional obligation to discharge those policies effectively, once they were decided and established. Berman (1999) found no major differences in the levels of professionalism expressed by public, private, and nonprofit managers, although he found indications of differences in the contexts that influence their professional orientations. This conception of professionalism among managers differs from the concept of highly professional occupations such as law and medicine, but Berman's finding makes the point, as do Brehm and Gates (1997), that professionalism can be an important motivating factor among many managers and employees in the public sector.

Management writers offer some useful suggestions about the management of professionals. They prescribe dual career ladders, which add to the standard career path for managers another for professionals, so that professionals can stay in their specialty (research, legal work, social work) but move up to higher levels of pay and responsibility. This relieves the tension over deciding whether one must give up one's profession and go into management. Some organizations rotate professionals in and out of management positions. The U.S. Geological Survey has a policy of rotating geologists in administrative positions back into professional research positions after several years. Some organizations also allow professionals to take credit for their accomplishments. For example, they allow them to claim authorship of professional research reports rather than requiring that they publish them anonymously in the name of the agency or company. Organizations can also pay for travel to professional conferences and in other ways support professionals in their desire to remain excellent in their field.

Researchers have not reported much research comparing professionals in the public and private sectors. Typically they treat issues involving professionals as generic, crossing the sectors. Government agencies have many professional employees, however, and a particular profession dominates many government agencies (Mosher, [1968] 1982), so the issues figure importantly in public management. For example, the Volcker Commission (1989) reported that the federal government faces grave difficulties in attracting highly qualified professionals because the private sector offers them such higher salaries. Conversely, work settings for some professionals in government appear to offer equal or superior intrinsic incentives. As noted earlier, Bozeman and Loveless (1987) found that public sector R&D labs have more positive work climates than private labs. Many public managers face a challenge in providing intrinsic incentives that can compete with the superior salaries available to some professionals in the private sector (Romzek, 1990).

## Motivation-Related Variables in Public Organizations

Researchers have made comparisons on a number of these variables between public and private samples, shedding some light on how the two categories compare.

***Role Ambiguity, Role Conflict, and Organizational Goal Clarity.*** For some work-related attitudes, researchers have found few differences between managers in public and private organizations. This has been the case with the most frequent observation in all the literature on the distinctive character of public management: public managers confront greater multiplicity, vagueness, and conflict of goals and performance criteria than managers in private organizations do (Rainey, 1989). These observations about vague, multiple goals in the public sector bear on classic questions about social control through politics or through markets (Lindblom, 1977). There is a fascinating divergence between political economists and organization theorists on the observations' validity. Political scientists and economists tend to regard this goal complexity as an obvious consequence or determinant of governmental (nonmarket) controls, while many organization theorists tend to regard it as a generic problem facing all organizations.

Beyond the observations of experienced executives, however, strikingly little comparative research directly addresses this issue. Rainey (1983) compared middle managers in government and business organizations about the role conflict and role ambiguity items described earlier, asking questions about the clarity of the respondents' goals in work, conflicting demands, and related matters. The government and business managers showed no differences on these questions nor on questions about whether they regarded the goals of their organization as clear and easy to measure. More recent surveys have confirmed these results (Bozeman and

Rainey, 1998; Rainey, Pandey, and Bozeman, 1995). One explanation may be that public managers clarify their roles and objectives by reference to standard operating procedures, whether or not the overall goals of the organization are clear and consistent. In addition, when researchers ask managers to describe their decision-making criteria, private managers mention financial performance criteria much more frequently than public managers do (Solomon, 1986; Schwenk, 1990).

The real issue, then, may not be whether managers perceive that goals are clear but rather what criteria and processes they use to clarify their goals, as well as just how valid those criteria are as sound measures of performance. Whatever the explanation, these limited findings point to important challenges for both researchers and practitioners in further analyzing such issues as how managers in various settings (public, private, and hybrid organizations) perceive objectives and performance criteria; how these objectives and criteria are communicated and validated, if they are; and whether these objectives and criteria do in fact coincide with the sorts of distinctions between public and private settings that are assumed to exist in our political economy. Wright (forthcoming) reports evidence that state government employees who perceive greater clarity of work and organizational goals also report higher levels of work motivation, so the frequent generalizations about vague goals in public organizations do not mean that leaders and managers in government cannot and should not continue efforts to clarify goals for organizational units and employees (see also Fletcher and Williams, 1996).

***Work Satisfaction.*** Many studies have found differences between respondents from the public and private sectors concerning other work-related attitudes and perceptions. In the United States and some other nations where such studies have been conducted, public employees and managers express high levels of general work satisfaction and other general attitudes about work, such as avoiding alienation and having a sense of worthwhile work, usually comparable to that reported by their private sector counterparts (Bozeman and Rainey, 1998; Cho and Lee, 2001; Davis and Ward, 1995; Gabris and Simo, 1995; Kilpatrick, Cummings, and Jennings, 1964; Light, 2002a; U.S. Office of Personnel Management, 1979, 2003). Some of these studies have found that public sector respondents express higher levels of satisfaction with certain facets of work, such as health benefits and job security. Large-scale surveys have shown that younger members of the public sector workforce show higher levels of general work satisfaction than younger private sector workers do (Steel and Warner, 1990) and that persons entering the public sector workforce are higher on certain measures of quality than entry-level private sector employees (Crewson, 1995a).

However, numerous studies across several decades that compared the work satisfaction of public and private sector employees, especially at managerial levels, have reported somewhat lower satisfaction among public sector employees in various specific facets of work (Buchanan, 1974; Bogg and Cooper, 1995; Bordia and Blau, 1998; Hayward, 1978; Kovach and Patrick, 1989; Lachman, 1985; Light, 2002a; Paine, Carroll, and Leete, 1966; Porter and Lawler, 1968; Rhinehart and others, 1969; Rainey, 1983; Solomon, 1986). These studies used different measures of satisfaction and varied samples, and this makes it hard to generalize about them. For example, Paine, Carroll, and Leete (1966) and Rhinehart and his colleagues (1969) found that groups of federal managers showed lower satisfaction than business managers on all categories of the Porter Needs Satisfaction Questionnaire, described earlier. Smith and Nock (1980), conversely, analyzing results of a large social survey, found that public sector blue-collar workers show more satisfaction with most aspects of their work than their private sector counterparts, but public sector white-collar workers show less satisfaction with coworkers, supervisors, and intrinsic aspects of their work. Hayward (1978) compared employees and managers in a diverse group of public and private organizations and found that satisfaction ratings were generally high among both groups. The public sector respondents, however, gave somewhat more unfavorable ratings concerning their job overall, their ability to make necessary decisions, the adequacy of the supplies in their organization, the amount of duplication with which they have to contend, and the amount of work they are expected to do. Rainey (1983) found that state agency managers scored lower than business managers on their satisfaction with promotion opportunities and with coworkers. Light (2002a) found that federal employees express higher satisfaction than private sector employees with job security and benefits and with the ability to accomplish something worthwhile, but the federal employees were lower on satisfaction with the public's respect for their work, with the extent to which their jobs were dead-end jobs, and with the degree to which they can trust their organizations. Illustrating the complications that can arise from changes in context, in contrast to Light's finding about the federal employees' sense that the public does not respect their work, Cho and Lee (2001) reported that in their Korean sample the public managers perceived higher levels of prestige in their jobs than did the private sector managers.

The findings of these studies vary a great deal and are not easily summarized. The public and private responses often did not differ greatly, yet it is hard to dismiss as accidental the consistent tendency of the public managers and employees to score lower on various satisfaction scales. Taken together, these studies reveal comparable levels of general or global satisfaction among respondents from the public and private sectors. The studies also indicate lower satisfaction with various intrinsic and extrinsic aspects of work in many public organizations than exists in many private ones. Some of the findings appear to reflect the sorts of administrative constraints described earlier—personnel system constraints (promotion and pay) and purchasing constraints (supplies). Others appear to reflect related frustrations with administrative complexities and complex political and policymaking processes, public sector realities that diminish some intrinsic rewards. The findings suggest that many public sector employees show high levels of satisfaction in their work, comparable to those of employees in the private and nonprofit sectors, and comparable or higher levels of satisfaction with certain facets of work, such as benefits and security, and sometimes with a sense that their work is important and socially valuable. Where public employees tend to express lower satisfaction with facets of work, they tend to be concerned over frustrating administrative and political constraints and complexities, and over certain extrinsic factors, such as constraints on pay and promotion.

***Organizational Commitment and Job Involvement.*** As mentioned earlier, there has been an interesting stream of research related to the topic of organizational commitment and job involvement in public organizations, much of it based on comparisons of public and private managers and employees. The research has produced some indications of particular frustrations in the public service. As with other topics, such as motivation and work satisfaction, however, the evidence is somewhat conflicting and complicated and leads us back to the conclusion that public organizations and managers may face particular challenges, but the situation in the public sector is not necessarily dire. The research further provides suggestions of approaches for public managers to take, and indications that public organizations and managers can take them effectively.

The stream of research began with studies by Buchanan (1974, 1975), who found that groups of federal executives expressed lower organizational commitment and job involvement than executives from private firms. He concluded that the public managers felt less commitment because they did not feel as strong a sense of having a personal impact on the organization, because the organization did not expect as much commitment, and because their work groups were more diverse and less of a source of attachment to the organization. Buchanan also suggested that the lower involvement scores indicated a frustrated service ethic, and he expressed concern that it reflected weak public service motivation on the part of the public managers. His evidence showed that the involvement responses resulted from a sense of holding a less challenging job, of working in less cohesive groups, and of having more disappointing experiences in the organization than the managers had expected when they joined it. These disappointments, he thought, might arise when idealistic, service-oriented entrants confront the realities of large government agencies, where they feel they have little impact.

More recently, Flynn and Tannenbaum (1993) also reported a study in which a sample of public managers expressed lower organizational commitment than a

sample of private sector managers. The public managers were lower on their ratings of the clarity, autonomy, and challenge of their jobs. Their lower scores on
clarity and autonomy appeared to be the strongest influences on their lower commitment scores. Brown (1996) conducted a meta-analysis of job involvement studies and found a modest relationship between employment in the public or private
sector and job involvement. For public sector respondents, several determinants
of job involvement, such as the job's motivating potential, pay satisfaction, and
participative decision making, were weaker. Moon (2000) reported survey results
in which a sample of public managers expressed lower organizational commitment than a sample of managers in private business.

Though they have not measured organizational commitment directly, other
studies and observations have indicated similar general characteristics of the public
sector work context. Boyatzis (1982) drew a conclusion similar to Buchanan's from
his comparisons of public and private managers, and Chubb and Moe (1990) found
a generally lower perceived sense of control and commitment among staff members and teachers in public schools than among their private school counterparts.

Case observations paint a similar picture. Michelson (1980) described examples of hardworking bureaucrats in "nonworking" bureaucracies. They work hard,
he observes, but the diffuse goals and haphazard designs of some programs make
their efforts futile. Cherniss (1980) observed that many public service professionals experience stress and burnout as a result of their frustrated motivation to help
their clients and because of the bureaucratic systems that aggravate their frustrations. Downs's observations about discouraged statesmen and increasing con-
servatism (1967), described in Chapter Nine, and Warwick's description of the
State Department (1975) have similar implications.

The large federal surveys mentioned earlier have also found a combination
of positive attitudes and frustration or discouragement among public employees.
The overwhelming majority of respondents to the federal employee attitude survey (U.S. Office of Personnel Management, 1979) said they feel that they do meaningful work, that what happens in their organization is important, and that their
organization performs effectively. Yet high percentages of these employees (more
than 45 percent), managers (35 percent), and executives (25 percent) expressed
concern that employees feel they cannot trust the organization. Many employees
expressed a sense of powerlessness and a lack of influence and participation in decision making (U.S. Office of Personnel Management, 1979, p. 36). In another
large survey, only a limited number of respondents felt that the opportunity to
have an impact on public affairs represents an important reason to stay in public
service (U.S. Merit Systems Protection Board, 1987). As described earlier, Light
(2002a) also reported survey results showing that federal employees, compared to
private business employees, expressed a mix of positive attitudes along with indi-

cations of fairly high levels of frustration or discouragement with certain facets of their work and work setting.

These research findings and observations support Buchanan's interpretation of well-motivated people encountering frustrations. Other studies, however, have found that public employees were not necessarily lower on organizational commitment (Balfour and Wechsler, 1990, 1991). Steinhaus and Perry (1996) analyzed data from a major national survey, the 1991 General Social Survey, and found that public sector employees showed no significant difference from private sector employees on a measure of organizational commitment. They found that the industry in which a person was employed predicted organizational commitment better than whether the person worked in the public or private sector. They concluded that a public versus private dichotomy is too simple a distinction for analyzing organizational commitment.

These mixed results raise some important challenges for public sector managers and researchers alike. First, they emphasize the intriguing and important question of whether all the assertions about the context of public organizations reviewed in earlier chapters influence an important variable like organizational commitment. The studies that found a public-private difference concentrated on managers, whereas those that did not, such as the Steinhaus and Perry study (1996), looked at all levels together, or mostly at nonmanagerial employees. This pattern suggests that the constraints and interventions that impinge on public organizations may have their greatest influence at managerial levels. The pattern of evidence also raises doubts about Buchanan's concerns about weakened motivation in government agencies. As noted in Chapter Nine, public service motivation is not the same as organizational commitment and job involvement. Public managers and employees may show lower scores on organizational commitment, for example, because they feel strongly committed to serving clients or to more general societal values and missions and do not regard the organization itself as the most important object of pride and loyalty (Romzek and Hendricks, 1982). In addition, the next chapter and Chapter Fourteen describe the growing body of work on highly committed administrative leaders and professionals in government (DiIulio, 1994; Riccucci, 1995). Low scores on commitment questions may reflect problems but not necessarily weak public service motives or low levels of general motivation and effort.

The evidence suggests that there are problems in the public sector, but public sector managers and employees do not show sharply lower levels of organizational commitment, work satisfaction, or other important attitudes. Where public managers and employees do show lower scores on organizational commitment, the responses appear to be linked to aspects of the public sector environment discussed in earlier chapters, such as constraining rules, complex goals, political intervention, turnover, and uncertainty. Surveys that find lower levels of organizational commitment and other important attitudes among people in the public sector also tend to find very positive attitudes as well, such as high ratings of the importance of the work, of serving clients, and of working hard. In addition, when people in public organizations express higher levels of organizational commitment, their responses tend to be based on desirable factors—such as a sense of meaningful public service or the opportunity to participate in important decisions—as opposed, for example, to whether the organization provides generous material benefits.

The mixed results in studies of organizational commitment in the public and private sectors actually move us toward suggestions for both managers and researchers. Balfour and Wechsler (1996) reported complex findings about variables related to their three dimensions of commitment described earlier. Generally, however, they found that four factors appeared to increase all three dimensions of commitment: more participation in decision making, lower political penetration (less external political influence on hiring, promotion, and treatment of clients), more respectful and supportive supervision, and more opportunity for advancement. In a similar vein, based on her own research and that of others, Romzek (1990) concluded that highly committed employees in government feel that their jobs are compatible with their ethics, values, and professional standards and that their families and friends support their affiliation with the organization for which they work. Although the studies reviewed here indicate difficulties in bringing about such conditions in some public organizations—probably in very complex, controversial, and highly politicized ones with diffuse mandates—public managers can often overcome these problems. As the research also shows, the problems in the public sector may not be more severe than those in the private sector, but rather simply different.

## The Challenge of Motivation in the Public Sector

Like the topics discussed before it, the topic of organizational commitment dramatizes the challenge for everyone concerned with effective public management. The research indicates the frustrations, constraints, and problems of working and managing in the public sector. It also reflects a strong current of motivation, effort, and constructive attitudes in public organizations. The challenge for leaders and managers involves dealing effectively with the complex environment of public organizations so as to support and make the most of the valuable human resources and potential. For all of us, the challenge is intensified by the absence of a conclusive, scientific solution to these problems in the research and theory of organizational behavior and related fields. Yet, as the review and examples here have shown, that body of knowledge does offer ideas, concepts, and methods that provide valuable support for those of us determined to pursue those challenges.

CHAPTER ELEVEN

# LEADERSHIP, MANAGERIAL ROLES, AND ORGANIZATIONAL CULTURE

All of the preceding chapters discuss topics that pose challenges for leaders at all levels in public organizations, and the framework presented in Chapter One implies the crucial role of leadership. As earlier chapters have discussed, some perspectives on organizations question whether leaders truly wield important influences or whether they are actually under the control of more powerful circumstances that determine the course of events. Recent research on leaders in private firms tends to find that there are weak relationships between leader behaviors and objective performance measures such as sales and profit margins, or at least that the effects of leadership are highly contingent on other factors (Klein and Kim, 1998; Waldman, Ramírez, House, and Puranam, 2001). Studies of leaders in the public sector, however, have recently been attributing a lot of influence to leader behaviors (such as Brudney, Hebert, and Wright, 1999; Hennessey, 1998; Kim, 2002; Thompson, 2000), and this chapter returns later to the question of whether leaders in the public sector make much difference given the shared power, politics, oversight, and other factors that can limit their impact in government. Whether or not leaders shape the destinies of their organizations and stride like titans over the rest of us, anyone who has served in an organization knows how much leaders can mean, or fail to mean, in the apparent direction and success of an organization and in the work lives of the people they purportedly lead. Yet in spite of such debates, the literature on leadership in the social sciences and elsewhere, including religious, literary, and philosophical discourse over the centuries, looms before us as a vast, complex body of human thought and effort (Kellerman and Webster, 2001) that, like other topics in the social sciences and related fields, ultimately plays out as rather confused and inconclusive.

As with previous topics, such as motivation, we are presented with the challenge of what to make of this body of work. This chapter takes the approach of first reviewing many of the theories and ideas about leadership and managerial roles that have developed in the field of organizational behavior and organizational psychology, and then examining concepts and ideas about organizational culture. Leaders need to influence organizational culture, which in the last several decades has become one of the most widely used (and misused) terms in popular discourse on management and organizations. Business firms cannot merge without setting off an explosion of discussion in business magazines and business sections of newspapers about whether the cultures of the two firms will clash. Governmental challenges, such as poor coordination among agencies and reorganizations such as the design of the Department of Homeland Security, spark heated discourse over the clashing cultures of different agencies. Lurie and Riccucci (2003) have described how proponents of the most significant reform of the social welfare system in the United States in recent history, the 1996 Temporary Assistance for Needy Families Act, envisioned the reform as a means of actually changing the culture of welfare agencies and the welfare system. Because of such significant applications of the concept, even though *organizational culture* has risen to buzzword status in popular discussion, it still represents an interesting, important topic (Khademian, 2002). People preparing for roles in and research on public management need to confront the basic literature and research on it, in part to retrieve it from the dustbin of buzzwords that have gone before it.

Although scholars and experts have repeatedly asserted that leaders in government agencies can have only weak influence on their organizations and related events, in the past several decades a genre of literature on influential, innovative, effective leaders in governmental administrative settings has developed. This chapter concludes with a review of this work that identifies, describes, and analyzes such leaders.

# Leadership Theories in Management and Organizational Behavior

An immense body of research on leadership in organizational settings offers a vast assortment of definitions and perspectives on leadership (Yukl, 2001). By leadership, most people mean the capacity of someone to direct and energize people to achieve goals. Faced with the challenge of understanding this topic, how have management researchers attacked the problem?

## Trait Theories

First, researchers have tried to determine those characteristics, or traits, that make a person an effective leader. Midcentury leadership researchers concentrated on this approach. They tried to identify the traits of effective leaders—physical characteristics such as height, intellectual characteristics such as intelligence and foresight, personality characteristics such as enthusiasm and persistence. They identified many important characteristics such as these, often demonstrating a relationship between these traits and effective leadership, and leadership characteristics of various sorts have remained an important element of leadership research. No one, however, has ever identified a common set of traits for excellent leaders. Leaders come in a variety of sizes, shapes, talents, and dispositions. The quest for universal traits has been replaced by other approaches.

## The Ohio State Leadership Studies

The social sciences developed rapidly during the middle of the twentieth century. More and more studies used new techniques such as questionnaires and computer analysis, and there was an increasing emphasis on systematic observations of human behavior. Drawing on samples from the military, schools, and other organizations, researchers at Ohio State University developed questionnaires that asked people to report on the behaviors of their superiors. After repeated analyses of the questionnaire results, they found that observations about leaders fell into two dimensions—*consideration* and *initiating structure*. These would become central issues, under various names, in much of the subsequent work on leadership. Consideration refers to a leader's concern for his or her relationships with subordinates. Questionnaire items pertaining to consideration ask whether the leader is friendly and approachable, listens to subordinates' ideas and makes use of them, cares about the morale of the group, and otherwise deals with subordinates in an open, communicative, concerned fashion. Initiating structure refers to a leader's emphasis on setting standards, assigning roles, and pressing for productivity and performance. The two dimensions tend to be related to each other, but only to a limited extent.

This research played a pivotal role in moving the field into empirical research on leadership. It drove the trait approach into disrepute by showing that effective leaders vary on these dimensions and do not display a uniform set of traits. It also set these two dimensions in place in the literature as two key aspects of leader behavior. Yet reviewers raised questions about the adequacy of the questionnaire measures and noted that the two dimensions do not make for a complete picture of leadership practice and effectiveness. Researchers moved off in search of more complete models.

## The Blake and Mouton Managerial Grid

The Ohio State leadership studies had a significant impact on Blake and Mouton's *managerial grid* approach (1984) to improving management practices. Blake and Mouton characterized organizations according to two dimensions with clear roots in the Ohio State studies—concern for people and concern for production. Organizations low on the former and high on the latter have *authority-obedience management.* Those high on concern for people and low on concern for production have *country club management.* Those low on both have *impoverished management.* This approach sought to move organizations toward high levels of both factors, or to *team management,* through open communication, participative problem solving and goal setting, confrontation of differences, and teamwork. This framework supported Blake and Mouton's popular organization development consulting method, which they applied in a broad range of government, business, and third sector organizations.

## Fiedler's Contingency Theory of Leadership

Researchers still sought more complete theories, especially theories that would better address the numerous situations that leaders face. Fiedler's contingency theory (1967) received a lot of attention because at the time it offered one of the best frameworks for examining the relationship between leadership style and organizational setting and how that relationship affects a leader's effectiveness. Fiedler used the *least preferred coworker* (LPC) scale to distinguish between types of leadership styles. The LPC scale asked a leader to think of the person with whom that leader could work least well and then to rate that person on about twenty numerical scales of personal characteristics, such as pleasant or unpleasant, tense or relaxed, boring or interesting, and nasty or nice. After repeated studies, Fiedler and his associates felt that the responses indicated two basic types of leaders: high-LPC leaders gave relatively favorable ratings to this least preferred associate, and low-LPC leaders rated the associate much more unfavorably. The responses of high-LPC leaders showed that they had more favorable dispositions toward coworkers and thus were relationship-oriented. The low-LPC leaders were task-oriented; they concentrated on task accomplishment over relationships with coworkers, and found less desirable coworkers more irritating because they hindered successful work.

Fiedler's theory holds that either type of leadership style can be effective, depending on whether it properly matches the contingencies facing the leader. According to the theory, the key contingencies, in order of their importance in determining effective leadership, are *leader-member relations,* marked by the degree of friendliness, trust, initiative, and cooperativeness of the leader and the subordinates; *task structure,* shaped by the clarity and specificity of what must be done; and *position power of the leader,* determined by the amount of formal power the leader has.

Leadership situations vary on each of these dimensions, from good to bad. Obviously, a leader enjoys the most favorable setting when all three are good and the least favorable when all three are bad. Moderately favorable settings have a mixture of good and bad conditions, such as good leader-member relations but an unstructured task setting and weak position power. Fiedler contended that low-LPC (task-oriented) leaders perform most effectively in the very favorable or very unfavorable settings, while high-LPC (relationship-oriented) leaders do best in the intermediate settings.

Fiedler's rationale for this conclusion evades easy explanation, but the logic appears to go like this: Low-LPC leaders do well in the best situations because everything is in place and the subordinates simply need to be given direction (and they accept the leader as authorized to give such direction). For example, the leader of an airplane crew who has the benefits of clear power, a strong task structure, and good relations with subordinates does best if he or she concentrates on giving orders to accomplish the task. The low-LPC type also does well in very bad situations that have so much potential disorder and disaffection anyway that worrying about establishing good personal relations simply wastes time. In such settings, the leader might as well go ahead and press for structure, order, and output. High-LPC leaders do best in the intermediate situations because an emphasis on good relations can overcome the one or two bad dimensions and take advantage of other favorable aspects of the setting. For example, a weakly empowered chair of a newly formed, poorly structured interdepartmental committee who has good relations with the committee members can take advantage of those good relations, encouraging participation and opinion sharing, to overcome the committee's other problems.

Fiedler argued that his theory shows that rather than trying to train leaders to fit a particular setting, organizations must alter the setting to fit the leader. He and his colleagues developed a *leader match* procedure, in which leaders use questionnaires to assess their own style and their leadership situation and then consider ways of changing the situation to make it better fit their style.

Critics questioned the adequacy of Fiedler's evidence and the methods he used. Clearly, the theory includes a very limited picture of the possible situational factors and variations in leadership styles. Still, it raises key issues about leadership processes and has advanced the effort to develop more complete theories.

## The Path-Goal Theory of Leadership

The path-goal theory of leadership draws on the expectancy theory of motivation described in Chapter Ten. Expectancy theory treats motivation as arising from expectations about the results of actions and the value of those results. Similarly, path-goal theory holds that effective leaders increase motivation and satisfaction among subordinates when they help them pursue important goals—that is, when they help them see the goals, the paths to them, and how to follow those paths effectively. Leaders must do this by showing subordinates the value of outcomes over which the leader has some control, by finding ways to increase the value to subordinates of those outcomes, by using appropriate coaching and direction to clarify the paths to those outcomes, and by removing barriers and frustrations to those paths.

The theory also considers a variety of leadership styles, characteristics of subordinates, and situational factors that affect the proper approach to a leader's path-goal work (House, 1971; House and Mitchell, 1974; Filley, House, and Kerr, 1976). House and Mitchell considered four leadership styles: *directive*, where the leader gives specific directions and expectations; *supportive*, marked by encouraging, sympathetic relations with subordinates; *achievement-oriented*, where the leader sets high goals and high expectations for subordinates' performance and responsibility; and *participative*, where the leader encourages subordinates to express opinions and suggestions.

Which style is best depends on various situational factors, such as whether the task is structured and provides clear goals, whether subordinates have well-developed skills and a sense of personal control over their environment (locus of control), how much formal authority the leader has, and whether the work group has strong norms and social relationships. When factors such as these provide weak path-goal indications and incentives, the proper leadership style can enhance them. The leader must avoid behaviors that impose redundancies and aggravations, however.

Researchers have predicted and tested relationships such as these:

- Directive leadership enhances satisfaction and expectancies if the task is ambiguous, but hurts them if the task is well structured and clear.
- Clear tasks already provide clear paths to goals, and subordinates may see more directions from a leader as redundant and irritating.
- Supportive leadership enhances satisfaction when tasks are frustrating and stressful, but can be inappropriate when the task, the work group, and the organization provide plenty of encouragement. In such situations the leader need only clarify directions as needed and set high standards.
- Achievement-oriented leadership increases performance on ambiguous tasks, either because those conditions allow (or require) ambitious goals more often than simple tasks do, or because achievement-oriented subordinates tend to select such tasks.
- Participative leadership works best for ambiguous tasks in which subordinates feel that their self-esteem is at stake, because participation allows them to influence decisions and work out solutions to the ambiguity. For clear tasks, however, participative leadership is effective only if subordinates value self-control and independence.

As these examples show, the theory weaves together leadership styles and situational factors to make sufficiently subtle predictions to capture some of the complex variations in real leadership settings. A lot of research based on the theory produced mixed results and much debate concerning its validity, however (Pinder, 1998, pp. 359–360; Yukl, 2001, pp. 212–216). House (1996) offers an elaborate reformulation of the theory, the adequacy of which remains to be established in research. Whether validated or not, the theory offers a number of interesting and useful suggestions for leaders to consider, about how to adapt leadership approaches to particular situations.

## The Vroom-Yetton Normative Model

Vroom and Yetton (1973; Vroom and Jago, 1974) proposed an elaborate framework for leaders to use in deciding how and how much to involve subordinates or subordinate groups in decisions. The framework takes the form of a decision tree that guides the leader through a series of questions about how important the quality of the decision will be, whether the leader has the necessary information to make a high-quality decision, whether the problem is well structured, whether acceptance of the decision by subordinates is important, and whether conflict among them is likely. The decision-making process guides the leader in selecting from various ways of handling the decision, such as delegating it or making it after consulting subordinates.

## Life-Cycle Theory

Hersey and Blanchard (1982) developed another form of contingency theory. Their life-cycle theory suggests that leadership styles must fit the level of maturity of the group being led. Mature groups have a higher capacity for accepting responsibility because they are well educated, experienced, and capable at accomplishing group tasks, and have well-developed relationships with one another and with the leader. With groups that are very low on these dimensions, however, leaders must engage in telling, emphasizing task directions over developing relationships with the group, to move the group toward better task capabilities. As the group moves higher on some dimensions of maturity but remains at a low level of maturity overall, the leader must do more selling, or heavy emphasizing of both tasks and relationships. As the group moves to moderately high maturity, participating becomes the most effective style. The leader relaxes the emphasis on task direction but still attends to relationships. Finally, for a very mature group, delegating becomes the effective approach. The leader deemphasizes his or her own role in directing tasks and maintaining relationships and shifts responsibility to group members.

Loosely defined concepts plague the theory, but they make important points. Leaders often face the challenge of assessing just how much delegation the group can accept (how much it needs someone to take charge and set directions), and determining how to move the group toward a greater capacity for handling tasks and relationships independently.

## Attribution Models

Social psychologists have developed a body of theory about how people make attributions about or attribute characteristics to one another. Some leadership researchers have applied this perspective to leadership and produced useful insights. They look at how leaders draw conclusions about how and why their subordinates are behaving and performing as they are, and how subordinates form impressions about leaders. Leaders interpret the apparent causes of subordinate behavior and performance in deciding how to respond. They take into account the uniqueness of the particular task to the performance, the consistency of the behaviors, and how the behaviors compare to those of other subordinates. Some of the research shows that when a subordinate performs poorly, leaders tend to attribute the problem to the subordinate if he or she has a bad record. If the person has a good record of past performance, however, leaders often conclude that the problem results from the situation surrounding the person and is not his or her fault. For their part, subordinates often attribute the lion's share of credit or blame for the group's performance and characteristics to the group's leader. If the group has performed well in the past, they tend more readily to give the leader credit for current successes, even rating him or her higher on certain leader behaviors and interpreting these as causes.

Attribution theories obviously offer a partial approach that does not cover the full topic of leadership, but they clearly point to important processes for leaders to keep in mind. Leaders always face the challenge of managing others' impressions of them and of trying to form valid impressions of their colleagues and subordinates. These attribution processes pertain especially to problems in public management, where political appointees come in at the top of agencies and must establish relations with career civil servants. Frequently the political appointees anticipate resistance and poor performance from the careerists, and the careerists anticipate amateurishness from the political appointee. When problems come up, the two types tend to interpret them according to their preconceptions about each other, aggravating the problem of developing effective working relationships. The careerists and appointees often come to respect each other, but attribution processes often slow this process (Golden, 2000; Heclo, 1978; Light, 1987; Ingraham, 1988).

## Leader-Member Exchange Theory

The leader-member exchange (LMX) theory of leadership concentrates on the dyadic relationships between a leader and individual subordinates, and on the development of low-exchange and high-exchange relationships (Dansereau, Graen, and Haga, 1975). Low-exchange relationships involve little mutual influence between the leader and subordinate, and the subordinate generally follows formal role requirements and receives standard benefits such as salary. According to the theory, leaders tend to establish high-exchange relationships with a small set of trusted subordinates, with whom they engage in mutually influential relations. These subordinates usually receive benefits in the form of more interesting assignments and participation in important decisions, but they incur more obligations such as meeting the leader's expectations of harder work, more loyalty, and more responsibility than is expected of those not included in the group. The leader, of course, incurs corresponding forms of obligation and benefit in these high-exchange relationships. Scholars developing this theory have devoted attention to measuring the existence of such relationships with questionnaires, analyzing the determinants of such relationships, and theorizing about how the relationships develop and mature over time. LMX theory has received more recent attention than a number of the other theories described previously and later in this chapter, but like all of them, it has sparked debate and criticism (Schriesheim, Castro, and Cogliser, 1999; Yukl, 2001, pp. 116–121). Researchers have used different definitions and measures, leaving a lot of unresolved questions about the definition and nature of the exchange relations, about how the relations develop and relate to group and individual performance. As with the other theories, however, LMX theory adds interesting suggestions about matters for leaders to consider in the leadership of individuals and groups.

## Operant Conditioning and Social Learning Theory Models

The operant conditioning and behavior modification perspectives described in Chapter Ten have found their way into the search for leadership theories. Some early behavior modification approaches emphasized reinforcement of outcomes over concern with internal mental states. Proponents argued that these approaches offered significant improvements for leadership techniques, for several reasons. They stressed observations of behavior rather than dubious inferences about what happens in a person's head. For example, they said that managers should look at behaviors and performance outcomes rather than at whether a person has a "good attitude." They called for close attention to the consequences of behavior, saying that leaders must attend to the behaviors they reinforce or extinguish by associating consequences with those behaviors. They emphasized positive reinforcement as the most effective approach.

Later approaches began to take into account developments in social learning theory. Albert Bandura (1978, 1997) and other psychologists demonstrated that operant conditioning models needed to expand to include forms of learning and behavioral change that are not tightly tied to some reinforcement. People learn by watching others, through modeling and vicarious learning. They use mental symbols, rehearsal, and memorization techniques to develop their behaviors. Taking these insights into account, social learning theory models of leadership have added analysis of internal mental states and social learning to their assessments of leadership (Kreitner and Luthans, 1987). This has led to additional suggestions about leadership practices. Because internal mental states and social learning (in addition to feedback and after-the-fact reinforcement) also affect behavior, leaders can use *feed-forward* techniques to influence behavior. They can anticipate problems and actively avoid them by clarifying goals. They can enhance employees' acceptance of goals by having them participate in their development, and through social cues (by acting as a good role model). They can also emphasize the development of self-efficacy and self-management, both for themselves and for their subordinates. This involves managing one's own environment by recognizing how environmental factors influence one's behavior, and through personal goal setting, rehearsal, self-instruction, and self-rewards (see, for example, Sims and Lorenzi, 1992).

## Cognitive Resource Utilization Theory

Researchers continue to work on additional theories. Among recent ones, Fiedler's cognitive resource utilization theory has received the most validation from supporting studies (Fiedler and Garcia, 1987). It extends the Fiedler contingency theory, specifying when directive (low-LPC) behaviors affect group performance, but also drawing in the effects of the leader's intelligence, competence, and stress level. Fiedler and Garcia reported the unexpected finding that considerate (high-LPC) leader behavior has little effect on group performance. If the group supports such a leader and the task requires cognitive abilities, then the cognitive abilities of the group determine its performance. If the group does not support the leader, then external factors, such as task difficulty, determine performance.

For directive leaders with much control over the situation, performance depends on whether the leader is free of stress, whether the task requires cognitive abilities, and whether the group supports the leader. If these conditions hold, the leader's intelligence strongly predicts performance. If the leader is under stress, however, the leader's experience becomes the best predictor of performance, because stress prevents the effective use of intelligence and brings experience more strongly into play. Also, if the task does not require cognitive skill or the group does not support the leader, then the leader's intelligence has little or no effect on performance. As the authors state, their theory and research suggest the "not surprising conclusion that directive leaders who are stupid give stupid directions, and if the group follows these directions, the consequences will be bad" (Fiedler and Garcia, 1987, p. 199). Directive leader behaviors result in good performance only if coupled with high leader intelligence and a supportive, stress-free setting. The theory offers useful new insights into such leadership process variables as stress, which leaders can strive to manage (House and Singh, 1987).

Scholars in organizational behavior and organizational psychology have developed other, less-prominent theories that this review does not cover (see Yukl, 2001). Yet arguably the most striking departure in leadership research in recent decades addresses transformational and charismatic leadership, and that body of research and theory needs attention. Before covering this approach, however, it is useful to review a body of research on managerial roles and behaviors to which the transformational leadership research reacts, and then to cover transformational and charismatic leadership, which have important linkages to the discussion of organizational culture that follows.

# The Nature of Managerial Work and Roles

As the research on leadership developed, there also emerged a body of work on the characteristics of managerial work, roles, and skills. This literature actually involves something of a trait approach. It seeks to develop general conceptions of managerial activities and competencies. Ever since the classical theorists began trying to define the role of the administrator, the approach of planning, organizing, staffing, directing, coordinating, reporting, and budgeting (POSDCORB) (described in Chapter Two), or some variant of it has served as a guiding conception of what managers must do. Often coupled with this view is the constantly repeated notion that managers in all settings must do pretty much the same general types of work. Allison (1983) illustrated the prevalence of the POSDCORB conception of managerial responsibilities when he used a form of it in one of the most widely reprinted and circulated articles ever written on public management (see Exhibit 11.1).

Not so preoccupied with what managers must do as with what they actually do, Mintzberg (1972) produced *The Nature of Managerial Work*, which now stands as a classic in the field. He did something that, remarkably, was considered quite original at the time. He closely observed the work of five managers who headed organizations by following them around and having them keep notebooks. He concluded that their work falls into the set of roles listed in Exhibit 11.1.

## EXHIBIT 11.1. MANAGERIAL ROLES AND SKILLS.

### Allison (1983): Functions of General Management

*Strategy*
Establishing objectives and priorities
Devising operational plans

*Managing internal components*
Organizing and staffing
Directing personnel and the personnel management system
Controlling performance

*Managing external constituencies*
Dealing with external units subject to some common authority
Dealing with independent organizations
Dealing with the press and the public

### Mintzberg (1972): Executive Roles

| *Interpersonal* | *Informational* | *Decisional* |
|---|---|---|
| Figurehead | Monitor | Entrepreneur |
| Leader | Disseminator | Disturbance handler |
| Liaison | Spokesperson | Resource allocator |
| | | Negotiator |

### Whetten and Cameron (2002): Management Skill Topics

| | |
|---|---|
| Self-awareness | Effective delegation and joint decision making |
| Managing personal stress | Gaining power and influence |
| Creative problem solving | Establishing supportive communication |
| Managing conflict | Improving group decision making |
| Improving employee performance, motivating others | |

### The Benchmarks Scales (McCauley, Lombardo, and Usher, 1989)

1a.  Resourcefulness
1b.  Doing whatever it takes
1c.  Being a quick study
2a.  Building and mending relationships
2b.  Leading subordinates
2c.  Compassion and sensitivity
3.  Straightforwardness and composure
4.  Setting a developmental climate
5.  Confronting problem subordinates
6.  Team orientation
7.  Balance between personal life and work
8.  Decisiveness
9.  Self-awareness
10.  Hiring talented staff
11.  Putting people at ease
12.  Acting with flexibility

Mintzberg also reported that when one actually watches what managers do, one sees the inaccuracy of some popular beliefs about their work. Managers do not play the role of systematic, rational planners but rather emphasize action over reflection. Their activities are characterized by brevity, variety, and discontinuity. While top-level managers are often told to plan and delegate and avoid regular duties, in reality they handle regular duties such as ceremonies, negotiations, and relations with the environment, such as meeting visitors and getting information from outside sources (to which they have the best access of anyone in the organization). They meet visiting dignitaries, talk with managers and officials from outside the organization, hobnob at charitable events, and preside over the annual banquet. While managers are sometimes told that they need aggregate, systematically analyzed information, they actually favor direct and interactive sources, such as telephone calls and face-to-face talks and meetings. While management increasingly has access to scientific supports and processes, managers still rely a great deal on intuition and judgment. Research has supported Mintzberg's observations about management and his typology of managerial roles (Kurke and Aldrich, 1983). Generally, the research finds his typology widely applicable to managers in many settings. Yet Mintzberg also found some characteristics unique to the public sector setting, and these too have been supported in recent research, as discussed later.

# Transformational Leadership

During the 1970s, researchers in the field expressed increasing concern about the inadequacy of their theories. Leadership theorists began to argue that research had concentrated too narrowly on the exchanges between leaders and their subordinates in task situations and on highly quantified models and analyses. Some researchers called for more attention to larger issues and other sources of leadership thought, such as political and historical analyses, and more qualitative research using interviews and case studies.

Political scientist James MacGregor Burns (1978) exerted a seminal influence on leadership thought in the management field. Concerned with major political and social leaders such as presidents and prime figures in social movements, he distinguished between *transactional leadership* and *transformational leadership*. Transactional leaders motivate followers by recognizing their needs and providing rewards to fulfill those needs in exchange for their performance and support. Transformational leaders raise followers' goals to higher planes, to a focus on transcendental, higher-level goals akin to the self-actualization needs defined by Maslow. In addition, they motivate followers to transcend their own narrow self-interest in pursuit of these goals, for the benefit of the community or the nation. Martin Luther King Jr. provides an example of a leader who did not simply offer to exchange benefits for support but also called for a new order of existence—a society of greater justice—and he inspired many people to work for this vision. Many others refrained from opposing it because of its moral rightness.

Management experts found these ideas provocative. As one of many examples of these adoptions of Burns's ideas, Bennis and Nanus (1985) reported a study of *transformative leaders.* Uncharitably, they said of the body of research on leadership, "Never have so many labored so long to say so little" (p. 4), a circumstance they did little to correct. They argued that our institutions and their leaders face increasing complexity and challenges to their credibility, requiring new conceptions of transformative leadership. This type of leadership relies on power, but not in a controlling, centralized way. These leaders possess an extraordinary talent for coupling visions of success to empowerment and motivation among their followers. Bennis and Nanus's observations about these leaders lack clarity and convincing validation. Still, they offer insights and thought-provoking perspectives on leadership that leaders at all levels can consider adapting and adopting.

Bennis and Nanus reported on their interviews with ninety outstanding leaders from business and the public sector (for example, a federal agency director, an orchestra leader, and a football coach). They drew a sharp distinction between leading and managing. The latter, they said, involves taking charge, accomplishing goals with efficiency, discharging the sort of functions listed by Mintzberg and other researchers on management functions (described earlier), and generally "doing things right" (p. 21). Leading involves guiding directions, actions, and opinions, or as they put it, "doing the right thing" (p. 21). Excellent leaders, they concluded, lead others largely by carefully managing themselves, through such strategies as the following:

- *Attention through vision.* They effectively create visions of successful futures, which focus their attention and that of their followers. They achieve this in part through transactions with followers that bring out the best in both leader and followers (Tichy and Ulrich, 1984).
- *Meaning through communication.* They effectively transmit this vision to others in ways that give meaning to their work and their quest. Bennis and Nanus described examples of even taciturn leaders who get their point across and communicate their purposes through symbols and drawings. The communication transmits not simply facts but, more important, reasons for and ways of learning and problem solving.
- *Trust through positioning.* Outstanding leaders show particular skill at choosing the best course, at knowing what is right and necessary. They choose direc-

tions and themes and adhere to them with constancy in ways that induce trust in their identity and integrity.

• *Deployment of self through positive self-regard.* Excellent leaders have high regard for their own skills and utilize them effectively. Yet they also remain aware of their own limitations and work to overcome them, often by attracting people who compensate for those limitations. They work with those people with respect, courteous attention, and trust, and they have the ability to do without constant approval.

• *The Wallenda factor.* Bennis and Nanus described one way that leaders pursue this deployment of self by pointing to the example of the famous tightrope walker Karl Wallenda. Wallenda put great energy and focus into his work; he did not obsess about past problems or prospects of failure. He finally lost his life in a major appearance before which he had been utterly preoccupied with not falling. Outstanding leaders encourage in themselves and others a spirit of development, experimentation, reasonable risk taking and adventure, and even tolerance for well-intentioned mistakes that lead to learning. They concentrate on succeeding and do not become obsessed with the possibility of failure.

• *Empowerment.* Successful leaders also expand their own capacity by empowering others, making them feel a sense of significance, community, competence, and even fun. Thus, the others strive to contribute not because of close direction and control by the leader but through empowerment.

Bass (1985, 1998; Bass and Avolio, 2002) presented a much more systematic analysis of transformational leadership, which adds too many additional points to be covered here. Like Burns, however, he sharply distinguished transactional from transformational leadership. He saw transformational leadership as uplifting. It shifts followers' focus from lower- to higher-order needs. It motivates them to sacrifice their own self-interest by showing followers that their self-interests are fulfilled or linked to community or higher-order needs. Bass agreed that there must be a shift in needs, but he pointed out that major leaders—Hitler, for instance— can have a transforming influence through a negative shift. Bass argued that the wrong kind of transformational leadership can damage followers and other groups.

Bass's analysis of transformational leadership points out that this form of leadership has an emotional and intellectual component. The emotional component involves charisma, an inspiring influence on followers. The intellectual component involves careful attention to individual followers, often of a benevolent, developmental, mentoring nature, as well as intellectual stimulation. The intellectual aspects can take various forms, such as manipulating symbols, using rational discourse, or evoking ideals, and can involve cognitive stimulation as much as intellectual teaching. Bass emphasized that leadership research has often underrated the importance of leaders' technical competence to their influence and effectiveness.

Followers often admire and follow leaders primarily because leaders are very good at what they do. Bass and colleagues (Bass, 1985, 1998) have developed a questionnaire instrument to analyze the component behaviors of transformational leadership, which according to this perspective include both transformational and transactional behaviors, as follows:

*Transformational Behaviors*

> *Idealized influence:* Arouses followers' emotional attachment to the leader and identification with him or her.
>
> *Intellectual stimulation:* Engages followers in recognizing and confronting challenges, and in viewing challenges from new perspectives.
>
> *Individualized consideration:* Provides support, encouragement, and coaching.
>
> *Inspirational motivation:* Communicates an appealing vision, using symbols to focus efforts, and modeling appropriate behaviors.

*Transactional Behaviors*

> *Contingent reward:* Clarifying the work required for rewards, and ensuring that rewards are contingent on appropriate behaviors.
>
> *Passive management by exception:* Punishments or other corrective actions in response to obvious deviations from acceptable standards.
>
> *Active management by exception:* Looking for mistakes and enforcing rules to avoid mistakes.

While Burns treated transactional and transformational leadership as two polar extremes, Bass argued that transformational leaders also engage in varying degrees of transactional interaction with followers. They have to provide rewards and reasonably clear goals and directions. But overemphasis on exchanges with followers, especially negative or punishing ones, can be harmful. The significance of transformational leadership derives from its capacity to lift and expand the goals of individuals, not by overemphasizing direct, extrinsic satisfaction of self-interest, but rather by inspiring new, higher aspirations. Hence comes the emphasis on relatively intangible, idealized influences through vision, empowerment, charisma, inspiration, individual consideration, and intellectual stimulation. Transformational leaders do not directly control their subordinates but rather seek to influence the climate in which they work. Thus, this view of leadership has connections with another recent trend, the emphasis on managing organizational culture.

## Charismatic Leadership

As part of the same trend that produced ideas about transformational leadership over the last several decades, leadership researchers have also developed theories of charismatic leadership that have similarities and overlaps with the concept of transformational leadership (Yukl, 2001, pp. 240–253; Shamir, Zakay, Breinin, and Popper, 1998). They have drawn on ideas from Max Weber's work (described in Chapter Two) on how leaders sometimes influence followers not just through traditional or formal authority, but through exceptional personal qualities that invoke strong confidence, loyalty, and commitment from followers. Those interested in this phenomenon have developed a number of different perspectives on it, two of the more prominent of which include an attributional theory or perspective, and a self-concept theory.

The attributional theory of charismatic leadership treats charisma as primarily a matter of the characteristics that followers attribute to their leader. When they attribute these qualities, they come to identify personally with the leader and to internalize values and beliefs that the leader espouses. They want to please and imitate the leader. According to this view of charismatic leadership, followers are more likely to react this way when the leader displays certain behaviors and skills, such as when the leader does the following:

- Advocates a vision that is different from the status quo, but still acceptable to followers
- Acts in unconventional ways in pursuit of the vision
- Engages in self-sacrifice and risk taking in pursuit of the vision
- Displays confidence in the leader's ideas and proposals
- Uses visioning and persuasive appeals to influence followers, rather than relying mainly on formal authority
- Uses the capacity to assess context and locate opportunities for novel strategies

Such leaders are most likely to emerge during a crisis, or in situations where the leader's exceptional behaviors and skills are a good match with a particular context.

The self-concept theory of charismatic leadership actually comes to some very similar conclusions, but it emphasizes more observable characteristics of the leader and followers. It also proceeds more from assumptions about the tendency of individuals to maintain their conception of themselves, including their social identities and their self-esteem, and the effects the leader has on such processes. Leaders have charismatic effects on followers when the followers feel that the leader's beliefs are correct, willingly obey the leader and feel affection for him or her, accept high performance goals for themselves, become emotionally involved in the mission of the group and feel that they contribute to it, and regard the leader as having extraordinary abilities. Charismatic leaders invoke such responses by articulating an appealing vision and using strong, imaginative forms of communication to express it. They take risks and engage in self-sacrifice to attain the vision. They express confidence in followers, set high expectations of them, and empower them. They build identification with the group or organization and carefully manage followers' impressions of them. When these behaviors invoke in followers the responses just described, the followers come to identify with the leader, to internalize the leader's beliefs and values, and to feel motivated to achieve tasks and goals that the leader espouses.

Charismatic leadership drew researchers' attention in part because of important examples of leaders in government, business, and nonprofit organizations who displayed such behaviors and such influences on followers, at least to some extent. For example, during his service as commissioner of the Internal Revenue Service, Charles Rossotti, regardless of whether he should be considered a charismatic leader, had a profound effect on the people who worked with him. In interviews, other executives in the IRS and in organizations such as unions and consulting firms that worked with the IRS would use terms such as *superhuman* to describe Rossotti's energy and acuity. These characterizations were all the more interesting because Rossotti is not a person of large stature or imposing physical presence (Thompson and Rainey, 2003).

Charismatic leadership obviously raises a lot of important questions about the nature and appropriateness of such forms of leadership. For example, if an organization becomes highly dependent on the special qualities of an individual leader, this raises challenges when the leader departs. Also, researchers on this topic have pointed out that there can be a dark side to charismatic leadership, and that there is a difference between *positive charismatics* and *negative charismatics*. Positive charismatics can exert the beneficial forms of influence implied in the perspectives just described. Hitler, however, immediately brings to mind a lot of the obvious problems of negative forms of charisma, such as excessive loyalty to evil and destructive ends. Researchers have noted that one does observe negative charismatics in organizations in the government and in the private sector. While not as heinous as Hitler, one hopes, such leaders can become self-absorbed, dependent on adulation, and excessively self-confident. They may take excessive risks and inhibit followers from suggesting improvements or pointing out problems.

As with the other theories, the research and thinking about transformational and charismatic leadership has raised controversies and criticisms about the adequacy of the theories and the research supporting them. Among many other issues, theorists dispute whether transformational and charismatic leadership are distinct or overlapping and related phenomena. Nevertheless, these streams of research and thought, besides being very interesting, raise for anyone in a leadership position some challenging considerations about a number of matters (see, for example, Yukl, 2001, 263–266), such as articulating a clear and appealing vision and showing how to attain it; displaying optimism and confidence in oneself and one's followers; using dramatic actions to emphasize key values; setting an example; and empowering people.

# Leadership and Organizational Culture

Transformational leaders avoid closely managing their subordinates and organizations. Rather, they exert their influence through *social architecture*, by working with the basic symbols and core values, or culture, of their organization. Writers on organizational culture have described the key roles that leaders play in forming, maintaining, and changing that culture (Khademian, 2002, pp. 15–42; Schein, 1992). Organizational analysts have been interested in similar themes for a long time, as suggested by the work of Chester Barnard and Philip Selznick described in Chapter Two. The topic really came alive in the management literature, however, when management experts began to find that leaders in excellent corporations in the United States and other nations placed heavy emphasis on managing the cultural dimensions of their firms (Collins and Porras, 1997; Ouchi, 1981; Peters and Waterman, 1982). In addition, researchers who study organizational cultures often use methods similar to those used by anthropologists to study the cultures of different societies. They argue that these methods provide deeper, more sensitive understanding of the realities of organizational life than do methods used by other researchers (Ott, 1989; Schein, 1992). They have proposed various definitions of culture and undertaken studies of basic values, symbols, myths, norms of behavior, and other elements of culture in organizations.

Some of these studies have focused on public organizations, and certainly the topic applies to them (see, for example, Lurie and Riccucci, 2003). Maynard-Moody, Stull, and Mitchell (1986) provide a rich description of the development and transformation of culture in the Kansas Department of Health and Environment. Early in the century, an influential secretary of the department instituted a culture that emphasized the use of professional expertise in the defense of public health, relative autonomy from political intrusion, strict rules, and adherence to the budget. Through slogans, pamphlets, symbolic political actions, and publicity campaigns, the secretary led the development of a well-established culture that predominated for decades. Much later, the governor and legislators, to bring the department under stronger political control, brought in an outsider as secretary. He and his followers led a reorganization that reduced the status of the adherents of the old culture and their beliefs and values, in part through constant denunciations of the old ways of doing things. The new culture, which emphasized different basic beliefs, such as the importance of political responsiveness and adherence to strict operating procedures, clashed with and eventually supplanted the older culture.

Previous chapters and later ones provide other illustrations of organizational culture in public organizations. The development of strategies and mission statements often draws on ideas about culture, and it seeks to shape culture in turn (see Chapter Seven and Exhibit 7.1). Chapter Seven described the efforts of an executive trying to manage aspects of the culture of a law enforcement agency, including its basic assumptions about communicative leadership and decision making. Chapters Thirteen and Fourteen provide further examples of leaders' efforts to influence culture in changing, revitalizing, and building excellence in public and private organizations. These examples force the question of what we mean by culture. Scholars use the term in diffuse ways, and journalists and managers often use it very loosely. If very careful, long-term observations are required for researchers to understand *culture*, will it not also be difficult for managers to understand it? If culture is a strong determinant of what happens in organizations, will it not be hard to change?

The literature provides guidance for confronting these challenges. One succinct definition, for example, says that organizational culture is the pattern of shared meaning in an organization (Trice and Beyer, 1993). In what sense, however, do shared meanings exist? Schein's conception of culture (1992), illustrated in Exhibit 11.2, provides some clarification. Schein contends that culture exists on various levels. The most basic and least observable level, often overlooked in other conceptions of culture, includes the basic assumptions on which the organization operates. Often invisible and unconscious, these assumptions are about the organization's relationship with its environment; about the nature of reality, time, and space; and about the nature of humans and their activities and relationships. The next level of culture involves more overtly expressed values about how things ought to be and how one ought to respond in general. Finally, the most observable level includes artifacts and creations, such as actual technological processes (purposely designed work processes and administrative procedures and instructions), art (symbols, logos, and creations), and behaviors (words used, communication patterns, significant outbursts, and rituals and ceremonies).

A policy about uniforms in a military unit illustrates Schein's three levels (Lewis, 1987). Admiral Hyman Rickover discouraged the wearing of uniforms in

## EXHIBIT 11.2. CONCEPTIONS AND DIMENSIONS OF CULTURE.

**Levels and Basic Assumptions of Organizational Culture (Schein, 1992)**

*Levels of Organizational Culture*

1. Artifacts and creations (the most observable level). Examples: the design of work processes and administrative procedures, art (logos and symbols), overt behaviors (words used, rituals, ceremonies, significant outbursts—such as something a top executive gets openly mad or happy about).

2. Basic values (a less observable level). Examples: values about how things ought to be and how one ought to respond and behave in general (for example, always help younger employees develop their skills and careers, always have strong relationships with key officials in the legislative branch).

3. Basic assumptions (the most basic, least observable level). Examples: basic assumptions on which people in the organization operate (for example, decisions should be made by people with the best brains, not the highest rank).

*Key Dimensions of the Basic Assumptions*

1. The organization's relation to its environment. Example: whether members see the organization as dominant or dominated.

2. The nature of reality and truth, and the basis for decisions. Example: whether decisions are based on tradition or on a scientific test. Subdimensions: the nature of time (for example, the length of cycles) and space (for example, perceived availability or constraints).

3. The nature of human nature. Examples: humans as bad or good, mutable or fixed.

4. The nature of human activity. Example: proactive versus reactive.

**Dimensions of Organizational Culture (Hofstede, Neuijen, Ohayv, and Sanders, 1990)**

*Member identity:* The degree to which individuals identify with the organization as a whole rather than some subgroup or specialization.

*Group emphasis:* The degree to which work is organized around groups rather than individuals.

*People focus:* The extent to which management considers the effects of their decisions on people in the organization.

*Unit integration:* The amount of encouragement of coordinated, interdependent activity among units.

*Control:* The degree to which rules and supervision are used to control employees.

*Risk tolerance:* The encouragement of risk and innovation.

*Reward criteria:* The extent to which rewards are based on performance rather than seniority or favoritism.

*Conflict tolerance:* The degree to which open airing of conflict is encouraged.

*Means-ends orientation:* The extent of managerial focus on outcomes and results rather than processes.

*Open-systems focus:* The amount of monitoring of external developments.

the project teams working in the U.S. Navy's nuclear program. Lower-ranking officers with more recent training often had the best knowledge. Uniforms carry symbols of hierarchical rank and authority (representing the first, most observable level of organizational culture). The absence of uniforms reduces the value of hierarchical rank and promotes the value of individuals' technical knowledge (the second level). At the third, most basic level, the underlying assumption is that those with the "best brains, not the highest rank" make the best decisions (Lewis, 1987, p. 107).

Other researchers have developed more elaborate sets of dimensions of organizational culture. Exhibit 11.2 summarizes the dimensions of organizational culture that Hofstede, Neuijen, Ohayv, and Sanders (1990) used in their study of twenty organizations. Leaders and teams working on the development of organizational culture can make pragmatic use of such dimensions, as well as of the measures of them described shortly. Researchers can work on further developing and confirming the role of such dimensions in public organizations.

## Variations Among Cultures

Analysts also emphasize variations among cultures. One such distinction points out that organizational cultures can vary from strong to weak. In organizations with strong cultures, the members share and strongly adhere to the organization's basic values and assumptions. In weak cultures, members feel little consensus and commitment. DiIulio (1994) described how some employees of the U.S. Bureau of Prisons feel a very strong commitment to the mission and values of the bureau, to the point that some retirees will rush to the scene of a crisis in the prison system to volunteer their services.

There may be multiple cultures and subcultures within an organization (Trice and Beyer, 1993, chaps. 5 and 6). Subcultures can form around occupational specializations, subunits or locations, hierarchical levels, labor unions, and counter-cultural groups such as rebellious units. Public agencies often have a single dominant occupational or professional specialization (Mosher, [1968] 1982; Warwick, 1975). Strong differences between cultures or subcultures obviously complicate the challenge of forging consensus on cultural changes and priorities.

Another source of variation is the role of external societal cultures and their influences on an organization. During the 1980s, for example, interest in the successes of Japanese management led to analyses of their more consensual decision-making processes, their group-oriented norms, and other characteristics of Japanese corporations that reflect their distinctive external societal culture (Ouchi, 1981).

## Assessing the Culture

As suggested earlier, the task of developing an understanding of an organization's culture imposes a major challenge on managers and researchers alike. The concepts and dimensions listed in Exhibit 11.2 can serve as focal points for such an assessment. Researchers use elaborate procedures for measuring and assessing culture. Exhibit 11.3 suggests references and sources for this undertaking.

Khademian (2002, pp. 42–47) proposes a *cultural roots framework* for analysis of public organizations. The cultural roots are three basic elements of every public agency or program: the public task to be done, the resources available to do it, and the environment in which the agency or program has to operate. These three elements become integrated in ways that produce commitments, or rules about how the job gets done. In order to influence the organization's culture, Khademian argues, public managers must concentrate on influencing the ways in which these basic elements or roots are integrated, using strategies described later.

## The Communication of Culture

Various forms that transmit an organization's culture serve as *sense-making mechanisms* for people in the organization as they interpret what goes on around them (Trice and Beyer, 1993, p. 80). The forms transmit information about the organization's basic values and assumptions. In analyzing their organization's culture,

---

### EXHIBIT 11.3. BACKGROUND REFERENCES
### FOR ASSESSING ORGANIZATIONAL CULTURE.

*Schein (1992, chap. 5).* Procedures and interview questions for assessing culture, including the dimensions of culture that his analysis emphasizes. *Methods:* Interviews focusing on surprises and critical incidents, and group interviews about the basic dimensions.

*Wilkins (1990).* Suggestions and interview questions for assessing "corporate character." Corporate character emphasizes "motivational faith" along two dimensions, fairness and ability. *Methods:* Interview and self-assessment questions for use in assessing faith in leaders' and their own fairness and in the organization's and their own abilities.

*Hofstede, Neuijen, Ohayv, and Sanders (1990).* Description of the measures of the cultural dimensions described in Exhibit 11.1. *Method:* Survey research questionnaires.

*Kotter and Heskett (1992).* Survey instrument and interview questions used in their study of the relations between corporate culture and performance in numerous business firms. *Method:* Organizational questionnaire survey and interviews.

*Ott (1989, chap. 5).* General review of methods of studying organizational culture.

---

leaders and teams must determine the current roles of these forms and the ways they need to be transformed.

***Symbols.*** Physical objects, settings, and certain roles within an organization convey information about its values and basic assumptions. The uniforms in the example about Rickover are one example. Goodsell (1977) studied 122 government agencies and found various physical conditions that symbolized either authority or service to clients. For example, flags, official seals, and physical distance between employees and clients symbolized authority. Symbols of a client service orientation included comfortable furniture and descriptions of services available.

Employees use symbols, too. In a large service center of the Social Security Administration, members of a problem-ridden subunit held a funeral for the subunit, complete with black balloons, a small black coffin, and the singing of hymns. Later, when the director had effectively resolved their concerns, the members gave him the coffin with the balloons deflated inside it, as a symbol that the problems were over.

Physical settings can have potent symbolic effects. Zalesny and Farace (1987), in a study of a public agency in a Midwestern state, found that a change to a more open office design—with no interior walls or partitions—had significant psychological effects on employees. Lower-level employees saw the change as promoting more democratic values. Managers felt they had lost status.

***Language.*** Slang, songs, slogans, jargon, and jokes can all carry the messages of a culture. Maynard-Moody, Stull, and Mitchell (1986) described the transformation of the culture of the Kansas Department of Health and Environment. One way that cultural changes were instituted was through derogatory references to "the old way of doing things" that debunked the assumptions and values of the former culture.

***Narratives.*** The people in an organization often repeat stories, legends, sagas, and myths that convey information about the organization's history and practices. Bennis and Nanus (1985) reported that in a large computer company, a manager lost a lot of money on an aggressive project. When he offered his resignation, his superior asked, "How can we fire you when we have just spent ten million dollars educating you?" Repeated around the organization, such a story can send a powerful message about the organization's support of reasonable risk taking and aggressiveness.

***Practices and Events.*** Repeated practices and special events, including recurrent or memorable one-time incidents, can transmit important assumptions and values. These events may include rites and ceremonies such as graduation ceremonies, induction and initiation ceremonies, annual meetings, annual banquets or holiday parties, and homecomings. Rites promote changes and goals such as passage, renewal, elevation, or degradation of individuals, conflict reduction, and integration of the group. Leaders' actions at times of crisis, memorable and widely noted speeches, and outbursts can all have such influences. Organizations have taken particular steps to support employees or customers during times of crisis or hardship, leading to legends and stories that symbolize and communicate organizational values.

# Leading Cultural Development

Experts on organizational culture heavily emphasize the crucial role of leadership in creating and upholding culture (Khademian, 2002; Schein, 1992; Trice and Beyer, 1993). Leaders create culture in new organizations and embody and transmit it in existing organizations. They can also integrate cultures in organizations that have multiple cultures by forging consensus. These different roles are important, because different types of leaders may play them. A long-term member of the organization, for example, often plays the strongest role in embodying and transmitting existing cultures. Nevertheless, leaders of high-performance organizations typically strive for an improved culture, even if the organization performs well already (Kotter and Heskett, 1992).

The concepts and points discussed earlier present challenges for leadership. Enhancing culture involves understanding its nature, assessing the particular culture of one's organization, dealing with multiple subcultures as necessary, understanding the different cultural forms in the organization, and using those forms to facilitate change. Leaders and leadership teams can use a variety of methods and strategies to lead the development of effective culture:

1. *Make clear what leaders will monitor, ignore, measure, or control.* For example, a leadership team can announce that a significant proportion of each manager's evaluation and bonus will be based on an assessment of how well the manager performed in developing subordinates' skills.

2. *React to critical incidents and organizational crises in ways that send appropriate cultural messages.* Crises provide opportunities for leaders to demonstrate fortitude, commitment to organizational members, and other values and basic assumptions. The computer firm manager who got the expensive "education," described earlier, provides an example. The Social Security Administration center director, also described earlier, when confronted with the funeral in the troubled subunit, reacted

not punitively but communicatively. He thus sent a message about the value he placed on communication and participation.

3. *Practice deliberate role modeling, teaching, and coaching.* Leaders can show, tell, and encourage values and behaviors they want employees to adopt. Chapter Thirteen describes a director of a state human services agency who led a transformation of the agency from a troubled, control-oriented organization to a more participative, quality-oriented one (Stephens, 1988). She led a participative process in which project teams developed a "blueprint for the future" aimed at improving organizational policies, designs, and procedures. She faithfully attended team meetings and made it clear that she would commit her time and the needed resources to the improvements. Her actions demonstrated her commitment to change and to the value of participation, teamwork, and new ideas and approaches. She presented herself as a role model as well as a teacher.

4. *Establish effective criteria for granting rewards and status, for selection and promotion of employees, and for dismissal or punishment.* The earlier example about introducing the development of subordinates as a criterion for managers' performance evaluations and bonuses shows that what an organization rewards its members for sends a powerful message about values and basic assumptions. Punishments send equally strong messages.

5. *Coordinate organizational designs and structures with cultural messages.* Without appropriate structural redesign, a leader's modeling and coaching about new approaches and values can evaporate into empty rhetoric and posturing (Golembiewski, 1985). If the leader's criteria for rewards conflict with features of the organization that impede the behaviors the leader wants to reward, role conflict and stress for members will surely result. Chapter Thirteen describes how, in the 1970s, large Social Security Administration service centers redesigned their structures and work processes. They changed from large units composed of specialists who worked on only one specific part of a case to work modules made up of different specialists who together handled each case as a whole. The change embodied strong messages about the values of teamwork and communication, and the removal of status differences among coworkers.

6. *Coordinate organizational systems and procedures with cultural messages.* Systems and procedures, such as technological systems, routine reporting requirements, performance evaluations, and group meetings, provide important messages about important values and basic beliefs. Bourgault, Dion, and Lemay (1993) described how a performance appraisal system for Canadian government executives has a team-building effect, in part because of its basis in shared values. Conversely, studies of pay-for-performance systems, including the Performance Management and Recognition System for middle managers in the U.S. federal government (discussed

in Chapter Ten), often illustrate how such systems fail to communicate useful information about important values (Perry, 1986; Perry, Petrakis, and Miller, 1989).

7. *Design physical spaces, including facades and buildings, to communicate the culture.* The study by Goodsell (1977), described earlier, suggests some of the aspects of physical setting and space that can communicate cultural information about public agencies.

8. *Employ stories about events and people.* Leaders can also make use of stories and accounts of past events and people as a way of promoting values and assumptions. Cooper (1987) described Gifford Pinchot's effective efforts to build support for the Forest Service and strong commitment among forest rangers by, in part, taking wilderness treks with foresters. These outings served to build his image as a person committed to his mission and richly appreciative of forest resources.

9. *Develop formal statements of the organizational philosophy or creed.* Formal credos and value statements promote an organization's values and generally commit the organization to them. Exhibit 7.1 provides examples. Denhardt (2000) provides numerous examples of such statements in public agencies in several different nations.

10. *Approach cultural leadership as comprehensive organizational change.* Leadership teams must approach the development of an effective organizational culture as they would any major, influential initiative. Chapter Thirteen covers successful organizational change, discussing how leadership teams can marshal resources, commitment, and consensus in a sustained, comprehensive fashion.

Khademian (2002) has recently contributed a somewhat different perspective on leading and managing culture, in which she proposes that public managers influence culture by concentrating on the basic elements, or roots, of culture—environment, resources, and task—and how their integration has developed commitments that form the culture. She proposes that managers follow a set of strategies for examining and influencing these commitments and their connections to the roots. These strategies include, for example, identifying the commitments that form the culture and their connections to the roots of culture, identifying and articulating what needs to change, practicing and demonstrating the desired changes, and approaching the changes as an inward, outward, and shared responsibility that involves internal management as well as management of environmental elements and the participation of organizational members and numerous external stakeholders.

As indicated earlier, Chapter Fourteen includes further examples of the importance of effective culture in public organizations. As suggested by Khademian's proposed strategies and at many points in earlier chapters, a major issue for public managers and researchers is the context of leadership in the public sector and how leaders have to work with it in developing culture and carrying out other management responsibilities.

# Leadership and Management in Public Organizations

A review of the management literature shows that researchers have treated leadership and management in the public sector as essentially the same as in other settings, including business. Many major contributions to the field, such as the Ohio State leadership studies and Fiedler's theories, were developed in part from research on military officers or government managers. Mintzberg's study (1972) included a public manager (a school system superintendent) and a quasi-public manager (a hospital administrator). Additional studies have found that Mintzberg's role categories apply to managers in government agencies (Lau, Pavett, and Newman, 1980). While Mintzberg and later researchers (Kurke and Aldrich, 1983) noted some special features of public managers' work, still others found that even these few distinctions do not always hold for all types of public managers (Ammons and Newell, 1989). Small wonder that leadership researchers typically regard a public-versus-private distinction as rather inconsequential. Leaders in all settings face the challenges and general tasks suggested by the theories we have reviewed.

## Generalizations About the Distinctive Context of Public Service

Although virtually everyone accepts the premise that all executives and managers face very similar tasks and challenges, a strong and growing body of evidence suggests that public managers operate within contexts that require rather distinctive skills and knowledge. For years, political scientists writing about public bureaucracies argued that the political processes and government institutions in which government managers work make their jobs very different from those of business executives. Those writers did not, however, do as much empirical research on leadership as the organizational behavior and management researchers did. Clear evidence of differences remained rather scarce, and many management scholars noted the evidence of similarities among all managerial roles and rejected such notions as crude stereotypes.

More recently, however, greater attention to the topic of public management has produced additional evidence concerning its distinctive nature. Some of this evidence comes from executives who have served in both business and government and have written about the differences they have seen between the two roles (Allison, 1983; Blumenthal, 1983; Chase and Reveal, 1983; Hunt, 1999; IBM Endowment for the Business of Government, 2002; Rumsfeld, 1983). Although their experiences and opinions have been diverse, they have agreed that the constraints, controls, and political and administrative processes in public organizations weighed heavily on their managerial behaviors. Though these elements of the context of leadership in the public sector have been discussed in earlier chapters, it may be useful here to review a number of them:

- Jurisdiction-wide rules for personnel, purchasing, budgeting, and other administrative functions, usually with an oversight agency administering them, which limit executive authority
- Legislative and interest-group alliances with subgroups and individuals within the organization, which dilute executives' authority over those groups or individuals
- Control by legislatures, chief executives, and oversight agencies over resource and policy decisions, and strong demands for accountability on the part of the agency head for all matters pertaining to the agency
- The influence of the press and the imperative that executives concern themselves with media coverage
- The short tenure of many top executives, which limits their time to accomplish goals and weakens their influence over careerists
- The absence of clear and accepted performance measures for their organizations and the activities within them, and the need to take a particularly broad range of interests and issues into account in decision making

Federal executives report from a very special perspective, of course. There are more than a dozen such reports (Hunt, 1999; Perry and Kraemer, 1983; IBM Endowment for the Business of Government, 2002; Shalala, 1998). Yet more structured academic research paints a similar picture. Various studies of public managers show a general tendency for their roles to reflect the context of political interventions and administrative constraints.

Much of this evidence comes not from studies of leadership practices but from analyses of managerial roles. In his seminal study, Mintzberg (1972) found that the work of all the managers fell into his now well-known role categories. Yet the public manager in the sample (a school administrator) and the quasi-public manager (a hospital administrator) spent more time in contacts and formal meetings with external interest groups and governing boards and received more external status requests than did the private managers. Later, Kurke and Aldrich (1983) replicated the study, including its findings about public management; they pointed to public-versus-private comparisons as an important direction for future research on managerial roles. Lau, Pavett, and Newman (1980), also using a technique based on Mintzberg's, found the roles of civilian managers in the U.S. Navy comparable to those of private manufacturing and service firm managers. Yet they also added the role of technical expert to the role categories for the navy managers and noted that these managers spend more time in crisis management and "fire drills" than private managers. Ammons and Newell (1989), conversely, conducted a survey of mayors and city managers using Mintzberg's categories and found somewhat different results. Comparing the sample of mayors and city managers to private sector samples from previous studies, Ammons and Newell found that these city officials spent no more time in formally scheduled meetings than did the private sector managers. This contradicts the findings of Mintzberg and of Kurke and Aldrich. Yet a closer look shows that the mayors and city managers did spend more time making phone calls and conducting tours than did the private sector managers. Ammons and Newell noted that they could not really say what the phone calls involved, and that they may well represent contacts with external groups and political actors.

A study by Porter and Van Maanen (1983) supports this interpretation. They compared city government administrators to industrial managers and found that the city administrators felt less control over how they allocated their own time, felt more pressed for time, and regarded demands from people outside the organization as a much stronger influence on how they managed their time. At the level of state government, Weinberg (1977) reported on a case study of the management of New Jersey state agencies by the governor, concluding that "crisis management" plays a central role in shaping public executives' decisions and priorities.

In an observational study of six bureau chiefs of large federal bureaus, Herbert Kaufman (1979) found that they spend much of their time in classic, generic management functions such as motivating employees, communicating, and decision making. The political environment figures crucially in their roles, however. Relations with Congress outweigh relations with the higher executives of their departments. Clearly, they operate within a web of institutional constraints on organizational structure, personnel administration, and other matters. Aberbach, Putnam, and Rockman's study of legislators and administrators in six countries (1981), described in Chapter Five, supports this depiction of congressional influence as stronger than that of agency heads.

Boyatzis (1982) conducted a study of managerial competencies that compared managers in four federal agencies and twelve large firms. He found that private managers were higher on "goal and action" competencies; he attributed this to clearer performance measures, such as profits, in the private sector (see Hooijberg and Choi, 2001, for a similar finding). The private managers also scored higher on competencies in "conceptualization" and "use of oral presentations." Boyatzis suggested that more strategic decision making in the private firms and more openness and standard procedures in the public sector account for this. Interestingly, Boyatzis's findings correspond to those of earlier studies. Like Guyot (1960), he found that public managers show higher levels of need for achievement and power. Yet their lower scores on goal and action competencies reflected less ability to fulfill such needs. Boyatzis's interpretation agreed with that of Buchanan (1975). They both regarded their findings as evidence that fairly ambitious and idealistic people come to managerial work in government but appear to experience constraints within complex government agencies and policymaking processes.

Chase and Reveal (1983) discussed the challenges of public management on the basis of Chase's extensive experience in government, especially in large urban agencies. Their depiction of the key challenges in managing a public agency concentrates on those challenges posed by the external political and institutional environment—dealing with elected chief executives who have shorter-term, more election-oriented priorities competing for a place on their agenda; coping with overhead agencies such as civil service commissions, budget bureaus, and general service agencies (for travel, purchasing, space allocation); dealing with legislators (including city councils); and managing relations with special-interest groups and the media.

While these studies differ in their findings, types of managers studied, and other important ways, they confirm the general observation that public managers carry out their work under conditions marked by constraints and interventions from the political and administrative environment. The form of influence or constraint may vary between mayors, public school superintendents, governors, and middle managers in federal agencies, but it shows up consistently in one form or another. Formal meetings with controlling groups, fire drills, crisis management, phone calls, external demands on time and priorities, the power of legislators, media, and interest groups—all are indications of the exposure of the public sector manager to the political process and to the administrative structures of government.

## Does Context Affect Performance and Behavior?

Clearly, the executives who reported on their experiences in both sectors in the studies just mentioned do not regard themselves as inferior managers. Yet sharper critiques raise crucial questions about whether the public sector context penalizes excellence in leadership or actually prevents it. From his case study of the U.S. State Department, Warwick (1975) concluded that federal executives and middle managers face strict constraints on their authority. Goals are vague. Congress and other elements of the federal system—including many politically appointed executives themselves—adhere to an administrative orthodoxy akin to the old principles of administration. They hold top executives accountable for all that happens in their agency and expect agencies to show clear lines of authority and accountability. The executives and middle managers have little control over career civil servants, yet they feel intense pressure to control them to avoid bad publicity or political miscues. Because of vague performance criteria, they try to control behavior rather than outcomes through a profusion of rules and clearance requirements. Paradoxically, this approach fails to exert real control on the lower levels and further complicates the bureaucratic system. Warwick referred to this drawing upward of authority as "escalation to the top"; he said that an "abdication at the bottom" mirrors it at lower levels, where careerists emphasize security and accept the rules. When they disagree, they simply "wait out" the executives' short tenure. Top executives also preoccupy themselves with external politics and public policy issues, abdicating any role in developing human resources or organizational support systems and processes, and otherwise developing the organization itself. Warwick cited Downs (1967) pointedly, and his view accords with Downs's and Niskanen's views described in Chapter Nine.

Lynn (1981) and Allison (1983) display much less pessimism but nevertheless express a similar concern about a performance deficit. Lynn laments the tendency of many federal executives to emphasize political showmanship over substantive management. He refers to the problem of "inevitable bureaucracy," in which higher levels try to control lower levels by disseminating new rules and directives, which simply add to the existing array of rules without exerting any real influence. Similarly, the report of the National Academy of Public Administration (1986) laments the complex web of controls and rules over managerial decisions in federal agencies and their adverse effect on federal managers' capacity and motivation to manage.

In addition, the Volcker Commission (1989) reported a quiet crisis at the higher levels of the career federal service. The poor image of the federal service, pay constraints and higher pay levels in the private sector, and pressures from political executives and appointees have damaged morale among these executives and increased their likelihood of leaving the federal service. Recruitment to replace them is hampered by the same factors that discourage these individuals. The loss and demoralization of experienced executives and difficulties in finding high-quality replacements will likely diminish effective leadership practices in the future.

## Surveys of Leadership Practices

A number of studies by government agencies and surveys of government employees that included their ratings of their supervisors have provided mixed evidence about the quality of leadership in government organizations (National Center for Productivity and Quality of Working Life, 1978; U.S. Merit Systems Protection Board, 1987; U.S. Office of Personnel Management, 1979, 2000, 2003).

These surveys and studies tend to find that generally, public sector employees and managers express favorable impressions of the leadership practices in their agencies. Yet the evidence also indicates some public sector problems and a degree of private sector superiority in developing leaders, participativeness of leaders, and some other leadership practices and conditions. For example, the survey reports sometimes compare government employees' responses to comparable responses to surveys of private employees, and a couple of them have found that about 10 to 15 percent more of the private employees give favorable ratings of the supervisors and leadership in their organizations (National Center for Productivity and Quality of Working Life, 1978; U.S. Office of Personnel Management, 2003). These results coincide generally with some of the concerns about constraints on leadership in government expressed by the authors cited earlier. Yet they also place those concerns in perspective by showing the inaccuracy of overstatements of the problem. While governments probably do face constraints in encouraging and developing excellent leadership practices, many excellent leaders and managers serve in government.

## Attention to Management and Leadership

Although many observers claim that public managers pay insufficient attention to leading and managing their organizations, the evidence clearly shows otherwise, at least in many specific cases. Critics say that public managers show too little attention to long-range objectives and internal development of their organization and human resources. But critics of business management, especially in recent years, complain that similar problems plague industry in the United States and that firms place too much emphasis on short-term profit. Critics also accuse business leaders of concentrating on achieving huge financial returns for themselves, even when the firm's performance lags. These criticisms of businesses and executives make it hard to depict government as inferior. Significantly, on the last day of 2002, the three main stories on the front page of the *Wall Street Journal* were concerned with scandals in the business sector, including one about the massive personal debt that one executive had piled up while guiding his firm into one of the largest bankruptcies in history, and another about fraudulent financial accounting and dealings that led to another huge bankruptcy. If business leadership is superior to leadership in government, that superiority is certainly not universally distributed in the business sector.

Moreover, abundant evidence shows that many government managers work very hard. Ammons and Newell (1989) reported that mayors, city managers, and their immediate executive assistants say they work about sixty to sixty-six hours per week. Executives from the private sector who have served in Washington regularly report their impressions of how hard the staff members and executives in the federal government work (Volcker Commission, 1989).

Do they spend much of this time on political gamesmanship, as some critics of federal executives suggest? At the city level, several surveys have asked city officials to report on the time they spend in managerial roles (staffing, budgeting, evaluating, directing, and so on), policymaking roles (forming policy about the future of the city, meeting with other city officials, and so on), and political roles (dealing with external political groups and authorities, such as state and federal officials and active community groups, and engaging in public relations activities such as speeches and ceremonies). Ammons and Newell (1989) found that the mayors, city managers, and executive assistants in their survey reported, on average, devoting 55 percent of their time to managerial roles, 28 percent to policy roles, and 17 percent to political roles. As might be expected, mayors ranged above these averages in their concentration on political activities, and assistants paid more attention to management tasks.

Ammons and Newell asked questions about the importance of the various roles to the officials' success. Most mayors placed the greatest importance on the political role, although 23 percent emphasized the managerial role as most important. The city managers emphasized the policy role more frequently than other roles, but they also heavily emphasized management; about 40 percent rated the managerial role as most important. The executive assistants overwhelmingly rated the managerial role as most important. In sum, city officials see themselves as devoting substantial amounts of time to managerial roles.

Similarly, the small sample of federal bureau chiefs in the Kaufman (1979) study noted earlier indicated that they spent much of their time in typical managerial activities, such as motivating the people in their bureaus. This orientation does not square with the complaints that public managers do not manage conscientiously. What explains this distance between various observers and researchers on a key point such as this?

## Contingencies and Variations

Obviously, many variations in context and in the individual officials surveyed account for these different views. The bureau chiefs that Kaufman studied tended to be longer-term career civil servants, at levels lower than the short-tenure political appointees who commonly head government agencies. The level of the manager and the institutional context make a lot of difference. As pointed out earlier, officials vary by elected versus appointed status, level in the agency hierarchy, distance from the political center (such as Washington, D.C., versus a district office, or the state capitol versus a state district office), political and institutional setting of the agency (such as executive and legislative authority in the jurisdiction; weak-mayor, strong-mayor, and council-manager structures at the local level), level of government, and other factors. These variations have great significance. At virtually all levels and in virtually all settings, public managers must to some degree balance managerial tasks with policymaking and with handling the political and institutional environment (oversight agencies, legislative and other executive authorities, clients and constituents, and the media). Yet some managers in public agencies (and in many private nonprofit agencies) face intense challenges of the latter sort, while others operate in virtual isolation from political intrusions.

Meyer (1979) provided one of many examples of the effects of the variations and contingencies in the contexts of public managers. He concluded from a large study of heads of state and local finance agencies that those in stronger positions politically—those who are elected or who are career civil servants rather than political appointees—show more ability to defend their agency against pressures for change in structure and against the loss of units to other agencies, apparently because of their greater ability to draw on support from political networks. As another example, Kotter and Lawrence (1974) reported an analysis of the variations in the contexts and behaviors of mayors. They concluded that effective mayors must "coalign" major components of their context. These include the mayor's own personal characteristics (cognitive and interpersonal skills, needs, and values), their agendas (tasks and objectives in the short and long run), their networks (the resources and expectations of city government members and their relationship to the mayor), and characteristics of the city itself (such as size and rate of change). For example, they argue that the mayor's cognitive style must align with the variety and variability of information about the city that must be processed. A technician orientation, emphasizing the analysis of discrete amounts of information, best aligns with a small, homogeneous, stable city, where information varies little and can be analyzed relatively easily. A professional orientation fits a large, heterogeneous city with unstable, hard-to-analyze information. The professional mayor emphasizes using his or her professional judgment and applying professional guidelines and knowledge. Between these extremes, an engineering mayor works best in a large, diverse, stable city where information is highly varied but analyzable. A craftsman most effectively deals with the less varied but less analyzable information in a small but unstable city. This typology draws on Perrow's ideas (1973) about information contingencies of tasks (see Chapter Eight).

Anderson, Newland, and Stillman (1983) also proposed a typology, one based more on a framework akin to Blake and Mouton's managerial grid (1984), described earlier in this chapter. They argued that cities have varied levels of demand for their officials to display either a people orientation or a technical orientation. Growth communities create high demand for both orientations and for a chief executive–type manager who works for change within regular organizational structures. Caretaker communities demand maintenance of existing services and an administrative caretaker, a leader with a technical orientation. Arbiter communities require much conflict resolution and therefore more of a people orientation than a technical one; a community leader mode of management best satisfies these requirements. A consumption community demands the most public services for the least cost and hence needs an administrative innovator who will follow the direction set by elected council members and seek innovations for the sake of efficiency and service delivery (that is, less emphasis on people, more on technical skill).

## Effective Leadership in Government

A growing body of research on effective and innovative leaders in government also breaks away from overgeneralizations about ineffectual managers struggling with an overwhelming political and administrative system. As mentioned in Chapter One, this stream of work has now developed into a genre in its own right (such as Allison, 1983; Ban, 1995; Barzelay, 1992; Behn, 1994; Borins, 1998; Cohen and Eimicke, 1998; Cooper and Wright, 1992; Denhardt, 2000; Doig and Hargrove, 1987; Hargrove and Glidewell, 1990; Holzer and Callahan, 1998; Ingraham, Thompson, and Sanders, 1998; Jones and Thompson, 1999; Light, 1998; Linden, 1994; Osborne and Gaebler, 1992; Popovich, 1998; Rainey and Steinbauer, 1999; Riccucci, 1995; Roberts and King, 1996; Thompson and Jones, 1994; Wolf, 1997). These studies provide numerous examples of innovative, influential, entrepreneurial leaders in government agencies and programs. For example, Lewis (1980) studied Hyman Rickover's development of the nuclear power program in the U.S. Navy, J. Edgar Hoover's impact on the FBI, and Robert Moses's transformation of the New York Port Authority. In each case, Lewis found an organization that was ineffective at achieving the major goals for which it presumably existed until it experienced a process of mentoring by an effective superior. In this process, the superiors developed appropriate goals and learned how to get things done. They then engaged in an "entrepreneurial leap" that changed the organization and its resource allocation in unforeseen ways, and they created an "apolitical shield" that defended their work from political intervention by casting it as nonpolitical and objectively necessary. Later phases involved struggling for autonomy, reducing environmental uncertainty, expanding the organization's domain, and fully institutionalizing the new organization (with consequent problems of "ultrastability"). Lewis's subjects stand as controversial titans who, through exceptional ambition, energy, and political and technical skill, took advantage of key political and technological developments to build effective organizations.

Other writers have described executives who played major roles in the development of the National Aeronautics and Space Administration, the Tennessee Valley Authority, major Department of Defense policies, the Social Security Administration, and the Forest Service. Doig and Hargrove (1987) concluded from a set of such studies that the innovative leaders in the public sector displayed similar general patterns. They identified new missions and programs for their agencies. They developed external and internal constituencies for these new initiatives, identified areas of vulnerability, and neutralized opposition. For their new missions, they enhanced the technical expertise of the agency and provided motivation and training for organizational members. The leaders followed a mixture of rhetorical strategy, involving evocative symbols and language, and coalition-building strategy, emphasizing the development of political support from many groups. Some leaders relied on both strategies; some primarily emphasized one over the other.

External conditions set the stage for these activities, according to Doig and Hargrove. The entrepreneurs actually took advantage of the diverse and fragmented governance structures often cited as reasons why public managers accomplish little. The difficulties of strong central control in such a system provided these leaders with opportunities to forge their own direction. They also took advantage of patterns of potential public support (for example, changing public attitudes during the 1930s supported a more active role for the federal government) and new technologies and alliances with elected political officials.

In their personalities and skills, the leaders displayed an "uncommon rationality," a remarkable ability to perceive effective means to ends. They were able to see the political logic in an emerging historical situation and link their initiatives to broader political and social trends. Doig and Hargrove also stressed the individual's motivation to make a difference, coupled with a sustained determination and optimism. Success depends, however, on the association of personal skills with organizational tasks and with favorable historical conditions, such as public and political support and timely technological possibilities.

Similarly, Riccucci (1995) profiled federal executives who fought heroically against corruption or on behalf of some program or policy to which they were dedicated, often using effective political tactics such as skillful use of the media and expert coalition-building, as well as effective organizational management techniques. Hargrove and Glidewell (1990) brought together authors who have provided biographical descriptions of determined and talented governmental executives struggling with jobs that are, in important senses, impossible.

Another important point about the ability of public managers to influence important developments is revealed in studies of policy entrepreneurs (Roberts and King, 1996). This conception of entrepreneurship focuses on people who influence policy, often from outside formal positions, by pressing for innovations in policies and programs. Some develop public support for the innovations, press legislators and administrators for support, and otherwise move the system by taking on a sustained role as a policy champion. Others may play the role of "policy intellectual," providing innovative ideas. As described earlier, public executives and managers can play such roles, but they sometimes face constraints on their independence to do so. They can also act as catalysts and sponsors, providing support, listening, and responding when policy champions with good ideas press for a hearing.

All these studies of entrepreneurship suggest ways we might reconcile the broad observations about indifferent public management with the evidence that many public managers have hammered out significant change. Marmor and Fellman (1986; Marmor, 1987), for example, offer a typology of public executives that concentrates more directly on the issue of internal program management and program accomplishment, and suggests key distinctions in leaders' motivation and objectives. They argue that public executives vary in managerial skills and commitment to program goals. Among those with low managerial skills are the *administrative survivors*, who also have low commitment to program goals and provide little effective leadership. *Program zealots* have high programmatic commitments but weak skills and also tend to be unsuccessful administrators. As for those with high managerial skills, *generalist managers* show low commitment to program goals. *Program loyalists*, highly skilled managers with strong programmatic commitments, serve as the most likely candidates for having entrepreneurial impact. Whether or not it is valid and complete, such a typology makes the important point, which should be obvious, that executives and managers in government vary widely in their motivations, energies, skills, and orientations. Such variations explain the success of some and the mediocrity of others, and should constantly remind us of the dangers of overgeneralizing about any category of human being.

## Modeling and Measuring Public Management

A very interesting and original recent approach to analyzing public sector leadership and management and variations related to it involves the development of a formal model and efforts to test the model with empirical data. Kenneth Meier and Laurence O'Toole (O'Toole and Meier, 1999) have developed and tested a model of the impact of public management on organizational performance. One of their focal questions, whether or not "management matters," has been a difficult issue in all management settings for a long time. Some of the major theories of organization, such as population-ecology theory (see Chapter Four), have in some ways implied that it does not matter what managers do. Events out of managers' control may determine organizational success and survival. As for the public sector, many observers have argued that the multiple constraints on managers described in Chapter Three and in this chapter diminish the importance of managers even more than in the private sector. Doig and Hargrove (1990, p. 2), for example, pointed out that Kaufman (1979), in an important study of federal executives, observed that "they make their mark in inches and not in miles" and achieve "modest, incremental accomplishments." Doig and Hargrove illustrate the controversy over this conclusion by presenting a set of biographies of influential, entrepreneurial leaders in government.

O'Toole and Meier (1999) add to this debate the first explicit and formal model of the influence of public management, and they test it with data from surveys of school district superintendents in Texas. While not easily summarized and possibly difficult for some readers, the model represents an unprecedented effort to develop such a model and test it with empirical evidence. This model needs attention from people seriously interested in public management.

The model employs concepts and initial assumptions about hierarchy and networks in the contexts of public managers:

- The authors posit the presence of some degree of hierarchy (and formal authority) that provides stability, acts as a buffer against external shocks, and helps coordinate the efforts of many actors to achieve a common purpose, although stability itself may or may not be related to performance.
- They also posit that public managers must deal with networks of other authorities and groups, particularly those in formation or in flux, which increase complexity and instability in the managerial environment.
- The model treats hierarchies (complete certainty in managerial relations) and networks (total structural fluidity and resulting uncertainty) as poles on a continuum.
- *Management* refers to "the set of conscious efforts to connect actors and resources to carry out established collective purposes" (p. 510). It involves motivating, coordinating, and providing stability, but also changing structure and exploiting opportunities in the environment in order to improve performance. Multiple actors can share the management task, so management includes the sum of all managerial efforts.

The authors then specify their model of management's impact on public program performance. They begin with a basic system:

$$O_t = \beta_0 O_{t-1} + \varepsilon$$

where current performance $(O_t)$ is the result of past performance $(O_{t-1})$ weighted by a rate of stability $(\beta_0)$ and a series of shocks to the system $(\varepsilon)$. Shocks $(\varepsilon)$ can come from either inside or outside the system. $\beta_0$ can range from 0 to 1. Hierarchy is associated with stability, so as hierarchy increases, $\beta_0$ approaches 1. When the administrative system involves more of a network, $\beta_0$ moves in the direction of 0 because networks are more unstable.

The authors also point out that a shock (symbolized by $X_t$) can get through the organization's buffering system:

$$O_t = \beta_0 O_{t-1} + \beta_2 X_t + \varepsilon_t$$

Thus, the authors divide $\varepsilon$ into some shock $(X_t)$ that gets through the organization's buffering system with initial impact $(\beta_2)$ and a random component $(\varepsilon_t)$.

They treat management as just another input to the system:

$$O_t = \beta_0 O_{t-1} + \beta_2 X_t + \beta_3 M + \varepsilon_t$$

with M representing management and $\beta_3$ its impact. A management coefficient $(\beta_3)$ significantly greater than zero would indicate that management matters. In other words, organizational performance at a given time is a function of performance at an earlier point multiplied by a stability factor, plus a shock to the system multiplied by a factor representing its influence, plus management times its impact, plus the random set of shocks around the system.

O'Toole and Meier then elaborate the model in various ways. For example, management can adopt a strategy of either buffering the system or actively seeking to exploit the environment for the benefit of the system. If the decision is to buffer the system from the environment, management interacts with the buffering process so that

$$O_t = \beta_1(H + M_1)O_{t-1} + \beta_2 X_t(1/HM_2) + \varepsilon_t$$

where $M_1$ is a maintenance function of management—the manager's efforts to add to hierarchy and structure—and $M_2$ is the management strategy for interacting with the environment. H is the extent of hierarchical stability. Management of the environment $(M_2)$ reduces the impact of environmental shocks while interacting with the extent of hierarchy. As $M_2$ increases, the factor $1/HM_2$, which is multiplied by the shock and its effect, $\beta_2 X_t$, goes down, because the manager's efforts to buffer the shock reduce its effects on performance. In other words, organizational performance depends on performance at a previous point in time, multiplied by the sum of hierarchy (which increases stability) and the manager's efforts to maintain the stability of the system, plus a factor representing any given external shock that the manager buffers $(1/HM_2)$, plus a random component $(\varepsilon_t)$. Organizational performance depends on previous performance and the degree to which hierarchy and the manager's maintenance behaviors affect performance, and the degree to which the manager buffers or defends the system from shocks.

Alternatively, if the manager's strategy is to exploit the environment (that is, not to buffer the system but to try to magnify some of the environmental influences), then

$$O_t = \beta_1(H + M_1)O_{t-1} + \beta_2 X_t(M_2/H) + \varepsilon_t$$

The first element in this equation, as in the previous one, means that as hierarchy and the manager's system maintenance actions increase, organizational performance tends to be consistent over time. The second factor has changed, so when $M_2$ increases, the amount that is multiplied by the shock factor $\beta_2 X_t$ increases, meaning that the manager's efforts to exploit the shock have increased its influence on organizational performance. So, more hierarchy and more managerial efforts to maintain the system can enhance performance, and more managerial efforts to exploit an external shock to the system cause that shock to have increased impact on performance.

One might develop the suspicion that Meier and O'Toole developed this model to give the rest of us severe headaches. It appears quite abstract, and some of us may have difficulty following it, so it becomes important to see if it leads to important empirical findings about the role and importance of public management. Meier and O'Toole (2001) conducted a survey of superintendents of Texas school districts and asked them, among other things, about their frequency of contact with school board administrators, business leaders, other superintendents, state legislators, and the Texas education agency. Meier and O'Toole regarded this measure of contact with important stakeholders and authorities as an indication of the superintendents' efforts at managing external networks, which in turn represents $M_2$ in the model just described, or the managers' efforts to exploit environmental opportunities and buffer the system from environmental shocks. With a variety of statistical tests, they found that this measure of network management showed a strong positive relationship to a measure of organizational performance—the pass rates for the districts on standardized tests that the state of Texas administers to all high school students each year. The statistical analysis included controls for important variables such as resources (for instance, teacher salaries and class size) and constraints (such as low-income students and ethnic minority students). Meier and O'Toole further found that higher levels of networking were associated with increasing impacts of resources on performance and decreasing impacts of constraints. They interpreted these results as evidence that the managers who engaged in more external network management were better able to exploit resources and mitigate constraints. While acknowledging limitations of the measures of the variables, Meier and O'Toole presented these results as a successful effort to analyze systematically the relation between management activities and organizational performance, and to demonstrate that the relationship is positive and that public management does matter.

In still another analysis, Meier and O'Toole (2002) developed a measure of managerial quality (on the part of the district superintendents) and showed that it positively relates to ten different measures of educational performance. The managerial quality measure is the amount of a superintendent's salary that is not accounted for by a set of variables that tend to influence salary, such as district size, personal characteristics such as education, and others (that is, the quality indicator is the residual of the regression of salary on the set of variables). Again, the results indicate that public management influences organizational performance, and they strengthen the evidence that high-quality public management has a positive influence on performance.

As indicated in the description of the models just presented, Meier and O'Toole predict that hierarchy and managers' maintenance behaviors will enhance organizational performance. This prediction goes against the grain of much contemporary thought in organization theory and management thought. As described in Chapter Two, the trend has moved strongly toward emphasis on flexibility and adaptiveness in organizations, rather than toward stability. O'Toole and Meier (2003) suggest, however, that stability can have important positive influences on organizational performance, through avoidance of turnover and disruptions, enhancement of valuable experience, and other ways. They provide evidence to support this view by using two measures of personnel stability (the tenure of the superintendent and the retention of teachers) to represent the hierarchy variable in their model. They find that these variables relate positively to organizational performance as represented by pass rates on the Texas standardized tests, and other indicators of educational performance of the school districts.

Meier and O'Toole's evidence represents school superintendents and school districts, which may differ from other public managers and public management settings, so the authors are testing the model with other populations, such as law enforcement administrators (Nicholson-Crotty and O'Toole, forthcoming). The measures of the variables have various limitations. For example, do pass rates on standardized tests adequately measure organizational performance? The major concepts in the model, such as hierarchy, maintenance behaviors, and networking behaviors, need more refinement. Nevertheless, the explicitness of the O'Toole-Meier model and their empirical tests sharpen these questions and make them salient for further research. Their stream of analyses represents a rare and original pattern of sustained, explicit, systematic analysis of major issues in public management, and in particular of whether public management "matters," indicating that it does and providing plausible evidence of why and how.

Even with all its descriptions and references, this chapter does not fully cover all the research and examples of effective public sector leadership and management. Chapters Thirteen and Fourteen provide more discussion of the leadership of change and of high-performance public organizations. Still, the theories and studies reviewed here provide valuable contributions to the analysis of organizational leadership and to the long-term challenge of developing a conception of public management that recognizes the skills and practices of the many effective managers of public organizations.

CHAPTER TWELVE

---

# TEAMWORK

---

## Understanding Communication and Conflict in and Among Groups

When the U.S. Internal Revenue Service went through the major transformation described at the beginning of Chapter Eight, it appointed twenty-four design teams to plan the new structures and processes the organization would need. Employees from all levels and many different locations came together to work in these teams, and they had to communicate effectively and confront and resolve conflicts. To emphasize the importance attached to these teams, the commissioner and the deputy commissioner of the IRS met with each of the teams in long, intensive sessions. The commissioner became virtually legendary within the organization for the attentiveness with which he prepared for the meetings by doing all the reading, with which he listened in the meetings, and with which he responded to each meeting with a "white paper," or written reaction to the information and ideas communicated in the meeting. Meanwhile, the commissioner also continued to communicate with the people in the IRS about the changes that were going on, through videotaped talks, the organizational newsletter, and other channels. As described in the next chapter, the Social Security Administration reorganized its public service centers into groups of about forty people in "modules" that would handle the processing of an individual client's claim from beginning to end. In effect these modules were work teams. During these changes, plenty of conflicts broke out, as they always do in any major organizational change.

The human group served as one of the founding topics in the social and administrative sciences. Teams, committees, task forces, work units, and other groupings make up the structure and activity of organizations. As the IRS and SSA examples illustrate, many organizational change and improvement efforts revolve around group processes, such as quality circles, or organizational development interventions, such as team-building exercises or problem-solving groups. Social scientists have studied groups so intensively for so many years that, as with other important topics such as motivation, the research has discovered more and more complexities. So many kinds of groups operate under so many different conditions that researchers must strain to understand all the variations. Yet group processes have never lost their significance for managers. If anything, they have become more significant recently. A recent trend toward *team-based organization* and *team-based management* has swept through many organizations, including public agencies (Katzenbach and Smith, 2001; Mohrman, Cohen, and Mohrman, 1995). The literature and practical applications of *high performance work systems* and *high performance organizations* in business firms now heavily emphasize the use of teams and the importance of constant communication (Appelbaum, Bailey, Berg, and Kalleberg, 2000; Lawler, 2003; Lawler, Mohrman, and Benson, 2001).

Organizational communications and conflict do not occur only within and between groups. As suggested in Chapter Five, in the discussion of managing relations with the media, public managers' communication responsibilities involve managing a complex range of channels and targets (Graber, 2003; Garnett, 1992). Yet much of the research on groups came about because people realized that groups influence communication and conflict among their members and between themselves and other groups. In addition, communication and conflict often intertwine. For example, suppose that members of the department of human services of a large state communicate to members of the state's department of labor that the labor department's opposition to a program to aid migrant laborers simply reflects its subservience to certain wealthy fruit growers. The labor department officials communicate back that the human services department is proposing an incompetently designed program just to build its own empire. Any skillful, highly trained social scientist might detect the presence of conflict in this situation. Conflict may cause or result from bad communication, and the way out of conflict usually emphasizes the establishment of effective communication. Researchers have examined many dimensions of communication and conflict in organizations. This chapter concentrates on certain fundamental points that figure importantly in discussions of organizational change and improvement. In addition, as usual, the discussion covers the application of these topics to public organizations.

# Groups in Organizations

Research has demonstrated that while groups often place strong pressures on their members to conform to others in their group, they also represent arenas for sharing and communicating. They affect the way we view ourselves and others, in and out of our groups, and the way we behave toward people. They influence our attitudes, including acceptance or rejection of new ideas. Chapter Two describes some of the classic research on groups, by Lewin, the Hawthorne researchers, Coch and French, and others, and how group processes have been a central topic in organizational development over the years. These and many other researchers have developed a number of important and lasting insights about groups. They have shown how groups can influence work habits and productivity, and they have shed light on the attitudes that group members maintain and how changes in those attitudes affect their behaviors. They have found that cohesion and commitment in groups can enforce attitudes and norms within the group and increase or decrease group performance and productivity, depending on the direction of group consensus. Group participation in decision making can enhance the quality of decisions and acceptance of change within an organization. Yet very cohesive groups can also clash with other groups, and groups can censor each other in harmful ways. Developing effective groups, then, involves a careful process of taking advantage of their potential without falling prey to their pitfalls. The literature now contains abundant guidance for the design and operation of groups and teams (Hackman, 2002; Harris, 2002; Katzenbach and Smith, 2001; Mohrman, Cohen, and Mohrman, 1995; Zander, 1994), so the discussion here concentrates on some basic topics about the nature of groups and their advantages and disadvantages.

## Group Formation, Norms, and Roles

The question of why and how groups form invites simple answers, such as "The assistant secretary appointed a representative of each major division in the agency." Yet in every group, unique informal patterns emerge that belie these simple answers. Groups may form through official appointments by leaders or under official rules or as a result of task imperatives such as the need for certain specializations. Some groups form entirely voluntarily, and even in formally established groups, members may decide how much to contribute or hold back, how much to cooperate or conflict, and so on. Groups vary in their attraction for members and in their influence over them. Members move into roles and levels of influence that may correspond little to those that are formally designated.

Earlier chapters discussed some of the reasons for these variations, including French and Raven's typology of power (1968)—reward power, coercive power, expert power, referent power, and legitimate power. French and Raven were group theorists and intended their typology for analyses of why groups vary in power to wield influence as a group, in attractiveness to their members, and in power over their members. Psychological experiments have shown that people often have fundamental impulses to group together with others. Psychologists interested in social comparison processes have pointed out that people often lack clear information about how they are doing and what they should do and thus draw on others as referents for their own behavior. Groups have a strong influence on people in this respect. Also, groups gain power and attractiveness as referents partly by dint of their other bases of power, such as their control of rewards, their expertness, and so on.

The controls that groups exert over their members have received much attention because of their obvious importance. As groups form, group norms and values develop. Some researchers find the concept of norms, or standards of behavior and attitudes shared by group members, to be elusive and vague. Whether or not the concept of norms perfectly captures the phenomenon, however, groups clearly display patterns of conformity to certain behaviors and beliefs.

Researchers have also analyzed the elaboration of various roles in groups, especially the psychological and social roles that may not follow formal assignments. Leadership obviously figures very importantly, and much of the work reviewed in Chapter Eleven, such as Fiedler's theory, pertains to group leadership. While leadership in groups obviously may follow from formal assignments and rank, informal leaders often emerge as well. Researchers who have intensively studied the development of leadership in newly formed groups report such findings as the importance of participation: those who participate most actively most often become the leaders in the eyes of other members. Researchers have also discovered, however, that although long-winded, assertive types sometimes come to be regarded as leaders early on, groups later turn more and more to less outspoken, more competent persons. In fact, multiple roles can emerge, with one or several people taking the lead in social and emotional matters, such as maintaining morale and harmony, and another person pressing for effective group structure and task accomplishment.

## Group Contexts, Structures, and Outcomes

Generalizations about groups, particularly from research on experimental groups, provide insights, but very diffuse ones. Researchers have worked on the implications of variations in group settings and characteristics to try to understand the effects of such contingencies as group size, tasks, communication patterns, and composition. Groups often have advantages over individuals (and larger groups over smaller groups) because of the availability of more talents, ideas, viewpoints, and other resources. Groups often outperform individuals at certain decision-making and problem-solving tasks. Yet larger groups can often suffer problems related to unwieldiness, diffusion of responsibility, and the presence of "free riders." Some research has also suggested that social relations tend to become more formal in larger groups and that their members tend to tolerate more impersonal, task-oriented behaviors by leaders.

Researchers have also intensively examined variations in group tasks, such as variations between individual and collaborative tasks and structured and unstructured tasks. Some researchers have produced evidence of the social facilitation of individual tasks, where the mere presence of another person enhances performance on familiar tasks. For more collaborative or group tasks, researchers and theorists have woven a complex array of concepts and relationships among group size and such task characteristics as homogeneity or heterogeneity and disjunctiveness or conjunctiveness. The material on contingency theories of organization (Chapter Eight) provides important implications for managers in relation to this topic, such as the need for subunits with more complex and variable tasks to have more flexible, interactive processes.

The structure and composition of groups also influence their processes, of course. Highly diverse groups whose members represent many different backgrounds and goals face particularly severe challenges in establishing smooth working relations. Examples include groups with an appointed member from each department in an organization or from each of a set of interest groups (such as a community advisory group for a government agency) and groups formed to carry out negotiations between labor and management. The communication structure imposed on a group can also determine many important outcomes. For example, Leavitt (1951) conducted research on communication networks in groups, comparing communication processes and outcomes in groups required to communicate in different patterns. In one pattern, the circle, members communicated with only two members (those adjacent to them), so information had to move around the group in a circle. In a chain pattern, members were arranged in a line, along which communication had to flow back and forth. In a wheel pattern, all communication had to flow through one member occupying the center, hub position. Other patterns included a fully interconnected group with all members able to communicate directly with all the others. The patterns determined numerous outcomes for the groups. The wheel produced the fastest transmission of information and good accuracy but low overall satisfaction, except for the person in the middle, who had a great time, usually emerging as the leader of a centralized process. The chain and circle produced slower communication, with less accuracy;

nobody liked the chain very much, but members expressed high satisfaction with the circle. In both the circle and the completely interconnected group, communication was often slow, but everyone got the word more effectively than with the other forms, and members felt higher satisfaction. The research thus dramatizes a trade-off faced by managers and groups that is also suggested by contingency theory. Many of the human relations–oriented models prescribe participation, and these experiments demonstrate that when people more actively participate, they understand more and feel better about the process. Yet the research also shows that such processes often move slowly, and a more centralized structure has some advantages in speed, accuracy, and leadership impact. Managers and groups have to choose the most important outcome.

## Advantages and Disadvantages of Groups

These sorts of findings from research and experience have made it clear that groups can serve as media for good or bad outcomes, depending on many factors. Managers must consider when and how groups can operate with the most value. Maier (1967) provided a list of pros and cons of using groups for problem solving, to which people often refer. Groups can bring in more knowledge, information, approaches, and alternatives than individuals. The participation of more people in group settings increases organization members' understanding and acceptance of decisions; members have a better idea of what the group decided and why, and they can carry this information back to people in the other units or groups to which they belong. But the social pressures in groups can bolster majority opinions regardless of their quality. Aggressive individuals or subgroups may stifle more capable members. As indicated by research described earlier, groups may press for conformity and move toward solutions too rapidly by stifling dissent. Some members may concentrate simply on winning, from their own or their unit's point of view.

Maier also pointed out that other factors can be good or bad, depending on the skill of the leader. Effective leaders can manage conflict and disagreement constructively and turn the relative slowness of group decision making to advantage, achieving good outcomes such as conflict resolution and more carefully discussed decisions. Groups may also make risky decisions. While exerting pressures for conformity, they often paradoxically create a dispersion of responsibility, where individuals shirk or evade responsibility for the group's actions or take social cues from others in the group that lead them to mistakenly underestimate the significance of a problem. Individuals may outperform groups when creativity and efficiency are paramount, acceptance of the decision is less crucial, the most qualified person is easy to identify, individuals are very unlikely to cooperate, or little time is available (Gordon, 2002).

## Groupthink

Irving Janis's work on groupthink (1971) reflects many of the elements of this body of research that have particular significance for managers, especially managers and leaders in government ('t Hart, 1990). Janis said he discovered groupthink not just in many organizational decision-making processes but also in some of the most immensely significant decisions, such as major strategic decisions by firms, and public policy decisions such as the bombing of North Vietnam during the Johnson administration and John Kennedy's decision to carry out the Bay of Pigs invasion. Janis argued that groups under the stress of making major decisions often exhibit the symptoms of groupthink. They need consensus and commitment to the course of action they choose, and the pressure for conformity leads members to see the group as invulnerable to opponents, to develop rationales to explain away or avoid serious consideration of apparent problems and threats, and to see themselves as morally right and stereotype their opponents as incapable or immoral. Pressure for agreement and unanimity falls on members who dissent, as others press them to agree and support the group and its leader. Members sometimes adopt the role of "mind guards," withholding information that might shake the group consensus, and engage in self-censorship, stifling their own impulse to disagree.

Janis described instances of groupthink primarily at lofty levels of authority, but managers encounter it in many settings. At the annual meeting of the county commissioners' association of a large state, for example, when the association's governing council convened, council members expressed outrage over new environmental protection regulations that the state legislature was imposing on the state's counties. Certain council members fulminated against the regulations, charging that they usurped the counties' rightful authority. As the discussion continued, members increasingly characterized the state legislators and agency executives behind the changes as tyrants and empire builders and depicted themselves as noble defenders of their constituents' right to govern themselves. They boldly proclaimed their intention to write a strong letter of protest to the legislators and agency officials (a step likely to prove ineffectual). These members reacted scornfully to suggestions that a more reasonable and moderate discussion of the situation would be more productive, as if those making such suggestions lacked courage. They thus displayed groupthink symptoms, such as stereotyping the opposition, overestimating one's own position, and stifling dissent.

Janis prescribed a number of steps leaders can take to help groups avoid groupthink:

- Encourage members to act as critical evaluators and impartial decision makers.
- Accept criticisms of your own actions.

- Invite outside experts to join the discussion.
- Require members to discuss the matter with others outside the group.
- Assign two or more groups to work on the problem separately.
- Assign a member to play devil's advocate.
- Break the group into two subgroups at key points.
- Set aside time to review threats to the group's decision and any possible weaknesses in it.
- At major decision points, hold "last chance" sessions in which members can air their reservations.

Later in this chapter we will consider an abundance of additional advice and procedures for managing groups. Before turning to those, however, it is useful to cover some basic ideas about communication and conflict.

## Communication in Organizations

Besides communication in and between groups, other forms and channels of communication play crucial roles in organizations. The ideas about power, strategy, structure, and leadership considered earlier are relevant here as well, because communication can occur through organizational rules and structures themselves, through formal written documents, and in one-on-one exchanges with superiors (Graber, 2003).

Discussions of organizational communication typically begin with a very general model of the communication process. According to such models, communication begins with the source from which a message originates. A transmitter encodes the message and sends it to a receiver, who decodes it and moves it to a destination. Noise influences the accuracy of the transmission. Other general conceptions depict a person as both a sender of messages, through particular channels, to another person, and a receiver of messages, back through the same or other channels, from that other person. Both people also communicate with other recipients and senders concomitantly. These fairly obvious models show what the research and theory emphasize—the nature of sources, senders, and recipients; the channels along which messages flow; and in particular, the problem of noise or distortion that impedes the accurate transmission of information (Downs, 1988).

Typical discussions also distinguish among horizontal communication, vertical (upward and downward) communication, and external (outward) communication with environmental components. Horizontal communications encounter difficulties as a result of conflict, competition, or other differences between subunits and groups. Vertical communications encounter difficulties as a result of hierarchical filtering and superior-subordinate relationships, including resistance, inattentiveness, misunderstanding, and reticence or withholding of information by lower levels. The distinction between formal and informal communications processes, already familiar by now, receives due notice, as does the research on communication networks described earlier.

## Communication Roles

Analysts of organizational communication have drawn on concepts from other areas of the social sciences to distinguish roles in the communication process (Rogers and Argawala-Rogers, 1976). *Gatekeepers* occupy positions where they can control the flow of information between units and groups. Others around *opinion leaders* look to them for information about the form their own opinions should take. People in *liaison* roles transmit information between two or more units or groups. *Cosmopolites* have many contacts outside the organization and bring a lot of external information into the organization.

## Communication Assessments and Audits

Beyond these generalizations, obviously, myriad dimensions of communication receive attention from researchers, as illustrated by the now numerous survey instruments and other procedures for assessing communication in organizations (Downs, 1988). Most of these tools ask individuals for their perceptions and evaluations of the information they receive in their organization and of its communication process. For example, the communications audit questionnaire of the International Communications Association asks about the amount of information the respondent sends and receives on an array of topics—job performance, pay and benefits, relationship of his or her own work to the overall organization, new procedures, organizational problems and policies, and so on. It also asks about the amount of information the respondent needs to send and receive. It asks similar questions about the amount of information sent to and received from various sources, such as top management, middle management, immediate supervisors, coworkers, and the grapevine. Other questions ask about respondents' satisfaction with the information they receive, the organization and extent of their organization's communication processes, how much follow-up on communications they need and receive, and the quality of the organizational and work climate. Other communication assessment procedures track specific messages through the organization and map the dissemination of information. Still others map actual communication networks in organizations, analyzing who communicates with whom and about what.

## Communication Problems

Obviously, the main issue in communications is getting it right, so the discussion often turns rapidly to what goes wrong. Exhibit 12.1 provides lists of communication difficulties. The exhibit first presents lists of communication barriers. These lists are typical of the way such problems are identified and expressed in the general management and organizational behavior literature. Then the exhibit presents a list of communication distortions that may occur in public bureaucracies, such as jargon, inflated prose, and the manipulation of information for political or bureaucratic purposes.

Some of the greatest literary and journalistic figures of the last two centuries have poured their talents into ridiculing and decrying these tendencies in government bureaucracies. Some of these critiques have become embodied in academic theories that posit that public bureaucracies and bureaucrats distort and manipulate information more aggressively than their counterparts in business. Before examining these and other theories and evidence about communication in public organizations, it is useful to cover the concept of conflict in organizations, which often intermingles with communication processes.

# Conflict in Organizations

Conflict has always represented a fundamental challenge for organizations and leaders. Frederick Taylor (1919) said that he pursued the principles of scientific management in part because he wanted to diminish conflicts between workers and managers by providing scientific solutions to the questions they regularly disputed. Lawrence and Lorsch (1967), in their seminal study of organizational design processes, found high levels of conflict in very effective organizations and very high investments in managing rather than avoiding conflict. Some of the most recent developments in organizational design, such as matrix designs and ideas about fluid and duplicating structures, intentionally design conflict into organizational structures. Research shows that well-managed conflict often improves decision making in organizations. Research also shows, however, that managers, especially in business organizations, tend to dislike conflict and seek to avoid it, even though such conflict avoidance may lead to less effective decision making (Schwenk, 1990).

In public and nonprofit organizations, one expects and even hopes for intense conflicts, although preferably not destructive ones. As noted earlier, public organizations often embody the unceasing political competition and public policy dilemmas of the nation. Government agencies and their subunits and managers compete for resources, for executive and legislative attention, and over their "turf"

## EXHIBIT 12.1. COMMUNICATION PROBLEMS AND DISTORTIONS.

### Barriers to Effective Communication

*Lack of feedback:* One-way communication, in which the receiver provides no return of information about whether and with what effect the information came across

*Noise in communication:* Interference with the message during its transmission, ranging from actual physical noise or distortion to distractions or interference from the presence of others, personal biases, or past experiences

*Misuse of language:* Excessively vague, inaccurate, inflammatory, emotional, positive, or negative language

*Listening deficiencies:* Receivers' listening inattentively, passively, or not at all

### Barriers to Effective Communication Between Groups

When two groups define a conflict between them as a win-or-lose conflict

When one or both groups seek to aggrandize their own power and emphasize only their own goals and needs

When they use threats

When they disguise their true positions and actively distort information

When they seek to exploit or isolate the other group

When they emphasize only differences and the superiority of their own position

### Communication Distortions in Public Bureaus

*Distorted perceptions:* Inaccurate perceptions of information that result from preconceived ideas or priorities or from striving to maintain self-esteem or cognitive consistency

*Erroneous translation:* Interpretation of information by receivers in ways not intended by the senders

*Errors of abstraction and differentiation:* Transmission of excessively abstract or selective information; underemphasis of differences in favor of similarities or excessive polarization of fairly similar positions

*Lack of congruence:* Ambiguity or inconsistency between elements of a message or between the particular message and other sources of information, such as conflicts between verbal and nonverbal cues or between officially communicated values and policies and other communications indicating that these policies and values do not hold

*Distrusted source:* Failure to accept an accurate message because of suspicions about bias or lack of credibility of the source

*Jargon:* Communication difficulties that result from highly specialized professional or technical language that confuses those outside the specialization (and often those within it). Some jargon has value, but officials may use inflated and pretentious language to appear knowledgeable or important, to intimidate or impede clients, to distort true intentions, or to evade accountability and scrutiny.

*Manipulating and withholding information:* Senders' actively distorting or withholding information in line with their own interests and related influences that they seek to impose on the receiver

*Source:* Johnson and Johnson, 1994; Gortner, Mahler, and Nicholson, 1987.

(Wilson, 1989). They share responsibilities for programs and policies but often have differing points of view and priorities. New administrations and newly elected and appointed officials enter the picture regularly and rapidly, claiming new mandates, attempting to forget or freeze programs into which people have poured their work lives, or setting out to do things differently and better. Ombudsmen, examiners, auditors, oversight agencies, and legislative committees and hearings have a duty to take a sharply questioning and often conflicting view of an agency's operations. Often at issue are the very lives or major living conditions of many people, and massive amounts of money, power, and influence. The separation of powers designed into the U.S. government actually calls for conflicting interests and authority as checks against one another. Yates (1985) observed that "Madisonian systems" with built-in contentions and divided authority abound in public and private organizations. Schwenk (1990) found that executives in nonprofit organizations see a positive relationship between conflict in the decision-making process and the quality of the resultant decisions, while executives in for-profit organizations regard conflict as damaging to the quality and clarity of decisions. The nonprofit executives, which included executives from government agencies, had to consider the needs of diverse constituents and groups. They found conflict unpleasant, but they regarded it as useful in clarifying the needs and goals of diverse groups.

One must expect conflict, then, and try to make a healthy form of it flow in government and its agencies. Keeping it healthy represents the key challenge. Research on organizations has focused on what types of conflict occur, what brings it about, how it proceeds, and as this chapter covers somewhat later, how to manage it constructively.

## Types of Conflict

Experts on organizational conflict point out that numerous types and forms of conflict occur in organizations. Conflict can exist within a person (as the concepts of role conflict and role ambiguity emphasize), between people, and within and between groups and organizational departments or divisions. Conflict can range horizontally, across levels of an organization. It can occur vertically, between higher and lower levels (the classic example is a dispute between management and labor; another common example is a battle within a geographically dispersed government agency or business firm between the people at headquarters and field or district personnel).

## Bases of Conflict

All types of conflict can originate in or be aggravated by organizational or subunit culture, values, goals, structures, tasks and functions, authority and leadership processes, and environmental pressures, as well as by the demographics and individual personalities of organizational or group members. You name it and it can cause a flare-up.

Researchers have provided useful lists of some of the most frequent sources of strife; these can help us sort through some of this complexity. They have cited differences in goals, values, cultures, and priorities, of course. The sociologists who began emphasizing dysfunctional bureaucracies around midcentury pointed out that the specialization of work and responsibility that bureaucracy involves, with its emphasis on reliable adherence to the rules and goals of specialized units, virtually ensures conflicts among units (for example, see the entry on Merton in Exhibit 2.1 in Chapter Two). Differences in power, status, rewards, and resources among people and groups can lead to feelings of inequity, or the simple need to compete with others can cause conflict. Where two groups' tasks or decision-making processes overlap, are intensely interdependent, or naturally compete, tensions can boil over. Not always mentioned in the research, but quite obvious, are the surprisingly frequent instances of significant conflict among high-level officials based simply on clashes of personal style and ego.

## Conflict Stages and Modes

Analysts of conflict have also noted what they call the phases of conflict episodes. Pondy's frequently cited classification (1967), for example, includes five stages:

1. *Latent conflict* exists when conditions have set the stage for conflict but it has not yet simmered to the surface.
2. *Perceived conflict* begins when the people involved begin to sense that conflict exists, even though they may attempt to downplay or deny it.
3. *Felt conflict* emerges when individuals begin to feel its effects—tension, anxiety, anger, or practical problems resulting from the conflict.
4. *Manifest conflict,* figuratively or actually, involves open warfare. People or groups try to frustrate, harm, or defeat one another. Either one group must win or lose; the conflict must continue, with destructive effects; or managers and members must effectively channel and manage the conflict toward constructive ends.
5. The *conflict aftermath* is the stage after the outbreak of conflict when some alternative and its results become evident.

As people and groups respond to the onset of conflict, their responses can take various forms. Thomas (1983) pointed out that people can respond through *avoidance* (trying to ignore or withdraw from the conflict). They can try *accommodation*, in which they cooperate and make concessions to the other party's demands or needs. *Compromise* involves an exchange of concessions and cooperative responses (without one side being more accommodating than the other). *Competing* involves simply trying to force, outdo, or defeat the other party without any appreciable accommodation or concern for its goals and needs. *Collaborating* occurs when two parties work together to meet both parties' needs mutually; it differs from compromise in that the two parties do not simply give up on certain goals and values but rather work to find ways to maximize returns for both.

Yates (1985) also offered useful suggestions for developing strategies and tactics for managing conflict. He described methods of fostering a competitive debate among conflicting parties, using neutral language to avoid escalating hostilities and behaving with civility and mutual respect. He suggested approaches that involve identifying mutual problems and avoiding enmity, win-or-lose situations, and long-term resentments. One does this partly through including all affected parties, providing complete information, and keeping communication channels open. Yates proposed a process of conflict management that has many similarities to the management of culture and transformational leadership described in Chapter Eleven. The conflict manager must understand the people involved, establish a sense of shared mission to give the parties an incentive to resolve the conflict, and adopt an incremental approach, focusing on winning concrete issues.

## Conflict Outcomes, Suppression, and Escalation

Experts on conflict have also detailed its outcomes and effects, though these are fairly obvious in much of the rest of the organizational behavior literature. Excessive conflict can induce stress, frustration, dissatisfaction, high turnover, absenteeism, and poor performance among employees. When poorly managed, it can damage organizations. The preceding discussion of types and modes of conflict provides a useful reminder that suppressed or poorly handled conflict can hurt an organization, in part because it can escalate more easily. Researchers point out that conflict can feed on itself, aggravating the sorts of barriers to communication described earlier—the use of charged language, bias in sending and receiving information, a tendency to interpret neutral statements from the other party as negative or aggressive, reduction of communication, and formation of we-they, win-lose perceptions of relationships. Severely entrenched, intense conflict can make an organization sick, like a mentally disturbed person who does irrational, self-destructive things.

Sometimes managers have to work with organizations facing severe challenges to effective communication and deal with people and groups that have many reasons to come into conflict. Researchers and consultants have developed a fairly rich fund of prescriptions for managing and improving group processes, communication, and conflict resolution processes in such organizations. After we look at these, the discussion will return to special considerations about public organizations.

# Managing Groups, Communication, and Conflict in Organizations

Earlier chapters covered many topics relevant to managing groups, communication, and conflict, and the following chapters will cover still more. The discussion of leadership in Chapter Eleven described propositions from Fiedler's contingency theory, path-goal theory, life-cycle theory, and other approaches to understanding how leaders should and do behave toward the groups they lead. These theories emphasize the many variations in leadership settings and styles among organizations and the need for setting and style to mesh. Keeping these many variations in mind, group theorists have suggested numerous general prescriptions for managing groups. The prescriptions for avoiding groupthink are one example. Leaders also have to try to enhance the attractiveness of group membership to increase group harmony, cohesiveness, and motivation (Zander, 1994). The typology of power offered by French and Raven (1968)—reward, coercive, expert, referent, and legitimate power—serves as a guide to some of the types of incentives that leaders can enhance and draw on to make groups effective. That typology implies additional incentives for group membership and motivation, such as prestige, a sense of having an impact or being important, conviviality, specialness of membership, and so on, that group theorists advise leaders to utilize. Many group theorists have a greater human relations orientation than leadership theorists. Prominent group theorists have typically argued that, in general, effective work groups require participative leaders who respect the dignity of group members and maintain harmony in groups (Zander, 1994).

This human relations emphasis probably comes from the close connections between group theory and the field of organization development (OD). Chapter Thirteen describes OD and some of the specific group techniques used to improve organizations, such as team building and T-group procedures, and to enhance effectiveness, communication, and conflict resolution in work groups. OD consultants also use a variety of techniques to enhance communication and resolve conflicts between different groups (Gordon, 2002). For example, they might use an organizational mirror procedure, in which other groups in the organization report their views of a particular group or unit to that group so that it can better assess its impact on and relations with others. A confrontation meeting brings two or more warring groups together to analyze and resolve the conflicts between them. Third-party interventions and interpersonal facilitator approaches have a person from outside the groups, and often outside the organization, come in to help with the conflict-resolution process. The latter involves a more central role for the facilitator in transmitting communications between the two groups (Blake and Mouton, 1984).

Most of these techniques involve ways of controlling the expression of hostility and aggression to prevent conflict from escalating. They usually try to provide a systematic way to uncover the nature of the conflict and discover a base for resolving it, through such procedures as image exchanges, in which members of the groups relate their views of the other group; sharing appreciation procedures, which call on group members to express appreciation of good things about the other group; and having the members list their expectations about the outcomes of the process. Management consultants may propose the use of a dialectical inquiry technique for managing and encouraging conflict in strategic decision-making processes. In this technique, the development of a strategic plan is followed by the development of a counterplan that questions the assumptions of the original plan. A devil's advocacy approach involves a critique of the basic assumptions of the strategic plan but does not propose a specific alternative (Schwenk, 1990).

Numerous other group procedures and techniques, not necessarily connected to OD practices, abound in organizations. The success of quality circles in Japan has led to their proliferation among organizations in the United States and other countries. A quality circle brings the members of a work group or organizational unit together for special group sessions on how to improve the quality of the unit's work and products. Organizations also typically employ special task forces, venture groups, policy committees, and other group-based approaches that explicitly seek to take advantage of group capacities. Several group decision-making procedures, such as the nominal group technique, brainstorming, and the Delphi technique, can facilitate communication and management of potential conflict within and among groups (Gordon, 2002). In the nominal group technique, each group member makes a list of responses to a focal question or issue—for example, What are the organization's most important goals? One by one, each group member reads aloud the first item on his or her list, then the second item, and so on. As the lists are read, the items are recorded and displayed for the group to see. The group then discusses the set of items—goals, in this example—to clarify them, discuss disagreements, and combine similar ones. They then follow any of several possible methods for coming to agreement on the final set of goals. (These kinds of group processes now have computer software to support them, and may take place in computer labs or technologically sophisticated conference rooms where the groups can use such technology.) The procedure thus allows each person to contribute, minimizes digression, and channels conflict into constructive patterns. Brainstorming sessions invite members to suggest all alternatives or possibilities about an issue or problem that they can think of. The group records all suggestions and then evaluates them and works toward a conclusion. In the Delphi technique, a smaller group prepares a questionnaire about a topic, circulates it to a larger group, and then uses the latter's responses to prepare a revised questionnaire. This second questionnaire is circulated along with information about the results of the first questionnaire, and the process is repeated until a consensus develops within the larger group.

In addition, communications experts commonly stress the usefulness of conducting organization-wide communications audits of the sort described earlier. They point to the crucial role of the climate or culture of an organization in fostering or stifling communication and in determining whether and how well people manage conflicts.

## Special Considerations for Public Organizations

The preceding review demonstrates that researchers have treated these topics as generally applicable across all organizations, with no need for any particular distinction among public, private, and nonprofit organizations. The review also indicates why they have taken this posture. They state the models and propositions at a high level of generality to make them applicable across groups and organizations. They see that managers in government, business, and nonprofit settings face common challenges in dealing with these dimensions of their work and can apply many of the proposed responses just as well in any of the sectors.

Still, some of the time-honored observations about government bureaucracies claim sharp distinctions between that domain and business firms in matters pertaining to groups, communication, and conflict. Many of these virtually classic views echo throughout some of the most prominent recent theoretical efforts. In many governmental settings, for example, an elaborate, diverse configuration of groups and authorities contests over organizational policies and decisions. As noted earlier, inside and outside government organizations, "Madisonian systems" operate (the product of laws that formally establish multiple authorities) or arise as a result of the activities of groups and individuals seeking to influence government policies—the pluralistic governmental processes long discussed by political scientists. Complex groups and interests outside an organization often mirror a corresponding complexity within, according to many people who write about government organizations. Interest groups, congressional committees, and elements of the executive branch form alliances with units and individuals inside a particular agency and jealously defend these relationships. Consequently, many large government agencies become highly diverse confederations of groups and units whose relative independence weakens the authority of the politically appointed executives at the top (Warwick, 1975; Seidman and Gilmour, 1986).

Observers also say that the fact that the goals of public agencies are multiple, hard to specify and measure, and conflicting adds to this complexity. Often, two government agencies or two bureaus within a particular agency pursue diametrically opposed goals—conserve natural resources and develop natural resources for economic and recreational uses, enhance international trade but prevent the sale of sensitive technology—or have sharply differing priorities for a program for which they share responsibility.

For all these reasons, government often involves a particularly high frequency of power-sharing situations (Bryson and Einsweiller, 1995; Kettl, 1993). Many commentators note that government managers need a particularly high level of tolerance for ambiguity and diversity and must frequently deal with conflicts among diverse groups. Public managers must also deal with a particularly wide array of interests and parties. At the same time, government heavily emphasizes control and accountability, but it does so within a context in which clear performance measures such as profits and sales are not available to aid in assessing accountability and performance. The greater diversity in public organizations, they say, aggravates their tendency to emphasize reporting, record keeping, and requests for clearances from higher hierarchical levels. Even smaller units in government face intense requirements to report to higher levels as a result of the federal system of grants and contracts, requirements imposed by larger agencies and jurisdictions, and so on. The system has become an elaborate array of "centrifugal and centripetal" forces (Warwick, 1975) and "inevitable bureaucracy" (Lynn, 1981). More and more diversity, coupled with pressures for accountability but few clear performance measures, breeds a profusion of rules, regulations, clearances, and reporting requirements.

All this implies that public management typically involves great information intensity and information traffic. The tasks that public organizations carry out, of course, tend to be service-oriented and information-intensive. Careful studies of information handling in the public and private sectors have shown that public organizations do in fact involve greater information intensity, with private service organizations such as banks and insurance companies coming close to resembling them but actually falling in an intermediate range between industrial firms and public agencies (Bretschneider, 1990).

Tullock (1965) developed a pessimistic theoretical argument about the effects of this governmental context on communication and the flow of information. He argued that the size and complexity of government bureaus create information leakage as lower-level officials communicate up the hierarchy. The officials must summarize the information they report upward and screen the information they receive from lower levels before transmitting it upward. This process deletes much of the information. And in addition to simply boiling down the information, they report the information that is most favorable to them and screen out unfavorable information. This leads to substantial distortions in upward communications in public bureaucracies, according to Tullock. He argued that private firms are better able to avoid such problems because their higher levels use such measures as sales and profits to prevent the lower levels from inaccurately reporting information about their activities.

Downs (1967) elaborated Tullock's observations into a more complex set of hypotheses. According to Downs, most communication in bureaus is *subformal*. Subformal communication increases with greater interdependence among activities, with uncertainty, and with time pressure, but decreases between subunits in sharp conflict with one another. Newer, fast-growing, changing bureaus have less effective communication networks than older, more stable ones. Information moving up the hierarchy becomes distorted for the reasons that Tullock described, and successful high-level officials use various strategies to counteract this distortion. They develop informal channels of information outside the bureau and set up overlapping responsibilities inside the bureau to create redundant internal channels. They employ *counterbiasing*, which means they adjust their own reactions to information from lower levels in ways that counter the biases they know the reports contain. For example, they reduce reliance on information about future events or qualitative factors. In agencies with many crises and much specialization, they bypass levels to get the "straight scoop" from lower levels. They seek to develop distortion-proof information systems, especially when precise accuracy and rapid transmission are very important and when there is a "tall" hierarchy and important variables are quantifiable. This characterization of the public sector setting, together with preceding ones, if correct, means that communications in the public sector are more intensive and difficult than in the private sector, with conflicts more likely to occur and more difficult to manage.

Yet little explicit comparative research has assessed this view. While researchers have examined communications in public agencies (Warwick, 1975), such studies cannot resolve the question of whether large private firms would show the same characteristics and processes. Searches performed for this book located few public-private comparative studies explicitly dealing with groups, communication, and conflict. In one, Boyatzis (1982) found that a sample of public managers showed lower levels of skill at managing group processes than private sector managers did. In another, Baum and James (1984) compared the responses of 2,300 employees from nine "clearly public" and five "clearly private" organizations to the International Communications Association communications audit survey questionnaire. On most of these questions, the respondents in the public organizations scored less favorably than did the private sector employees. On almost every item about information received and sent, they felt they received and sent less and needed to send and receive more than the private sector respondents. They also scored lower on each of thirty-two questions about organizational climate (concerning relations with coworkers, supervisors, and subordinates; satisfaction with work, pay, communication, and other factors; and quality of products and services). As with the satisfaction studies discussed in Chapter Ten, the public sector respondents expressed reasonably high satisfaction on many of these items but scored lower than private sector respondents. Baum and James concluded that public managers face greater challenges in establishing effective communications and must work harder at it.

Schwenk (1990) compared the perceptions of forty executives from for-profit (FP) and not-for-profit (NFP) organizations regarding conflict surrounding decision making in their organizations. All the executives found conflict unpleasant, but the FP executives felt that conflict diminished the quality and clarity of decisions, and they found it more unpleasant than the NFP executives. The NFP executives reported a positive association between conflict and the quality and clarity of decisions. In describing their decisions, the FP executives much more frequently mentioned criteria related to financial performance—a finding consistent with that of Solomon (1986)—while the NFP managers more often mentioned the needs of constituents and the speed and effectiveness of service delivery.

Schwenk (1990) also analyzed the executives' descriptions of their decisions using the decision framework developed by Mintzberg, Raisinghani, and Theoret (1976), described in Chapter Seven. He found that conflict in the NFP organizations more often occurred in the early phases of the decision-making process (the phases concerned with problem recognition and diagnosis) and that NFP decision-making processes involved more steps and more "recycles," in which the decision process cycles back to an earlier phase. In the FP decision-making processes, conflict tended to occur later, in the phase involving evaluation and choice of alternatives. The NFP executives apparently regarded conflict as useful in clarifying diverse criteria and the demands of diverse interests and constituencies, particularly in the recognition and diagnosis of problems. While the sample for the Schwenk study was not large, the findings tend to reflect the organizational context of public organizations described earlier in this and in other chapters. They also tend to concur with other researchers' findings about decision-making processes in public organizations compared to private ones (Hickson and others, 1986; Solomon, 1986).

In sum, much theory and some expert observation hold that public organizations face greater complexity and more potential problems in group relations, communication, and conflict resolution than private organizations. Little direct comparative evidence supports these observations, but the few studies that do provide evidence about them tend to show greater complexity and problems. This conclusion should not be overstated and overgeneralized, however. The interpretation that the private sector performs better on these dimensions is too simple and easy. Previous chapters, and Chapters Thirteen and Fourteen, show numerous examples of effective public management involving strong and productive communication. The public sector may face greater challenges precisely because of the nature of government as an arena for the complex policymaking decisions and political choices of an advanced political economy. Yet, as the review in this chapter has shown, the literature phrases the issues and prescriptions at a high level of generality, making them applicable to public, private, and nonprofit organizations. Public managers may not need knowledge and skills significantly different from those covered here, but they do need particularly well-developed knowledge and skills in this area. For effective communication in public agencies, there are now well-developed frameworks, guidelines, and advice for public managers (Graber, 2003; Garnett, 1992).

PART THREE

# STRATEGIES FOR MANAGING AND IMPROVING PUBLIC ORGANIZATIONS

# CHAPTER THIRTEEN

# MANAGING ORGANIZATIONAL CHANGE AND DEVELOPMENT

If, as Chapter Six asserts, organizational effectiveness is the fundamental issue in organizational analysis, then the challenge of changing organizations is a strong candidate for second place. A sprawling literature addresses organizational change and innovation, with much of it focused on how to change organizations for the better. As earlier chapters point out, controversy simmers over whether public organizations and their employees resist change. The truth is that researchers and experts often note a paradoxical aspect of change in public organizations. Far from being isolated bastions of resistance to change, they change constantly. This pattern may sometimes impede substantial long-term change, however. In many public organizations, the politically appointed top executives and their own appointees come and go fairly rapidly. In federal agencies, the agency heads stay less than two years on average. Shifts in the political climate cause rapid shifts in program and policy priorities. This can make it hard to sustain implementation of major changes. Conversely, we now have an abundance of examples of successful change in public organizations, and this chapter describes some of them.

## Relatively Natural Change: Organizational Life Cycles

Members of organizations plan and carry out some changes purposefully. Other changes occur more spontaneously or naturally as organizations pass through phases of development or respond to major shifts in their environment. The two types of change intermingle, of course, as managers and other members respond to shifting circumstances. In the last two decades, in their writing and research on organizational life cycles, birth, and decline, scholars have turned more attention to externally imposed and naturally evolving change processes (Aldrich, 1999; Baum and McKelvey, 1999; Kimberly, Miles, and Associates, 1980; Cameron, Sutton, and Whetten, 1988). Much of this work concentrates on business firms but applies to public organizations as well (for example, Van de Ven, 1980; Quinn and Cameron, 1983). Years ago, Simon, Smithburg, and Thompson (1950) noted that public organizations become distinct by the nature of their birth. An influential set of interests must support the establishment of a public organization as a means of meeting a need that those interests perceive, and they must express that need politically. Public agencies are born of and live by the satisfaction of interests that are sufficiently influential to maintain the agencies' political legitimacy and the resources that come with it.

Later, Downs (1967) suggested a number of more elaborate ways in which public bureaus form. For one of these ways, Max Weber coined the phrase "routinization of charisma," in which people devoted to a charismatic leader press for an organization that pursues the leader's goals. Alternatively, as Simon, Smithburg, and Thompson (1950) pointed out, interested groups press for the formation of a bureau to carry out a function for which they see a need. A new bureau can split off from an existing one, as did the Department of Education from what used to be the Department of Health, Education, and Welfare (Radin and Hawley, 1988). Also, entrepreneurs may gain enough support to form a new bureau. Admiral Hyman Rickover became a virtual legend by building an almost autonomous program for the development of nuclear propulsion in the nuclear power branch of the navy's Bureau of Ships and the nuclear reactor branch of the Atomic Energy Commission (Lewis, 1987).

## The Stages of Organizational Life

Downs also said that bureaus have a three-stage life cycle. The earliest stage involves a struggle for autonomy. "Zealots" and "advocates" dominate young bureaus and struggle to build political support for their bureau's legitimacy and resource requests. Once a bureau has established itself and ensured its survival, it enters a stage of rapid expansion, in which its members emphasize innovation. Ultimately, it enters a deceleration phase, in which the administrators concentrate on elaborating rules and ensuring coordination and accountability. Downs associated this process with what he called the *rigidity cycle* for bureaus. He said that as bureaus grow older and larger and enter the deceleration stage, the zealots and advocates either depart for more active, promising programs or settle into the role of "conservers." Conservers come to dominate the bureau, and it ossifies. Others have pointed out that over time many bureaus form strong alliances with interest groups and legislators—especially legislators on the committees that oversee them. These allies guard the bureaus' access and influence and stave off many change attempts (Warwick, 1975; Seidman and Gilmour, 1986).

Yet Downs oversimplifies the foot-dragging bureaucracy. Large, old organizations change markedly, as has been recognized in recent life-cycle models. Quinn and Cameron (1983) developed a framework based on similarities among models that others have proposed. Their framework conceives of four stages of organizational life cycle—the entrepreneurial, collectivity, formalization and control, and elaboration stages.

In the *entrepreneurial stage*, members of the new organization concentrate on marshaling resources and establishing the organization as a viable entity. An entrepreneurial head or group usually plays a strong leading role, pressing for innovation and new opportunities and placing less emphasis on planning and coordination. Quinn and Cameron illustrate this stage by describing a newly created developmental center for the mentally disabled in a state department of mental health (DMH). The energetic center director led a push for new treatment methods that involved deinstitutionalizing clients and developing their self-reliance. The center began to receive expanded support from federal grants, the DMH, and the legislature. In this stage, the center emphasized the open-systems model of organization.

Out of the first stage develops the second, the *collectivity stage*. In this stage the members of the center developed high cohesion and commitment. They operated in a flexible, team-based mode, exhibiting high levels of effort and zeal for the center's mission. This type of shift represents an expanded emphasis on teamwork, marked by adherence to the human relations model as well as to the open-systems component of the competing values framework described in Chapter Six.

The research on life cycles points out that crises sometimes push organizations into new stages. About six years after the formation of the center, a major newspaper ran articles attacking the DMH for inefficiency, poor treatment of clients, and loose administrative practices. The articles cited critical reports from oversight agencies citing inadequacies in such control mechanisms as organizational charts, records, job descriptions, policy manuals, and master plans. The DMH conducted a special investigation and instructed the center director to move toward a more traditional organizational structure and more traditional controls. The director left, and the new director emphasized clear lines of authority, rules, and accountability. Staff commitment fell, and many staff members left. The center had clearly moved into the *formalization and control stage*. In competing values terms, the rational control model predominated, and the importance of open systems and human relations criteria declined.

The case ended at this point, but the life-cycle framework includes a fourth stage, involving *structural elaboration and adaptation*. Confronting the problems of extensive control and bureaucracy that develop during the third stage, the organization moves toward a more elaborate structure to allow more decentralization but also corresponding coordination processes. The organization seeks new ways to adapt, to renew itself, and to expand its domain. A large corporation may become more of a conglomerate, multiplying its profit centers, or it may adopt a matrix design (Mintzberg, 1979). It appears to be difficult for public agencies to decentralize in these ways, however (Mintzberg, 1989). They have no sales and profit indicators to use in establishing profit centers, and they face stronger external accountability pressures. Note that in the DMH case the press and the oversight agencies both pressed for traditional bureaucratic structures—charts, manuals, job descriptions. Some public agencies also reconfigure in later stages, however, as described shortly.

## Organizational Decline and Death

Many older, supposedly entrenched organizations face intense pressure to renew themselves. During the 1970s and 1980s, such pressures rose to particular intensity in the United States. Businesses faced surging international competition and swings in the price of oil and other resources. Government agencies faced tax revolts and skepticism about government. This climate bolstered the Reagan administration's efforts to cut the federal budget, including funding for many agencies and for federal support to state and local governments, many of which also faced state and local initiatives to force tax cuts (Levine, 1980a). In the 1990s, these pressures eased in certain ways because of a strong economy, and research on decline in public agencies slackened. Nevertheless, many factors continued to pressure public organizations in many nations to do more with less. In the United States, a drive to reduce taxes and the federal deficit continued. The Clinton administration's National Performance Review eliminated 324,580 jobs from the federal workforce, bringing federal employment to its lowest level since 1950. As the new century got under way the Bush administration issued the *President's Management Agenda,* which criticized the Clinton administration for making these employment reductions in an across-the-board, poorly planned way that did not take into account strategic human resource needs. At the same time, however, the management agenda announced that *competitive sourcing* would be one of the primary emphases of the administration. This involves conducting competitive assessments to determine whether government jobs and tasks should be outsourced, or contracted out to private organizations (U.S. Office of Management and Budget, 2002). The administration further announced the objective of considering more than 800,000 federal jobs for outsourcing, and the Department of the Army announced a plan to contract out more than 200,000 jobs. In many other nations, reforms as part of the *New Public Management* movement often emphasized using more businesslike arrangements in government, including contracting out and privatizing governmental activities. So, the challenge of reductions, declines, and cutbacks looms very large for people in government.

Even before these recent pressures, organizational researchers realized that while such pressures may have intensified during the period, they actually reflected ongoing processes of decline and demise that had received little attention in organizational research (Kimberly, Miles, and Associates, 1980; Cameron, Sutton, and Whetten, 1988). Bankruptcy rates among business firms have always been high, and all organizations, including public ones, tend to have low survival rates (Starbuck and Nystrom, 1981). Organizations may decline at various rates and in various patterns, for a number of reasons (Levine, 1980b). They may atrophy, their performance declining due to internal deterioration. They may become rigid, inefficient, and plagued with overstaffing and ineffective structures and communications. As described later, the Social Security Administration (SSA) once became so backlogged in processing client requests that everyone involved agreed that something had to be done. Very recently, the IRS undertook a major transformation in response to performance problems and public criticisms (Thompson and Rainey, 2003).

*Vulnerability and Loss of Legitimacy.* Organizations, especially new ones, can be quite vulnerable to the loss of resources or support from their environment. Shifts in consumer preferences can undercut businesses. Government organizations face an analogous problem when voters resist taxes. This issue is related to another reason for decline, the loss of legitimacy. Private firms, such as tobacco companies, can suffer when the public or public officials question the legitimacy of their products or activities. Legitimacy figures even more crucially for public organizations. Public and oversight authorities often impose stricter criteria on public organizations for honest, legitimate behaviors, as in the example of the HUD scandal described in Chapter Seven.

*Environmental Entropy.* An organization's environment can simply deteriorate in its capacity to support the organization. Resources may dry up. Political support may wane. Public organizations often lose support because of the waning of the social need they address (Aldrich, 1999; Levine, 1980a).

*Responses to Decline.* Organizations respond to decline with greater or lesser aggressiveness and with more or less acceptance of the need for change (Whetten,

1988; Daft, 2001, pp. 512–515). Some organizations take a negative, resistant disposition toward the pressures for change. They may aggressively strike a preventive posture or passively react in a defensive mode. They may try to prevent pressures for change by manipulating the environment. Public agencies may try to develop or maintain legislation that rules out competition from other agencies or private providers of similar services. Public employee unions sometimes attack privatization proposals because public employees may find them threatening. Conversely, organizations may adopt a less proactive defense against cuts, citing statistics showing the need for their programs and working to persuade legislators that their programs meet important social needs.

Other organizations take a more receptive approach to the need for change, either by reacting or by generating change and adaptation. Many public agencies react with across-the-board cuts in subunit budgets, layoffs, or other reductions in their workforce. Conversely, organizations can also adapt through flexible, self-designing structures and processes. They may allow lower-level managers and employees to redesign their units when they feel the need (Whetten, 1988).

The pressures for reduced government just described have led to a rich discussion of tactics for responding to funding cutbacks. Table 13.1 summarizes Charles Levine's description of some of those tactics (1980b). Rubin (1985) analyzed the Reagan administration's cutbacks in five federal agencies. She found that the agencies' responses in some ways matched what one would expect from the public administration literature and in some ways differed markedly. The president was fairly successful in achieving cutbacks in the agencies. His strong popular support blunted interest-group opposition to the cuts in the early phases. Still, agencies with interest-group support more effectively resisted the cutbacks. Yet Rubin found no evidence of strong "iron triangles" (tight alliances of agencies, interest groups, and congressional committees, as discussed in Chapter Five) protecting the agencies.

The agencies were not nearly so self-directed and uncontrollable as is sometimes claimed. Agency heads tended to comply with the president's cutback initiatives and usually did not work aggressively to mobilize interest-group support. Career personnel carried out many of the cuts as part of their responsibility to serve the president. Some of the agencies, particularly central administrative and regulatory agencies, had no strong interest-group support and were more vulnerable to cuts. Golden (2000) analyzed the career civil servants' reactions to policy changes that Reagan appointees sought in four federal agencies and found that the careerists put up little strong resistance. Their tendency to resist and their manner of doing so depended on many factors, such as professional background. Attorneys in one agency argued more with the Reagan appointees, but felt that it was part of their professional responsibility to carry out their duties conscientiously even when they disagreed with the priorities of the Reaganites.

## TABLE 13.1. ORGANIZATIONAL DECLINE AND CUTBACK MANAGEMENT: TACTICS FOR RESPONDING TO DECLINE AND FUNDING CUTS.

| | Tactics to Resist Decline | Tactics to Smooth Decline |
|---|---|---|
| External political (problem depletion) | 1. Diversify programs, clients, and constituents<br>2. Improve legislative liaison<br>3. Educate the public about the agency's mission<br>4. Mobilize dependent clients<br>5. Become "captured" by a powerful interest group or legislator<br>6. Threaten to cut vital or popular programs<br>7. Cut a visible and widespread service a little to demonstrate client dependence | 1. Make peace with competing agencies<br>2. Cut low-prestige programs<br>3. Cut programs to politically weak clients<br>4. Sell and lend expertise to other agencies<br>5. Share problems with other agencies |
| External economic/ technical (environmental entropy) | 1. Find a wider and richer revenue base (for example, metropolitan reorganization)<br>2. Develop incentives to prevent disinvestment<br>3. Seek foundation support<br>4. Lure new public- and private-sector investment<br>5. Adopt user charges for services where possible | 1. Improve targeting on problems<br>2. Plan with preservative objectives<br>3. Cut losses by distinguishing between capital investments and sunk costs<br>4. Yield concessions to taxpayers and employers to retain them |
| Internal political (political vulnerability) | 1. Issue symbolic responses, such as forming study commissions and task forces<br>2. "Circle the wagons"—develop a siege mentality to retain esprit de corps<br>3. Strengthen expertise | 1. Change leadership at each stage in the decline process<br>2. Reorganize at each stage<br>3. Cut programs run by weak subunits<br>4. Shift programs to another agency<br>5. Get temporary exemptions from personnel and budgetary regulations that limit discretion |
| Internal economic/ technical (organizational atrophy) | 1. Increase hierarchical control<br>2. Improve productivity<br>3. Experiment with less costly service-delivery systems<br>4. Automate<br>5. Stockpile and ration resources | 1. Renegotiate long-term contracts to regain flexibility<br>2. Install rational choice techniques such as zero-based budgeting and evaluation research<br>3. Mortgage the future by deferring maintenance and downscaling personnel quality<br>4. Ask employees to make voluntary sacrifices such as taking early retirements and deferring raises<br>5. Improve forecasting capacity to anticipate future cuts<br>6. Reassign surplus facilities to other users<br>7. Sell surplus property, lease back when needed<br>8. Exploit the exploitable |

*Source:* Levine, 1980b. Reproduced by permission of Chatham House Publishers, Inc.

These analyses establish some extremely important points. Agency responses to decline are more complex and perhaps less politically resistant than depicted in the general literature—agencies do change, and they do not necessarily resist change as forcefully as stereotypes and some theories suggest. Still, politics figures very importantly in change and cutback attempts and can severely impede them. Understanding when and how one can effect change becomes the major challenge, to which we return later.

***The Ultimate Decline: Organizational Death.*** A conclusion similar to Rubin's comes from a debate over whether public agencies can "die." Kaufman (1976) investigated the question of whether government organizations are immortal, in view of the many assertions about their staunch political support and their intransigence against pressures for change, reduction, or elimination. He noted many threats to an agency's survival. They face competition from other agencies, loss of political support, and the constant reorganization movements that keep officials continuously hunting for ways to reshape government, especially ways that appear more efficient. Kaufman reviewed statistics on the death rates of federal agencies and concluded that such rates are not negligible. Generally, however, federal agencies have a strong tendency to endure. Of the agencies that existed in 1923, he said, 94 percent had lineal descendants in 1974.

Later, Starbuck and Nystrom (1981) mounted a fascinating challenge to this conclusion. They pointed out that Kaufman had classified agencies as lineal descendants even if they had changed organizational locations, names, or personnel or had substantially different functions. When agencies merged, he treated the new agency as a descendant of both of the former ones. Starbuck and Nystrom pointed out that studies of death rates of industrial organizations typically treat mergers between corporations as resulting in only one existing organization. When a corporation goes bankrupt and employees start a similar new one, analysts do not count this as a continuation. Difficult issues exist, then, in defining organizational death. Starbuck and Nystrom reanalyzed Kaufman's data, using criteria more akin to those used in studies of industry; they found that government agencies and industrial corporations have similar death and survival rates. A large proportion of both government agencies and business firms do not survive very long. The analysis turns on whether one uses criteria biased toward organizational change or against it.

Peters and Hogwood (1988) also report finding a great deal of organizational change in the U.S. federal bureaucracy. Their analysis shows, however, what other organization theorists have seen when they have studied public organizations (Meyer, 1979): public organizations may be quite change-resistant and intransigent in some ways, and steering them in new and innovative directions can be a major challenge for society. Yet they do, in fact, change a great deal, including undergoing the ultimate change of passing out of existence. As described in later sections, they can also revitalize themselves after periods of decline.

More recently, Daniels (1997) has analyzed the termination of public programs, pointing out that programs do get terminated. Termination, he concludes, is hard to achieve, involves a great deal of political conflict, and presents an American political paradox in that "everyone supports it, and everyone opposes it" (p. 70). Similarly, but with more emphasis on the likelihood of agency termination, Lewis (2002) reported a study of government agency mortality between 1946 and 1997 and concluded that 62 percent of agencies created since 1946 have been terminated. He also emphasized the major role of political processes, concluding that agencies face the greatest likelihood of mortality when shifts in the political climate bring their critics and opponents into power.

## Innovation and Organizations

Another response to pressures on organizations, a response that they need in order to survive, is innovation. Innovations in society and in organizations figure so importantly in social progress that a body of research focused specifically on such processes has developed in the last several decades. Some of it addresses the broad topic of diffusion of innovations in societies and across levels and units of government. Numerous studies have explored such topics as the adoption of birth control methods in overpopulated countries, new agricultural methods in less developed countries, and different ways of providing firefighting, garbage collection, and teaching services in governments across the United States. Some studies have also analyzed general measures of innovativeness in a certain type of organization, such as the number of health-related innovations adopted by county health departments. According to Rogers and Kim (1985), the vast majority of these innovation studies have focused on public organizations or public programs, and their application to business organizations remains open to question. They also point out that many of these studies followed what they called the *classical diffusion model*, which includes the following components: characteristics of the innovation itself (see Exhibit 13.1), communication channels in the social system being studied, time (for example, rate of adoption of innovations), and members of the social system (the characteristics of its individuals and groups and how those characteristics influence their response to innovation). Students of innovation have also developed process models emphasizing initiation and implementation processes in which people perceive a performance gap and match an innovation to a perceived problem, and then implement the innovation through restructuring and institutionalization. Exhibit 13.1 offers a simplified look at this important topic and all the work on it, but it has

## EXHIBIT 13.1. ATTRIBUTES OF INNOVATIONS THAT AFFECT THEIR IMPLEMENTATION.

1. Cost—initial and continuing; financial and social
2. Returns on investment
3. Efficiency—improvements in efficiency offered by innovation
4. Risk and uncertainty
5. Communicability—clarity of the innovation and its results
6. Compatibility—similarity to existing product or process
7. Complexity
8. Scientific status
9. Perceived relative advantage—whether potential advantages can be demonstrated or made visible
10. Point of origin—from inside or outside the organization; from what person, unit, or institution
11. Terminality—whether the innovation has a specific end point
12. Reversibility and divisibility—whether the innovation can be reversed or divided into steps or components so that the organization can return to the status quo if necessary
13. Commitment—the degree of behavioral and attitudinal commitment required for success
14. Interpersonal relations—how the innovation influences personal relations
15. Public- versus private-good attributes—whether the innovation provides public benefits or restricts benefits to a smaller set of individuals
16. Gatekeepers—how the innovation is related to various influential persons or groups that can block or initiate the innovation
17. Adaptability—whether users can modify and refine the innovation
18. Successive innovations—prospects for leading to additional innovations

*Source:* Adapted from Zaltman, Duncan, and Holbek, 1973.

potential use for practicing managers as well as researchers thinking about the characteristics of an innovation that can influence its success.

Organizational researchers have also studied innovation within organizations, of course. Mone, McKinley, and Barker (1998), for example, argued for a contingency perspective on the relationship between innovation and organizational decline. They proposed that organizations will respond to decline with more innovation when power is more widely diffused in the organization, and when the organization's mission is not strongly "institutionalized." Other studies tend to concentrate on private sector organizations, involving variables related to market share and competition, in ways that make their application to many government agencies difficult to interpret (see, for example, Greve and Taylor, 2000).

### Innovation in Public and Nonprofit Organizations

In something of a revolt against the literature and stereotypes that cast government organizations as rigid and change-resistant, a stream of research and discussion about innovative government organizations has burgeoned in the last decade or so (see, for example, Behn, 1994; Borins, 1998; Cohen and Eimicke, 1998; Holzer and Callahan, 1998; Ingraham, Thompson, and Sanders, 1998; Levin and Sanger, 1994; Light, 1998; Linden, 1990, 1994). The studies vary widely from one another and offer complex conclusions, making it difficult to summarize them without producing a blurring array of lists of their conclusions. The following examples, nevertheless, offer a picture of some of these contributions.

Linden (1990), on the basis of a set of case observations, drew conclusions about how an innovative manager can make an organization more effective. Innovative managers, he found, share seven characteristics: strategic action, holding on and letting go, creating a felt need for change, starting with concrete change, using structural changes, dealing with risk, and using political skills. Innovation involves both rational and intuitive thinking, and successful innovation is a function of many small starts and pilots. Successful innovation also tends to involve the use of multifunction teams, and occurs where leaders and sponsors provide time, freedom, flexibility, and access to resources, and where they offer autonomy and support for committed champions, while preventing an emphasis on "turf" protection. Linden (1994) later described a set of cases of successful process reengineering initiatives in government organizations, which involved moving away from organizing around functional groupings and toward being "seamless."

Borins (1998) conducted an elaborate analyses of 217 state and local government programs that had won awards in the Ford Foundation and Kennedy School of Government's Innovations in American Government Awards program. Borins found an array of factors that tended to characterize the programs that had made award-winning innovations. The successful innovations, he concluded, occurred where there was systematic thinking and planning for change, where the programs delivered multiple services, and where they were partnered with other organizations. Effective innovation also tended to occur where the programs applied new technology, undertook process improvements and organizational redesign, and emphasized empowerment, incentives instead of regulation, prevention instead of remediation, and use of the private sector, voluntarism, and internal competition. As for when and why successful innovation takes place, Borins's analysis indicated three main paths: politicians responding to crises, newly appointed agency heads restructuring organizations, and midlevel and frontline workers responding to internal problems and taking advantage of opportunities. Interestingly, Borins found that about half of the persons initiating the award-winning innovations were career civil servants below the agency-head level.

Light (1998) conducted a questionnaire and case analysis of twenty-six public and nonprofit organizations in Minnesota that he identified as innovative, to determine how and why they were innovative. He chose the organizations because of their diversity in mission, size, age, and other factors. He discussed how people need to release creativity in the organization by lowering or removing internal and external barriers and debunking myths. He concluded from his observations that innovative organizations must work with and manipulate four factors that make up the organizational "ecosystem" on which long-term, sustained innovation depends: the external environment, the internal structure, leadership, and internal management systems. For each of these components he suggested a lengthy list of "preferred states" most conducive to innovation. For example, concerning the external environment, the organization should "center on mission," "embrace volatility," lower barriers to external collaboration by working with stakeholders and clients, and "harvest external support." Concerning internal structure, the organization should "stay thin" by avoiding too many layers, push authority downward and democratize to maximize participation, encourage collaboration, and provide resources to support innovation and innovative thinking. Leadership should, among other emphases, issue a call for ideas, give permission to fail, communicate to excess, and keep faith and inspiration alive. Preferred states for management systems include downplaying pay, measuring performance, celebrating success, and constantly listening and learning. Light found that relatively small nonprofit organizations tend to be the organizations most likely to sustain innovations and innovativeness. He saw no single path to innovation, and observed that organizations show different mixtures of states. He concluded that core values, such as honesty, trust, rigor, and faith play a strong role in this process.

Other studies, described in later sections and chapters, also reflect on successful innovation and other forms of change in public organizations.

## Large-Scale Planned Change

Besides facilitating individual innovations and patterns of innovativeness, organizations also undergo major, large-scale transformations and planned processes of development, such as the transformation of the Internal Revenue Service mentioned at several points earlier. A vast literature presents many different perspectives, models, and research issues about major organizational change (for example, Armenakis and Bedeian, 1999; Burke, 2002; Pettigrew, Woodman, and Cameron, 2001; Van de Ven and Poole, 1995). Rather than attempting to cover this range of material, the discussion here concentrates on certain key issues, such as resistance to change, types of change, and perspectives on the leadership and management of change and development, including organizational development, some analyses of successful leadership of change, and examples of successful and unsuccessful change leadership in public organizations. The perspective on successful large-scale organizational change developed here is highly consistent with conclusions about the topic in recent overviews (Armenakis and Bedeian, 1999).

## Resistance to Change

From the beginning, management and organization theorists have recognized the problem of resistance to change in organizations. Many authors have argued that traditional bureaucratic forms of organization inhibit change. They assign people to positions and departments on the basis of rules and job descriptions, require people to adhere to them, and reward them for doing so. This aggravates the normal human tendency to resist change for all the reasons implied by analysis of the characteristics of innovations (Exhibit 13.1): change can be costly, troublesome, unfamiliar, threatening, and difficult to understand and accomplish.

## Good Reasons to Resist Change

Human resistance to change can be one of the most destructive, dangerous tendencies in life, but managers and researchers often appear to forget that people have good reasons to resist change. Fairly typically, a new manager enters an organization with a desire to have an impact and not simply to serve as a caretaker. Employees sometimes throw objections and obstacles in the way of the new manager's proposals. Quite often, the new manager expresses frustration with longtime employees' commitment to the status quo.

Certainly, the new manager may have good reason to complain, but he or she may also cripple effective change by too readily assuming that resistance means laziness, selfishness, or stupidity. People may have well-justified reasons to resist. Some ideas are simply bad ideas, and the people with the most experience realize it. The *New Yorker* magazine once ran a cartoon in which two employees of a fast-food restaurant watched a family stopped in their car at the drive-through window of the restaurant. The family members were leaning out of the car with tongs in hand, struggling to serve themselves out of a large salad bowl perched on the windowsill of the drive-through window. Cherry tomatoes bounced like Ping-Pong balls on the pavement. Lettuce floated in the wind. One employee was saying to the other, "Well, it looks as if the drive-through salad bar is an idea whose time has not yet come." Some ideas are bad ideas. They deserve to be resisted.

Unsuccessful ideas abound in government and industry. As one prominent example, Lyndon Johnson directed that the planning and program budgeting system (PPBS) be adopted in all federal agencies. Within a few years the directive was withdrawn. Many elected officials and politically appointed executives at all levels of government initiate new programs, reforms, or legislation but show a disinclination to become too deeply involved in implementing them. They often feel that their duty involves setting policy and directing the bureaucracy rather than closely following its management. Many of them do not stay very long in their positions. Their mandate is often far from clear, no matter how much they claim that it is. This can deprive the change process of essential support and leadership.

The point is not to defend the prerogative of the public bureaucracy to resist change but rather to emphasize a dilemma about organizational change in government. As described later, successful organizational change usually requires sustained support from leaders, participative planning, and flexible implementation. Government managers achieve these conditions more often than many people suppose, but much of the literature nevertheless suggests their scarcity in the public sector. What we learn from the management literature on change makes the point that, in the example just provided, the reason for the failure of PPBS was not necessarily that it was a bad idea. It was a well-intentioned innovation advocated by many experts on public administration. Good ideas are not simply born, however; they are made—developed and nurtured—through appropriate change processes. Too negative a view of resistance to new initiatives and ideas can cloud the message that people may have reasonable objections that can make a dubious idea into a better one. The challenge for public managers is to find ways to overcome obstacles to such participation and flexibility amid the political complexities and accountability pressures in government.

## Types of Change

Many types, levels, and degrees of change complicate the discussion of the change process. Researchers have not thoroughly incorporated these variations into their models; instead they have moved to highly general frameworks that broadly cover many types of change. Still, the variations bear noting and have implications that are taken up in later sections.

Daft (2001) points out that organizations undergo at least four types of change:

- Technology changes occur in production processes and equipment, as in the installation of computerized client information systems or word processing systems.
- Administrative changes include new performance-appraisal systems, such as the Performance Management and Recognition System for all middle managers in the federal civil service; pay-for-performance systems, such as those that state and local agencies have tried to implement; and affirmative action programs.
- Changes in products and services abound in all types of organizations. As described later, the SSA has struggled for the last several decades with steady increases in the number and nature of social security services mandated by Congress.
- Human resource changes occur as a result of training, development, and recruitment efforts aimed at improving leadership and human relations practices or upgrading employee skills.

While each of these different domains may undergo limited change relatively independently, they frequently intertwine. In fact, for major changes, the challenge is to coordinate them. Tichy (1983) argued that most approaches to organizational change have concentrated on one of three primary dimensions: the political, technical, or cultural aspects of change. Strategic change, as Tichy called it, involves moving beyond these more fragmented approaches and coordinating these three dimensions to effect large-scale transformations in an organization's relationship to its environment.

Golembiewski (1986) introduced the conception of three types of change that can occur in individual responses in organizations. *Alpha change* involves the change from one level to another along a measure of some dimension, such as job satisfaction. *Beta chang*e involves a similar change in degree, except that the significance that people attach to intervals on the measure may change as well. *Gamma change,* however, involves a general change in state rather than just a change in degree. A person may shift to a redefinition or new conception of reality such that the meaning of the dimension fundamentally changes for that person. In their research, Golembiewski and his colleagues found that virtually all the people in the most advanced stages of "burnout" fall at a point on a measure of work satisfaction that is almost the exact opposite of the point at which virtually all of those in the earliest phases fall. This suggests that once a person moves into the more serious phases of burnout, he or she also moves to a fundamentally different state, in which the meaning and nature of job satisfaction change radically. Differences in responses to job satisfaction measures do not fully capture this shift, which raises major issues for both research and practice pertaining to organizational change, because it complicates the measurement and assessment of change in challenging ways.

There are a variety of strategies and tactics for leading and managing these different types and degrees of change (Daft, 2001, chap. 10). Before covering examples of frameworks and suggestions about leading major change processes, it is useful to explore the topic of organizational development, a well-established subfield of organization theory that concentrates on changing the human relations aspects of organizations for the better

# Organization Development

Writers and practitioners in organization development (OD) work to improve the functioning of organizations, especially along human relations and social dimensions, by applying social scientific theory and techniques. OD consultants or "change agents" work with people in organizations to improve communication, problem solving, renewal and change, conflict airing and resolution, decision making, and trust and openness. They often go into organizations to help them diagnose and overcome problems they have in these areas. Ideally, they seek to leave the organization better able to manage such processes effectively. A mountain of books, articles, and professional journals, as well as a number of professional associations, deliberate about OD, and large corporations and government agencies sometimes have OD offices or bureaus that minister to the other parts of the organization.

As this description suggests, OD has firm roots in the human relations orientation in organization studies and in the group dynamics movement. It also draws on various elements of social science and organizational behavior, such as theories of motivation, leadership, and systems, and techniques such as survey research. OD theory and practice vary widely but tend to have common basic values and assumptions about organizations and the people in them. French and Bell (1999) point out that OD involves common assumptions about people, groups, and organizations:

- People have a drive to grow and develop, especially if they are provided with an encouraging environment. They want to make a greater contribution to their organization than most organizational settings permit.
- For most people, the work group is a very important factor. People value acceptance and cooperation in work groups. Leaders cannot provide for all leadership needs, so members of groups must assist one another.
- Suppressed feelings are detrimental to satisfaction, trust, and cooperation. Most groups and organizations induce suppressed feelings more than they should. Solutions to most problems in groups must be transactional, involving changes in people's relationships.
- The leadership style and culture at higher levels tend to pervade the organization, shaping levels of trust and teamwork throughout.
- Win-lose conflict management strategies usually do harm in the long run.
- Collaborative effort has value. The welfare of all members of the system is important and should be valued by those who are most powerful in the system.

OD practitioners tend to value personal growth and a richer, more meaningful, more enjoyable, more effective life for people in organizations, especially through allowing peoples' feelings and sentiments to have a legitimate value. They also value commitment to both action and research, and democratization and power equalization in organizations. One can begin to guess some of the controversies that these assumptions and values engender among management experts. Before looking at them, however, it is useful to consider how OD interventions in organizations tend to proceed.

## OD Interventions and Change Processes

OD consultants take a variety of approaches, but the action-research model shown in Exhibit 13.2 illustrates a typical pattern. Key executives perceive a problem or performance gap. They bring in a consultant, who conducts a diagnosis of the organization and the problem, often using interviews, surveys, and group meetings. The consultant feeds the results back to the clients and works with them in interpreting the results and developing plans for the OD program, including objectives, problems to be addressed, and techniques to be used. The consultant continues gathering information for use in the activities, using such tools as group problem-solving and team-building sessions. Further planning takes place as new ideas arise from the activities, and the consultant continues to gather information to assess the newly planned activities and their effects. The consultant continues this developmental process for a time, until eventually he or she leaves the people in the organization to continue it on their own. Similar models include an ultimate phase, consisting of institutionalizing the changes that the OD project has developed and terminating the relationship with the consultant (Burke, 1994; French and Bell, 1999; French, Bell, and Zawacki, 2000).

### EXHIBIT 13.2. PHASES OF AN ACTION RESEARCH MODEL FOR ORGANIZATIONAL DEVELOPMENT.

1. Performance gap: Key executives perceive problems.
2. Executives confer with an organizational consultant.
3. Diagnosis: The consultant begins a process of diagnosis and data gathering.
4. Feedback: The consultant communicates the results to key clients and client groups.
5. Joint action planning: The consultant works with client groups in planning the objectives and procedures (such as team building) for the OD program.
6. Further data gathering: The consultant continues to monitor perceptions and attitudes.
7. Further feedback: In team-building sessions or other settings, the organizational members address the problems identified in the diagnostic work.
8. The client groups discuss and work on the data from the diagnosis and earlier sessions. New attitudes emerge.
9. Action planning: The groups set objectives for further development and develop plans for getting there.
10. Action: The plans are carried out, and new behaviors develop.
11. Further data gathering.
12. Further feedback.
13. Further action planning.
14. Continuation and consultant departure: The cycle of diagnosis, feedback, planning, and action continues until the appropriate point for the departure of the consultant.

*Source:* Burke, 1982; French and Bell, 1999.

## OD Intervention Techniques

OD consultants can draw from an array of responses to the problems they help an organization identify. The literature in the field provides a variety of models, typologies, and tables suggesting the type and level of intervention that the people in the organization and the consultant might select (Burke, 1994; French and Bell, 1999). For example, if the organization wants to focus on problems at the level of individual organizational members, it might work on new approaches to recruitment and selection, training and development, counseling, and job design. At the broader organizational level, OD may involve organization-wide survey-feedback processes, grid OD projects, quality-of-work-life programs, management by objectives projects, or intergroup conflict-management procedures.

For the development of group processes, an OD project might employ team-building techniques that work groups can use to develop more effective relationships. Team-building exercises typically focus on setting goals for the group, analyzing members' roles and responsibilities and the work processes of the team, and examining the relationships among the members. The OD consultant might draw on various techniques to support these efforts, such as a role negotiation process in which members list the things they feel each other member should do more or less of in the group. Then the members negotiate agreements about the changes and confirm these agreements with a written contract.

OD consultants also employ a technique they call *process consultation*. The consultant observes the work groups and other activities; gathers observations and information about key processes such as communication, teamwork, and interpersonal conflict handling; and consults with the members on interpreting and improving these processes.

OD projects in the past often employed T-groups, encounter groups, or sensitivity sessions. All are group sessions intended to develop communication and understanding among the members of the group and enhance each member's sensitivity to the feelings and viewpoints of the other members. These approaches grew out of the work of Kurt Lewin and his colleagues described in Chapter Two. Such groups engage in intensive discussions aimed at helping participants learn more about how other people see them and respond to them and how they perceive others. The sessions follow a diverse array of approaches, often involving such exercises as having members take turns expressing perceptions of other members. In some versions, these techniques become highly confrontational and emotional, and participants often find the experience exhilarating. These techniques were widely used during the 1960s, but their use has dwindled, apparently because of controversy about whether they had much long-term impact, and evidence that when they did have an impact it often appeared to be damaging to some participants (Back, 1972).

## OD Effects and Controversies

Just how a consultant selects, combines, and uses all these procedures depends on his or her experience and skill. No organizing theory links the aspects of OD or systematically guides its practice. OD consultants play a role much like that of clinicians in psychology or psychiatry in that they have no clear, uncontested theory or guide for practice. They operate on the basis of their experience and intuition, choosing from an array of loosely defined procedures. The complexity of organizations and their problems makes it hard for OD consultants to establish and prove clear successes. Critics sometimes attack OD for this lack of substantive theory and theory-based research. They say that OD's concentration on human relations issues can lead to misdiagnosing an organization's problems when they involve other dimensions, such as the accounting system or production processes. Some critics, for example, argue that OD concentrates on human resource issues in organizations when large-scale strategic change requires coordinating those issues with strategies for improving the organization's technical and political dimensions. OD adherents respond that they know their efforts are often valuable, even if they cannot always produce simple, clear evidence of marked improvements in profits or other performance criteria. They also argue that other areas of organization theory hardly provide managers with beautifully crafted guides to changing and improving their organization, and that they are justified in trying to go out and do what they can to apply behavioral science knowledge to the problems that organizations face.

## OD in the Public Sector

Despite these controversies, OD remains a widely used approach for improving and changing public and nonprofit organizations (Carnevale, 2003). OD experts who work with public sector organizations regularly discuss whether public and private organizations differ in ways that affect the application of OD. That discussion has an interesting history.

In a leading contribution to this debate, Golembiewski (1969; see also 1985) cited greater challenges in the public sector as a result of factors much like those discussed in earlier chapters. He said that five primary structural constraints complicate the application of OD in government:

1.  Multiple actors have access to multiple authorities, thus presenting a complex array of possible supporters or resisters for an OD project. For example, the State Department began Project ACORD (Action for Organizational Development) after a career official with strong ties to key members of Congress pushed for it. Yet the project stalled when other prominent actors—the department head and officials in the budget and personnel bureaus—attacked it. The newspapers even got into the act, with editorials calling for the State Department to leave its long-term civil servants alone and not pester them with a dubious program.

2.  Conflicting interests and reward structures complicate the problem. Different congressional committees, legislators, and administrators may respond to different incentives. For example, some actors may press for improved organizational operations, while others may seek to defend political alliances.

3.  The administrative hierarchy is fragmented and weakened by these competing affiliations, thus making it harder to sustain the implementation of OD projects. Administrative officials may have stronger ties to congressional allies and stronger commitment to their programs than to the top executives in their department or to the president.

4.  Weak relationships between career civil servants and politically appointed executives produce a similar problem of diffuse authority.

5.  Golembiewski agreed with Kaufman (1969) that the political system continually shifts its emphasis among several goals for the executive branch—representativeness, executive leadership, and politically neutral competence. During a period of emphasis on the first two, such as President Reagan's drive to master and reduce the federal bureaucracy, the climate for OD deteriorates.

Golembiewski argued that these factors interact with managerial "habits" in government in ways that hinder OD. Higher-level executives tend to avoid delegating authority and tend to establish multiple layers of review and approval because of their tenuous authority over lower levels. Legislative and legal strictures constrain many dimensions that OD often seeks to reform, such as reward systems and job classifications. Government agencies, more often than business firms, have secrecy and security requirements. People in government show more "procedural regularity and caution." The role of the professional manager is poorly developed in government compared to business, according to Golembiewski. He suggests that this results in part from the difficulty of enhancing public managers' sense of ownership of organizational objectives and values, due to the public nature of the organizations they lead. This in turn poses greater challenges in enhancing managers' commitment to their agency.

Golembiewski concluded that these conditions create differences in the culture that predominates in public agencies. Unlike in other settings such as private business firms, managers in public organizations face more constraints and have fewer supports and rewards for inventiveness, risk taking, and effort. Not surprisingly, some public managers are cautious about supporting initiatives in their organization.

Most other authors who have examined this issue agree with Golembiewski in general but make variations in his analysis. Davis (1983), for example, offered a similar analysis of the effects of the external political environment on the use of OD in the public sector. Yet he more heavily emphasized the problem of public agencies' pursuit of multiple goals with vague programs and performance criteria (perhaps because he drew on an OD project in a human services agency, the area of government where these problems are probably severest).These writers and others (Carnevale, 2003) have nevertheless emerged from these discussions with the conclusion that OD certainly can succeed in the public sector. While their depictions of the public sector environment have made some common notions of bureaucratic rigidity sound positively optimistic, these OD experts treat the public sector context as perhaps more challenging than the private sector but ultimately manageable, as presenting a set of conditions for which one can be prepared.

Golembiewski (1985) reported evidence that OD projects in the public sector enjoy a relatively impressive success rate, apparently in line with that of projects in the private sector. First, he and his colleagues reviewed numerous published reports of OD initiatives in public organizations and classified the difficulties they apparently encountered. They found that in 270 reports of OD applications, the writers frequently mentioned the sort of constraints that Golembiewski had described. They noted external constraints such as procedural rigidity (in 124 cases), diversity of interests and values (111 cases), public scrutiny (87 cases), and the "volatile political/administrative interface"—the rocky relationship between legislative and administrative units and between career officials and political officials (62 cases). They also mentioned internal constraints such as lack of professionalism (78 cases), weak chains of command (70 cases), complex objectives (61 cases), and short time frames (52 cases). In addition, the reports for city governments were generally similar to those for other levels of government. Although the reports cited these complications, Golembiewski noted that the large number of initiatives reported—especially considering that agencies carry out many efforts that are not reported in the professional literature—suggests that "the constraints may be tougher in the public sector, but they are not that tough" (p. 67).

Golembiewski also analyzed studies that have sought to assess the effectiveness of OD applications in both sectors. One of his students assessed the success of the 270 OD initiatives mentioned earlier, using procedures similar to those used in previous studies of OD success rates, and found that most of the reports indicated either positive effects (43 percent) or highly positive effects (41 percent), with only 7 percent indicating no effect and 9 percent reporting negative effects (p. 82). The results also suggested that the public sector initiatives included a healthy percentage of the most demanding OD applications; furthermore, they did not indicate that the success rate in public agencies resulted from a tendency to try more limited forms of OD interventions in government. In addition, Golembiewski had independent observers do similar ratings of forty-four OD applications in city governments and found even higher success rates. These success rates are very similar to those reported for the private sector, Golembiewski concluded, and indicate that despite the apparent constraints of the government context, OD practitioners do fairly well at adapting to them.

Gortner, Mahler, and Nicholson (1987) raised some challenging questions about Golembiewski's conclusions. They argued that his methodology has weaknesses because people report the successful cases but not the unsuccessful ones, that when they write articles, they describe their projects in the best possible light. In addition, they suggest, the OD application may fade over time.

More recently, however, Robertson and Seneviratne (1995) reported on a study that generally supported Golembiewski's conclusions. Robertson and Seneviratne performed a general analysis (a *meta-analysis*) of about fifty studies of planned change interventions in public and private organizations. They found that OD interventions in public and private organizations showed similar rates of success in such areas as work setting and organizational outcomes. They found some differences in more specific areas, however. The evidence indicated that change efforts in the private organizations led to positive changes in four components of work settings—organizing arrangements, social factors, technology, and physical setting. In the public organizations, however, the change efforts appeared to have a positive effect only on organizing arrangements and social factors, not on technology and physical setting. In addition, even though change efforts showed positive effects on organizing arrangements in both sectors, these effects were significantly stronger in the private sector. Also, change efforts in both sectors showed positive influences on a general measure of organizational outcomes, with no significant difference between the sectors. Change interventions in the public organizations, however, showed a significantly stronger relationship to one dimension of the organizational outcomes measure—improved organizational performance—than change efforts in the private organizations. These results support many of the observations about public and private organizations cited in previous chapters—such as the greater constraints on organizational structures in public organizations. They also generally support Golembiewski and his colleagues' conclusion that public agencies may face certain challenges. Generally, however, planned change initiatives appear to succeed about as often in public organizations as they do in private organizations. In spite of stereotypes and some academic assertions based more on simplistic theory than on systematic evidence, organizational change initiatives occur with frequency and apparent success throughout government.

# Success and Failure in Large-Scale, Planned Organizational Change

The evidence of successful change initiatives in public organizations illustrates the importance of how the members of an organization manage and implement change. Organizations have always periodically undertaken large-scale planned change processes that are well beyond the scope of OD initiatives. In recent decades, challenges from international competition and other pressures have caused many U.S. corporations to undergo thorough overhauls. The management literature began to resound with terms such as *transformation, reinvention,* and *reengineering,* all referring to strategies for large-scale planned change in organizations. Under the pressures described earlier and in previous chapters, governments have followed suit (Gore, 1993; U.S. Office of Management and Budget, 2002). As noted earlier, the literature on large-scale organizational change is quite diverse and difficult to summarize succinctly. Two articles, however, in which the authors summarize patterns of organizational change and transformation provide particularly valuable observations about analyzing and managing successful initiatives. Although they were published some thirty years apart, they have some interesting similarities, and according to recent overviews of the topic, they also show similarities to the perspectives of other organizational change theorists and researchers (Armenakis and Bedeian, 1999).

About three decades ago, Greiner (1967) analyzed eighteen major organizational change attempts and drew conclusions about the patterns of successful change. He noted that some frequently used approaches to change often seem to founder. Examples include unilateral actions, such as top-down decrees or commands for structural changes; limited attempts at power sharing through group decision making; and efforts to encourage delegation of authority through T-group training. The successful change efforts that Greiner observed involved much more comprehensive approaches, as illustrated in Exhibit 13.3.

As the table suggests, Greiner's observations about successful patterns of change emphasize the following conditions and steps:

- Pressure for improvement is felt widely among people within the organization and among relevant actors outside it.
- A new person is brought in as head of the organization or as a consultant to lead the change effort.

## EXHIBIT 13.3. PATTERNS OF SUCCESSFUL ORGANIZATIONAL CHANGE.

**Phase I: Pressure and Arousal**

1. *There is significant external and internal pressure for change.* There is a widespread perception of performance gaps and of a need for change, placing pressure on top management.

**Phase II: Intervention and Reorientation**

2. *A new person enters as change leader.* The person has a record as a successful change agent and enters as a leader of the organization or as a consultant working with the leader.
3. *The new person leads a reexamination of past practices and current problems.* The newcomer uses his or her objective, external perspective to encourage examination of old views and rationalizations and attention to "real" problems.
4. *Top management becomes heavily involved in the reexamination.* The head of the organization and his or her immediate subordinates assume a direct, heavily involved role in the reexamination.

**Phase III: Diagnosis and Recognition**

5. *The change leader engages multiple levels in diagnosis.* The change leader involves multiple levels and units in collaborative, fact-finding, problem-solving discussions to identify and diagnose current problems. The diagnosis involves significant power sharing.

**Phase IV: Invention and Commitment**

6. *The change leader stimulates a widespread search for creative solutions, involving many levels.*

**Phase V: Experimentation and Search**

7. *Solutions are developed, tested, and proven on a small scale.* Problems are worked out and solved. Experimentation is encouraged.

**Phase VI: Reinforcement and Acceptance**

8. *Successes are reinforced and disseminated and breed further success.* People are rewarded. Successes become accepted and institutionalized.

*Source:* Adapted from Greiner, 1967.

- Top executives involve themselves heavily in beginning and sustaining the change process.
- The change agent (the new head or consultant), with the involvement of top executives, initiates a general diagnosis.
- The change agent leads this diagnostic process using multilevel, collaborative fact-finding and problem-solving sessions to identify and diagnose the key problems. Representatives of many units and levels participate. The human resources unit is heavily involved.
- Participants develop solutions. The solutions are tested first on a small scale, then on a wider scale, and finally implemented.
- Participants use successes to reinforce results, and the results become widely accepted.

As indicated in step 5 (Phase III) of Exhibit 13.3, and implied in other phases, Greiner emphasized the key role of power sharing in successful patterns of change. He concluded that success requires power sharing and that it must occur through a developmental process. The failures he observed involved more unilateral pressures for change, with an illogical sequence of steps.

About thirty years later, Kotter (1995), a prominent author on leadership, organizational change, and other topics, published an article on organizational change in the same journal in which Greiner's article had appeared, the *Harvard Business Review*. In the article, Kotter presented a number of reasons for the failure of organizational *transformations* (a currently fashionable term for large-scale, comprehensive change efforts). Exhibit 13.4 turns Kotter's reasons for failure around, transposing them into requirements for success. Kotter's observations about organizational change differ from Greiner's in important ways. Kotter refers

### EXHIBIT 13.4. STEPS FOR
### SUCCESSFUL ORGANIZATIONAL TRANSFORMATION.

1. *Establish a sense of urgency.*
   - Examine market and competitive realities.
   - Identify crises and opportunities.
2. *Form a powerful guiding coalition.*
   - Assemble a group with enough power to lead the change effort.
   - Encourage the group to work as a team.
3. *Create a vision.*
   - Create a vision to help direct the change effort.
   - Develop strategies for achieving that vision.
4. *Communicate the vision.*
   - Use all available means to communicate the new vision and strategy.
   - Have the guiding coalition teach the necessary new behaviors by example.
5. *Empower others to act on the vision.*
   - Remove obstacles to change.
   - Change systems or structures that present obstacles.
6. *Create short-term wins.*
   - Plan for visible performance improvements.
   - Create those improvements.
   - Recognize and reward employees involved in those improvements.
7. *Consolidate improvements and produce further change.*
   - Use increased credibility to change systems, structures, and policies to pursue the vision.
   - Hire and develop employees who can implement the vision.
8. *Institutionalize the new approach.*
   - Articulate the connection between the new behaviors and organizational success.
   - Ensure leadership development and succession.

*Source:* Adapted from Kotter, 1995.

to *vision,* a contemporary and much discussed topic in management theory today. He also emphasizes the role of a *guiding coalition,* in contrast to Greiner's focus on a change leader who comes in from the outside (a later section in this chapter describes a successful change in the SSA that did not involve a change leader from the outside). Kotter's phrasing is consistent with other research on large-scale change in organizations that emphasizes the essential role of shared values (which can equate to vision in important ways) and leadership teams rather than individual, heroic leaders (see, for example, Huber and Glick, 1993).

The similarities between the two views, offered thirty years apart, and their similarity to other current perspectives (Armenakis and Bedeian, 1999), are striking and provide a simple but deceptively demanding framework for large-scale organizational change:

- Widespread belief in the need for change
- Clear, sustained leadership, including support from top executives
- Broad participation in diagnosing problems and planning the change
- Flexible, incremental implementation, involving experimentation, feedback, adaptation, and building on prior success to institutionalize change

These elements appear luxurious to public sector managers, because so many public organizations face frequent turnover of top executives, interventions and constraints from external authorities, and other conditions that might block some of these steps. Nevertheless, the following sections note examples of the effective adoption of many of these elements of successful change in public agencies.

## Successful Revitalization in Public Agencies

Many of these conditions and steps, together with an emphasis on transforming organizational culture, characterize successful revitalization efforts in public organizations that had declined. Poister (1988b), for example, provided a compilation of case studies of such efforts. In one of these studies, Holzer (1988) described a marked enhancement in the productivity of the New York City Department of Sanitation, with improved labor-management cooperation and teamwork, enhanced productivity and information management, technical innovations in refuse collection, and the upgrading of managerial talent and organization (which involved contending with stringent civil service regulations and trying to modify them).

Decker and Paulson (1988) describe how a multifaceted performance-improvement system vastly improved the performance of the Jacksonville Electric Authority. The system included efforts to improve work planning and information management and to transform the organizational culture to place more emphasis on consultative team management, strategic planning and identification of corporate goals, and well-developed management systems to achieve them.

Stephens (1988) described how a new director of the Alabama Division of Rehabilitation and Crippled Children Service led the division through a transformation from a troubled, control-oriented organization to a more quality-oriented, participative one. She led a widely participative process to develop the division's "Blueprint for the Future" and to improve agency policies, performance evaluation, quality assurance, and organization. The process also aimed to make supervisors more oriented to coaching and consultation and to involve project teams in reviewing agency policies. The director used aspects of managing culture similar to those described in Chapter Eleven. She faithfully met and spoke with the teams. She posted the Blueprint for the Future on her office wall. She redesigned the organization chart, placing Alabama's disabled children and adults at the top of the chart to dramatize her emphasis on client service.

Poister and Larson (1988) described the revitalization of the Pennsylvania Department of Transportation, which involved a reorganization to make the agency less top-heavy and to place greater emphasis on merit selection to improve the professional capabilities and management capacity of the agency's personnel. The agency's leaders also mounted a campaign to build political support. They worked to improve financial and programmatic control and to develop the organization through quality circles, participative management, and the identification of guiding values.

Poister (1988a) pointed out that all these efforts reflect multifaceted processes of strategic change, involving many policy, managerial, technological, and political initiatives and a series of strategies that developed over time. While diverse, they all emphasize developing a shared vision and mission, strategic planning, and developing the organization's leadership and culture. They involve redistributions of power toward more active involvement of the agency's members. Yet they also emphasize enhancements of management systems, such as financial, productivity-measurement, and information-management systems. Effective revitalization campaigns also required the agency managers to develop and maintain effective political support, to provide resources and a mandate for the changes. Thus, successful revitalizations occur in different types of public organizations, often in patterns very similar to those in private firms. Yet success requires more than skillful employment of generic principles of organizational change—it requires skill in dealing with the political context and administrative features of public organizations. These skillful applications and the conditions supporting them can be further clarified by a comparison between a successful and an unsuccessful attempt at large-scale change in public agencies. Besides these examples and those described earlier in this chapter, there are many additional examples of successful leadership of change and development in public organizations (for example, Behn, 1994; Denhardt, 2000; Svara, 1994; Thompson and Jones, 1994; Thompson and Rainey, 2003).

## Two Contrasting Cases

Reviewing two cases of large-scale change in government agencies helps to clarify the applicability of Greiner's and Golembiewski's observations. Warwick (1975) reported on a failed attempt in the U.S. Department of State to do what everyone would love to do—reduce bureaucracy. The SSA, however, succeeded in a similar effort. When the SSA faced extreme problems with administrative foul-ups and delays in processing claims, the people in the agency responded with a successful redesign of the organization and its claims processing system, and improved performance. These cases illustrate the validity of the many observations about the ways in which the political and institutional context of government and the internal cultures of public agencies can impede change. Yet they also support the claim that, under the right circumstances, applying sound principles of change, skillful public managers and employees can carry out major changes effectively.

***The "O Area" Reforms in the Department of State.***  Warwick (1975) described a fascinating case in which a well-intentioned undersecretary in the State Department initiated an unsuccessful effort to decentralize decision making and eliminate levels of hierarchy. An administrative area known as the O Area had become a complex array of hierarchical layers and diverse offices. The undersecretary's reforms eliminated six hierarchical levels (including 125 administrative positions) and started a process of management by objectives and programs. According to the undersecretary's plan, the program managers at the levels below the eliminated layers would manage more autonomously—without so many administrators above them and with more direct lines to the deputy undersecretary. They would also follow a management by objectives program in which they would specify objectives, target dates, and needed resources.

Although the undersecretary's ideas for reform were heavily influenced by McGregor's concept of Theory Y management (1960), other managers commented that he sought to apply Theory Y using Theory X methods. The undersecretary made the changes fairly unilaterally and then called together a large group of managers and employees to announce them. Rumors had gone around about the reforms, but the nature of them, according to Warwick (1975, p. 37), caught "even the most reorganized veterans off guard."

Yet Warwick devotes most of his analysis to the factors hindering change in the State Department, which he tends to generalize to all government agencies.

Externally, congressional relations and related politics played a major role. Some of the administrators whose positions were targeted for elimination had strong allies in Congress and among interest groups that opposed the changes. The State Department had several different personnel systems (foreign service officers and others), which complicated the change process. A bill that would have unified the systems, however, did not pass in Congress. A civil service union opposed it, a powerful senator felt that it would dilute the foreign service, and the chair of the Senate Foreign Relations Committee gave it little support because he wanted better cooperation from the secretary of state on matters pertaining to the war in Vietnam. The secretary of state became concerned about the wide span of control that the reduction in the hierarchy created (with many program managers reporting to the undersecretary).

Warwick argued that an administrative orthodoxy prevails in Washington and elsewhere in government. Legislators and political executives expect traditional chains of command and hierarchical arrangements and worry that their absence means disorganization. The secretary of state was facing a great deal of political pressure from Congress and the public over decisions about the Vietnam War and did not want to waste political capital on any controversy over the administration of the State Department.

Warwick argued that career civil servants are accustomed to turnover among top political executives every two or three years. Motivated by caution and security, they can easily build defenses against the repetitive cycles of reform and change that the political executives attempt during their short stays in public agencies. The careerists can simply wait out the top executives by doing nothing, or they can mobilize opposition in Congress and among interest groups. Like many public agencies, the State Department also had internal conflicts among units and specialists, including a tradition of rivalry between foreign service officers and other groups of State Department employees and between units organized by function and units organized by geographical regions of the world. These internal conflicts complicated change efforts, especially because the participants often had external political allies.

The undersecretary implemented his changes with some good effect. The changes appeared to have beneficial results for the autonomy, willingness to experiment, and motivation of some of the units and managers. Yet coordination appeared to suffer, and internal and external resistance mounted. Not long after attempting the changes, the undersecretary left the State Department. His successor derided the reforms, and within about nine months he eliminated most of them. Some useful remnants endured, according to Warwick, and some of the lessons learned proved valuable in later change efforts. Yet Warwick concluded that the reforms had clearly failed.

More generally, Warwick suggested that the conditions he found in the State Department tend to sustain complex bureaucracy in all government agencies. Congress and interest groups often resist change because they develop alliances with agencies and their subunits. They jealously guard against reorganizations that threaten those arrangements. Rapid turnover at the tops of agencies has the effects already noted. The diversity and interrelations of government agencies complicate change efforts. Any one public policy arena tends to involve many different agencies (for example, the Departments of Agriculture and Commerce and many other agencies are involved in foreign affairs). Because legislation and policymaking decisions may involve many agencies, consensus and support become elusive. Statutes and systemwide rules govern many aspects of organization and procedure, sometimes dictating the actual agency structure and placing constraints on job descriptions, purchasing, space procurement, personnel decisions, and many other processes. Administrative orthodoxy, coupled with diffuse agency goals, reinforces the tendency to impose classic bureaucratic control.

Warwick noted conditions particular to the State Department that had a lot to do with the outcome of the reforms—the problems of the Vietnam War during this period, a history of complex political influences on the department, internal rivalries, the particularly great need for secure communications, and the worldwide scope of operations. Still, he moved toward gloomy conclusions about prospects for changing public bureaucracies. Almost as if he was determined not to end on such a note, however, he offered suggestions about reducing and changing bureaucracy that echo those of Greiner and the OD experts. He pointed out that facile prescriptions for participative management in public agencies face some sharp challenges. Many of the conditions described earlier weigh against prospects for highly participative processes, but to facilitate successful change, government managers must deal with these conditions. Warwick argued that one cannot eliminate bureaucracy by decimation—by firing people or merging or cutting units—or by top-down demands for reform. Effective debureaucratization, he concluded, must have strong roots within the agency. The people in the agency must see the changes as important and useful to them. All significant internal constituencies must participate in considering the problem. There must be a careful, collaborative diagnosis, followed by broad-based discussions about concrete alternatives for change. Then proponents of the change must seek support from external controllers and allies. To avoid the problem of rapid turnover among top executives, a coordinating body should monitor and sustain the change, and this body should include more than one senior political appointee.

### Modularization of Claims Processing in the Social Security Administration.

While the very words *modularization of claims processing* summon up the impulse to doze off, this example represents an effective attempt to do something similar to what the State Department reforms failed to do—to reform bureaucracy in the direction of decentralized control over the work and an enriched work environment. In the 1960s, the SSA became overloaded and backlogged in processing claims for Old-Age and Survivors Insurance (that is, social security payments). Clients complained to the SSA and to members of Congress, who passed the heat along to the agency. At one point, the SSA struggled with a backlog of one million claims. Something had to be done.

The problem had developed largely because Congress had added new programs and new forms of coverage to the original social security program, such as extending coverage to dependents, farmers, the self-employed, and the disabled. Along with population growth, these additions continually expanded the number of claims to be processed. Also, because of the different programs and the complications of individual cases, some of the claims could raise confounding difficulties. A claimant might have worked under multiple aliases, for example, and have a degenerative brain disease and no memory of his or her original name and birth date.

The organizational system for handling the claims proved more and more ineffective at responding to the load. The SSA had several major functional bureaus—for the retirement and survivors' insurance (RSI) program, for disability insurance, for data processing and records, and for supervising the district offices. The district offices, located around the country, took in claims from clients applying for their benefits. For the RSI program, they then forwarded the claims to one of six program service centers (PSCs). These were located in six regions of the country. Each had about two thousand employees. When a claim arrived at a PSC from the district office, a clerical support unit would prepare a folder for the claimant and forward it to a claims unit. There, a claims authorizer would determine the type and degree of eligibility for social security payments. The folder would then be forwarded to a payments unit, where a benefit authorizer would compute the amount of the benefit payment and do some paperwork necessary to begin processing the payment through the computer. The folder would then go to an accounts unit, which assembled and coded information about the case, then to another unit for entry into the computer, then to a records maintenance unit for storage. In some of these units, hundreds of people worked at desks in long rows, receiving deliveries of stacks of folders from shopping carts, with coffee and lunch breaks announced by the ringing of bells. Control clerks and supervisors, emphasizing the technical issues and production rates of their unit, spot-checked the work for accuracy.

Any incomplete information or disagreements among the technical specialists would delay a claim, because it would have to be sent back to the earlier point in the process for clarification or correction. Communication about the problem usually had to be in writing. There was no provision for getting a problem claim back to the same person who had done the earlier work. The increasing number of claims and the complications of many of the claims increasingly clogged the system. The system created incentives for employees to "cream" the cases by avoiding the very difficult ones or even slipping them to the next phase to get them off their desk. Problem cases piled up.

Robert Ball, the long-term, highly respected commissioner of the SSA, appointed an experienced SSA official, Hugh McKenna, as director of the RSI bureau, with a mandate to correct the problems. McKenna initiated an open-ended process of change, with some four years of research, development, experimentation, and morale building. Several task forces with internal and external representation studied management processes, case handling, and labor relations. A consulting firm analyzed the case-management process. Large team-building and morale-boosting meetings were held between managers and staff from the PSCs, district offices, and the RSI central office. The office staff worked with the PSCs to develop training courses on participatory management. Interestingly, someone made a comment about McKenna similar to the one made about the State Department undersecretary—that he "ordered participatory management." He did, but there was obviously a crucial difference in the way that order was imposed.

Out of these efforts emerged the concept of modular claims-processing units. The planning staff in the central office suggested setting up smaller units—composed of fifty employees—containing all the technical specialists needed to process a claim and letting them handle claims from beginning to end. Claiming to draw on the ideas of McGregor, Herzberg, Likert, and Maslow (described in Chapters Two and Ten), the proponents of the module concept argued that it would provide job enrichment and participatory management. Individuals would identify with their tasks more and see their clients as individuals, they would have easier access to supervisors and managers, and they would have more control over the process and their part in it.

One of the PSCs tried out one such unit on an experimental basis and then created a total of six modules. Problems arose. At one point, productivity dropped in the modules, and termination of the experiment was seriously considered. However, the staff decided that the problems could be corrected. Managers apparently had some trouble adjusting to the new system. In one instance, two module managers tried to merge their modules to create combined functional units for files, accounts, claims, and so on. The central staff had to urge them back to the original concept. The blending of clerical staff and technical specialists in the modules caused some racial and status conflicts. Relations with other agencies, such as the Civil Service Commission (now the Office of Personnel Management), required skillful handling to obtain new space and to receive approval of new personnel structures. Ultimately, other PSCs adopted the modules, with some modifications. In one module, the specialists involved in processing a claim sat around a desk together, working through individual cases in direct contact with one another. The modular approach was also adopted by the Disability Insurance Bureau, although with more employees per module.

The modular concept became widely accepted in the agency as a success. At one point, processing time for new claims in the PSCs had dropped by 50 percent, to an average of twenty days, and it later dropped further, to an average of fifteen days, with very few long-delayed cases. Some employee surveys showed increased job satisfaction in the modules. The picture was not all rosy, however. Some long-standing employees disliked the change. Problems with computer systems complicated matters. Morale later suffered badly when the agency began a process of eliminating seventeen thousand employees in the 1980s, which apparently made it difficult to properly staff some of the modules. Nevertheless, many people in the agency regarded the modular concept as successful. Today, the PCSs are all organized into modules, and the employees regard them not as an innovation but as a standard feature of the centers. Recent developments, such as computerization of claims processing, are causing some problems for the modular design. Some of the centers are experimenting with new forms of organizing the claims-processing work. As they do so, managers and employees frequently express concern about moving away from the modular design—a sign of just how successful this change has been.

The success may simply reflect the proper application of some of the generic principles of change. The change was widely recognized as necessary, it had support from the top, and there was flexible implementation, with adaptation, feedback, and experimentation, and a realistic strategy for achieving the agency's objectives. The change did, in a sense, have a top-down character, but in this case it appears to illustrate what the experts mean by "support from the top." There must be sponsors and champions of the change with sufficient authority and resources to see it through.

Some particulars about the SSA case distinguish it from the State Department case; these are summarized in Exhibit 13.5. SSA had as chief executive a long-term career civil servant who had enjoyed trust and support from key congressional figures and thus could gain a grant of authority to solve the agency's problems without interference. SSA has strong support from a large clientele receiving a specific service, and the agency's tasks tend to be clear and mechanistic. The people in the agency were able to encapsulate their work processes and management methods and seal them off from political intervention.

While such factors may have provided SSA with advantages, the case suggests some key additional considerations about successful change in public organizations (Rainey, 1990). SSA had a durable, skillful power center that was committed

## EXHIBIT 13.5. CONDITIONS FOR A SUCCESSFUL CHANGE IN A FEDERAL AGENCY.

1. *A durable power center, committed to successful change*
   - Strong, stable leadership by career civil servants
   - An internal change agent (career agency executive) with sufficient authority and resources
   - Active, creative bureau staff
2. *Appropriate timing for collective support*
   - A political "window of opportunity"
   - Political overseers (congressional committee heads) who are supportive but not interventionist
   - Political sophistication of agency leaders and staff—effective management of relations with Congress and oversight agencies (OPM, GSA)
   - Strategies that blend sincere employee involvement with decisive exercise of authority
3. *A comprehensive, clear, realistic alternative process*
   - A long-term change strategy, using group processes to develop new structures
   - A major structural reform, focused on measurable outputs, that decentralizes operational responsibility
   - Reasonable clarity about the nature and objectives of the new structure and process

*Source:* Rainey and Rainey, 1986.

to successful change. Ironically, for all the stereotypes about career bureaucrats resisting change, in this case the long-term civil servants were the champions of change. In one instance, they even had to outwit a conservative political appointee who sought to undercut the reforms because he thought they would result in "grade creep"—that is, employees might get higher salary grade classifications because of increased responsibilities in the modules. The leaders of the change effort hurried through an approval of the new personnel structure by the Civil Service Commission to prevent any blockage of the reforms. In this and many other ways, they utilized their knowledge of the political and administrative systems to sustain the change. Also, they were not leaving soon. They had the career commitment to the agency to want the changes to succeed, and they and others knew they would be there for the duration.

In addition, the SSA change took place at the appropriate time for it to garner collective support. (See the section on the agenda-setting process in Chapter Five for a discussion of the concept of windows of opportunity in the political process.) As noted earlier, the reform at the State Department was hindered by the Vietnam War and by other problems with the timing of the change. Of course, the SSA enjoys no inherent immunity from political interference; many agencies that do mechanistic work with clear outputs get buffeted by external political forces. The timing was right for this change at the SSA, however, in that no distracting crises or controversies weighed against it. The need for change was widely recognized both inside and outside the SSA. In part this reflects luck, and in part it reflects the skill of experienced public managers and staff members who knew when and how to work for better alternatives.

Indeed, they did develop a better alternative, one that was comprehensive, clear, and realistic. Rather vague, prepackaged models, such as management by objectives, will fail if they are not adapted to fit the particular structural and cultural conditions within an organization. The sponsors and champions of the change in the SSA applied relatively firm, consistent pressure for a reasonably clear, realistic idea, while allowing a degree of experimentation and variation in its implementation.

Other aspects of the social security program and related policies can be debated at length. Nevertheless, in this case, experienced career civil servants in the SSA brought about an effective improvement in a process essential to one of the largest single categories of disbursement from the federal budget of the United States, and that very directly affects the lives of at least sixty million Americans. The public has heard little about this. News reporters have overlooked it. But perhaps it should not receive heroic treatment—it represents only one of many instances of skillful change and management that go on in government continually.

CHAPTER FOURTEEN

# ADVANCING EFFECTIVE MANAGEMENT IN THE PUBLIC SECTOR

Public organizations perform crucial functions, and it is imperative that they perform them effectively. All of the previous chapters have in some way described possibilities for effective management of public organizations. This chapter covers some more summative approaches to the topic, including general issues about the performance of public organizations, and reviews profiles of well-performing organizations in both the private and public sectors. It then reviews some recent trends in management reform and the pursuit of high performance that have had important influences on public management. Finally, the chapter explores one of the most prominently discussed and frequently employed strategies for enhancing the performance of government—privatization of governmental services, especially through contracting out. Despite its long history of use in government, proponents of privatization still propose it as an innovative solution for public organizations. The main objective of this section, however, is not to analyze privatization. Primarily, it illustrates ways in which the topics and ideas from the framework for organizational analysis presented in Figures 1.1 and 1.2, as elaborated in the previous chapters, can be brought to bear in pursuing new (or renewed) alternatives in public management. It attempts to illustrate a systematic approach to organizing and managing in order to confront a task such as establishing a well-organized approach to privatization, or many other imperatives and challenges that people in public organizations must effectively manage.

# The Performance of Public Organizations

Criticism of government and its components, such as government officials, organizations, and employees, is a thriving industry in the United States and in many other nations that allow freedom of expression. Many people make their living in whole or in part in this industry, and virtually all citizens contribute to it in some way. Like other industries, it creates problems, such as information pollution—that is, distortions and excesses in reporting and analysis of government. At the same time, it is an absolutely crucial industry, because we control government in part by scrutinizing and criticizing it. This industry also illustrates the point that the history and culture of the United States have in many ways drawn on the fundamental assumption that public organizations are beset with performance problems, such as red tape and inefficiency, while private business firms perform more efficiently and effectively. This assumption is widespread but not universal: surveys show that a majority of Americans share it, but not all (see, for example, Light, 2002a; Lipset and Schneider, 1987). Surveys have also found that some Americans are suspicious of private business but have a strong, deep-seated support for—if not confidence in—their government's institutions (Lipset and Schneider, 1987). The final section of this chapter examines the evidence and debate on the performance of public organizations relative to the performance of the private sector, leading to the conclusion that in spite of the assumption to the contrary, many public organizations and managers perform very well.

Chapter Two described how the literature on organizations and management increasingly emphasizes the complexity and turbulence confronting organizations, with more and more discussion of paradoxes, conflicting values, and even the chaos facing all organizations (see, for example, Daft, 2001; Kiel, 1994; Peters, 1987; Quinn, 1988). For public organizations, the pressures include public and political hostility, funding reductions, and other challenges that many officials and experts depict as crises affecting all levels of government (Gore, 1993; National Commission on the Public Service, 1989, 2003; Partnership for Public Service, 2002; Thompson, 1993; U.S. Office of Management and Budget, 2002; U.S. Senate, Committee on Governmental Affairs, 2001; U.S. General Accounting Office, 2002a).

Somewhat paradoxically, in view of all the references to crisis and pressure, a growing literature has concentrated on successful organizations. Peters and Waterman's *In Search of Excellence* (1982), which described many excellent corporations, became one of the best-selling popular books about management in history. It appears to have been the starting point for a profusion of similar books about successful corporate management that have been pouring out ever since (see, for example, Collins and Porras, 1997).

Similarly, pressures on the public sector have prompted many authors and officials to defend the value and the record of government (Esman, 2000; Glazer and Rothenberg, 2001; Light, 2002b; Neiman, 2000) and public organizations (Milward and Rainey, 1983). In the leading book mounting the case in favor of government organizations, Goodsell (1994) pointed to substantial evidence that public organizations and employees frequently perform well and defy many of the negative stereotypes that echo in the media, popular opinion, and political and academic discourse. As described in previous chapters and later in this one, so many other writers have described effective public managers and organizations that books and articles on this topic represent a genre in the literature on administration (see, for example, Ban, 1995; Beam, 2001; Behn, 1994; Borins, 1998; Cohen and Eimicke, 1995; Denhardt, 2000; DiIulio, 1989, 1994; Doig and Hargrove, 1987; Gold, 1982; Halachmi and Bouckaert, 1995; Hargrove and Glidewell, 1990; Holzer and Callahan, 1998; Jriesat, 1997; Kelman, 1987; La Porte, 1995; Light, 1997; Linden, 1994; Moore, 1995; Poister, 1988b; Popovich, 1998; Porter, Sargent, and Stupak, 1986; Riccucci, 1995; Tierney, 1988; Wilson, 1989; Wolf, 1993, 1997).

The debate over whether public organizations perform well—or as well as private firms—has many complexities. Previous chapters have discussed the many constraints on public organizations that can hamper their performance—complex sets of goals and difficulties in measuring performance, political interventions and turnover, externally imposed rules, inadequate resources and funding, policies and programs that are poorly designed by policymakers in the executive and legislative branches, and many others. Research fairly commonly finds that when public services are directly compared to privately delivered forms of the same service, the private sector displays more efficiency (Savas, 2000)—but not always (Donahue, 1990; Hodge, 2000; Sclar, 2000). In fact, Downs and Larkey (1986) described one national study that found that federal agencies showed higher rates of increase on productivity measures during the late 1960s than did a large sample of private firms. Individual agencies provide further examples. Studies have found that the U.S. Postal Service, the target of criticism and the brunt of jokes for decades, shows a much higher level of productivity per worker than any other postal service in the world, coupled with lower first-class mail rates than all but two other nations—Belgium and Switzerland—in spite of contending with greater geographic distances and other complexities. In addition, as Chapters Nine and Thirteen illustrate, there are many examples of innovative behaviors in public organizations and of studies that have found receptivity to change among public employees and no difference between the public and private sectors in general innovativeness.

In fact, the population of private and nonprofit organizations displays abundant weaknesses in many ways. Scholarly analyses and media reports regularly detail failures and bankruptcies, massive expensive blunders, and patterns of fraud and abuse in many of these organizations, sometimes in the most prestigious and reputable of them. In the first several years of the twenty-first century, such reports reached a crescendo. At times the litany of problems is so long that one wonders whether these sectors can serve as useful guiding models for the public sector. Conversely, just as with the public sector, the list of successes by business and nonprofit organizations is long and impressive, often involving accomplishments that would have seemed miraculous to people living even a few decades ago.

The point, then, is not to belabor invidious questions about whether one sector is better than another, but to underscore the challenge of pursuing excellence in all managerial settings. Many public and private organizations perform very well. What can we learn from studies of them?

## Profiles of Corporate Excellence

To examine some of these profiles, we might delve back into the recent history of the management literature. Peters and Waterman's *In Search of Excellence* (1982), now somewhat dated, apparently became so popular because it forged beyond complicated debates about organizational effectiveness and put forth stimulating observations about management in excellent firms (although the authors' conclusions actually echo much of the earlier literature on human relations in organizations and organizational responses to complexity). Peters and Waterman described these firms as placing a heavy emphasis on "productivity through people" (p. 14). They did not merely mouth that value, the authors said, they "live their commitment to people" (p. 16), and they "achieve extraordinary results with ordinary people" (p. xxv). They definitely try to attract and reward excellent performers, but they also emphasize both autonomy and teamwork.

The firms studied by Peters and Waterman devoted careful attention to managing their organizational culture. They developed coherent philosophies about product quality, business integrity, and fair treatment of employees and customers. Along with the stories and slogans that flourished in these companies, these philosophies emphasized the shared values that guided major decisions and motivated and guided performance. The firms nurtured the philosophies through heavy investments in training and socialization. "Without exception," the authors noted, "the dominance and coherence of culture proved to be an essential quality of the excellent companies" (p. 75). The firms behaved as if they accepted the principle that "soft is hard," that is, that the intangible issues of culture, values, human relations—matters that many managers regard as fuzzy and unmanageable—can and must be skillfully managed.

The successful firms sought coherence in their approach to management, with the shared values of the culture guiding the relationships between staff characteristics, skills, strategies, structure, and management systems. In so doing, they accepted ambiguity and paradox as part of the challenge. Organizing involves paradoxes, where one tries to do conflicting things at the same time, under conditions that often provide little clarity. The paradoxical aspects are evident in some of these companies' approaches to management, which Peters and Waterman describe in these terms:

• *A bias for action.* These companies tended toward an approach that one executive described as "ready, fire, aim." They avoided analyzing decisions to death and took action aggressively.

• *Staying close to the customer.* Deeply concerned about the quality of their products and services, people in these companies sought to stay in close touch with their customers and to be aware of their reactions.

• *Valuing autonomy and entrepreneurship.* Many of these companies provided autonomy in work and encouraged people to engage in entrepreneurial behaviors. They often tolerated the failure of well-intended, aggressive initiatives.

• *Enhancing productivity through people.* As noted earlier, the companies emphasized motivating and stimulating their people through respect, participation, and encouragement. They often used imagery, language, symbols, events, and ceremonies to do this.

• *A hands-on, value-driven approach.* The people in these firms devoted much attention to clarifying and stating the primary beliefs and values that guided the organization, to clarifying what the company "stands for."

• *Sticking to the knitting.* The companies stayed focused on the things they did well and avoided ill-advised forays into activities that diluted their efforts and goals.

• *A simple form and lean staff.* The companies often had relatively simple structures and small central staffs. Some massive corporations achieved this by decentralizing into fairly autonomous business units, each like a smaller company in itself.

• *Simultaneous loose and tight properties.* The companies balanced the need for direction and control with the need for flexibility and initiative. They might have had "tight" general guidelines and commitments to certain values, but they allowed considerable flexibility within those general values and guidelines. The approach that the Social Security Administration took when it adopted its modular work units (described in Chapter Thirteen) appears to fit this pattern. The change followed a clear, general concept—modularization—with firm commitment from the top, yet units could adopt the concept experimentally and flexibly. They could make reasonable adaptations, but not radically depart from the basic idea. This example suggests the ways in which many of these approaches mesh together. A relatively clear idea for a change, coupled with relatively clear and appealing values expressed as part of that idea, provides both a source of motivation and direction and a reasonable framework that higher levels can firmly insist on, without being rigid or dictatorial.

At about the same time as Peters and Waterman's book appeared, Americans became increasingly interested in the success of Japanese firms, which had been competing so effectively against American companies in many key industries. Observations of these firms revealed similarities to the particularly successful American companies. In one prominent book on the topic, Ouchi (1981) observed that many Japanese firms offered lifetime employment and avoided layoffs in hard times. They expressed a holistic concern for their employees. They moved slowly in evaluating and promoting personnel. They used more implicit control mechanisms, such as social influences on employees. They practiced collective decision making and collective responsibility, and developed relatively nonspecialized career paths.

The Japanese companies sought to develop trust on the part of their employees so they would have the confidence to contribute to the organization in many ways. They emphasized work groups as the basis for collective decisions and responsibilities. The companies emphasized the development of philosophies or styles that guide organizational objectives, operating procedures, and major decisions, such as new product lines. They supported these philosophies through extensive training programs. Ouchi noted that some successful American corporations, such as IBM, Procter & Gamble, Hewlett Packard, and Eastman Kodak (which were included in Peters and Waterman's study), had orientations similar to some of these aspects of Japanese management.

The appearance of books such as these, especially the Peters and Waterman book and several sequels and television programs on the same theme, produced a movement within management circles in the United States. Numerous similar books appeared, and many corporations took steps to emulate the purported patterns of excellence. More and more annual reports proclaimed a company philosophy, typically including sonorous expressions of devotion to employees, customers, and high-quality products. The annual report of one high-tech firm described the company as a "closely knit family" of forty thousand.

Predictably, controversy followed this material on corporate excellence and Japanese management. The generalized observations about the characteristics of successful firms leave some questions about just how valid they are and how closely they apply to any particular organization. It is not always clear how one carries out some of the prescriptions these books offer—especially how one weaves them all together. Also, Peters and Waterman themselves noted that some managers told them that culture is only one of many important aspects of their organization. Other features, such as sound technical and production systems, can figure just as crucially. Some of the supposedly excellent companies that Peters and Waterman studied encountered difficulties later. A strong downsizing trend among corporations in the United States soon began to erode any claims that successful corporations placed great value on their people. Nevertheless, there are important reasons to look back at Peters and Waterman and Ouchi as representative and leading examples of the wave of books on corporate excellence. For one reason, these books make valuable and fascinating points, including the importance of people and organizational culture, the inevitability of paradox and ambiguity and the necessity to manage them, and the feasibility of managing complex organizations successfully. Many of these points and themes still echo in the management literature and in the professed philosophies of many organizations, and they echo in the accounts of effective public management reviewed in earlier chapters and in this one. However, many of the studies of effective public management have followed a similar pattern of providing general case descriptions of purportedly effective, innovative, and high-performance public managers and organizations. This raises many of the same issues about how clear, valid, and widely practiced the authors' conclusions are about the values and practices they report.

## Research on Effective Public Organizations

Strikingly, the corporate excellence literature turned on their heads some frequent observations about the problems of public organizations. The Civil Service Reform Act of 1978 institutionalized the belief that weak links between pay, firing, and performance cause public organizations to perform poorly, and this belief has continued to play a strong role in discussions of governmental reforms (Rainey and Kellough, 2000). The writers on corporate excellence said that while the best profit-oriented firms tried very hard to recognize and reward excellent performers, they also emphasized a culture of communication, shared values, and mutual loyalty and support between the organization and its employees, as well as decentralization, flexibility, and adaptiveness. Although governmental reforms have sometimes claimed to pursue such conditions, and sometimes have involved efforts to do so, the reforms tend to mix such themes with the message that dysfunctional government agencies and many poor performers in them need to be fixed through such measures as pay-for-performance schemes and streamlined procedures for firing and discipline (Rainey and Kellough, 2000; Walters, 2002). This raises the question of how government can actually pursue enlightened reforms in a context of constant criticism and skepticism, a question all the more important as government confronts the apparent human capital crisis described shortly. At the same time, it makes attention to the reports of effective government organizations important, because in many of these reports one finds applications of some of the important values and philosophies that successful private corporations reportedly apply.

In one of the earliest examples of research on government organizations, resembling the approach of Peters and Waterman, Gold (1982) studied ten successful organizations, five public and five private. He chose healthy organizations with well-respected products or services that appeared to be good places to work, including the U.S. Forest Service, the U.S. Customs Service, the U.S. Passport Office, and the city governments of Sunnyvale, California, and Charlotte, North Carolina. The private organizations included a regional theater organization, the Dana Corporation (an automobile parts manufacturer), Hewlett Packard, L. L. Bean, and Time, Inc. He found that the ten organizations had certain common characteristics:

- They emphasized clear missions and objectives that are widely communicated and understood throughout the organization.
- The people in the organization saw it as special because of its products or services, and took pride in this.
- Management placed great value on the people in the organization, on treating them fairly and respectfully, and on open, honest, informal communication with them.
- The managers did not see their organization as particularly innovative, but they emphasized innovative ways of managing people.
- Management emphasized delegation of responsibility and authority as widely and as far down in the organization as possible. They involved as many people as possible in decision making and other activities.
- Job tasks and goals were clear, and employees received much feedback. Good performance earned recognition and rewards.
- The handling of jobs, participation, and the personnel function was aimed at challenging people and encouraging their enthusiasm and development.

Gold did find some distinctions between the public and private organizations, however. The public organizations did not articulate their mission as clearly and consistently as the private ones did. Apparently the private organizations' focus on profit as an element of their objectives helped in this regard. The managers in the public organizations, however, talked about excellence in the professionalism of the staff and about smoothly run operations and processes. The public organizations also had a harder time promoting from within, an approach that the private firms emphasized as a way of building experience, knowledge, and commitment among their employees.

As indicated by the many references cited earlier in this chapter and in previous ones, these types of studies have continued to appear. At one point, Hale (1996) summarized the conclusions of some of the most recent studies of high-performance public agencies. She concluded that in high-performance organizations, leaders define their key role as providing conditions that support employee productivity and that support employees in providing the organizations' customers with what they want and need from the organization. These organizations, and their leaders, typically hold the following values:

- *Learning.* They support learning, risk taking, training, communication, and work measurement.
- *A focused mission.* They emphasize clarifying their mission and communicating it to the members of the organization, its customers, and other stakeholders.
- *A nurturing community.* They provide a supportive culture, with a focus on teamwork, participation, flexible authority, and effective reward and recognition processes.
- *Enabling leadership.* They facilitate learning, communication, flexibility, sharing, and the development of a vision and commitment to it.

Later, Rainey and Steinbauer (1999) sought to develop further the sort of summary that Hale undertook. They bluntly asserted that public organizations can be very successful and effective, by reasonable standards, and as effective as business firms. They pointed to various examples of effective performance of government agencies, such as the low administrative expenses of the SSA, which represent only about 0.8 percent of the total benefits that the SSA disburses (Eisner, 1998). They sought to pull together the studies of high performance and excellent government organizations and looked for common patterns and generalizations, as illustrated in Table 14.1. As that table indicates, and as summaries of these types of studies here and in Chapter Thirteen also show, these studies vary widely in their methods, in the concepts and terms they use, in the degree to which they provide clear evidence in support of their conclusions, and in other ways. This makes it a difficult task to describe and summarize them, and it takes a lot of time and space to do so. Exhibit 14.1, however, provides a set of propositions that Rainey and Steinbauer offered as a result of the review.

Obviously one can criticize this set of propositions and debate its adequacy on many grounds, such as the clarity of the concepts and the adequacy of the evidence supporting them. It does make the point, however, that numerous researchers and authors are advancing evidence of successful, effective organizations and management in public organizations. This in turn suggests that many public organizations are managed as well as or better than private ones, and that many public managers perform very effectively. These propositions raise the challenge of continuing to develop our knowledge of how public organizations achieve these effective performances and change for the better.

# Trends and Developments in the Pursuit of Effective Public Management

Besides the research on effective public organizations, a number of trends and developments related to the pursuit of effective public management are worthy of attention. A vast array of such activities and initiatives goes on constantly and previous chapters have covered many of them, such as the Government Performance Project, applications of the Balanced Scorecard in the public sector, and the Government Performance and Results Act and the efforts at strategic planning that it required (all covered in Chapter Six). It is difficult to decide which additional developments to cover, but everyone interested in public management should be aware of the developments covered here. They serve to illustrate certain points about the context and dynamics of the theory and practice of management in general and of public management.

## Total Quality Management

In the last two decades, organizations throughout the public and private sectors have undertaken Total Quality Management (TQM) programs. The widespread implementation of these programs makes it important for public managers and students of public management to be aware of TQM. As we will see, TQM also raises challenging alternatives for management, and it has clearly influenced the objectives of current government reform efforts described later in this chapter (for example, focusing on the customer, the use of teams, and continuous improvement) and the literature on public management (for example, Beam, 2001). It also

## TABLE 14.1. CHARACTERISTICS OF
## HIGH-PERFORMANCE GOVERNMENT ORGANIZATIONS.

|  | Gold (1982) | Hale and Williams (1989) | Wilson (1989) |
|---|---|---|---|
| Mission/ Public Orientation | Emphasize clear mission and objectives. | Increase contact with customers to better understand their needs. | Mission is clear and reflects a widely shared and warmly endorsed organizational culture. Political support is from external stakeholders. |
| Leadership/ Managing Employees | Employees take pride in the organization and its product. Focus is on treating employees fairly and respectfully through honest and open communication. Emphasis is on delegating responsibility and authority as widely as possible. Management aims at challenging and encouraging people. Management emphasizes innovative ways of managing. | Increase discretionary authority for managers and employees for greater control over accountability. Increased employee participation taps their knowledge, skills, and commitment. | Executives command loyalty, define and instill a clear sense of mission, attract talented workers, and make exacting demands of subordinates. Leaders make peer expectations serve the organization. Discretionary authority for operators is maximized. Executive takes responsibility for organizational maintenance. Implementation perspective is bottom up. |
| Task Design/ Work Environment | Great value is placed on the people in the organization. Job tasks and goals are clear. | Partnerships allow the sharing of knowledge, expertise, and other resources. Employ state-of-the-art productivity improvement techniques. Improve work measurements to provide a base for planning and implementing service improvements and worker evaluation. | Goals are clearly defined. There is widespread agreement on how critical tasks are performed. Agency is given autonomy to develop operational goals from which tasks are designed. Agency is able to control or keep contextual goals in proper perspective. |

*Source:* Portions of this table are adapted from Rainey and Steinbauer, 1999, p. 359; and from Hale, 1996, p. 139.

| Denhardt (2000) | Popovich (1998) | Hale (1996) | Holzer and Callahan (1998) |
|---|---|---|---|
| Dedication to public service and understanding public intent. Serving the public, which represents democratic values. | Aim for mission clarity and understanding. Maintain open and productive communication among stakeholders. | Mission is focused, clarified, and communicated to organization members. | Organization is customer focused. Partnerships are built with public and private organizations and citizens. |
| Leader demonstrates commitment to mission. Manager builds sense of community in organization. Manager clearly articulates values. Managers insist on high ethical standards. Leadership is empowered and shared. Employees accept responsibility and performance accountability. | Employees are empowered. Organizations allocate resources for continuous learning. Employees accept accountability to achieve results with rewards and consequences. People are motivated and inspired to succeed. | Enabling leadership emphasizes learning, communication, flexibility, sharing, and vision development. | Leaders manage for quality using long-term strategic planning, with support from top leadership. Human resources are developed and employees are empowered through team building, systematic training, recognition, and a balance between employee and organizational needs. |
| Change is seen as natural, appropriate (pragmatic incrementalism). Approach to change is creative and humane. Commitment is to values. | Outcomes are defined and focus is on results (performance measures). New work processes are instituted as necessary. Organization adjusts flexibly and nimbly to new conditions. Organization is competitive in terms of performance. Work processes are restructured to meet customer needs. | Learning is emphasized, and learning, risk taking, training, communication, and work measurement are carefully supported. Nurturing-community culture is supportive and emphasizes teamwork, participation, flexible authority, and effective reward and recognition. | Technologies that are adapted include open access to data, automation for productivity, cost-effective applications, and cross-cutting techniques that deliver on public demands. Performance is measured by establishing goals and measuring results, justifying and allocating resource requirements as necessary, and developing organizational improvement strategies. |

## EXHIBIT 14.1. PROPOSITIONS
## ABOUT EFFECTIVE PUBLIC ORGANIZATIONS.

Public agencies are more likely to perform effectively when there are high levels of the following conditions:

Effective relations with oversight authorities (legislative, executive, judicial). Authorities are:
- Attentive
- Demanding
- Supportive
- Delegative

Effective relations with other stakeholders
- Favorable public opinion and general public support
- Multiple, influential, mobilizable constituent and client groups
- Effective relations with partners and suppliers
      Effective management of contracting and contractors
      Effective utilization of technology and other resources
      Effective negotiation of networks

Responsive autonomy in relation to political oversight and influence

Mission valence (the attractiveness of the mission)
- Difficult but feasible
- Reasonably clear and understandable
- Worthy/worthwhile/legitimate
- Interesting/exciting
- Important/influential
- Distinctive

Strong organizational culture, linked to mission

Effective leadership
- Stability of leadership
- Multiplicity of leadership—a cadre of leaders, teams of leaders at multiple levels
- Leadership commitment to mission
- Effective goalsetting in relation to task and mission accomplishment
- Effective coping with political and administrative constraints

Effective task design
- Intrinsically motivating tasks (interest, growth, responsibility, service, and mission accomplishment)
- Extrinsic rewards for task accomplishment (pay, benefits, promotions, working conditions)

Effective development of human resources
- Effective recruitment, selection, placement, training, and development
- Values and preferences among recruits and members that support task and mission motivation

High levels of professionalism among members
- High levels of special knowledge and skills related to task and mission accomplishment
- Commitment to task and mission accomplishment
- High levels of public service professionalism

High levels of motivation among members
- High levels of public service motivation among members
- High levels of mission motivation among members
- High levels of task motivation among members

*Source:* Adapted from Rainey and Steinbauer, 1999.

provides an interesting and significant example of the dissemination of ideas and techniques in public and private management (Berman and West, 1995).

The term *Total Quality Management* refers more to a general movement or philosophy of management than to a specific set of management procedures. Different authors take different approaches to TQM. W. Edwards Deming, one of the founders of this movement, who developed many of the original ideas behind it, did not refer to his approach as Total Quality Management. In fact, he disapproved of this label. Yet a review of some of Deming's seminal ideas provides a useful introduction to TQM (Dean and Evans, 1994; Deming, 1986; Juran, 1992).

Deming was an industrial statistician. Writing in the 1950s, he advocated using statistical measures of the quality of a product during all the phases of its production. He called for this approach to replace the quality-control procedures often used in industry, which assessed the product only at the end of the production process. Deming included this commitment to statistical quality control in his general philosophy of management. He put together fourteen tenets of his approach. These tenets, frequently quoted in the TQM literature, include the following:

- Publish a statement of company aims and purposes for all employees to see, and demonstrate commitment to the statement on the part of management.
- Have everyone in the company learn and adopt the new philosophy.
- Constantly improve the production system.
- Institute training, teach leadership skills, and encourage self-improvement.
- Drive out fear and create trust and a climate of innovation.
- Use teams to pursue optimal achievement of company goals.
- Eliminate numerical production quotas and management by objectives, and concentrate on improving processes and on methods of improvement.
- Remove barriers to pride of workmanship.

Although some of these tenets sound simple, many have profound implications for an organization's basic approach to organizing and managing. For example, these principles led Deming to oppose individualized performance appraisals because they damage teamwork, fail to focus on serving the customer, and usually emphasize short-term results. Compare his orientation to the themes in civil service reforms and government pay reforms described in Chapter Ten (for example, pay-for-performance plans based on individual performance appraisals, and the streamlining of procedures for firing and disciplining employees). In contrast, Deming argued that to make the commitment to improving quality work, people have to feel free to contribute their ideas about problems and improvements. Hence, the leaders of the organization must "drive out fear."

Deming argued that his approach to management represented a general philosophy that must receive total commitment from the organization. Measures of quality should be used at all phases of production and should be the basis for continuous efforts to improve quality. The organization should strive to improve relative to its own previous quality measures as well as to those of comparable organizations. The quality measures should be based on the preferences and point of view of the organization's customers.

When Deming first began to advance his ideas, they received little attention from managers in the United States. The Japanese, however, embraced his ideas enthusiastically, and the Deming Award became a very prestigious award in Japan for excellence in management. As Japanese firms joined the list of the most successful firms in the world and began outcompeting with U.S. firms in many markets, managers in the United States decided that they needed to pay some attention to what this fellow Deming had to say. For example, Deming was instrumental in the Ford Motor Company's adoption of a corporate strategy and philosophy based on a commitment to quality (Dean and Evans, 1994). The general acceptance and adoption of these programs became so widespread that by 1987 Congress passed legislation establishing the Malcolm Baldrige National Quality Award Program (named for a former U.S. secretary of commerce), which annually recognizes organizations with excellent quality management programs and achievements.

Well-developed TQM programs tend to involve such conditions and principles as the following (Dean and Evans, 1994; Cohen and Brand, 1993):

- An emphasis on defining quality in terms of customer needs and responses.
- Working with suppliers to improve their relationship to the quality of the organization's production processes and products.
- Measurement and assessment of quality at all phases of production, with commitment to continuous improvement in quality. Quality measures are often benchmarked against similar measures for similar organizations as a way of assessing improvement and general level of performance.
- Teamwork, trust, and communication in improving quality; use of decision-making and quality improvement teams involving participants from many areas and levels of the organization that are involved in the production process.
- Well-developed training programs to support teamwork and quality assessment and improvement.
- A broad organizational commitment to the process, from the top-executive ranks on down, that encompasses strategy, cultural development, communication, and other major aspects of the organization.

In well-developed programs, top executives demonstrate commitment and leadership. Symbols, language, communication, and training are coordinated around the quality program. In some of the companies, for example, every employee receives sixty days of quality training within two weeks of joining the organization, and everyone, including the CEO, takes the training. The training often involves coverage of a fairly standard set of analytical procedures, including such techniques as cause-and-effect ("fishbone") diagrams, flowcharts, and procedures for counting and tabulating data related to production quality, and for analyzing causes and interpretations.

Although the TQM movement originally focused on industry, it swept through government as well, with applications in many different types of agencies and at all levels of government (Council of State Governments, 1994). Consistent with the theme of this book, the basic principles of TQM emphasize that successful total quality efforts depend heavily on commitment and strategic implementation (Cohen and Brand, 1993). The principles of TQM are often general, stressing leadership, culture, incentives and motivation, groups and teams, and many of the other topics covered in previous chapters. Failed TQM efforts often display the opposite of these qualities—insufficient leadership, weak culture, weak management of the change process, and poor provisions for motivation and teamwork.

TQM has its detractors, who criticize it as one more management fad that will soon be supplanted by another. Significantly, early in the twenty-first century, fewer and fewer organizations appeared to be implementing TQM programs, and many organizations appeared to be abandoning them, although many similar approaches, such as high-performance work systems and high-performance organizations, continued in various ways (Appelbaum, Bailey, Berg, and Kalleberg, 2000; Lawler, Mohrman, and Benson, 2001). TQM obviously has very challenging and interesting features, however, especially for government. It proposes a management philosophy quite opposed to the one that has prevailed in many government reforms in recent years (Peters and Savoie, 1994; Rainey and Kellough, 2000). Also, its history illustrates the need for comprehensive, strategic approaches to many innovations in management—approaches that apply many of the ideas covered in previous chapters.

## The Reinventing Government Movement

Osborne and Gaebler's book *Reinventing Government* (1992) became a best-seller during the early 1990s and influenced many government reforms in the years since its publication (Brudney and Wright, 2002; Brudney, Hebert, and Wright, 1999; Gore, 1993; Hennessey, 1998; Kearney, Feldman, and Scavo, 2000). Its approach and its success resemble those of Peters and Waterman's *In Search of Excellence* and one can appropriately characterize it as the public sector equivalent of that book. Like the other studies of excellence in public management described earlier, it provides provocative and challenging ideas about approaches to public management and the delivery of government services. Interestingly, however, its perspective on the state of performance in the public sector was mixed. The authors introduced the book with the claim that in many ways government is failing and breaking down. Yet they also argued that government plays an essential role in society and has to define and carry out that role effectively—hence the need for reinvention. In particular, the authors attacked the old-fashioned, centralized, bureaucratic model that dominated many government agencies and programs. They called for more entrepreneurial activities to supplant that approach.

Significantly, however, to support their call for a more entrepreneurial approach in government, they cited many government practices they had observed around the country that were already quite effective, such as decentralizing, encouraging privatization, encouraging control of programs at the community level, increasing attention to the "customers" of government programs, finding ways for government to make money on its operations ("enterprising government"), and increasing competition among government programs and between government and the private sector. Exhibit 14.2 summarizes their strategies for more entrepreneurial government. They illustrated the use of these strategies through numerous examples from government programs.

Their proposals had a rapid, major impact, including the establishment of the Clinton administration's National Performance Review, described later. *REGO* (reinventing government) became a widely used term in the federal government and in other government circles. The REGO trend heavily influenced a broad array of developments, including the reinvention of the civil service system of the state of Florida and an entrepreneurial effort at getting a hotel built in downtown Visalia, California. These two examples are quite significant, because according to some observers they were unsuccessful. Wechsler (1994) concluded that the civil service reform efforts in Florida had little important effect. Gurwitt (1994) reported that the Visalia episode had bad results. There, government officials wanted a hotel built downtown to support economic development efforts. Pursuing entrepreneurial strategies, they tried to avoid spending government funds to subsidize the development of the hotel. They bought land and worked out an arrangement with a developer to lease the land from the city and build a hotel on it. This way, the city would make money on the arrangement through the lease payments. Unfortunately, the developer folded, and rather than give up on the project and take a loss, the city assumed more than $20 million of the developer's debts.

Several studies have sought to assess the implementation of REGO reforms at different levels of government. Brudney, Hebert, and Wright (1999) found limited implementation in state governments of reforms representing REGO ideas, except for fairly widespread efforts at strategic planning, but a later survey showed some increase in the implementation of REGO reforms (Brudney and Wright, 2002). Kearney, Feldman, and Scavo (2000) surveyed 912 city managers and found

# EXHIBIT 14.2. OSBORNE AND GAEBLER'S STRATEGIES FOR REINVENTING GOVERNMENT.

*Catalytic Government*

"Leverage" government authority and resources by using private- and nonprofit-sector resources and energies, through such strategies as privatization of public services and public-private partnerships.

Government should "steer" rather than "row," by emphasizing directions and priorities but letting private and nonprofit organizations deliver services and carry out projects.

*Community-Owned Government*

Empower local communities and groups. Allow more local control through such strategies as community policing and resident control of public housing.

*Competitive Government*

Introduce more competition between government and private organizations, within government, and between private organizations through such strategies as competitive contracting, private competition with public services, and school choice and voucher programs.

*Mission-Driven Government*

Focus government programs on their missions rather than on bureaucratic rules and procedures, through such strategies as flexible budgeting procedures (such as expenditure control budgets) and more flexible personnel rules and procedures (such as broader, more flexible pay categories, as studied in the China Lake Experiments).

*Results-Oriented Government*

Place more emphasis on outcomes rather than inputs, through greater investment in performance measures, including using them in budgeting and evaluation systems.

*Customer-Driven Government*

Give customers of public programs and services more influence over them. Pay more attention to customers through procedures such as customer surveys, toll-free numbers, TQM programs, and complaint tracking. Give customers more choice through voucher systems and competition among service providers.

*Enterprising Government*

Find ways to earn money through user fees, profitable uses of government resources and programs, and innovative cost-saving and privatization projects.

*Anticipatory Government*

Prevent problems before they occur rather than curing them after they do, through strategic planning, futures commissions, long-range budgeting, interdepartmental planning and budgeting, and innovative prevention programs in environmental protection, crime, fire, and other service areas.

*Decentralized Government*

Decentralize government activities through such approaches as relaxing rules and hierarchical controls, participatory management, innovative management, employee development, and labor-management partnerships.

*Market-Oriented Government*

Use economic market mechanisms to achieve public policy goals and deliver public services, through such techniques as pollution taxes, deposit fees on bottles, user fees, tax credits, and vouchers.

*Source:* Adapted from Osborne and Gaebler, 1992.

high levels of agreement with principles and ideas similar to those proposed by Osborne and Gaebler. The city managers, however, were less likely to have taken action to implement the principles and ideas than they were to express agreement with them. Interestingly, studies of reinvention initiatives have tended to find that leadership support played a strong role in the their implementation (see, for example, Brudney and Wright, 2002; Hennessey, 1998).

As these examples and studies show, the REGO ideas have been influential, but also controversial. For example, some critics have raised concerns about thinking of citizens as customers of public organizations. In addition, many of the REGO proposals, such as efforts to privatize public services, have been going on for centuries, and Frederickson (1996), a leading scholar in public administration, has likened them to "old wine in new bottles." Yet, like many new approaches, the proposals can also be regarded as stimulating and challenging, and the research and examples just described underscore a main theme of this book: challenging new ideas require effective implementation, and in government, implementation requires effective public management.

## The National Performance Review

The REGO movement influenced the Clinton administration's National Performance Review (NPR). As with the other recent developments described in this chapter, NPR deserves attention as a major recent reform effort in public management. Some experts regarded the NPR as unprecedented in terms of the activity it generated and the attention it received (Kettl, 1993). The NPR involved a review of federal operations by a staff in Washington under the leadership of Vice President Gore. Among other activities, Gore conducted meetings with employees in federal agencies, ostensibly to gather ideas about problems and solutions, but also with the obvious intent of making a symbolic statement.

In many ways, the NPR's tenor was similar to that of the reinventing government movement (see Exhibit 14.3). The first report (Gore, 1993) argued that the federal government needed a drastic overhaul to improve its operations, a reinvention similar to that in many corporations that had reformed themselves in the face of international competition in the 1980s. Yet the report—and Gore, in his public statements and actions (such as his meetings with agency employees)—took the position that federal employees were not to blame for the problems in government. The structures and systems were the problems, the report said, and it emphasized the importance of listening to federal employees' ideas and observations. The report announced numerous initiatives to reform the structure and operations of the federal government, as well as many change efforts within federal agencies. Exhibit 14.3 summarizes some of the major priorities and initiatives

## EXHIBIT 14.3. THE NATIONAL PERFORMANCE REVIEW: MAJOR PRIORITIES AND INITIATIVES.

1. Cut Red Tape
   - *Streamline the budget-making process.* Use biennial budgeting; relax OMB categories and ceilings; allow agencies to roll over 50 percent of funds not spent.
   - *Decentralize personnel policy.* Eliminate the *Federal Personnel Manual;* allow departments to conduct their own recruiting, examining, evaluation, and reward systems; simplify the classification system; reduce the time to terminate employees and managers for cause and to deal with poor performers.
   - *Streamline procurement.* Simplify procurement regulations; decentralize GSA authority for buying information technology; allow agencies to buy where they want; rely on the commercial marketplace.
   - *Reorient the inspectors general.* Reorient them from strict compliance auditing to evaluating management control systems.
   - *Eliminate regulatory overkill.* Eliminate 50 percent of internal agency regulations; improve interagency coordination of regulations; allow agencies to obtain waivers from regulations.
   - *Empower state and local governments.* Establish an enterprise board for new initiatives in community empowerment; limit the use of unfunded mandates; consolidate grant programs into more flexible categories; allow agency heads to grant states and localities selective waivers from regulations and mandates; give control of public housing to local housing authorities with good records.

2. Put Customers First
   - *Give customers "voice" and "choice."*
   - *Make service organizations compete.*
   - *Create market dynamics and use market mechanisms.*

3. Empower Employees to Get Results
   - *Decentralize decision making.*
   - *Hold federal employees accountable for results.*
   - *Give federal workers the tools they need.*
   - *Enhance the quality of work life.*

4. Cut Back to Basics
   - *Eliminate what we don't need.*
   - *Collect more.*
   - *Invest in productivity and reengineer to cut costs.*

*Source:* Adapted from Gore,1993.

announced in the first report of the NPR. As the table suggests, the NPR emphasized the need to reform many of the constraints on federal agencies discussed in this book. The reforms would decentralize and relax personnel and procurement regulations, for example.

Many of the NPR reforms also reflect the management trends described in this book—including the prescriptions of Peters and Waterman, TQM, REGO, and others—with an emphasis on serving the customer, decentralization, empowerment, and relaxed controls. The report thus provides an interesting example of the infusion into government reform of trends and ideas in business management.

Predictably, the NPR was controversial in public administration circles, in terms of whether it was well conceived and whether it would have lasting and beneficial effects. Without question, however, it caused a lot of activity in federal agencies. Among other steps, the NPR announced and carried out a major reduction of the federal workforce, mentioned in several previous chapters (U.S. Office of Management and Budget, 2002). This gave rise to questions about whether such cuts were really the result of an ulterior motive behind the glowing discourse about reforms, and whether the NPR was simply part of the recent trend of presidents' attacking the bureaucracy for political effect (Arnold, 1995). In addition, many of the NPR initiatives were implemented by executive order, including one instructing federal agencies to reduce their internal regulations by 50 percent and one eliminating the elaborate federal personnel manual. Such measures seemed to have little impact.

Subsequent NPR reports announced additional reforms. An executive order directed federal agencies to publish customer service standards, and a great many did (Clinton and Gore, 1995). Follow-up reports announced indications of progress, such as reductions in regulations, cost savings of $58 billion, and a variety of steps in different agencies to improve operations and services (Gore, n.d.). One of the efforts under the NPR involved a presidential directive ordering federal agencies to set up so-called reinvention laboratories to work on improving their procedures. Some of these reinvention labs reported successes in finding improved and innovative ways of carrying out their agency's business, although they also encountered many obstacles to change (Sanders and Thompson, 1996).

Thompson (2000) assessed the impact of the NPR by examining results of surveys of employees and other sources of evidence, and through an in-depth case study of its implementation in the SSA. He concluded that NPR did effect impacts in the major reduction in federal jobs, in reducing administrative costs in the federal government, in reforming the federal procurement system, in empowering frontline managers and employees, and in establishing labor-management partnerships. He found little evidence of impacts in the reform of the civil service system in order to decentralize it, in enhancing service delivery to the public, and in reengineering and streamlining work processes in agencies. He also found very limited impacts within the SSA.

It was easily predictable, moreover, that the success of NPR would depend on the political fortunes of the administration that sponsored it. As if to provide a perfect example of one of the frequently noted obstacles to change and reform in government, Vice President Gore lost the presidential election to George W. Bush, and soon the activities associated with NPR were terminated. A search for its Web site now takes you to a "cybercemetary" at North Texas State University, where its documents are archived.

Ultimately, NPR illustrated many of the obstacles to reform in government. At the same time, however, it represented a historic initiative in the pursuit of improved public management. Whether or not it was the right thing to do, a massive reduction in federal employees represents a major impact. Also, reforms of the procurement system and the reductions in federal administrative expenses represent important accomplishments. The NPR, in addition, documented many examples of effective public management. It received relatively strong support from top executives (the president and vice president), it made an effort to involve organizational members (the federal employees) in change and to enlist their support, and it advanced measures for decentralized diagnosis and incremental improvement of performance problems (the reinvention labs). Significantly, it clearly exerted far more influence on the federal government and its agencies than did Reagan-era reform efforts like the Grace Commission.

## The President's Management Agenda

The second President Bush is the first president to have a management degree, and early in his administration he indicated an interest in management by issuing the *President's Management Agenda*. The Agenda announced five primary government-wide initiatives: Strategic Management of Human Capital, Competitive Sourcing (employing competition to decide whether federal employees or private contractors should provide federal services), Improved Financial Performance, Expanded Electronic Government, and Budget and Performance Integration. The U.S. Office of Management and Budget (OMB) then issued *agency scorecards* to twenty-five major federal agencies based on discussions with experts in government and universities (U.S. Office of Management and Budget, 2002). The scorecards use a "traffic light" grading system for each of the five government-wide initiatives. A green light means success, yellow means mixed results, and red means unsatisfactory. In the early phases of this process, of the 130 traffic lights awarded to the twenty-six agencies on the five initiatives, only nineteen were yellow, one was green, and the rest were red. OMB then began to publish an additional listing of the agencies, awarding green, yellow, and red lights on the basis of the progress they were making in the five areas. The five agenda priorities reflect important management issues in the federal government and at other levels that have advocates other than the Bush administration. In some ways they reflect priorities that the NPR and other reform efforts have also emphasized. How much reform and progress the agenda and the traffic lights accomplish will also be an agenda item for researchers and observers in public management in coming years.

## The Human Capital Movement

As mentioned earlier, other people besides members of the Bush administration advocate reforms and improvements in the five areas that the *President's Management Agenda* targets. The issue of *human capital* has origins and imperatives similar to the human capital issues in many state governments (see, for example, Abramson and Gardner, 2002). This emphasis amounts to a movement at the federal level that responds in part to a purported crisis.

The term *human capital* has attracted its share of ridicule. A Dilbert cartoon in 2002 portrayed Dogbert, one of the usual characters, talking to Dilbert's boss, who is always insensitive and inept, about human capital. Dogbert asked if the boss preferred to refer to the employees as *human capital* or *livestock*. The boss said he preferred *human capital* because if they were to use the term *livestock*, the employees might demand hay. *Human capital* may sound somewhat dehumanizing because it conjures up the image of using human beings like machines or other capital stock. Proponents of this movement, however, intend totally opposite implications. They call for leaders to regard the human beings in their organizations as their most valuable asset. They argue that in the information age, when human knowledge and intellectual skills play such a crucial role in organizational success, leaders need to realize the value of investing in human beings in their organizations and to help people develop their knowledge and skills. Moreover, organizations need to strategize, plan, and invest in making sure that this human-capital emphasis infuses the organization's operations and its long-term development.

In addition to the OMB, David M. Walker, comptroller general of the United States, has served as one of the main proponents of the human capital focus (Walker, 2001; U.S. General Accounting Office, 2002a, 2002b). Also, Senator Voinovich of Ohio advanced legislation on human capital issues that was included in the legislation authorizing the Department of Homeland Security, but Voinovich's legislation applied the requirements to all federal agencies. The legislation requires, for example, that each federal agency appoint a chief human capital officer to be responsible for strategic planning for human capital, aligning the strategic planning with the agency's mission, and fostering a culture of performance and improvement.

The human capital movement has been driven in part by concerns over a growing crisis in human capital in the federal government, a crisis that the situation in the states tends to mirror. The Senate Governmental Affairs Committee (U.S. Senate, 2001), as well as other sources, described the growing crisis as involving several developments. As of 2002, 53 percent of the federal workforce will be eligible for retirement by 2004, 71 percent of senior managers will be eligible for retirement by 2006, and 58 percent of GS-15 managers will be able to retire by 2007. At the same time, a survey found that good students in universities tended to have an unfavorable view of the federal government as a place to work. In the survey, one out of ten members of Phi Beta Kappa rated the federal government as a good place to work. In addition, the federal workforce had been downsized by about 325,000 between 1993 and 2000, with new hires decreasing sharply during that period as well, and with critics complaining that the downsizing was "nonstrategic," or poorly planned and executed in relation to long-term human resource needs (Partnership for Public Service, 2002; U.S. Office of Management and Budget, 2002). As still another challenge, the rapid changes in information technology and other areas have forced changes in the sorts of skills and personnel needed in all types of organizations. These changes usually involve imperatives for bringing in more highly educated, trained, and skilled employees, for which organizations in the public, nonprofit, and private sectors compete aggressively.

In response to these developments, the players in this movement have so far concentrated on exhorting or pressuring federal agencies to take human capital seriously, advising them on how to do it, and recommending or crafting legislation to set in place some of the structures and requirements to support it (such as chief human capital officers). The General Accounting Office (GAO), for example, has issued frameworks, checklists, and a model to guide agency efforts (U.S. General Accounting Office, 2002a, 2002b). The GAO model provides a conceptual framework, guidelines, and pointers on how to achieve success in establishing four "human capital cornerstones":

1. *Leadership:* to establish a commitment to human capital management and to establish the role of the human capital function
2. *Strategic human capital planning:* to achieve integration and alignment of the human capital function with the organization's strategy, mission, and operations, and to produce data-driven human capital decisions
3. *Acquiring, developing, and retaining talent:* making targeted investments in people to ensure that human capital approaches are tailored to meet organizational needs
4. *Results-oriented organizational culture:* involving empowerment and inclusiveness to ensure that unit and individual performance are linked to organizational goals

Obviously, the long-term influence of the legislation, admonitions, traffic lights, frameworks, and guidelines coming from the human capital movement remains to be seen. The imperatives moving this activity along, however, manifest at the state and local levels. According to recent analyses, 42 percent of the 15.7 million state and local government employees in the United States in 1999 were from forty-five to sixty-four years old. Between 2000 and 2015, two-fifths of state and local government employees will be eligible to retire. This outflow of talent and knowledge has disastrous potential for numerous reasons, among them, that state and local governments need to play a major role in homeland security, and that they face increasing pressures to upgrade information and communication systems for improved service delivery in many areas. Thus, state governments face pressures to develop and improve human capital, and to consider ways to respond flexibly and rapidly to this imperative, including the possibility of bringing in people who have not moved up through the state civil service system.

## Research on Governance

Another important stream of activity, primarily on the research front rather than in the realm of practice, involves a growing body of research on "governance" that seeks to incorporate more of the full complexity of governmental activity. As previous chapters in this book and as many other authors have pointed out, government involves a vast complex of levels and networks of activities and relationships. Sprawling literature on public administration, public policy, and political science refers to the many programs, policies, organizations, and authorities involved in producing government services and outputs. Lynn, Heinrich, and Hill (2000) have sought to advance a conceptual framework that captures this complexity and to use it to guide explicit empirical research. They define governance as "regimes of laws, administrative rules, judicial rulings, and practices that constrain, prescribe, and enable government activity, where such activity is broadly defined as the production and delivery of publicly supported goods and services." (Lynn, Heinrich, and Hill, 2000, p. 3). The central question of research on governance, they say, is "how can public-sector regimes, agencies, programs, and activities be organized and managed to achieve public purposes?" (p. 1).

To pursue this question, they propose a general model that encourages attention to the broad patterns of relationships involved in governance, as opposed to focusing on isolated elements of it (such as an individual organization in the policy system), and that also seeks to encourage empirical research:

$$O = f(E, C, T, S, M)$$

In this model,

$O$ = outputs/outcomes at the individual and/or organizational levels, measured by "precisely defined, empirically measured variables" (Lynn, Heinrich, and Hill, 2000, p. 16)

E = environmental factors, such as political structures, external authority and monitoring, and funding constraints and dependencies

C = client characteristics

T = treatments (primary work processes or technologies), such as organizational missions and objectives, and program treatments and technologies

S = structures, such as organizational type, centralization of control, administrative rules and incentives, and contractual arrangements

M = managerial roles and actions, such as leadership practices, professionalism, and control mechanisms such as performance standards.

As some of the descriptions of "excellent" and "high-performing" government organizations in earlier sections of this chapter illustrate, such descriptions often take the form of case examples of "best practices" to follow. While often richly descriptive and suggestive about alternatives to pursue, these case examples often lack a basis of rigorous empirical evidence for their conclusions. While acknowledging the value of such observations and suggestions, Heinrich and Lynn (2000a) wanted to bring together scholars trying to develop explicit models of the performance of public programs, especially models containing organizational and managerial variables, and to subject them to quantitatively rigorous empirical tests. Under a grant from the Pew Charitable Trusts, a special research symposium for this purpose was held at the School of Public Administration and Policy at the University of Arizona, where the papers presented became the chapters for their book, *Governance and Performance: New Perspectives.*

Heinrich and Lynn (2000b; Heinrich, 2000) demonstrate their efforts to analyze governance activities at multiple levels by analyzing the earnings in the first year after training among people who receive employment training under the Job Training Partnership Act (JTPA). They use a technique called hierarchical linear modeling that analyzes data in a way that helps the researcher understand the different roles of variables at different levels in a hierarchical system. They analyze variables at both the site level (the location of the training program) and the individual level (the characteristics of the trainees) and find effects of variables at both levels. For example, at the individual level, a trainee's gender and level of education showed strong relations to earnings after the training program. The results also show, moreover, very strong relations between certain characteristics of the way the programs were structured and managed at the site level. The sites vary in the degree to which "Private Industry Councils" (PICs) have administrative control over the program, and the results show higher post-program earnings when the PICs have more control. Managerial decisions, such as the emphasis on such performance standards as the rate of employment after the program also had an important influence on trainees' earnings after the program. In this way, the researchers draw conclusions about the effects of variables at different levels in the program.

Other chapters in *Governance and Performance* illustrate similar multilevel analyses. Roderick, Jacob, and Bryk (2000) provide another HLM analysis, of a program to end social promotion in the Chicago schools. They find that governance variables show important relations to outcomes for students. Jennings and Ewalt (2000) report a multivariate analysis of welfare policies in forty-four states aimed at reducing welfare caseloads. They find a strong influence of states' policy choices and administrative actions on caseload declines. Analyzing welfare-to-work programs in counties in Michigan, Sandfort (2000) assesses the role of managerial variables by showing that the counties' choices of service delivery structures and technologies influence the success of the program. Riccio, Bloom, and Hill (2000) then provide a description of their plans for a study of welfare-to-work programs using large data sets and HLM analysis similar to that of Heinrich and Lynn, and including measures of organizational climate and managerial processes. Knott and Hammond (2000) develop a formal "spatial" model that posits conditions under which congressional committees can foster or block changes in government policies, and apply the model to four case studies of deregulation policies. Their chapter also illustrates the application of multilevel models to public management, by showing how legislative committees can figure as important influences on public managers. Along with the chapter by Heinrich and Lynn, these chapters provide evidence of the value of trying to model and analyze public policies and programs with as much attention as possible to their full complexity and multilevel nature.

Other chapters in *Governance and Performance* show that Lynn, Heinrich, and Hill's (2000) approach to governance has similarities to approaches described in earlier sections and chapters of this book, such as the Government Performance Project, research on networks (Provan and Milward, 1995), and the O'Toole-Meier model and studies of public management. Milward and Provan (2000) contribute to *Governance and Performance* a chapter on governing networks that emphasizes the distinction between governance through contractual relations as opposed to governance through trust and collaboration, and the importance of a network's stability to its effectiveness. O'Toole and Meier (2000) present a formal model that includes a distinction between networks and hierarchies, and emphasizes the role of managers in exploiting "shocks" from the environment, but also in buffering the organization from shocks. Ingraham and Donahue (2000) describe the model of governmental management capacity that they developed for the Government Performance Project (described in Chapter Six). Their model posits that management capacity depends on the performance of four management subsystems—the financial, human resources, capital, and information technology subsystems—and the presence of a system of "managing for results." They further propose sets of assessment criteria for each of these subsystems.

Besides the one advanced by Lynn, Heinrich, and Hill (2000), there are other uses of the term "governance" and other approaches to the topic (Frederickson and Smith, 2003, chap. 9). Reviewers of the Lynn, Heinrich, and Hill approach express various concerns about it, such as pointing out the challenges that the inherent complexities of the goals of government programs pose for those who would model and measure governmental performance (Ellwood, 2000; see also Lowery, 2002). Nevertheless, this research on governance presents one of the very interesting and important current streams of research activity in relation to public management.

# Managing Major Initiatives and Priorities: Privatization and Contracting Out

These recent developments illustrate the point that effective management and organization in the public sector remains a crucial, dynamic challenge, a challenge that becomes especially apparent when we observe the implementation (or failed implementation) of new initiatives in government. As a concluding effort in this book, this section applies the framework shown in Figures 1.1 and 1.2, and the topics included in that framework, which have been elaborated on throughout the book, to the topic of organizing for and managing a very recent trend in public management, the increasing emphasis on privatization of public services. As mentioned at the beginning of this book, effective management and leadership require sustained, careful, comprehensive approaches to the challenges of organizing and managing. The discussion that follows suggests how the conceptual framework presented at the outset, together with the concepts and ideas from the preceding chapters, can support the development of such an approach to this topic, and in doing so, suggest how it can be applied to other important topics, such as the management of volunteer programs (Brudney, 1990), of information technology initiatives, and many other issues.

Although it has a long history in the United States and other nations, privatization has received greater emphasis lately as a strategy for dealing with tightened budgets in the public sector (and the consequent need for reducing costs and increasing efficiency) and for escaping alleged weakness of government through innovative and flexible ways of delivering public services. Yet proponents of privatization often overlook the point that privatization increases the imperative for effective public management rather than relaxing or easing it.

## Managing Privatization

Government contracts with private providers are nothing new in the United States, but privatization has increased a great deal in the last several decades, with governments at all levels sharply increasing their contracts with the private sector (Cooper, 2003; Greene, 2002; Chi, 1994). In addition, privatization has increased in service areas where it has been rare in the past, such as the operation of prisons. As Chapters Five and Six mentioned, the expansion of privatization has raised questions about the "hollow state," third-party government, and the changing nature of government and public management (Kettl, 1993, 2002; Milward, 1996; Moe, 1996; Smith and Lipsky, 1993). Privatization, then, is a widely and increasingly utilized mode of service delivery that imposes problems on public managers but also offers them strategic options (Cohen, 2001). Managing privatization effectively thus represents one aspect of excellence in public management.

During the last two decades, a wave of privatization initiatives have swept the globe, with nations on all continents trying to transfer government activities to private operators. Most nations have many more government-owned enterprises than the United States, and in most of these countries, privatization was concerned with how to sell or transfer such enterprises to private owners and operators. In the United States, by contrast, privatization primarily involves government contracts with private or nonprofit organizations to deliver public services and carry out public policies. Actually, privatization of public services can take many forms besides selling the operation or contracting it out, including the following:

- Granting a franchise to private operators
- Providing vouchers to service recipients to purchase services from private providers
- Using volunteers (for staff support or service delivery, for example)
- Providing subsidies and financial incentives to private operators, such as tax incentives, grants, and subsidization of startup costs
- Initiating self-help or coproduction programs, in which citizens perform services for their own benefit or share in providing them
- Selling off or shedding activities to private operators, or simply ceasing them so that private operators can take them over (Zahra, Ireland, Gutierrez, and Hitt, 2000)

For the most part, however, privatization in the United States involves contracts with nongovernmental organizations. As mentioned, contracts and similar arrangements such as grants and franchises have been part of government for a long time. Eli Whitney, the famous inventor, received a contract from the government in 1798 to provide ten thousand muskets in two years. It took him ten years to finish the project (Dean and Evans, 1994, p. 5).

## Privatization Pitfalls and Ironies

The example of Whitney's overrun suggests one of the many pitfalls of privatization. In recent years, proponents of privatization, some of whom show an obvious ideological bias toward private business and against government activity, have promoted privatization as a bold new initiative. Yet the Whitney example and thousands of similar ones remind us that privatization is as old as the republic and that, while it has produced many benefits, its history has been fraught with scandals and problems. In addition, rather than offering a private sector alternative to government, privatization can lead to governmentalization of the private sector, in which government increasingly draws segments of the private sector into its sphere of activity (Moe, 1996). Private contractors and service providers can then become just one more interest group, lobbying for government policies favorable to themselves and their industry or service area (Smith and Lipsky, 1993). The greatest irony of privatization, however, is that it increases demands for excellence in public management rather than alleviating them. Proponents tout it as a cure for bad government, but it takes excellent government to make it work. The discussions of third-party government in earlier chapters point out that contracting out and other forms of privatization, grant programs, and operation of government services by nongovernmental organizations strain the lines of management and accountability. Public managers become increasingly responsible for programs and services over which they have less control. They can influence the outcomes of such programs and services only through the vehicles spelled out in their contracts with private service providers, rather than through direct administrative control. Major issues, such as the legal liability of government and public managers, can become more complex and uncertain (Cooper, 2003). As the history of privatization has shown, private service providers may perform poorly or even illegally. As Sclar (2000) points out, "you don't always get what you pay for" (see also Kuttner, 1997). Armed only with relatively loose lines of control and accountability, government officials nevertheless share responsibility for such failures. Strong advocates of privatization continue to claim that it produces more efficient and effective delivery of public services (Savas, 2000). Conversely, Hodge (2000) reports a meta-analytic study of hundreds of studies of privatization in many different nations and concludes that privatization can lead to modestly lower costs; such gains, however, tend to concentrate in certain service areas, such as refuse collection and building maintenance, with no appreciable gains apparent in other service areas. In spite of such controversies over just how beneficial privatization can be, it persists as an option, not only because some ideologues simplemindedly promote it, but in part because it can offer a valuable alternative for government managers. It can produce savings and efficiencies, flexibility in management, and other strategic advantages. Thus, to avoid the problems and take advantages of the promise, successful privatization requires skillful public management.

What does successful management of privatization involve? We now have a well-developed literature on privatization and contracting out that considers their pros and cons and what needs to happen for such strategies to work well (Brown and Potoski, 2003; Chi, 1994; Cooper, 2003; Council of State Governments, 1993; Donahue, 1990; Romzek and Johnston, 2002; Savas, 2000; Sclar, 2000; Rehfuss, 1989; Van Slyke, 2003; Warner and Hebdon, 2001). Exhibit 14.4 presents some of the conditions that should be in place for successful privatization and contracting out, according to the professional literature. As noted, proponents make very strong claims for privatization as a panacea for the alleged ills of government. They point to a fairly consistent set of research findings that indicate that private organizations often provide services at lower costs per unit of output compared to government agencies. Other authors, however, point to some problems with many of these studies and to the complication introduced by the fact that government organizations often have to pursue different goals and values than private organizations, even in the same service areas (for example, see the sections in Exhibit 14.4 on goals and values and on performance and effectiveness). In addition to not focusing on the many examples of problems with private sector contracts and how to avoid them, these studies, frequently conducted by economists, tend to overlook the issue of management.

A growing body of experience and research has increasingly documented the problems that can occur and the conditions that need to be in place for effective contracting out. These authors implicitly present a contingency theory of privatization in that they suggest the contingencies that managers have to deal with in successful privatization initiatives. As suggested in Exhibit 14.4, they tend to emphasize such contingencies as the following:

- Having a range of contractors submit competitive bids for the contract, to avoid monopolistic bidding situations
- Effectively managing strong employee or union opposition to the contract (see "People" in Exhibit 14.4)
- Carrying out effective precontract planning and analysis, including such precautions as well-developed cost comparisons and meetings with potential bidders
- Establishing effective contracts, with clear stipulation of goals and performance criteria and provisions for monitoring, evaluation, incentives, and sanctions, which must include consideration of equity, effects on the community, social goals, and other typical public sector issues

# EXHIBIT 14.4. CONDITIONS FOR SUCCESSFUL PRIVATIZATION AND CONTRACTING OUT.

The conditions necessary for successful privatization, especially through contracting out, organized by the components in Figure 1.1:

## 1. Environment

*Bidders.* There must be a set of competitive bids for the contract. Bidders need to be experienced in the service area, have a good record, and be qualified on such criteria as having the capacity to operate in the geographic area where the service is needed and in the manner required by the size and scope of the required operation.

*Political environment.* The environment should be free of inappropriate political pressure for privatization, especially pressure to select a particular provider.

*Resource support.* Authorities should be willing to provide resources to support the provisions for privatization listed in the sections that follow.

*Legal and institutional environment.* The privatization initiative must conform to federal and state government mandates. Examples: federal statutes may require payment of prevailing wages; state laws may limit contracts to the present fiscal year. Liability issues should be carefully reviewed.

## 2. Goals/Values

The privatization initiative should support the agency's mission and its primary goals and values. Governments should usually avoid contracting out certain core functions, such as those involving public safety and security, deadly force, and the handling of public funds.

The goals and values of the privatized activity should be clear (see Performance and Effectiveness at end of exhibit).

## 3. Leadership/Strategy/Culture

Agency leaders should be carefully involved with privatization policies and activities, including their coordination with agency strategies and culture.

## 4. Structure

*Specialization and responsibility.* Responsibility for privatization and contracting out should be clearly defined. Qualified personnel need to be hired, trained, and otherwise set in place to supervise and run the process. Examples: agencies need expertise in contracting processes, in legal issues related to contracting out (or vouchers, franchising, or other modes), and in accounting and financial issues, such as cost accounting and comparisons of the cost of in-house service provision versus contracting out—all coordinated with expertise in the policy or service area involved. Responsibilities for contract development and monitoring need clear definition.

*Departmentalization or subunits.* Agencies should have effective organizational structures for contracting out, with effective locations of offices and units with expertise and responsibility. Example: small agencies may have a central contracting office as well as contracting officers in an administrative services unit; larger agencies may have contracting and privatization units in larger subunits. Departments may place subunits in charge of monitoring contracts.

Agencies may need to maintain the capacity to take over the activity if the contractor goes bankrupt or the contracting process otherwise encounters problems. The responsible units need to be clearly designated and provided with appropriate resources (for example, to maintain the necessary equipment and personnel).

# EXHIBIT 14.4. CONDITIONS FOR SUCCESSFUL PRIVATIZATION AND CONTRACTING OUT, Cont'd.

*Hierarchy and centralization.* Accountability, reporting, and authority relationships should be effectively designed, with clear arrangements for reporting and review of contracts and contracting-out processes and for involvement and awareness of appropriate managers and executives.

*Rules and regulations.* Appropriate rules and procedures should be in place for the provisions mentioned previously (reporting, review, taking back the contracted activity) and subsequently (precontracting procedures, monitoring).

## 5. Process

*Power relationships.* Authority and power relationships related to issues of contracting out should be clarified. Authority and accountability relationships with the contractor, and the responsibilities of the contractor, should be clear and carefully reviewed and specified. (For example, details such as the responsibility for maintaining equipment and machinery should be clarified. Required approvals, such as agency authority to approve the contractor's decision to raise user fees, should be clear. Quality control and review procedures should be clarified). Incentives for effective performance and sanctions for poor performance should be clear and effective.

*Decision-making processes.* Precontracting and contract selection and supervision processes should be well developed. Precontracting processes should involve careful specification of needs and requirements and of the pros and cons of contracting out, including cost comparisons. Meetings and communications with potential bidders about RFP details and goals should be carefully planned. Processes for monitoring and evaluation, and for related evaluative decisions and actions (sanctions and incentives), should be clear and well developed.

*Communications.* As suggested above, communications with potential bidders and contractors and among responsible agency personnel should be well planned, with responsibilities and procedures well clarified.

*Change and innovation.* The role of contracting out and privatization in relation to change and innovation should be carefully developed, to make use of the advantages of these strategies for gaining access to new flexibility, technologies, personnel, and other opportunities.

*People.* The effects on agency personnel should be assessed. Often new contracting-out initiatives should not go forward if there is sharp employee resistance, without effective plans for responding to the resistance.

Effective plans for existing employees should include provisions for supportive discharge of those employees as necessary (that is, effective management of downsizing). Contractors can sometimes offer existing employees attractive alternatives, and contracts can sometimes include provisions that the contractor will hire some existing employees. Analysis of the costs of contracting out should include consideration of the costs to the jurisdiction of layoffs or reduced employment.

## 6. Performance and Effectiveness

Privatization initiatives should have performance measures associated with them that are monitored and used in evaluation, with incentives and sanctions attached, as feasible.

These measures should include public sector performance criteria, such as equity, representativeness, responsiveness, and community and social goals (see Goals/Values above).

The professional literature emphasizes contingencies such as these as well as the others indicated in Exhibit 14.4. Not all of them apply in all situations. For example, there may be situations in which effective relations with a single long-term contractor provide better results than soliciting competitive bids from many providers. Still, we now have a growing consensus on a set of contingencies to be managed in successful contracting out.

Recognizing and managing such contingencies thus becomes one part of excellence in public management. As suggested earlier, however, a more general objective of Exhibit 14.4 is to illustrate an approach to privatization that involves a comprehensive and well-developed approach to organizing for the challenge and managing it. The suggestions in the table are limited by space and time and could be richly expanded with ideas from the earlier chapters. For example, one could approach privatization initiatives as matters of change management, drawing on the ideas in Chapter Thirteen about managing successful change. One could combine change management with a strategic planning process that focuses on privatization and contracting out specifically, or one could draw those topics into a broader strategic plan to coordinate privatization with the overall organizational strategy. In dealing with how privatization affects the culture of one's organization, one could draw on the discussion in Chapter Eleven about leadership and culture, with its ideas about how leaders can influence such matters as employee concerns about privatization initiatives and how they mesh with their agency's mission and values. In these and many other ways, the framework for the book, and the deeper treatment of its components, illustrate another view of privatization (perhaps a limited one that managers and researchers will revise or even discard in favor of a better one) as a challenge to excellence in organizing and managing in the public sector.

# Conclusion

The foregoing discussion of the management of privatization initiatives and programs emphasizes the general point that while the concepts, theories, and ideas covered in this book do not offer a scientific solution, they can certainly support the development of a well-conceived, well-informed orientation toward excellence in public organization and management.

It is consistent with the theme repeatedly stated in this book that its conclusion should be brief. Effective understanding and management of public organizations do not sum up neatly into a set of snappy aphorisms. The preceding examples are intended to illustrate ideas and topics developed in earlier chapters of the book, which have been applied as comprehensively as possible to management initiatives.

The framework offered in this book may need some improvements for some people and for various situations, but knowledge of the ideas and materials in this book should still be valuable to those with a sustained commitment to excellence in public management. Ultimately, it is the general determination to maintain and improve public management that remains essential.

The government of the United States, including all of its levels and adjoining private activities, amounts to one of the great achievements in human history. Like private and nonprofit organizations, public organizations routinely provide beneficial services that would have been considered miracles a century ago. Yet they also have the capacity to do great harm and impose severe injustice. The viability and value of government depend on legions of managers, employees, supporters—and critics—who share a determination that this great institution will perform well, and that through its performance the nation will prosper.

# REFERENCES

Aberbach, J. D., Putnam, R. D., and Rockman, B. A. *Bureaucrats and Politicians in Western Democracies.* Cambridge, Mass.: Harvard University Press, 1981.

Aberbach, J. D., and Rockman, B. A. *In the Web of Politics: Three Decades of the U.S. Federal Executive.* Washington, D.C.: Brookings Institution Press, 2000.

Abney, G., and Lauth, T. *The Politics of State and City Administration.* Albany: State University of New York Press, 1986.

Abramson, M. A., and Gardner, N. W. (eds.). *Human Capital 2002.* Lanham, Md.: Rowman & Littlefield, 2002.

Abramson, M. A., and Kamensky, J. M. (eds.). *Managing for Results 2002.* Lanham, Md.: Rowman & Littlefield, 2001.

Adams, G. B., and Balfour, D. L. *Unmasking Administrative Evil.* Thousand Oaks, Calif.: Sage, 2001.

Adams, J. S. "Inequity in Social Exchange." In L. Berkowitz (ed.), *Advances in Experimental and Social Psychology.* Orlando, Fla.: Academic Press, 1965.

Aharoni, Y. *The Evolution and Management of State-Owned Enterprises.* New York: Ballinger, 1986.

Alderfer, C. P. *Existence, Relatedness, and Growth: Human Needs in Organizational Settings.* New York: Free Press, 1972.

Aldrich, H. E. *Organizations and Environments.* Upper Saddle River, N.J.: Prentice Hall, 1979.

Aldrich, H. E. *Organizations Evolving.* Thousand Oaks, Calif.: Sage, 1999.

Allison, G. T. "Public and Private Management: Are They Fundamentally Alike in All Unimportant Respects?" In J. L. Perry and K. L. Kraemer (eds.), *Public Management.* Mountain View, Calif.: Mayfield, 1983.

Alonso, P., and Lewis, G. B. "Public Service Motivation and Job Performance." *American Review of Public Administration,* 2001, *31,* 363–380.

American Customer Satisfaction Index. "Special Report: Government Satisfaction Scores." Ann Arbor: University of Michigan Business School, 2001. [www.theasci.com].

Ammons, D. N., and Newell, C. *City Executives: Leadership Roles, Work Characteristics, and Time Management.* Albany: State University of New York Press, 1989.

Anderson, W. F., Newland, C., and Stillman, R. *The Effective Local Government Manager.* Washington, D.C.: International City Management Association, 1983.

Angle, H., and Perry, J. L. "An Empirical Assessment of Organizational Commitment and Organizational Effectiveness." *Administrative Science Quarterly,* 1981, *26,* 1–13.

Antonsen, M., and Jorgensen, T. B. "The 'Publicness' of Public Organizations." *Public Administration,* 1997, *75,* 337–357.

Appelbaum, E., Bailey, T., Berg, P., and Kalleberg, A. L. *Manufacturing Advantage: Why High-Performance Work Systems Pay Off.* Ithaca, N.Y.: Cornell University Press, 2000.

Argyris, C. "The Individual and Organization: Some Problems of Mutual Adjustment." *Administrative Science Quarterly,* 1957, *2,* 1–24.

Argyris, C. *The Applicability of Organizational Sociology.* London: Cambridge University Press, 1972.

Armenakis, A. A., and Bedeian, A. G. "Organizational Change: A Review of Theory and Research in the 1990s." *Journal of Management,* 1999, *25,* 293–315.

Arnold, P. E. "Reform's Changing Role." *Public Administration Review,* 1995, *55,* 407–417.

Atkinson, S. E., and Halversen, R. "The Relative Efficiency of Public and Private Firms in a Regulated Environment: The Case of U.S. Electric Utilities." *Journal of Public Economics,* 1986, *29,* 281–294.

Back, K. *Beyond Words.* New York: Russell Sage Foundation, 1972.

Backkx, M., Carney, M., and Gedajlovic, E. "Public, Private, and Mixed Ownership and the Performance of International Airlines." *Journal of Air Transport Management,* 2002, *8,* 213–220.

Baldwin, J. N. "Perceptions of Public Versus Private Sector Personnel and Informal Red Tape: Their Impact on Motivation." *American Review of Public Administration,* 1990, *20,* 7–28.

Balfour, D. L., and Wechsler, B. "Organizational Commitment: A Reconceptualization and Empirical Test of Public-Private Differences." *Review of Public Personnel Administration,* 1990, *10,* 23–40.

Balfour, D. L., and Wechsler, B. "Organizational Commitment: Antecedents and Outcomes in Public Organizations." *Public Productivity and Management Review,* 1996, *19,* 256–277.

Ban, C. "The Crisis of Morale and Federal Senior Executives." *Public Productivity Review,* 1987, *11,* 31–49.

Ban, C. *How Do Public Managers Manage? Bureaucratic Constraints, Organizational Culture, and the Potential for Reform.* San Francisco: Jossey-Bass, 1995.

Bandura, A. *Principles of Behavior Modification.* Austin, Tex.: Holt, Rinehart and Winston, 1969.

Bandura, A. *Social Learning Theory.* Upper Saddle River, N.J.: Prentice Hall, 1978.

Bandura, A. *Social Foundations of Thought and Action: A Social Cognitive Theory.* Upper Saddle River, N.J.: Prentice Hall, 1986.

Bandura, A. "Self-Regulation of Motivation and Action Through Internal Standards and Goal Systems." In L. A. Pervin (ed.), *Goal Concepts in Personality and Social Psychology.* Hillsdale, N.J.: Erlbaum, 1989.

Bandura, A. *Self-Efficacy: The Exercise of Control.* New York: W. H. Freeman, 1997.

Barnard, C. I. *The Functions of the Executive.* Cambridge, Mass.: Harvard University Press, 1938.

Barrett, K., and Green, R. *Powering Up: How Public Managers Can Take Control of Information Technology.* Washington, D.C.: CQ Press, 2001.

Bartol, K. M. "Professionalism as a Predictor of Organizational Commitment, Role Stress, and Turnover: A Multidimensional Approach." *Academy of Management Journal,* 1979, *22,* 815–826.

Barton, A. H. "A Diagnosis of Bureaucratic Maladies." In C. H. Weiss and A. H. Barton (eds.), *Making Bureaucracies Work.* Thousand Oaks, Calif.: Sage, 1980.

Barzelay, M. *Breaking Through Bureaucracy.* Berkeley: University of California Press, 1992.

Barzelay, M. *The New Public Management.* Berkeley: University of California Press, 2001.

Bass, B. M. *Leadership and Performance Beyond Expectations.* New York: Free Press, 1985.

Bass, B. M. *Transformational Leadership: Industrial, Military, and Educational Impact.* Mahwah, N.J.: Lawrence Erlbaum Associates, 1998.

Bass, B. M., and Avolio, B. J. (eds.). *Developing Potential Across a Full Range of Leadership: Cases on Transactional and Transformational Leadership.* Mahwah, N.J.: Lawrence Erlbaum Associates, 2002.

Baum, E., and James, A. C. "Communication in Public and Private Sector Organizations." Paper presented at the annual meeting of the Academy of Management, Boston, 1984.

Baum, J.A.C., and McKelvey, B. (eds.). *Variations in Organization Science.* Thousand Oaks, Calif.: Sage, 1999.

Beam, G. *Quality Public Management.* Chicago: Burnham Publishers, 2001.

Beck, P. A., Rainey, H. G., and Traut, C. "Disadvantage, Disaffection, and Race as Divergent Bases for Citizen Fiscal Policy Preferences." *Journal of Politics,* 1990, *52,* 71–93.

Behn, R. D. *Leadership Counts.* Cambridge: Harvard University Press, 1994.

Behn, R. D. "The Big Questions of Public Management." *Public Administration Review,* 1995, *55,* 313–324.

Bellante, D., and Link, A. N. "Are Public Sector Workers More Risk Averse Than Private Sector Workers?" *Industrial and Labor Relations Review,* 1981, *34,* 408–412.

Bendor, J., and Moe, T. M. "An Adaptive Model of Bureaucratic Politics." *American Political Science Review,* 1985, *79,* 755–774.

Bendor, J., Moe, T. M., and Shotts, K. W. "Recycling the Garbage Can: An Assessment of the Research Program." *American Political Science Review,* 2001, *95,* 169–190.

Benn, S. I., and Gaus, G. F. *Public and Private in Social Life.* New York: St. Martin's Press, 1983.

Bennis, W., and Nanus, B. *Leaders: The Strategies for Taking Charge.* New York: HarperCollins, 1985.

Berman, E. M. "Professionalism Among Public and Nonprofit Managers: A Comparison." *American Review of Public Administration,* 1999, *29,* 149–166.

Berman, E., and Wang, X. "Performance Measurement in U. S. Counties: Capacity for Reform." *Public Administration Review,* 2000, *60,* 409–420.

Berman, E. M., and West, J. P. "Municipal Commitment to Total Quality Management: A Survey of Recent Progress." *Public Administration Review,* 1995, *55,* 57–66.

Berman, S. L., Wicks, A. C., Kotha, S., and Jones, T. M. "Does Stakeholder Orientation Matter? The Relationship Between Stakeholder Management Models and Firm Financial Performance." *Academy of Management Journal,* 1999, *42,* 488–506.

Berry, F. S., Berry, W. D., and Foster, S. K. "The Determinants of Success in Implementing an Expert System in State Government." *Public Administration Review,* 1998, *58,* 293–305.

Berry, F. S., and Wechsler, B. "State Agencies' Experience with Strategic Planning: Findings from a National Survey." *Public Administration Review,* 1995, *55,* 159–168.

Beyer, J. M., and Trice, H. M. "A Reexamination of the Relations Between Size and Various Components of Organizational Complexity." *Administrative Science Quarterly,* 1979, *24,* 48–64.

Blais, A., and Dion, S. (eds.). *The Budget-Maximizing Bureaucrat.* Pittsburgh: University of Pittsburgh Press, 1991.

Blake, R. R., and Mouton, J. S. "Overcoming Group Warfare." *Harvard Business Review,* 1984, *62,* 98–108.

Blau, P. M., and Schoenherr, R. A. *The Structure of Organizations.* New York: Basic Books, 1971.

Blau, P. M., and Scott, W. R. *Formal Organizations.* Novato, Calif.: Chandler & Sharp, 1962.

Block, P. *The Empowered Manager: Positive Political Skills at Work.* San Francisco: Jossey-Bass, 1987.

Blumenthal, J. M. "Candid Reflections of a Businessman in Washington." In J. L. Perry and K. L. Kraemer (eds.), *Public Management.* Palo Alto, Calif.: Mayfield, 1983.

Bogg, J., and Cooper, C. "Job Satisfaction, Mental Health, and Occupational Stress Among Senior Civil Servants." *Human Relations,* 1995, *48,* 327–341.

Bordia, P., and Blau, G. "Pay Referent Comparison and Pay Level Satisfaction in Private Versus Public Sector Organizations in India." *International Journal of Human Resource Management,* 1998, *9,* 155–167.

Borins, S. *Innovating with Integrity: How Local Heroes Are Transforming American Government.* Washington, D.C.: Georgetown University Press, 1998.

Boschken, H. L. *Strategic Design and Organizational Change: Pacific Rim Seaports in Transition.* Tuscaloosa: University of Alabama Press, 1988.

Bourgault, J., Dion, S., and Lemay, M. "Creating a Corporate Culture: Lessons from the Canadian Federal Government." *Public Administration Review,* 1993, *53,* 73–80.

Bowsher, C. A. "OMB Management Leadership: Testimony Before the Committee on Governmental Affairs, U.S. Senate, Oct. 31, 1990." (T-GGD-91–1.) Washington, D.C.: U.S. General Accounting Office, 1990.

Boyatzis, R. E. *The Competent Manager.* New York: Wiley, 1982.

Bozeman, B. *All Organizations Are Public: Bridging Public and Private Organizational Theories.* San Francisco: Jossey-Bass, 1987.

Bozeman, B. (ed.). *Public Management: State of the Art.* San Francisco: Jossey-Bass, 1993.

Bozeman, B. *Bureaucracy and Red Tape.* Upper Saddle River, N.J.: Prentice-Hall, 2000.

Bozeman, B. "Public-Value Failure: When Efficient Markets May Not Do." *Public Administration Review,* 2002a, *62,* 145–161.

Bozeman, B. *Government Management of Information Mega-Technology: Lessons from the Internal Revenue Service's Tax Systems Modernization.* Arlington, Va.: IBM Endowment for the Business of Government, 2002b.

Bozeman, B., and Bretschneider, S. "The 'Publicness Puzzle' in Organization Theory: A Test of Alternative Explanations of Differences Between Public and Private Organizations." *Journal of Public Administration Research and Theory,* 1994, *4,* 197–223.

Bozeman, B., and Kingsley, G. "Risk Culture in Public and Private Organizations." *Public Administration Review,* 1998, *58,* 109–118.

Bozeman, B., and Loveless, S. "Sector Context and Performance: A Comparison of Industrial and Government Research Units." *Administration and Society,* 1987, *19,* 197–235.

Bozeman, B., and Rainey, H. G. "Organizational Rules and Bureaucratic Personality." *American Journal of Political Science,* 1998, *42,* 163–189.

Brehm, J., and Gates, S. *Working, Shirking, and Sabotage: Bureaucratic Response to a Democratic Public.* Ann Arbor: University of Michigan Press, 1997.

Breton, A., and Wintrobe, R. *The Logic of Bureaucratic Conduct.* Cambridge: Cambridge University Press, 1982.

Bretschneider, S. "Management Information Systems in Public and Private Organizations: An Empirical Test." *Public Administration Review,* 1990, *50,* 536–545.

Bretschneider, S., and Wittmer, D. "Organizational Adoption of Microcomputer Technology: The Role of Sector." *Information Systems Research,* 1993, *4,* 88–108.

Brewer, G. A., and Selden, S. C. "Whistle Blowers in the Federal Civil Service: New Evidence of the Public Service Ethic." *Journal of Public Administration Research and Theory,* 1998, *8,* 413–439.

Brewer, G. A., Selden, S. C., and Facer, R. L. "Individual Conceptions of Public Service Motivation." *Public Administration Review,* 2000, *60,* 254–264.

Brief, A. P. *Attitudes in and Around Organizations.* Thousand Oaks, Calif.: Sage, 1998.

Brown, S. P. "A Meta-Analysis and Review of Organizational Research on Job Involvement." *Psychological Bulletin,* 1996, *120,* 235–255.

Brown, T. L., and Potoski, M. "Managing Contract Performance: A Transaction Costs Approach." *Journal of Policy Analysis and Management,* 2003, *22,* 275–297.

Brudney, J. L. *Fostering Volunteer Programs in the Public Sector: Planning, Initiating, and Managing Voluntary Activities.* San Francisco: Jossey-Bass, 1990.

Brudney, J. L., and Hebert, F. T. "State Agencies and Their Environments: Examining the Influence of Important External Actors." *Journal of Politics,* 1987, *49,* 186–206.

Brudney, J. L., Hebert, F. T., and Wright, D. S. "Reinventing Government in the American States: Measuring and Explaining Administrative Reform." *Public Administration Review,* 1999, *59,* 19–30.

Brudney, J., Hebert, F., and Wright, D. "From Organizational Values to Organizational Roles: Examining Representative Bureaucracy in State Administration." *Journal of Public Administration Research and Theory,* 2000, *10,* 491–513.

Brudney, J. L., O'Toole, L. J., and Rainey, H. G. (eds.). *Advancing Public Management: New Developments in Theory, Methods, and Research.* Washington, D.C.: Georgetown University Press, 2000.

Brudney, J. L., and Wright, D. S. "Revisiting Administrative Reform in the American States: The Status of Reinventing Government During the 1990s." *Public Administration Review,* 2002, *62,* 353–361.

Bryant, A. "Business Advice from the Sidelines." *New York Times,* Mar. 6, 1996, p. C1.

Bryson, J. M. *Strategic Planning for Public and Nonprofit Organizations: A Guide to Strengthening and Sustaining Organizational Achievements.* San Francisco: Jossey-Bass, 1995.

Bryson, J. M., and Einsweiler, R. C. (eds.). *Shared Power.* Lanham, Md.: University Press of America, 1995.

Bryson, J. M., and Roering, W. D. "Strategic Planning Options for the Public Sector." In J. L. Perry (ed.), *Handbook of Public Administration.* (2nd ed.) San Francisco: Jossey-Bass, 1996.

Buchanan, B. "Government Managers, Business Executives, and Organizational Commitment." *Public Administration Review,* 1974, *35,* 339–347.

Buchanan, B. "Red Tape and the Service Ethic: Some Unexpected Differences Between Public and Private Managers." *Administration and Society,* 1975, *6,* 423–438.

Burke, W. W. *Organization Development.* (2nd ed.) Reading, Mass.: Addison-Wesley, 1994.

Burke, W. W. *Organization Change: Theory and Practice.* Thousand Oaks, Ca.: Sage, 2002.

Burns, J. M. *Leadership.* New York: HarperCollins, 1978.

Burns, T., and Stalker, G. M. *The Management of Innovation.* London: Tavistock, 1961.

Burrell, G., and Morgan, G. *Sociological Paradigms and Organizational Analysis.* London: Heinemann, 1980.

Bush, G. W., "Freedom to Manage Act Legislative Proposal." Washington, D.C.: The White House, Office of the Press Secretary, October 17, 2001.

Cameron, K. "Measuring Organizational Effectiveness in Institutions of Higher Education." *Administrative Science Quarterly,* 1978, *23,* 604–632.

Cameron, K., Sutton, R. I., and Whetten, D. A. (eds.). *Readings in Organizational Decline.* New York: Ballinger, 1988.

Cameron, K., and Whetten, D. A. (eds.). *Organizational Effectiveness: A Comparison of Multiple Models.* Orlando, Fla.: Academic Press, 1983.

Campbell, J. P. "On the Nature of Organizational Effectiveness." In P. S. Goodman, J. M. Pennings, and Associates, *New Perspectives on Organizational Effectiveness.* San Francisco: Jossey-Bass, 1977.

Campbell, J. P., and Pritchard, R. D. "Motivation Theory in Industrial and Organizational Psychology." In M. D. Dunnette (ed.), *Handbook of Industrial and Organizational Psychology.* New York: Wiley, 1983.

Carnevale, D. G. *Organizational Development in the Public Sector.* Boulder, Colo.: Westview Press, 2003.

Carroll, G. R., Delacroix, J., and Goodstein, J. "The Political Environments of Organizations: An Ecological View." In B. M. Staw and L. L. Cummings (eds.), *Research in Organizational Behavior,* Vol. 10. Greenwich, Conn.: JAI Press, 1988.

Chackerian, R., and Abcarian, G. *Bureaucratic Power in Society.* Chicago: Nelson-Hall, 1984.

Chase, G., and Reveal, E. C. *How to Manage in the Public Sector.* Reading, Mass.: Addison-Wesley, 1983.

Cherniss, G. *Professional Burnout in Human Service Organizations.* New York: Praeger, 1980.

Chi, K. "Privatization in State Government: Trends and Issues." Paper presented at the National Conference of the American Society for Public Administration, Kansas City, July 23–27, 1994.

Child, J. "Organizational Structure, Environment, and Performance: The Role of Strategic Choice." *Sociology,* 1972, *6,* 1–22.

Cho, K., and Lee, S. "Another Look at Public-Private Distinction and Organizational Commitment: A Cultural Explanation." *International Journal of Organizational Analysis,* 2001, *9,* 84–102.

Chubb, J. E., and Moe, T. M. "Politics, Markets, and the Organization of Schools." *American Political Science Review,* 1988, *82,* 1065–1088.

Chubb, J. E., and Moe, T. M. *Politics, Markets, and America's Schools.* Washington, D.C.: Brookings Institution, 1990.

Clark, P. B., and Wilson, J. Q. "Incentive Systems: A Theory of Organizations." *Administrative Science Quarterly,* 1961, *6,* 129–166.

Clausewitz, C. V. *On War* (M. Howard and P. Paret, eds. and trans.). Princeton, N.J.: Princeton University Press, 1986.

Clinton, B., and Gore, A. *Putting Customers First '95: Standards for Serving the American People.* Washington, D.C.: U.S. Government Printing Office, 1995.

Coch, L., and French, J.R.P. "Overcoming Resistance to Change." *Human Relations*, 1948, *1*, 512–532.

Cohen, M. D., March, J. G., and Olsen, J. P. "A Garbage Can Model of Organizational Choice." *Administrative Science Quarterly*, 1972, *17*, 1–25.

Cohen, S. "A Strategic Framework for Devolving Responsibility and Functions from Government to the Private Sector." *Public Administration Review*, 2001, *61*, 432–440.

Cohen, S., and Brand, R. *Total Quality Management in Government: A Practical Guide for the Real World*. San Francisco: Jossey-Bass, 1993.

Cohen, S., and Eimicke, W. *The New Effective Public Manager: Achieving Success in a Changing Government*. San Francisco: Jossey-Bass, 1995.

Cohen, S., and Eimicke, W. *Tools for Innovators: Creative Strategies for Managing Public Sector Organizations*. San Francisco: Jossey-Bass, 1998.

Collins, J. C., and Porras, J. I. *Built to Last: Successful Habits of Visionary Companies*. New York: HarperCollins, 1997.

Cook, J. D., Hepworth, S. J., Wall, T. D., and Warr, P. B. *The Experience of Work*. London: Academic Press, 1981.

Cooper, J. M. "Gifford Pinchot Creates a Forest Service." In J. W. Doig and E. C. Hargrove (eds.), *Leadership and Innovation*. Baltimore: Johns Hopkins University Press, 1987.

Cooper, P. J. "Understanding What the Law Says About Administrative Responsibility." In J. L. Perry (ed.), *Handbook of Public Administration*. (2nd ed.) San Francisco: Jossey-Bass, 1996.

Cooper, P. J. *Public Law and Public Administration*. Itasca, Ill.: Peacock, 2000.

Cooper, P. J. *Governing by Contract: Challenges and Opportunities for Public Managers*. Washington, D.C.: CQ Press, 2003.

Cooper, T. L., and Wright, N. D. *Exemplary Public Administrators: Character and Leadership in Government*. San Francisco: Jossey-Bass, 1992.

Council of State Governments. "Privatization." *State Trends and Forecasts*, 1993, *2*, 1–36.

Council of State Governments. "Total Quality Management." *State Trends and Forecasts*, 1994, *3*, 1–35.

Coursey, D., and Rainey, H. G. "Perceptions of Personnel System Constraints in Public, Private, and Hybrid Organizations." *Review of Public Personnel Administration*, 1990, *10*, 54–71.

Crane, D. P., and Jones, W. A. *The Public Manager's Guide*. Washington, D.C.: Bureau of National Affairs, 1982.

Cranny, C. J. (ed.). *Job Satisfaction*. San Francisco: New Lexington Books, 1992.

Crewson, P. E. "A Comparative Analysis of Public and Private Sector Entrant Quality." *American Journal of Political Science*, 1995a, *39*, 628–639.

Crewson, P. E. "The Public Service Ethic." Unpublished doctoral dissertation, American University, Washington, D.C., 1995b.

Crewson, P. E. "Public-Service Motivation: Building Empirical Evidence of Incidence and Effect." *Journal of Public Administration Research and Theory*, 1997, *7*, 499–518.

Crow, M., and Bozeman, B. "R&D Laboratory Classification and Public Policy: The Effects of Environmental Context on Laboratory Behavior." *Research Policy*, 1987, *16*, 229–258.

Cyert, R. M., and March, J. G. *A Behavioral Theory of the Firm*. Upper Saddle River, N.J.: Prentice Hall, 1963.

Daft, R. L. *Organization Theory and Design*. (7th ed.) Cincinnati, Ohio: South-Western College, 2001.

Dahl, R. A., and Lindblom, C. E. *Politics, Economics, and Welfare*. New York: HarperCollins, 1953.

Daniels, M. R. *Terminating Public Programs: An American Political Paradox*. Armonk, N.Y.: M. E. Sharpe, 1997.

Dansereau, F., Jr., Graen, G., and Haga, W. J. "A Vertical Dyad Linkage Approach to Leadership within Formal Organizations: A Longitudinal Investigation of the Role Making Process." *Organizational Behavior and Human Performance*, 1975, *13*, 46–78.

Davis, D., and Ward, E. "Health Benefit Satisfaction in the Public and Private Sectors: The Role of Distributive and Procedural Justice." *Public Personnel Journal*, 1995, *25*, 255–271.

Davis, S. M., and Lawrence, P. R. *Matrix*. Reading, Mass.: Addison-Wesley, 1977.

Davis, T.R.V. "OD in the Public Sector: Intervening in Ambiguous Performance Environments." In J. L. Perry and K. L. Kraemer (eds.), *Public Management*. Palo Alto, Calif.: Mayfield, 1983.

Dawes, S. S. "Government and Technology: User, Not Regulator." *Journal of Public Administration Research and Theory*, 2002, *12*, 627–630.

Dean, J. W., and Evans, J. R. *Total Quality*. St. Paul, Minn.: West, 1994.

Decker, J. E., and Paulson, S. K. "Performance Improvement in a Public Utility." *Public Productivity Review*, 1988, *11*, 52–66.

Demerath, N., Marwell, G., and Aiken, M. *Dynamics of Idealism*. San Francisco: Jossey-Bass, 1971.

Deming, W. E. *Out of Crisis*. Cambridge, Mass.: MIT Center for Advanced Engineering Study, 1986.

Denhardt, R. B. *Theories of Public Organizations*. (3rd ed.) Pacific Grove, Calif.: Brooks/Cole, 1999.

Denhardt, R. B. *The Pursuit of Significance*. (2nd ed.) Prospect Heights, Ill.: Waveland Press, 2000.

Denhardt, R. B., and Jennings, E. T. *The Revitalization of the Public Service*. Columbia: Extension Publications, University of Missouri, 1987.

Dess, G. G., and Beard, D. W. "Dimensions of Organizational Task Environment." *Administrative Science Quarterly*, 1984, *29*, 52–73.

Dewey, J. *The Public and Its Problems*. Chicago: Swallow Press, 1927.

DiIulio, J. J. "Recovering the Public Management Variable: Lessons from Schools, Prisons, and Armies." *Public Administration Review*, 1989, *49*, 127–133.

DiIulio, J. J. "Managing a Barbed-Wire Bureaucracy: The Impossible Job of Corrections Commissioner." In E. C. Hargrove and J. C. Glidewell (eds.), *Impossible Jobs in Public Management*. Lawrence: University Press of Kansas, 1990.

DiIulio, J. J. "Principled Agents: The Cultural Bases of Behavior in a Federal Government Bureaucracy." *Journal of Public Administration Research and Theory*, 1994, *4*, 277–320.

DiMaggio, P. J., and Powell, W. R. "The Iron Cage Revisited: Institutional Isomorphism and Collective Rationality in Organizational Fields." *American Sociological Review*, 1983, *48*, 147–160.

Dobbin, F. R., and others. "The Expansion of Due Process in Organizations." In L. G. Zucker (ed.), *Institutional Patterns and Organizations*. New York: Ballinger, 1988.

Doig, J. W., and Hargrove, E. C. (eds.). *Leadership and Innovation*. Baltimore: Johns Hopkins University Press, 1987.

Doig, J. W., and Hargrove, E. C. (eds.). *Leadership and Innovation*. (abridged ed.) Baltimore: Johns Hopkins University Press, 1990.

Dolan, J. "The Senior Executive Service: Gender, Attitudes, and Representative Bureaucracy." *Journal of Public Administration Research and Theory,* 2000, *10,* 513–529.

Dolan, J. "The Budget-Minimizing Bureaucrat? Empirical Evidence from the Senior Executive Service." *Public Administration Review,* 2002, *62,* 42–50.

Donahue, J. D. *The Privatization Decision.* New York: Basic Books, 1990.

Donahue, J. D. Presentation to the Executive Session on the Future of Public Service, John F. Kennedy School of Government, April 29, 2002.

Donaldson, L. *The Contingency Theory of Organizations.* Thousand Oaks, Calif.: Sage, 2001.

Downs, A. *Inside Bureaucracy.* New York: Little, Brown, 1967.

Downs, C. W. *Communication Audits.* Glenview, Ill.: Scott, Foresman, 1988.

Downs, G. W., and Larkey, P. *The Search for Government Efficiency: From Hubris to Helplessness.* New York: Random House, 1986.

Drake, A. W. "Quantitative Models in Public Administration: Some Educational Needs." In A. W. Drake, L. Keeney, and P. M. Morse (eds.), *Analysis of Public Systems.* Cambridge, Mass.: MIT Press, 1972.

Dunn, D. D. *Politics and Administration at the Top: Lessons from Down Under.* Pittsburgh, Pa.: University of Pittsburgh Press, 1997.

Dunn, D. D., and Legge, J. L. "Politics and Administration in U.S. Local Governments." *Journal of Public Administration Research and Theory,* 2002, *12,* 401–422.

Durant, R. F. *The Administrative Presidency Revisited.* Albany: State University of New York Press, 1992.

Eadie, D. C. "Leading and Managing Strategic Change." In J. L. Perry (ed.), *Handbook of Public Administration.* (2nd ed.) San Francisco: Jossey-Bass, 1996.

Earley, P. C., and Lituchy, T. R. "Delineating Goal and Efficacy Effects: A Test of Three Models." *Journal of Applied Psychology,* 1991, *76,* 81–98.

Eisner, R. A. "Cut Social Security? No, Expand It." *Wall Street Journal,* Dec. 16, 1998, p. 22.

Elling, R. C. "The Relationships Among Bureau Chiefs, Legislative Committees, and Interest Groups: A Multistate Study." Paper presented at the annual meeting of the American Political Science Association, Washington, D.C., 1983.

Elling, R. C. "Civil Service, Collective Bargaining, and Personnel-Related Impediments to Effective State Management: A Comparative Assessment." *Review of Public Personnel Administration,* 1986, *6,* 73–93.

Ellwood, J. W. "Prospects for the Study of the Government of Public Organizations and Policies." In C. J. Heinrich and L. Lynn (eds.), *Governance and Performance: New Perspectives.* Washington, D.C.: Georgetown University Press, 2000.

Emery, F. E., and Trist, E. L. "The Causal Texture of Organizational Environments." *Human Relations,* 1965, *18,* 21–32.

Emmert, M. A., and Crow, M. M. "Public-Private Cooperation and Hybrid Organizations." *Journal of Management,* 1987, *13,* 55–67.

Emmert, M. A., and Crow, M. M. "Public, Private, and Hybrid Organizations: An Empirical Examination of the Role of Publicness." *Administration and Society,* 1988, *20,* 216–244.

Esman, M. J. *Government Works: Why Americans Need the Feds.* Ithaca, N.Y.: Cornell University Press, 2000.

Etzioni, A. "Mixed Scanning: A 'Third' Approach to Decision Making." *Public Administration Review,* 1967, *27,* 385–392.

Etzioni, A. A. *Comparative Analysis of Complex Organizations.* New York: Free Press, 1975.

Etzioni, A. "Mixed Scanning Revisited." *Public Administration Review,* 1986, *46,* 8–14.

Evans, M. G. "Organizational Behavior: The Central Role of Motivation." *Journal of Management*, 1986, *12*, 203–223.

Ferlie, E., Pettigrew, A., Ashburner, L., and Fitzgerald, L. *The New Public Management in Action.* Oxford: Oxford University Press, 1996.

Fiedler, F. E. *A Theory of Leadership Effectiveness.* New York: McGraw-Hill, 1967.

Fiedler, F. E., and Garcia, J. E. *New Approaches to Leadership: Cognitive Resources and Organizational Performance.* New York: Wiley, 1987.

Filley, A. C., House, R. J., and Kerr, S. *Managerial Process and Organizational Behavior.* Glenview, Ill.: Scott, Foresman, 1976.

Fletcher, C., and Williams, R. "Performance Management, Job Satisfaction, and Organizational Commitment." *British Journal of Management*, 1996, *7*, 169–180.

Flynn, D. M., and Tannenbaum, S. I. "Correlates of Organizational Commitment: Differences in the Public and Private Sector." *Journal of Business and Psychology*, 1993, *8*, 103–116.

Follett, M. P. "The Giving of Orders." In J. S. Ott (ed.), *Classic Readings in Organizational Behavior.* Pacific Grove, Calif.: Brooks/Cole, 1989. (Originally published 1926.)

Fottler, M. D. "Management: Is It Really Generic?" *Academy of Management Review*, 1981, *6*, 1–12.

Fountain, J. *Building the Virtual State: Information Technology and Institutional Change.* Washington D.C.: Brookings Institution, 2001.

Francois, P. "'Public Service Motivation' as an Argument for Government Provision." *Journal of Public Economics*, 2000, *78*, 275–299.

Frederickson, H. G. "Comparing the Reinventing Government Movement with the New Public Administration." *Public Administration Review*, 1996, *56*, 263–270.

Frederickson, H. G., and Hart, D. K. "The Public Service and the Patriotism of Benevolence." *Public Administration Review*, 1985, *45*, 547–553.

Frederickson, H. G., and Johnston, J. M. *Public Management Reform and Innovation: Research, Theory, and Application.* Tuscaloosa: University of Alabama Press, 1999.

Frederickson, H.G., and Smith, K. B. *The Public Administration Theory Primer.* Boulder, Colo.: Westview Press, 2003.

French, J.R.P., and Raven, B. "The Bases of Social Power." In D. Cartwright and A. Zander (eds.), *Group Dynamics.* New York: HarperCollins, 1968.

French, W. L., and Bell, C. H. *Organization Development: Behavioral Science Interventions for Organization Improvement.* (6th ed.) Upper Saddle River, N.J.: Prentice Hall, 1999.

French, W. L., Bell, C. H., and Zawacki, R. A. *Organization Development and Transformation: Managing Effective Change.* (5th ed.) Boston: Irwin/McGraw-Hill, 2000.

Fried, R. C. *Performance in American Bureaucracy.* New York: Little, Brown, 1976.

Frumkin, P., and Galaskiewicz, J. "Institutional Isomorphism and the Public Sector." *Journal of Public Administration Research and Theory*, 2003, *13*, forthcoming.

Fry, B. R. *Mastering Public Administration.* Chatham, N.J.: Chatham House, 1989.

Gabris, G. T. (ed.). "Why Merit Pay Plans Are Not Working: A Search for Alternative Pay Plans in the Public Sector—A Symposium." *Review of Public Personnel Administration*, 1987, *7*, 9–90.

Gabris, G. T., and Simo, G. "Public Sector Motivation as an Independent Variable Affecting Career Decisions." *Public Personnel Management*, 1995, *24*, 33–51.

Galbraith, J. R. *Organizational Design.* Reading, Mass.: Addison-Wesley, 1977.

Galbraith, J. *Designing Organizations.* San Francisco: Jossey-Bass, 2002.

Galbraith, J., Downey, D., and Kates, A. *Designing Dynamic Organizations.* New York: American Management Association, 2002.

Gallup Organization. "Measuring and Improving Employee Engagement." Princeton, New Jersey: The Gallup Organization, 2003. [www.gallup.com/management].

Garnett, J. L. *Communicating for Results in Government: A Strategic Approach for Public Managers.* San Francisco: Jossey-Bass, 1992.

Garson, G. D., and Overman, E. S. *Public Management Research Directory,* Vols. 1 and 2. Washington, D.C.: National Association of Schools of Public Affairs and Administration, 1981, 1982.

Gawthorp, L. C. *Bureaucratic Behavior in the Executive Branch.* New York: Free Press, 1969.

Gerth, H., and Mills, C. W. *From Max Weber: Essays in Sociology.* New York: Oxford University Press, 1946.

Glazer, A., and Rothenberg, L. S. *Why Government Succeeds and Why It Fails.* Cambridge, Mass.: Harvard University Press, 2001.

Gold, K. A. "Managing for Success: A Comparison of the Public and Private Sectors." *Public Administration Review,* 1982, *42,* 568–575.

Gold, S. D., and Ritchie, S. "Compensation of State and Local Employees: Sorting Out the Issues." In F. J. Thompson (ed.), *Revitalizing State and Local Public Service: Strengthening Performance, Accountability, and Citizen Confidence.* San Francisco: Jossey-Bass, 1993.

Golden, M. M. *What Motivates Bureaucrats? Politics and Administration During the Reagan Years.* New York: Columbia University Press, 2000.

Golembiewski, R. T. "Civil Service and Managing Work." *American Political Science Review,* 1962, *56,* 964–969.

Golembiewski, R. T. "Organization Development in Public Agencies: Perspectives on Theory and Practice." *Public Administration Review,* 1969, *29,* 367–368.

Golembiewski, R. T. *Humanizing Public Organizations.* Mount Airy, Md.: Lomond, 1985.

Golembiewski, R. T. "Contours in Social Change: Elemental Graphics and a Surrogate Variable for Gamma Change." *Academy of Management Review,* 1986, *11,* 550–566.

Golembiewski, R. T. *Practical Public Management.* New York: Dekker, 1995.

Golembiewski, R. T., Proehl, C. T., and Sink, D. "Success of OD Applications in the Public Sector: Totting Up the Score for a Decade, More or Less." *Public Administration Review,* 1981, *41,* 679–682.

Goodsell, C. T. "Bureaucratic Manipulation of Physical Symbols: An Empirical Study." *American Journal of Political Science,* 1977, *21,* 79–91.

Goodsell, C. T. *The Case for Bureaucracy.* Chatham, N.J.: Chatham House, 1994.

Gordon, J. R. *Organizational Behavior: A Diagnostic Approach.* Upper Saddle River, N.J.: Prentice Hall, 2002.

Gore, A. *Common Sense Government: Works Better and Costs Less.* Third Report of the National Performance Review. Washington, D.C.: U.S. Government Printing Office, n.d.

Gore, A. *From Red Tape to Results: Creating a Government That Works Better and Costs Less.* Report of the National Performance Review. Washington, D.C.: U.S. Government Printing Office, 1993.

Gortner, H. F., Mahler, J., and Nicholson, J. B. *Organization Theory: A Public Perspective.* Florence, Ky.: Dorsey Press, 1987.

Graber, D. A. *The Power of Communication: Managing Information in Public Organizations.* Washington, D.C.: CQ Press, 2003.

Greenberg, J., and Cropanzano, R. (eds.). *Advances in Organizational Justice.* Palo Alto, Calif.: Stanford University Press, 2001.

Greene, J. D. *Cities and Privatization.* Upper Saddle River, N.J.: Prentice Hall, 2002.

Greiner, L. E. "Patterns of Organizational Change." *Harvard Business Review,* 1967, *45,* 119–128.

Greve, H. R., and Taylor, A. "Innovations as Catalysts for Organizational Change: Shifts in Organizational Cognition and Search." *Administrative Science Quarterly,* 2000, *45,* 54–80.

Grizzle, G. A., and Pettijohn, C. D. "Implementing Performance-Based Program Budgeting: A System-Dynamics Perspective." *Public Administration Review,* 2002, *62,* 51–62.

Gross, B. M. "What Are Your Organization's Objectives?" In W. R. Nord (ed.), *Concepts and Controversy in Organizational Behavior.* Pacific Palisades, Calif.: Goodyear, 1976.

Gruneberg, M. M. *Understanding Job Satisfaction.* London: Macmillan, 1979.

Guion, R. M., and Landy, F. J. "The Meaning of Work and Motivation to Work." *Organizational Behavior and Human Performance,* 1972, *7,* 308–339.

Gulick, L. "Notes on the Theory of Organization." In L. Gulick and L. Urwick (eds.), *Papers on the Science of Administration.* New York: Institute of Public Administration, 1937.

Guralnick, D. B. (ed.). *Webster's New World Dictionary of the American Language.* New York: Simon & Schuster, 1980.

Gurwitt, R. "The Entrepreneurial Gamble." *Governing,* 1994, *7,* 34–40.

Guy, M. E. "Productivity and Gender." *Public Productivity and Management Review,* 1995, *19,* 125–127.

Guyot, J. F. "Government Bureaucrats Are Different." *Public Administration Review,* 1960, *20,* 195–202.

Haas, J. E., Hall, R. H., and Johnson, N. J. "Toward an Empirically Derived Taxonomy of Organizations." In R. V. Bowers (ed.), *Studies of Behavior in Organizations.* Athens: University of Georgia Press, 1966.

Hackman, J. R. *Leading Teams: Setting the Stage for Great Performances.* Boston, Mass.: Harvard Business School Press, 2002.

Hackman, J. R., and Oldham, G. R. *Work Redesign.* Reading, Mass.: Addison-Wesley, 1980.

Hage, J., and Aiken, M. "Routine Technology, Social Structure, and Organizational Goals." *Administrative Science Quarterly,* 1969, *14,* 366–376.

Halachmi, A., and Bouckaert, G. *The Enduring Challenges in Public Management: Surviving and Excelling in a Challenging World.* San Francisco: Jossey-Bass, 1995.

Hale, S. J. "Achieving High Performance in Public Organizations." In J. L. Perry (ed.), *Handbook of Public Administration.* (2nd ed.) San Francisco: Jossey-Bass, 1996.

Hale, S. J., and Williams, M. M. (eds.). *Managing Change.* Washington, D.C.: Urban Institute Press, 1989.

Hall, R. H. *Organizations: Structure and Process.* (8th ed.) Upper Saddle River, N.J.: Prentice Hall, 2002.

Hammond, T. H. "In Defense of Luther Gulick's 'Notes on the Theory of Organizations.'" *Public Administration,* 1990, *68,* 143–173.

Hannan, M. T., and Freeman, J. *Organizational Ecology.* Cambridge, Mass.: Harvard University Press, 1989.

Hansen, J. R. "Scientific Management Goes Golfing: When Frederick W. Taylor Applied His Principle of the 'One Best Way' to Golf, the Acclaim Was Less Than Unanimous." *Invention & Technology,* Spring 1999, pp. 200–227.

Haque, M. S. "The Diminishing Publicness of Public Service Under the Current Mode of Governance." *Public Administration Review,* 2001, *61,* 65–82.

Hargrove, E. C., and Glidewell, J. C. (eds.). *Impossible Jobs in Public Management.* Lawrence: University Press of Kansas, 1990.

Harris, T. E. *Small Group and Team Communication.* Boston: Allyn and Bacon, 2002.

Harrison, J. S., and Freeman, R. E. "Stakeholders, Social Responsibility, and Performance: Empirical Evidence and Theoretical Perspectives." *Academy of Management Journal*, 1999, *42*, 479–485.

Hartman, R., and Weber, A. *The Rewards of Public Service*. Washington, D.C.: Brookings Institution, 1980.

Hayward, N. *Employee Attitudes and Productivity Differences Between the Public and Private Sectors*. Washington, D.C.: Productivity Information Center, National Technical Information Center, U.S. Department of Commerce, 1978.

Heclo, H. "Issue Networks and the Executive Establishment." In A. King (ed.), *The New American Political System*. Washington, D.C.: American Enterprise Institute, 1978.

Hedge, D., and Johnson, R. J. "The Plot That Failed: The Republican Revolution and Congressional Control of the Bureaucracy." *Journal of Public Administration Research and Theory*, 2002, *12*, 333–352.

Heinrich, C. J. "Organizational Form and Performance: An Empirical Investigation of Nonprofit and For-Profit Job-Training Service Providers." *Journal of Policy Analysis and Management*, 2000, *19*, 233–261.

Heinrich, C. J., and Lynn, L. (eds.). *Governance and Performance: New Perspectives*. Washington, D.C.: Georgetown University Press, 2000a.

Heinrich, C. J., and Lynn, L. "Governnance and Performance: The Influence of Program Structure and Management on Job Training Partnership Act (JTPA) Program Outcomes." In C. J. Heinrich and L. Lynn (eds.), *Governance and Performance: New Perspectives*. Washington, D.C.: Georgetown University Press, 2000b.

Heintze, T., and Bretschneider, S. "Information Technology and Restructuring in Public Organizations: Does Adoption of Information Technology Affect Organizational Structures, Communications, and Decision-Making? *Journal of Public Administration Research and Theory*, 2000, *10*, 801–830.

Hellriegel, D., Woodman, R. W., and Slocum, J. W. *Organizational Behavior*. Cincinnati, Ohio: South-Western College, 2000.

Hennessey, T. J., Jr. ""Reinventing" Government: Does Leadership Make the Difference?" *Public Administration Review*, 1998, *58*, 522–532.

Henry, N. "Is Privatization Passé? The Case for Competition and the Emergence of Intersectoral Administration." *Public Administration Review*, 2002, *62*, 374–378.

Hersey, P., and Blanchard, K. H. *Management of Organizational Behavior*. Upper Saddle River, N.J.: Prentice Hall, 1982.

Herzberg, F. "One More Time: How Do You Motivate Employees?" *Harvard Business Review*, 1968, *46*, 36–44.

Herzberg, F., Mausner, B., Peterson, R. O., and Capwell, D. F. *Job Attitudes: Review of Research and Opinion*. Pittsburgh: Psychological Service of Pittsburgh, 1957.

Hickson, D. J., and others. "A 'Strategic Contingencies' Theory of Interorganizational Power." *Administrative Science Quarterly*, 1971, *16*, 216–229.

Hickson, D. J., and others. *Top Decisions: Strategic Decision Making in Organizations*. San Francisco: Jossey-Bass, 1986.

Hill, L. B. (ed.). *The State of Public Bureaucracy*. Armonk, N.Y.: Sharpe, 1992.

Hinnant, C. C. "Managerial Perceptions of Technology Acceptance: Examining the Adoption of E-Government Technologies by State Agencies." Paper presented at the American Political Science Association Conference, San Francisco, Aug. 30–Sept. 2, 2001.

Hirschman, A. O. *Shifting Involvements*. Princeton, N.J.: Princeton University Press, 1982.

Hjern, B., and Porter, D. O. "Implementation Structures: A New Unit of Administrative Analysis." *Organization Studies*, 1981, *2*, 211–227.

Hodge, G. A. *Privatization: An International Review of Performance.* Boulder, Colo.: Westview Press, 2000.

Hofstede, G., Neuijen, B., Ohayv, D. D., and Sanders, G. "Measuring Organizational Cultures: A Qualitative and Quantitative Study Across Twenty Cases." *Administrative Science Quarterly*, 1990, *35*, 286–316.

Holdaway, E., Newberry, J. F., Hickson, D. J., and Heron, R. P. "Dimensions of Organizations in Complex Societies: The Educational Sector." *Administrative Science Quarterly*, 1975, *20*, 37–58.

Holzer, M. "Productivity In, Garbage Out: Sanitation Gains in New York." *Public Productivity Review*, 1988, *11*, 37–50.

Holzer, M., and Callahan, K. *Government at Work: Best Practices and Model Programs.* Thousand Oaks, Calif.: Sage, 1998.

Hood, C., and Dunsire, A. *Bureaumetrics: The Quantitative Comparison of British Central Government Agencies.* Tuscaloosa: University of Alabama Press, 1981.

Hooijberg, R., and Choi, J. "The Impact of Organizational Characteristics on Leadership Effectiveness Models: An Examination of Leadership in a Private and a Public Sector Organization." *Administration and Society*, 2001, *33*, 403–431.

House, R. J. "A Path-Goal Theory of Leader Effectiveness." *Administrative Science Quarterly*, 1971, *16*, 321–338.

House, R. J. "Path-Goal Theory of Leadership: Lessons, Legacy, and a Reformulated Theory. *Leadership Quarterly*, 1996, *7*, 323–352.

House, R. J., and Mitchell, T. R. "Path-Goal Theory of Leadership." *Journal of Contemporary Business*, 1974, *3*, 81–97.

House, R. J., and Rizzo, J. R. "Role Conflict and Ambiguity as Critical Variables in a Model of Organizational Behavior." *Organizational Behavior and Human Performance*, 1972, *7*, 467–505.

House, R. J., and Singh, J. V. "Organizational Behavior: Some New Directions in I/O Psychology." *Annual Review of Psychology*, 1987, *38*, 619–718.

Houston, D. J. "Public-Service Motivation: A Multivariate Test." *Journal of Public Administration Research and Theory*, 2000, *10*, 713–727.

Huber, G. P., and Glick, W. H. (eds.). *Organizational Change and Redesign.* New York: Oxford University Press, 1993.

Hult, K. M. "Feminist Organization Theories and Government Organizations: The Promise of Diverse Structural Forms." *Public Productivity and Management Review*, 1995, *19*, 128–142.

Hummel, R. *The Bureaucratic Experience.* New York: St. Martin's Press, 1994.

Hunt, A. "Reflections of a Heavyweight." *The Wall Street Journal*, July 1, 1999, p. A23.

IBM Endowment for the Business of Government. "A Conversation with Charles Rossotti, Commissioner, Internal Revenue Service." *The Business of Government*, Winter 2002, pp. 13–17. Arlington, Va.: IBM Endowment for the Business of Government.

Ingraham, P. W. "Transition and Policy Change in Washington." *Public Productivity Review*, 1988, *12*, 61–72.

Ingraham, P. W. "Of Pigs in Pokes and Policy Diffusion: Another Look at Pay-for-Performance." *Public Administration Review*, 1993, *53*, 348–356.

Ingraham, P. W., and Donahue, A. K. "Dissecting the Black Box Revisited: Characterizing Government Management Capacity." In C. J. Heinrich and L. Lynn (eds.), *Governance and Performance: New Perspectives.* Washington, D.C.: Georgetown University Press, 2000.

Ingraham, P. W., Thompson, J. R., and Sanders, R. P. *Transforming Government: Lessons from the Reinvention Laboratories.* San Francisco: Jossey-Bass, 1998.

Janis, I. L. "Groupthink." *Psychology Today,* Nov. 1971, p. 43.

Jennings, E. T., Jr., and Ewalt, J.A.G. "Driving Caseloads Down: Welfare Policy Choices and Administrative Action." In C. J. Heinrich and L. Lynn (eds.), *Governance and Performance: New Perspectives.* Washington, D.C.: Georgetown University Press, 2000.

Johnson, D. W., and Johnson, F. P. *Joining Together: Group Theory and Group Skills.* Needham Heights, Mass.: Allyn & Bacon, 1994.

Johnson, L. K. *America's Secret Power: The CIA in a Democratic Society.* New York: Oxford University Press, 1989.

Jones, B. D. "Bounded Rationality." *Annual Review of Political Science,* 1999, *2,* 297–321.

Jones, L. R., and Thompson, F. *Public Management: Institutional Renewal for the Twenty-First Century.* Stamford, Connecticut: JAI Press, 1999.

Jriesat, J. E. *Public Organization Management: The Development of Theory and Process.* Westport, Conn.: Quorum, 1997.

Juran, J. M. *Juran on Quality by Design: The New Steps for Planning Quality into Goods and Services.* New York: Free Press, 1992.

Jurkiewicz, C. L., and Brown, R. G. "GenXers vs. Boomers vs. Matures: Generational Comparisons of Public Employee Motivation." *Review of Public Personnel Administration,* 1998, *18,* 18–37.

Jurkiewicz, C. L., Massey, T. K., and Brown, R. G. "Motivation in Public and Private Organizations." *Public Productivity and Management Review,* 1998, *21,* 230–250.

Kahn, R. F., and others. *Organizational Stress: Studies in Role Conflict and Ambiguity.* New York: Wiley, 1964.

Kalleberg, A. L., Knoke, D., and Marsden, P. V. "The National Organizations Survey (NOS) 1996–1997." Ann Arbor, Michigan: Inter-university Consortium for Political and Social Research, 2001. (ICPSR 3190).

Kalleberg, A. L., Knoke, D., Marsden, P. V., and Spaeth, J. L. "The National Organizations Study: An Introduction and Overview." *American Behavioral Scientist,* 1994, *37,* 860–871.

Kalleberg, A. L., Knoke, D., Marsden, P. V., and Spaeth, J. L. *Organizations in America: Analyzing Their Structures and Human Resource Practices.* Thousand Oaks, Calif.: Sage, 1996.

Kanter, R. M. "Power Failure in Management Circuits." In J. M. Shafritz and J. S. Ott (eds.), *Classics of Organization Theory.* Florence, Ky.: Dorsey Press, 1987.

Kaplan, R. S., and Norton, D. P. *The Balanced Scorecard: Translating Strategy into Action.* Boston: Harvard Business School Press, 1996.

Kaplan, R. S., and Norton, D. P. *The Strategy-Focused Organization: How Balanced-Scorecard Companies Thrive in the New Business Environment.* Boston: Harvard Business School Press, 2000.

Karl, K. A., and Sutton, C. L. "Job Values in Today's Workforce: A Comparison of Public and Private Sector Employees." *Public Personnel Management,* 1998, *27,* 515–527.

Kast, F. E., and Rosenzweig, J. E. (eds.). *Contingency Views of Organization and Management.* Chicago: Science Research Associates, 1973.

Katz, D., Gutek, B. A., Kahn, R. L., and Barton, E. *Bureaucratic Encounters: A Pilot Study in the Evaluation of Government Services.* Ann Arbor: Survey Research Center, Institute for Social Research, University of Michigan, 1975.

Katz, D., and Kahn, R. L. *The Social Psychology of Organizations.* New York: Wiley, 1966.

Katzell, R. A., and Thompson, D. E. "Work Motivation: Theory and Practice." *American Psychologist,* 1990, *45,* 144–153.

Katzenbach, J. R., and Smith, D. K. *The Discipline of Teams.* New York: Wiley, 2001.

Kaufman, H. *The Forest Ranger.* Baltimore: Johns Hopkins University Press, 1960.

Kaufman, H. "Administrative Decentralization and Political Power." *Public Administration Review,* 1969, *29,* 3.

Kaufman, H. *Are Government Organizations Immortal?* Washington, D.C.: Brookings Institution, 1976.

Kaufman, H. *Red Tape: Its Origins, Uses, and Abuses.* Washington, D.C.: Brookings Institution, 1977.

Kaufman, H. *The Administrative Behavior of Federal Bureau Chiefs.* Washington, D.C.: Brookings Institution, 1979.

Kearney, R. C., Feldman, B. M., and Scavo, C.P.F. "Reinventing Government: City Manager Attitudes and Actions." *Public Administration Review,* 2000, *60,* 535–548.

Keeley, M. "Impartiality and Participant-Interest Theories of Organizational Effectiveness." *Administrative Science Quarterly,* 1984, *29,* 1–12.

Keiser, L. R., Wilkins, V. M., Meier, K. J., and Holland, C. A. "Lipstick and Logarithms: Gender, Institutional Context, and Representative Bureaucracy." *American Political Science Review,* 2002, *96,* 553–564.

Kellerman, B., and Webster, S. W. "The Recent Literature on Public Leadership Reviewed and Considered." *The Leadership Quarterly,* 2001, *12,* 484–514.

Kellough, J. E., and Lu, H. "The Paradox of Merit Pay in the Public Sector." *Review of Public Personnel Administration,* 1993, *13,* 45–64.

Kellough, J. E., and Nigro, L. C. "Pay for Performance in Georgia State Government: Employee Perspectives on Georgia Gain After 5 Years." *Review of Public Personnel Administration,* 2002, *22,* 146–166.

Kelman, S. "The Grace Commission: How Much Waste in Government?" *Public Interest,* 1985, *78,* 62–82.

Kelman, S. *Making Public Policy.* New York: Basic Books, 1987.

Kelman, S. "The Making of Government Good Guys." *New York Times,* July 2, 1989, Business Section, p. 1.

Kelman, S. *Procurement and Public Management.* Washington, D.C.: AEI Press, 1990.

Kenny, G. K., and others. "Strategic Decision Making: Influence Patterns in Public and Private Sector Organizations." *Human Relations,* 1987, *40,* 613–631.

Kerr, D. L. "The Business of Government: The Balanced Scorecard in the Public Sector." *Perform,* 2001, *1,* 4–9.

Kerr, S. "On the Folly of Rewarding A, While Hoping for B." In J. S. Ott (ed.), *Classic Readings in Organizational Behavior.* Pacific Grove, Calif.: Brooks/Cole, 1989.

Kettl, D. F. *Government by Proxy.* Washington, D.C.: CQ Press, 1988.

Kettl, D. F. "The Image of the Public Service in the Media." In Volcker Commission, *Leadership for America: Rebuilding the Public Service.* Lexington, Mass.: Heath, 1989.

Kettl, D. F. *Sharing Power.* Washington, D.C.: Brookings Institution, 1993.

Kettl, D. F. *The Transformation of Governance: Public Administration for the Twenty-First Century.* Baltimore: Johns Hopkins University Press, 2002.

Kettl, D. F., and Milward, H. B. (Eds.). *The State of Public Management.* Baltimore: Johns Hopkins University Press, 1996.

Khademian, A. M. *Working with Culture: The Way the Job Gets Done in Public Organizations.* Washington, D.C.: CQ Press, 2002.

Khojasteh, M. "Motivating the Private vs. Public Sector Managers." *Public Personnel Management,* 1993, *22,* 391–399.

Kiel, L. D. *Managing Chaos and Complexity in Government: A New Paradigm for Managing Change, Innovation, and Organizational Renewal.* San Francisco: Jossey-Bass, 1994.

Kilpatrick, F. P., Cummings, M. C., and Jennings, M. K. *The Image of the Federal Service.* Washington, D.C.: Brookings Institution, 1964.

Kim, S. "Participative Management and Job Satisfaction: Lessons for Management Leadership." *Public Administration Review,* 2002, *62,* 231–241.

Kimberly, J. R. "Organizational Size and the Structuralist Perspective: A Review, Critique, and Proposal." *Administrative Science Quarterly,* 1976, *21,* 577–597.

Kimberly, J. R., Miles, R. H., and Associates. *The Organizational Life Cycle: Issues in the Creation, Transformation, and Decline of Organizations.* San Francisco: Jossey-Bass, 1980.

Kingdon, J. W. *Agendas, Alternatives, and Public Policies.* New York: HarperCollins, 1995.

Klein, H. J. "An Integrated Control Theory Model of Work Motivation." *Academy of Management Review,* 1989, *14,* 150–172.

Klein, H. J., and Kim, J. S. "A Field Study of the Influence of Situational Constraints, Leader-Member Exchange, and Goal Commitment on Performance." *Academy of Management Journal,* 1998, *41,* 88–95.

Klein, J. I. "Feasibility Theory: A Resource-Munificence Model of Work Motivation and Behavior." *Academy of Management Review,* 1990, *15,* 646–665.

Kleinbeck, U., Quast, H. H., Thierry, H., and Harmut, H. (eds.). *Work Motivation.* Hillsdale, N.J.: Erlbaum, 1990.

Knott, J. H., and Hammond, T. H. "Congressional Committees and Policy Change: Explaining Legislative Outcomes in Banking, Trucking, Airlines, and Telecommunications Deregulation." In C. J. Heinrich and L. Lynn (eds.), *Governance and Performance: New Perspectives.* Washington, D.C.: Georgetown University Press, 2000.

Knott, J. H., and Miller, G. J. *Reforming Bureaucracy.* Upper Saddle River, N.J.: Prentice Hall, 1987.

Koenig, H., and O'Leary, R. "Eight Supreme Court Cases That Have Changed the Face of Public Administration." *International Journal of Public Administration,* 1996, *19,* 5–22.

Koppel, J.G.S. "Hybrid Organizations and the Alignment of Interests: The Case of Fannie Mae and Freddie Mac." *Public Administration Review,* 2001, *61,* 468–482.

Kotter, J. P. "Leading Change: Why Transformation Efforts Fail." *Harvard Business Review,* Mar.–Apr. 1995, pp. 59–67.

Kotter, J. P., and Heskett, J. L. *Corporate Culture and Performance.* New York: Macmillan, 1992.

Kotter, J. P., and Lawrence, P. R. *Mayors in Action.* Somerset, N.J.: Wiley-Interscience, 1974.

Kovach, K. A., and Patrick, S. L. "Comparisons of Public and Private Subjects on Reported Economic Measures and on Facet Satisfaction Items for Each of Three Organizational Levels." Paper presented at the annual meeting of the Academy of Management, Washington, D.C., 1989.

Kraemer, K. L., and Dedrick, J. "Computing and Public Organizations." *Journal of Public Administration Research and Theory,* 1997, *7,* 89–112.

Kraemer, K. L., and Perry, J. L. "Institutional Requirements for Research in Public Administration." *Public Administration Review,* 1989, *49,* 9–16.

Kreitner, R., and Luthans, F. "A Social Learning Approach to Behavioral Management." In J. R. Gordon (ed.), *Organizational Behavior.* (2nd ed.) Needham Heights, Mass.: Allyn & Bacon, 1987.

Kurke, L. E., and Aldrich, H. E. "Mintzberg Was Right! A Replication and Extension of the Nature of Managerial Work." *Management Science,* 1983, *29,* 975–984.

Kurland, N. B., and Egan, T. D. "Public vs. Private Perceptions of Formalization, Outcomes, and Justice." *Journal of Public Administration Research and Theory,* 1999, *9,* 437–458.

Kuttner, R. *Everything for Sale: The Virtues and Limits of Markets.* New York: Knopf, 1997.

Lachman, R. "Public and Private Sector Differences: CEOs' Perceptions of Their Role Environments." *Academy of Management Journal,* 1985, *28,* 671–679.

Ladd, E. C. "What the Voters Really Want." In J. L. Perry and K. L. Kraemer (eds.), *Public Management.* Mountain View, Calif.: Mayfield, 1983.

Landy, F. J., and Becker, W. S. "Motivation Theory Reconsidered." In L. L. Cummings and B. M. Staw (eds.), *Research in Organizational Behavior,* Vol. 9. Greenwich, Conn.: JAI Press, 1987.

Landy, F. J., and Guion, R. M. "Development of Scales for the Measurement of Work Motivation." *Organizational Behavior and Human Performance,* 1970, *5,* 93–103.

Langbein, L. I., "Ownership, Empowerment, and Productivity: Some Empirical Evidence On the Causes and Consequences of Employee Discretion." *Journal of Policy Analysis and Management,* 2000, *19,* 427–449.

Langbein, L. I., and Lewis, G. B. "Pay, Productivity, and the Public Sector: The Case of Electrical Engineers." *Journal of Public Administration Research and Theory,* 1998, *8,* 391–412.

La Porte, T. "Regulatory Compliance and the Ethos of Quality Enhancement: Surprises in Nuclear Power Plant Operations." *Journal of Public Administration Research and Theory,* 1995, *5,* 109–137.

Larkin, J. "Spreading the Word: Improving Government/Media Relations Means a Better Image for Public Service." *PA Times,* 1992, *15,* 3.

Larson, M. *The Rise of Professionalism.* Berkeley: University of California Press, 1977.

Lasko, W. "Executive Accountability: Will SES Make a Difference?" *Bureaucrat,* 1980, *9,* 6–7.

Lau, A. W., Pavett, C. M., and Newman, A. R. "The Nature of Managerial Work: A Comparison of Public and Private Sector Jobs." *Academy of Management Proceedings,* 1980, 339–343.

Lawler, E. E., III. *Pay and Organizational Effectiveness.* New York: McGraw-Hill, 1971.

Lawler, E. E., III. *Strategic Pay: Aligning Organizational Strategies and Pay Systems.* San Francisco: Jossey-Bass, 1990.

Lawler, E. E., III. *Treat People Right! How Organizations and Individuals Can Propel Each Other into a Virtuous Spiral of Success.* San Francisco: Jossey-Bass, 2003.

Lawler, E. E., III, and Hall, D. T. "Relationship of Job Characteristics to Job Involvement, Satisfaction, and Intrinsic Motivation." *Journal of Applied Psychology,* 1970, *54,* 305–312.

Lawler, E. E., III, Mohrman S. M., and Benson, G. *Organizing for High Performance: Employee Involvement, TQM, Reengineering, and Knowledge Management in the Fortune 1000: The CEO Report.* San Francisco: Jossey-Bass, 2001.

Lawrence, P. R., and Lorsch, J. W. *Organization and Environment.* Cambridge, Mass.: Harvard University Press, 1967.

Leavitt, H. J. "Some Effects of Certain Communication Patterns on Group Performance." *Journal of Abnormal and Social Psychology,* 1951, *46,* 38–50.

Lee, G., and Perry, J. L. "Are Computers Boosting Productivity? A Test of the Paradox in State Governments." *Journal of Public Administration Research and Theory,* 2002, *12,* 77–102.

Lee, M., and Shin, W. "An Empirical Analysis of the Role of Referent Point in Justice Perception in R&D Setting in Korea." *Journal of Engineering and Technology Management,* 2000, *17,* 175–191.

Lerner, A. W., and Wanat, J. "Fuzziness and Bureaucracy." *Public Administration Review,* 1983, *43,* 500–509.

Levin, M. A., and Sanger, M. B. *Making Government Work: How Entrepreneurial Executives Turn Bright Ideas into Real Results.* San Francisco: Jossey-Bass, 1994.

Levine, C. H. (ed.). *Managing Fiscal Stress.* Chatham, N.J.: Chatham House, 1980a.

Levine, C. H. "Organizational Decline and Cutback Management." In C. H. Levine (ed.), *Managing Fiscal Stress.* Chatham, N.J.: Chatham House, 1980b.

Lewis, D. E. "The Politics of Agency Termination: Confronting the Myth of Agency Immortality." *Journal of Politics,* 2002, *64,* 89–107.

Lewis, E. B. *Public Entrepreneurship.* Bloomington: Indiana University Press, 1980.

Lewis, E. B. "Admiral Hyman Rickover: Technological Entrepreneurship in the U.S. Navy." In J. W. Doig and E. C. Hargrove (eds.), *Leadership and Innovation.* Baltimore: Johns Hopkins University Press, 1987.

Lichter, R. S., Rothman, S., and Lichter, L. *The Media Elite.* Bethesda, Md.: Adler and Adler, 1986.

Light, P. C. "When Worlds Collide: The Political-Career Nexus." In G. C. Mackenzie (ed.), *The In-and-Outers.* Baltimore: Johns Hopkins University Press, 1987.

Light, P. C. *The Tides of Reform: Making Government Work.* New Haven, Conn.: Yale University Press, 1997.

Light, P. C. *Sustaining Innovation.* San Francisco: Jossey-Bass, 1998.

Light, P. C. *The Troubled State of the Federal Public Service.* Washington D.C.: Brookings Institution, 2002a.

Light, P. C. *Government's Greatest Achievements from Civil Rights to Homeland Defense.* Washington, D.C.: Brookings Institution, 2002b.

Likert, R. *The Human Organization.* New York: McGraw-Hill, 1967.

Lindblom, C. E. "The Science of Muddling Through." *Public Administration Review,* 1959, *19,* 79–88.

Lindblom, C. E. *Politics and Markets.* New York: Basic Books, 1977.

Linden, R. M. *From Vision to Reality: Strategies of Successful Innovators in Government.* Charlottesville, Va.: LEL Enterprise, 1990.

Linden, R. M. *Seamless Government: A Practical Guide to Re-engineering in the Public Sector.* San Francisco, Calif.: Jossey-Bass, 1994.

Linsky, M. *Impact: How the Press Affects Federal Policymaking.* New York: Norton, 1986.

Lipset, S. M., and Schneider, W. *The Confidence Gap: Business, Labor, and Government in the Public Mind.* Baltimore: Johns Hopkins University Press, 1987.

Lipsky, M. *Street-Level Bureaucracy.* New York: Russell Sage Foundation, 1980.

Locke, E. A. "What Is Job Satisfaction?" *Organizational Behavior and Human Performance,* 1969, *4,* 309–336.

Locke, E. A. "The Myth of Behavior Modification in Organizations." *Academy of Management Review,* 1977, *2,* 543–553.

Locke, E. A. "The Nature and Causes of Job Satisfaction." In M. D. Dunnette (ed.), *Handbook of Industrial and Organizational Psychology.* New York: Wiley, 1983.

Locke, E. A. "The Motivation to Work: What We Know." In P. Pintrich and M. Maehr (eds.), *Advances in Motivation and Achievement,* vol. 10. Greenwich, Conn.: JAI Press, 1999.

Locke, E. A. "Motivation by Goal Setting." In R. T. Golembiewski (ed.), *Handbook of Organizational Behavior.* (2nd ed.) New York: Marcel Dekker, 2000.

Locke, E. A., and Henne, D. "Work Motivation Theories." In C. L. Cooper and I. Robertson (eds.), *International Review of Industrial and Organizational Psychology.* New York: Wiley, 1986.

Locke, E. A., and Latham, G. P. *A Theory of Goal Setting and Task Performance.* Upper Saddle River, N.J.: Prentice Hall, 1990a.

Locke, E. A., and Latham, G. P. "Work Motivation: The High Performance Cycle." In U. Kleinbeck and others (eds.), *Work Motivation.* Hillsdale, N.J.: Erlbaum, 1990b.

Long, N. E. "Power and Administration." *Public Administration Review,* 1949, *9,* 257–264.

Lowi, T. *The End of Liberalism.* New York: Norton, 1979.

Lowery, D. "Improving Governance." *Journal of Public Administration Research and Theory,* 2002, *12,* 293–297.

Lueck, S. "Chief Justice's Daughter Lands in Hot Seat." *Wall Street Journal,* Nov. 11, 2002, p. A4.

Lurie, I., and Riccucci, N. M. "Changing the 'Culture' of Welfare Offices: From Vision to the Front Lines." *Administration & Society,* 2003, *35,* 653–677.

Luttwak, E. N. *The Pentagon and the Art of War: The Question of Military Reform.* New York: Simon and Schuster, 1984.

Lynn, L. E. *Managing the Public's Business.* New York: Basic Books, 1981.

Lynn, L. E. *Managing Public Policy.* New York: Little, Brown, 1987.

Lynn, L. E. *Public Management as Art, Science, and Profession.* Chatham, N.J.: Chatham House, 1996.

Lynn, L. E., Jr., Heinrich, C. J., and Hill, C. J. "Studying Governance and Public Management: Why? How?" In C. J. Heinrich and L. Lynn (eds.), *Governance and Performance: New Perspectives.* Washington, D. C.: Georgetown University Press, 2000.

MacAvoy, P. W., and McIssac, G. S. "The Performance and Management of United States Federal Government Enterprises." In P. W. MacAvoy, W. T. Stanbury, G. Yarrow, and R. J. Zeckhauser (eds.), *Privatization and State-Owned Enterprises.* Boston: Kluwer, 1989.

MacDonald, F. "Economic Freedom and the Constitution." *Florida Policy Review,* 1987, *3,* 38–44.

Macy, J. W. *Public Service: The Human Side of Government.* New York: HarperCollins, 1971.

Maier, N.R.F. "Assets and Liabilities in Group Problem Solving: The Need for an Integrative Function." *Psychological Review,* 1967, *74,* 239–249.

Mainzer, L. C. *Political Bureaucracy.* Glenview, Ill.: Scott, Foresman, 1973.

Maitland, L. "Focus of H.U.D. Inquiry: An Obscure and Influential Woman." *New York Times,* May 31, 1989, p. 11.

March, J. G. "The Business Firm as a Political Coalition." *Journal of Politics,* 1962, *24,* 662–678.

March, J. G., and Olsen, J. P. (eds.). *Ambiguity and Choice in Organizations.* Bergen, Norway: Universitetsforlaget, 1976.

March, J. G., and Olsen, J. P. "Garbage Can Models of Decision Making in Organizations." In J. G. March and R. Weissinger-Baylon (eds.), *Ambiguity and Command.* White Plains, N.Y.: Pitman, 1986.

March, J. G., and Simon, H. A. *Organizations.* New York: Wiley, 1958.

Marmor, T. R. "Entrepreneurship in Public Management: Wilbur Cohen and Robert Ball." In J. W. Doig and E. C. Hargrove (eds.), *Leadership and Innovation.* Baltimore: Johns Hopkins University Press, 1987.

Marmor, T. R., and Fellman, P. "Policy Entrepreneurship in Government: An American Study." *Journal of Public Policy,* 1986, *6,* 225–253.

Marsden, P. V., Cook, C. R., and Kalleberg, A. L. "Organizational Structures: Coordination and Control." *American Behavioral Scientist,* 1994, *37,* 911–929.

Mascarenhas, B. "Domains of State-Owned, Privately Held, and Publicly Traded Firms in International Competition." *Administrative Science Quarterly,* 1989, *34,* 582–597.

Mashaw, J. L. *Bureaucratic Justice.* New Haven, Conn.: Yale University Press, 1983.

Maslow, A. H. *Motivations and Personality.* New York: HarperCollins, 1954.

Maslow, A. *Eupsychian Management.* Burr Ridge, Ill.: Irwin, 1965.

Maynard-Moody, S., Stull, D. D., and Mitchell, J. "Reorganization as Status Drama: Building, Maintaining, and Displacing Dominant Subcultures." *Public Administration Review,* 1986, *46,* 301–310.

McCauley, C. D., Lombardo, M. M., and Usher, C. H. "Diagnosing Management Development Needs: An Instrument Based on How Managers Develop." *Journal of Management,* 1989, *15,* 389–404.

McClelland, D. C. *The Achieving Society.* New York: Free Press, 1961.

McClelland, D. C. *Power: The Inner Experience.* New York: Irvington, 1975.

McClelland, D. C., and Winter, D. G. *Motivating Economic Achievement.* New York: Free Press, 1969.

McCurdy, H. E., and Cleary, R. "Why Can't We Resolve the Research Issue in Public Administration?" *Public Administration Review,* 1984, *44,* 49–55.

McGregor, D. *The Human Side of Enterprise.* New York: McGraw-Hill, 1960.

McGuire, M. "Managing Networks: Propositions on What Managers Do and Why They Do It." *Public Administration Review,* 2002, *62,* 599–609.

McKelvey, B. *Organizational Systematics.* Berkeley: University of California Press, 1982.

Meier, K. J. *Politics and the Bureaucracy.* (4th ed.) New York: Harcourt College Publishers, 2000.

Meier, K. J., and O'Toole, L. J. "Managerial Strategies and Behavior in Networks: A Model with Evidence from U.S. Public Education." *Journal of Public Administration Research and Theory,* 2001, *11,* 271–93.

Meier, K. J., and O'Toole, L. J. "Public Management and Organizational Performance: The Impact of Managerial Quality." *Journal of Public Policy Analysis and Management,* 2002, *21,* 629–643.

Melkers, J., and Willoughby, K. "The State of the States: Performance-Based Budgeting Requirements in 47 out of 50." *Public Administration Review,* 1998, *58,* 66–73.

Merton, R. K. "Bureaucratic Structure and Personality." *Social Forces,* 1940, *18,* 560–568.

Meyer, J. W., and Rowan, B. "Institutionalized Organizations: Formal Structure as Myth and Ceremony." In J. W. Meyer and W. R. Scott (eds.), *Organizational Environments: Ritual and Rationality.* Thousand Oaks, Calif.: Sage, 1983.

Meyer, M. W. *Change in Public Bureaucracies.* Cambridge: Cambridge University Press, 1979.

Meyer, M. W. "'Bureaucratic' vs. 'Profit' Organization." In B. L. Staw and L. L. Cummings (eds.), *Research in Organizational Behavior.* Greenwich, Conn.: JAI Press, 1982.

Meyers, M. K., Riccucci, N. M., and Lurie, I. "Achieving Goal Congruence in Complex Environments: The Case of Welfare Reform." *Journal of Public Administration Research and Theory,* 2001, *11,* 165–201.

Michelson, S. "The Working Bureaucrat in the Nonworking Bureaucracy." In C. H. Weiss and A. H. Barton (eds.), *Making Bureaucracies Work.* Thousand Oaks, Calif.: Sage, 1980.

Miles, R. E., and Snow, C. C. *Organizational Strategy, Structure, and Process.* New York: McGraw-Hill, 1978.

Miles, R. H. "A Comparison of the Relative Impacts of Role Perceptions of Ambiguity and Conflict by Role." *Academy of Management Journal,* 1976, *19,* 25–35.

Miles, R. H. *Macro Organization Behavior.* Glenview, Ill.: Scott, Foresman, 1980.

Miles, R. H., and Petty, M. M. "Relationships Between Role Clarity, Need for Clarity, and Job Tension and Satisfaction for Supervisory Roles." *Academy of Management Journal,* 1975, *18,* 877–883.

Miller, J. C. "A Presidential Veto for Pork Spending." *Wall Street Journal,* Jan. 30, 1990, p. A18.

Miller, W., Kerr, B., and Reid, M. "A National Study of Gender-Based Occupational Segregation in Municipal Bureaucracies: Persistence of Glass Walls?" *Public Administration Review,* 1999, *59,* 218–230.

Milward, H. B. "The Changing Character of the Public Sector." In J. L. Perry (ed.), *Handbook of Public Administration.* (2nd ed.) San Francisco: Jossey-Bass, 1996.

Milward, H. B., and Provan, K. G. "Principles for Controlling Agents." *Journal of Public Administration Research and Theory,* 1998, *8,* 203–221.

Milward, H. B., and Provan, K. G. "How Networks Are Governed." In C. J. Heinrich and L. Lynn (eds.), *Governance and Performance: New Perspectives.* Washington, D.C.: Georgetown University Press, 2000.

Milward, H. B., Provan, K. G., and Else, B. A. "What Does the 'Hollow State' Look Like?" In B. Bozeman (ed.), *Public Management: State of the Art.* San Francisco: Jossey-Bass, 1993.

Milward, H. B., and Rainey, H. G. "Don't Blame the Bureaucracy." *Journal of Public Policy,* 1983, *3,* 149–168.

Milward, H. B., and Wamsley, G. "Interorganizational Policy Systems and Research on Public Organizations." *Administration and Society,* 1982, *13,* 457–478.

Miner, J. B. *Theories of Organizational Behavior.* Orlando, Fla.: Dryden, 1980.

Mintzberg, H. *The Nature of Managerial Work.* New York: HarperCollins, 1972.

Mintzberg, H. *The Structuring of Organizations.* Upper Saddle River, N.J.: Prentice Hall, 1979.

Mintzberg, H. *Power in and Around Organizations.* Upper Saddle River, N.J.: Prentice Hall, 1983.

Mintzberg, H. *Mintzberg on Management.* New York: Free Press, 1989.

Mintzberg, H., Raisinghani, D., and Theoret, A. "The Structure of Unstructured Decisions Processes." *Administrative Science Quarterly,* 1976, *21,* 266–273.

Mitnick, B. M. *The Political Economy of Regulation.* New York: Columbia University Press, 1980.

Moe, R. C. "Managing Privatization: A New Challenge to Public Administration." In B. G. Peters and B. A. Rockman (eds.), *Agenda for Excellence 2: Administering the State.* Chatham, N.J.: Chatham House, 1996.

Moe, R. C. "The Emerging Federal Quasi Government: Issues of Management and Accountability." *Public Administration Review,* 2001, *61,* 290–312.

Mohrman, S. A., Cohen, S. G., and Mohrman, A. M. *Designing Team-Based Organizations: New Forms for Knowledge Work.* San Francisco: Jossey-Bass, 1995.

Molnar, J. J., and Rogers, D. L. "Organizational Effectiveness: An Empirical Comparison of the Goal and System Resource Approaches." *Sociological Quarterly,* 1976, *17,* 401–413.

Mone, M. A., McKinley, W., and Barker, V. L., III. "Organizational Decline and Innovation: A Contingency Framework." *Academy of Management Journal,* 1998, *23,* 115–132.

Moon, M. J. "Organizational Commitment Revisited in New Public Management: Motivation, Organizational Culture, Sector, and Managerial Level." *Public Performance and Management Review,* 2000, *24,* 177–194.

Moon, M. J., and Bretschneider, S. "Does the Perception of Red Tape Constrain IT Innovativeness in Organizations? Unexpected Results from a Simultaneous Equation Model and Implications." *Journal of Public Administration Research and Theory,* 2002, *12,* 273–292.

Mooney, J. D. "The Scalar Principle." In J. D. Mooney and A. C. Reiley (eds.), *The Principles of Organization.* New York: HarperCollins, 1930.

Moore, M. H. "Police Leadership: The Impossible Dream." In E. C. Hargrove and J. C. Glidewell (eds.), *Impossible Jobs in Public Management.* Lawrence: University Press of Kansas, 1990.

Moore, M. H. *Creating Public Value: Strategic Management in Government.* Cambridge, MA: Harvard University Press, 1995.

Moore, M. H. "Managing for Value: Organizational Strategy in For-Profit, Nonprofit, and Governmental Organizations." *Nonprofit and Voluntary Sector Quarterly,* 2000, *29,* 183–204.

Morrisey, G. L. *Management by Objectives and Results in the Public Sector.* Reading, Mass.: Addison-Wesley, 1976.

Morse, P. M., and Bacon, L. W. (eds.). *Operations Research for Public Systems.* Cambridge, Mass.: MIT Press, 1967.

Morton, N. O., and Lindquist, S. A. "Revealing the Feminist in Mary Parker Follett." *Administration & Society,* 1997, *29,* 348–372.

Mosher, F. *Democracy and the Public Service.* New York: Oxford University Press, 1982. (Originally published 1968.)

Mott, P. E. *The Characteristics of Effective Organizations.* New York: HarperCollins, 1972.

Mowday, R. T., Porter, L. W., and Steers, R. M. *Employee-Organization Linkages.* Orlando, Fla.: Academic Press, 1982.

Murray, H. A. *Explorations in Personality.* New York: Oxford University Press, 1938.

Murray, M. A. "Comparing Public and Private Management: An Exploratory Essay." *Public Administration Review,* 1975, *35,* 364–371.

Murray, D., Schwartz, J., and Lichter, R. S. *It Ain't Necessarily So: How the Media Remake Our Picture of Reality.* Lanham, Md.: Rowman & Littlefield, 2001.

Musolf, L., and Seidman, H. "The Blurred Boundaries of Public Administration." *Public Administration Review,* 1980, *40,* 124–130.

Naff, K. C., and Crum, J. " Working for America: Does Public Service Motivation Make a Difference?" *Review of Public Personnel Administration,* 1999, *19,* 5–16.

National Academy of Public Administration. *Revitalizing Federal Management.* Washington, D.C.: National Academy of Public Administration, 1986.

National Academy of Public Administration. *The Transforming Power of Information Technology.* Washington, D.C.: National Academy of Public Administration, 2001.

National Center for Productivity and Quality of Working Life. *Employee Attitudes and Productivity Differences Between the Public and Private Sectors.* Washington, D.C.: National Center for Productivity and Quality of Working Life, 1978.

National Commission on the Public Service. *Leadership for America: Rebuilding the Public Service.* Washington, D.C.: National Commission on the Public Service, 1989.

National Commission on the Public Service. *Urgent Business for America: Revitalizing the Federal Government for the 21st Century.* Washington, D.C.: The Brookings Institution, January, 2003.

National Council of Social Security Management Associations. "Survey of Management." Hackensack, N.J.: National Council of Social Security Management Associations, Feb. 2002. [www.ncssma.org].

Neiman, M. *Defending Government: Why Big Government Works.* Upper Saddle River, N.J.: Prentice Hall, 2000.

Nicholson-Crotty, S., and O'Toole, L. J. "Testing a Model of Public Management and Organizational Performance: The Case of Law Enforcement Agencies." *Journal of Public Administration Research and Theory,* forthcoming.

Niskanen, W. A. *Bureaucracy and Representative Government.* Hawthorne, N.Y.: Aldine de Gruyter, 1971.

Nutt, P. C. "Public-Private Differences and the Assessment of Alternatives for Decision Making." *Journal of Public Administration Research and Theory,* 1999, *9,* 305–349.

Nutt, P. C. "Decision-Making Success in Public, Private, and Third Sector Organizations: Finding Sector Dependent Best Practice." *Journal of Management Studies,* 2000, *37,* 77–108.

Nutt, P. C., and Backoff, R. W. *Strategic Management of Public and Third-Sector Organizations: A Handbook for Leaders.* San Francisco: Jossey-Bass, 1992.

Nutt, P. C., and Backoff, R. W. "Strategy for Public and Third-Sector Organizations." *Journal of Public Administration Research and Theory,* 1995, *5,* 189–211.

Nye, J. S., Jr. "Information Technology and Democratic Governance." In E. C. Kamarck and J. S. Nye (eds.), *Democracy.com? Governance in a Networked World.* Hollis, N.H.: Hollis Publishing Company, 1999.

Office of Economic Cooperation and Development, Public Management Committee. "The Challenges of Retirement Departures in the Public Service." *Focus: Public Management Newsletter,* 2002, *24,* p. 4.

O'Leary, R. "The Expanding Partnership Between Personnel Management and the Courts." In P. W. Ingraham and B. S. Romzek (eds.), *New Paradigms for Government: Issues for the Changing Public Service.* San Francisco: Jossey-Bass, 1994.

O'Leary, R., and Straussman, J. D. "The Impact of Courts on Public Management." In B. Bozeman (ed.), *Public Management: State of the Art.* San Francisco: Jossey-Bass, 1993.

Olsen, J. P. "Garbage Cans, New Institutionalism, and the Study of Politics." *American Political Science Review,* 2001, *95,* 191–198.

Olshfski, D. F. "Politics and Leadership: Political Executives at Work." *Public Productivity and Management Review,* 1990, *13,* 225–244.

Osborne, D., and Gaebler, T. *Reinventing Government.* Reading, Mass.: Addison-Wesley, 1992.

Ospina, S. M. "Realizing the Promise of Diversity." In J. L. Perry (ed.), *Handbook of Public Administration.* (2nd ed.) San Francisco: Jossey-Bass, 1996.

O'Toole, L. J. "Treating Networks Seriously: Practical and Research-Based Agendas in Public Administration." *Public Administration Review,* 1999, *57,* 45–52.

O'Toole, L. J. "Research on Policy Implementation: Assessment and Prospects." *Journal of Public Administration Research and Theory,* 2000, *10,* 263–288.

O'Toole, L. J., and Meier, K. J. "Modelling the Impact of Public Managment: Implications of Structural Context." *Journal of Public Administration Research and Theory,* 1999, *9,* 505–526.

O'Toole, L. J., and Meier, K. J. "Networks, Hierarchies, and Public Management: Modeling the Nonlinearities." In C. J. Heinrich and L. Lynn (eds.), *Governance and Performance: New Perspectives.* Washington, D.C.: Georgetown University Press, 2000.

O'Toole, L. J., and Meier, K. J. "Plus ça Change: Public Management, Personnel Stability, and Organizational Performance." *Journal of Public Administration Research and Theory,* 2003, *13,* 43–64.

Ott, J. S. *The Organizational Culture Perspective.* Pacific Grove, Calif.: Brooks/Cole, 1989.

Ouchi, W. *Theory Z: How American Business Can Meet the Japanese Challenge.* Reading, Mass.: Addison-Wesley, 1981.

Paine, F. T., Carroll, S. J., and Leete, B. A. "Need Satisfactions of Managerial Level Personnel in a Government Agency." *Journal of Applied Psychology*, 1966, *50*, 247–249.

Pandey, S. K., and Kingsley, G. A. "Examining Red Tape in Public and Private Organizations: Alternative Explanations from a Social Psychological Model." *Journal of Public Administration Research and Theory*, 2000, *10*, 779–800.

Pandey, S. K., and Scott, P. G. "Red Tape: A Review and Assessment of Concepts and Measures." *Journal of Public Administration Research and Theory*, 2002, *12*, 553–580.

Parkinson, C. N. *Parkinson's Law*. Boston: Houghton Mifflin, 1957.

Partnership for Public Service. *News from the Partnership*, 2002, *1*(2). [www.ourpublicservice.org].

Patchen, M., Pelz, D., and Allen, C. *Some Questionnaire Measures of Employee Motivation and Morale*. Ann Arbor: Survey Research Center, Institute for Social Research, University of Michigan, 1965.

Patterson, T. E. *The American Democracy*. (5th ed.) New York: McGraw-Hill, 2001.

Perrow, C. "The Analysis of Goals in Complex Organizations." *American Sociological Review*, 1961, *26*, 688–699.

Perrow, C. "Departmental Power and Perspective in Industrial Firms." In M. N. Zald (ed.), *Power in Organizations*. Nashville, Tenn.: Vanderbilt University Press, 1970a.

Perrow, C. *Organizational Analysis*. Belmont, Calif.: Wadsworth, 1970b.

Perrow, C. "A Framework for Comparative Analysis of Organizations." In F. E. Kast and J. E. Rosenzweig (eds.), *Contingency Views of Organization and Management*. Chicago: Science Research Associates, 1973.

Perry, J. L. "Merit Pay in the Public Sector: The Case for a Failure of Theory." *Review of Public Personnel Administration*, 1986, *7*, 57–69.

Perry, J. L. "Measuring Public Service Motivation: An Assessment of Construct Reliability and Validity." *Journal of Public Administration Research and Theory*, 1996, *6*, 5–24.

Perry, J. L. "Bringing Society in: Toward a Theory of PSM." *Journal of Public Administration Research and Theory*, 2000, *10*, 471–488.

Perry, J. L., and Kraemer, K. L. (eds.). *Public Management*. Mountain View, Calif.: Mayfield, 1983.

Perry, J. L., and Miller, T. K. "The Senior Executive Service: Has It Worked?" Paper presented at the annual meeting of the American Political Science Association, San Francisco, Aug. 1990.

Perry, J. L., Petrakis, B. A., and Miller, T. K. "Federal Merit Pay, Round II: An Analysis of the Performance Management and Recognition System." *Public Administration Review*, 1989, *49*, 29–37.

Perry, J. L., and Porter, L. W. "Factors Affecting the Context for Motivation in Public Organizations." *Academy of Management Review*, 1982, *7*, 89–98.

Perry, J. L., and Rainey, H. G. "The Public-Private Distinction in Organization Theory: A Critique and Research Strategy." *Academy of Management Review*, 1988, *13*, 182–201.

Perry, J. L., and Wise, L. R. "The Motivational Bases of Public Service." *Public Administration Review*, 1990, *50*, 367–373.

Pervin, L. A. (ed.). *Goal Concepts in Personality and Social Psychology*. Hillsdale, N.J.: Erlbaum, 1989.

Peters, B. G., and Hogwood, B. W. "The Death of Immortality: Births, Deaths, and Metamorphoses in the U.S. Federal Bureaucracy, 1933–1982." *American Review of Public Administration*, 1988, *18*, 119–133.

Peters, B. G., and Savoie, D. J. "Civil Service Reform: Misdiagnosing the Patient." *Public Administration Review,* 1994, *54,* 418–425.

Peters, T. J. *Thriving on Chaos.* New York: Knopf, 1987.

Peters, T. J. "Restoring American Competitiveness: Looking for New Models of Organizations." *Academy of Management Executive,* 1988, *2,* 104–110.

Peters, T. J., and Waterman, R. H. *In Search of Excellence: Lessons from America's Best-Run Companies.* New York: HarperCollins, 1982.

Petter, J., and others. "Dimensions and Patterns in Employee Empowerment: Assessing What Matters to Street-Level Bureaucrats." *Journal of Public Administration Research and Theory,* 2002, *12,* 377–400.

Pettigrew, A. M., Woodman, R. W., and Cameron, K. S. "Studying Organizational Change and Development: Challenges for Future Research." *Academy of Management Journal,* 2001, *44,* 697–714.

Petty, M. M., McGee, G. W., and Cavender, J. W. "A Meta-Analysis of the Relationship Between Individual Job Satisfaction and Individual Performance." *Academy of Management Review,* 1984, *9,* 712–721.

Pfeffer, J. *Power in Organizations.* Boston: Pitman, 1981.

Pfeffer, J. *Organizations and Organization Theory.* Boston: Pitman, 1982.

Pfeffer, J. *Managing with Power.* Boston: Harvard Business School Press, 1992.

Pfeffer, J., and Salancik, G. R. *The External Control of Organizations.* New York: HarperCollins, 1978.

Pfiffner, J. P., and Brook, D. A. (eds.). *The Future of Merit: Twenty Years After the Civil Service Reform Act.* Washington, D.C.: Woodrow Wilson Center Press; Baltimore: Johns Hopkins University Press, 2000.

Pinder, C. C. *Work Motivation in Organizational Behavior.* Upper Saddle River, N.J.: Prentice Hall, 1998.

Pitt, D. C., and Smith, B. C. *Government Departments: An Organizational Perspective.* London: Routledge, 1981.

Poister, T. H. "Crosscutting Themes in Public Sector Agency Revitalization." *Public Productivity Review,* 1988a, *11,* 29–35.

Poister, T. H. (ed.). "Success Stories in Revitalizing Public Agencies." *Public Productivity Review,* 1988b, *11,* 27–103.

Poister, T. H., and Larson, T. D. "The Revitalization of PennDOT." *Public Productivity Review,* 1988, *11,* 85–103.

Pollitt, C., and Bouckaert, G. *Public Management Reform: A Comparative Perspective.* Oxford: Oxford University Press, 2000.

Pondy, L. R. "Organizational Conflict: Concepts and Models." *Administrative Science Quarterly,* 1967, *12,* 296–320.

Popovich, M. G. (ed.). *Creating High-Performance Government Organizations.* San Francisco, Calif.: Jossey-Bass, 1998.

Porter, E. A., Sargent, A. G., and Stupak, R. J. "Managing for Excellence in the Federal Government." *New Management,* 1986, *4,* 24–32.

Porter, L. W. "Job Attitudes in Management: Perceived Deficiencies in Need Fulfillment as a Function of Job Level." *Journal of Applied Psychology,* 1962, *46,* 375–384.

Porter, L. W., and Lawler, E. E., III. *Managerial Attitudes and Performance.* Burr Ridge, Ill.: Irwin, 1968.

Porter, L. W., and Van Maanen, J. "Task Accomplishment and the Management of Time." In J. L. Perry and K. L. Kraemer (eds.), *Public Management*. Mountain View, Calif.: Mayfield, 1983.

Porter, M. E. *Competitive Advantage*. New York: Free Press, 1998.

Posner, B. T., and Schmidt, W. H. "The Values of Business and Federal Government Executives: More Different Than Alike." *Public Personnel Management*, 1996, *25*, 277–289.

Provan, K. G., and Milward, H. B. "A Preliminary Theory of Interorganizational Network Effectiveness: A Comparative Study of Four Community Mental Health Systems." *Administrative Science Quarterly*, 1995, *40*, 1–33.

Provan, K. G., and Milward, H. B. "Do Networks Really Work? A Framework for Evaluating Public-Sector Organizational Networks." *Public Adiministration Review*, 2001, *61*, 414–423.

Pugh, D. S., Hickson, D. J., and Hinings, C. R. "An Empirical Taxonomy of Work Organizations." *Administrative Science Quarterly*, 1969, *14*, 115–126.

Putnam, R. D. *Making Democracy Work: Civic Traditions in Modern Italy*. Princeton: Princeton University Press, 1993.

Quinn, J. B. *Strategies for Change: Logical Incrementalism*. Homewood, Ill.: Irwin, 1990.

Quinn, R. E. *Beyond Rational Management: Mastering the Paradoxes and Competing Demands of High Performance*. San Francisco: Jossey-Bass, 1988.

Quinn, R. E., and Cameron, K. "Organizational Life Cycles and Shifting Criteria of Effectiveness: Some Preliminary Evidence." *Management Science*, 1983, *29*, 33–51.

Quinn, R. E., and Rohrbaugh, J. "A Spatial Model of Effectiveness Criteria: Towards a Competing Values Approach to Organizational Analysis." *Management Science*, 1983, *29*, 363–377.

Raab, J. "Where Do Policy Networks Come From?" *Journal of Public Administration Research and Theory*, 2002, *12*, 581–622.

Radin, B. A. "The Government Performance and Results Act and the Tradition of Federal Management Reform: Square Pegs in Round Holes?" *Journal of Public Administration Research and Theory*, 2000, *10*, 111–135.

Radin, B. A. *The Accountable Juggler: The Art of Leadership in a Federal Agency*. Washington, D.C.: CQ Press, 2002.

Radin, B. A., and Hawley, W. D. *The Politics of Federal Reorganization: Creating the U.S. Department of Education*. New York: Pergamon Press, 1988.

Rainey, G. W. "Implementation and Managerial Creativity: A Study of the Development of Client-Centered Units in Human Service Programs." In D. J. Palumbo and D. J. Calista (eds.), *Implementation and the Policy Process*. Westport, Conn.: Greenwood Press, 1990.

Rainey, G. W., and Rainey, H. G. "Breaching the Hierarchical Imperative: The Modularization of the Social Security Claims Process." In D. J. Calista (ed.), *Bureaucratic and Governmental Reform* (JAI Research Annual in Public Policy Analysis and Management). Greenwich, Conn.: JAI Press, 1986.

Rainey, H. G. "Perceptions of Incentives in Business and Government: Implications for Civil Service Reform." *Public Administration Review*, 1979, *39*, 440–448.

Rainey, H. G. "Reward Preferences Among Public and Private Managers: In Search of the Service Ethic." *American Review of Public Administration*, 1982, *16*, 288–302.

Rainey, H. G. "Public Agencies and Private Firms: Incentive Structures, Goals, and Individual Roles." *Administration and Society*, 1983, *15*, 207–242.

Rainey, H. G. "Public Management: Recent Research on the Political Context and Manager-ial Roles, Structures, and Behaviors." *Yearly Review of Management of the Journal of Management*, 1989, *15*, 229–250.

Rainey, H. G. "Toward a Theory of Goal Ambiguity in Public Organizations." In J. L. Perry (ed.), *Research in Public Administration*, Vol. 2. Greenwich, Conn.: JAI Press, 1993.

Rainey, H. G. "The 'How Much Process is Due?' Debate: Legal and Managerial Perspectives." In P. J. Cooper (ed.), *Public Law and Administration*. San Francisco: Jossey-Bass, 1997.

Rainey, H. G. "Work Motivation." In R. T. Golembiewski (ed.), *Handbook of Organizational Behavior*. (2nd ed.) New York: Marcel Dekker, 2000.

Rainey, H. G. *A Weapon in the War for Talent: Using Special Hiring Authorities to Recruit Crucial Personnel*. Arlington, Va.: IBM Endowment for the Business of Government, 2002.

Rainey, H. G., Backoff, R. W., and Levine, C. L. "Comparing Public and Private Organizations." *Public Administration Review*, 1976, *36*, 233–246.

Rainey, H. G., Facer, R., and Bozeman, B. "Repeated Findings of Sharp Differences Between Public and Private Managers' Perceptions of Personnel Rules." Paper presented at the 1995 Annual Meeting of the American Political Science Association, Chicago, Aug. 31–Sept. 3, 1995.

Rainey, H. G., and Kellough, J. E. "Civil Service Reform and Incentives in the Public Service." In J. Pfiffner and D. Brook (eds.), *The Future of Merit: Twenty Years After the Civil Service Reform Act*. Washington, D.C.: The Woodrow Wilson Center Press and Baltimore: Johns Hopkins University Press, 2000.

Rainey, H. G., and Milward, H. B. "Public Organizations: Policy Networks and Environments." In R. H. Hall and R. E. Quinn (eds.), *Organizational Theory and Public Policy*. Thousand Oaks, Calif.: Sage, 1983.

Rainey, H. G., Pandey, S., and Bozeman, B. "Public and Private Managers' Perceptions of Red Tape," *Public Administration Review*, 1995, *55*, 567–574.

Rainey, H. G., and Steinbauer, P. J. "Galloping Elephants: Developing Elements of a Theory of Effective Public Organizations." *Journal of Public Administration Research and Theory*, 1999, *9*, 1–32.

Rainey, H. G., Traut, C., and Blunt, B. "Reward Expectancies and Other Work-Related Attitudes in Public and Private Organizations: A Review and Extension." *Review of Public Personnel Administration*, 1986, *6*, 50–73.

Rawls, J. R., Ullrich, R. A., and Nelson, O. T. "A Comparison of Managers Entering or Reentering the Profit and Nonprofit Sectors." *Academy of Management Journal*, 1975, *18*, 616–622.

Rehfuss, J. *The Job of the Public Manager*. Florence, Ky.: Dorsey Press, 1989.

Rhinehart, J. B., and others. "Comparative Study of Need Satisfaction in Governmental and Business Hierarchies." *Journal of Applied Psychology*, 1969, *53*, 230–235.

Riccio, J., Bloom, H. S., and Hill, C. J. "Management, Organizational Characteristics, and Performance: The Case of Welfare-to-Work Programs." In C. J. Heinrich and L. Lynn (eds.), *Governance and Performance: New Perspectives*. Washington, D.C.: Georgetown University Press, 2000.

Riccucci, N. M. *Unsung Heroes: Federal Executives Making a Difference*. Washington, D.C.: Georgetown University Press, 1995.

Ring, P. S. "Strategic Issues: What Are They and Where Do They Come From?" In J. M. Bryson and R. C. Einsweiller (eds.), *Strategic Planning*. Chicago: Planners Press, 1988.

Ring, P. S., and Perry, J. L. "Strategic Management in Public and Private Organizations: Implications of Distinctive Contexts and Constraints." *Academy of Management Review*, 1985, *10*, 276–286.

Ripley, R. B., and Franklin, G. A. *Congress, the Bureaucracy, and Public Policy*. Florence, Ky.: Dorsey Press, 1984.

Rizzo, J. R., House, R. J., and Lirtzman, S. E. "Role Conflict and Ambiguity in Complex Organizations." *Administrative Science Quarterly*, 1970, *15*, 150–163.

Roberts, N. C., and King, P. J. *Transforming Public Policy: Dynamics of Policy Entrepreneurship and Innovation*. San Francisco: Jossey-Bass, 1996.

Robertson, P. J., and Seneviratne, S. J. "Outcomes of Planned Organizational Change in the Public Sector: A Meta-Analytic Comparison to the Private Sector." *Public Administration Review*, 1995, *55*, 547–558.

Rocheleau, B., and Wu, L. F. "Public Versus Private Information Systems—Do They Differ in Important Ways? A Review and Empirical Test." *American Review of Public Administration*, 2002, *32*, 379–397.

Roderick, M., Jacob, B. A., and Bryk, A. S. "Evaluating Chicago's Efforts to End Social Promotion." In C. J. Heinrich and L. Lynn (eds.), *Governance and Performance: New Perspectives*. Washington, D.C.: Georgetown University Press, 2000.

Rodgers, R. R., and Hunter, J. E. "A Foundation of Good Management Practice in Government: Management by Objectives." *Public Administration Review*, 1992, *52*(1), 27–39.

Roessner, J. D. "Incentives to Innovate in Public and Private Organizations." In J. L. Perry and K. L. Kraemer (eds.), *Public Management*. Palo Alto, Calif.: Mayfield, 1983.

Roethlisberger, F. J., and Dickson, W. J. *Management and the Worker*. Cambridge, Mass.: Harvard University Press, 1939.

Rogers, E. M., and Argawala-Rogers, R. *Communication in Organizations*. New York: Free Press, 1976.

Rogers, E. M., and Kim, J. "Diffusion of Innovations in Public Organizations." In R. L. Merrit (ed.), *Innovation in the Public Sector*. Thousand Oaks, Calif.: Sage, 1985.

Rohrbaugh, J. "Operationalizing the Competing Values Approach: Measuring Performance in the Employment Service." *Public Productivity Review*, 1981, *5*, 141–159.

Rokeach, M. *The Nature of Human Values*. New York: Free Press, 1973.

Romzek, B. S. "Employee Investment and Commitment: The Ties That Bind." *Public Administration Review*, 1990, *50*, 274–382.

Romzek, B. S. "Accountability of Congressional Staff." *Journal of Public Administration Research and Theory*, 2000, *10*, 413–446.

Romzek, B. S., and Dubnick, M. J. "Accountability in the Public Sector: Lessons from the Challenger Tragedy." *Public Administration Review*, 1987, *47*, 227–239.

Romzek, B. S., and Hendricks, J. "Organizational Involvement and Representative Bureaucracy: Can We Have It Both Ways?" *American Political Science Review*, 1982, *76*, 75–82.

Romzek, B. S., and Johnston, J. M. "Effective Contract Implementation and Management: A Preliminary Model." *Journal of Public Administration Research and Theory*, 2002, *12*, 423–453.

Rosen, B. *Holding Government Bureaucracies Accountable*. Westport, Conn.: Praeger, 1998.

Rosenbloom, D. H., Kravchuck, R. S., and Rosenbloom, D. G. *Public Administration*. New York: McGraw Hill, 2001.

Rosenbloom, D. H., and O'Leary, R. *Public Administration and Law*. New York: Dekker, 1997.

Rourke, F. E. *Bureaucracy, Politics, and Public Policy*. New York: Little, Brown, 1984.

Rubin, I. S. *Shrinking the Federal Government: The Effect of Cutbacks on Five Federal Agencies.* White Plains, N.Y.: Longman, 1985.

Rubin, M. S. "Sagas, Ventures, Quests, and Parlays: A Typology of Strategies in the Public Sector." In J. M. Bryson and R. C. Einsweiller (eds.), *Strategic Planning.* Chicago: Planners Press, 1988.

Rumsfeld, D. "A Politician-Turned-Executive Surveys Both Worlds." In J. L. Perry and K. L. Kraemer (eds.), *Public Management.* Mountain View, Calif.: Mayfield, 1983.

Ruttenberg, S. H., and Gutchess, J. *Manpower Challenge of the 1970s: Institutions and Social Change.* Baltimore: Johns Hopkins University Press, 1970.

Salamon, L. M. (ed.). *The State of Nonprofit America.* Washington, D.C.: Brookings Institution Press, 2002.

Salamon, L. M., and Elliot, O. V. (eds.). *The Tools of Government: A Guide to the New Governance.* Oxford: Oxford University Press, 2002.

Saltzstein, G. H. "Explorations in Bureaucratic Responsiveness." In L. B. Hill (ed.), *The State of Public Bureaucracy.* Armonk, N.Y.: Sharpe, 1992.

Sandeep, P. "Why Government Can't Always Get the Best." *Government Executive,* Mar. 1989, p. 64.

Sanders, R. P. "The 'Best and Brightest': Can the Public Service Compete?" In Volcker Commission, *Leadership for America: Rebuilding the Public Service.* Lexington, Mass.: Heath, 1989.

Sanders, R. P., and Thompson, J. D. "The Reinvention Revolution." *Government Executive,* 1996, *28,* 1–12.

Sandfort, J. R. "Examining the Effect of Welfare-to-Work Structures and Services on a Desired Policy Outcome." In C. J. Heinrich and L. Lynn (eds.), *Governance and Performance: New Perspectives.* Washington, D. C.: Georgetown University Press, 2000.

Savas, E. S. *Privatization and Public-Private Partnerships.* New York: Seven Bridges Press/Chatham House, 2000.

Schay, B. W. "Effects of Performance-Contingent Pay on Employee Attitudes." *Public Personnel Management,* 1988, *17,* 237–250.

Schein, E. H. *Organizational Culture and Leadership: A Dynamic View.* (2nd ed.) San Francisco: Jossey-Bass, 1992.

Schott, R. L. "The Professions in Government: Engineering as a Case in Point." *Public Administration Review,* 1978, *38,* 126–132.

Schriesheim, C. A., Castro, S., and Cogliser, C. C. "Leader-Member Exchange Research: A Comprehensive Review of Theory, Measurement, and Data-Analytic Procedures." *Leadership Quarterly,* 1999, *10,* 63–113.

Schuler, R. S. "Role Perceptions, Satisfaction, and Performance Moderated by Organizational Level and Participation in Decision Making." *Academy of Management Level,* 1977, *20,* 159–165.

Schumann, R., and Fox, R. "Gender and Local Government: A Comparison of Women and Men City Managers." *Public Administration Review,* 1999, *59,* 231–242.

Schuster, J. R. "Management Compensation Policy and the Public Interest." *Public Personnel Management,* 1974, *3,* 510–523.

Schwartz, J. E. *America's Hidden Success: A Reassessment of Twenty Years of Public Policy.* New York: Norton, 1983.

Schwenk, C. R. "Conflict in Organizational Decision Making: An Exploratory Study of Its Effects in For-Profit and Not-for-Profit Organizations." *Management Science,* 1990, *36,* 436–448.

Sclar, E. D. *You Don't Always Get What You Pay for: The Economics of Privatization.* Ithaca, N.Y.: Cornell University Press, 2000.

Scott, W. R. "The Adolescence of Institutional Theory." *Administrative Science Quarterly,* 1987, *32,* 493–511.

Scott, W. R. *Organizations: Rational, Natural, and Open Systems.* (5th ed.) Upper Saddle River, New Jersey: Prentice Hall, 2003.

Scott, P. G., and Falcone, S. "Comparing Public and Private Organizations: An Exploratory Analysis of Three Frameworks." *American Review of Public Administration,* 1998, *28,* 126–145.

Seidman, H. "Public Enterprises in the United States." *Annals of Public and Cooperative Economy,* 1983, *54,* 3–18.

Seidman, H., and Gilmour, R. *Politics, Position, and Power.* New York: Little, Brown, 1986.

Selden, S. C. *The Promise of Representative Bureaucracy.* Armonk, N.Y.: Sharpe, 1997.

Selden, S. C., Brudney, J. L., and Kellough, J. E. "Bureaucracy as a Representative Institution: Toward a Reconciliation of Bureaucratic Government and Democratic Theory." *American Journal of Political Science,* 1998, *42,* 717–744.

Selznick, P. *Leadership and Administration.* New York: HarperCollins, 1957.

Selznick, P. *TVA and the Grass Roots.* New York: HarperCollins, 1966.

Shalala, D. E. "Are Large Public Organizations Manageable?" *Public Administration Review,* 1998, *58,* 284–289.

Shamir, B., Zakay, E., Breinin, E., and Popper, M. "Correlates of Charismatic Leader Behavior in Military Units: Subordinates' Attitudes, Unit Characteristics, and Superiors' Appraisals of Leader Performance." *Academy of Management Journal,* 1998, *41,* 387–409.

Sharkansky, I. "The Overloaded State." *Public Administration Review,* 1989, *49,* 201–203.

Sherman, W. M. *Behavior Modification.* New York: HarperCollins, 1990.

Siegel, G. B. "Who Is the Public Employee?" In W. B. Eddy (ed.), *Handbook of Organization Management.* New York: Dekker, 1983.

Sikula, A. F. "The Values and Value Systems of Governmental Executives." *Public Personnel Management,* 1973a, *2,* 16–22.

Sikula, A. F. "The Values and Value Systems of Industrial Personnel Managers." *Public Personnel Management,* 1973b, *2,* 305–309.

Simon, C. A., and Wang, C. "The Impact of AmeriCorps Service on Volunteer Participants: Results from a Two-Year Study in Four Western States." *Administration & Society,* 2002, *34,* 522–540.

Simon, H. A. "The Proverbs of Administration." *Public Administration Review,* 1946, *6,* 53–67.

Simon, H. A. *Administrative Behavior.* New York: Free Press, 1948.

Simon, H. A. "On the Concept of Organizational Goal." In F. E. Kast and J. E. Rosenzweig (eds.), *Contingency Views of Organization and Management.* Chicago: Science Research Associates, 1973.

Simon, H. A. "Organizations and Markets." *Journal of Public Administration Research and Theory,* 1995, *5,* 273–294.

Simon, H. A. "Why Public Administration?" *Journal of Public Adminstration Research and Theory,* 1998, *8,* 1–12.

Simon, H. A., Smithburg, D. W., and Thompson, V. A. *Public Administration.* New York: Knopf, 1950.

Simon, M. E. "Matrix Management at the U.S. Consumer Product Safety Commission." *Public Administration Review,* 1983, *43,* 357–361.

Sims, H. P., and Lorenzi, P. *The New Leadership Paradigm.* Thousand Oaks, Calif.: Sage, 1992.

Skinner, B. F. *Science and Human Behavior.* New York: Free Press, 1953.

Smith, F. J. "Index of Organizational Reactions." *JSAS Catalogue of Selected Documents in Psychology,* 1976, *6,* 54.

Smith, M. P., and Nock, S. L. "Social Class and the Quality of Life in Public and Private Organizations." *Journal of Social Issues,* 1980, *36,* 59–75.

Smith, S. R., and Lipsky, M. *Nonprofits for Hire: The Welfare State in the Age of Contracting.* Cambridge, Mass.: Harvard University Press, 1993.

Solomon, E. E. "Private and Public Sector Managers: An Empirical Investigation of Job Characteristics and Organizational Climate." *Journal of Applied Psychology,* 1986, *71,* 247–259.

Stajkovic, A. D., and Luthans, F. "Differential Effects of Incentive Motivators on Work Performance." *Academy of Management Journal,* 2001, *4,* 580–590.

Starbuck, W. H., and Nystrom, P. C. "Designing and Understanding Organizations." In P. C. Nystrom and W. H. Starbuck (eds.), *Handbook of Organizational Design.* New York: Oxford University Press, 1981.

Steel, B. S., and Warner, R. L. "Job Satisfaction Among Early Labor Force Participants: Unexpected Outcomes in Public and Private Sector Comparisons." *Review of Public Personnel Administration,* 1990, *10,* 4–22.

Steinhaus, C. S., and Perry, J. L. "Organizational Commitment: Does Sector Matter?" *Public Productivity and Management Review,* 1996, *19,* 278–288.

Stephens, J. E. "Turnaround at the Alabama Rehabilitation Agency." *Public Productivity Review,* 1988, *11,* 67–84.

Stevens, J. M., Wartick, S. L., and Bagby, J. *Business-Government Relations and Interdependence: A Managerial and Analytical Perspective.* New York: Praeger, 1988.

Stewart, R. B. "The Reformation of American Administrative Law." *Harvard Law Review,* 1975, *88,* 1667–1711.

Stillman, R. *The American Bureaucracy.* Chicago: Nelson-Hall, 1996.

Svara, J. H., and Associates. *Facilitative Leadership in Local Government: Lessons from Successful Mayors and Chairpersons.* San Francisco: Jossey-Bass, 1994.

Swiss, J. E. *Public Management Systems.* Upper Saddle River, N.J.: Prentice Hall, 1991.

Taylor, F. W. *The Principles of Scientific Management.* New York: HarperCollins, 1919.

Tehrani, M., Montanari, J. R., and Carson, K. R. "Technology as Determinant of Organization Structure: A Meta-Analytic Review." In L. R. Jauch and J. L. Wall (eds.), *Proceedings of the Annual Meeting of the Academy of Management,* 1990.

't Hart, P. *Groupthink in Government: A Study of Small Groups and Policy Failure.* Amsterdam: Swetz and Zeitlinger, 1990.

Thomas, K. W. "Conflict and Conflict Management." In M. D. Dunnette (ed.), *Handbook of Industrial and Organizational Psychology.* New York: Wiley, 1983.

Thompson, F., and Jones, L. R. *Reinventing the Pentagon: How the New Public Management Can Bring Institutional Renewal.* San Francisco: Jossey-Bass, 1994.

Thompson, F. J. *Personnel Policy in the City.* Berkeley: University of California Press, 1975.

Thompson, F. J. "Managing Within Civil Service Systems." In J. L. Perry (ed.), *Handbook of Public Administration.* San Francisco: Jossey-Bass, 1989.

Thompson, F. J. (ed.). *Revitalizing State and Local Public Service: Strengthening Performance, Accountability, and Citizen Confidence.* San Francisco: Jossey-Bass, 1993.

Thompson, J. D. "Common and Uncommon Elements in Administration." *Social Welfare Forum,* 1962, *89,* 181–201.

Thompson, J. D. *Organizations in Action.* New York: McGraw-Hill, 1967.

Thompson, J. R., and Rainey, H. G. *Modernizing Human Resource Management in the Federal Government: The IRS Model.* Arlington, Va.: IBM Endowment for the Business of Government, 2003.

Thompson, J. R. "Reinvention as Reform: Assessing the National Performance Review." *Public Administration Review,* 2000, *60,* 508–521.

Tichy, N. M. *Managing Strategic Change.* New York: Wiley, 1983.

Tichy, N. M., and Ulrich, D. "The Leadership Challenge: A Call for the Transformational Leader." *Sloan Management Review,* 1984, *26,* 59–68.

Tierney, J. T. *The U.S. Postal Service.* Westport, Conn.: Auburn House, 1988.

Tolbert, P. S. "Resource Dependence and Institutional Environments: Sources of Administrative Structure in Institutions of Higher Education." *Administrative Science Quarterly,* 1985, *30,* 1–13.

Tolbert, P. S., and Zucker, L. G. "Institutional Sources of Change in the Formal Structure of Organizations: The Diffusion of Civil Service Reform, 1880–1935." *Administrative Science Quarterly,* 1983, *28,* 22–39.

Tolchin, M. "Sixteen States Failing to Pay Required Medicare Costs." *New York Times,* Mar. 9, 1989, p. 45.

Trice, H. M., and Beyer, J. M. *The Cultures of Work Organizations.* Upper Saddle River, N.J.: Prentice Hall, 1993.

Trist, E. L., and Bamforth, K. W. "Some Social and Psychological Consequences of the Longwall Method of Coal Getting." *Human Relations,* 1951, *4,* 3–38.

Tullock, G. *The Politics of Bureaucracy.* Washington, D.C.: Public Affairs Press, 1965.

U.S. General Accounting Office. *Social Security: Actions and Plans to Reduce Agency Staff.* (GAO/HRD-86–76BR.) Washington, D.C.: U.S. General Accounting Office, 1986.

U.S. General Accounting Office. *Federal Pay: Comparisons with the Private Sector by Job and Locality.* (GAO/GGD-90–81FS.) Washington, D.C.: U.S. General Accounting Office, 1990.

U.S. General Accounting Office. *Military Personnel: Preliminary Results of DOD's 1999 Survey of Active Duty Members.* Washington, D.C.: U.S. General Accounting Office. GAO/T-NSIAD-00–110, March 8, 2000.

U.S. General Accounting Office. *Managing for Results: Using Strategic Human Capital Management to Drive Transformational Change.* (GAO-02–940T.) Washington, D.C.: U.S. General Accounting Office, July 15, 2002a.

U.S. General Accounting Office. *A Model of Strategic Human Capital Management.* (GAO-02–373SP.) Washington, D.C.: U.S. General Accounting Office, Mar. 2002b.

U.S. General Accounting Office. *Results-Oriented Cultures: Modern Performance Management Systems Are Needed to Effectively Support Pay for Performance.* Washington, D.C.: U.S. General Accounting Office. GAO-03–612T. April 1, 2003.

U.S. Merit Systems Protection Board. *Working for the Federal Government: Job Satisfaction and Federal Employees.* Washington, D.C.: U.S. Merit Systems Protection Board, 1987.

U.S. Office of Management and Budget. *The President's Management Agenda.* Washington, D. C.: U.S. Office of Management and Budget, 2002. [http://www.whitehouse.gov/omb/budget/fy2002/mgmt].

U.S. Office of Personnel Management. *Federal Employee Attitudes.* Washington, D.C.: U.S. Office of Personnel Management, 1979, 1980, 1983.

U.S. Office of Personnel Management, *Poor Performers in Government: A Quest for the True Story.* Washington, D.C.: U.S. Office of Personnel Management, 1999.

U.S. Office of Personnel Management. *Survey of Federal Employees.* Washington, D.C.: U.S. Office of Personnel Management, 2000.

U.S. Office of Personnel Management. *Human Resources Flexibilities and Authorities in the Federal Government.* Washington, D.C.: U.S. Office of Personnel Management, 2001.

U.S. Office of Personnel Management. *The Federal Human Capital Survey.* Washington, D.C.: U.S. Office of Personnel Management, 2003.

U. S. Senate, Committee on Governmental Affairs. "Report to the President: The Crisis in Human Capital," 2000. [http://govt-aff.senate.gov/humancapital].

U.S. Senate, Committee on Governmental Affairs. Subcommittee on Oversight of Government Management, Restructuring, and the District of Columbia. *High Risk: Human Capital in the Federal Government:* Hearing before the Oversight of Government Management, Restructuring, and the District of Columbia Subcommittee of the Committee on Governmental Affairs, United States Senate, One Hundred Seventh Congress, first session, February 1, 2001. Washington, D.C.: U.S. Government Printing Office.

U.S. Social Security Administration. *Social Security Vision 2010.* Washington, D.C.: U.S. Social Security Administration, 2000.

U. S. Social Security Administration, *Fiscal Year (FY) 2003 Annual Performance Plan.* Washington, D.C.: U.S. Social Security Administration, 2003. www.ssa.gov/performance/2003/

Van de Ven, A. H. "Review of H. E. Aldrich, Organizations and Environments." *Administrative Science Quarterly,* 1979, *24,* 320–326.

Van de Ven, A. H. "Early Planning, Implementation, and Performance of New Organizations." In J. R. Kimberly, R. H. Miles, and Associates, *The Organizational Life Cycle: Issues in the Creation, Transformation, and Decline of Organizations.* San Francisco: Jossey-Bass, 1980.

Van de Ven, A. H., Delbecq, A. L., and Koenig, R. "Determinants of Coordination Modes Within Organizations." *American Sociological Review,* 1976, *41,* 322–338.

Van de Ven, A. H., and Ferry, D. L. *Measuring and Assessing Organizations.* New York: Wiley-Interscience, 1980.

Van de Ven, A. H., and Poole, M. S. "Explaining Development and Change in Organizations." *Academy of Management Review,* 1995, *20,* 510–540.

Van Riper, P. P. "Luther Gulick on the Efficiency of Democracy: In Introduction." *Administrative Theory & Praxis,* 1998, *20,* 78–90.

Van Slyke, D. M., "The Mythology of Privatization in Contracting for Social Services." *Public Administration Review,* 2003, *63,* 296–315.

Vigoda, E. "From Responsiveness to Collaboration: Governance, Citizens, and the Next Generation of Public Administration." *Public Administration Review,* 2002, *62,* 527–540.

Volcker Commission. *Leadership for America: Rebuilding the Public Service.* Lexington, Mass.: Heath, 1989.

Vroom, V. H. *Work and Motivation.* New York: Wiley, 1964.

Vroom, V. H., and Jago, A. J. "Decision-Making as a Social Process: Normative and Descriptive Models of Leader Behavior." *Decision Sciences,* 1974, *5,* 743–769.

Vroom, V. H., and Yetton, P. W. *Leadership and Decision-Making.* Pittsburgh: University of Pittsburgh Press, 1973.

Waldman, D. A., Ramírez, G. G., House, R. J., and Puranam, P. "Does Leadership Matter? CEO Leadership Attributes and Profitability Under Conditions of Perceived Environmental Uncertainty." *Academy of Management Journal,* 2001, *44,* 134–143.

Waldman, S., Cohn, B., and Thomas, R. "The HUD Ripoff." *Newsweek,* Aug. 7, 1989, pp. 16–22.

Waldo, D. *The Administrative State*. New York: Holmes & Meier, 1984. (Originally published 1947.)

Walker, David M. *Human Capital: Taking Steps to Meet Current and Emerging Human Capital Challenges*: Statement of David M. Walker, Comptroller General of the United States, before the Subcommittee on Oversight of Government Management, Restructuring, and the District of Columbia, Committee on Governmental Affairs, U.S. Senate. Washington, D.C.: United States General Accounting Office, 2001. GAO-01-965T.

Walsh, A. H. *The Public's Business: The Politics and Practices of Government Corporations*. Cambridge, Mass.: MIT Press, 1978.

Walters, J. "Flattening Bureaucracy." *Governing*, 1996, *9*, 20–24.

Walters, J. *Life After Civil Service: The Texas, Georgia, and Florida Experiences*. Arlington, Va.: IBM Endowment for the Business of Government, 2002.

Wamsley, G. L., and Zald, M. N. *The Political Economy of Public Organizations*. Lexington, Mass.: Heath, 1973.

Wamsley, G. L., and others. *Refounding Public Administration*. Thousand Oaks, Calif.: Sage, 1990.

Warner, M., and Hebdon, R. "Local Government Restructuring: Privatization and Its Alternatives." *Journal of Policy Analysis and Management*, 2001, *20*, 315–336.

Warwick, D. P. *A Theory of Public Bureaucracy*. Cambridge, Mass.: Harvard University Press, 1975.

Wechsler, B. "Reinventing Florida's Civil Service System: The Failure of Reform." *Review of Public Personnel Administration*, 1994, *14*, 64–75.

Wechsler, B., and Backoff, R. W. "Policy Making and Administration in State Agencies: Strategic Management Approaches." *Public Administration Review*, 1986, *46*, 321–327.

Wechsler, B., and Backoff, R. W. "The Dynamics of Strategy in Public Organizations." In J. M. Bryson and R. C. Einsweiller (eds.), *Strategic Planning*. Chicago: Planners Press, 1988.

Weick, K. E. *The Social Psychology of Organizing*. Reading, Mass.: Addison-Wesley, 1979.

Weidenbaum, M. L. *The Modern Public Sector: New Ways of Doing the Government's Business*. New York: Basic Books, 1969.

Weinberg, M. W. *Managing the State*. Cambridge, Mass.: MIT Press, 1977.

Weisbrod, B. A. "The Future of the Nonprofit Sector: Its Entwining with Private Enterprise and Government." *Journal of Policy Analysis and Management*, 1997, *16*, 541–555.

Weisbrod, B. A. (ed.). *To Profit or Not to Profit: The Commercial Transformation of the Nonprofit Sector*. Cambridge: Cambridge University Press, 1998.

Weiss, D. J., Dawis, R. V., England, G. W., and Lofquist, L. H. *Manual for the Minnesota Satisfaction Questionnaire*. Minneapolis: Industrial Relations Center, University of Minnesota, 1967.

Weiss, H. L. "Why Business and Government Exchange Executives." In J. L. Perry and K. L. Kraemer (eds.), *Public Management*. Palo Alto, Calif.: Mayfield, 1983.

Welch, E. W., and Wong, W. "Global Information Technology Pressure and Government Accountability: The Mediating Effect of Domestic Context on Web Site Openness." *Journal of Public Administration Research and Theory*, 2001a, *11*, 509–538.

Welch, E. W., and Wong, W. "Effects of Global Pressures on Public Bureaucracy: Modeling a New Theoretical Framework." *Administration & Society*, 2001b, *32*, 371–402.

West, J. P. (ed.). "Symposium Issue: Civil Service Reform in the State of Georgia." *Review of Public Personnel Administration*, 2002, *22*, 79–93.

West, W. F. *Controlling the Bureaucracy*. Armonk, N.Y.: Sharpe, 1995.

Whetten, D. A. "Sources, Responses, and Effects of Organizational Decline." In K. Cameron, R. I. Sutton, and D. A. Whetten (eds.), *Readings in Organizational Decline*. New York: Ballinger, 1988.

Whetten, D. A., and Cameron, K. S. *Developing Management Skills.* (5th ed.) Upper Saddle River, N.J.: Prentice-Hall, 2002.

White, J. D., and Adams, G. B. *Research in Public Administration: Reflections on Theory and Practice.* Thousand Oaks, Calif.: Sage, 1994.

Whorton, J. W., and Worthley, J. A. "A Perspective on the Challenge of Public Management: Environmental Paradox and Organizational Culture." *Academy of Management Review,* 1981, *6,* 357–361.

Wildavsky, A. *Speaking Truth to Power.* New York: Little, Brown, 1979.

Wildavsky, A. *The New Politics of the Budgetary Process.* Glenview, Ill.: Scott, Foresman, 1988.

Wilkins, A. L. *Developing Corporate Character: How to Successfully Change an Organization Without Destroying It.* San Francisco: Jossey-Bass, 1990.

Williamson, O. E. *Markets and Hierarchies.* New York: Free Press, 1975.

Williamson, O. E. "The Economics of Organizations: The Transaction Cost Approach." *American Journal of Sociology,* 1981, *87,* 548–577.

Williamson, O. E. (ed.). *Organization Theory: From Chester Barnard to the Present and Beyond.* New York: Oxford University Press, 1990.

Williamson, O. E. "Transaction Cost Economics and Public Administration." In P. B. Boorsma (ed.), *Public Priority Setting.* Netherlands: Kluwer Academic Publishers, 1997, 19–37.

Williamson, O. E. "Public and Private Bureaucracies: A Transaction Cost Economics Perspective," *Journal of Law, Economics, and Organization,* 1999, *15,* 306–342.

Wilson, J. Q. *Political Organizations.* New York: Basic Books, 1973.

Wilson, J. Q. *Bureaucracy.* New York: Basic Books, 1989.

Wise, C. R., and Nader, R. "Organizing the Federal System for Homeland Security: Problems, Issues, and Dilemmas." *Public Administration Review,* 2002, *62,* 44–57.

Wittmer, D. "Serving the People or Serving for Pay: Reward Preferences Among Government, Hybrid Sector, and Business Managers." *Public Productivity and Management Review,* 1991, *14,* 369–384.

Wolf, P. J. "Why Must We Reinvent the Federal Government? Putting Historical Developmental Claims to the Test." *Journal of Public Administration Research and Theory,* 1997, *7*(3), 353–388.

Wolf, P. J. "A Case Survey of Bureaucratic Effectiveness in U.S. Cabinet Agencies: Preliminary Results." *Journal of Public Administration Research and Theory,* 1993, *3*(2), 161–181.

Woll, P. *American Bureaucracy.* New York: Norton, 1977.

Wood, B. D., and Waterman, R. W. *Bureaucratic Dynamics.* Boulder, Colo.: Westview Press, 1994.

Woodward, J. *Industrial Organization: Theory and Practice.* Oxford: Oxford University Press, 1965.

Wright, B. E. "Public-Sector Work Motivation: A Review of the Current Literature and a Revised Conceptual Model." *Journal of Public Administration Research and Theory,* 2001, *11,* 559–586.

Wright, B. E. "The Role of Work Context in Work Motivation: A Public Sector Application of Goal and Social Cognition Theories." *Journal of Public Administration Research and Theory,* forthcoming.

Yates, D., Jr. *The Politics of Management: Exploring the Inner Workings of Public and Private Organizations.* San Francisco: Jossey-Bass, 1985.

Yuchtman, E., and Seashore, S. E. "A System Resource Approach to Organizational Effectiveness." *American Sociological Review,* 1967, *32,* 891–903.

Yukl, G. *Leadership in Organizations.* (5th ed.) Upper Saddle River, N.J.: Prentice Hall, 2001.

Zaffane, R. "Patterns of Organizational Commitment and Perceived Management Style: A Comparison of Public and Private Sector Employees." *Human Relations,* 1994, *47,* 977–1010.

Zahra, S. A., Ireland, R. D., Gutierrez, I., and Hitt, M. A. "Privatization and Entrepreneurial Transformation: Emerging Issues and a Future Research Agenda." *Academy of Management Review,* 2000, *25,* 509–524.

Zalesny, M. D., and Farace, R. V. "Traditional Versus Open Offices: A Comparison of Sociotechnical, Social Relations, and Symbolic Meaning Perspectives." *Academy of Management Journal,* 1987, *30,* 240–259.

Zaltman, G., Duncan, R., and Holbek, J. *Innovations and Organizations.* New York: Wiley, 1973.

Zander, A. *Making Groups Effective.* (2nd ed.) San Francisco: Jossey-Bass, 1994.

# NAME INDEX

## A

Abcarian, G., 11
Aberbach, J. D., 103, 119, 318
Abney, G., 109, 118
Abramson, M. A., 129, 412
Adams, G. B., 10, 11
Adams, J. S., 250, 255, 256
Aharoni, Y., 71
Aiken, M., 45, 188, 246
Alderfer, C. P., 231, 234
Aldrich, H. E., 46, 80, 85, 86, 87, 88, 89, 190, 301, 316, 317, 318, 356, 359
Allen, C., 226, 227
Allison, G. T., 9, 11, 106, 134, 176, 205, 267, 299, 300, 316, 320, 324
Alonso, P., 246
Ammons, D. N., 316, 318, 321, 322
Anderson, W. F., 323
Angle, H., 279
Antonsen, M., 69
Appelbaum, E., 333, 405
Argawala-Rogers, R., 340
Argyris, C., 39, 40, 48, 189

Armenakis, A. A., 366, 377, 380
Arnold, P. E., 30, 100, 410
Ashburner, L., 60
Atkinson, S. E., 73
Avolio, B. J., 303

## B

Back, K., 36, 38, 373
Backkx, M., 73
Backoff, R. W., 9, 74, 171, 173, 174
Bacon, L. W., 161
Bagby, J., 62
Bailey, T., 333, 405
Baldwin, J. N., 272
Balfour, D. L., 11, 279, 288, 287
Ball, R., 386
Bamforth, K. W., 42
Ban, C., 11, 16, 85, 222, 223, 270, 324
Bandura, A., 262, 264, 265, 266, 268, 298
Barker, V. L., III, 364
Barnard, C. I., 33–34, 35, 47, 52, 155, 228, 232, 235, 307
Barrett, K., 214
Bartol, K. M., 281

Barton, A. H., 7, 9, 133, 184, 224, 238
Barton, E., 104
Barzelay, M., 16, 60, 71, 324
Bass, B. M., 303, 304
Baum, E., 350, 351
Baum, J.A.C., 80, 356
Beam, G., 392, 399
Beard, D. W., 85
Beck, P. A., 104
Becker, W. S., 267, 268
Bedeian, A. G., 366, 377, 380
Behn, R. D., 16, 101, 134, 220, 267, 324, 365, 382, 392
Bell, C. H., 370, 371, 372
Bellante, D., 272
Bendor, J., 163, 169, 238
Benn, S. I., 65
Bennis, W., 302, 303, 312
Benson, G., 333, 405
Berg, P., 333, 405
Berman, E. M., 129, 281, 403
Berman, S. L., 84
Berry, F. S., 169, 171, 175
Beyer, J. M., 48, 189, 308, 310, 311, 313
Blais, A., 163, 238

# SUBJECT INDEX

Government agency names are sorted under the first word following the jurisdiction, for example, Department of Defense (U.S.).

## A

Absenteeism, 277
Access, public vs. private, 65
Accommodation, 344
Accountability, 59–60, 96–97
Achievement, 253–255
Achievement-oriented leadership, 294
Action for Organizational Development (Project ACORD), 374
Action-planning systems, 196, 197
Action research, 37
Adaptation, 43–44, 54, 358
Adhocracy, 199
Administrative Behavior (Simon), 35
Administrative changes, 368
"Administrative man," 36
Administrative management school: context for, 30; Follett and, 31; generic aspects, 57; government reform and, 30; Gulick and, 28–31; homogeneity principle,

28; organizational structure and, 185–186; overview, 50; POSDCORB, 29, 299; scalar principle, 29, 50; span of control (*See* Span of control); specialization in, 28–29
Administrative Procedures Act, 92
Administrative survivors, 326
Advocates, 237, 356
Affective motives, 244
Affiliation commitment, 279
Afghanistan, 127
Agencies: organizational continuum and, 66, 67f; political authority of, 90; public vs. private, 65; scorecards, 411. *See also* Public organizations
Agriculture, innovation in, 363
Alabama Division of Rehabilitation and Crippled Children Service, 381
Alpha change, 369
Altruism, 246
Ambiguities, role-related, 133–134, 277–278, 282–283
Ambivalence toward government, 6–7, 104

Analyzers, 175
Antigovernment trends, 5–7, 21
Appointments, political, 113
Arbiter communities, 324
Architecture, 312, 314–315
Astuteness, political, 119
Atomic Energy Commission, 356
Attentive publics, 101
Attitude, work-related: job involvement and, 278; job satisfaction and, 274–277; motivation-related, 220, 273–288; openness to change, 272; organizational commitment and, 278–279; professionalism and, 279–282; risk aversion, 272; role conflict and ambiguity in, 277–278; self-reported motivation, 271–273
Attribution, 296, 305
Authority: administrative principles, 185; budgeting, 114; decentralization of, 84; in decision-making, 151–152, 156, 160; economic, 68–69, 70f; escalation to the top, 319–320; formal, 110–111; hierarchy of, 194; of legislative bodies,